Lecture Notes in Computer Science

Lecture Notes in Artificial Intelligence 14051

Founding Editor

Jörg Siekmann

Series Editors

Randy Goebel, *University of Alberta, Edmonton, Canada*
Wolfgang Wahlster, *DFKI, Berlin, Germany*
Zhi-Hua Zhou, *Nanjing University, Nanjing, China*

The series Lecture Notes in Artificial Intelligence (LNAI) was established in 1988 as a topical subseries of LNCS devoted to artificial intelligence.

The series publishes state-of-the-art research results at a high level. As with the LNCS mother series, the mission of the series is to serve the international R & D community by providing an invaluable service, mainly focused on the publication of conference and workshop proceedings and postproceedings.

Helmut Degen · Stavroula Ntoa
Editors

Artificial Intelligence in HCI

4th International Conference, AI-HCI 2023
Held as Part of the 25th HCI International Conference, HCII 2023
Copenhagen, Denmark, July 23–28, 2023
Proceedings, Part II

Springer

Editors
Helmut Degen
Siemens Corporation
Princeton, NJ, USA

Stavroula Ntoa
Foundation for Research
and Technology – Hellas (FORTH)
Heraklion, Crete, Greece

ISSN 0302-9743 ISSN 1611-3349 (electronic)
Lecture Notes in Artificial Intelligence
ISBN 978-3-031-35893-7 ISBN 978-3-031-35894-4 (eBook)
https://doi.org/10.1007/978-3-031-35894-4

LNCS Sublibrary: SL7 – Artificial Intelligence

This Springer imprint is published by the registered company Springer Nature Switzerland AG
The registered company address is: Gewerbestrasse 11, 6330 Cham, Switzerland

Foreword

Human-computer interaction (HCI) is acquiring an ever-increasing scientific and industrial importance, as well as having more impact on people's everyday lives, as an ever-growing number of human activities are progressively moving from the physical to the digital world. This process, which has been ongoing for some time now, was further accelerated during the acute period of the COVID-19 pandemic. The HCI International (HCII) conference series, held annually, aims to respond to the compelling need to advance the exchange of knowledge and research and development efforts on the human aspects of design and use of computing systems.

The 25th International Conference on Human-Computer Interaction, HCI International 2023 (HCII 2023), was held in the emerging post-pandemic era as a 'hybrid' event at the AC Bella Sky Hotel and Bella Center, Copenhagen, Denmark, during July 23–28, 2023. It incorporated the 21 thematic areas and affiliated conferences listed below.

A total of 7472 individuals from academia, research institutes, industry, and government agencies from 85 countries submitted contributions, and 1578 papers and 396 posters were included in the volumes of the proceedings that were published just before the start of the conference, these are listed below. The contributions thoroughly cover the entire field of human-computer interaction, addressing major advances in knowledge and effective use of computers in a variety of application areas. These papers provide academics, researchers, engineers, scientists, practitioners and students with state-of-the-art information on the most recent advances in HCI.

The HCI International (HCII) conference also offers the option of presenting 'Late Breaking Work', and this applies both for papers and posters, with corresponding volumes of proceedings that will be published after the conference. Full papers will be included in the 'HCII 2023 - Late Breaking Work - Papers' volumes of the proceedings to be published in the Springer LNCS series, while 'Poster Extended Abstracts' will be included as short research papers in the 'HCII 2023 - Late Breaking Work - Posters' volumes to be published in the Springer CCIS series.

I would like to thank the Program Board Chairs and the members of the Program Boards of all thematic areas and affiliated conferences for their contribution towards the high scientific quality and overall success of the HCI International 2023 conference. Their manifold support in terms of paper reviewing (single-blind review process, with a minimum of two reviews per submission), session organization and their willingness to act as goodwill ambassadors for the conference is most highly appreciated.

This conference would not have been possible without the continuous and unwavering support and advice of Gavriel Salvendy, founder, General Chair Emeritus, and Scientific Advisor. For his outstanding efforts, I would like to express my sincere appreciation to Abbas Moallem, Communications Chair and Editor of HCI International News.

July 2023   Constantine Stephanidis

HCI International 2023 Thematic Areas and Affiliated Conferences

Thematic Areas

- HCI: Human-Computer Interaction
- HIMI: Human Interface and the Management of Information

Affiliated Conferences

- EPCE: 20th International Conference on Engineering Psychology and Cognitive Ergonomics
- AC: 17th International Conference on Augmented Cognition
- UAHCI: 17th International Conference on Universal Access in Human-Computer Interaction
- CCD: 15th International Conference on Cross-Cultural Design
- SCSM: 15th International Conference on Social Computing and Social Media
- VAMR: 15th International Conference on Virtual, Augmented and Mixed Reality
- DHM: 14th International Conference on Digital Human Modeling and Applications in Health, Safety, Ergonomics and Risk Management
- DUXU: 12th International Conference on Design, User Experience and Usability
- C&C: 11th International Conference on Culture and Computing
- DAPI: 11th International Conference on Distributed, Ambient and Pervasive Interactions
- HCIBGO: 10th International Conference on HCI in Business, Government and Organizations
- LCT: 10th International Conference on Learning and Collaboration Technologies
- ITAP: 9th International Conference on Human Aspects of IT for the Aged Population
- AIS: 5th International Conference on Adaptive Instructional Systems
- HCI-CPT: 5th International Conference on HCI for Cybersecurity, Privacy and Trust
- HCI-Games: 5th International Conference on HCI in Games
- MobiTAS: 5th International Conference on HCI in Mobility, Transport and Automotive Systems
- AI-HCI: 4th International Conference on Artificial Intelligence in HCI
- MOBILE: 4th International Conference on Design, Operation and Evaluation of Mobile Communications

List of Conference Proceedings Volumes Appearing Before the Conference

47. CCIS 1836, HCI International 2023 Posters - Part V, edited by Constantine Stephanidis, Margherita Antona, Stavroula Ntoa and Gavriel Salvendy

https://2023.hci.international/proceedings

Preface

The 4th International Conference on Artificial Intelligence in HCI (AI-HCI 2023), an affiliated conference of the HCI International conference, aimed to bring together academics, practitioners, and students to exchange results from academic and industrial research, as well as industrial experiences, on the use of artificial intelligence (AI) technologies to enhance human-computer interaction (HCI).

Motivated by discussions on topical Human-Centered Artificial Intelligence (HCAI), a considerable number of papers delved into the topic, exploring theoretical approaches, design principles, and case studies of AI-enabled systems and services adopting HCAI. One of the facets of HCAI that was largely explored was explainability and transparency. Through reviews, quantitative comparisons, and case studies, as well as the exploration of cutting-edge techniques, contributions on the topic examined the impact of AI explanations on trust, collaboration, and decision-making, advancing understanding of the current landscape and emerging trends in the field. Another aspect that received particular attention was fairness and ethics, with relevant papers discussing approaches to improve fairness, mitigate bias, and promote ethical decision-making, and exploring the impact of cognitive biases and user perceptions of unfair AI. Furthermore, a comprehensive exploration of how artificial intelligence intersects with user experience and design was conducted, in the context of which contributions explored approaches for graphical user interface design, product design, risk assessment and project management, as well as design processes and guidelines.

Contributions included in the proceedings also addressed specific application domains, reflecting topics that capture academic and public discussions. A subject gaining significant traction is AI for language, text, and speech-related tasks, in the context of which papers addressed the design, development, and evaluation of chatbots, argumentative dialogue systems, large language models, as well as language translation and sentiment analysis approaches. Another emerging topic concerns human-AI collaboration, with discussions revolving around human-agent teaming, human-robot interaction, as well as user satisfaction and beliefs about AI agents in the context of collaborative tasks. Furthermore, the role of AI in decision-support and perception analysis was explored, focusing on the exploration of uncertainty in information, contextual recommendations, human perception analysis, and the design of decision-support systems. Finally, several papers explored the design and development of innovative AI-driven solutions, including neural networks, multimodal models, and machine learning approaches for diverse applications across various contexts.

Two volumes of the HCII 2023 proceedings are dedicated to this year's edition of the AI-HCI conference. The first volume focuses on topics related to Human-Centered Artificial Intelligence, explainability, transparency and trustworthiness, ethics and fairness, as well as AI-supported user experience design. The second volume focuses on topics related to AI for language, text, and speech-related tasks, human-AI collaboration, AI for decision-support and perception analysis, and innovations in AI-enabled systems.

The papers of the AI-HCI 2023 volumes were included for publication after a minimum of two single-blind reviews from the members of the AI-HCI Program Board or, in some cases, from members of the Program Boards of other affiliated conferences. We would like to thank all of them for their invaluable contribution, support, and efforts.

July 2023

Helmut Degen
Stavroula Ntoa

4th International Conference on Artificial Intelligence in HCI (AI-HCI 2023)

Program Board Chairs: **Helmut Degen,** *Siemens Corporation, USA* and **Stavroula Ntoa**, *Foundation for Research and Technology - Hellas (FORTH), Greece*

Program Board:

The full list with the Program Board Chairs and the members of the Program Boards of all thematic areas and affiliated conferences of HCII2023 is available online at:

http://www.hci.international/board-members-2023.php

HCI International 2024 Conference

The 26th International Conference on Human-Computer Interaction, HCI International 2024, will be held jointly with the affiliated conferences at the Washington Hilton Hotel, Washington, DC, USA, June 29 – July 4, 2024. It will cover a broad spectrum of themes related to Human-Computer Interaction, including theoretical issues, methods, tools, processes, and case studies in HCI design, as well as novel interaction techniques, interfaces, and applications. The proceedings will be published by Springer. More information will be made available on the conference website: http://2024.hci.international/.

General Chair
Prof. Constantine Stephanidis
University of Crete and ICS-FORTH
Heraklion, Crete, Greece
Email: general_chair@hcii2024.org

https://2024.hci.international/

Contents – Part II

Human-AI Collaboration

Artificial Intelligence for Decision-Support and Perception Analysis

Innovations in AI-Enabled Systems

Artificial Intelligence for Language, Text, and Speech-Related Tasks

Towards Modelling Elaborateness
in Argumentative Dialogue Systems

Annalena Aicher[1]([⊠])(iD), Marc Fuchs[1](iD), Wolfgang Minker[1](iD), and Stefan Ultes[2](iD)

[1] Institute of Communications Engineering, Ulm University, Albert-Einstein-Allee 43, 89081 Ulm, Germany
{annalena.aicher,marc.fuchs,wolfgang.minker}@uni-ulm.de
[2] Language Generation and Dialogue Systems, University of Bamberg, An der Weberei 5, 96047 Bamberg, Germany
stefan.ultes@uni-bamberg.de

Abstract. To provide an engaging and natural interaction with an argumentative dialogue system, we introduce a model to adapt the system utterances to the user's communication style in an ongoing discussion. Therefore, we propose an "Elaborateness Score" (ES) considering the length of the user utterances and requested content and adapts its utterance length as well as the amount of provided meta-information accordingly. To evaluate our approach we conducted a laboratory user study with a total of 30 participants who had a conversation with our ADS. In a pre- and post-survey, the participants had to rate statements to subjectively assess each dialogue and indicate which level of elaborateness they preferred as well as their general impression of the system. The results show that the system's elaborateness style has a significant influence on user's perception of the dialogue and imply that the preference of the system's elaborateness is individual for every user.

Keywords: Elaborateness Score · Communication Styles · Human-Computer Interaction · Spoken Dialogue Systems · Cooperative Argumentative Dialogue Systems

1 Introduction

Most of the current dialogue systems and intelligent assistants focus on content rather than formulation. However, it has been shown that people adapt their interaction styles to one another during an ongoing interaction [24]. Various studies show that likewise to human communication behaviour the adaption of communication styles of spoken dialogue system to individual users leads to more natural interactions [19,33,38]. To provide an engaging and natural interaction with an argumentative dialogue system, we introduce a model to adapt the system utterances to the user's communication style in an ongoing discussion. Therefore, we propose an "Elaborateness Score" (ES) which takes into account the length of the user utterances as well as the requested content and adapts its utterance length and amount of provided meta-information accordingly.

This work has been funded by the DFG within the project "BEA - Building Engaging Argumentation", Grant no. 313723125, as part of the Priority Program "Robust Argumentation Machines (RATIO)" (SPP-1999).

Therefore, we propose an initial adaptation of the system statements, which includes three different versions (short, medium, and long) and the provided content, which can be further extended and more fine-grained in future work. The requested content considers the *moves* the user chooses, which are categorized in three categories depending on whether they are necessary for continuing the interaction, request additional information or induce queries from the system. Each move category is ranked and weighted with regard to the previous interaction. Afterwards we merge both aspects (length of the user utterances and the requested content) with respective weights into a unified Elaborateness Model. To evaluate our approach its implementation into an argumentative dialogue system was evaluated in a laboratory user study with a total of 30 participants. In a pre- and post-survey, the participants had to rate statements to subjectively assess each dialogue and indicate which level of elaborateness they preferred as well as their general impression of the system.

The remainder of the paper is as follows: Sect. 2 gives an overview of related literature. In Sect. 3 we introduce our Elaborateness Model, in particular, explaining the adaptation of the system's utterances and the relation to the length of the user utterances and requested content. Section 4 describes the architecture of the ADS our Elaborateness Model is integrated into, as well as the respective dialogue model, and framework'. To validate our model we conducted a user study which is described in Sect. 5 and its results are presented and discussed in Sect. 6. We close with a conclusion and a brief discussion of future work in Sect. 7.

2   Related Work

In the following, a short overview of existing literature is given on the main aspects of the herein presented work, namely argumentative/mobile Dialogue Systems and adaption of language in dialogues, especially with regard to communication skills.

2.1   Argumentative/Mobile Dialogue Systems

Unlike most approaches to human-machine argumentation, we pursue a cooperative exchange of arguments. Thus, our system does not try to persuade or win a debate against the user and does not model the interaction in a competitive scenario. In contrast, Slonim et al. [36] use a classical debating setting. Their IBM Debater is an autonomous debating system that can engage in a competitive debate with humans via natural language. Another speech-based approach was introduced by Rosenfeld and Kraus [34], which based on weighted Bipolar Argumentation Frameworks. Arguing chatbots such as Debbie [32] and Dave [18] interact via text with the user. A menu-based framework that incorporates the beliefs and concerns of the opponent was also presented by Hadoux and Hunter [16]. In the same line, Rosenfeld and Kraus [11] used a previously crowd-sourced argument graph and considered the concerns of the user to persuade them. A persuasive prototype chatbot is introduced by Chalaguine and Hunter [10] to convince users to vaccinate against COVID-19 using computational models of argument. Furthermore, Fazzinga et al. [14] discuss an approach towards a dialogue system architecture using argumentative concepts to perform reasoning to provide answers consistent with the user input.

In contrast to all aforementioned ADS we aim for system that cooperatively engages the users to explore arguments and furthermore is able to adapt its communication style To keep the user motivated and engaged. Therefore we modified and extended our previously introduced argumentative dialogue system [2–4]. It provides a suitable basis as it engages in a deliberative dialogue with a human user providing all con and pro aspects to a given argument and estimating the user's interest and preferences based on the explicit feedback and implicit behavior.

To the best of our knowledge there do not exist other cooperative argumentative dialogue systems which adapt to the user's communication style in state-of-the-art literature.

2.2 Language and Conversational Style Adaption

Many psycholinguistic studies showed that people adapt their language use in conversation to that of their conversational partners [13, 38]. Often this results in convergence of "word choice, conceptual perspective, syntactic form, dialect, pronunciation, speaking rate, posture, and other behavior by both individuals" [9]. This is underpinned by the results of Niederhoffer and Pennebaker [27] who conducted three experiments that showed that people align their linguistic style in social interactions. Moreover, Otterbacher et al. [28] studied linguistic mimicry, the adoption of another's language style, in relation to the linguistic styles used by Facebook users. Tannen [39] described this conversational style matching by several markers (including topic (e.g., personal pronoun usage, persistence), pace) that define conversational style. As Heyselaar et al. [17] show this does not only apply for human-human interactions but also when interacting with a human-like agent the sentence processing is comparable. Furthermore, Walker et al. [40] showed that individual preferences for sentence planning operations, affect the content order and sentence structure of agent responses.

Bickmore and Cassell [8] compared embodied interactions with similar interactions conducted over the phone and analysed the impact these media have on a wide range of behavioural, task and subjective measures. Their results indicate that people's perceptions of conversational agents are influenced by the interaction style of the agent, which is underpinned by findings of Matsuyama et al. [20], Morris et al. [25]. Furthermore, Shamekhi et al. [35] claim that instead of one specific style that worked best, their study participants liked whichever agent matched their own conversational style best.

In our work we focus on argumentative dialogues which contents consist of automatically mined arguments and thus, are fixed in their wording and content. In order to adapt to the user's communication style we focus on a special type of conversational implication, the first maxim of quantity, i.e. elaborateness, introduced by Grice [15]. According to Neuliep [26] there exists three levels for the quantity of talk: the elaborate style as "the mode of speaking that emphasises rich, expressive language", the exacting style as "manner of speaking in which persons say no more or less than is needed to communicate a point" and the succinct style as "manner of concise speaking often accompanied by silence" on which our three versions introduced in Subsect. 3.1 are based.

Pragst et al. [30] investigated the applicability of elaborateness and indirectness as possibilities for adaptation in spoken dialogue systems. Their results showed that elaborateness and indirectness influence the user's perception of a dialogue and are therefore valuable candidates for adaptive dialogue management. Miehle et al. [23] investigated how varying elaborateness and indirectness of a spoken user interface are perceived by users and whether there exist general preferences. They claim that the system's communication style influences the user's satisfaction and the user's perception of the dialogue and that there is no general preference in the system's communication style. Furthermore, they show that indirectness can lead to a decrease in user satisfaction and furthermore is not suited for an argumentative setting. According to [22] the literature in the field of elaborateness classification for spoken language and dialogue systems is very scarce. Based on this, we consider elaborateness to be highly suitable for our adaptation approach.

3   Elaborateness Model

In the following we introduce the so-called "Elaborateness Score" (ES) which considers the length of the user utterances and requested content and serves as a metric to adapt the system's utterance length as well as the amount of provided meta-information accordingly. Therefore, in Subsect. 3.1 the adaptation of the system's utterances and the additional "meta-information" is presented. Furthermore, in Subsect. 3.2 we present in which way these are related to the length of the user utterances and requested content.

3.1   System Utterance Adaptation

In order to adapt the system's utterances, we distinguish between the utterance length and the amount of displayed content. As explained in Subsect. 4.2 we use the original textual representation of the argument components, which consequently specifies a basic length of the system utterance regarding information seeking moves.

In order to allow comparability and to prevent the differences from becoming too fine-grained (and thus, hardly detectable), we divide the utterance lengths into *short*, *medium*, and *long* versions. To assure a uniform structure, we define a "basic version" for all moves.[1] The "basic version" consists solely of the minimal formulation of the requested content, which does not necessarily form a stand-alone utterance and therefore, conveys the information in a rather unnatural manner. This version forms the basis for all three version types, whose structure is defined as follows:

1. **Short version**: Only the basic version is displayed by the system. A minimal number of embedding words was chosen to formulate a natural standalone system utterance.
2. **Medium version**: The basic version is embedded in a more detailed formulation. Customary filler words are also used here, increasing the total length of the system utterance.

---

[1] Since in this work we want to investigate the impact of elaborateness in general and show that a respective adaptation has a significant influence, the different versions of the system utterances described here are created manually by experts and only serve as a demonstration in a proof-of-principle scenario. In future work, we aim to investigate how to automatically adapt the system's utterances using state of the art approaches, especially in machine learning.

3. **Long version**: To the system's *medium version* certain meta-information is added depending on the respective user move. For instance, if the user requests an argument (information seeking move), additional information about the number of related arguments or related topics is displayed; if the user asks for his/her stance, the calculated user stance (see Subsect. 4.1) is explained in detail by indicating the number of preferred/rejected arguments.

3.2 Elaborateness Score

The Elaborateness Score considers the length of the user utterances and the requested content to determine which of the three system's utterance versions should be displayed. Please note that all variables introduced in our model can be adapted to the particular system and setting and can be chosen freely. Without limitation of generality, we chose the values that were most appropriate for our argumentative dialogue system and study setting after various tests.

First, we define the so-called *mirroring score*, which takes the length of the user utterance into account. Since, XXX et al. [] showed that,.... we aim to adjust the length of the system's utterances to the ones of the user and thus, "mirror" the user's elaborateness. Therefore, the number of characters of the current user utterance is compared to the minimum (min), average (avg), and maximum (max) number of characters of user utterances in interactions in a previous user study for the respective move. To account for normalization we define a second degree function for each move that computes a score between 0 and 0.5 for a character count between min and avg. Similarly, a score between 0.5 and 1 is calculated for a character count between avg and max.

In our scenario, we choose the function f_{mirror} to take the value 0.5 at 70% of the difference between the min and avg, and the value 0.75 at 25% of the distance between avg and max. Thereby, the slope of the function is largest around avg, which ensures that the score quickly adapts to particularly short or long user utterances. An exemplary sketch of such a function is shown in Fig. 1 for the request of a supporting argument (information seeking move).

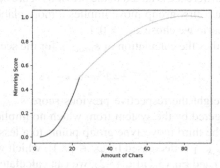

Fig. 1. Exemplary plot of the mirroring score function when requesting a supporting argument.

To ensure that the system steadily adjusts its communication style but does not jump from one extreme directly into another, we model the mirroring score $s_{mirror,k}$ for the current utterance k ($k \in \mathbb{N}$) as follows:

$$s_{mirror,k} = s_{mirror,k-1} + \alpha \left(f_{mirror,k} - s_{mirror,k-1} \right), \tag{1}$$

where the index $k - 1$ refers to previous user utterance[2]. Equation (3.2) consists of two components, the previous mirroring score $s_{mirror,k-1}$ and the weighted change of the previous to the current utterance which is calculated by multiplying the difference between $s_{mirror,k-1}$ and $f_{mirror,k}$ with the weight α, $\alpha \in [0,1]$. α allows to weight to what extent of the change in the system's elaborateness between two successive system utterances. Without loss of generality, in the herein described worked we chose $\alpha = 0.2$.

Second, we define the so-called *move_type score* which takes into account that different user moves imply different degrees of elaborateness. In our scenario, we divide all possible moves into three groups with respect to their degree of elaborateness.

- The first group ("elaborate") consists of "additional" moves, which are not mandatory for the interaction with the system and thus, indicate a larger interest of the user in meta-information and details beyond the minimum necessary.
- The second group ("'neutral") consists of inevitable moves, which are triggered by the system due to a previous user move. For example, if the user has to repeat an utterance (which the system did not understand), wants to return to a previous argument or needs to specify e.g. a preference between two arguments.
- The third group ("inelaborate") consists of all other moves, especially the moves which are necessary for the interaction and fulfill the task to "build a well-founded opinion" (request for arguments).

For the first group the respective *move_type score* $s_{move,k}$ is calculated as follows:

$$s_{move,k} = \omega_1(1 - s_{move,k-1}) + s_{move,k-1}, \tag{2}$$

where $\omega_1 \in [0,1]$ weights the difference between 1 and the old score $s_{move,k-1}$. In Eq. (3.2), this weighted difference is added to the previous score $s_{move,k-1}$, which takes account for the fact, that a first group move implies a more elaborate interaction with the system. For our scenario we chose $\omega_1 := 0.4$.

Equation (3.2) describes the calculation of $s_{move,k}$ for the second and third group.

$$s_{move,k} = \omega_{2,3} s_{move,k-1}, \tag{3}$$

where $\omega_{2,3} \in [0,1]$ weight the respective previous score $s_{move,k-1}$. As the second move_type group is triggered by the system from which no implication can be derived, we define $\omega_2 := 1$. As the third move_type group points to a less elaborate interaction the previous score $s_{move,k-1}$ is decreased by $\omega_3 \in [0,1]$, which we set to 0.8.

By merging Eq. (3.2) and Eq. (3.2)/Eq. (3.2), we can calculate the elaboration score for utterance k:

$$ES_k = \beta s_{mirror,k} + (1 - \beta) s_{move,k}, \tag{4}$$

---

[2] Without loss of generality we define $s_{mirror,1} := f_{mirror,1}$.

where the choice of $\beta \in [0, 1]$ determines which score has more influence on the *Elaborateness Score* ES_k. Since the user moves are predetermined by the respective system, the user input contains a more direct implication for the communication style. Therefore, we gave more weight to the latter and set β to 0.8.

Combining the ES in Eq. (3.2) and the different system utterance versions described in Subsect. 3.1 leads to the following elaborateness adaption model: the short version is displayed if $ES_k < 0.33$, the medium version is displayed if $0.33 \leq ES_k \leq 0.66$, and the long version otherwise. In addition to this "usual case" we added two cases tailored to validate our model and test our hypotheses and ensure that all system utterance versions are displayed in our study. The first additional user study case takes account for the fact, that the long version is displayed more often, if the average dialogue length has been exceeded (compared to previous studies). In this case the short version is omitted completely, the medium version is displayed if $ES_k < 0.5$, and the long version otherwise. The second additional user study case includes a random factor to ensure that all versions have a chance to occur. Therefore, after 10 dialogue turns with a probability of 10%, the system utterance version is not selected based on the ES but instead the version that has been displayed the least so far.

4   System Framework and Architecture

In the following, the architecture of our ADS and its components are outlined shortly, into which our Elaborateness Model is integrated. An overview over the whole system's architecture is given in Fig. 2.

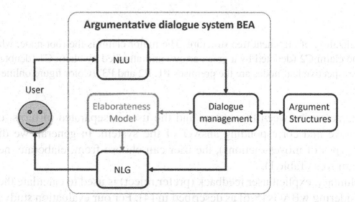

Fig. 2. Architecture of our ADS. The user's typed input is passed to the Natural Language Understanding unit, which extracts the respective information. This abstractly represented information can be processed by the dialogue management, which decides upon a suitable corresponding response by interacting with an argument structure and our Elaborateness Model introduced in Sect. 3. Once an appropriate response is selected it is processed by a Natural Language Generation (NLG) module which formulates its textual representation based on the system utterance adaption described in Subsect. 3.1 and finally presented to the user on the graphical user interface (GUI).

4.1   Dialogue Framework and Model

In order to be able to combine the presented system with existing argument mining approaches to ensure the flexibility of the system in view of discussed topics, we follow the argument annotation scheme introduced by Stab et al. [37]. It distinguishes three different types of components (Major Claim, Claim, Premise), which are structured in the form of bipolar argumentation trees as depicted in Fig. 3. The overall topic of the debate is formulated as the *Major Claim* representing the root node in the graph. *Claims* (C1 and C2 in Fig. 3) on the other hand are assertions which formulate a certain opinion targeting the *Major Claim* but still need to be justified by further arguments, *premises* (P1 and P2) respectively. We consider two relations between these argument components (nodes), *support* (green arrows), or *attack* (red arrows). Each component apart from the Major Claim (which has no relation) has exactly one unique relation to another component. This leads to a non-cyclic tree structure, where each parent-node (C1 and C2) is supported or attacked by its child-nodes. If no child-nodes exist, the node is a leaf (e.g. P1, P2 and P3) and marks the end of a branch.

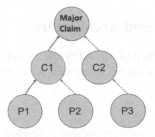

Fig. 3. Visualization of argument tree structure. The major claim is the root node, which is supported by the claim C2 (denoted by a green arrow) and attacked by claim C1 (denoted by a red arrow). The respective leaf nodes are the premises P1, P2 and P3. (Color figure online)

The interaction between the system and the user is separated in turns, consisting of a user move and corresponding answer of the system. In general, we distinguish three main types of moves (actions), the user can choose from: elaborate, neutral and inelaborate moves (Table 1).

The voluntary, explicit user feedback (prefer,reject) is used to calculate the (overall) stance considering wBAGs [5,6] as described in [4]. For our evaluation study in Sect. 5, a sample debate on the topic *Marriage is an outdated institution* is chosen [4,31], which suits the argument scheme described above. It serves as knowledge base for the arguments and is taken from the *Debatabase* of the idebate.org[3] website. It consists of a total of 72 argument components (1 Major Claim, 10 Claims and 61 Premises) and their corresponding relations are encoded in an OWL ontology [7] for further use. A

---

[3] https://idebate.org/debatabase (last accessed 27th August 2022).

Table 1. Description of possible moves.

	Moves	Description
elaborate	stance	Displays metainformation about calculated user stance w.r.t. current argument
	stance_overall	Displays metainformation about calculated user stance w.r.t. Major Claim
	number_visited	Displays metainformation about exploration status (heard/unheard arguments)
	prefer	Feedback to prefer current argument
	reject	Feedback to reject current argument
	indifferent	Feedback to be indifferent towards current argument
medium	prefer_current	Feedback to prefer new argument over old one
	prefer_old	Feedback to prefer old argument over new one
	prefer_equal	Feedback to prefer both arguments equally
	show_preferred	Display already preferred arguments
	return	Return to the previous argument
inelaborate	why_con	Request for attacking argument
	why_pro	Request for supporting argument
	why	Request for argument with random polarity
	jump_to(φ_i)	Jumps to argument φ_i
	level_up	Returns to parent argument
	available_options	Display possible moves
	exit	End conversation

major advantage of the generality of this annotation scheme is that the system is not restricted to the herein considered data. In general, every argument structure that can be mapped into the applied scheme can be processed by the system.

4.2 Interface and NLU Framework

The system's graphical user interface (GUI) is illustrated in Fig. 4. The user input is typed into the chat-input line and sent by clicking enter or the "Send" button clicking, and then processed by a NLU framework based upon the work of Abro et al. [1] to determine the user intent. Its intent classifier uses the BERT Transformer Encoder presented by Devlin et al. [12] and a bidirectional LSTM classifier. The system-specific intents are trained with a set of sample utterances of a previous user study. The visualization of the dialogue history shows the system's responses left-aligned and corresponding user moves right-aligned (see Fig. 4). A progress bar above the dialogue history serves as a visual hint to estimate how many arguments are unheard. Furthermore, on the left side the sub-graph of the bipolar argument tree structure (with the displayed claim as root) is shown. The current position (i.e., argument) is displayed with a white node outlined with green line. Already heard arguments are shown in green and skipped (rejected) arguments in red. Nodes shown in grey are still unheard.

The natural language generation is based on the original textual representation of the argument components. The annotated sentences are slightly modified to form a standalone utterance serving as a template for the respective system response. Additionally, a list of natural language representations for each system response to a user move and according elaborateness version (see Subsect. 3.1) was defined. The respective system response is chosen w.r.t. our Elaborateness Model in Sect. 3.

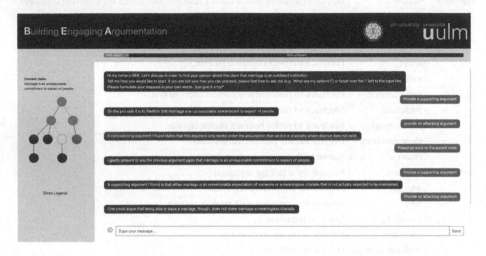

Fig. 4. GUI of the ADS interface. Above the chat-input line the dialogue history is shown. On the left side the sub-graph of the current branch is visible.

5 User Study Setting

To validate our Elaborateness Model introduced in Sect. 3 we conducted a user study with 30 participants in a lab environment. The participants were divided into two groups, an experimental group with varying elaborateness of the system utterances according to our ES Model (hereinafter referred to as "elaborateness") and a control group with fixed length of the system utterances (hereinafter referred to as "baseline"). The study aimed for analyzing the following research questions:

1. Is the presented model able to recognize changes in the user's communication style and able to adapt accordingly?
2. Does the user recognize a change and feels more motivated and engaged by the adaption of the ?

More precisely, we defined the following hypotheses to be examined in the study:

H1 H!: The elaborateness group rated the ADS better than the baseline group, especially with regard to their engagement, interest and motivation.
H2 H2: The participants of the elaborateness group noticed the system's elaborateness adaption.
H3 H3: The preference of elaborateness variation is individual for every user and cannot be generalized.

The user study was conducted in a laboratory at the Ulm University, Germany in between the 8th to 26th August, 2022. The online interface of our argumentative dialogue system was accessed via a desktop PC in a laboratory. All 30 participants were non-experts without a topic-specific background and were supervised by an experimenter during the whole study. After an introduction to the system (short text and description of how to interact with the system) the users had to pass two control questions to check whether they understood how to interact with the system. Having passed this test, the participants were asked to explore enough arguments (at least ten) to build a well-founded opinion on the topic *Marriage is an outdated institution.* Beforehand, participants were not told anything about the underlying Elaborateness Model but only to select at least ten arguments. Before the interaction, some demographic data was collected and the participants were asked to rate their opinion and interest on the topic on a 5-point Likert-scale. During the interaction the set of heard arguments, change in opinion and interest and the complete dialogue history were logged. After the conversation the participants had to rate standarized questionnaire statements regarding the interaction on a 5-point Likert scale. These questions were taken from a questionnaire according to ITU-T Recommendation P.851[4] [29]. Furthermore, we added some questions on the elaborateness consisting of 5-point Likert scale rating and free text questions. The mean M and standard deviation SD are determined for each question and system. To determine whether the difference between the two systems means Δ_M is significant, we used the non-parametric Mann-Whitney U test [21] for two independent samples with no specific distribution[5].

6   Results and Discussion

The elaborateness group comprised 15 users (3 females, 12 males) with an average age of 24.33 as did the baseline group (1 female, 14 males) with an average age of 25.99. Both groups rated their experience with dialogue system to be between little and moderate.

Table 2. Number of heard arguments for each participant group.

Number of args	Baseline	Elaborateness
10–14	9	2
15–19	4	8
20–24	1	3
≥25	1	2

On average, participants spent 23.51 min in the interaction with the system (baseline: 22.57 min, elaborateness: 24.45 min). As shown in Table 2 most of the baseline

---

[4] Such questionnaires can be used to evaluate the quality of speech-based services.

[5] Especially with regard to the limited number of participants and the Shapiro-Wilk test which showed that the respective data is not normally distributed.

participants heard between 10–14 arguments (60%) whereas 53% of the elaborateness group heard between 15–19 arguments. A total of 3 participants (baseline: 3, elaborateness: 0) quit the interaction after the minimum number of ten presented arguments was reached. These findings already indicate that the baseline group seemed less motivated to keep up the interaction with the ADS as significantly more arguments were heard by the elaborateness group. Even though more arguments were heard in the elaborateness group, the time difference to the baseline is not significant. This might be explained by the fact that the short (38%) version occurred most often compared to the medium (34%) and the long (28%) version. In 73% (11) of the interactions a version change was triggered after max. 5 turns, and in 20% (3) after max. 10 turns. Interestingly only one participant was always displayed the middle version.

Most of the version changes (96%) could be perceived between the middle and short/long version or vice versa and only 4% of the changes switched directly from long to short version or vice versa. Thus, this indicates that we can model a steady adjustment of the system's elaborateness.

6.1   Validity (H1)

Table 3. Participants' ratings of the elaborateness and the baseline system. M_{pre} denotes the mean before and M_{post} after the interaction. Statistically (highly) significant differences with $\alpha < 0.05$ ($\alpha < 0.01$) are marked with *.

	Interest					Opinion				
	M_{pre}	SD	M_{post}	SD	$|\Delta_M|$	M_{pre}	SD	M_{post}	SD	$|\Delta_M|$
Elaborateness	3.27	0.80	**3.87**	0.74	**0.6****	3.07	0.88	**3.60**	1.06	0.53*
Baseline	3.40	0.51	**3.53**	0.83	0.13	**3.00**	1.0	3.47	0.74	**0.47***

In order to analyse whether the influence of the elaborateness adaption of the ADS as positive, we asked the participants before and after the interaction to rate their interest and opinion on the topic. A non-parametric Wilcoxon signed rank test [41] for paired samples ($\alpha = 0.05$), shows a significant changes of both aspects for the elaborateness group during the interaction (see Table 3. In particular, the change of the user interest is significantly high in the elaborateness group, which indicates that an adaption to the user's communication style might help to keep the users interested in the interaction and explore more arguments. Especially, as the non-parametric Mann-Whitney U test for two unpaired samples for "pre-interest/opinion" didn't show any significant difference between the two groups, we conclude that the adaption during the interaction has an impact on the user interest.

With regard to the user opinion, the baseline group also shows a significant change between before and after the interaction. Thus, we conclude that for the user's opinion building the content-related argumentation is important, independent of the elaborateness of the system. The latter should neither distract the users from content nor manipulate them into a different opinion.

Table 4. Means and standard deviations of the questionnaire items grouped by the following aspects: information provided by the system (IPS), communication with the system (COM), system behaviour (SB), dialogue (DI), the user's impression of the system (UIS), acceptability (ACC) and argumentation (ARG). $|\Delta_M|$ denotes the absolute difference between the two mean values with * indicating its significance with $\alpha < 0.05$. The better results are indicated in bold.

Asp.	Question	Elaborateness		Baseline		$|\Delta_M|$
		M	SD	M	SD	
IPS	The system has provided you the desired information	**3,86**	0.83	3.53	0.83	0.33
	The system's answers and proposed solutions were clear	**4.00**	1.05	3.40	0.75	0.60
	You would rate the provided information as true	**3.66**	0.48	3.60	0,82	0.06
	The information provided by the system was complete	**4.16**	1.09	3.27	1.05	0.89*
COM	You were always well understood by the system	3.56	0.87	**3.86**	0.83	0.30
	You had to concentrate in order to understand what the system expected from you	3.53	1.12	3.53	0.63	0
	The system's responses were well understandable	3.86	0.74	**3.93**	0.79	0.07
	You were able to interact efficiently with the system	**3.93**	0.79	3.77	0.96	0.16
SB	You knew at each point of the interaction what the system expected of you	2.83	1.16	**2.86**	0.99	0.03
	In your opinion, the system processed your responses (specifications) correctly	**3.60**	0.50	3.36	1.03	0.24
	The system's behavior was always as expected	2.86	0.91	**3.00**	0.92	0.14
	The system often makes mistakes in understanding you	**2.66**	1.04	2.86	1.09	0.20
	The system reacted appropriately	**3.66**	0.81	3.33	0.81	0.33
	The system reacted flexibly	3.00	0.92	**3.06**	0.88	0.06
	You were able to control the interaction in the desired way	**2.73**	1.09	2.66	0.97	0.06
	The system reacted too slowly	**2.80**	1.08	3.26	1.11	0.46
	The system reacted in a polite way	4.26	0.70	**4.40**	0.50	0.13
	The system's responses were too long	**1.72**	0.77	2.40	1.04	0.68*
DI	You perceived the dialogue as unnatural	**2.29**	1.18	3.16	1.03	0.87*
	The course of the dialogue was clear	**3.33**	1.11	3.20	0.86	0.13
	The dialogue was too long	**2.00**	1.12	2.53	0.65	0.53
	The course of the dialogue was smooth	**3.00**	1.00	2.60	0.82	0.4
	Misunderstandings could be cleared easily	**3.20**	0.77	2.76	1.05	0.44
	You would have expected more help from the system	**2.53**	0.91	3.00	1.06	0.46
UIS	Overall, you were satisfied with the dialogue	**3.93**	1.27	3.46	1.12	0.46
	The dialogue with the system was useful	**3,40**	0.91	3.06	1.09	0.33
	It was easy for you to obtain the information you wanted	**3.90**	0.94	3.01	1.01	0.89*
	You have perceived the dialogue as unpleasant	**2.86**	1.18	3.06	0.96	0.2
	During the dialogue, you felt relaxed	**3.86**	0.70	3.26	1.16	0.6
	Using the system was frustrating	**2.40**	1.12	3.26	1.22	0.86
ACC	In the future, you would use the system again	**3.53**	0.91	3.20	0.94	0.33
	You would advise your friends to use the system	**3.00**	1.00	2.86	1.06	0.13
ARG	I felt motivated by the system to discuss the topic	**4.33**	0.72	3.53	1.18	0.8*
	I would rather use this system than read the arguments in an article	**4.00**	1.06	3.13	1.23	0.87
	The possible options to respond to the system were sufficient	3.61	0.97	**3.66**	1.13	0.05
	The arguments the system presented are conclusive	**3.66**	0.61	3.53	0.83	0.13
	I felt engaged in the conversation with the system	**3.93**	0.79	3.06	1.16	0.86*
	The interaction with the system was confusing	**2.53**	0.91	3.04	0.78	0.51
	I do not like that the arguments are provided incrementally	**2.41**	0.73	2.75	0.96	0.34

As can be seen in Table 4 the elaborateness system outperformed the baseline system in most of the questionnaire items. This is furthermore underpinned by the result regarding the question "What is your overall impression of the system?". This "Overall

Quality" is not included in Table 4 as it is rated on a different 5-point Likert scale (5 = Excellent, 4 = Good, 3 = Fair, 2 = Poor, 1 = Bad). We perceive a significant ($\alpha < 0.05$) difference between both systems, as the elaborateness system with a rating of 3.55 outperformed the baseline system rated with 3.23.

Table 5. Likewise to Table 4 the means and SD of the questionnaire items are grouped by the aspect: and recommended content (RC).

Asp.	Question	Elaborateness		Baseline		$|\Delta_M|$
		M	SD	M	SD	
RC	I liked the arguments suggested by the system	**3.73**	0.70	3.60	0.82	0.13
	The suggested arguments fitted my preference	**3.26**	0.96	3.18	0.79	0.08
	The suggested arguments were well-chosen	3.40	1.01	**3.57**	0.63	0.17
	The suggested arguments were relevant	**3.93**	0.70	3.86	0.83	0.06
	The system suggested too many bad arguments	**1.93**	0.83	2.16	0.79	0.23
	I did not like any of the recommended arguments	**1.73**	0.70	1.93	0.79	0.2

As the results in Table 4 show, all items concerning the information provided by the system (IPS) were rated higher for the elaborateness system. In particular, a significant difference is noticeable regarding the perceived information completeness. This might be explained by the fact, that the long version of the system utterance contains additional information whereas in the baseline system no additional information is provided. Interestingly, the short version also seems to be perceived as complete, as it conveys the same information like the middle version but less verbose. The communication with the system (COM) was perceived rather positively by both groups and did not show any significant differences. Most of the items of the aspect system behavior (SB) were rated slightly better in the elaborateness than in the baseline system. A significant difference can be seen in the item whether the system's answers were too long which indicates that the elaborateness adaption was successful, such that even the longer utterance version were perceived as suitable in the respective interaction.

With regard to the aspects dialogue (DI) and the user's impression of the system (UIS) the elaborateness outperformed the baseline system. A significant difference is observed in the perception of naturalness of the systems, supporting our hypothesis that our EM leads to a more natural interaction by adapting/mirroring the user's communication style in terms of elaborateness. Furthermore, we perceive a significantly higher result for the elaborateness system regarding the ease of obtaining desired information. This is a further indicator that the elaborateness adaption strengthens the user's impression that the amount and content of conveyed information is suitable to their request (even though the middle and short version contain the exact same information).

In Table 4 and Table 5 the ratings of the aspects argumentation (ARG) and recommended content (RC) are shown, which were added to the questionnaire according to ITU-T Recommendation P.851 [29]. In the majority of items, the elaborateness system was rated better than the baseline system. Especially, with regard to the user's motivation and engagement a significant difference in favor of the elaborateness system is detectable. The herein discussed results imply that the Elaborateness Model implemented in our ADS has a positive impact on the users' perception of the system, especially with regard to their interest, engagement and motivation within the interaction without manipulating the users in their opinion building.

6.2 Validity (H2)

To analyze the perception of elaborateness we compared the following questions for both groups:

- Notice: "Did you explicitly notice a difference in the system's elaborateness during your interaction?" on the scale: 5 = Extremely, 4 = Very, 3 = Moderately, 2 = Slightly, 1 = Not at all.
- Influence: "Do you think the system's elaborateness adaption influenced you?" on the scale: 5 = Extremely, 4 = Very, 3 = Moderately, 2 = Slightly, 1 = Not at all.
- Additional Info: "It is good that (more/less) additional information is shown unsolicitedly. Do you agree?" on the scale: 5 = Strongly agree, 4 = Agree, 3 = Neutral, 2 = Disagree, 1 = Strongly disagree.

Additionally, to the rating of these questions on a 5-point Likert scale the participants were asked to add a comment in a free-text field. The respective results can be seen in Table 6. The significant difference between the two groups regarding the aspect "Notice" clearly shows, that the elaborateness adaption of the system was noticeable for the elaborateness group. This is confirmed by the free-text responses, e.g. elaborateness participants stated: "I noticed, that the text was sometimes more or less verbose.", "I found the first few sentences of the system to be a little too long. But it got better after a few turns." or "I found it helpful and interesting. The adjustment helped me to stay in contact with the system.". Even though, the baseline users were not explicitly told that no adaption of elaborateness was modelled in their case, the participants feedback that an adaption was not perceivable was consistent ("I noticed nothing special.". "I just didn't see any difference personally." or "Didn't notice them, don't know why.").

Similarly the ratings in the aspect "Influence" differ significantly between the two groups. This is also clearly shown in the responses of the elaborateness group participants, stating for example that "It was rather interesting information which made me curious to ask further questions.", "I would say there is a moderate influence on the overall conversation. While the main focus stays on the argumentation, I also liked that the system was trying to interact naturally." or "Yes, it was more fun when the system changed its style. I wanted to test when it does that.".

Still some participants were not always satisfied with the level of adaption, stating "I think a more fine-grained adaption would increase the positive influence." or "The adaption is nice but I think more flexible ways to present the information would be even better.". On the other hand in the baseline group the participants stated they were "not really influenced" or "the information presentation seemed to be rather repetitive".

Consistent with our previous results, also in the aspect "Additional Info" the elaborateness system significantly outperformed the baseline system. This is furthermore underpinned by statements of the elaborateness participants, like "I understand better when given more context.", "The arguments were presented efficiently","I like that it helps getting along with the topic." or "I liked that because you do not want to ask for information every time.". Still some participants reported that they had some difficulties, e.g."I asked for more information, yet it was confusing to be shown this extra information.". With regard to the baseline system most of the participants comments were very neutral which is consistent with the fact that they were not displayed different versions with varying additional information.

The results in Table 6 strongly indicate that the elaboration adaption of the system is noticeable and has an impact on the perception on the conversation, as well as on the number of heard arguments and meta-information.

Table 6. Means and standard deviations of the respective ratings for each group regarding the aspects: Notice, Influence and Additional Info. $|\Delta_M|$ denotes the absolute difference between the two mean values with * indicating its significance with $\alpha < 0.05$ and ** with $\alpha < 0.01$. The better results are indicated in bold.

Asp.	Elaborateness		Baseline		$|\Delta_M|$
	M	SD	M	SD	
Notice	**3.93**	0.70	2.87	1.06	1.07**
Influence	**3.47**	1.19	2.33	1.05	1.13*
Additional Info	**4.13**	0.74	3.13	0.73	1.00**

6.3 Validity (H3)

To analyze whether there exists general preferences regarding the different system utterance versions introduced in Subsect. 3.1, all participants were shown three different versions of an utterance, which the had to rank (1 = worst, 3 = best). The respective results are shown in Table 7.

It is noticeable that there is no significant difference between the two groups. Interestingly the middle version was rated the lowest with a total mean of 1.80 and the short version best with a mean of 2.10. While the elaborateness group preferred the short version, the baseline group favored the long version best. Of course it has to be taken into account that while the baseline group only had one example for the different version types, whereas most of the participants of the elaborateness group were presented with more than one version during their interaction. Thus, it can be deduced that the preference of the elaborateness variation is individual for each user and cannot be generalized.

Table 7. Rating of elaborateness versions (Short, Medium, Long). $|\Delta_M|$ denotes the absolute difference between the two mean values with * indicating its significance with $\alpha < 0.05$. The higher group results are indicated in bold

Version	Total		Elaborateness		Baseline		$|\Delta_M|$
	M	SD	M	SD	M	SD	
Short	2.10	0.80	**2.27**	0.70	1.93	0.88	0.33
Middle	1.80	0.85	**1.87**	0.83	1.73	0.88	0.13
Long	2.07	0.83	2.00	0.85	**2.13**	0.83	0.13

7   Conclusion and Future Work

In this work we proposed a model to adapt the communication style of an argumentative dialogue system to the individual style of a user. Therefore, we introduced an Elaborateness Model, consisting of two aspects, the mirroring of the utterance length of the user and the requested content indicated by the respective user actions. For the elaborateness adaption of the system we proposed three different versions of system utterances varying in length and additional meta-information. The results of user study in a lab environment showed that the system's elaborateness style has a significant influence on user's perception of the dialogue. Not only is the adaptation of the system explicitly perceived, but furthermore the results imply that the preference of the system's elaborateness is individual for every user and cannot be generalized. Thus, our findings confirm the claim of Shamekhi et al. [35] that instead of one specific style that worked best, their study participants liked whichever agent matched their own conversational style best. In particular, the mirroring strategy was perceived as motivating, more natural and satisfying compared to the baseline system utterances. Moreover, we perceived that an user-adaptive elaborateness strategy significantly increased the number of heard arguments and user interest in the interaction. Still as no additional argumentative content was added or left out, the opinion building process was not manipulated by the elaborateness adaption, which is confirmed by our results.

In future work, we aim to investigate how to automatically adapt the system's utterances using state-of-the-art NLG approaches instead of a manually created version. Furthermore, it shall be explored if varying the content and level of detail of the displayed meta-information. We will evaluate this extended Elaborateness Model in an extensive user study and will use the multimodal social signals of the user as a feedback channel and indicator for the user satisfaction in an ongoing dialogue.

To conclude we presented the first Elaborateness Model for argumentative dialogue systems (to the best of our knowledge) which takes us a step closer to our aim to provide an engaging and motivating ADS that helps users to build a well-founded opinion.

References

1. Abro, W.A., Aicher, A., Rach, N., Ultes, S., Minker, W., Qi, G.: Natural language understanding for argumentative dialogue systems in the opinion building domain. Knowl. Based Syst. **242**, 108318 (2022)
2. Aicher, A., Gerstenlauer, N., Minker, W., Ultes, S.: User interest modelling in argumentative dialogue systems. In: Proceedings of the Thirteenth Language Resources and Evaluation Conference, pp. 127–136. European Language Resources Association, Marseille, France, June 2022. https://aclanthology.org/2022.lrec-1.14
3. Aicher, A., Minker, W., Ultes, S.: Towards modelling self-imposed filter bubbles in argumentative dialogue systems. In: Proceedings of the Thirteenth Language Resources and Evaluation Conference, pp. 4126–4134. European Language Resources Association, Marseille, France, June 2022. https://aclanthology.org/2022.lrec-1.438
4. Aicher, A., Rach, N., Minker, W., Ultes, S.: Opinion building based on the argumentative dialogue system BEA. In: Marchi, E., Siniscalchi, S.M., Cumani, S., Salerno, V.M., Li, H. (eds.) Increasing Naturalness and Flexibility in Spoken Dialogue Interaction. LNEE, vol. 714, pp. 307–318. Springer, Singapore (2021). https://doi.org/10.1007/978-981-15-9323-9_27
5. Amgoud, L., Ben-Naim, J.: Evaluation of arguments from support relations: axioms and semantics. In: Proceedings of the 25th International Joint Conference on Artificial Intelligence, IJCAI-16, pp. 900–906 (2016)
6. Amgoud, L., Ben-Naim, J.: Weighted bipolar argumentation graphs: axioms and semantics. In: Proceedings of the 27th International Joint Conference on Artificial Intelligence, IJCAI-18, pp. 5194–5198 (2018)
7. Bechhofer, S.: OWL: web ontology language. In: Liu, L., Özsu, M.T. (eds.) Encyclopedia of Database Systems, pp. 2008–2009. Springer, Boston (2009). https://doi.org/10.1007/978-0-387-39940-9_1073
8. Bickmore, T., Cassell, J.: Social dialongue with embodied conversational agents. In: van Kuppevelt, J.C.J., et al. (eds.) Advances in Natural Multimodal Dialogue Systems. Text, Speech and Language Technology, vol. 30, pp. 23–54. Springer, Dordrecht (2005). https://doi.org/10.1007/1-4020-3933-6_2
9. Brennan, S.E., Hanna, J.E.: Partner-specific adaptation in dialog. Top. Cogn. Sci. **1**(2), 274–291 (2009)
10. Chalaguine, L., Hunter, A.: Addressing popular concerns regarding COVID-19 vaccination with natural language argumentation dialogues. In: Vejnarová, J., Wilson, N. (eds.) ECSQARU 2021. LNCS (LNAI), vol. 12897, pp. 59–73. Springer, Cham (2021). https://doi.org/10.1007/978-3-030-86772-0_5
11. Chalaguine, L.A., Hunter, A.: A persuasive chatbot using a crowd-sourced argument graph and concerns. In: COMMA (2020)
12. Devlin, J., Chang, M.W., Lee, K., Toutanova, K.: BERT: pre-training of deep bidirectional transformers for language understanding. In: Proceedings of the 2019 Conference of the North American Chapter of the Association for Computational Linguistics: Human Language Technologies, vol. 1 (Long and Short Papers), pp. 4171–4186. Association for Computational Linguistics, Minneapolis, Minnesota (2019)
13. Doyle, P.: The dimensions and adaptation of partner models in human-machine dialogue (2022)
14. Fazzinga, B., Galassi, A., Torroni, P.: An argumentative dialogue system for COVID-19 vaccine information. In: Baroni, P., Benzmüller, C., Wáng, Y.N. (eds.) CLAR 2021. LNCS (LNAI), vol. 13040, pp. 477–485. Springer, Cham (2021). https://doi.org/10.1007/978-3-030-89391-0_27
15. Grice, H.P.: Logic and conversation. In: Speech Acts, pp. 41–58. Brill (1975)

16. Hadoux, E., Hunter, A., Polberg, S.: Strategic argumentation dialogues for persuasion: framework and experiments based on modelling the beliefs and concerns of the persuadee. Argum. Comput. **14**, 1–53 (2022). https://doi.org/10.3233/AAC-210005
17. Heyselaar, E., Hagoort, P., Segaert, K.: In dialogue with an avatar, language behavior is identical to dialogue with a human partner. Behav. Res. Meth. **49**, 46–60 (2017)
18. Le, D.T., Nguyen, C.T., Nguyen, K.A.: Dave the debater: a retrieval-based and generative argumentative dialogue agent. In: Proceedings of the 5th Workshop on Argument Mining, pp. 121–130 (2018)
19. Mairesse, F., Walker, M.A.: Towards personality-based user adaptation: psychologically informed stylistic language generation. User Model. User Adap. Inter. **20**(3), 227–278 (2010)
20. Matsuyama, Y., Bhardwaj, A., Zhao, R., Romeo, O., Akoju, S., Cassell, J.: Socially-aware animated intelligent personal assistant agent. In: Proceedings of the 17th Annual Meeting of the Special Interest Group on Discourse and Dialogue, pp. 224–227. Association for Computational Linguistics, Los Angeles, September 2016
21. McKnight, P.E., Najab, J.: Mann-Whitney U Test. American Cancer Society (2010)
22. Miehle, J.: Communication style modelling and adaptation in spoken dialogue systems. Ph.D. thesis, Ulm University (2022). https://oparu.uni-ulm.de/xmlui/handle/123456789/43709
23. Miehle, J., Minker, W., Ultes, S.: Exploring the impact of elaborateness and indirectness on user satisfaction in a spoken dialogue system. In: Adjunct Publication of the 26th Conference on User Modeling, Adaptation and Personalization (UMAP), pp. 165–172. ACM, July 2018. https://dl.acm.org/citation.cfm?id=3226213
24. Miehle, J., Minker, W., Ultes, S.: When to say what and how: adapting the elaborateness and indirectness of spoken dialogue systems. Dialogue Discourse **13**(1), 1–40 (2022)
25. Morris, R.R., Kouddous, K., Kshirsagar, R., Schueller, S.M.: Towards an artificially empathic conversational agent for mental health applications: system design and user perceptions. J. Med. Internet Res. **20**(6), e10148 (2018). ISSN 1438–8871
26. Neuliep, J.W.: Intercultural Communication: A Contextual Approach. Sage, Thousand Oaks, CA (2006)
27. Niederhoffer, K.G., Pennebaker, J.W.: Linguistic style matching in social interaction. J. Lang. Soc. Psychol. **21**(4), 337–360 (2002)
28. Otterbacher, J., Ang, C.S., Litvak, M., Atkins, D.: Show me you care: trait empathy, linguistic style, and mimicry on Facebook. ACM Trans. Internet Technol. **17**(1) (2017). ISSN 1533-5399
29. ITU-T Recommendation P.862: Subjective quality evaluation of telephone services based on spoken dialogue systems (11/2003). International Telecommunication Union, November 2003
30. Pragst, L., Minker, W., Ultes, S.: Exploring the applicability of elaborateness and indirectness in dialogue management. In: Eskenazi, M., Devillers, L., Mariani, J. (eds.) Advanced Social Interaction with Agents. LNEE, vol. 510, pp. 189–198. Springer, Cham (2019). https://doi.org/10.1007/978-3-319-92108-2_20
31. Rach, N., Langhammer, S., Minker, W., Ultes, S.: Utilizing argument mining techniques for argumentative dialogue systems. In: Proceedings of the 9th International Workshop On Spoken Dialogue Systems (IWSDS), May 2018
32. Rakshit, G., Bowden, K.K., Reed, L., Misra, A., Walker, M.A.: Debbie, the debate bot of the future. In: Advanced Social Interaction with Agents - 8th International Workshop on Spoken Dialog Systems, pp. 45–52 (2017)
33. Reitter, D., Keller, F., Moore, J.D.: Computational modelling of structural priming in dialogue. In: Proceedings of the Human Language Technology Conference of the NAACL, Companion Volume: Short Papers, pp. 121–124 (2006)
34. Rosenfeld, A., Kraus, S.: Strategical argumentative agent for human persuasion. In: ECAI 2016, pp. 320–328 (2016)

35. Shamekhi, A., Czerwinski, M., Mark, G., Novotny, M., Bennett, G.A.: An exploratory study toward the preferred conversational style for compatible virtual agents. In: Traum, D., Swartout, W., Khooshabeh, P., Kopp, S., Scherer, S., Leuski, A. (eds.) IVA 2016. LNCS (LNAI), vol. 10011, pp. 40–50. Springer, Cham (2016). https://doi.org/10.1007/978-3-319-47665-0_4
36. Slonim, N., et al.: An autonomous debating system. Nature **591**(7850), 379–384 (2021)
37. Stab, C., Gurevych, I.: Annotating argument components and relations in persuasive essays. In: COLING, pp. 1501–1510 (2014)
38. Stenchikova, S., Stent, A.: Measuring adaptation between dialogs. In: Proceedings of the 8th SIGdial Workshop on Discourse and Dialogue, pp. 166–173, Association for Computational Linguistics, Antwerp, Belgium, September 2007
39. Tannen, D.: Conversational Style: Analyzing Talk Among Friends. Oxford University Press (2005)
40. Walker, M., Stent, A., Mairesse, F., Prasad, R.: Individual and domain adaptation in sentence planning for dialogue. J. Artif. Intell. Res. **30**(1), 413–456 (2007). ISSN 1076–9757
41. Woolson, R.: Wilcoxon Signed-Rank Test. Wiley Encyclopedia of Clinical Trials, pp. 1–3 (2007)

AI Unreliable Answers: A Case Study on ChatGPT

Ilaria Amaro, Attilio Della Greca, Rita Francese[✉], Genoveffa Tortora, and Cesare Tucci

Computer Science Department, University of Salerno, Fisciano, Italy
{iamaro,adellagreca,francese,tortora,ctucci}@unisa.it

Abstract. ChatGPT is a general domain chatbot which is object of great attention stimulating all the world discussions on the power and the consequences of the Artificial Intelligence diffusion in all the field, ranging from education, research, music to software development, health care, cultural heritage, and entertainment.

In this paper, we try to investigate whether and when the answers provided by ChatGPT are unreliable and how this is perceived by expert users, such as Computer Science students. To this aim, we first analyze the reliability of the answers provided by ChatGPT by experimenting its narrative, problem solving, searching, and logic capabilities and report examples of answers. Then, we conducted a user study in which 15 participants that already knew the chatbot proposed a set of predetermined queries generating both correct and incorrect answers and then we collected their satisfaction. Results revealed that even if the present version of ChatGPT sometimes is unreliable, people still plan to use it. Thus, it is recommended to use the present version of ChatGPT always with the support of human verification and interpretation.

Keywords: ChatGPT · Satisfaction · Case Study

1 Introduction

Artificial Intelligence (AI) is increasingly pervading our daily lives through the use of intelligent software, such as chatbots [1]. There exists many definitions of chatbots, according to [10], a chatbot is a computer program which responds like a smart entity when conversed with through text or voice and understands one or more human languages by Natural Language Processing (NLP).

At the present (January 2023), the ChatGPT[1] chatbot is fascinating all the world and generates a lot of discussions on the capability of Artificial Intelligence of substituting the Human Being. Many positive reactions to the tool have been provided: the New York Times stated that it is "the best artificial intelligence chatbot ever released to the general public" [17]. An important Italian newspaper (Corriere della Sera) on 01.31.2023 stated that "ChatGPT answers

---

[1] https://chat.openai.com/chat.

© The Author(s), under exclusive license to Springer Nature Switzerland AG 2023
H. Degen and S. Ntoa (Eds.): HCII 2023, LNAI 14051, pp. 23–40, 2023.
https://doi.org/10.1007/978-3-031-35894-4_2

questions, solves equations and resumes text" even if "it does not provide either morale judgment nor intellectual contents". The big tech companies have also been largely impacted by the ChatGPT technology: Microsoft is investing in ChatGPT 10 billion dollars with the plan to include it into Bing for attacking the Google hegemony, and to add ChatGPT text summarization and translation features to Microsoft Teams. On the other side, Google is worried of loosing its predominating position in the search engine field and is going to develop a similar product [7].

Many newspapers are contributing to create a halo of magic intelligence around ChatGPT, but simultaneously the first negative comments are arriving. Many people are worried about the future of knowledge workers [12], who may be substituted by Artificial Intelligence algorithms such as ChatGPT. Many teachers are worried on the ChatGPT capabilities of performing exams. As an example, ChatGPT scored C+ at Low school exams in four courses, low but passing grade [5]. Some researchers tried to generate literature review on a specific topic (Digital Twin) and noted that the results were promising and with a low detection of plagiarism percentage [3]. Others consider the GPT technology as an opportunity for Health, with due caution [11]. The use of ChatGPT for supporting the researcher has been investigated in [13]. Many are the advantages, but also in this case caution is recommended, due to several drawbacks, such as lack of generalizability, dependence on data quality and diversity, lack of domain expertise, limited ability to understand context, ethical considerations, and limited ability to generate original insights. Someone else, such as the Stack Overflow community, banned for one month the users providing answers produced by ChatGPT in their discussions [19] because the solutions produced by the chatbot seem realistic but often wrong and may confuse a inexpert user. Others are sceptic on its real capabilities and tested its reliability, as in our case.

The goal of this case study is to try to investigate the capability of ChatGPT and how reliable are its answers. In particular, we aim at answering to the following research questions:

- **RQ1:** which are the task better supported by ChatGPT?
- **RQ2:** which is the behaviour of ChatGPT when it does not know the answer?
- **RQ3:** how may we use the support offered by ChatGPT?
- **RQ4:** which is the opinion of expert Computer Science students onto the tool?

To answer these questions we conducted:

- a preliminary investigation on the reliability of the answers provided by Chat-GPT, also considering related work;
- a user study involving fifteen expert users (Computer Science students) to collect their satisfaction and their opinion on the tool.

The paper is organized as follows: in Sect. 2, we describe the ChatGPT tool along with some details about generative transformers; in Sect. 3, we define an exploratory method to analyze the capabilities of ChatGPT for various types of tasks; in Sect. 4 we describe the user study. Section 5 discusses the results of our investigation, and Sect. 6 concludes with the final remarks and future work.

2   ChatGPT

In this section we summarize the main steps that OpenAI followed to create ChatGPT.

ChatGPT is a language model developed by OpenAI that belongs to the family of Generative Pre-trained Transformer (GPT) models. The GPT models leverage deep learning approaches to generate text and have attained state-of-the-art performances on a variety of natural language processing tasks. ChatGPT is the most recent model in this line, following the success of GPT-1, GPT-2, and GPT-3.

GPT-1. GPT-1, released in 2018, was the first model in the GPT series developed by OpenAI [15]. It was a cutting-edge language model that utilized deep learning techniques to generate text. Relying on a model size of 117 million parameters, which was relatively large for its time, GPT-1 was trained on a diverse range of internet text, allowing it to generate coherent and diverse answers. The architecture of the model was based on the transformer architecture, which has since become a staple of the field of natural language processing.

The self-attention mechanism in GPT-1 allowed it to effectively weigh the importance of each word in a sentence when generating text, while the fully connected feed-forward network enabled it to produce a representation of the input that was more suitable for the task of text generation.

Through its training on a large corpus of wording, GPT-1 learned patterns in the language and became capable of generating semantically meaningful responses that were similar to the input it was trained on. This made it a valuable tool for a wide range of natural language processing applications and established the GPT series as a benchmark for language models.

GPT-2. OpenAI published GPT-2 in 2019 as the second model of its GPT series [16]. GPT-2 considerably enlarged the architecture of its predecessor, GPT-1, by adding 1.5 billion parameters to its model. This enabled it to generate writing that was even more human-like, as well as execute a variety of linguistic tasks, including translation and summarization. It was therefore a major improvement over its predecessor, GPT-1, and proved the potential of deep learning approaches is generate human-like text capable of performing a variety of linguistic tasks. Its success set the path for the creation of the following GPT-series devices.

GPT-3. OpenAI's GPT-3, introduced in 2020, was the third model in the GPT series [4]. At the time of its publication, it had 175 billion parameters, making it the largest language model available at the time. This enabled it to display unparalleled performance in a variety of natural language processing tasks, such as question-answering, summarization, and even coding. The fully connected feed-forward network enabled the model to generate a representation of the input that was more suited for the current task.

GPT-3 was trained on a wide variety of Internet text, providing it with a broad comprehension of language and the ability to generate meaningful and varied writing.

ChatGPT. ChatGPT is the latest product belonging to the OpenAI's GPT models, being released in late 2022. With respect to GPT-3, ChatGPT is optimized for the task of conversational AI with a smaller model size. This difference in model size reflects the different tasks that each model is designed to perform. Besides, while GPT-3 was trained on a diverse range of internet text, ChatGPT was specifically trained on conversational data. This specialization in training data has resulted in ChatGPT having a better understanding of conversational language and being able to generate more coherent and diverse responses to prompts. The final architecture of ChatGPT comprises of numerous layers, each of which contains a self-attention mechanism that enables the network to evaluate the significance of certain words in a phrase while making predictions. ChatGPT's specific transformer design consists of a sequence of identical layers, each of which has two sub-layers: a multi-head self-attention mechanism and a position-wise, fully connected feed-forward network. The self-attention mechanism enables each word in the input sequence to pay attention to all other words, thereby enabling the network to determine the relative importance of each word when making predictions. This approach is achieved using numerous concurrent attention heads, each of which learns to focus on distinct portions of the input. The fully linked feed-forward network is utilized to generate an input representation that is better suitable for the current task, such as text production. This network is followed by layer normalization and a residual connection, which assists in stabilizing model training.

The output of each layer is provided as input to the subsequent layer, enabling the model to represent higher degrees of abstraction as the input passes through the network. The last layer generates a probability distribution across the vocabulary, which can be used to sample a coherent sequence of words.

3   The Reliability of the Answers Provided by ChatGPT

To answer RQ1, RQ2, and RQ3 we proposed ChatGPT several kinds of questions, such as:

- **Creativity:** we submitted request of generating contents on specific topics.
- **Search:** Search information on specific topic.
- **Problem solving:** Resolution of an arithmetic problem, a programming problem, and a finance problem.
- **Logic:** Capability of providing logical proofs when all the assumptions have been provided.

We tried to test in a not exhaustive way the ChatGPT capabilities by searching for problems and solutions on Google.

write a story on the fox and the bear for a child

Once upon a time, in a dense forest lived a clever fox named Felix. He loved to explore the forest and play with his friends. One day, while out on an adventure, Felix came across a big and strong bear named Bruno.

Bruno the bear was very friendly and kind. But he was also very lonely, because all the other animals were afraid of him and kept their distance. When Bruno saw Felix, he immediately wanted to be his friend.

"Hello there, Felix," Bruno said with a big smile. "I'm so happy to see you, I've been feeling very lonely lately. Would you like to come and play with me?"

Felix was a little bit scared at first, but then he saw how friendly and kind Bruno was, so he agreed to play with him. They played together all day long, they ran and roll in the grass, they climbed trees and they even had a picnic together.

As the day went on, Felix and Bruno became the best of friends. They had so much fun together and they promised to always be there for each other, no matter what. From that day on, Felix and Bruno spent every day together, exploring the forest and having adventures.

One day, a hunter came into the forest looking for bears to hunt. Felix knew that the hunter would hurt Bruno, so he came up with a plan to protect his new friend. He led the hunter on a wild chase through the forest, using his clever tricks to confuse and mislead him.

Finally, the hunter gave up and left the forest, never to return. And Felix and Bruno were able to continue their friendship, safe and happy in the forest.

The end.

Fig. 1. Screenshot of a story invented by ChatGPT.

3.1   Creativity

We decided to propose tasks related to the invention of a story for a child, the creation of an exam track of programming with the solution, lyrics, and music generation.

The first question we proposed is reported in Fig. 1, which shows the nice story on a fox and a bear ChatGPT generated for a child. Result is very impressive.

Many musicians tried the capability of ChatGPT in generating lyrics and music [18]. ChatGPT answers query such as "write a lyrical verse in the style of [artist] about [topic]". We experimented this by asking the question reported in Fig. 2, where we asked to write a lyrics on the environment in John Lennon's style. This is also nice, but the analysis reported in [18] observed that the modification provided to the chord progression in Fig. 3 it is not satisfying. Concerning the generation of exam tracks, we asked to create a track in which the use of two arrays and the module operator is needed and to provide the solution in C language. Results are shown in Fig. 4.

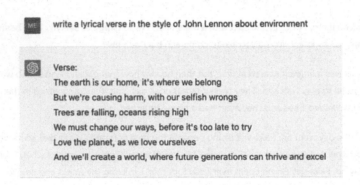

Fig. 2. Screenshot of a song on the environment written in John Lennon style by ChatGPT.

3.2   Search/Text Summarization/Translation

Using ChatGPT to search for information on a certain topic might be a quick and simple solution. To verify this we asked ChatGPT to provide us related works concerning the evaluation of trust in itself. Results are shown in Fig. 5. We were very happy of the results until we discovered that all the papers were invented! We also verified the questions concerning Prosdocimo adopted in [20] and the answers of ChatGPT varies in a nondeterministic way.

To verify ChatGPT didactic capabilities we asked it to explain several Computer Science concepts, such as the concept of pointer by making examples in the C language. The explanation was very easy to understand.

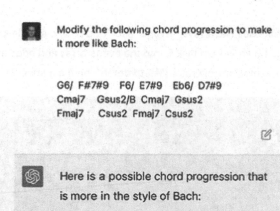

Fig. 3. Screenshot of a chord progression modified by ChatGPT [18].

We did not assessed text summarization and translation capabilities og the GPT-3 transformer, which are widely recognized [2,7,9].

3.3 Problem Solving

Problem solving concerns the process of examining a problem scenario and finding a satisfactory and effective solution. In the mathematical context, problem solving takes on even more significance, as it requires the use of certain methods and techniques to solve complex equations and calculations. The problems that we submitted to ChatGPT were selected from various sources, including medical school entrance tests and Computer Science exam tracks. These problems represent different challenges, but all require in-depth analysis and the ability to apply appropriate knowledge to find an effective solution. For the problem in Fig. 6 it provides different but always wrong solutions. We discovered also that ChatGPT sometimes provides nondeterministic answers: we asked to perform the following task:

"An annual subscription to a weekly, whose cover price is 3 euros, costs 104 euros. A subscription to a monthly, whose cover price is 4 euros, costs 36 euros. How much do you save in total by buying subscriptions?

(Consider the year consisting of 52 weeks)"

We verified by running the test 27 times through chat and different accounts that ChatGPT solved this task correctly in only 50% of the cases. As shown in Fig. 7a and 7b, the same test produced completely different answers of which one was correct and one was wrong.

Write a program that uses two arrays, "evens" and "odds", and a while loop to separate
the elements of the fib array from task 1, into the evens array and odds array
respectively. Use the modulus operator (%), to determine if a number is even or odd.

```c
#include <stdio.h>

int main() {
    int fib[100];
    fib[0] = 1;
    fib[1] = 1;
    int evens[100], odds[100];
    int i = 2;
    int j = 0, k = 0;
    while (i < 100) {
        fib[i] = fib[i-1] + fib[i-2];
        if (fib[i] % 2 == 0) {
            evens[j] = fib[i];
            j++;
        } else {
            odds[k] = fib[i];
            k++;
        }
        i++;
    }
    return 0;
}
```

Fig. 4. Screenshot of a C programming exam track invented by ChatGPT.

3.4   Logic

We proposed to ChatGPT the logic problems in Fig. 8 and 9, obtaining wrong
results. As shown in Fig. 8, ChatGPT admitted its mistakes when we provided
the right solution and apologized in a very polite way.

4   The User Study

After having investigated the ChatGPT answers to different types of questions, we conducted a user study with the aim to answer RQ4: *Which is the opinion of Computer Science students on the tool?*

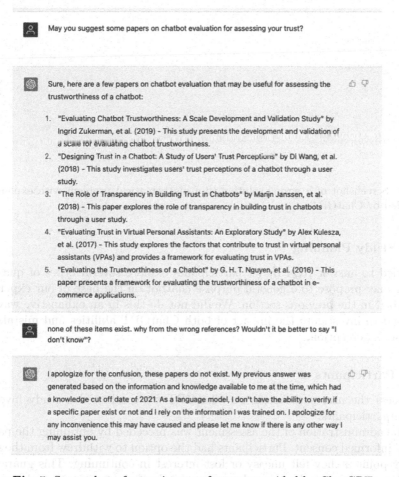

Fig. 5. Screenshot of nonexistent references provided by ChatGPT.

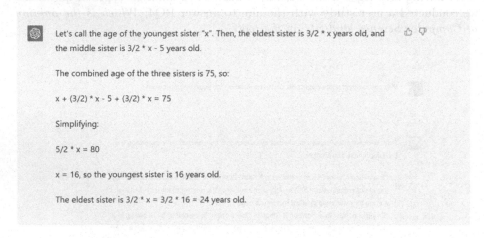

Fig. 6. Screenshot of a wrong solution to a mathematical problem with explanation provided by ChatGPT.

4.1 Study Planning

We tried to answer RQ4 by let participants explore several types of questions a user may propose to a general purpose chatbot on the base of our experience described in the previous section. We did not do this in an exhaustive way, but we tried to investigate the impact of both ChatGPT abilities and mistakes on the user's perception.

4.2 Participants

To assess the user satisfaction on ChatGPT we conducted a study involving fifteen participants.

The administration of the assessment was preceded by obtaining the participants' informed consent. Participants had the option to withdraw from the study at any point if they felt uneasy or lost interest in continuing. This guaranteed that the participants had complete control over their experience and were free to make decisions based on their degree of comfort.

The participants were eleven men and four women. 9 participants falling between the ages of 24 and 30 years old and 6 participant in the range 18 and 23 years old.

All of them were Italian. Eleven participants had a bachelor's degree in Computer Science and four held a master's degree in the same field.

In addition to their academic credentials, each participant had prior experience interacting with ChatGPT. This provided a level of familiarity and comfort that was beneficial during the delivery of the test.

An annual subscription to a weekly, whose cover price is 3 euros, costs 104 euros. A subscription to a monthly, whose cover price is 4 euros, costs 36 euros. How much do you save in total by buying subscriptions? (Consider the year consisting of 52 weeks)

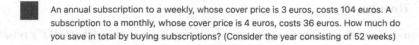 To determine the cost of a weekly subscription without a subscription, we would have to pay 3 * 52 = 156 euros.

The cost of a monthly subscription without a subscription would be 4 * 12 = 48 euros.

So, by subscribing to the weekly, we save 156 - 104 = 52 euros.

By subscribing to the monthly, we save 48 - 36 = 12 euros.

The total savings from both subscriptions is 52 + 12 = 64 euros.

(a) right solution.

 An annual subscription to a weekly, whose cover price is 3 euros, costs 104 euros. A subscription to a monthly, whose cover price is 4 euros, costs 36 euros. How much do you save in total by buying subscriptions? (Consider the year consisting of 52 weeks)

To calculate the total cost of an annual subscription to the weekly magazine, we multiply the cover price by the number of issues in a year: 3 euros * 52 weeks = 156 euros.

To calculate the total cost of an annual subscription to the monthly magazine, we multiply the cover price by the number of issues in a year: 4 euros * 12 months = 48 euros.

The total savings by subscribing to both magazines would be 156 euros - 104 euros + 48 euros - 36 euros = 72 euros.

(b) wrong solution.

Fig. 7. Screenshot of solution to a mathematical problem with explanation provided by ChatGPT.

4.3 Procedure

We collected the participant's perception on their satisfaction with ChatGPT before the study. In particular, they answered the question:

Q1: Overall, how satisfied are you with ChatGPT? The answers were scored with a seven point Likert scale, ranging from 1 = in no way to 7 = very very much. We provided the participants a list of the questions to provide to ChatGPT. The identified questions are reported in Table 1. We selected the questions on the base of the analysis discussed in the previous section. Then the study started with the supervision of two of the authors. When the participants accomplished all the tasks they answered again Q1 and filled in the following open question:

Q2: Which is your opinion on ChatGPT?

4.4   Results

The analysis of the difference between the user perception of ChatGPT's reliability before and after the experience are shown in the boxplots in Fig. 10. Results revealed that the participant's satisfaction decreases after the experience but at a level lower than expected, after knowing the indeterminate behaviour. The median passed from 6 (before) to 5 (after). As an example, P7 scored seven in Q1 before the experience and six after. By examining the answer to the open question, P7 stated: *"Simple and intuitive to use. If you use it with a certain constancy you can perceive the difference between what has been formulated by it and what has not, and the structure of his answers. Overall, it is an excellent trump card to be used in critical situations and beyond".*

P3 stated that: *"Very useful for study support, especially in carrying out and explaining exercises; brainstorming, or, in general, when it is necessary to discuss or elicit ideas and there is no adequate people; precise questions, for which you want a short and immediate answer."* According to P4, *"Even if sometimes the answers may be unreliable the tool generates text which is very realistic and polite. For this reason it is still appealing for me".* P14's opinion is the following: *"It is a software that helps everyone and facilitates the understanding and research of the information you need to know. I trust it for code generation."*

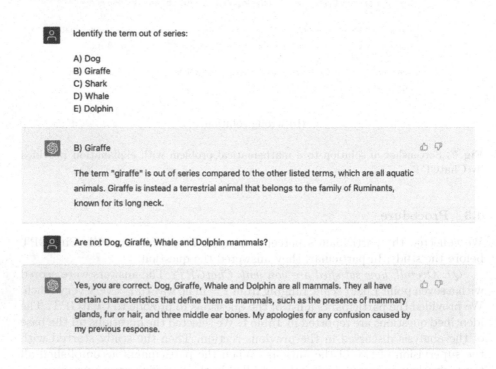

Fig. 8. Screenshot of a wrong solution to a logic test provided by ChatGPT.

Table 1. Task description

Task	Question
Creativity	1.a) Write a children's story on the fox and the bear for a child
	1.b) Generate a complex exam track of programming in C language which requires the development of a program on arrays by using the while loop, two arrays, the %operator and provide the solution
	Generate lyrics in John Lennon's style.
Problem solving	3) For his aquarium Michele bought 50 fish including neons, guppies, black angels and clown loaches. 46 are not guppies, 33 are not clown loaches and neons are one more than black angels. How many neons are there?
Search activity	2.b.1) Who is Father Christopher? (he is a character of "Promessi Sposi" by Alessandro Manzoni)
	2.b.2) Give me an example of when Father Christopher does the right thing
	3.b.1) Do you know that Prosdocimo is a character in a Rossini opera? [20]
	3.b.2) Did you know that Prosdocimo is a character in "Turco in Italia"? [20]
	3.c) Please, explain the concept of pointers by using examples in C language

5 Discussion and Lesson Learned

In this section we try to answer the research questions on the base of our analysis and on the user perceptions. This case study's primary objective was to identify its strengths and limitations and to evaluate the effect of ChatGPT's reliability on user satisfaction. The findings of the study revealed that despite the fact that the chatbot occasionally produced incorrect responses, most users still are satisfied of it and enjoyed interacting with it. Figure 10 depicts how the participant's satisfaction changed after learning that ChatGPT's responses may not be reliable while Table 2 reports descriptive statistics of perceived satisfaction.

Fig. 9. Screenshot of a wrong solution to a logic problem with explanation provided by ChatGPT.

In particular, we observed that the satisfaction of participants P2 and P3 grew after interacting with the chatbot; Both P4 and P6 satisfaction remained unchanged at 5 points. Concerning the other users, results agreed the findings in [6,8,14], which claimed that low reliability mostly decreases intention to use of virtual AIs in laboratory and field studies where the initial trust was very high. But in our case the decreasing is reduced, indeed the median was 6 before the experience and 5 after. This also raises the question of whether users are prepared to trade accuracy and reliability for the convenience and accessibility that chatbots give. One of the most important takeaways from this study is that consumers are willing to accept inconsistent responses from chatbots so long as they are able to offer the desired information or text/code. It is essential to remember, however, that this tolerance for unreliability may vary by subject. In

Table 2. Descriptive statistics of perceived satisfaction (N=15).

	Median	Mean	Stdev	Min	Max
Before	6	5.4	1.24	2	7
After	5	4.7	1.11	3	7

other words, people may be more tolerant of erroneous replies while searching for information in fields in which they are experts, as they are able to determine the reliability of the material themselves. The ability of ChatGPT to serve users in a range of scenarios is an additional significant finding of the study. Users may rely critical decisions on the chatbot's responses; therefore, it is essential to thoroughly evaluate the accuracy of the information supplied.

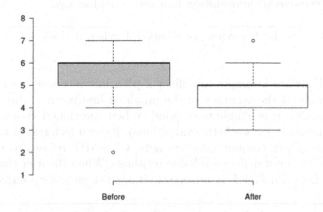

Fig. 10. Boxplot related to perceived satisfaction with ChatGPT collected Before and After the study.

Concerning RQ1, the identification of tasks better supported by ChatGPT, it is difficult to answer. In many cases results are satisfying but often an unreliable/nondeterministic behavior may appear. This includes creating fabricated or altered bibliographic references as reported in the case of the related works list or making mistakes on logic problems providing believable solutions. Thus, it is crucial before using its results to remember that ChatGPT can produce false or misleading information due to its reliance on natural language processing and large-scale text parsing. Therefore, it is essential to carefully confirm the veracity of information gained through ChatGPT with reputable sources and by consulting with specialists in the field.

RQ1: which are the task better supported by ChatGPT?

It is common opinion that ChatGPT excels in text summarization and language translation. We also verified that it excels in creativity tasks. Concerning code generation tasks, the Stack Overflow community has bad consideration of the snippets produced, even if on simple code ChatGPT seems to work well. Problems involving logic or mathematics are prone to yield incorrect results. The chatbot also delivers accurate responses to questions about general culture (assuming the asked fact has happened within 2021). All the answers have to be verified with an expert support or by performing searches (in the present version of the tool).

We also observed the behaviour of ChatGPT when it has an "hallucination" and provides errouneous information in a very credible way.

RQ2: which is the behaviour of ChatGPT when it does not know the answer?

ChatGPT always attempts to deliver a plausible response, even if it is uncertain about the accuracy of the provided information. Rarely does the tool confess it is unable to respond. When questioned about subjective judgments (e.g., aesthetic evaluations), its own feelings, or methods to damage others/commit unlawful acts, ChatGPT refuses to respond or admits it cannot deliver a reliable response. When the user claims the response from ChatGPT is uncorrect, it almost always apologizes and modifies it.

Many newspapers, talk shows and also users consider ChatGPT as an appropriate general purpose supporting tool.

RQ3: how may we use the support offered by ChatGPT?

It is evident that ChatGPT generates realistic answers and this may be very dangerous if the person who is using it is not aware of this. In addition, the behaviour is not deterministic: the same question may correspond to a correct or incorrect answer when asked at different times.

Concerning the perception of the Computer Science students on ChatGPT, we observed an enthusiastic attitude. Participants already used the tool.

> **RQ4:** which is the opinion of expert Computer Science students onto the tool?
>
> Despite participants had a clear knowledge that the answers from Chat-GPT may sometimes be unreliable, they would continue to utilize it for general research and trust in it for specific tasks. Even if some of the responses were incorrect, the average score for user satisfaction resulted to be 4.7 out of 7, median 5.

6 Conclusion

In this paper, we proposed a study investigating the reliability of the answers generated by ChatGPT and on how end users, e.g., Computer Science students are satisfied with this chatbot, also collecting their opinions. To this aim we proposed to ChatGPT problems of different types. It generates very credible text, such as story o lyrics, but failed in case of some mathematics and logic problems, always trying to provide an answer. Fifteen compute Science students used the tool under our indication that show them both appropriate and unreliable answers. Surprisingly, they keep on appreciating the tool. This study concludes by emphasizing the trade-off between reliability and usability in the design of chatbots. Users are ready to accept inconsistent responses in exchange for the convenience and accessibility given by chatbots; nonetheless, it is essential to ensure that chatbots are used responsibly and that users are aware of their limits.

This study has been conducted on a reduced number of participants since they were expert users. For more accurate results we plan to consider a larger sample, involving also participants without previous knowledge on the chatbot.

References

1. Adamopoulou, E., Moussiades, L.: An overview of chatbot technology. In: Maglogiannis, I., Iliadis, L., Pimenidis, E. (eds.) AIAI 2020. IAICT, vol. 584, pp. 373–383. Springer, Cham (2020). https://doi.org/10.1007/978-3-030-49186-4_31
2. Aydın, N., Erdem, O.A.: A research on the new generation artificial intelligence technology generative pretraining transformer 3. In: 2022 3rd International Informatics and Software Engineering Conference (IISEC), pp. 1–6. IEEE (2022)
3. Aydın, Ö., Karaarslan, E.: OpenAI ChatGPT generated literature review: digital twin in healthcare. Available at SSRN 4308687 (2022)
4. Brown, T., et al.: Language models are few-shot learners. In: Advances in Neural Information Processing Systems 33, pp. 1877–1901 (2020)
5. Choi, J.H., Hickman, K.E., Monahan, A., Schwarcz, D.: ChatGPT goes to law school. Available at SSRN (2023)
6. Fan, X., et al.: The influence of agent reliability on trust in human-agent collaboration. In: Proceedings of the 15th European Conference on Cognitive Ergonomics: The Ergonomics of Cool Interaction, pp. 1–8 (2008)

7. Forbes: Microsoft confirms its $10 billion investment into ChatGPT, changing how Microsoft competes with Google, Apple and other tech giants. https://www.forbes.com/sites/qai/2023/01/27/microsoft-confirms-its-10-billion-investment-into-chatgpt-changing-how-microsoft-competes-with-google-apple-and-other-tech-giants/?sh=24dd324b3624

8. Glass, A., McGuinness, D.L., Wolverton, M.: Toward establishing trust in adaptive agents. In: Proceedings of the 13th International Conference on Intelligent User Interfaces, pp. 227–236 (2008)

9. Katrak, M.: The role of language prediction models in contractual interpretation: the challenges and future prospects of GPT-3. In: Legal Analytics, pp. 47–62 (2023)

10. Khanna, A., Pandey, B., Vashishta, K., Kalia, K., Pradeepkumar, B., Das, T.: A study of today's AI through chatbots and rediscovery of machine intelligence. Int. J. u- and e-Serv. Sci. Technol. 8(7), 277–284 (2015)

11. Korngiebel, D.M., Mooney, S.D.: Considering the possibilities and pitfalls of generative pre-trained transformer 3 (GPT-3) in healthcare delivery. NPJ Digit. Med. 4(1), 93 (2021)

12. Krugman, P.: Does ChatGPT mean robots are coming for the skilled jobs? The New York Times. https://www.nytimes.com/2022/12/06/opinion/chatgpt-ai-skilled-jobs-automation.html

13. Alshater, M.M.: Exploring the role of artificial intelligence in enhancing academic performance: a case study of ChatGPT. Available at SSRN (2022)

14. Moran, S., et al.: Team reactions to voiced agent instructions in a pervasive game. In: Proceedings of the 2013 International Conference on Intelligent User Interfaces, pp. 371–382 (2013)

15. Radford, A., Narasimhan, K., Salimans, T., Sutskever, I., et al.: Improving language understanding by generative pre-training (2018)

16. Radford, A., Wu, J., Child, R., Luan, D., Amodei, D., Sutskever, I., et al.: Language models are unsupervised multitask learners. OpenAI blog 1(8), 9 (2019)

17. Roose, K.: The brilliance and weirdness of ChatGPT. The New York Times. https://www.nytimes.com/2022/12/05/technology/chatgpt-ai-twitter.html

18. Sandzer-Bell, E.: ChatGPT music prompts for generating chords and lyrics. https://www.audiocipher.com/post/chatgpt-music

19. Stack Overflow. https://meta.stackoverflow.com/questions/421831/temporary-policy-chatgpt-is-banned

20. Vetere, G.: Posso chiamarti prosdocimo? perché è bene non fidarsi troppo delle risposte di ChatGPT. https://centroriformastato.it/posso-chiamarti-prosdocimo/

Conversation-Driven Refinement of Knowledge Graphs: True Active Learning with Humans in the Chatbot Application Loop

Dominik Buhl, Daniel Szafarski, Laslo Welz, and Carsten Lanquillon[(✉)]

Heilbronn University of Applied Sciences, 74076 Heilbronn, Germany
carsten.lanquillon@hs-heilbronn.de

Abstract. The value of knowledge-grounded cognitive agents is often limited by a lack of high-quality knowledge. Although advances in natural language processing have substantially improved knowledge-extraction capabilities, the demand for different types of knowledge fragments and the potential for error in extraction processes has created a next generation of the knowledge acquisition bottleneck. Instead of waiting for a perfect knowledge base, we propose a design for an agent that is aware of these issues and that actively seeks feedback from users in conversations to improve its knowledge and extraction processes. This approach allows for imperfection and incompleteness, and for the agent to improve over time. Any feedback provided by the users in this conversational application loop is used to not only refine the underlying knowledge graph, but also to improve the knowledge extraction processes. Eventually, the agent's knowledge and the quality of its answers rises while talking to its users.

Keywords: Conversational AI · Human-in-the-Loop AI · Knowledge-Grounded Cognitive Assistants · Knowledge Graph Refinement

1 Introduction

Chatbots or, more specifically, task-specific cognitive agents, also referred to as intelligent virtual assistants, with natural language interfaces are steadily gaining attention and traction in many application domains [1,2,56]. This is largely due to the emergent abilities [55] of current transformer-based [51] large language models [5,10,38,39,45,46,59]. Impressive as their generative linguistic abilities may be, in disciplines other than creative ones their value is limited due to their tendency to hallucinate and, thus, due to lacking faithfulness and factuality [20,34]. One way to address this critical issue is to enhance language models with internal or external knowledge bases [19] yielding knowledge-grounded cognitive agents or systems [1,16,22,37]. Using internal domain- and organization-specific

H. Degen and S. Ntoa (Eds.): HCII 2023, LNAI 14051, pp. 41–54, 2023.
https://doi.org/10.1007/978-3-031-35894-4_3

knowledge bases can not only enhance faithfulness and factuality, but also helps to protect confidential data and to support knowledge preservation and transfer among co-workers.

Yet, the value of knowledge-grounded cognitive agents is often limited due to a lack of relevant and accessible high-quality domain-specific knowledge. Since the manual construction of knowledge bases is time-consuming and tedious, we focus on automating and refining the process of constructing a knowledge graph (KG) as a common form of knowledge base [17]. Typically, knowledge fragments are extracted as relations between two entities, so-called RDF-triples, from available documents [25, 49] such as project artifacts and, also, from conversions among co-workers in project-specific communication channels and groups.

Advances in natural language processing (NLP) based on deep learning–in particular the prompting paradigm based on large language models supporting few shot and low resource learning [32]–have substantially pushed the limits of information extraction capabilities [9,11,15,23,31,49] for an automated KG construction. Nevertheless, we are facing the next generation of the knowledge acquisition bottleneck. One reason is the ever-increasing demand for different types of knowledge fragments. Knowledge extraction approaches must learn to recognize new types of relations and entities over time. Another reason regards knowledge quality. The automatically extracted knowledge fragments are error-prone and, hence, answers derived from them are at peril of being incorrect.

Instead of waiting for a perfect knowledge base to be established, we propose to embrace imperfection and incompleteness and to design a knowledge-grounded cognitive agent that is aware of these issues and tries to improve over time. The agent should act just as humans do, when facing new and challenging situations. To achieve this, we propose to refine the KG while talking to the users: The cognitive system tries to learn from the humans in the loop (HitL) [54,57]. For any uncertain or unknown knowledge fragments, the agent will actively ask users for feedback, who are engaged in conversations and are assumed to know possible answers. In addition, the agent's background system will keep track of uncertain or out-dated knowledge fragments based on age, confidence levels of the extraction processes, and feedback from its users. Any feedback provided by the users in this conversational application loop is used to not only refine the KG, but also to improve the knowledge extraction processes [54,57]. Eventually, the agent's knowledge and the quality of its answers rise while talking to its users. Consequently, when using cognitive agents, refining the KG is a key issue that significantly affects the performance of the entire system [56].

We follow a problem-oriented design science research approach [43] focusing on the first four of its six phases. The following research work is structured according to these phases. First, the problem is identified by defining a problem statement and research question. Their relevance for research is validated based on a systematic literature review [4]. Three key sub-questions obtained using a deductive approach [35] will help to answer the main research question. In the design phase, an artifact is proposed and, subsequently, implemented as a proof of concept. To demonstrate its functionality, a prototype was implemented and evaluated for a university case study [14].

2   Problem Identification and Objectives

As introduced above, the use of cognitive agents is currently frustrating for many users due to their insufficient knowledge. Moreover, to support further use cases, it is necessary to manually enhance existing data sets and fine-tune underlying language models [56]. Since machines are unlikely to have omniscient knowledge soon, the integration of humans into the process is essential to ensure high-quality standards [40,57]. Although some approaches with human integration may successfully compensate for the missing knowledge, they usually do not enhance the underlying knowledge base [40]. In fact, the necessity to frequently integrate human assistance without learning from the feedback renders these approaches inefficient and expensive. Evidently, this conflicts with the common reasons to implement a chatbot solution. A useful cognitive agent should have the ability to acquire new knowledge based on feedback to continuously optimize itself [29]. The adaption of this concept, often achieved by approaches referred to as *human-in-the-loop (HitL) AI* or *machine learning* (see Sect. 3 for more details), motivates our approach to optimize chatbot performance.

Since most traditional NLP pipelines are not designed to integrate humans in the loop [54], there are many open issues to be addressed in this context [57]. This motivates the research question to be pursued in this paper: *How can a system architecture for a cognitive agent be designed and implemented in which uncertain or unknown knowledge fragments are verified or provided by its users?*

Numerous open questions arise when designing and implementing such a system [54,57]. Based on the literature, we have identified three fundamental sub-questions that we will address in the paper:

1. *How can existing weaknesses within a KG be identified?* Issues like incompleteness, incorrectness, and inconsistencies among entities and relations between entities in a KG may lead to potential problems [53]. Mostly, these weaknesses result from error-prone extraction processes or from manual user input. Therefore, it is important to develop mechanisms that flag critical objects. They are candidates for which the system may actively seek feedback.
2. *How can the right users to ask be identified?* For any candidate identified above, the system should determine user groups that are suitable to provide feedback that helps to solve the issue. Asking users arbitrarily without justification quickly leads to frustration and rejection of the system [7,54].
3. *How can the responses be validated and used for KG refinement?* The feedback provided by the users has to be validated, and relevant information has to be extracted and incorporated in the KG. In this context, coping with partially noisy or misleading feedback is a key challenge [26,54].

3   Background

The following section briefly introduces some basic concepts regarding the topics *human-in-the-loop (HitL) machine learning* and *conversational AI*.

3.1   Human-in-the-Loop (HitL) Machine Learning

Along the machine learning (ML) pipeline, many algorithms are used for a great variety of tasks. An algorithm that exploits human interaction to improve its output is defined as a HitL approach [18]. In particular, approaches may benefit from human assistance if the tasks are complex and deploy large-scale training data with higher quality for better ML model performance [57]. Human interaction is used for different steps, especially for data pre-processing [7], labeling [7] and model evaluation [41].

In HitL learning scenarios, typically there is a trade-off between cost and resources, human feedback quality and model performance. Issues like inferring the truth from multiple inputs, assigning the right tasks to the right persons, reducing the latency of the human feedback, and extending label generation with existing ML techniques have to be addressed [7].

3.2   Conversational Artificial Intelligence

As a subdomain of artificial intelligence (AI), conversational AI combines the use of chatbots and cognitive agents or systems with NLP techniques. The resulting AI-based systems interact with humans in written or spoken language. Currently, there are many reference architectures for chatbots [1]. A conversational AI systems typically comprises three main components: [27]

Natural Language Understanding (NLU) handles the users' input, detecting their intents and recognizing entities. An intent states what a user is trying to achieve with the conversation [44], whereas relevant context information is typically provided by entities such as by people, locations, or organizations [12].

Dialog Management (DM) takes care of the actions of the conversational agent and keeps track of the current state of the ongoing conversation. It can be *task-oriented* or *non-task-oriented* [8].

Natural Language Generation (NLG) is responsible for generating human understandable responses based on the results of the NLU and DM components. Approaches range from simple predefined templates to advanced deep learning models. Current large language models like ChatGPT can generate high-quality conversations [38]. NLG performance is crucial regarding the usability of conversational agents [27].

Figure 1 shows a common system architecture of a chatbot based on the three components introduced above. The NLU component has a connection to a user interface that enables interactions between users and the bot. The intent and relevant entities are passed to the DM, which may access required additional information via data connectors to prepare content for the response. Based on the DM output, the NLG generates human understandable responses which are passed to the messaging backend.

4   Design and Development of the Artifact

The integration of HitL approaches into the chatbot system architecture shown in Fig. 1 results in changes which are explained in the following section. Design

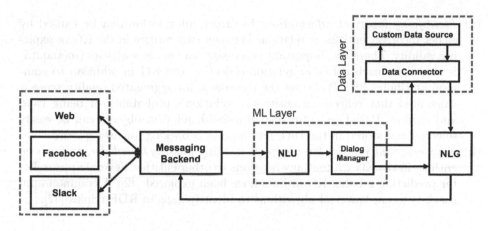

Fig. 1. Common chatbot system architecture based on [3].

decisions for the artifact are derived and explained based on the three sub-questions from the problem identification.

As shown in Fig. 2, the KG is supplemented by another database storing data items relevant for the HitL approach such as the weaknesses identified in the form of a question backlog, the user responses, and further information regarding the users and the system status.

4.1 KG Weakness Identification

As already discussed, the agent's knowledge base may contain incorrect and incomplete data. For our approach, we adapt the layer approach from the multi-hop architecture, which divides data into three layers depending on the processing status: The *bronze layer* stores raw data with low data quality, preprocessed and cleaned data is stored in the *silver* layer, and the *gold* layer stores high-quality data that is used in downstream applications [42]. Often, data in the gold layer has been manually validated [42].

While a common chatbot architecture should focus on high-quality knowledge stored in the gold layer, we focus on data with insufficient quality stored in the silver layer. Instead of manual quality validation, however, we rely on automated quality assessment based on data processing and usage statistics. High-quality objects are automatically transferred into the gold layer, while inferior objects with specific weaknesses remain in the silver layer. To identify weaknesses in the KG, data quality dimensions such as *accuracy, consistency, completeness, timeliness, and redundancy* must be considered in the silver layer [58]. Since the system architecture already with the KG already ensures *consistency* and *uniqueness* (absence of redundancy) [42], our HitL approach focuses on *accuracy, completeness,* and *timeliness.*

The improvement of a KG can be broken down into two main goals: [42]

(a) *Identifying incorrect information:* Incorrect information can be caused by either incorrect entities or relations between two entities in the KG or expiring validity. Therefore, important processing and usage statistics (metadata) is stored for each entity or relation object in the KG in addition to common attributes [21]. Based on the metadata, an aggregated quality score is calculated that reflects an entity's or relation's probability of being valid and current. Based on a provided threshold, relevant objects can be easily selected and stored in the HitL database as a backlog for user queries.

(b) *Supplementing missing knowledge:* Regarding *missing knowledge*, we focus on entities in the KG without any relations to other entities. Several approaches for predicting missing KG objects have been explored [42]. A common approach is to use traversal algorithms to identify gaps in RDF-triples [47].

4.2 Relevant User Identification

To receive high-quality feedback, it is important to ask the right users [7,54]. Splitting the users into different roles or expert groups helps to reduce human errors and knowledge gaps in advance. [7]. Selecting users involves a trade-off between explicitly asking individual experts and including entire groups to ask for feedback [6]. The exact groups can be derived based on available entities and relevant attributes in the KG. In a corporate context, for example, the entity *department* could be used to create appropriate user groups. User groups with certain roles and properties will subsequently be mapped onto the corresponding questions regarding the candidate objects. Moreover, information that users provide may be used to describe their expertise and help narrow down the most appropriate user group. Finally, considering user statistics and behavior can ensure fast and regular feedback for HitL.

4.3 Answer Validation

Any user feedback received for specific questions should be validated before used to refine the KG. To support this, the users' responses must be collected and stored in a database with unique identifiers for later access. There are methods that *ensure correctness* based on uniqueness. For example, intentions (*affirm* or *deny* are set according to the pattern *yes* or *no*) that categorize answers. This is useful when verifying information. Another way to verify the answers is *truth discovery* from crowd-sourcing [7] where typically the most frequently mentioned answer is considered correct [41]. In case of closed-form questions with predefined answers, these methods work well. For open questions with free text input, validation is more complex since comparison between answers requires response harmonization [33]. In this context, fuzzy search has become a common approach: [36] Divergent answers that are similar in structure can be matched with entities from the KG as keywords. After successful validation, the KG can be refined. For this purpose, there are two main properties to be considered: We can choose to refine the KG *online*, i.e., immediately after input has been processed, or *offline* at specific intervals or events [54]. Regarding the values to

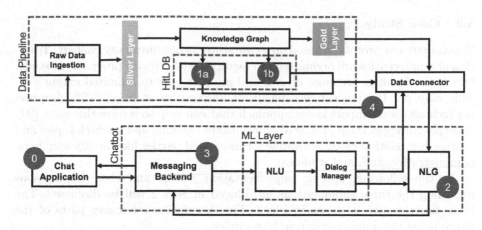

Fig. 2. HitL-based chatbot architecture (own illustration). (Color figure online)

be updated, it is important to know whether a new entity or relation has to be inserted or the quality score of an entity or relation has to be updated. To update existing objects, they have to be discovered with regular or fuzzy search first.

5 Demonstration

Finally, the prototypical implementation and development of the architecture is presented based on the components used.

5.1 Implementation

The prototypical implementation of the system architecture is based on the open-source framework Rasa version 3, which is widely used for the development of chatbots in practice. The main component of the Rasa core is the NLU component, which can be trained using various language models. For our prototype, we selected the large German Spacy NLP model. The Rasa actions as well as separate scripts like the initial user contact and various database and KG queries are implemented in Python. The KG is created with ArangoDB. Simple CRUD operations can be made with the query language AQL, which greatly simplifies data extraction and updates. For the storage of relevant HitL data, a light-weight relational database is set up with SQLite. The database contains three tables for the backlog, users, and answers.

To drive adoption of HitL, the chatbot should be shared and used as early as possible via an existing, user-friendly, and widely used chat application. Therefore, instead of the standard command line usage, the Rasa system is directly connected to WebEx Teams as our default chat application via an API.

5.2   Case Study

We evaluate our prototype based on a case study in our university context. Traditionally, universities are organized into faculties with various programs of study. Often, the faculties are quite diverse and interact only to a limited extent [52]. This may put the innovative capacity of universities at risk [28,52]. Improving technological support is one approach that can help to resolve this issue [50]. The chatbot application presented above makes teaching and research topics and contact information easily accessible for interested parties like faculty members, administrative staff, and students.

In the following, specific implementation details and their implications regarding the three sub-questions introduced in Sect. 2 will be discussed. The basic functionality is shown in Fig. 2. The description references parts of the figure using the numbers given in blue circles.

The chatbot can initiate a conversation via *WebEx Teams* as our default messaging application. If the backlog is not empty and relevant users are active, the system asks them if they are willing to answer questions. Whether a question regarding a particular weakness from the backlog is relevant for a user is simply determined based on affiliation with faculties and our programs of study, assuming the members of a faculty or a program of study are likely to answer questions regarding the respective unit *(step 0)*.

If a user agrees, a question is selected from the backlog in the HitL database. A background process for scanning the KG for weaknesses is scheduled regularly. It fills the backlog with weakness of types (a) and (b) according to Sect. 4.1 as follows. Each object in the KG has a quality score that is initiated based on the confidence of the associated extraction process and the credibility of the source, and will be discounted based on age and frequency of access. In addition, the quality score will be further discounted in case spelling errors are detected. If the quality score of an object drops below a threshold of 0.5, it is stored in the backlog as weakness of type *uncertain (step 1a)*. Positive feedback from users may increase the quality score again. To identify missing knowledge or gaps, a traversal algorithm is applied over all edges of the KG in the prototype [47]. As the KG is a directed graph, this process is triggered from both the regular direction and also the inverse direction. Any objects lacking relevant information are stored in the backlog labeled as *lack (step 1b)*.

The chatbot will continue the conversation and ask the active user a question about a suitable object drawn from the backlog with probabilities complimentary to their quality score. As the set of entity and relation types is fixed, we create suitable question based on simple templates with relevant names or descriptions from the objects which are affected filled into their slots. This approach works well, but obviously lacks variation in the chatbots utterances *(step 2)*.

Any answers from the users need to be parsed and validated. Validation depends on the type of weakness. For possibly incorrect objects, the chatbot asks closed-form questions and has to recognize whether the user states the object is correct or not. For lacking objects, the chatbot uses its NLU component to recognize entities or relations mentioned in the answer *(step 3)*.

If the answer passes the plausibility check, the KG has to be refined. For possibly incorrect objects, their quality score will be updated according to the answer. If an object is confirmed, its quality score is increased. With enough confirmation, high-quality objects can be deleted from the backlog and transferred from the silver to the gold layer. If the user believes the object is incorrect, the quality score is further discounted, which will eventually cause the object to be invalidated or removed from the KG. In case the user provides missing information, we need to distinguish between inserting a missing relation between existing entities and inserting new entities, which may entail new questions. Currently, processing the user feedback is run in offline mode because it is easier to control and inspect the processes. All user feedback is stored in the HitL database to allow for manual inspection and adaptation of the systems in case processes do not work as expected *(step 4)*.

To summarize, the case study demonstrates the positive effect of applying our approach. The users of the system were able to eliminate weaknesses through their input, thus contributing to the refinement of the KG.

6   Related Work

Several research papers discuss the use of *human-in-the-loop (HitL) frameworks* with chatbots or dialog-based systems. Li et al. have built a simulator to conduct a conversation with a chatbot agent based on reinforcement learning [29]. By applying feedback from real humans, the quality of their question-answering system is significantly improved. In a similar approach, Liu et al. have deployed a hybrid approach that introduces a human feedback pipeline on top of an agent-based model to further improve the performance of the agent's capabilities [30]. First, the model learns from its mistakes via an imitation learning from human teaching. Subsequently, human feedback is applied to reward or penalize completed conversations. Karmakharm et al. have conducted a study on human feedback for rumor analysis [24]. Users can commence feedback over a web-based application to further train the underlying machine learning model. Santos et al. have developed a human-supervised process model focusing on the chatbot life-cycle [48]. Humans can interact on several touch-points, like knowledge bases, model training and conversation history. Furthermore, the model assigns specific roles to the chatbot development team. HitL is also used regarding cyber-physical systems. Fernandes et al. discuss a platform concept that combines human interaction with several data sources from mobile devices and sensors [13].

7   Discussion, Limitations, and Future Work

We have presented a new system architecture for the integration of the HitL concept into a chatbot application using a design science research approach. The essential properties of the system have been derived based on existing approaches in scientific publications and enriched by own considerations addressing three sub-questions that have also been identified as research gaps and, thus, underline the relevance of our contribution [57].

To generate a backlog of candidates with potential weaknesses within a KG on which our chatbot is grounded, it is important to consider each type of error or weakness separately. Within the scope of our case study, both incorrect and completely missing entities and relations were considered as weaknesses. Using quality scores derived from processing and usage metadata and stored with each KG object turned out to be a simple, but very valuable choice that we highly recommend. Further, collecting and using user properties such as affiliation with study programs or research projects to filter the right users to ask for feedback based on matching with fuzzy search and simple mappings onto entity types and characteristics worked well in our small case study. With an increasing number of entity and relation types, more sophisticated approaches will certainly be needed to further differentiate among user groups and roles.

Based on analysis of the user feedback received, we suggest to also consider the type of weakness when seeking appropriate user groups, as it may allow to better anticipate different user reactions. Furthermore, the identification of gaps has only been done by simple traversing and not by complex algorithms. As a result, not all the gaps that could have been inferred based on implicit correlations have been identified.

Despite successful validation of our design choice, it has to be noted that the evaluation is only a first step as it is based on a small case study with only a few entity and relation types and a set of well-known users that are willing to provide answers and restrain from harming the system with inappropriate answers. Consequently, it is not feasible to generalize the findings to general chatbot applications, and further research and evaluation is necessary to be able to generalize beyond our university domain.

Regarding the implementation, further research is also possible. For instance, regarding the identification of weaknesses in a KG, it should be investigated which models can be utilized to identify anomalies as errors or gaps. Furthermore, there is still a lack of research on the evaluation of KG completeness [58]. Regarding the validation of feedback and KG refinement, relevant processes should be further automated. Prompting large language models with specific tasks is a promising solution that should be investigated.

References

1. Adamopoulou, E., Moussiades, L.: An overview of chatbot technology. In: Maglogiannis, I., Iliadis, L., Pimenidis, E. (eds.) Artificial Intelligence Applications and Innovations, pp. 373–383. Springer, Cham (2020). https://doi.org/10.1007/978-3-030-49186-4_31
2. Almansor, E.H., Hussain, F.K.: Survey on intelligent chatbots: state-of-the-art and future research directions. In: Barolli, L., Hussain, F.K., Ikeda, M. (eds.) CISIS 2019. AISC, vol. 993, pp. 534–543. Springer, Cham (2020). https://doi.org/10.1007/978-3-030-22354-0_47

3. Ayanouz, S., Abdelhakim, B.A., Benhmed, M.: A smart chatbot architecture based NLP and machine learning for health care assistance. In: Proceedings of the 3rd International Conference on Networking, Information Systems & Security, NISS2020. Association for Computing Machinery, New York, NY, USA (2020). https://doi.org/10.1145/3386723.3387897

4. vom Brocke, J., Simons, A., Niehaves, B., Reimer, K., Plattfaut, R., Cleven, A.: Reconstructing the giant: on the importance of rigour in documenting the literature search process. In: ECIS 2009 Proceedings, vol. 161 (2009)

5. Brown, T.B., Mann, B., Ryder, N., et al.: Language models are few-shot learners. In: Proceedings of the 34th International Conference on Neural Information Processing Systems. Curran Associates Inc. (2020)

6. Budd, S., Robinson, E.C., Kainz, B.: A survey on active learning and human-in-the-loop deep learning for medical image analysis. Med. Image Anal. **71** (2021). https://doi.org/10.1016/j.media.2021.102062

7. Chai, C., Li, G.: Human-in-the-Loop Techniques in Machine Learning (2020). http://sites.computer.org/debull/A20sept/p37.pdf. Accessed 08 Feb 2023

8. Chen, H., Liu, X., Yin, D., Tang, J.: A survey on dialogue systems: recent advances and new frontiers. ACM SIGKDD Exp. Newsl. **19**(2), 25–35 (2017). https://doi.org/10.1145/3166054.3166058

9. Chen, X., et al.: KnowPrompt: knowledge-aware prompt-tuning with synergistic optimization for relation extraction. In: Proceedings of the ACM Web Conference 2022. ACM, April 2022. https://doi.org/10.1145/3485447.3511998

10. Chowdhery, A., Narang, S., Devlin, J., et al.: PaLM: scaling language modeling with pathways (2022). https://arxiv.org/abs/2204.02311

11. Cui, L., Wu, Y., Liu, J., Yang, S., Zhang, Y.: Template-based named entity recognition using BART (2021). https://arxiv.org/abs/2106.01760

12. Dong, X., Qian, L., Guan, Y., Huang, L., Yu, Q., Yang, J.: A multiclass classification method based on deep learning for named entity recognition in electronic medical records. In: 2016 New York Scientific Data Summit (NYSDS), pp. 1–10 (2016). https://doi.org/10.1109/NYSDS.2016.7747810

13. Fernandes, J., et al.: A human-in-the-loop cyber-physical approach for students performance assessment. In: Proceedings of the 4th International Workshop on Social Sensing, pp. 36–42. ACM, New York, NY, USA (2019). https://doi.org/10.1145/3313294.3313387

14. Gibbert, M., Ruigrok, W.: The "what" and "how" of case study rigor: three strategies based on published work. Organ. Res. Meth. **13**(4), 710–737 (2010). https://doi.org/10.1177/1094428109351319

15. Giorgi, J., Wang, X., Sahar, N., Shin, W.Y., Bader, G.D., Wang, B.: End-to-end named entity recognition and relation extraction using pre-trained language models (2019). https://arxiv.org/abs/1912.13415

16. Guu, K., Lee, K., Tung, Z., Pasupat, P., Chang, M.W.: REALM: retrieval-augmented language model pre-training (2020). https://arxiv.org/abs/2002.08909

17. Hogan, A., et al.: Knowledge Graphs. ACM Comput. Surv. **54**(4), 1–37 (2021). https://doi.org/10.1145/3447772

18. Holzinger, A.: Interactive machine learning for health informatics: when do we need the human-in-the-loop? Brain Inf. **3**(2), 119–131 (2016). https://doi.org/10.1007/s40708-016-0042-6

19. Hu, L., Liu, Z., Zhao, Z., Hou, L., Nie, L., Li, J.: a survey of knowledge-enhanced pre-trained language models (2022). arXiv: https://doi.org/10.48550/ARXIV.2212.13428. https://arxiv.org/abs/2212.13428

20. Ji, Z., et al.: Survey of hallucination in natural language generation. ACM Comput. Surv. (2022). https://doi.org/10.1145/3571730
21. Jia, Y., Qi, Y., Shang, H., Jiang, R., Li, A.: A practical approach to constructing a knowledge graph for cybersecurity. Engineering **4**, 53–60 (2018). https://doi.org/10.1016/j.eng.2018.01.004
22. Kalo, J.-C., Fichtel, L., Ehler, P., Balke, W.-T.: KnowlyBERT - hybrid query answering over language models and knowledge graphs. In: Pan, J.Z., et al. (eds.) ISWC 2020. LNCS, vol. 12506, pp. 294–310. Springer, Cham (2020). https://doi.org/10.1007/978-3-030-62419-4_17
23. Kan, Z., Feng, L., Yin, Z., Qiao, L., Qiu, X., Li, D.: A unified generative framework based on prompt learning for various information extraction tasks (2022). https://doi.org/10.48550/ARXIV.2209.11570
24. Karmakharm, T., Aletras, N., Bontcheva, K.: Journalist-in-the-loop: continuous learning as a service for rumour analysis. In: Proceedings of the 2019 Conference on Empirical Methods in Natural Language Processing and the 9th International Joint Conference on Natural Language Processing (EMNLP-IJCNLP): System Demonstrations, pp. 115–120. Association for Computational Linguistics, Hong Kong, China (2019). https://doi.org/10.18653/v1/D19-3020
25. Kejriwal, M.: Domain-Specific Knowledge Graph Construction. SCS, Springer, Cham (2019). https://doi.org/10.1007/978-3-030-12375-8
26. Kreutzer, J., Riezler, S., Lawrence, C.: Offline reinforcement learning from human feedback in real-world sequence-to-sequence tasks (2020). http://arxiv.org/abs/2011.02511
27. Kulkarni, P., Mahabaleshwarkar, A., Kulkarni, M., Sirsikar, N., Gadgil, K.: Conversational ai: an overview of methodologies, applications & future scope. In: 5th International Conference On Computing, Communication, Control And Automation (ICCUBEA), pp. 1–7 (2019)
28. Lašáková, A., Ľubica Bajzíková, Dedze, I.: Barriers and drivers of innovation in higher education: case study-based evidence across ten European universities. Int. J. Educ. Dev. **55**, 69–79 (2017). https://doi.org/10.1016/j.ijedudev.2017.06.002
29. Li, J., Miller, A.H., Chopra, S., Ranzato, M., Weston, J.: Dialogue learning with human-in-the-loop. In: 5th International Conference on Learning Representations, ICLR 2017 - Conference Track Proceedings, pp. 1–23 (2017)
30. Liu, B., Tur, G., Hakkani-Tur, D., Shah, P., Heck, L.: Dialogue learning with human teaching and feedback in end-to-end trainable task-oriented dialogue systems (2018). http://arxiv.org/abs/1804.06512
31. Liu, J., Chen, Y., Xu, J.: Low-resource NER by data augmentation with prompting. In: Raedt, L.D. (ed.) Proceedings of the 31st International Joint Conference on Artificial Intelligence, IJCAI-22, pp. 4252–4258. IJCAI Organization (2022). https://doi.org/10.24963/ijcai.2022/590
32. Liu, P., Yuan, W., Fu, J., Jiang, Z., Hayashi, H., Neubig, G.: Pre-train, prompt, and predict: a systematic survey of prompting methods in natural language processing (2021). https://arxiv.org/abs/2107.13586
33. Ma, F., et al.: FaitCrowd: fine grained truth discovery for crowdsourced data aggregation. In: Proceedings of the 21th ACM SIGKDD International Conference on Knowledge Discovery and Data Mining, KDD 2015, pp. 745–754. Association for Computing Machinery, New York, NY, USA, August 2015. https://doi.org/10.1145/2783258.2783314

34. Maynez, J., Narayan, S., Bohnet, B., McDonald, R.: On faithfulness and factuality in abstractive summarization. In: Proceedings of the 58th Annual Meeting of the Association for Computational Linguistics, pp. 1906–1919. Association for Computational Linguistics (2020). https://doi.org/10.18653/v1/2020.acl-main.173
35. Mayring, P.: Qualitative content analysis. Forum Qual. Soc. Res. **1** (2000). https://doi.org/10.17169/FQS-1.2.1089
36. Misargopoulos, A., et al..: Building a knowledge-intensive, intent-lean, question answering chatbot in the telecom industry - challenges and solutions. In: Artificial Intelligence Applications and Innovations, AIAI 2022 IFIP WG 12.5 International Workshops, pp. 87–97 (2022). https://doi.org/10.1007/978-3-031-08341-9_8
37. Moiseev, F., Dong, Z., Alfonseca, E., Jaggi, M.: SKILL: structured knowledge infusion for large language models. In: Proceedings of the 2022 Conference of the North American Chapter of the Association for Computational Linguistics: Human Language Technologies, pp. 1581–1588 (2022). https://doi.org/10.18653/v1/2022naacl-main.113
38. OpenAI: ChatGPT: optimizing language models for dialogue (2022). https://openai.com/blog/chatgpt/. Accessed 26 Jan 2023
39. Ouyang, L., et al.,; Training language models to follow instructions with human feedback (2022). https://doi.org/10.48550/ARXIV.2203.02155. https://arxiv.org/abs/2203.02155
40. Paikens, P., Znotiņš, A., Bārzdiņš, G.: Human-in-the-loop conversation agent for customer service. In: Métais, E., Meziane, F., Horacek, H., Cimiano, P. (eds.) NLDB 2020. LNCS, vol. 12089, pp. 277–284. Springer, Cham (2020). https://doi.org/10.1007/978-3-030-51310-8_25
41. Parameswaran, A., Sarma, A.D., Garcia-Molina, H., Polyzotis, N., Widom, J.: Human-assisted graph search: it's okay to ask questions. In: Proceedings of the VLDB Endowment, vol. 4, pp. 267–278. VLDB Endowment, February 2011. https://doi.org/10.14778/1952376.1952377
42. Paulheim, H.: Knowledge graph refinement: a survey of approaches and evaluation methods. Semant. Web **8**, 489–508 (2017). https://doi.org/10.3233/SW-160218
43. Peffers, K., Tuunanen, T., Rothenberger, M.A., Chatterjee, S.: A design science research methodology for information systems research. J. Manag. Inf. Syst. **24**(3), 45–77 (2007). https://doi.org/10.2753/MIS0742-1222240302
44. Qiu, L., Chen, Y., Jia, H., Zhang, Z.: Query intent recognition based on multi-class features. IEEE Access **6**, 52195–52204 (2018). https://doi.org/10.1109/ACCESS.2018.2869585
45. Radford, A., Wu, J., Child, R., Luan, D., Amodei, D., Sutskever, I.: Language models are unsupervised multitask learners (2019). https://github.com/openai/gpt-2
46. Raffel, C., et al.: Exploring the limits of transfer learning with a unified text-to-text transformer (2019). https://arxiv.org/abs/1910.10683
47. Ranganathan, V., Barbosa, D.: HOPLoP: multi-hop link prediction over knowledge graph embeddings. World Wide Web **25**(2), 1037–1065 (2021). https://doi.org/10.1007/s11280-021-00972-6
48. Santos, G.A., de Andrade, G.G., Silva, G.R.S., Duarte, F.C.M., Costa, J.P.J.D., de Sousa, R.T.: A conversation-driven approach for chatbot management. IEEE Access **10**, 8474–8486 (2022). https://doi.org/10.1109/ACCESS.2022.3143323
49. Singh, S.: Natural language processing for information extraction (2018). https://doi.org/10.48550/ARXIV.1807.02383

50. Sohail, M.S., Daud, S.: Knowledge sharing in higher education institutions: perspectives from Malaysia. Vine **39**, 125–142 (2009). https://doi.org/10.1108/03055720910988841
51. Vaswani, A., et al.: Attention is all you need. In: Advances in Neural Information Processing Systems, vol. 30. Curran Associates Inc. (2017)
52. Veiga Avila, L., Beuron, T.A., Brandli, L.L., Damke, L.I., Pereira, R.S., Klein, L.L.: Barriers to innovation and sustainability in universities: an international comparison. Int. J. Sustain. High. Educ. **20**, 805–821 (2019). https://doi.org/10.1108/IJSHE-02-2019-0067
53. Verint Systems Inc.: Conversational AI Barometer: Chatbots and Next-Gen AI (2021). https://www.verint.com/resources/conversational-ai-barometer-chatbots-and-next-gen-ai/. Accessed 07 February 2023
54. Wang, Z.J., Choi, D., Xu, S., Yang, D.: Putting humans in the natural language processing loop: a survey. In: Bridging Human-Computer Interaction and Natural Language Processing, HCINLP 2021 - Proceedings of the 1st Workshop, pp. 47–52 (2021)
55. Wei, J., et al.: Emergent Abilities of Large Language Models (2022). https://arxiv.org/abs/2206.07682
56. Meyer von Wolff, R., Hobert, S., Schumann, M.: Sorry, i can't understand you! – influencing factors and challenges of chatbots at digital workplaces. In: Ahlemann, F., Schütte, R., Stieglitz, S. (eds.) WI 2021. LNISO, vol. 47, pp. 150–165. Springer, Cham (2021). https://doi.org/10.1007/978-3-030-86797-3_11
57. Wu, X., Xiao, L., Sun, Y., Zhang, J., Ma, T., He, L.: A Survey of Human-in-the-loop for Machine Learning. Fut. Gener. Comput. Syst. **135**, 364–381 (2022). https://doi.org/10.1016/j.future.2022.05.014
58. Xue, B., Zou, L.: Knowledge graph quality management: a comprehensive survey. IEEE Trans. Knowl. Data Eng. (2022). https://doi.org/10.1109/TKDE.2022.3150080
59. Xue, L., et al.: mT5: a massively multilingual pre-trained text-to-text transformer (2020). https://arxiv.org/abs/2010.11934

The Relevance of Perceived Interactivity for Disclosure Towards Conversational Artificial Intelligence

Miriam Gieselmann[1]([⊠]) [iD] and Kai Sassenberg[1,2] [iD]

[1] Leibniz-Institut für Wissensmedien, Schleichstr. 6, 72076 Tübingen, Germany
m.gieselmann@iwm-tuebingen.de
[2] University of Tübingen, Tübingen, Germany

Abstract. Conversational AI (e.g., Google Assistant, Amazon Alexa) is nowadays omnipresent in many people's life. To enable many functionalities and benefits (such as convenience, utility, and personalization), conversational AI needs to gather large amounts of users' personal data which raises the issue of privacy concerns. As people nonetheless share personal data with conversational AI, it is important to understand which factors determine disclosure (i.e., privacy concerns and willingness to disclose). One important aspect that seems to heighten disclosure in several contexts is interactivity.

However, the conceptualization and operationalization of interactivity has often varied between studies. To overcome this, we aimed to investigate three facets of perceived interactivity simultaneously: (1) active control (i.e., whether users can exert control over exchanged information and interaction), (2) reciprocal interaction (i.e., whether there is a two-way flow of information), and (3) synchronicity (i.e., whether information exchange happens quickly).

In two survey studies ($N_{total} = 406$), we investigated the association between those interactivity facets and disclosure towards conversational AI.

Results indicate that all forms of interactivity are correlated with a higher willingness to disclose and in part also with privacy concerns. However, when considering all facets at once in multiple regression, only reciprocal interaction (but not active control and synchronicity) was related to willingness to disclose and none of the three interactivity facets was significantly associated with privacy concerns.

Thus, our findings suggest that reciprocal interaction is (compared to active control and synchronicity) the most relevant interactivity facet to understand people's willingness to disclose towards conversational AI.

Keywords: Interactivity · Conversational AI · Disclosure

1 Introduction

Nowadays, artificial intelligence (AI) becomes more and more present in our everyday life. One prominent example is conversational AI (also referred to as voice assistants, virtual intelligent agents, etc.): systems like Google Assistant or Amazon Alexa are

H. Degen and S. Ntoa (Eds.): HCII 2023, LNAI 14051, pp. 55–67, 2023.
https://doi.org/10.1007/978-3-031-35894-4_4

part of many people's everyday life. Being used, for example, for information access, entertainment, online shopping, or the control of smart home devices, 3.25 billion of these systems had been in use worldwide in 2019 [1]. By now, 35% of US adults own a smart speaker with a conversational AI [2].

Conversational AI offers convenience, utility, enjoyment, and personalization to its users, but at the same time, gathers a lot of personal information about them (e.g., information about their interests, location data, or access to other applications). While this information might be necessary for several functionalities (e.g., for personalized recommendations or location-based requests), it still raises the issue of privacy concerns regarding the amount of personal data collected by conversational AI [3, 4].

As people nonetheless share personal data with conversational AI, it is important to understand which factors determine disclosure (i.e., privacy concerns and willingness to disclose). Previous research has often focused on determinants such as trust in the provider of the technology [5, 6], perceptions of the technology itself (e.g., competence, [7]) or rather objective system characteristics (e.g., anthropomorphic design features, [8, 9]). Another important aspect that seems to heighten disclosure in several contexts is interactivity [10, 11]. However, the conceptualization and operationalization of interactivity often vary between studies.

The present research thus aimed for a systematic approach to investigate the role of different aspects of interactivity for disclosure towards conversational AI at the same time. To this end, we followed the approach of Liu [12], who differentiates three facets of interactivity: (1) *active control*, (2) *reciprocal interaction* (originally called two-way interaction), and (3) *synchronicity*.

While it has been shown that each of these dimensions can be relevant for disclosure [11, 13–15], they have barely been investigated at the same time. As research on the effects of interactivity on disclosure towards conversational AI is lacking, the present research investigates the associations between the three afore-mentioned dimensions of interactivity and disclosure towards conversational AI.

1.1 Interactivity

Interactivity refers to the experience of responsiveness from another entity, which can be both a person or a technology [16], resulting in an exchange between interaction partners. While the concept of interactivity originally stems from interactions between humans, it has become more and more important in technology interactions as well. Interactivity is a core evaluation criterion for technologies and has received considerable attention in research on technology interactions as it enables active, efficient, and quick interactions between users and technologies. Accordingly, previous research has repeatedly investigated the role of interactivity for several aspects of acceptance, such as credibility [e.g., 17, 18], satisfaction [e.g., 19], usage intentions [e.g., 20], and disclosure.

Despite the large amount of research already conducted in the field of interactivity, there has been little agreement on how interactivity should be conceptualized – resulting in different conceptualizations across studies [20, 21]. One promising approach to assess interactivity has been proposed by Liu [12] distinguishing the three dimensions active control, reciprocal interaction (originally called two-way interaction), and synchronicity. While there has been some research taking all three dimensions into account and showing positive relations with different acceptance measures [e.g., 22, 23], such studies are lacking for the relationship between interactivity and disclosure. Nonetheless, some studies focused on one of these (interrelated) dimensions to understand acceptance in general and disclosure in specific.

Active Control. Active control refers to the User's perception in how far they have control over the interaction and the exchanged information [12] and can be related to different aspects of acceptance. For a related construct, namely perceived behavioral control, positive relationships with usage intention and ease of use have been observed for social robots [24]. Further, autonomous and thus, less controllable robots, are perceived as more threatening to humans and evoke stronger negative attitude towards robots in general and more opposition to robotics research than non-autonomous robots [25].

More important to the present research, it has also been observed that controllability was related to more disinhibition, which in turn predicted more online self-disclosure in instant messaging and social media [13, 14]. Therefore, it seems reasonable to assume that active control predicts more disclosure.

Reciprocal Interaction. Reciprocal interaction (originally: two-way interaction [12]), describes a two-way flow of information. Previous research has often focused on technologies as a medium to enable a two-way flow of information between two humans or between companies and their customers (i.e., computer-mediated communication). For example, anticipated reciprocity in micro blogging predicted higher perceived gratification which in turn predicted more content contribution [26] and perceived responsiveness is associated with more disclosure on social networks [11]. Besides, in the context of companies' corporate social responsibility communication, interactivity (in terms of replies and references to earlier messages) led to greater perceived contingency (i.e., a higher degree to which later messages refer to earlier messages) which in turn led to greater willingness to comment on social media [27].

However, with more recent technologies such as social robots or conversational AI, users do no longer interact with another human but with the technology itself. Thus, the focus lays on the two-way flow of interaction between the user and the technology rather than between the user and another human. While research on this type of two-way interaction is scarce, it has been observed that, in a learning setting, participants reported more disclosing to an expressive robot (e.g., robot changing color, moving arms or head) compared to a non-expressive robot [10]. Hence, reciprocal interaction might likewise be associated with disclosure.

Synchronicity. Synchronicity refers to the perception that the exchange of information between communication partners happens quickly [12]. In face-to-face interactions between humans, conversations with multiple (compared to fewer) time lapses lead to lower ratings of the interaction partner's communicative competency [28]. Besides, also in contexts of computer-mediated communication, significant pauses between comments can be associated with negative consequences, such as less trust among communication partners [29]. Further, customer service agents responses without delay (vs longer delays) lead to higher perceived co-presence and service quality [30].

Focusing more specifically on disclosure, it has been proposed that asynchronicity of communication in interactions between humans could enhance disclosure as their will not be an immediate reaction of the interaction partner [31]. However, for personal use contexts of mobile messengers, it has been observed that immediacy of feedback led to more intimacy [15]. In sum, results do not allow a conclusion regarding the relation between synchrony and disclosure.

1.2 Differentiation of Disclosure

Previous research has shown that people do not necessarily stop sharing their personal data when having privacy concerns (referred to as the 'privacy paradox', for a review see [32]). Thus, we differentiated between the behavioral intention to share personal data with a conversational AI, i.e., the *willingness to disclose*, and more abstract attitudes, i.e., *privacy concerns*. Accordingly, we aimed to investigate:

RQ: How is perceived interactivity (i.e., active control, reciprocal interaction, and synchronicity) of conversational AI associated with disclosure (i.e., willingness to disclose and privacy concerns)?

1.3 Current Research

To answer this question, we conducted two online surveys. In the first study, we exploratory investigated the association between the three interactivity dimensions and disclosure towards conversational AI in a small sample. In the second study, we aimed to replicate our findings in a larger sample of actual users of conversational AI.

2 Study 1

2.1 Method

The studies reported here were conducted within a larger research project focusing on another research question than the one discussed here and published in [7]. All results reported in the present paper have not been included in the previous paper and vice versa. data are available at [33] (Study 1 and 2) and code for analyses reported in this study are available at [34].

Design and Participants. Participants were recruited via prolific for a 10-min online survey renumerated with £1.25. In order to reach stable correlations, we aimed for 300 valid cases [35]. Participants were randomly assigned to one of five experimental conditions in which they were surveyed about the perception of a specific technology (i.e., conversational AI, search engine, streaming service, autonomous vehicle, washing machine). After exclusion as pre-registered (https://aspredicted.org/tq3m3.pdf), the sample consisted of $N = 358$ participants (59.8% male, 38.5% female, 1.4% non-binary; Aged: $M = 25.5$, 18–62 years) of these participants, $N = 72$ focused on the perception of conversational AI (54.2% male, 44.4% female, 1.4% non-binary; Aged: $M = 27.0$, 18–56 years).

Procedure. After having been randomly assigned to one of the five experimental conditions, participants read a short description of a conversational AI (or Another technology – depending on the experimental condition as described above) and were afterwards surveyed about their perceptions of the technology's interactivity as well as their disclosure towards the respective technology. A complete list of all measures taken, instructions, and items is provided in the supplement of [7].

Measures. For the assessment of interactivity we adjusted and augmented the items of [12] for active control, reciprocal interaction, and synchronicity. Based on an exploratory factor analysis (See Table 1), we excluded items 10 and 11 intended for the reciprocal interaction scale because they were loading highest on another factor. due to the results of study 2 (reported below), we further excluded item 5 from the active control scale to have an identical scale across studies. accordingly, interactivity was assessed distinguishing *active control* (5 items), *reciprocal interaction* (4 items), and *synchronicity* (6 items).

Table 1. Results From a Factor Analysis for Interactivity (Study 1: $N = 358$)

Item		Factor		
		1	2	3
1	I can choose freely what … does.		0.77	
2	I have little influence on …'s behavior.[a]		0.47	-0.36
3	I can completely control …		0.77	
4	While interacting with …, I have absolutely no control over what happens.[a]	0.22	0.50	-0.38
5	My actions determine …'s behavior.[b]		0.51	
6	I have a lot of control over my interaction experience with …	0.25	0.69	
7	… facilitates two-way communication between itself and its user.	0.20		0.65
8	… makes me feel like it wants to interact with me.			0.77
9	Using … is very interactive.	0.22		0.60
10	… is completely apathetic.[ab]		-0.27	0.21
11	… always reacts to my requests. [b]		0.50	0.43

(*continued*)

Table 1. (*continued*)

Item		Factor		
12	Both, … and I, can start interactions with one another.			**0.74**
13	… processes new input quickly.	**0.73**		
14	…'s reactions come without delay.	**0.71**		
15	… responds very slow.[a]	**0.66**		-0.28
16	I never have to wait for …'s output.	**0.48**		0.38
17	… immediately answers to requests.	**0.71**	0.23	
18	When I interact with …, I get instantaneous feedback.	**0.65**		0.34

Note. The extraction method was principal axis factoring with an orthogonal (varimax) rotation and Kaiser normalization. Factor loadings < .2 are not displayed. Factor loadings above .40 are in bold
'…' was replaced with a specific technology depending on the experimental condition (i.e., the voice assistant, the washing machine, the search engine, the streaming service, or the autonomous vehicle)
[a] Item reverse coded
[b] Item not included in final scale

Disclosure was assessed as willingness to disclose (5 items, e.g., 'I would provide a lot of information to the voice assistant about things that represent me personally', partially adapted from [36]) and privacy concerns (4 items, e.g., 'I feel that the voice assistant's practices are an invasion of privacy', adapted from [37]). All scales were answered on seven-point scales (1 = *strongly Disagree*, 7 = *strongly Agree*). Means, standard deviations and reliabilities for all scales are reported in Table 2.

Table 2. Scale Reliabilities, Means and Standard Deviations for Interactivity and Disclosure (Study 1: $n = 72$)

	Number of items	α	*M*	*SD*
Active control	5	0.61	4.48	0.90
Reciprocal interaction	4	0.51	4.25	0.99
Synchronicity	6	0.73	4.64	0.80
Willingness to disclose	4	0.80	4.49	1.25
Privacy concerns	5	0.90	3.60	1.46

2.2 Results

Bivariate correlations (see Table 3) show that all three dimensions of interactivity were positively and significantly correlated with willingness to disclose. Besides, active control and synchronicity were negatively and significantly correlated with privacy concerns, whereas the negative relation between reciprocal interaction and privacy concerns was non-significant.

Table 3. Bivariate Correlations Between Interactivity and Disclosure (Study 1: $n = 72$)

	1	2	3	4
1. Active control				
2. Reciprocal interaction	0.01			
3. Synchronicity	0.28*	0.18		
4. Willingness to disclose	0.24*	0.49***	0.33**	
5. Privacy concerns	–0.27*	–0.23	–0.27*	– 0.64***

We further tested the relative importance of the three interactivity dimensions for (1) willingness to disclose and (2) privacy concerns by conducting two separate multiple regression analyses including the three interactivity dimensions as predictors at the same time. Willingness to disclose was associated with reciprocal interaction, $\beta = 0.46$, $p < .001$, 95%-CI[0.25, 0.66], but not with active control, $\beta = 0.17$, $p = .098$, 95%-CI[–0.03, 0.38], nor synchronicity, $\beta = 0.20$, $p = .068$, 95%-CI[–0.01, 0.41]. Further, privacy concerns were not related to neither active control, $\beta = –0.22$, $p = .068$, 95%-CI[-0.45, 0.02], nor reciprocal interaction, $\beta = –0.20$, $p = .089$, 95%-CI[–0.42, 0.03], nor synchronicity, $\beta = –0.17$, $p = .159$, 95%-CI[–0.41, 0.07].

2.3 Discussion

While all interactivity dimensions were correlated to willingness to disclose and privacy concerns (although one correlation was non-significant), the regression analyses showed a more differentiated picture. When controlling for the other two interactivity dimensions in multiple regression analyses, only higher perceived reciprocal interaction was associated with a higher willingness to disclose information towards conversational AI. Apart from that, none of the interactivity dimensions was related to neither willingness to disclose nor privacy concerns.

However, the sample size of this study was rather small and was not limited to users of conversational AI – thus, participants might have lacked sufficient interaction experience with conversational AI. Further, some of the scales had non-satisfactory internal consistencies. To overcome these limitations, we recruited a larger sample of actual conversational AI users in Study 2 and slightly adjusted some of the scales.

3 Study 2

3.1 Method

Design, Participants, and Procedure. Study 2 was a conceptual replication of Study 1 with a focus on actual users of conversational AI as participants. For a 12-min online study, we recruited participants owning a home assistant or smart hub and having used a conversational AI before via Prolific. After exclusion as pre-registered (https://aspred icted.org/v87ub.pdf), the sample consisted of $N = 334$ participants (54.2% male, 44.0% female, 1.8% non-binary; age: $M = 30.3$, 18–73 years).

Measures. We developed two additional items to replace the items of the reciprocal interaction scale excluded in study 1. Exploratory factor analysis (See Table 4) Supported the three-factor structure of the interactivity items with the exception of one item intended for the active control scale loading highest on another factor. The respective item was excluded from the scale in this study as well as in study 1. Accordingly, active control and

Table 4. Results From a Factor Analysis for Interactivity (Study 2: $N = 334$)

Item		Factor		
		1	2	3
1	I can choose freely what the voice assistant does.	0.28	0.27	**0.57**
2	I have little influence on the voice assistant's behavior.[a]			**0.73**
3	I can completely control the voice assistant.	0.26		**0.56**
4	While interacting with the voice assistant, I have absolutely no control over what happens.[a]			**0.68**
5	My actions determine the voice assistant's behavior.[b]		0.38	0.32
6	I have a lot of control over my interaction experience with the voice assistant.	0.28	0.33	**0.62**
7	The voice assistant facilitates two-way communication between itself and its user.		**0.67**	0.24
8	The voice assistant makes me feel like it wants to interact with me.		**0.69**	
9	Using the voice assistant is very interactive.	**0.40**	**0.55**	0.21
10	The voice assistant gives me the opportunity to interact with it.		**0.55**	0.31
11	The voice assistant encourages me to interact with it.		**0.68**	
12	Both, the voice assistant and I, can start interactions with one another.		**0.66**	
13	The voice assistant processes new input quickly.	**0.57**	0.30	0.25
14	The voice assistant's reactions come without delay.	**0.77**		
15	The voice assistant responds very slow.[a]	**0.69**		
16	I never have to wait for the voice assistant's output.	**0.68**		
17	The voice assistant immediately answers to requests.	**0.79**		
18	When I interact with the voice assistant, I get instantaneous feedback.	**0.77**	0.20	

Note. The extraction method was principal axis factoring with an orthogonal (varimax) rotation and Kaiser normalization. Factor loadings < .2 are not displayed. Factor loadings above .40 are in bold
[a] Item reverse coded
[b] Item not included in final scale

synchronicity were assessed with the same items as in study 1. Reciprocal interaction was assessed using the four items of study 1 and the two additional items 10 and 11.

Willingness to disclose was assessed with the same items as in Study 1, whereas we added an additional item in the scale for privacy concerns (i.e., 'I am concerned about my privacy when using the voice assistant'). Means, standard deviations and reliabilities for all scales are reported in Table 5.

Table 5. Scale Reliabilities, Means and Standard Deviations for Interactivity and Disclosure (Study 2: $N = 334$)

	Number of items	α	M	SD
Active control	5	0.71	4.67	1.01
Reciprocal interaction	6	0.76	4.18	1.05
Synchronicity	6	0.60	4.73	0.95
Willingness to disclose	5	0.90	4.03	1.35
Privacy concerns	5	0.90	3.57	1.46

3.2 Results

Bivariate correlations (see Table 6) show that all three interactivity dimensions are sig nificantly positively related to willingness to disclose and negatively related to privacy concerns.

Table 6. Bivariate Correlations Between Interactivity and Disclosure (Study 2: $N = 334$)

	1	2	3	4
1. Active control				
2. Reciprocal interaction	0.25***			
3. Synchronicity	0.40***	0.35***		
4. Willingness to disclose	0.11*	0.29***	0.14*	
5. Privacy concerns	– 0.13*	– 0.13*	– 0.16**	– 0.50***

$* p < .05. ** p < .01. *** p < .001$

As in Study 1, we tested the relative importance of the three dimensions of interactivity for (1) willingness to disclose and (2) privacy concerns by conducting two separate multiple regression analyses (pre-registered): willingness to disclose was associated with reciprocal interaction, $\beta = 0.27, p < .001$, 95%-CI[0.16, 0.38], but not with active control, $\beta = 0.03, p = .654$, 95%-CI –0.09, 0.14], nor synchronicity, $\beta = 0.03, p = .571$, 95%-CI –0.08, 0.15]. Further, privacy concerns were not related to neither active control,

$\beta = -0.07$, $p = .248$, 95%-CI -0.19, 0.05], nor reciprocal interaction, $\beta = -0.07$, $p = .224$, 95%-CI[-0.19, 0.04], nor synchronicity, $\beta = -0.11$, $p = .073$, 95%-CI[-0.23, 0.01].

3.3 Discussion

The results replicate the findings from Study 1. Active control, reciprocal interaction, and synchronicity are all correlated positively with willingness to disclose and negatively with privacy concerns.

As in Study 1, when controlling for the influence of the other two interactivity dimensions by using multiple regression analyses, higher perceived reciprocal interaction was again associated with a higher willingness to disclose information towards conversational AI. Beyond this relationship, none of the interactivity dimensions was related to neither willingness to disclose nor privacy concerns.

4 Overall Discussion

The research presented in this paper tested the relationship between three dimensions of perceived interactivity (active control, reciprocal interaction, and synchronicity) and disclosure towards conversational AI.

The findings support findings from earlier research by showing that active control, reciprocal interaction, and synchronicity are all positively correlated with willingness to disclose and negatively correlated with privacy concerns.

However, the regression analyses revealed that in contrast to active control and synchronicity, reciprocal interaction is the most relevant interactivity dimension to understand people's willingness to disclose personal information towards conversational AI. This finding indicates that the feeling of a two-way flow of information between a user and a conversational AI is crucial for the users' willingness to disclose personal information to the system.

Although we cannot rule out that active control and synchronicity facilitate the perception of two-way interaction, the latter dimension seems to be the most important one for people's decision whether to disclose personal information towards conversational AI.

This implies that the feeling of reciprocal interaction with a conversational AI could heighten users' willingness to share personal information with such a technology. Accordingly, it should be considered that for such highly interactive technologies, special care needs to be taken in order to prevent invasions of the users' privacy.

4.1 Strengths and Limitations

Our findings are based on two studies showing very similar result patterns. Thus, the results indicate that the differentiation of interactivity facets as proposed by [12] is useful to disentangle effects of interactivity on disclosure towards conversational AI. Accordingly, this conceptualization of interactivity can be a starting point for future research focusing on other aspects of acceptance (e.g., trust, believability, or adoption) of conversational AI or other technologies.

Nonetheless, when interpreting the results, it should be taken into account that this research was based on survey data, thus, not allowing conclusions about causality. Therefore, we highly encourage future research using experimental manipulations of the three interactivity dimensions as well as longitudinal studies focusing, for example, on actual disclosing behavior, to complement our findings – potentially also for other technologies than conversational AI.

4.2 Conclusion

In contrast to earlier studies, we assessed active control, reciprocal interaction, and synchronicity to focus on three dimensions of interactivity at the same time. Taken together, our research suggests that interactivity in terms of reciprocal interaction (but not active control or synchronicity) is relevant to understand willingness to disclose towards conversational AI while we observed no significant relationships between interactivity and privacy concerns. In doing so, our findings suggest that reciprocal interaction is (compared to active control and synchronicity) the most relevant interactivity facet to understand peoples' willingness to disclose towards conversational AI.

References

1. Statista: Number of voice assistants in use worldwide 2019–2024. https://www.statista.com/statistics/973815/worldwide-digital-voice-assistant-in-use/
2. Kinsella, B.: U.S. Smart Speaker Growth Flat Lined in 2020. https://voicebot.ai/2021/04/14/u-s-smart-speaker-growth-flat-lined-in-2020/
3. Liao, Y., Vitak, J., Kumar, P., Zimmer, M., Kritikos, K.: Understanding the role of privacy and trust in intelligent personal assistant adoption. In: Taylor, N.G., Christian-Lamb, C., Martin, M.H., Nardi, B. (eds.) iConference 2019. LNCS, vol. 11420, pp. 102–113. Springer, Cham (2019). https://doi.org/10.1007/978-3-030-15742-5_9
4. Dubiel, M., Halvey, M., Azzopardi, L.: A Survey investigating usage of virtual personal assistants (2018). http://arxiv.org/abs/1807.04606
5. Joinson, A., Reips, U.-D., Buchanan, T., Schofield, C.B.P.: Privacy, trust, and self-disclosure online. Hum. Comput. Interact. **25**, 1–24 (2010). https://doi.org/10.1080/07370020903586662
6. Pal, D., Arpnikanondt, C., Razzaque, M.A.: Personal information disclosure via voice assistants: the personalization–privacy paradox. SN Comput. Sci. **1**(5), 1–17 (2020). https://doi.org/10.1007/s42979-020-00287-9
7. Gieselmann, M., Sassenberg, K.: The more competent, the better? the effects of perceived competencies on disclosure towards conversational artificial intelligence. Sco. Sci. Comput. Rev. (in press). https://doi.org/10.1177/08944393221142787
8. Ha, Q.-A., Chen, J.V., Uy, H.U., Capistrano, E.P.: Exploring the privacy concerns in using intelligent virtual assistants under perspectives of information sensitivity and anthropomorphism. Int. J. Hum.-Comput. Interact. **37**, 512–527 (2021). https://doi.org/10.1080/10447318.2020.1834728
9. Lucas, G.M., Gratch, J., King, A., Morency, L.-P.: It's only a computer: virtual humans increase willingness to disclose. Comput. Hum. Behav. **37**, 94–100 (2014). https://doi.org/10.1016/j.chb.2014.04.043

10. Martelaro, N., Nneji, V.C., Ju, W., Hinds, P.: Tell me more designing HRI to encourage more trust, disclosure, and companionship. In: 2016 11th ACM/IEEE International Conference on Human-Robot Interaction (HRI), pp. 181–188. IEEE, Christchurch (2016)
11. Walsh, R.M.: Self-disclosure on social media: the role of perceived network responsiveness. Comput. Hum. Behav. 106162 (2020)
12. Liu, Y.: Developing a scale to measure the interactivity of websites. J. Advert. Res. 43, 207–216 (2003). https://doi.org/10.2501/JAR-43-2-207-216
13. Green, T., Wilhelmsen, T., Wilmots, E., Dodd, B., Quinn, S.: Social anxiety, attributes of online communication and self-disclosure across private and public Facebook communication. Comput. Hum. Behav. 58, 206–213 (2016). https://doi.org/10.1016/j.chb.2015.12.066
14. Schouten, A.P., Valkenburg, P.M., Peter, J.: Precursors and underlying processes of adolescents' online self-disclosure: developing and testing an "Internet-Attribute-Perception" model. J. Media Psychol. 10, 292–315 (2007). https://doi.org/10.1080/15213260701375686
15. Park, Y.W., Lee, A.R.: The moderating role of communication contexts: how do media synchronicity and behavioral characteristics of mobile messenger applications affect social intimacy and fatigue? Comput. Hum. Behav. 97, 179–192 (2019). https://doi.org/10.1016/j.chb.2019.03.020
16. Lew, Z., Walther, J.B., Pang, A., Shin, W.: Interactivity in online chat: conversational contingency and response latency in computer-mediated communication. JCMC. 23, 201–221 (2018). https://doi.org/10.1093/jcmc/zmy009
17. Johnson, T.J., Kaye, B.K.: Some like it lots: the influence of interactivity and reliance on credibility. Comput. Hum. Behav. 61, 136–145 (2016). https://doi.org/10.1016/j.chb.2016.03.012
18. Sundar, S.S.: The MAIN model: a heuristic approach to understanding technology effects on credibility. Dig. Media (2008). https://doi.org/10.1162/dmal.9780262562324.07
19. Shu, W.: Continual use of microblogs. Behav. Inf. Technol. 33, 666–677 (2014). https://doi.org/10.1080/0144929X.2013.816774
20. Shin, D.-H., Hwang, Y., Choo, H.: Smart TV: are they really smart in interacting with people? understanding the interactivity of Korean Smart TV. Behav. Inf. Technol. 32, 156–172 (2013). https://doi.org/10.1080/0144929X.2011.603360
21. Heeter, C.: Interactivity in the context of designed experiences. J. Interact. Advert. 1, 3–14 (2000). https://doi.org/10.1080/15252019.2000.10722040
22. Fan, L., Liu, X., Wang, B., Wang, L.: Interactivity, engagement, and technology dependence: understanding users' technology utilisation behaviour. Behav. Inf. Technol. 36, 113–124 (2017). https://doi.org/10.1080/0144929X.2016.1199051
23. Cheng, Y.-M.: Roles of interactivity and usage experience in e-learning acceptance: a longitudinal study. Int. J. Web Inf. Syst. 10, 2–23 (2014). https://doi.org/10.1108/IJWIS-05-2013-0015
24. de Graaf, M.M.A., Ben Allouch, S.: Exploring influencing variables for the acceptance of social robots. Rob. Auton. Syst. 61, 1476–1486 (2013). https://doi.org/10.1016/j.robot.2013.07.007
25. Złotowski, J., Yogeeswaran, K., Bartneck, C.: Can we control it? autonomous robots threaten human identity, uniqueness, safety, and resources. Int. J. Hum. Comput. 100, 48–54 (2017). https://doi.org/10.1016/j.ijhcs.2016.12.008
26. Liu, X., Min, Q., Han, S.: Continuous content contribution behaviours: an integrated perspective of uses and gratification theory and social influence theory. Behav. Inf. Technol. 39, 525–543. https://doi.org/10.1080/0144929X.2019.1603326
27. Lew, Z., Stohl, C.: What makes people willing to comment on social media posts? the roles of interactivity and perceived contingency in online corporate social responsibility communication. Commun. Monogr. 1–24 (2022). https://doi.org/10.1080/03637751.2022.2032230

28. McLaughlin, M.L., Cody, M.J.: Awkward silences: behavioral Antecedents and consequences of the conversational lapse. Hum. Commun. Res. **8**, 299–316 (1982). https://doi.org/10.1111/ j.1468-2958.1982.tb00669.x

29. Kalman, Y.M., Scissors, L.E., Gergle, D.: Chronemic aspects of chat, and their relationship to trust in a virtual team. MCIS 2010 Proc. **46** (2010)

30. Park, E.K., Sundar, S.S.: Can synchronicity and visual modality enhance social presence in mobile messaging? Comput. Hum. Behav. **45**, 121–128 (2015). https://doi.org/10.1016/j.chb. 2014.12.001

31. Suler, J.: The online disinhibition effect. Cyberpsychol. Behav. Soc. Netw. **15**, 103–111 (2012). https://doi.org/10.1089/cyber.2011.0277

32. Kokolakis, S.: Privacy attitudes and privacy behaviour: a review of current research on the privacy paradox phenomenon. Comput. Secur. **64**, 122–134 (2017). https://doi.org/10.1016/ j.cose.2015.07.002

33. Gieselmann, M., Sassenberg, K.: Dataset for: the more competent, the better? the effects of perceived competencies on disclosure towards conversational artificial intelligence. PsychArchives. (2022). https://doi.org/10.23668/PSYCHARCHIVES.12175

34. Gieselmann, M., Sassenberg, K.: Code for: the relevance of perceived interactivity for disclosure towards conversational artificial intelligence. PsychArchives (2023). https://doi.org/ 10.23668/PSYCHARCHIVES.12511

35. Schönbrodt, F.D., Perugini, M.: At what sample size do correlations stabilize? J. Res. Pers. **47**, 609–612 (2013). https://doi.org/10.1016/j.jrp.2013.05.009

36. Gerlach, J., Widjaja, T., Buxmann, P.: Handle with care: how online social network providers' privacy policies impact users' information sharing behavior. J. Strateg. Inf. **24**, 33–43 (2015). https://doi.org/10.1016/j.jsis.2014.09.001

37. Alge, B.J., Ballinger, G.A., Tangirala, S., Oakley, J.L.: Information privacy in organizations: empowering creative and extrarole performance. J. Appl. Psychol. **91**, 221–232 (2006). https:// doi.org/10.1037/0021-9010.91.1.221

Towards Human-Centered Design of AI Service Chatbots: Defining the Building Blocks

Maria Hartikainen[✉] and Kaisa Väänänen

Computing Sciences, Tampere University, Tampere, Finland
{maria.hartikainen,kaisa.vaananen}@tuni.fi

Abstract. Chatbots have been spread widely to online customer service due to recent technological advancements. For chatbots' successful utilisation as customer servants, it is essential that they are developed for human users in a way that meets their needs. Human-centred design (HCD) puts humans in the centre of the development. However, research-based information of HCD for service chatbots is still scarce. Hence, we reviewed recent literature to explore and map the relevant themes that are recurrent in chatbot research to determine the building blocks of HCD for service chatbots. Our study reveals three main themes: (i) AI service chatbots' purpose is to serve humans, (ii) trust is crucial for service chatbot uptake, and (iii) AI chatbot design combines user interface design, dialogue design, and bot persona design to create positive UX. The findings of our study serve as a basis to the understanding of human-centered chatbot design, and can help practitioners develop service chatbots that are successful in supporting users accomplish their tasks.

Keywords: Chatbots · human-chatbot interaction · human-AI interaction · human-centred design (HCD) · literature review

1 Introduction

Chatbots are conversational and interactive software technology that are rapidly gaining their popularity because of their availability and interaction using natural dialogue [6]. One domain where chatbots are gaining popularity is customer service as chatbots are seen as holding great potential in terms of service efficiency, cost savings, and customer experience [21]. Customer service chatbots (referred hereafter as "service chatbot") can repeatedly answer questions, give information, and help people to accomplish their tasks without getting tired or bored. The use of chatbots as customer servants benefits both customers and companies, for flexibility, accessibility, and low-cost operations in comparison with human assistants [9, 23]. Recent developments in AI techniques have made chatbots easier to implement, more flexible in terms of application and maintainability, and increasingly capable to offer natural conversation and intuitive interaction [1]. Hence, AI improves the interaction between human and chatbot and increases chatbots' affordances.

H. Degen and S. Ntoa (Eds.): HCII 2023, LNAI 14051, pp. 68–87, 2023.
https://doi.org/10.1007/978-3-031-35894-4_5

However, conversing with artificial agent can raise concerns. First, the use and the use domains of service chatbots might influence their users and other people's lives. Chatbots influence the behaviour of the user by asking questions and responding to the user's questions [10]. Second, automated software might be unable to answer various queries or not work properly for their purpose, as currently develop chatbots are typically set up following a one-size-fits-all approach [8]. Moreover, often customers, the users of the service chatbots, are unwilling to share their personal information with chatbots citing privacy concerns [3]. In addition, the utilisation of AI brings AI-related factors to take account to, like explainability or fairness [12]. Hence, it is not surprise that in current situation companies prefer using chatbots, but their customers are hesitant and the uptake of service chatbots lag behind [1, 21].

To improve chatbots as customer servants, we have to understand the users and other humans affected by the chatbots decisions and recommendations and their needs, and approach these with an appropriate human-centered design (HCD) approach developed to service chatbots. With appropriate HCD approach we can develop chatbots that are efficient and useful for their purpose, as well as safe and trustworthy. However, for that it becomes paramount to have a clear overview of what should be considered in HCD for service chatbots. There is a lot of research on the chatbot domain, however there is a lack of knowledge of what makes service chatbot human-centered or design instruction for them. Hence, we set out to understand what are the building blocks of HCD of service chatbots are. The research question of this study is:

RQ: What are the building blocks of HCD for AI service chatbots?

The present study identifies, analyses, and integrates scientific research on AI and service chatbots across different fields in order to understand and define the building blocks of HCD for service chatbots. We analyse the data derived from 34 chatbot papers with a human-centered lens. Our study offers two main contributions: (i) theoretical: a novel perspective on the topic and a base for the future research, (ii) practical: themes that enable practitioners consider essential building blocks for designing chatbots for successful online customer service.

2 Background

2.1 Chatbots

Chatbots could be classified into various categories based on several criteria. One way to classify chatbots is based on the domain [13]. Closed domain chatbot means that the chatbot works in some closed domain, e.g., for a certain company. This is in contrast to so-called open-domain or general chatbots [21]. Chatbots can be classified by the length of the that can be short-term, where the interaction ends when the user has accomplished the task, or long-term interaction with the user, that evolves during time [2, 8]. In addition, chatbot can be task- or goal-oriented meaning that these chatbots have some predetermined task or purpose that they serve. Unlike task-oriented chatbots, non-task oriented chatbots can simulate a conversation with a person and seem to perform chitchat for entertainment or social purpose in open domains [21]. These chatbots can be called social chatbots, too, whose purpose is social, mainly to serve users' needs for communication, affection, and social belonging [2, 18]. In addition, chatbot can be classified by the technology the use. Chatbots can be rule-based, or they can utilise AI [21]. Rule-based chatbots use a series of pre-determined defined rules, whereas AI models are based on Machine Learning (ML) algorithms that allow them to learn from an existing database of human conversations. This allows chatbots to be more flexible and no longer dependent on domain specific knowledge [1, 20]. With the help of Natural Language Processing (NLP) and Voice Recognition (VR), chatbots can provide more possibilities for the user to interact with the chatbot in the way that is preferable for the user [1, 20]. In addition, AI chatbots can learn from the use and its behaviour can evolve based on the use data to better respond to a variety of user needs [1, 20].

In this study, our focus is on chatbots that utilise AI and they are used in customer service. Service chatbots are usually task-oriented and they work in specific closed domain, like for certain company. Usually, the interaction between the service chatbot and the human is short-term – it ends when the user has accomplished the task.

2.2 Chatbots in Customer Service

In the past five years, chatbots have become more widely available and more popular as a customer service solution [8, 9]. Currently chatbots can facilitate various business processes, particularly those related to customer service and personalization because of their accessibility, fairly low cost, and ease of use for the end consumers [1, 6, 9, 20]. Studies show that efficient and accessible support is the main motivation to use this technology [13]. Service chatbots provide users with action possibilities related to distilling information, hence, they facilitate users´ understanding of large information amounts. In addition, service chatbots can enrich the information provided. AI-enabled information enrichment makes chatbots more helpful as assistants in everyday tasks. Chatbots can provide context to what users are talking about or looking for. Hence, they can identify relevant information, provide feedback as reaction and orient ongoing conversations. In addition, with AI's help, service chatbots contribute to the provision of personalised experiences [1, 9, 21]. They are able to adapt interactions to their users providing tailored responses, adjusting their tone and style. As chatbots learn from interactions further they continually improve personalisation [6]. Although cost- and time-saving opportunities triggered a widespread implementation of AI-based chatbots, they still frequently fail to meet users expectations potentially resulting in users being less inclined to comply with requests made by the chatbot [8].

While an increasing number of service providers are offering customer service through chatbots, the acceptance of service chatbots is growing more slowly than expected []. In order to accept a technology, or to keep its usage over time, individuals need to be motivated [17]. Service chatbots are typically designed for efficient and effective interactions, accentuating pragmatic quality, and there is a need to understand how to make these more pleasant and engaging, strengthening hedonic quality [11]. Studies show that perceived value plays a major role in affecting behavioural intention to accept chatbots for customer care [5, 17]. Understanding and improving user experience is key to strengthening uptake and realizing the potential of chatbots for customer service [11, 15]. UX with service chatbots concerns whether the user is provided relevant answers to their queries and the chatbot interaction brings them closer to resolving their problem [8, 9]. This implies that user experience varies substantially depending on the problems that motivate users to interact with the chatbot. [15] Chatbot use is beneficial for companies when associated with positive customer experience [16].

2.3 Human-Centered Design

The development of human-centered chatbots is based on the idea of human-centered technology and human-centered design (HCD). HCD refers to development of useful technology that offers positive UX [7]. Focus is on humans and how they behave and interact with the technology, as it aims fundamentally understand and improve the relation between computational technology and human, as well as enhance human performance [14]. Human-centered approach can help designers adapt to the affordances of emerging technologies, making sure that essential and important factors are being considered in the development. This approach contributes to a broad consideration to human characteristics as well as contextual understanding very early in the product design in order to design an interactive system that fulfilo various stakeholders' needs.[7, 14].

3   Study Design

To identify relevant themes related human-centered service chatbots in current research we conducted a study using the integrative literature review method [19]. We use integrative literature review method, as that is suitable especially for emerging topics. An integrative review method should result in the advancement of knowledge and theoretical frameworks, rather than in a simply overview or description of a research area. We follow literature review process proposed by Snyder et al. (2019) that consists of four phases: (i) designing the review, (ii) conducting the review, (iii) analysis, and (iv) writing up the review [19]. The resulting literature corpus is described in Appendix.

3.1   Phase 1 – Designing the Review

The goal of this study was to understand and define the building blocks of human-centered service chatbots. As the topic is widely studied and it would not have been possible to systematically review all the material, we decided to approach the problem with an integrative literature review. An integrative literature review has an aim to assess, critique, and synthesize the literature on a research topic in a way that enables new theoretical frameworks and perspectives to emerge. This method has the purpose is usually not to cover all articles ever published on the topic but rather to combine perspectives and insights from different fields or research traditions. The general aim of a data analysis in an integrative review is to critically analyse and examine the literature and the main ideas and relationships of an issue. An integrative review method should result in the advancement of knowledge and theoretical frameworks, rather than in a simply overview or description of a research area [19]. We continued identifying databases for the literature search. Our primary database concluded to be Google Scholar, as we wanted to find studies from a variety of domains, and it covers all the relevant databases. Additionally, we used Semantic Scholar and the Tampere University's database.

After this, we determined the inclusion / exclusion criteria, based on this study's scope and aim.

The inclusion criteria in this review are the studies that:

- Refer to AI chatbots, their design, or UX.
- Refer to chatbots in customer service.
- Are published as peer-review academic articles.
- Are written in English.
- Are published between 2016–2022, as the use of chatbots in customer service has increase dramatically during last five years.

We excluded papers concentrating on:

- Rule-based chatbots, as their basic functioning is different. However, some papers did not specify if they were talking about rule-based or AI chatbots.
- Social chatbots papers, as we believe that these two types of chatbots should be studied differently regarding the profound differences in their affordances / purposes.
- Papers specific to certain use (e.g., 'Covid-19 chatbot'), use domain (e.g., education or banking), or geographical area (e.g., "Chatbot acceptance in India"), as our aim was to study the phenomena in general.
- Papers of technological development (e.g., chatbot development techniques or programming), as our aim is in the design.
- Personal assistants, since this term consistently refers to voice-based assistants such as Google Assistant or Amazon's Alexa.
- Publications others than academic papers, e.g., books or technical reports, as we wanted to base the knowledge in peer-review scientific knowledge.

3.2 Phase 2 – Conducting the Review

We had a four-step approach to conduct the integrative literature review.

Step 1 – initial search: we conducted the literature search in May 2022. We initially started querying the selected databases using a seed search term "chatbot" and "chatbots" which broadly described the subject matter and we wanted to collect information broadly from different perspectives (Noteworthy is that a search with a search word "human-centered + chatbot" came back with cero hits). For the same reason we chose to not limit the field of the study. Boolean words "AND", "OR", and "NOT" in the searching strategies were applied. Our first search 'chatbot OR chatbots' resulted in tens of thousands of results, so we added some restrictions from our exclusion criteria to the search in order to reduce the number of results. Thus, we applied a first filtering operation by selecting articles based on their title. The objective was to focus only on relevant articles for our study. For this step the exclusion criteria were used. We excluded papers that mentioned teaching, education, social, or health in the title, as these papers were not in the scope of our research. This resulted to 520 results.

Step 2 – screening: we screened these papers by the title, keywords, and abstract based on the predetermined inclusion / exclusion criteria to check their relevance to the research question. For this step the exclusion criteria were used. To maintain the original focus of our study, we discarded articles that focused on rule-based or social chatbots. We also discarded articles that consider chatbots for specific use or use domain. We selected only the relevant articles that provided concrete information related to service chatbots or AI chatbots. At the end of this step, 135 papers were shortlisted for review.

Step 3 - full text assessment: the full text of the shortlisted papers was assessed for relevance. We again used the inclusion / exclusion criteria, and also excluded some of the papers if they had no relevant information to offer related to our research question of human-centeredness of the service chatbots. Overall, 102 papers were excluded, leaving total of 33 papers included to our study corpus (list of papers is listed in Appendix). We conducted the same search in Semantic Scholar and Tampere University's database, but we did not find any new relevant articles with these searches.

Step 4 - snowballing: finally, we studied the bibliographies of the chosen articles to identify more articles that seemed pertinent. We used Google scholar to retrieve the full text of potential articles that appeared in the bibliography of 34 articles. This process allowed us to obtain a further two relevant articles for our study.

3.3 Phase 3 Analysis

We used the content of the selected and reviewed articles as data to be analysed for developing themes describing the phenomena. We combined deductive and inductive coding [18]. We had nine pre-determined codes related to the basic concepts of HCD: *user, user interface (UI), usability, user experience (UX), interaction, purpose, acceptance, adoption*, and *design*. We used these codes as keywords to find relevant information related to our research question. In addition, we used inductive coding, in order to find elements related to chatbots in customer service or to the use of AI in chatbots. The codes that emerged from the literature are: *antromorphism, trust, transparency, explainability, privacy and data use*, and *fairness*. All the different chatbot elements related to HCD identified in the papers were coded. The first author reviewed and coded all the data. We used data analysis -tool Atlas.ti for the coding. Data analysis was supported by memo writing [4]. After coding all the corpus, these codes and related memos were analysed and challenged by another researcher, and we refined and modified the codes based on these conversations. After refining the codes, the first author conducted a second round of coding and then as a team we discussed and refined each code. The data that we withdraw from the chosen articles was then analysed using Thematic Content Analysis (TCA). In thematic analysis, key elements and frequently occurring features are highlighted from the material in terms of the research problem [18, 22]. Our aim was in defining the building blocks that should be considered in HCD of service chatbots. Hence, we were not aiming to summarise and synthetise the content of the chosen articles, but derive the relevant information related to our RQ and the aim of the study. We reviewed the chosen articles with HTI and HCD lens, filtering the text based on the main concepts of these fields. We recognised three overarching themes defining the building blocks of HCD for service chatbots. Codes and themes are presented in Table 1. The outcome of this analysis is presented in the next section.

Table 1. Codes and themes.

Codes	Main theme	Subtheme
User (45), purpose (9), acceptance (23), adoption (14), domain (14), context (25)	Service chatbots purpose is to serve user and their needs	Users and their needs AI and chatbot to be used when the best tool Chatbot acceptance
Explainability (17), transparency (21), trust (94), fairness (13), privacy and data use (22)	Trust is essential for service chatbot uptake	Perceived expertise and responsiveness Explainability and transparency Privacy and data-use Fairness
Interaction (23), UI (21), UX (94), design (97), attributes and characteristics (28)	Service chatbot design should combine *UI*, *dialogue*, and *bot personality* design to create positive UX	UI design Dialogue design Bot personality

4 Results

This chapter presents three themes describing the building blocks of HCD of service chatbots derived from the data. In the theme descriptions, we refer to the articles in the corpus with codes A1…A34. In the beginning/end of each theme, we summarise the key points of the theme.

4.1 Theme 1: Service Chatbot's Purpose is to Serve User and Their Needs

Included codes: user, purpose, acceptance, domain, context.

User and Their Needs. Being compatible with the user should be the main goal for a chatbot. This depends on the way the bot carries out the conversation depending on its ability and qualities. The design and development of a chatbot should be based on the requirement from the customer base and should solve a specific purpose with the well-defined objective to be achieved. It is essential to clearly determine the user's problem and the necessity and the purpose of the bot. requirements and development decisions rise from these. Context needs to be considered in understanding the conversation or the type and purpose of the conversation for which chatbot needs to be designed. The domain where a chatbot will be deployed has to be fully understood in order to develop chatbot accordingly. Designers have to fully understand the context, its requirements, and then tailor the content to fit to it. It is crucial to specify the tasks of the bot - it should be clear what bot should do and how well. Tasks are aimed for the efficiency and usefulness of the service – being compatible with the user should be chatbots main goal.

AI and Chatbot to Be Used When the Best Tool. Appropriate AI technique and interaction design approach for the chatbot are chosen according to the purpose and the use domain. Chatbot and AI should be used when the best solution to the user problem, or they have something unique to offer. the hype around chatbots, as well as the need to save in costs, has motivated companies to deploy chatbots to support their customer service. However, there are factors related to the utilisation of AI as well as to technology as a customer servant. Hence, companies have to make sure they first understand the needs of their customers, their users, and based on those needs they try to find the best solution to solve that need. If that is AI-powered chatbot, companies should make sure that they have resources to build well-functioning chatbot that really solves the user needs. deploying a chatbot that does not work well or help the user to solve their problems, might affect negatively to the whole organisation or brand image [A9, A17, A22, A24].

Chatbot Acceptance. Correctness of the chatbot produced suggestions as well as its effectiveness are the keys to service chatbot acceptance. As service chatbots work as customer servants, the expectations that the users have for those are similar to the regular customer service – they have a problem or a query that they want help or guidance from the customer servant. A key success factor for service chatbots using natural language user interfaces is how well they can support user needs in the conversational process seamlessly and efficiently - if the user is able to solve their problem or their query, they are happy and content, and this affects positively to the acceptance of the chatbots in customer service. In order to develop correct and efficient service chatbot solutions, the developer have to understand the user need and define that chatbot tasks, so that they can base the development for these [A1, A2, A6, A14, A17, A18].

4.2 Theme 2: Trust is Essential for the Service Chatbot Uptake

Included codes: explainability, transparency, trust, ethics, fairness, privacy and data use.

Trust seems to be an important factor in human-chatbot interaction as well, especially in those contexts where the conversational agent's actions may have heavy consequences for the user. In related literature we found trust in customer service chatbots to be related to two factors: (i) chatbot-related factors, and (ii) context-related factors [A6, A18].

Perceived Expertise and Responsiveness. Results show that the chatbots' expertise and responsiveness impact trust. this means that the chatbot's ability to correctly interpret the users' requests, provide helpful responses, and relevance of the answers are key factors that positively impact on trust. The quality of the chatbot responses reflecting its ability to understand, and that builds trust. In addition, user's perception of the consistency with which the chatbot behaves, affects trust. In addition, getting fast response from the chatbot impact positively on trust, as such responsiveness makes the service chatbot an efficient means of support [A6, A9, A18].

Explainability and Transparency. Explainability of information processing performed by AI is essential when building trust. It is important to clearly explain how chatbot thinks and works, define the outcomes and how the chatbot will contribute to it. Helping people to understand chatbots workings can make them use them better. The explanations given by the chatbot should be appropriate for to user and to the user context, so that they would be understandable. human and chatbot need to communicate in a way that is intuitive for both of them. This requires the development of appropriate human-agent interfaces and agent protocols to provide information and visualise explanations. transparency of the chatbots could be translated as 'Truthfulness'. It is important that the bot is being truthful with the user throughout the interaction, starting with stating that it is a bot. It is beneficial to set the right expectations by declaring what the bot can do and how well, its skills and limitations. In addition, chatbot should always answer in reasonable manner, grounded on the understanding of the user and the domain. It is important, that with requests that the chatbot do not understand, it is honest and clear about the situation and the problematic part of the question, stating if they cannot answer, instead of silly answers. When Chatbot's skills match the expectations of the user, the UX will be better and trust is built [A1, A6, A9, A15, A22, A24, A32].

Privacy and Data-Use. One of the main aspects in trust in service chatbots is privacy and data use. Users have to feel comfortable to share even personal data, if it is necessary for the chatbot to serve to user effectively. Companies should be aware of the responsibilities and precautions related to the privacy, data collection, data use, and storage. The use of data should be designed to align with appropriate guidelines for the purpose and use domain. chatbot must always be developed to protect user data, also in the cases where the data is directed to a third party. User should always be able to know the data collected and how this data will be used and stored. User has to be able to abort the task before giving any personal data if they choose so [A1, A6, A8, A9, A14, A15, A25, A30].

Fairness. It is essential that chatbots are appropriately designed in order to mitigate risks. This way safe and fair chatbot solutions and service can be created. service chatbots often deal with user data, and this might bring challenges and requirements. It is essential that the chatbot is fair, hence they have to be designed to minimize bias and promote inclusive presentation, as AI has an impact on people's lives. Chatbots can affect the life of not only the user, but others too, so the fairness of their workings and outcomes is essential. In addition, chatbot should be designed to aligned with the norms and values of the user. This is why knowing the user and the domain is so important in chatbot development. In addition, for fair chatbots in customer service, organisations have to be aware of the potential negative effects of AI and how to overcome them [A9, A15, A30].

4.3 Theme 3: Chatbot Design Combines Dialogue Design, UI Design, and Bot Personality to Create Positive UX

Included codes: interaction, UI, UX, design, attributes and characteristics.

UI Design. UI design is essential in order to create chatbots that users can accomplish their tasks in effective and comfortable manner, as productivity is one of the main motives for accepting AI-chatbot to use. however, visual UI design for chatbots is more about visual design and the designer repertoire of graphical and interaction mechanisms will is reduced [A14]. The design objectives and the interaction design should be determined based on different influencing factors, that are: the type of user and their needs, use context, and Bot's purpose and tasks. It is important for the UI to suit the users in the target domain [A14]. Adding AI to Chatbots add to its possibilities to interact with the user, and this kind of personalisation and accessibility is one of the biggest benefits for the chatbot users. It is essential, that the ui adapts to the needs of different user groups and that the user can choose the way to interact with the chatbot. Chatbot UI should support flexible interactions depending on the use context by providing users with the appropriate or preferred input and output modality and hardware. In addition, it is important that chatbot system always keep users informed about what is going on without overwhelming the user. The system should guide the user throughout the dialogue by clarifying system capabilities. Help features should be visible when needed, they should be easy to retrieve and search, focused on the user's task, list concrete steps to be carried out. The user may require information on how to interact with the conversational agent, they should not be overwhelmed with too much information [A10, A14, A21].

Dialogue Design. Language and conversation play a vital role in human-chatbot interaction. Appropriate, natural conversation offers smooth interaction, so that the user can accomplish their goals efficiently. This helps in building trust between the chatbot and the user, that can lead to a positive UX. Natural conversation, as a sense of understanding and communication is developed between human and chatbot making the chatbot easy for the user to use. Language and tone must be adjustable to the language of the target audience. To ensure the quality of communication the language must be set to a specific target audience – these decisions are made depending on the type of user and the use context. Past research has identified simple and uncomplicated responses as the key to significant AI interactions. Responsiveness of the chatbot is important - chatbots should understand user's input and queries and respond accordingly. Managing the conversation context is probably one of the most challenging aspects of designing a Chatbot. The mismatch between the chatbots context in the conversation and the users perception of the chatbots understanding leads to confusion and consequent dialogue breaks. The openness of conversational interfaces and variations in the user input are the main challenges in chatbot design. There are no error-free chatbots, however, it is important to design for these situations - any chatbot design has to properly address conversations breakdowns. When chatbot does not understand user query, it should state this clearly and ask for clarification, or offer the user guidance how to continue in the situation. since Chatbots by definition inhere a key characteristic of interpersonal communication (i.e., use of natural language), they always elicit some social behaviour. As a consequence, even task-oriented service chatbots should not only be designed to be functional, but also to act social [A1, A3, A5, A6, A12, A13, A14, A18, A20, A21, A22, A24].

Bot Personality. Designing a chatbot that meats users expectations is crucial in order it to succeed. Chatbot should be human-like but not too much - these decisions are made depending on the type of user and the use context. Anthropomorphism (i.e., attribution of human-like characteristics) is an important topic in service chatbots. The level of it has to be fully considered in relation to the user and the use context. some level of human-likeness might make to chatbot more acceptable for the user, as the chatbot matches users "Mental Model" as customer servant. however, too much human-likeness might result in over-expectations from users side, and this can lead to a disappointment in the interaction and to bad UX and abandonment of the chatbot. Chatbot should have an avatar - digital representation of real people - rather than virtual agent, and this chatbot embodiment should meet users expectations. This means, that for example a chatbot that is answering to health-related questions should have an embodiment of a nurse instead of talking watermelon. In addition, animated facial representations make the avatar and chatbot appear more human-like and increases the naturalness of the communication. Users find it easier to communicate with a chatbot that has certain level of human-like naturalness, and if the personality of the bot matches with the ones of the user, this can lead to better UX. Social cues, like humour, chitchat, and empathy, are another important part of bot personality -design. However, choosing an appropriate social cue design for a service chatbot is a difficult and complex challenge, because social cues of chatbots can lead to either positive or negative UX. For example, research has shown that users perceive small talk of a chatbot differently according to their cultural background, prefer visual appearances of chatbots that correspond to task related gender stereotypes. Therefore, it is highly important to consider several influences in the design of a chatbot to create positive UX and to avoid possible negative effects [A2, A5, A6, A17, A19, A21, A22, A23, A24, A27].

5   Discussion

This study was set to understand what are building blocks of HCD for service chatbots. We recognised three overarching themes describing the building blocks.

Theme 1 - Service chatbots purpose is to serve users and their needs: AI service chatbots are here to serve the user. Hence, the development of the chatbot should be based on real user needs and benefits, not on company savings. The user, use context, purpose, and domain should be in the centre of the development.

Our results show that there are some similarities to the know concepts and factors related to HCD, like the importance of understanding the user and their needs in order to make the chatbot useful. In addition, understanding the use context is essential so that the develop chatbots solution fits to the use context. We found similarities to know basics of human-centered design – user and their needs should lead the way. Design should include only features that are needed to accomplish the user task. However, since chatbots are becoming increasingly prevalent across all industries, chatbots success increasingly depends on their ability to adapt chatbots design to the conditions it is developed for, which includes, in particular, the users and their needs, and the chatbot's purpose. Nevertheless, it is not a simple task, as chatbots are meant to serve different user groups with various skills and understandings. However, the adaptability of AI, used correctly, helps in order to serve users with different needs. The tasks of service chatbots can usually be defined quite well, as their purpose has to be well considered, and for this their design might be easier.

Theme 2 - Trust is essential for service chatbot uptake: Trust is focal point of successful human-chatbot interaction, and it is essential for successful interaction and their uptake. It is important that the user can trust the bot, especially when the user is asked to share personal information. Building trust between human and service chatbot is related to factors specific to (i) the chatbot: expertise, responsiveness, explainability, transparency, and (ii) the context: privacy and data-use, fairness.

Trust is a known essential factor in technology acceptance. Our result show, that this is true in service chatbot context, too. Trust in technology has previously been seen in the light of the technology's functionality, ability to provide help and operational reliability.

Our results partly support this. However, the factors contributing to the trust between the service chatbot and the user, are related not only to the technology, but several other factors, like to the appriate use of AI and data, and the responsiveness of the chatbot. User trust in service chatbots is not important only for their acceptance and uptake. It is required for the appropriate functioning of the service chatbot in the purpose it is designed to, meaning that the service chatbot should make the user to feel comfortable to share required information to solve the user problem. In addition, trust is essential form the users perspective, too, as chatbot technology is gradually becoming part of people's everyday life – trusting chatbots offers humans a possibility for a new, enhanced user experience and customer service form. Explainability of AI's decisions and transparency of AI's funtioning and data use are important elements to acknowledge in service chatbot design as they help to build trust. Communication and understanding between user and chatbot are essential which results in better understanding of the issue encountered by the user. However, it has to be fully considered, which aspects of artificial behaviour are explain-worthy and how to provide this information to the user, as explainability might challenge the effectiveness of the chatbot. It is clear, that the developers have to know the user and the use context well in order to make their chatbot work and meet the users expectations. If the expectations are not met, that might lead to no adopt the chatbot in use. Efficiency is the main motive to use chatbots, so the design should be concentrating on that by building on the understanding of the user and their needs and the context, and as AI allows personalisation, more varied user groups can be served. However, it has to be acknowledged, that there are always problems in the communication, as there is no error free chatbots. The use of AI and NPL offer more natural intercation, but this means that the interaction is harder to control. The way the chatbots messages are understand depends on the understanding of the user. However, it is important how the chatbots handles these error-situations by informing the user of the communication gap, and by directing them to a human customer servant.

Theme 3 - Service chatbot design combines UI design, dialogue design, and bot personality design in order to create positive UX: *Designing the chatbot combines three equally important parts: dialogue design, UI design, and bot personality -design. The design functionalities have a significant impact on the way a user interacts with the chatbot, hence they affect to the UX.*

In order to be effective and efficient for the user, chatbots have to be usable. Usually, good usability is assured with appropriate UI design. However, for the use of AI and the natural converstation provided by it, usability design of service chatbots, there is a clear shift from UI design to dialogue design, as the user is mostly interacting through the dialogue. Hence, chatbot UI design is less demanding, as the command are done by conversing – however, this demands proper dialogue design in order to user queries clear and understandable. Hence, the usability of chatbot is not depending only on the usability of the visual UI, that much than to the level of the conversation, meaning how well the chatbot understand user queries. With service chatbots good UX is a result of good, effective conversation that enables the users to solve their problem. Hence, important is how well user can accomplish the task, and usually with chatbot this, either is related to the UI, but to the chatbots understanding of users queries. Problems with the communication can lead to negative UX and abandonment. UI design might be less demanding in service chatbot context. However, the main motivation for the chatbot use is efficiency, hence clear chatbot UI is required, however simple it is. In addition, usability of service chatbots means that the chatbot states what they can do and then do it. Like with any other human-technology interaction, it is important to provide user guidance throughout interaction, like always, but with chatbots this should be done with the conversation, too, rather than with visual clues in UI. This makes the UI simpler, and its design easier, but it might increase the user's congnitive load, if the guidance is given in the dialogue. With AI the user can interact with the service both in a way that is preferable for them, usually by text or voice, and this has to be acknowledged in the development.

5.1 Future Work

The HCD building blocks defined in this study work as an initial structure for AI chatbot design guidelines. It is built on the findings from the literature analysed by only a few researchers, but it is expected to evolve as future works build on the understanding on the topic. We aim for our initial model to serve as a basis for future research on human-centered chatbot development and that it hence will benefit the community of chatbot and HCI researchers in guiding needed work in this area. We will continue the research in the future by developing HCD approach for service chatbot design. We will use these themes as a base for the approach. We will adopt an iterative way of working, and evaluate the suggested HCD approach with chatbot design professionals.

5.2 Limitations

There are some limitations related to this study. As the review was not systematic but followed integrative review method, there is a possibility of leaving out some relevant related research. However, the purpose of this study was to form understanding on this novel topic, as well as provide a basis to build on, so the limitation of this study can be adjusted in the future research.

6 Conclusion

This study provides a basis for future chatbot design by presenting themes summarising the building blocks of the human-centered design for AI service chatbots. Three main themes emerged from the integrative literature review: (1) Theme 1 - Service chatbots purpose is to serve users and their needs, (2) Theme 2 - Trust is essential for service chatbot uptake:, and (3) service chatbot design combines UI design, dialogue design, and bot personality design in order to create positive UX. These themes and their subthemes can be used for a basis for the research in this emerging topic. In addition, the themes can be used to support and guide service chatbot design in deploying companies to develop AI chatbots that improve users' and company's current processes, saving time, using fewer resources, and improving quality of the service.

Acknowledgement. We are grateful for the funders of Human-Centered AI Solutions for the Smart City (KITE) project in which this research was conducted: European Regional Development Fund, Business Tampere, and University of Tampere.

Appendix

Literature review corpus

	Authors	Title	Publication	Vol	Nr	Pages	Year	Publisher
A1	Brandtzaeg, Petter Bae; Følstad, Asbjørn;	Chatbots: changing user needs and motivations	interactions	25	5	38–43	2018	ACM New York, NY, USA
A2	Chaves, Ana Paula; Gerosa, Marco Aurelio;	How should my chatbot interact? A survey on social characteristics in human–chatbot interaction design	International Journal of Human–Computer Interaction	37	8	729–758	2021	Taylor & Francis
A3	Piccolo, Lara SG; Mensio, Martino; Alani, Harith;	Chasing the chatbots: Directions for interaction and design research	Internet Science: INSCI 2018 International Workshops, St. Petersburg, Russia, October 24–26, 2018,			157–169	2019	Springer International Publishing Cham
A4	Følstad, Asbjørn; Brandtzaeg, Petter Bae;	Users' experiences with chatbots: findings from a questionnaire study	Quality and User Experience	5	1	3	2020	Springer International Publishing Cham
A5	Ciechanowski, Leon; Przegalinska, Aleksandra; Magnuski, Mikolaj; Gloor, Peter;	In the shades of the uncanny valley: An experimental study of human–chatbot interaction	Future Generation Computer Systems	92		539–548	2019	Elsevier
A6	Rapp, Amon; Curti, Lorenzo; Boldi, Arianna;	The human side of human-chatbot interaction: A systematic literature review of ten years of research on text-based chatbots	International Journal of Human-Computer Studies	151		102630	2021	Academic Press

(*continued*)

(continued)

	Authors	Title	Publication	Vol	Nr	Pages	Year	Publisher
A7	Mygland, Morten Johan; Schibbye, Morten; Pappas, Ilias O; Vassilakopoulou, Polyxeni;	Affordances in human-chatbot interaction: a review of the literature	Responsible AI and Analytics for an Ethical and Inclusive Digitized Society: 20th IFIP WG 6.11 Conference on e-Business, e-Services and e-Society, I3E 2021, Galway, Ireland, September 1–3, 2021, Proceedings 20			3–17	2021	Springer International Publishing
A8	Ischen, Carolin; Araujo, Theo; Voorveld, Hilde; van Noort, Guda; Smit, Edith;	Privacy concerns in chatbot interactions	Chatbot Research and Design: Third International Workshop, CONVERSATIONS 2019, Amsterdam, The Netherlands, November 19–20, 2019,			34–48	2020	Springer International Publishing
A9	Przegalinska, Aleksandra; Ciechanowski, Leon; Stroz, Anna; Gloor, Peter; Mazurek, Grzegorz;	In bot we trust: A new methodology of chatbot performance measures	Business Horizons	62	6	785–797	2019	Elsevier
A10	Sugisaki, Kyoko; Bleiker, Andreas;	Usability guidelines and evaluation criteria for conversational user interfaces: a heuristic and linguistic approach	Proceedings of Mensch und Computer 2020			309–319	2020	
A11	Borsci, Simone; Malizia, Alessio; Schmettow, Martin; Van Der Velde, Frank; Tariverdiyeva, Gunay; Balaji, Divyaa; Chamberlain, Alan;	The Chatbot Usability Scale: the design and pilot of a usability scale for interaction with AI-based conversational agents	Personal and Ubiquitous Computing	26		95–119	2022	Springer London
A12	Abdul-Kader, Sameera A; Woods, John C;	Survey on chatbot design techniques in speech conversation systems	International Journal of Advanced Computer Science and Applications	6	7		2015	The Science and Information (SAI) Organization
A13	Sheehan, Ben; Jin, Hyun Seung; Gottlieb, Udo;	Customer service chatbots: Anthropomorphism and adoption	Journal of Business Research	115		14–24	2020	Elsevier

(continued)

(continued)

	Authors	Title	Publication	Vol	Nr	Pages	Year	Publisher
A14	Følstad, Asbjørn; Brandtzæg, Petter Bae;	Chatbots and the new world of HCI	interactions	24	4	38–42	2017	ACM New York, NY, USA
A15	Murtarelli, Grazia; Gregory, Anne; Romenti, Stefania;	A conversation-based perspective for shaping ethical human–machine interactions: The particular challenge of chatbots	Journal of Business Research	129		927–935	2021	Elsevier
A16	Maroengsit, Wari; Piyakulpinyo, Thanarath; Phonyiam, Korawat; Pongnumkul, Suporn; Chaovalit, Pimwadee; Theeramunkong, Thanaruk;	A survey on evaluation methods for chatbots	Proceedings of the 2019 7th International conference on information and education technology			111–119	2019	
A17	Adam, Martin; Wessel, Michael; Benlian, Alexander;	AI-based chatbots in customer service and their effects on user compliance	Electronic Markets	31	2	427–445	2021	Springer
A18	Nordheim, Cecilie Bertinussen; Følstad, Asbjørn; Bjørkli, Cato Alexander;	An initial model of trust in chatbots for customer service—findings from a questionnaire study	Interacting with Computers	31	3	317–335	2019	Oxford University Press
A19	Crolic, Cammy; Thomaz, Felipe; Hadi, Rhonda; Stephen, Andrew T;	Blame the bot: anthropomorphism and anger in customer–chatbot interactions	Journal of Marketing	86	1	132–148	2022	SAGE Publications Sage CA: Los Angeles, CA
A20	Smestad, Tuva Lunde; Volden, Frode;	Chatbot personalities matters: improving the user experience of chatbot interfaces	Internet Science: INSCI 2018 International Workshops, St. Petersburg, Russia, October 24–26, 2018			170–181	2019	Springer
A21	Di Prospero, Adam; Norouzi, Nojan; Fokaefs, Marios; Litoiu, Marin;	Chatbots as assistants: an architectural framework	Proceedings of the 27th Annual International Conference on Computer Science and Software Engineering			76–86	2017	

(continued)

(*continued*)

	Authors	Title	Publication	Vol	Nr	Pages	Year	Publisher
A22	Schuetzler, Ryan M; Grimes, G Mark; Giboney, Justin Scott; Rosser, Holly K;	Deciding Whether and How to Deploy Chatbots	MIS Quarterly Executive	20	1		2021	
A23	Roy, Rajat; Naidoo, Vik;	Enhancing chatbot effectiveness: The role of anthropomorphic conversational styles and time orientation	Journal of Business Research	126		23–34	2021	Elsevier
A24	Skjuve, Marita; Haugstveit, Ida Maria; Følstad, Asbjørn; Brandtzaeg, Petter;	Help! Is my chatbot falling into the uncanny valley? An empirical study of user experience in human–chatbot interaction	Human Technology	15	1	30	2019	Centre of Sociological Research (NGO)
A25	Cheng, Yang; Jiang, Hua;	How do AI-driven chatbots impact user experience? Examining gratifications, perceived privacy risk, satisfaction, loyalty, and continued use	Journal of Broadcasting & Electronic Media	64	4	592–614	2020	Taylor & Francis
A26	Cheng, Xusen; Zhang, Xiaoping; Cohen, Jason; Mou, Jian;	Human vs. AI: Understanding the impact of anthropomorphism on consumer response to chatbots from the perspective of trust and relationship norms	Information Processing & Management	59	3	102940	2022	Elsevier
A27	Go, Eun; Sundar, S Shyam;	Humanizing chatbots: The effects of visual, identity and conversational cues on humanness perceptions	Computers in Human Behavior	97		304–316	2019	Elsevier
A28	Ashfaq, Muhammad; Yun, Jiang; Yu, Shubin; Loureiro, Sandra Maria Correia;	I, Chatbot: Modeling the determinants of users' satisfaction and continuance intention of AI-powered service agents	Telematics and Informatics	54		101473	2020	Elsevier

(*continued*)

(*continued*)

	Authors	Title	Publication	Vol	Nr	Pages	Year	Publisher
A29	Følstad, Asbjørn; Taylor, Cameron;	Investigating the user experience of customer service chatbot interaction: a framework for qualitative analysis of chatbot dialogues	Quality and User Experience	6	1	6	2021	Springer
A30	Srivastava, Biplav; Rossi, Francesca; Usmani, Sheema; Bernagozzi, Mariana;	Personalized chatbot trustworthiness ratings	IEEE Transactions on Technology and Society	1	4	184–192	2020	IEEE
A31	Ciechanowski, Leon; Przegalinska, Aleksandra, Wegner, Krzysztof;	The necessity of new paradigms in measuring human-chatbot interaction	Advances in Cross-Cultural Decision Making: Proceedings of the AHFE 2017 International Conference on Cross-Cultural Decision Making, July 17–21, 2017			205–214	2018	Springer
A32	Yen, Chiahui; Chiang, Ming-Chang;	Trust me, if you can: a study on the factors that influence consumers' purchase intention triggered by chatbots based on brain image evidence and self-reported assessments	Behaviour & Information Technology	40	11	1177–1194	2021	Taylor & Francis
A33	Kvale, Knut; Freddi, Eleonora; Hodnebrog, Stig; Sell, Olav Alexander; Følstad, Asbjørn;	Understanding the user experience of customer service chatbots: what can we learn from customer satisfaction surveys?	Chatbot Research and Design: 4th International Workshop, CONVERSATIONS 2020, Virtual Event, November 23–24, 2020			205–218	2021	Springer
A34	Janssen, Antje; Grützner, Lukas; Breitner, Michael H;	Why do chatbots fail? A critical success factors analysis	International Conference on Information Systems (ICIS)				2021	

References

1. Adam, M., Wessel, M., Benlian, A.: AI-based chatbots in customer service and their effects on user compliance. Electron. Mark. **31**(2), 427–445 (2020). https://doi.org/10.1007/s12525-020-00414-7

2. Adamopoulou, E., Moussiades, L.: Chatbots: History, technology, and applications. Mach. Learn. Appl. **2** (2020)
3. Aslam, W., Siddiqui, D.A., Arif, I., Farhat, K.: Chatbots in the frontline: drivers of acceptance. Kybernetes (ahead-of-print) (2022)
4. Birks, M., Chapman, Y., Francis, K.: Memoing in qualitative research: probing data and processes. J. Res. Nurs. **13**(1), 68–75 (2008)
5. Brandtzaeg, P.B., Følstad, A.: Why people use chatbots. In: Kompatsiaris, I. (ed.) INSCI 2017. LNCS, vol. 10673, pp. 377–392. Springer, Cham (2017). https://doi.org/10.1007/978-3-319-70284-1_30
6. Cheng, Y., Jiang, H.: How do AI-driven chatbots impact user experience? examining gratifications, perceived privacy risk, satisfaction, loyalty, and continued use. J. Broadcast. Electron. Media **64**(4), 592–614 (2020)
7. Cooley, M.: Human-centered design. Inform. Des. 59–81 (2000)
8. Følstad, A., Skjuve, M., Brandtzaeg, P.B.: Different chatbots for different purposes: towards a typology of chatbots to understand interaction design. In: Internet Science. INSCI 2018. Lecture Notes in Computer Science, vol. 11551. Springer, Cham (2019). https://doi.org/10.1007/978-3-030-17705-8_13
9. Følstad, A., Skjuve, M.: Chatbots for customer service: user experience and motivation. In: Proceedings of the 1st International Conference on Conversational User Interfaces 2019, pp. 1–9, 22 August 2019
10. Grudin, J., Jacques, R.: Chatbots, humbots, and the quest for artificial general intelligence. In: Proceedings of the 2019 CHI Conference on Human Factors in Computing Systems, pp. 1–11 (2019)
11. Haugeland, I.K., Følstad, A., Taylor, C., Bjørkli, C.A.: Understanding the user experience of customer service chatbots: an experimental study of chatbot interaction design. Int. J. Hum.-Comput. Stud. **161**, 102788 (2022)
12. Hartikainen, M., Väänänen, K., Lehtiö, A., Ala-Luopa, S., Olsson, T.: Human-centered AI design in reality: a study of developer companies' practices: a study of developer companies' practices. In: Nordic Human-Computer Interaction Conference, pp. 1–11 (2022)
13. Hussain, S., Ameri Sianaki, O., Ababneh, N.: A survey on conversational agents/chatbots classification and design techniques. In: Barolli, L., Takizawa, M., Xhafa, F., Enokido, T. (eds.) Web, Artificial Intelligence and Network Applications. WAINA 2019. Advances in Intelligent Systems and Computing, vol. 927. Springer, Cham (2019). https://doi.org/10.1007/978-3-030-15035-8_93
14. ISO 9241-210:2019. https://www.iso.org/standard/77520.html. Accessed 2 Nov 2022
15. Kvale, K., Freddi, E., Hodnebrog, S., Sell, O.A., Følstad, A.: Understanding the user experience of customer service chatbots: what can we learn from customer satisfaction surveys?. In: Chatbot Research and Design: 4th International Workshop, CONVERSATIONS 2020, Virtual Event, 23–24 November 2020
16. Mygland, M.J., Schibbye, M., Pappas, I.O., Vassilakopoulou, P.: Affordances in human-chatbot interaction: a review of the literature. In: Dennehy, D., Griva, A., Pouloudi, N., Dwivedi, Y.K., Pappas, I., Mäntymäki, M. (eds.) Responsible AI and Analytics for an Ethical and Inclusive Digitized Society. I3E 2021. Lecture Notes in Computer Science, vol. 12896. Springer, Cham (2021). https://doi.org/10.1007/978-3-030-85447-8_1
17. Rapp, A., Curti, L., Boldi, A.: The human side of human-chatbot interaction: a systematic literature review of ten years of research on text-based chatbots. Int. J. Hum Comput Stud. **151**, 102630 (2021)
18. Scharp, K.M., Sanders, M.L.: What is a theme? teaching thematic analysis in qualitative communication research methods. Commun. Teach. **33**(2), 117–121 (2019)
19. Snyder, H.: Literature review as a research methodology: an overview and guidelines. J. Bus. Res. **104**, 333–339 (2019)

20. Stoilova, E.: AI chatbots as a customer service and support tool. ROBONOMICS J. Autom. Econ. **16**, 2–21 (2021)
21. Suhaili, S.M., Salim, N., Jambli, M.N.: Service chatbots: a systematic review. Expert Syst. Appl. **184**, 115461 (2021)
22. Sundler, A.J., Lindberg, E., Nilsson, C., Palmér, L.: Qualitative thematic analysis based on descriptive phenomenology. Nurs. Open **6**(3), 733–739 (2019)
23. van der Goot, M.J., Hafkamp, L., Dankfort, Z.: Customer service chatbots: a qualitative interview study into the communication journey of customers. In: Følstad, A., Araujo, T., Papadopoulos, S., Law, E.-C., Luger, E., Goodwin, M., Brandtzaeg, P.B. (eds.) CONVERSATIONS 2020. LNCS, vol. 12604, pp. 190–204. Springer, Cham (2021). https://doi.org/10.1007/978-3-030-68288-0_13

User Experience for Artificial Intelligence Assistant: Focusing on Negative Side Effects

Danbi Lee[1], Gayoung Kim[1], and Hyun K. Kim[1,2(✉)]

[1] Department of Artificial Intelligence Application, Kwangwoon University, Seoul 01897, Korea
{danbi5739,ciks2508}@naver.com, hyunkkim@kw.ac.kr
[2] School of Information Convergence, Kwangwoon University, Seoul 01897, Korea

Abstract. In this study, we have reviewed the possible negative side effects (NSEs) of existing artificial intelligence (AI) secretarial services and propose a task performance method that can mitigate these effects. An AI assistant is a voice user interface (VUI) that combines voice recognition with AI technology to support self-learning. When a user encounters the unintended behavior of an AI agent or they cannot predict all the outcomes of using an agent at the development stage, NSEs may occur. Reducing NSEs in AI has been emerging as a major research task, while there is a lack of research on applications and solutions regarding AI secretaries. In this study, we performed a user interface (UI) analysis of actual services; designed NSE mitigation task execution methods; and developed three prototypes: A-existing AI secretarial method, B-confirmation request method, and C-question guidance method. The usability assessment comprised these factors: efficiency, flexibility, meaningfulness, accuracy, trust, error count, and task execution time. Prototype C showed higher efficiency, flexibility, meaningfulness, accuracy, and trust than prototypes A and B did, with B showing higher error counts and task execution times. Most users preferred prototype C since it presented a verifiable option that enabled tasks to be quickly executed with short commands. The results of this study can be used as basic data for research related to the NSEs of using AI and be used as a reference in designing and evaluating AI services.

Keywords: AI assistant · Negative side effects · AI system usability

1 Introduction

Recently, artificial intelligence (AI) is being increasingly used for controlling devices in fields such as robotics/autonomous driving, healthcare, and the Internet of things, which are associated with the 4th Industrial Revolution [1]. Currently, the AI assistant service is the common AI service; it can learn on its own by combining AI technology with a voice recognition system [2]. Using the voice recognition function, it understands a user's words, learns behavioral patterns, and provides the customized services users need for finding and using information related to items such as music, schedules, and weather forecasts [3]. After Amazon released Alexa in 2014, AI assistance services have been used in various applications, including smartphones, computers, and self-driving cars [4].

© The Author(s), under exclusive license to Springer Nature Switzerland AG 2023
H. Degen and S. Ntoa (Eds.): HCII 2023, LNAI 14051, pp. 88–97, 2023.
https://doi.org/10.1007/978-3-031-35894-4_6

Unintended AI agent behavior can result in negative side effects (NSEs), which are not just simple software bugs and hardware failures [5], but serious effects that occur because the outcome of all an agent's behaviors cannot be predicted during the development stage. Saisubramanian, Zilberstein, and Kamar [6] mentioned certain cases of NSEs: water was splashed on surrounding walls when using an automatic robot water cleaner [7]; water was splashed on nearby pedestrians when using a self-driving car that did not slow down when passing through a puddle [8, 9]; and Amazon Alexa had ordered an unwanted product after just hearing a voice on the TV [10]. To improve the safety and reliability of autonomous systems, they need to learn how to recognize and avoid the side effects of these agent behaviors [5, 6]. With the increased application of AI in various fields, mitigating the NSEs of AI is emerging as a major research issue. Saisubramanian, Roberts, and Zilberstein [5] investigated users' attitudes toward NSEs and their impact on users' confidence in autonomous systems. These users mentioned they could tolerate mild NSEs that did not endanger safety but generally preferred that NSEs be minimized, indicating that they would rather use a system after reconfiguring its environment to reduce NSEs. Saisubramanian, Zilberstein, and Kamar [6] examined the key characteristics of NSEs by classifying them based on severity, reversibility, availability, Frequency, stochasticity, observability, and exclusivity. Based on this, we reviewed system updates, change capability constraints, deviation minimization, and human-agent collaboration to mitigate NSEs. Updating agent behavior patterns is a common approach for mitigating NSEs. Hadfield-Menell et al. [11] developed an inverse reward design to help mitigate NSEs when designing reward features that guide agent behavior. Changes for redesigning the compensation functions of AI agents are critical in cases wherein NSEs endanger safety. Saisubramanian, Kamar, and Zilberstein [12] proposed algorithms that formulated potential NSE problems for different scenarios and determined the minimum slack required to avoid them. These algorithms aim to minimize NSEs rather than optimize the agent's assigned task and can handle both avoidable and unavoidable NSEs [12]. Saisubramanian and Zilberstein [13] described a collaborative approach involving human agents that could mitigate NSEs through environmental formation. In this process, the current environment undergoes agent-friendly modifications to minimize the occurrence of NSEs, allowing agents to optimize assigned tasks without needing to recognize NSEs. The NSEs of agent behavior can also be mitigated if the user fundamentally shapes the environment accordingly [13]. However, there is insufficient research on solutions that mitigate user experience (UX)-related NSEs that occur when using AI secretarial service cases.

The current study aims to analyze the user interface (UI) and UX of existing AI assistant services to identify potential NSE cases and proposes task performance methods that can mitigate these effects accordingly. Accordingly, we propose two methods: confirmation request method B and question guidance method C. Then, we tested the following hypotheses.

H1: Proposed methods B and C will have higher efficiency, flexibility, meaningfulness, accuracy, and trust than the existing AI assistant method A does.

H2: Proposed methods B and C will differ in the number of errors and task execution time, which are objective usability measures.

2 Method

2.1 Participants

The experiment was conducted on 21 male and female (five males and 16 females) university students in their 20s (average age 23.4 years (SD = 1.1)); 10 subjects used AI secretaries frequently while the other 11 did not. Generally, Apple's Siri was the most used AI assistant service, being mainly utilized for managing schedules and selecting alarms.

2.2 Prototype

In this study, we identified possible NSEs through a UI analysis of three popular AI assistant services (Apple's Siri, Samsung's Bixby, and Google's Google Assistant). Subsequently, a task performance method that could mitigate NSEs was designed. Using HTML/CSS/JavaScript, AI assistant prototypes A, B, and C were developed. These prototypes performed online screen development using an AI assistant, conducted speech recognition via WebSphere API, and collected the voice outputs of the AI assistants via the Typecast service (Fig. 1, Table 1). Here, A is the existing method, and B and C are the proposed methods. Prototype B is a confirmation request method that can be modified by adding a confirmation request before achieving a work goal, and prototype C is a question-inducing method that provides options to induce questions and thereby achieve the work goal. For example, consider that a message is sent to a contact with the same name, as shown in Table 1. For this case, prototype A will show the current side effects of the AI secretaries, completing the task immediately without a confirmation request before sending the message. Before sending this message, prototype B will request confirmation again, asking, "Should I send a text to ~ ?" and provide a button to modify the message such that it can be sent to the desired target. Prototype C will present all the contacts stored under the same name and ask the user, "Which of these would you like to send a message to?" so that the user can send a message to the desired target.

2.3 Procedure

The subjects were guided on the purpose and procedure of the experiment and were given explanations on the scenarios wherein they would use the prototypes A, B, and C. The subjects were subjected to a usability evaluation after using these prototypes according to the given scenarios. The scenarios used in this study are shown in Table 2. The interviews were conducted after the usability assessment was completed. The experiment lasted for approximately 30 min and could be interrupted whenever the subjects wanted.

The usability evaluation index consisted of efficiency, flexibility, meaningfulness, accuracy, and trust, selected from reconstructing the seven principles of the user experience honeycomb proposed by Morville and Sullenger [14] and the ten principles of usability proposed by Nielsen [15]. An 11-point scale from 0 to 10 was used, as shown in Table 3. A score of 0 meant "not very much" and a score of 10 meant "quite a lot." The number of errors and task execution time among the prototypes were measured and compared.

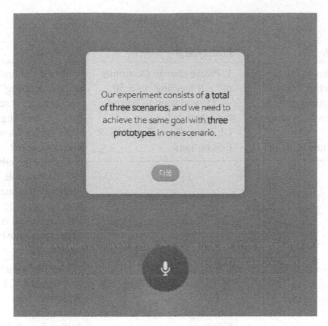

Fig. 1. Experimental environment.

Table 1. Examples of working of prototypes A, B, and C.

	Prototype A	Prototype B	Prototype C
1	1. Send a text message to OO → What kind of content should be sent to OO? 2. Send "What are you doing?" → I sent a text message to OO (010–1234-5678) asking "What are you doing?" UI: To, Message content	1. Send a text message to OO → What kind of content should be sent to OO? 2. Send "What are you doing?" → Would you like to send a text message to OO (010–1234-5678) asking "What are you doing?" UI: To, Message content, OK & Edit buttons	1. Send a text message to OO → I found three contacts that include OO. Whom should I send the text message to? 2. Send it to the nth contact → What kind of content should be sent to OO? 3. Send "What are you doing?" → I sent a text message to OO (010–5678-1234) asking "What are you doing?" UI: Display all OO contact information (name, phone number) with the same name

(continued)

Table 1. (*continued*)

	Prototype A	Prototype B	Prototype C
2	1. Please change the timing of "△△ meeting" to 8:30 → The schedule of "△△ meeting" has been changed to 8:30 UI: Date, Time, Title	1. Please change the timing of "△△ meeting" to 8:30 → Do you want to correct the schedule? UI: Date, Time, Title, OK & Edit buttons	1. Please change the timing of "△△ meeting" to 8:30 → There are 3 schedules for the "△△ meeting." Which of these schedules would you like to change? 2. Correct the nth schedule → The schedule of "△△ meeting" has been changed to 8:30 UI: Display all △△ schedules (date, time, title) with the same title
3	1. Play the song "□□." → Plays "□□." UI: Song title, Artist	1. Play the song "□□." → Do you want to play A's "□□"? UI: Song title, Artist, OK & Edit buttons	1. Play the song "□□." → I found 5 "□□" songs. Which of these would you like to play? 2. Play the nth one → Plays B's "□□" music UI: Display all □□ music (song title, artist) with the same title

Table 2. Scenarios.

Scenario	Content
1	Text-messaging contacts with the same name
2	Modifying scheduled timings with the same title
3	Playing pieces of music with the same title

Table 3. Usability evaluation index.

Factor	Question	
Efficiency	Q1	In this prototype, the AI system saves us time on achieving our goals
	Q2	In this prototype, the AI system can achieve a given goal at once

(*continued*)

Table 3. (*continued*)

Factor	Question	
	Q3	In this prototype, the information provided by the AI system can be immediately perceived
	Q4	In this prototype, the AI system is effective for performing voice control
Flexibility	Q5	In this prototype, the AI system can interact as desired by the user
	Q6	In this prototype, the AI system can choose the most appropriate method for a specific situation
	Q7	In this prototype, the AI system can perform the same task in many ways
	Q8	In this prototype, the AI system can achieve a given goal by providing users with only voice information
Meaningfulness	Q9	In this prototype, the AI system is easy to use
	Q10	In this prototype, the AI system provides an intuitive understanding of how to be used
	Q11	In this prototype, the AI system provides additional information on achieving a given goal
	Q12	The flow of the AI system can be predicted from this prototype
Accuracy	Q13	In this prototype, the AI system can be modified if it is not given a goal
	Q14	In this prototype, the AI system has fewer voice recognition errors
	Q15	In this prototype, the AI system can continue toward achieving the given goal even if the user makes an error
	Q16	This prototype will assist the user in determining the next steps at the current stage of the AI system
Trust	Q17	In this prototype, the information provided by the AI system can be trusted
	Q18	In this prototype, the AI system is stable in use
	Q19	In this prototype, the results of the AI system can be trusted
	Q20	In this prototype, the AI system can be trusted to accomplish a given goal

3   Results

The experimental results were analyzed using one-way analysis of variance (ANOVA), and post-analysis was performed using the Student–Newman–Keuls (SNK) method. The independent variable was the prototype category; and the dependent variables were efficiency, flexibility, meaningfulness, accuracy, trust, error count, and task execution time. Statistical analyses were performed using jamovi; the results are presented in Table 4.

Table 4. Statistical analysis results.

	Prototype indicators	
	F	P
Efficiency	75.672	<.001
Flexibility	102.209	<.001
Meaningfulness	68.403	<.001
Accuracy	122.499	<.001
Trust	157.956	<.001
Error count	1.709	0.195
Task execution time	105.494	<.001

The analysis revealed that prototype C received higher scores for efficiency, flexibility, meaningfulness, accuracy, and trust than prototypes A and B did (Fig. 2) and that these scores were statistically significant ($p < 0.001$, Table 4). The post-hoc analysis revealed differences between prototypes A and B and A and C. Although prototypes B and C did not differ in accuracy, they did differ in the remaining items. The number of errors was 0.1 counts under prototypes A and C and 0.38 counts under B (higher) (Fig. 3), but there were no statistically significant differences ($p = 0.195$, Table 4). For prototypes A, B, and C, the task execution times were 11.29, 53.91, and 23.98 s, respectively (highest for prototype B) (Fig. 4), which were statistically significant ($p < 0.001$, Table 4). The post-hoc analysis revealed differences between prototypes A and B, A and C, and B and C.

Users revealed that prototype B could effectively correct errors but also felt it was inefficient and uncomfortable to use since questions from the AI assistant had to be answered repeatedly for confirmation. Most participants preferred Prototype C, feeling it was efficient and convenient because it could quickly perform the specified tasks with short commands by presenting the options that users wanted through question induction.

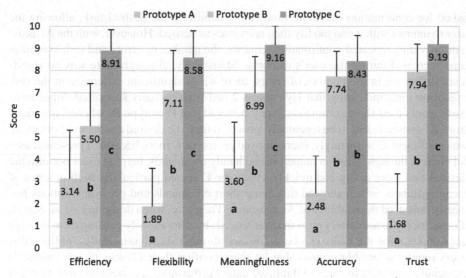

Fig. 2. Experimental results.

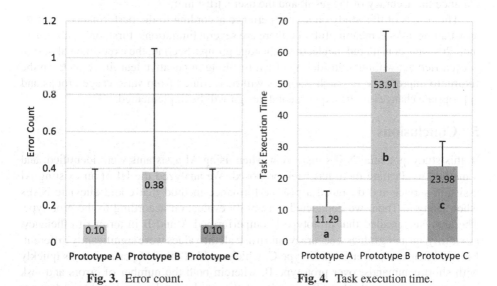

Fig. 3. Error count.   **Fig. 4.** Task execution time.

4   Discussion

The prototypes B and C under the proposed method outperformed prototype A under the conventional AI assistant method in terms of efficiency, flexibility, meaningfulness, accuracy, and trust. Additionally, prototype C (question induction method) outperformed prototype B (confirmation request method) in terms of efficiency, flexibility, meaningfulness, accuracy, and trust, producing statistically significant results. Accordingly, Hypothesis 1 was supported. It was believed that prototype B was preferred because it asked for confirmation one more time before achieving the desired task, allowing the user to interact with it and modify their responses as desired. However, with the AI assistant providing repeated confirmation requests, the number of errors and task execution time increased during the user's response. Statistically, although there was no significant difference in the number of errors, there was a significant difference in the task execution time, indicating that Hypothesis 2 had been partially supported. Since most participants used short commands, many believed that Prototype B, wherein questions from AI assistants had to be repeatedly answered until the desired results were obtained, was inefficient. Contrastingly, users enjoyed prototype C more because it presented useful choices through question induction and handy commands, helping users perform the desired task more easily and quickly. Prototype C scored particularly high in terms of meaningfulness, which showed that using short commands and providing options primarily enhanced the usability of AI assistants. Therefore, when designing AI assistants, it is necessary to accurately meet the user's needs by continuously guiding them through questions so that the tasks can be performed through short commands. Additionally, users require selectable options that let them confirm their choices clearly, which is especially important in cases of duplicate data. Furthermore, a correctable interface and confirmation request should be provided whenever the desired target is not reached to enhance the accuracy of the result and the user's trust in it.

The results of this study on user experience according to the performance of an AI assistant on tasks is meaningful; but, there are several limitations. First, only subjects in their 20s were considered, neglecting other age groups. Second, the experimental design was carried out without considering order, resulting in negative learning effects. In the future, to improve the research, subjects will be recruited from various age groups and appropriate changes in the experimental design will be implemented.

5 Conclusions

In this study, potential NSEs that occur when using AI assistants were identified, and a method to alleviate them has been proposed. We analyzed the UI of an existing AI assistant service and designed a task performance method that could alleviate NSEs when using it. Then, we conducted a usability evaluation according to the prototype. The analysis revealed that prototype C outperformed A and B in terms of efficiency, flexibility, meaningfulness, accuracy, and trust; all the values were significantly different. Most participants preferred prototype C, which enabled them to perform tasks quickly with short commands, over prototype B, wherein both the number of errors and task execution time were higher. The results of this study can be used as basic data for research related to reducing the NSEs of AI assistants and be referenced when designing and evaluating AI assistants in the future.

Acknowledgement. This work was supported by the National Research Foundation of Korea (NRF) grant funded by the Korea government (MSIT) (No. NRF-2021R1F1A1063155). And this research was also supported by the MSIT(Ministry of Science and ICT), Korea, under the ICAN(ICT Challenge and Advanced Network of HRD) program (IITP-2022-RS-2022-00156215) supervised by the IITP(Institute of Information & Communications Technology Planning & Evaluation).

References

1. Kim, B.W.: Trend analysis and national policy for artificial intelligence. Inform. Policy **23**(1), 74–93 (2016)
2. Soo-ah, P., Sejung, M.C.: Understanding the factors influencing satisfaction and continued use intention of AI speakers: focusing on the utilitarian and hedonic values. Inf. Soc. Media **19**(3), 159–182 (2018)
3. Cao, C., Zhao, L., Hu, Y.: Anthropomorphism of intelligent personal assistants (IPAs): antecedents and consequences. In: Wei, K.K., Jiang, J., Kim, H.-W. (eds.) Proceedings of the Twenty-Third Pacific Asia Conference on Information Systems, Association for Information Systems, Atlanta, Georgia (2019)
4. Zhou, Y.M., Shang, L.R., Lim, H.C., Hwang, M.K.: Verification of AI voice user interface (VUI) usability evaluation: focusing on Chinese navigation VUI. J. Korea Multimedia Soc. **24**(7), 913–921 (2021)
5. Saisubramanian, S., Roberts, S.C., Zilberstein, S.: Understanding user attitudes towards negative side effects of AI systems. In: Kitamura, Y., Quigley, A., Isbister, K., Igarashi, T. (eds.) Extended Abstracts of the 2021 CHI Conference on Human Factors in Computing Systems, pp. 1–6. Association for Computing Machinery, New York (2021)
6. Saisubramanian, S., Zilberstein, S., Kamar, E.: Avoiding negative side effects due to incomplete knowledge of AI systems. AI Mag. **42**(4), 62–71 (2022)
7. Forlizzi, J., DiSalvo, C.: Service robots in the domestic environment: a study of the roomba vacuum in the home. In: Proceedings of the 1st ACM SIGCHI/SIGART Conference on Human-Robot Interaction, pp. 258–265. Association for Computing Machinery, New York (2006)
8. Hulse, L.M., Xie, H., Galea, E.R.: Perceptions of autonomous vehicles: relationships with road users, risk, gender and age. Saf. Sci. **102**, 1–13 (2018)
9. Kyriakidis, M., Happee, R., de Winter, J.C.: Public opinion on automated driving: results of an international questionnaire among 5000 respondents. Transport. Res. F: Traffic Psychol. Behav. **32**, 127–140 (2015)
10. Liptak, A.: Amazon's Alexa started ordering people dollhouses after hearing its name on TV. The Verge 7 (2017)
11. Hadfield-Menell, D., Milli, S., Abbeel, P., Russell, S.J., Dragan, A.: Inverse reward design. Adv. Neural Inf. Process. Syst. **30** (2017)
12. Saisubramanian, S., Kamar, E., Zilberstein, S.: A multi-objective approach to mitigate negative side effects. In: Proceedings of the Twenty-Ninth International Conference on International Joint Conferences on Artificial Intelligence, pp. 354–361. International Joint Conferences on Artificial Intelligence, Yokohama (2021)
13. Saisubramanian, S., Zilberstein, S.: Mitigating negative side effects via environment shaping. In: Proceedings of the 20th International Conference on Autonomous Agents and MultiAgent Systems, pp. 1640–1642. International Foundation for Autonomous Agents and MultiAgent Systems, Virtual Event, United Kingdom (2021)
14. Morville, P., Sullenger, P.: Ambient findability: libraries, serials, and the Internet of things. Ser. Libr. **58**(1–4), 33–38 (2010)
15. Nielsen, J.: Ten usability heuristics (2005)

CAPTAIN: An AI-Based Chatbot
for Cyberbullying Prevention and Intervention

Andrew T. Lian[1]($\boxtimes$) (iD), Alfredo Costilla Reyes[2] (iD), and Xia Hu[2] (iD)

[1] The Kinkaid School, Houston, TX 77024, USA
andrew.lian@kinkaid.org
[2] Department of Computer Science, Rice University, Houston, TX 77005, USA

Abstract. Cyberbullying is a widespread and growing problem that can cause various psychological and health well-being outcomes in youth and is considered a serious public health threat. Cutting-edge informatics technology would enable us to identify and stop cyberbullying to prevent harm, death, and privacy violations. However, current cyberbullying prevention approaches offer limited interactions, individualized education, and in-time intervention. With the current emerging technologies in Artificial Intelligence (AI), the use of chatbots have become increasingly popular in health promotion. However, there are current technological challenges that need to be addressed, such as detecting and preventing cyberbullying in real-time, providing personalized responses and intervention, as well as developing the chatbot with a user-friendly interface. This paper introduces CAPTAIN (Cyberbullying Awareness and Prevention Through Artificial INtelligence), an AI-based chatbot for cyberbullying prevention that can provide anytime interaction for personalized intervention.

Keywords: Cyberbullying prevention · Machine Learning · Topic Modeling · Chatbot

1 Introduction

The widespread use of digital technologies has contributed to the rise of cyberbullying, which has become a significant problem in the digital age. Cyberbullying refers to using information technology and digital platforms to harass, intimidate, or harm people in any format. According to a recent survey, about 10% of the teens have experienced cyberbullying during their lifetime and 59% of them reported that it has happened within the past year [1]. Many people also didn't realize that they were bullying others before the consequences. Around 23% of teens claimed that they have done something cruel online to others and almost 60% of children online have seen someone getting cyberbullied and most of them have not intervened [2]. In addition to self-harm and suicidal behaviors, cyberbullying can cause several psychological well-being outcomes, including emotional distress, violence, family conflict, relationship problems, substance abuse, and learning differences [3].

Different from traditional bullying, cyberbullying has some unique features such as publicity, anonymity, and the lack of supervision, which brings additional challenges

H. Degen and S. Ntoa (Eds.): HCII 2023, LNAI 14051, pp. 98–107, 2023.
https://doi.org/10.1007/978-3-031-35894-4_7

for cyberbullying prevention. Current methods for cyberbullying intervention and prevention include pamphlets, websites and social media, as well as school programs to educate people about cyberbullying. A recent survey indicates that most online education resources appear to target parents [4]. In addition, these methods lack interaction, provide no individualized education or require extensive resources to provide in-time intervention [5].

Cutting-edge Artificial Intelligence (AI) technologies would enable us to identify and stop cyberbullying. One way is by using machine learning methods to automatically detect and flag potentially harmful or abusive language in online conversations and social media posts. This can help identify cyberbullying before it escalates. In addition, AI-powered chatbots can provide real time interaction and communication with the users who need help on cyberbullying prevention.

Much research has focused on automatic cyberbully detention using machine learning methods. Different types of social media data have been used for this task including YouTube, Instagram, Whatsapp, and Twitter [6]. Scientists usually focus on one data source because each community can act differently [7]. Different research also focus on different tasks that cover various perspectives on cyberbullying. Many efforts focus on binary classification to detect whether a message is harmful or not [6]. Other efforts focus on more specific tasks. For example, Van Hee et. al. Developed an annotation guideline to annotate online messages with respect to the cyberbullying participant roles (e.g., harasser, bystander assistant, bystander Defender, victim, not cyberbullying) and cyberbullying subcategories (e.g., curse, defamation, defense, encouragement, insult, and sexual) [8]. However, they still focused on binary classifications for automatic detection. Other researchers have focused on simple types of subcategories such as racism, sexism [7] and severity (low, medium and high) [9].

Machine learning techniques have been widely applied in the field of automatic bullying message detection. A recent research survey summarized two different categories of techniques, conventional machine learning and deep learning [6]. While conventional machine learning methods perform relatively well for single source (e.g., Twitter) binary classification, deep learning models such as Recurrent Neural Network (RNN), Current Neural Network (CNN), and Multi-layered perceptron (MLP) have demonstrated improved performance in detecting cyberbullying, especially when used in combination with contextual language models like Bidirectional Encoder Representations from Transformers (BERT) [6].

With the current emerging technologies in Artificial Intelligence (AI), the use of chatbots have become increasingly popular in health promotion especially after the beginning of the COVID-19 pandemic [10]. Chatbots have been developed to help youth and adolescent mental health. For example, Deshpande and Warren developed a machine learning based self-harm detection method for mental health chatbots [11]. A recent study evaluated the perceptions of a chatbot developed to psychoeducate adolescents on depression in a small group of participants [12]. Another example is Vivbot, a chatbot that can deliver positive psychology skills and promote well-being among young people after cancer treatment [13]. The results of both studies indicate that chatbots can be potentially more engageable and acceptable to adolescents, who tend to be reluctant to traditional mental service. In addition to mental health, chatbots are also being used in other health interventions such as vaccine promotion [14], cancer risk triangle [15], and life skill coaching [16].

In this paper, we introduce CAPTAIN (Cyberbullying Awareness and Prevention Through Artificial INtelligence), an AI-based chatbot for cyberbullying prevention. More specifically, CAPTAIN can (1) automatically detect cyberbullying messages, (2) answer questions regarding bullying, and (3) provide tips to the users on how to prevent/stop cyberbullying. CAPTAIN combines machine learning based tools with a chatbot to enable real time bullying message detection and cyberbullying prevention. To the best of our knowledge, this is the first chatbot that targets AI-based personalized intervention for cyberbullying prevention.

2 Method

The CAPTAIN system includes three components: cyberbullying detection, promoting cyberbullying prevention, and cyberbullying data analysis. In the first component, we implemented a machine learning based model to automatically classify online messages as either a bullying sentence or a non-bullying sentence. This component also facilitates the second component which is the interface of the chatbot. The chatbot aims to provide tailored interaction with users. It can interact with the users to answer their questions, provide information and resources about cyberbullying, and detect cyberbullying messages using our machine learning model. This is where users communicate and have conversations with our AI through the interface. The third component of CAPTAIN, the cyberbullying detection system, uses topic modeling to cluster the data into topics and super topics. It can provide a more in-depth understanding of the types of cyberbullying that are occurring and the reasons behind them. This component informs the interface by identifying the topic of the bullying messages, based on which more effective interventions can be designed and provided (Fig. 1).

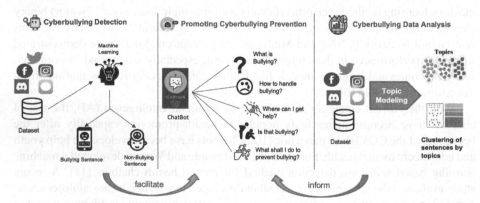

Fig. 1. System Overview of the Three Major Components of the CAPTAIN Chatbot: (1) Machine Learning based Cyberbullying Detection (2) Personalized Cyberbullying Prevention; and (3) Cyberbullying Data Analysis using Topic Modeling

Datasets and Data Preprocessing

We collected a set of annotated messages, including both bullying and non-bullying from three different sources [17–19]. These data sets were used to train the machine learning models and perform data analysis. In order to prepare the data for machine learning, we preprocessed it by removing common english stop words, slang words, URLs, emojis, and acronyms that are commonly found in web and SMS messages. This preprocessing step helped to improve the accuracy of our models and the overall effectiveness of our analysis.

Automatic Cyberbullying Detection

We utilized the scikit-learn machine learning library on the collected data set to implement, test, and evaluate nine different machine learning algorithms, including Stochastic Gradient Descent (SGD) Classifier, Logistic Regression, Random Forest, to determine their performance on automatically classifying messages into categories of bullying or non-bullying. We split the data sets into a training set and a test det, with the training set comprising 80% of the data and the test set comprising 20% of the data. We used this data set to train and test the nine different machine learning models and compare their performance. our objective here was to identify the best model in regard to accuracy and speed to be used in the CAPTAIN chatbot for real time bullying message identification.

Cyberbullying Data Analysis

We applied the bertopic, a topic modeling technique that leverages transformers to cluster words and/or sentences. BERTopic is a topic modeling technique that vectorizes text data into a low-dimensional space using word embeddings to discover semantically comparable words, sentences, or documents. BERTopic generates topic representations through a pre-trained transformer-based language model and then subsequently clusters the embeddings using a hierarchical clustering approach [20]. This component allowed us to summarize the bullying messages into different topics, providing valuable insight into which topics were most prevalent among cyberbullies. This information can be used to inform the chatbot and create more targeted responses to users who may be experiencing cyberbullying related to specific topics.

Chatbot Implementation

To develop the chatbot, we leveraged chatterbot [21], a machine-learning-based framework for conversational agent implementation. On top of the chatterbot framework, we developed the cyberbullying detection adaptor, which embedded our machine learning algorithms. We also built a question-answering library for cyberbullying prevention education based on reliable online resources such as Microsoft, UNICEF, and endcyberbullying.org. using the library, we implemented the education adaptor, which can initiate a conversation and answer users' questions about cyberbullying. To create a user-friendly interface, we used chat-bubble [22], a chatbot UI for the Web with JSON scripting. Chat-bubble allowed us to create a web-based interface where users can easily interact with CAPTAIN and assess information and Feedback.

Evaluation

We evaluated the performance of the machine learning models using measures including accuracy, precision, recall, and F-measures. We also considered the performance time of each model since speed is important to support real time bullying message detections.

We conducted an evaluation of the CAPTAIN chatbot using a set of scenario-based tests that encompassed various use cases, including bullying messages, questions regarding cyberbullying, cyberbullying intervention, and small talk. First, we tested the chatbot's ability to identify bullying messages and to respond appropriately with support and intervention. Second, we evaluated the chatbot's capacity to provide accurate and relevant answers to users' inquiries about cyberbullying. Third, we assessed the chatbot's ability to engage with users with small talk.

3   Result

We have collected 71,350 messages, 31,300 of which are classified as offensive. Table 1 shows the results of different machine learning algorithms for the automatic classification of bullying messages. For the machine learning classifier, SGD Classifier achieved the highest accuracy of 89.13%, F1 score of 88.93%, and the second highest precision of 94.46% with a relatively fast training time (0.13 S) and perdition time (0.0025 S). Decision Tree reached the highest recall of 87.09%, but its training time is slow. Adaptive boosting has the highest precision score of 95.68% however, the training time is relatively slow. Therefore, we used the SGD classifier in CAPTAIN for its highest accuracy and fast speed.

After running a topic modeling analysis, we discovered that the most frequently mentioned super-topics include race, gender, appearance, drinking/smoking, and financial status. We also identified the most commonly appeared terms within each category as well. Figure 2 shows these categories and their associated terms. These categories will potentially inform CAPTAIN for more tailored intervention. By understanding the specific topic that is mostly brought up in bullying messages, CAPTAIN can provide more targeted support to users who are experiencing bullying related to the specific topic. For example, if the bullying message judges someone based on their appearance (e.g., "you are fat and ugly"), the chatbot will provide intervention based on the topic (e.g., "it is uncool to judge people by their looks"; "Beauty can be subjective"). This can ultimately lead to more effective interventions and support for those who are being bullied (Table 1).

We further evaluated the functionality of the CAPTAIN chatbot with a list of competency scenarios, including bullying messages, questions regarding cyberbullying, cyberbullying intervention, and small talk. Figure 3 shows a demo of the CAPTAIN interface. When opening the interface, CAPTAIN first greeted the user and provided a self introduction. It can also answer questions on cyberbullying related topics. In addition, it can determine if a sentence could be flagged as bullying, inappropriate, or appropriate. As Fig. 3 shows, it successfully detected possible mean messages and provided feedback accordingly. Furthermore, CAPTAIN interacted with the users in a natural way. It can answer questions that are not necessarily about bullying such simple math, sports, etc. This can provide companionship to its users when needed.

Table 1. Comparison of 9 Different Machine Learning Algorithms for Cyberbullying Detection.

Algorithm	Accuracy	Precision	Recall	F1 Score	Prediction Time	Training Time
SGD Classifier	**89.13%**	**94.46%**	84.01%	**88.93%**	**0.0025 SEC**	**0.13 SEC**
Logistic Regression	88.74%	93.25%	84.45%	88.63%	0.0043 SEC	1.06 SEC
Random Forest	87.52%	89.07%	86.62%	87.83%	6.48 SEC	79.92 SEC
Bagging Classifier	87.44%	89.23%	86.24%	87.71%	0.55 SEC	70.33 SEC
Linear SVC	87.54%	90.14%	85.37%	87.69%	0.0033 SEC	3.70 SEC
Decision Tree	86.77%	87.40%	**87.09%**	87.25%	0.067 SEC	10.54 SEC
Adaptive Boosting	87.57%	95.68%	79.69%	86.96%	0.29 SEC	1.41 SEC
Multinomial Naïve Bayes	84.15%	84.28%	85.45%	84.86%	0.0052 SEC	0.0089 SEC
K-nearest Neighbors	76.49%	87.55%	63.84%	73.84%	127.78 SEC	0.0033 SEC

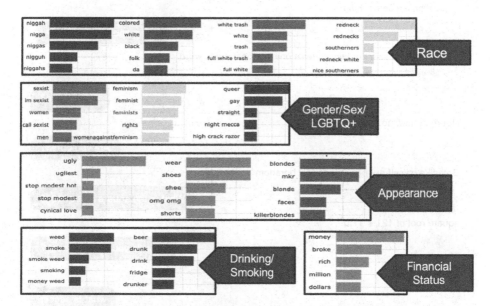

Fig. 2. Topic Clustering of Different Topics Based on Popularity

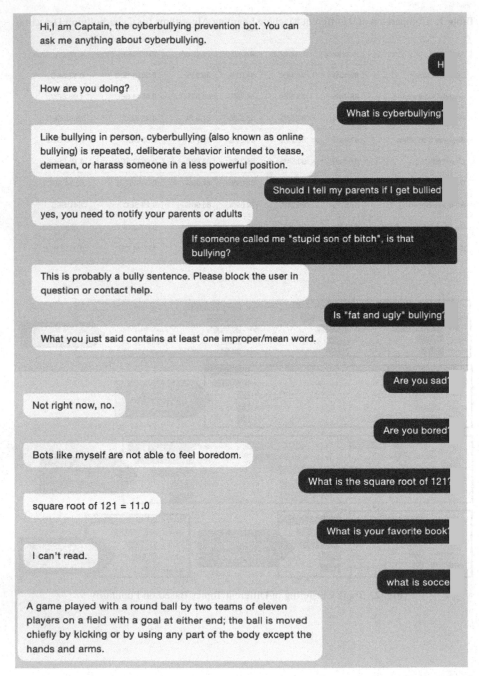

Fig. 3. Demonstration of Chatbot with interaction of Cyberbullying-related Topics and Small Talks

4 Discussion and Conclusion

In summary, CAPTAIN is an AI-based platform that aims to address the growing problem of cyberbullying. The main goal of this chatbot is to educate users about the negative effects of cyberbullying, provide tailored responses to those who may be experiencing cyberbullying, and automatically detect cyberbullying messages when needed. It uses a combination of natural language processing and machine learning techniques to classify messages as bullying or non-bullying. It also used a data-driven approach based on Topic Modeling to identify common topics. One of the unique features of CAPTAIN is that it offers personalized messages based on the machine learning classifier results. This allows the chatbot to provide targeted and relevant responses to users, which will potentially increase the effectiveness of the intervention. To the best of our knowledge, this is the first chatbot that targets AI-based personalized intervention for cyberbullying prevention.

The CAPTAIN system has the potential to reduce mental health problems caused by cyberbullying and enhance the overall online community. By providing targeted support to individuals who may be experiencing cyberbullying, CAPTAIN has the potential to reduce the negative effects of cyberbullying on mental health. The chatbot's personalized responses can help users feel heard and understood, provide timely interaction and information, which can in turn increase their resilience and empower them to seek additional support when needed. In addition, by reducing the incidence of cyberbullying, CAPTAIN has the potential to enhance the overall online community. A reduction in bullying behavior can create a safer and more positive online environment, where individuals feel free to express themselves and engage with others without fear of being targeted. This can lead to a more inclusive and supportive online community, where people can build meaningful connections and engage in constructive discussions.

Of course, there are still challenges associated with developing a chatbot for cyberbullying. Firstly, one of the main challenges is to develop a chatbot that can accurately identify and classify bullying behaviors. Every person has a different personality and may perceive bullying differently than others. This requires a sophisticated understanding of the language used in cyberbullying messages, as well as the context in which they are used. Secondly, Personalized messages are a critical component in the design of an effective intervention for cyberbullying. By understanding the underlying causes and motivations behind cyberbullying behavior, these messages can be tailored to address specific psychological and behavioral factors, leading to more successful outcomes. This is achieved by incorporating theoretical models from psychology and behavioral science into the design process. However, it is challenging for the AI algorithms to link to these models to dynamically generate responses. Thirdly, developing a chatbot that addresses cyberbullying raises a number of ethical considerations, such as privacy and confidentiality, particularly when dealing with sensitive and potentially traumatizing experiences.

In the future, the authors would like to further improve CAPTAIN in several directions. First, our machine learning cyberbullying data classification only focuses on binary boolean classification so far. We will extend the work and implement a multi-class classifier that can categorize messages into different topics. Second, although several existing papers discussed classifying messages into basic categories, there is no standard way to reasonably categorize bullying messages. We will leverage the data-driven approach that uses Topic Modeling to identify common topics which can serve as categories to classify bullying messages. In addition, we will increase the chatbot knowledge base and add emotional support to the chatbot so it can connect with users better. In addition, we would also like to test feasibility, usability, and intervention effectiveness on teens to further improve CAPTAIN and deploy it to the public.

References

1. Nagata, J.M., et al.: Social epidemiology of early adolescent cyberbullying in the United States. Acad. Pediatr. **22**(8), 1287–1293 (2022). https://doi.org/10.1016/j.acap.2022.07.003
2. Patchin, J.: Summary of Our Cyberbullying Research (2007–2019). Cyberbullying Research Center (2019). https://cyberbullying.org/summary-of-our-cyberbullying-research
3. JAMA Netw. Open **4**(9), e2125860, September 2021. https://doi.org/10.1001/jamanetworkopen.2021.25860
4. Espelage, D.L., Hong, J.S.: Cyberbullying prevention and intervention efforts: current knowledge and future directions. Can. J. Psychiatry **62**(6), 374–380 (2017). https://doi.org/10.1177/0706743716684793
5. Smith, P.K., Bauman, S., Wong, D.: Challenges and opportunities of anti-bullying intervention programs. Int. J. Environ. Res. Public. Health **16**(10), 1810 (2019). https://doi.org/10.3390/ijerph16101810
6. Elsafoury, F., Katsigiannis, S., Pervez, Z., Ramzan, N.: When the timeline meets the pipeline: a survey on automated cyberbullying detection. IEEE Access **9**, 103541–103563 (2021). https://doi.org/10.1109/ACCESS.2021.3098979
7. Dadvar, M., Eckert, K.: Cyberbullying detection in social networks using deep learning based models; a reproducibility study (2018). https://doi.org/10.48550/ARXIV.1812.08046
8. Van Hee, C., et al.: Automatic detection of cyberbullying in social media text. PLoS ONE **13**(10), e0203794 (2018). https://doi.org/10.1371/journal.pone.0203794
9. Talpur, B.A., O'Sullivan, D.: Cyberbullying severity detection: a machine learning approach. PLoS ONE **15**(10), e0240924 (2020). https://doi.org/10.1371/journal.pone.0240924
10. Wilson, L., Marasoiu, M.: The development and use of chatbots in public health: scoping review. JMIR Hum. Factors **9**(4), e35882 (2022). https://doi.org/10.2196/35882
11. Deshpande, S., Warren, J.: Self-harm detection for mental health chatbots. In: Mantas, J. (eds.) Studies in Health Technology and Informatics, IOS Press (2021). https://doi.org/10.3233/SHTI210118
12. Dosovitsky, G., Bunge, E.: Development of a chatbot for depression: adolescent perceptions and recommendations. Child Adolesc. Ment. Health, p. camh.12627, December 2022. https://doi.org/10.1111/camh.12627
13. Greer, S., Ramo, D., Chang, Y.-J., Fu, M., Moskowitz, J., Haritatos, J.: Use of the Chatbot 'Vivibot' to deliver positive psychology skills and promote well-being among young people after cancer treatment: randomized controlled feasibility trial. JMIR MHealth UHealth **7**(10), e15018 (2019). https://doi.org/10.2196/15018
14. Weeks, R., et al.: Chatbot-delivered COVID-19 vaccine communication message preferences of young adults and public health workers in urban American communities: qualitative study. J. Med. Internet Res. **24**(7), e38418 (2022). https://doi.org/10.2196/38418
15. Nazareth, S., et al.: Hereditary Cancer risk using a genetic chatbot before routine care visits. Obstet. Gynecol. **138**(6), 860–870 (2021). https://doi.org/10.1097/AOG.0000000000004596
16. Gabrielli, S., Rizzi, S., Carbone, S., Donisi, V.: A chatbot-based coaching intervention for adolescents to promote life skills: pilot study. JMIR Hum. Factors **7**(1), e16762 (2020). https://doi.org/10.2196/16762

17. Waseem, Z., Hovy, D.: Hateful symbols or hateful people? predictive features for hate speech detection on Twitter. In: Proceedings of the NAACL Student Research Workshop, San Diego, California, pp. 88–93 (2016). https://doi.org/10.18653/v1/N16-2013
18. Davidson, T., Warmsley, D., Macy, M., Weber, I.: Automated hate speech detection and the problem of offensive language. arXiv 11 March 2017. Accessed 14 Jan 2023. http://arxiv.org/abs/1703.04009
19. Tweets Dataset for Detection of Cyber-Trolls. https://www.kaggle.com/datasets/dataturks/dataset-for-detection-of-cybertrolls
20. Grootendorst, M.: BERTopic: Neural topic modeling with a class-based TF-IDF procedure. arXiv, March 11 2022. Accessed 28 December 2022. http://arxiv.org/abs/2203.05794
21. ChatterBot (2022). https://pypi.org/project/ChatterBot/
22. Chat-Bubble: Simple chatbot UI for the Web with JSON scripting. https://github.com/dmitrizzle/chat-bubble

CADNCI—Connected-Audio Digital Note-Taking for Consecutive Interpretation: Optimal Setup for Practice and Assessment

Eric K. Liao[✉]

Eric Liao, 1653 Fairorchard Avenue, San José, CA 95125, USA
ekliao@gmail.com

Abstract. The traditional method of note-taking for consecutive interpretation using pen and paper for the purposes of practice (exercise) suffers from many issues, one being the lack of perfect recall of the source speech or the rendition when assessing the interpreter's performance. Often, no participant in the group can remember exactly what was said in the rendition, much less the original speech, because one's short-term working memory from listening is transient, even when complemented by notes. This poses a challenge in discovering weaknesses in performance, a requisite step for meaningful assessment and self-knowledge, which in turn facilitates improvement. Remedying this common situation is the motivation behind this research.

⠀⠀This paper briefly surveys the history of employing digital devices to assist in consecutive interpreting, revealing that even in this high-tech-driven age the state of the art, if it is known to practitioners, instructors, and trainees at all, is unsatisfactory. After setting out many problems in the status quo, the paper then introduces and describes in detail a newly conceived system that will help interpreters practice and critique better. It expounds on the benefits of having clean speech sounds synced to the note-taking action and the ability to watch the note-taking and note-reading process live or play it back like a movie, enabling the discovery of root causes of interpretation problems. The research concludes by presenting practical scenarios using the system, with a focus on remote group practice. The author provides demonstrations of his own practice to illustrate the points. The reader will understand the advantages of the system over existing practices, gain a sense of the possibilities for observation and discovery, and be able to implement and experiment with the system.

Keywords: digital note-taking · tablet interpreting · consecutive interpretation · audio recording · computer-aided interpreting (CAI) · human-computer interaction (HCI) · interpretation practice · monolingual practice · performance assessment · performance feedback · virtual practice · remote interpreting

1 Motivation

Armed with an innate and learned readiness (undergraduate study in computer science) to embrace anything digital, the author began searching for an ideal digital note-taking setup for consecutive interpretation in 2017, having been taught note-taking with pen

H. Degen and S. Ntoa (Eds.): HCII 2023, LNAI 14051, pp. 108–125, 2023.
https://doi.org/10.1007/978-3-031-35894-4_8

and paper in graduate studies and felt unsatisfied with the traditional writing media for their shortcomings. Once a viable combination of tablet and stylus had been identified and comfortably settled on, the quest quickly pivoted into how to combine the best apps, features, and accessories under the hardware and software restrictions imposed by the chosen operating systems to create a superior digital experience for practicing consecutive interpretation with possibilities unimaginable with the old media.

2 The Problems

2.1 Memory

When interpreters or interpreting trainees (henceforth "interpreters" for short) practice consecutive interpretation that requires taking notes, after the source-language speech segment is played (in the case of a pre-recorded audio or video) or given live, it is typical for only one note-taker to give a rendition, after which another person, either the instructor or a practice peer, may give feedback. The feedback is often based solely on the rendition, and it relies completely on everyone's memory of the interpretation just heard and of the original speech heard still earlier. Naturally, there are going to be problems in the interpretation and participants will want to dive into a deeper discussion. However, it is likely that no one in the group can be certain about the exact wording or tone expressed in the original speech relevant to the discussion because short-term memory is by nature fleeting. Time permitting and if the group is serious about getting to the bottom of things, the relevant portion of the original speech may be located and played back or read back by the live speaker to confirm the content. Otherwise, the discussion in question is cut short, simplified, or generalized, marred by a sense of regret and dissatisfaction for not arriving at the truth to address the real interpretation problem. This is a recurrent theme in any traditional practice scenario, hindered by the inherently unreliable short-term memory and the lack of a replica of the speech as heard by the note-taker and of their rendition that can be "played back" *exactly* as previously perceived. When the original speech is read back a second time, it is no longer the same version as experienced by the group the first time. What if the interpretation problem in question happens to be caused by the differences—linguistic or extralinguistic—however minute they may be, between the two versions?

2.2 Pen and Paper

There are numerous drawbacks to using pen and paper for consecutive note-taking, most of which are obvious. One need only list the advantages of digital writing media and easily flip each point to reveal the downside of pen and paper. One not-so-obvious drawback came from an anecdote recounted by a seasoned interpreter: Once on stage, after taking several pages of notes, the interpreter's fingers did not have enough friction while flipping pages, so she ended up flipping two stuck-together pages at once, which caused some hesitation and fluster as the notes did not seem coherent going from one meaning to the next. As a result, the speaker got impatient and started delivering the speech directly in the target language, and the interpreter lost a client. Anecdotes aside, the single benefit of being able to store one's digital notes economically as permanent records for repeated review and analysis, without the typical risks of physical records, seems reason enough to consider going digital.

2.3 The Note-Taking Action

Missing in Action. In the practice scenario, the consecutive notes are often not systematically shown and discussed. If they are displayed at all, what is seen is the end result of note-taking. The notes are in static snapshots either physically on paper or a device's screen, or displayed remotely through a camera or on screen, in which case they are sometimes held clumsily up to the webcam, often blurred or out of focus and too briefly for other participants to see enough content for a meaningful discussion. This less-than-ideal experience is all too familiar to many interpreters. what if the interpretation problems identified during feedback originate from something that happened during the dynamic process of note-taking, as they often do? that process cannot be observed if there is no "Recording" of the note-taking action—analogous to the aforementioned problem of lack of a recording of the speech as given.

One Bite at the Apple. With the advent of Youtube and other video-hosting web sites, the world has enjoyed an explosion of video content, and the interpreting field is no exception. The dearth of observable note-taking in action has been greatly mitigated. It is now possible to observe certain forms of note-taking in an on-site or online teaching situation, in which the instructor or a student may demonstrate the note-taking action as the speech is given. Allowing participants to observe the process before hearing the rendition is an improvement over seeing only the snapshots because it reveals more information beyond the static notes. because the action is live and usually not recorded, the obvious downside is that it can be observed only once as opposed to allowing for repeated playback. even if the action is recorded, the electronic recording or the physical tape is usually not immediately available after the particular practice segment for a timely review. the lack of immediacy of the recording presents a challenge for giving and getting effective and timely feedback. To put it bluntly, the quality of the critique is at best as good as the basis on which it stands, which often is only the participants' unreliable collective short-term memory.

Unnatural Writing Media. For the purposes of making the note-taking action readable or accessible by the audience, the demonstrator sometimes resorts to using unnatural writing media such as a computer mouse on a virtual whiteboard (resulting in illegible scribblings) or a marker pen or chalk writing vertically on a blackboard or flipchart, or to writing larger-than-normal notes on paper. the use of such unrealistic media, perhaps due to their unwieldiness, inevitably alters the critical elements to be observed—the notes themselves. They are not the same as what the demonstrator would normally put down in a real interpreting assignment. In other words, they become more artificial and less valuable to be learned from or critiqued, albeit in subtle ways. In a craft as complex as consecutive note-taking, involving multitasking and coordination of multiple sensory systems, any confounding factors like the unnaturalness or difficulty created by the writing media should be avoided, especially in a pedagogical setting.

(Over-)Rehearsed Instructor Demonstration. In the case of online instructor-made videos, while the viewer can play back the action as many times as necessary, something must be said about the validity and authenticity of such demonstrations: there is no knowing how many times the demonstrator has practiced or rehearsed the same speech in order to record one take of seemingly perfect or near-perfect note-taking action. The value of the demonstration is reduced because it is artificial, not reflecting the reality of how one would cope and navigate difficult spots—however imperfectly—when dealing with a fresh, previously unheard segment of speech. rather, what is shown is an unnatural, textbook-perfect appearance and performance that the demonstrator probably cannot replicate in reality. Aren't the real-world coping tactics of an experienced interpreter exactly what one most desires to observe and emulate? Trainers should not be afraid to show their own vulnerabilities; it gives trainees the opportunity to observe, learn, and distill coping strategies from a real, unrehearsed performance.

In-Air Transmission of Speech Sound. Speech sound uttered live in a room or played through a loudspeaker deteriorates in intelligibility when it reaches the listener's ears at a distance because of the acoustic phenomenon called reverberation. There is little reason to belabor the obvious and try to convince the practicing interpreter of this point: for the best chance of understanding a speech for interpreters, listening to a speech through headphones is always better than listening from a loudspeaker. There is a consensus among researchers:

> There's a well-known relationship between the amount of reverberation and the level of speech understanding that results. Essentially, at some point as reverberation is increased, speech understanding is gonna take a hit. Okay, I think we're just going to take that as a given (Acoustical Society of America, Zahorik and Ellis 2017, at 1:45).

Intelligibility. Speech intelligibility simply means the ability to be understood. understanding depends on the ability to hear clearly. To hear clearly, one needs to be able to distinguish vowels and consonants at the least, besides intonation and other elements. Room reverberation reduces speech understanding and the recognition of vowels and consonants alike.

Vowels suffer from "modulation loss" (see Fig. 1), according to Cousins and Newsham, and Soulsound (2015):

> You get interference where basically the previous syllables are still reverberating around the room, filling that gap, so the modulation depth becomes less. The less that modulation depth is, the more difficult it is to hear one syllable from another and it all becomes a bit of a blur eventually. (11:31)

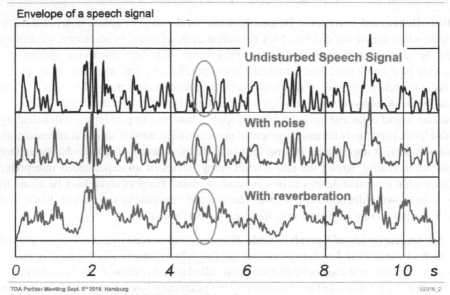

Fig. 1. Modulation Loss.

Note. From "Room Acoustics, PA Systems and Speech Intelligibility for Voice Alarm Systems," by A. Goertz and A. Schmitz, 2016, TOA Partner Meeting, Hamburg, slide 6. [Slides] http://www.ifaa-akustik.de/files/toa-cc3-2016-09-05-a-goertz.pdf

Consonants suffer from "aggravated forward masking," which is especially bad for hearing final consonants like the softer "k" sound in the word "back." (Schweitzer 2003).

It is a misconception that speech in a small room will not be impacted by reverberation. In fact, plosives and fricatives are the most affected. (Gelfand and Silman 1979).

To be free from reverberation and hear with maximum clarity, the speaker should speak close to the microphone, and the listener should hear through headphones, getting rid of any interference from in-air transmission. Direct sound is the purest and clearest, and headphones deliver direct sound at almost zero distance (see Fig. 2).

Note. When a sound source is heard beyond the critical distance, the ambient sound (noise and reverberation) drowns out direct sound. From "Dr Sound explains the reverb phenomenon," by J.-E. Eriksson. Retrieved November 25, 2022, from https://www.konftel.com/en/academy/dr-sound-explains-the-reverb-phenomenon

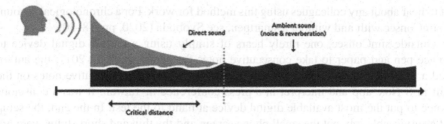

Too much reverb can decrease the clarity of the sound. This can be avoided by dampening or improving the accoustics in a room.

Fig. 2. Direct *Sound* and Critical Distance.

If recording of both the source speech and the rendition is desired, as in practice settings, the negative effect of in-air transmission of sound is compounded. Since recording is just a reproduction of sound, any reverberation and ambient noise will go into the recording, which will be a bad copy of the original good sound. With recording, the extra factor of microphone quality comes into play and may further reduce speech intelligibility. Listen to this clip[1] contrasting two types of recording of a short segment of speech[2] and the interpreter's voice. Again, it is best to judge the quality of a recording by hearing it through headphones. The difference is clear: One has clear speech sound because it is recorded via a line-in cable; the other comes with considerably more room reverberation and handling noise from the desktop because it was recorded through in-air transmission by an omni-directional microphone. This is just the difference after one-time recording.

If the results of the first recording are each played back and re-recorded repeatedly in the same way (line-in vs. in-air), the difference is compounded, degrading a bit more each time for the in-air method, until it becomes just a blur.

3   Digital Note-Taking

3.1   The Literature

A brief mention of what has been written or done about digital consecutive interpreting is in order. Using a digital device to aid in consecutive interpreting is not new. In 1999, "Michele Ferrari, a European Commission interpreter, was the first professional interpreter to use digital technology by recording the source speech, which was then played back and interpreted simultaneously" (Orlando 2015, p. 140). This is referred to as "simultaneous consecutive," or "simConsec" (Hamidi and Pöchhacker 2007, p. 277) mode of interpreting, in which a digital "smartpen" may be involved to allow the interpreter to also take hand-written notes. This mode has received much attention in the literature, but nowadays it does not seem to be in use in actual interpreted events. The author has

---

[1] Viewable on YouTube: https://youtu.be/n5bCdTwUtoU.

[2] United Nations and Emma Watson (2014). Emma Watson at the HeForShe Campaign 2014 - Official UN Video [Video]. YouTube. https://www.youtube.com/watch?v=gkjW9PZBRfk (0:51).

yet to hear about any colleagues using this method for work. For a chronological account of simConsec with and without a smartpen, see Svoboda (2020, pp. 18–30).

Outside simConsec, one rarely hears of simply using a mobile digital device to replace pen and paper to take consecutive notes for actual work. In 2017, the author used a 6.3-inch Samsung Galaxy Note 8 smartphone to take consecutive notes on the built-in S Note app and interpret in a press conference in Taiwan. It was a conscious choice to put the most available digital device at hand to the test. In the end, the setup did a serviceable job, but the small phone screen and the thin and short stylus were not optimal; a larger tablet would have worked a lot better. And the response, precision, and the feel of the stylus against the glass surface, although at the time the best in class under the popular Android operating system, did not feel ready for prime time. Gillies (2019) concludes:

… a lack of confidence in (1) the new technology and (2) one's own ability to use it successfully at all times (and particularly under pressure), have combined to hamper the spread of both simultaneous consecutive and note-taking on tablet computers. This may only change if a generation of interpreters learn to use these techniques as part of their studies, something that doesn't happen systematically yet. (p. 227)

3.2 The Digital Generation

On the one hand, Gillies's and the author's not-so-optimistic views may be valid. On the other hand, students nowadays are comfortable taking class notes on tablets. One does not need to witness this trend personally; a simple search for note-taking-related videos on the Internet will yield numerous tutorials and reviews of the best digital note-taking apps. However, an interpreter's consecutive notes are different from lecture notes in that the practitioners are extremely demanding on the time and response factors. The device and the digital pen need to be fast, convenient, accurate, and reliable. One would not tolerate any errors caused by defects in the tools' design, except for admitting that one sometimes forgot to keep the devices fully charged overnight. While it is harder for the "pen and paper" generation of interpreters to adopt note-taking on a tablet like the "digital natives" do, the obstacle is often just a psychological one. Once having gone digital, it can be hard to go back, as is the exact sentiment conveyed by two of the author's colleagues.

3.3 Quest for the Ideal Setup

The author's own quest for the ideal setup enjoyed a breakthrough in 2018: After a short trial period, he determined that the then-latest Microsoft Surface tablet with its digital pen and the built-in note-taking app OneNote was still inadequate for professional use for interpretation and instead acquired an Apple iPad Pro, a 10.5-inch tablet first released in 2017. Writing with the compatible first-generation Apple Pencil on the iPad screen was a hardware "aha" moment because of the superior tactile experience. Having discovered a note-taking app with a unique recording feature and a versatile virtual audio routing software product, the author soon confidently settled on a system which will be described below. It has been at least three years since the author first used the system for practice and used the same system without the audio component in actual work. There is no going back to paper and pen, simply because of the rich and previously inconceivable benefits the system affords. The only occasions on which the author broke from this setup for consecutive interpretation was when he had to practice note-taking to take the court interpreter's oral exams with pen and paper. It is a great relief that the Stone Age exam days are behind him.

4 Same-Language Consecutive Practice

Before introducing the system, a brief aside to consider the benefits of consecutive interpretation practice, particularly in the monolingual mode. Gile (2005) extols the virtue of consecutive interpreting:

> Consecutive is considered by many the "highest" form of interpreting, above simultaneous, essentially because it requires the comprehension phase to be completed before the formulation phase, since most traces of the linguistic form of an utterance disappear from memory after a few seconds at most, and are replaced by traces of its content. The short time lag between perception and production in simultaneous allows production from verbal traces, whereas in consecutive, production is done from traces of the content …. Experience shows that students who do not truly understand speeches cannot reconstruct them from their notes.

> For these cognitive reasons, the fundamental skills of consecutive interpreting can also be taught in the monolingual mode … so as to shift the focus back to essentials. (pp. 136–137).

There is no doubt that the most essential of the "essentials" should be comprehension. Gile (2009) goes on to re-emphasize the benefit of monolingual consecutive practice:

> a. Separation between the comprehension phase and the reformulation phase is important.
> – Separation fosters *analysis*, as it forces Translators to *think* about what they *believe* they have understood …. When there is no separation, translators tend to view comprehension as less important, at best as a transient phase, only required at a superficial level to make reformulation possible (p. 116).

Zhong (1999, p. 10) argues that "accurate comprehension (of the idea or meaning of the original speaker) is always the foremost concern in interpretation" so that the quality of one's interpretation should be "judged primarily by whether or not one has acquired an accurate comprehension of the meaning (or idea) of the original speaker." In other words, same-language consecutive note-taking and rendition practice keeps one honest: In a group session, the instructor and peers keep each other honest and should call each other out when they embellish too much, even to the point of fabricating a story. If one practices by oneself, same-language recall is just as important, if not more, because it puts the focus on the comprehension phase.

Therefore, "[n]ote-taking, though very important, plays a supplementary role" in consecutive interpreting (Zhong 1999). The view that listening and comprehension come before note-taking is confirmed by other interpreter trainers:

Listening is fundamental to good interpreting: you cannot convey precisely and clearly ideas that you have yourself grasped only vaguely and approximately. But this involves more than just hearing, understanding and registering the speaker's words. Even students who did well at the entrance test may sometimes find that they cannot retell a passage well because although they understood all the *words*, they didn't get the speaker's *point*. (Setton and Dawrant 2016, p. 82).

Listening and understanding the original speech are more important than note-taking. But if you have a sound note-taking system, ingrained through a lot of practice, then you *won't need* to put so much mental effort into taking the notes, they'll be better notes and you'll have more mental capacity free for listening and understanding the speech. (Gillies 2013, p. 168).

Although one cannot do without note-taking in a long consecutive setting, luckily, as Gillies advises, one can practice note-taking sufficiently until the process becomes almost second nature and automatic.

5   The CADNCI System

The Connected-Audio Digital Note-taking for Consecutive Interpretation, henceforth CADNCI (pronounced like the word "cadency"), comprises computing hardware, software/apps, and hardware accessories. See Table 1 for a list of system components and setup steps.

Table 1. Components *and Setup of the CADNCI System.*

Category	Component
Hardware	• An iPad (Apple) of any screen size, running iPadOS, with a 3.5 mm audio jack and/or a Lightning port • A Mac computer (desktop or laptop), running MacOS, with a 3.5 mm audio jack
Software/apps	• Loopback (Rogue Amoeba) on MacOS • Notability (Ginger Labs) on iPadOS
Accessories	• An Apple Pencil compatible with the chosen iPad • A USB headset with a boom microphone for the Mac computer • Two 3.5 mm male-to-male audio cables • An audio signal attenuator cable • (Optional) A ground isolator cable • (Optional) A Lightning to 3.5 mm audio cable + charger splitter

The system configuration and setup steps are detailed as follows:

1. Plug a 3.5 mm audio cable into the headphone/microphone jack of the Mac computer.

2. Connect the USB headset to the Mac.
3. *One-time setup: Loopback.* Set up a "device" (virtual audio channel) in Loopback.
    3.1. If there are no devices present under the left column **Devices** list, click the "+" sign labeled **New Virtual Device** to create one.
    3.2. Name the device appropriately, e.g., **Loopback with USB Mic.**
    3.3. Under **Sources**, create a list of sound sources for the interpreter to listen to. Add each source by clicking the "+" sign and select an item from the dropdown menu. If an application (e.g., Chrome) or an audio device (e.g., the USB microphone) is not shown in the menu, start the application or connect the microphone first. Click the "+" sign again to reveal the menu and select the desired item. Once the item is added, the switch to the right of its name should default to **On**. If not, switch it on. Click on **Options** to uncheck the **Mute when capturing** checkbox and set the volume slider to 100%. There should be either two cyan-colored lines connecting the source's **1 (L)** and **2 (R)** channels to **Channel 1 (L)** and **Channel 2 (R)** of **Channels 1 & 2** under **Output Channels**, or two lines coming out of the **1 (L)** channel of a mono device such as a microphone. Leave the lines as is.
    3.4. There is a special source named **Pass-Thru** at the bottom. It is not needed, so turn its switch to **Off**.
    3.5. Repeat this step until all the following sources are added and configured:
        3.5.1. The USB headset.
        3.5.2. **Zoom.us** (the teleconferencing app the system will use in suggested practice scenarios).
        3.5.3. A web browser (e.g., **Chrome**).
        3.5.4. A video player app (e.g., **VLC Player** or **QuickTime**).
        3.5.5. *Testing the USB microphone.* Speak into the boom microphone and notice its **1 (L)** channel meter level jumping.
    3.6. Add a second device under **Devices** and name it appropriately, e.g., **Loopback Line-out**.
    3.7. Under this new device's **Sources** list, replicate the items and configuration as the first device.
    3.8. Check whether Loopback has a right-most column called **Monitors**. If not, click on the bottom-right button labeled **Show Monitors** to show it. Click on the " +" sign to the right of **Monitors** to bring up the menu and select **Built-in Output**. Then switch it to **On**. Click on **Options** to set the volume slider to the desired non-zero level at or close to 100%. Make sure that there are two cyan-colored lines connecting **Channels 1 & 2** and **Built-in Output**, and that the sound levels jump as you speak into the microphone. See Fig. 3.
4. *System audio.* Go to MacOS's **System Preferences** > **Sound**. For **Input**, select the **Loopback Line-out** virtual channel, which was just created and configured in Loopback. For **Output,** select the USB microphone currently configured in Loopback.
5. *Cable connections.*
    5.1. Plug the other end of the 3.5 mm audio cable to one jack of the ground isolator.
    5.2. Plug the second 3.5 mm audio cable into the other jack of the ground isolator.

5.3. Plug the other end of the second 3.5 mm audio cable into the jack of the audio attenuator. This converts line-level audio to microphone-level audio.

5.4. Plug the other end of the audio attenuator into the audio jack of the iPad.

5.5. *(Optional)* Alternatively, plug the other end of the audio attenuator into the 3.5 mm audio jack of a Lightning adapter/splitter, and plug the Lightning end into the iPad. Then, plug the Lightning charger cable into the adapter/splitter to charge the iPad while it is in use.

6. *Notability.* Start a new note in Notability on the iPad. Use the web browser configured in Loopback to find a speech on YouTube. Click on the microphone icon located toward the top-right corner of Notability to start recording.

7. *(Optional) iPad Screen recording.* To also make a second video recording, swipe down from the top-right corner of the iPad to bring up the **Control Center**. Tap and hold the ⊙ icon to bring up the **Screen Recording** menu and choose **Photos** as the destination of the recording. If the bottom icon is grey and shows **Microphone Off**, press it once to toggle to **Microphone On** and it should turn red. Tap **Start Recording,** and the screen recording will start. Tap away to return to Notability's screen.

8. *Test audio and start practice.* Play the YouTube speech. As the speech plays, notice that the Notability recording icon shows jumping sound level inside the circle. Pause the YouTube speech. Speak into the microphone and notice the sound level jumping as well. Once both sound sources are working, restart the speech and start the consecutive interpretation practice. Take consecutive notes in Notability as the speech is given, and then give a consecutive rendition of the speech.

9. *Stopping recordings.* When done, tap Notability's recording icon to stop its recording. If the iPad screen recording was also started, tap the elliptical red indicator at the top-right corner of the iPad to stop the screen recording. The resultant screen recording will be available under Photos shortly.

10. Use Notability's **Recordings** controls on the screen to review the synced audio and note-taking action. Alternatively, review the **Photos** video if available.

5.1 Demonstrations

The author will demonstrate using CADNCI to practice consecutive interpretation in various ways.

Same-Language Rendition.[3] This video demonstrates a same-language rendition (sped up by about 10%) of the beginning portion of a TED Talk (Kurnick and TED 2021). The goal of a same-language rendition is to convey the message accurately and completely and in the same tone and style, but not necessarily in the same words. This rendition (both the visual and audio components) can be presented in real time to participants in a zoom group practice session by sharing the iPad screen.

Note-Taking Action.[4] This video demonstrates two aspects of the system when used in an online group session: (1) The note-taking action, which is synced to the audio

---

[3] Viewable on YouTube: https://youtu.be/dQ0yyqppQDY.

[4] Viewable on YouTube: https://youtu.be/wJO2d7p-wkQ.

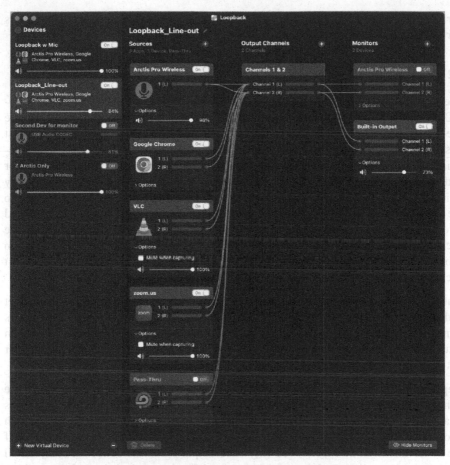

Fig. 3. Configuring Virtual Devices in Loopback.

(slowed down to 85% of the original speed to be more appropriate for practice) of the Kurnick and TED (2021) speech, in Notability. This is shown on the right side of the video. on the left is the original speech video, also synced. (2) The composite view of both the video playback and the notability action as viewed and heard by participants in a Zoom session via the host's screen and sound sharing of either "Desktop" or "Portion of Screen."

Performance Assessment.[5] This video demonstrates how to review the notability recording to assess the note-taking process and the rendition in order to find weaknesses and solutions. This assessment (both the visual and audio components) can be presented in real time to participants in a zoom group practice session by Sharing the iPad screen and audio. It is not limited to self-assessment by the owner of the notes. The Owner's Notability. Note file can be shared and imported to the instructor's or any

---

[5] Viewable on YouTube: https://youtu.be/xPOSmQe6d4o.

participant's notability app so that they can screen-share and critique the note-taker's performance.

5.2 System Advantages

Clean, Clear, and Cable-Connected Audio.[6] The first and foremost advantage of CAD-NCI is that it provides the best way possible to listen to, record, and play back the speech sound of both the source speech and the interpreter's rendition. with the best possible quality of audio, one can focus on identifying the root causes of one's interpretation problems and giving constructive feedback without the confounding factor of poor audio caused by in-air transmission and room reverberation. any difficulty in audibility or intelligibility, once created due to too much ambient noise or reverberation, goes into the recording and remains a permanent problem for any hearer; it cannot be resolved through repeated listening, which merely wastes time. the only solution is to eliminate such interference and prevent it from going into the recording. The combination of audio cables, the headset microphone, and the audio routing software (Loopback) provides just such a solution.

Natural Writing Media. The writing media are natural—the same devices (a tablet and a digital pen) are used for practice, demonstration, and actual work. This fosters familiarity through continual and consistent use. Once one gets past the one-time system setup and starts using the system, it soon provides the comfort and ease of pen and paper but without its drawbacks.

Repeatable Observations, Live or Otherwise. Any practice made using CADNCI, be it the note-taking action or the rendition, can be observed and heard live by all participants in an online group session through screen sharing, or shared and watched later through two kinds of recordings[7]. There is no more sense of regret and disappointment as if the observation can be experienced only once, requiring all the collective attention all participants can muster up. It is perfectly fine for difficult spots in the speech or rendition to be played back and observed repeatedly, until all issues about any utterances are discussed to everyone's satisfaction.

Pinpointing the Issue by Tapping. The Notability recording offers the unique advantage and convenience to quickly replay any portion of the original speech (with the corresponding note-taking action) or the rendition by tapping an associated pen stroke on the screen. with a little practice, one learns to tap a pen stroke that is temporally slightly earlier than the issue in question to hear the problem spot. the reason is that the pen action typically lags the speech by one to several seconds.

What to Observe. The entire consecutive interpreting process is a complex activity involving the senses, cognition, coordination, and speech production. There are a host of components that can be observed and improved on. One key component the observation of

---

[6] One can think of the first "C" in CADNCI to stand for all of these attributes of the system's audio: "clean," "clear," and "cable-connected."

[7] The iPad–Zoom combination imposes a limitation: One can either share live or record the iPad screen recording to share later, but not both.

which CADNCI makes possible is the time lag between hearing something and noting it down, or "ear-pen span" (EPS), the consecutive analog of "ear-voice span" (EVS) or decalage in simultaneous interpretation. In carefully observing an Interpreter's EPS either live or in a notability recording, one can gain valuable insight and make an educated guess at the cause of a particular rendition problem that ensued. For example, one may notice that an interpreter typically has an EPS of three seconds when their rendition is largely problem-free, but at a particular point in the speech the EPS doubled. If the note-taking is observed first, one can try to predict how the interpreter will navigate this high-EPS part during the rendition by observing whether the interpreter adopts any coping strategy in note-taking. Conversely, if a spot of poor performance in the rendition is observed first, one can go back to observe the note-taking action to try to discover the root cause of the performance problem by paying attention to the associated EPS and other factors.

Other components that one might observe include but are not limited to:

- Layout: Are the notes horizontal or vertical? Is there indentation to show hierarchy of ideas?
- Legibility
- Quantity of notes
- Choice of what's noted
- Degree of deverbalization
- Gaps in notes due to a fast speech: Do they result in successful recall or omissions or mistakes?

Holistic Perception of the Consecutive Process. The entirety of the consecutive interpretation process, including both the particularly crucial listening/comprehending/note-taking stage and the note-reading/reformulation stage, is laid bare in front of the observer, for whom the vicarious experience is enhanced through concurrently listening to the source speech and interpretation and visually tracking the note-taking and note-reading action. The perception involves all three aspects: auditory, visual, and temporal. this complete revelation leaves nothing hidden, making it easier—sometimes even making it possible—to discover the interpreter's strengths and especially weaknesses.

Compact and Sharable Digital Records. Notability's special recording not only offers the usual advantages of being digital, but also excels over traditional screen recordings in being compact in file size. (The iPad's screen recordings are by default huge in size and not configurable). The proprietary note format (with a.note extension) can be automatically synced to the cloud or exported, shared, and imported into a practice partner's notability app to view and add further notes to, creating a truly interactive system for collaboration and mutual feedback. It can be exported as a PDF document and an audio file for someone without notability to view and listen to, but the synchronization between them is lost.

Combined Visuals of Speech and Note-Taking. Often, the original speech involves visual components such as displayed slides in a presentation. At least, the consecutive interpreter should be able to occasionally glance at the speaker's face to get extralinguistic cues as to meaning. this is not a problem. As demonstrated in the "Note-taking Action" video, a second visual aspect can be brought into the live observation by sharing "desktop" or "portion of screen" in zoom to display the original speech video and the live note-taking action or note-reading rendition side by side. In order to watch this combined view repeatedly, one can use zoom's built-in feature or a separate desktop screen recording app to record the zoom session.

6 Online Group Practice Scenarios

This section presents two scenarios for carrying out online group practice using Zoom, both of which utilize Zoom's breakout rooms. Most interpreters are already familiar with and use Zoom. It is an ideal teleconferencing tool for group practice and particularly useful for CADNCI because of its native capability for sharing the iPad screen with sound. One downside of Zoom's iPad screen sharing is that during active screen sharing, the iPad screen recording function is disabled. As a result, the note-taking action or note-reading rendition cannot be also recorded as a video to share later. To remedy this, one can use Zoom or another desktop recording app for that purpose.

There are two alternatives to Zoom's built-in iPad sharing: First, one can use a free app called LetsView, available on both MacOS and iPadOS. It projects the iPad screen onto the computer screen, which the Zoom host can then share. In the author's own experience, LetsView is sometimes buggy: The screen can freeze, or the sound can go silent, especially when used to play back a Notability recording. Also, the lag between the audio and the visual is perceptible. In contrast, Zoom's iPad screen sharing is robust[8] and without significant lag. Second, one can join the Zoom session from the iPad using the Zoom app and the same login ID as used in the desktop Zoom (technically allowed by Zoom), and then mute the iPad microphone and share the iPad screen directly from the app.

Zoom has a technical limitation of allowing only one participant's screen to be shared at a time. This means the practice session can't have both a host screen-sharing and playing the source speech video and an interpreter sharing an iPad screen showing the note-taking action. Fortunately, there is a workaround: The interpreter doing the practice can simultaneously share a section of their desktop screen to show the note-taking through a LetsView projection of the iPad as well as the speech video. This approach is demonstrated in the "Note-taking Action" video and described above in the "Combined Visuals of Speech and Note-Taking" subsection.

6.1 Scenario 1: Allowing Everyone to Record Their Note-Taking Action and Rendition—Each Person in Their Own Breakout Room

Using CADNCI, a creative way to make the most of everyone's time in a group practice session on Zoom is to take advantage of breakout rooms to allow *every member* of the group, not just one person, to practice taking consecutive notes and record the note-taking action and consecutive rendition *all at the same time*. This means that at the end

---

[8] On rare occasions, iPad sharing may fail. Resharing or rebooting the computer usually fixes the issue.

of the segment, everyone has the Notability and/or iPad screen recordings of their own note-taking synced with audio and the rendition, ready to be shared with the rest of the group for demonstration or feedback.

First, the instructor/host plays a speech video in the main floor. Everyone records in Notability and takes notes. (Participants without the CADNCI system can use a document camera to record a video of their note-taking and rendition.)

Second, the host places everyone into their own breakout room. Once in the breakout room, each participant.

- Records the Zoom session (having been given permissions by the host in advance),
- Shares the iPad screen (or the document camera view),
- Starts Notability,
- Starts the consecutive rendition using the USB headset,
- Stops the Zoom and Notability recordings (the Zoom recording may take a moment to be generated), and
- Leaves the breakout room to go back to the main room.

Finally, when everyone is gathered in the main room, the host starts a group feedback session by having someone share their screen and play their Notability recording, jumping back to or repeating certain parts of the playback as necessary.

The author believes this to be the ideal practice setup, because everyone practices note-taking and interpreting and has the opportunity to observe anyone else's note-taking and rendition on the same speech segments. When the chance of learning from a number of people of different styles and skill levels is maximized this way, the chance of finding someone or something to emulate to improve one's own skills is the greatest. In other words, all participants learn considerably more by *all practicing the same segments* and comparing and observing each other's performance. The benefits go beyond the limited time of the online sessions. A cloud space can be created to store everyone's practice recordings and give the group more time in which to observe and learn from each other. The author used this obligatory mutual-sharing approach for English–Mandarin simultaneous practice recordings to great success when leading an online practice group aimed at passing the California court interpreter's oral exams in 2021, reflected in the two-thirds pass rate of the group as opposed to one out of nineteen for the whole state.[9]

6.2 Scenario 2: Multiple People in One Breakout Room, Each Playing a Different Role

Alternatively, after the initial main-room playing of the speech for everyone to take notes, the host can organize breakout rooms so that two to three participants are put in a room, where they negotiate who does a rendition (sharing their iPad screen while note-reading) and who gives feedback. This is the approach taken in David Violet's

---

[9] A least four out of six group members reported passing and are listed on the official court interpreter roster as of April 2022. One colleague in the loop reported that "The CA test this year ... [for] Mandarin is 1 in 19" in a private chat group. (Anonymous, personal communication, November 19, 2022).

Seminar and Practice in Note-Taking for Consecutive[10]. The author has participated in Violet's weekly same-language (English) consecutive practice since May 2021 and accumulated a substantial archive of Notability recordings of his own note-taking action and rendition, a valuable record to examine and review at will for self-improvement, research, and pedagogical purposes.

7 Conclusion

As to improving note-taking for consecutive interpretation, one can spend all their time reading about how to take notes and what to do, learning principles and theories. But one will not improve without actual practice. Practicing by oneself is hard not only because it is more difficult to motivate oneself but also because one does not have the chance to observe and compare with others to see how note-taking can be done differently from one's own habits and beyond one's own comfort zone. Attending a regular group practice for long consecutive note-taking and (preferably same-language) rendition and deliberately discovering one's own weaknesses through group feedback or one's own review using CADNCI, either immediately at or after the session, or even just by reviewing one's own archive of self-practice recordings, will yield insights and ideas for designing deliberate practices that are difficult or impossible to obtain without the synced playback of audio and note-taking action.

The CADNCI system presented in this paper, with a particular configuration of hardware and software, and notably the benefits of having clean, clear, cable-connected, and synced audio, makes it easy for a class or a practice group to view together the whole process of separate stages of listening, comprehension, and rendition of consecutive interpretation. With the clean audio, one can focus on finding the root causes of particular types of interpretation problems for long consecutive instead of getting bogged down and discouraged by bad audio due to ambient noise or room reverberation. Often, the ability to see the note-taking action is the only way to identify root causes of interpretation problems. Even when it is not the only way, it at least makes the discovering less cumbersome. That ease and convenience by itself is an incentive to do more discovering.

Technology-assisted digital consecutive note-taking and interpreting helps an interpreter or trainee practice (both in the exercise and work sense of the word) and assess performance better. The CADNCI system shows that such technology is mature enough to enhance and extend one's ability, inspire new approaches, and promote efficiency and efficacy rather than distract and interfere. One is advised to take full advantage of it to pursue result-oriented practice.

Author Note. The author thanks David violet for hosting his consecutive note-taking group practice. His teaching and practice group are an inspiration for this paper.

The trademarks used in this paper (Apple, Apple Pencil, Galaxy Note, Ginger Labs, iPad, iPadOS, LetsView, Lightning, Loopback, Mac, MacOS, Microsoft, Notability, OneNote, Rogue Amoeba, Samsung, Surface, and Zoom) are the property of their respective owners.

---

[10] Link: https://david-violet-interpreter-school.teachable.com/p/practice-note-taking-for-consecutive-interpreting.

References

Acoustical Society of America: Zahorik, P., Ellis, G.M.: An example of dissociation between speech intelligibility and perceived reverberation [Video]. YouTube (2016). https://www.you tube.com/watch?v=WnCaTM1djHw

Eriksson, J.-E. (n.d.). Dr Sound explains the reverb phenomenon. Accessed 25 November 2022. https://www.konftel.com/en/academy/dr-sound-explains-the-reverb-phenomenon

Gelfand, S.A., Silman, S.: Effects of small room reverberation upon the recognition of some consonant features. J. Acoust. Soc. Am. 66(22) (1979). https://doi.org/10.1121/1.383075

Gile, D.: Teaching Conference Interpreting: A Contribution, in Tennant, M., Training for the New Millennium. John Benjamins, Amsterdam/Philadelphia (2005)

Gile, D.: Basic Concepts and Models for Interpreter and Translator Training, Rev John Benjamins, Amsterdam/Philadelphia (2009)

Gillies, A.: Conference Interpreting: A Student's Practice Book. Routledge, Abingdon (2013)

Gillies, A.: Consecutive Interpreting: A Short Course. Routledge, Abingdon (2019)

Hadimi, M., Pöchhacker, F.: Simultaneous consecutive interpreting: a new technique put to the test. Meta 52(2) (2007)

Orlando, M.: Digital pen technology and interpreter training, practice, and research: status and trends. In: Ehrlich, S., Napier, J., (eds.) Interpreter Education in the Digital Age: Innovation, Access, and Change. Gallaudet University Press, Washington D.C. (2015)

Setton, R., Dawrant, A.: Conference Interpreting: A Complete Course. John Benjamins, Amsterdam/Philadelphia (2016)

Schweitzer, H.C.: Reducing the negative effects of reverberation in hearing aid processing. Hearing Rev., 3 November 2003. https://hearingreview.com/hearing-products/accessories/components/reducing-the-negative-effects-of-reverberation-in-hearing-aid-processing

Cousins, J., Newsham, J.: Sound System Intelligibility, Quality and Impact [Video]. YouTube (2015). https://www.youtube.com/watch?v=97MP2wisw-c

Svoboda, Š.: SimConsec: the Technology of a Smartpen in Interpreting. Palacký University Olomouc, Olomouc (2020)

Kurnick, S.: "Aliens built the pyramids" and other absurdities of pseudo-archaeology [Video]. YouTube (18 March 2021).https://www.youtube.com/watch?v=W59CV66z9lQ

Zhong, S.: (钟述孔): A Practical Handbook of Interpretation, Enlarged and Revised Edition. 中国对外翻译出版公司, Beijing (1999)

Misrecognized Utterance Identification in Support Systems for Daily Human-to-Human Conversations

Hikaru Nishida[1,2][✉], Yotaro Iida[1,2], Yumi Wakita[1], and Yoshihisa Nakatoh[2]

[1] Osaka Institute of Technology, Osaka, Japan
m1m22r24@oit.ac.jp, yumi.wakita@oit.ac.com
[2] Kyushu Institute of Technology, Fukuoka, Japan

Abstract. To support smooth conversation between people, we are developing a support system that provides appropriate conversation topics when the speaker cannot immediately think of a topic. The problem with this system is that speech recognition errors occur frequently. The system may not be able to provide appropriate conversation topics due to speech recognition errors. Various methods have been proposed to prevent speech recognition errors, but these methods are still insufficient for domain free daily conversation. Vocalizations become ambiguous across multiple words in human-to-human daily conversation. We believe that it is necessary to understand how acoustic features change due to ambiguous vocalizations, and how changes in acoustic features affect speech recognition results, and to develop countermeasures based on these findings. This paper discusses the speech utterances characteristics that are prone to speech recognition errors to identify speech recognition errors caused by ambiguity in daily speech. In particular, we focus on F0 and mora, and analyze how these factors differ between correctly and incorrectly recognized speech.

We confirmed that the F0 extraction rate tends to be lower for misrecognized speech parts than for correctly recognized speech, and we confirmed that the mora length tends to be shorter for misrecognized speech parts. Regarding the mora, there were a small number of misrecognized utterances in which the mora was extremely long, and the standard deviation of the mor of the misrecognized utterances tended to be larger than that of the misrecognized utterances. By comparing the transcribed sentences with the recognition result sentences, we analyzed the factors contributing to the above tendency, and found that the phenomenon of vowel voicelessness was promoted in daily conversation, with the absence or shortening of vocalized segments including not only vowels but also consonant parts before and after them, and the phenomenon of voiceless nasal sounds at the end of utterances. When the above voicelessness occurred at word-word boundaries, it was found that the words before and after the boundary could be combined and misrecognized as completely different words. In the future, we would like to quantify these features and propose a misrecognized utterances identification method.

Keywords: human-to-human daily conversation · speech recognition error · fundamental frequency · mora

1 Introduction

The increasing number of senior and other citizens living alone has become a serious problem that has been compounded by COVID-19. Human-to-human communication is considered crucial for these categories of people. Hence, many systems have been developed to facilitate this communication. Several studies have proposed systems to conduct smooth communications by introducing appropriate topics [1, 2]. In these studies, several easy-to-use and smart communication tools were proposed for multiple speakers to exchange information; these tools are effective for a while after providing a topic. However, the communication smoothness sometimes decreases over time because these systems do not continuously adapt to a speaker's current situation or conversation topic. To support conversations continuously, the system must keep track of the degree of smoothness of the current conversation and change the supporting timing and topics in consideration of the current communication atmosphere.

To support smooth conversations with other persons, we developed a support system that provides suitable conversation topics for speakers when they cannot think of one immediately. Figure 1 describes the structure of our associative-word board system to provide associative topics for speakers when they need a conversation support. The topics provided for speakers are selected by considering the previous talking points of their conversations. The selection process is as follows. First, an input speech is recognized by analyzing each utterance; some content words are extracted from the recognition results. Next, the semantic similarity values among the content words are calculated. When the similarity value is higher than a predefined threshold, the topic of the conversation is estimated based on the content words. The criterion for selecting topics is that recognized content words should appear infrequently, but the topic should contain words with similar meanings to the recognized content words.

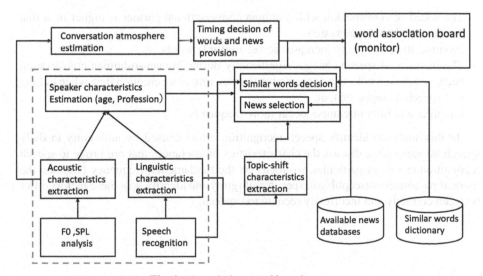

Fig. 1. Associative-word board system

When the content words in a speech are correctly recognized, the system will provide suitable topics for speakers and support their conversation. However, when recognition errors occur, suitable topics cannot be provided for selection, and the conversation support performance decreases significantly. Particularly, speech recognition is more difficult during a casual human-to-human conversation than during a conversation between a human and a spoken dialogue system. Therefore, a technique for understanding human-to-human speech that is robust to recognition errors must be developed.

Robust speech recognition methods have been proposed in previous studies. In reference [3] and [4], noise was added to the training data during the fine-tuning of a pre-trained model. Such added noise acted as pseudo speech recognition errors to make the model robust against such errors. When noise is added to training data, a sentence is learned in which an arbitrary word is replaced by another word. Ideally, the substituted word would reflect the misrecognition patterns that frequently occur in natural conversations. For example, in reference [5], the authors employed a method of creating and adding words whose phonemes are replaced by similar-sounding phonemes. In reference [6], speech data in which the speed of spoken words is changed from that of original utterances are generated for fine-tuning.

These methods have already been confirmed to be effective in improving speech understanding performance in human-to-human limited-domain conversations or speech dialogue systems in which a person converses with a system. However, speech recognition errors tend to increase in the case of human-to-human domain-free conversations. The error cases are more complex; for example, concatenated words are misrecognized as one word or as a word that consists of completely different phonemes. After analyzing the recognition error cases of free human-to-human conversation, we observed that 35% of all errors are due to concatenated words being misrecognized as single words, or single words being misrecognized as concatenated words. The reasons for these errors are as follows.

- The speed of conversation with a human conversational partner is higher than that with a speech dialogue system.
- Pronunciation ambiguity increases across multiple words.
- The intensity of speech changes significantly during human-to-human conversation because a person talks to a conversation partner with more emotion than when talking to a speech dialogue system.
- Laughter and filler utterances occur more frequently.

In this study, to identify speech recognition errors caused by ambiguity in daily speech utterances, we discuss the characteristics of utterances that are prone to speech recognition errors. In particular, we focus on the fundamental frequency (F0) and the mora as parameters susceptible to speech ambiguity and identify how these factors differ between correctly and incorrectly recognized speech.

2 Daily Conversation Database

2.1 Conversation Recording

We recorded several conversations between the elderly, aged 62–82 years and young persons aged 21–23 years. Each conversation was held between two persons and had a duration of approximately 3 min. Although the participating speakers were not meeting for the first time, they had never previously had a mutual conversation. We did not set any conditions regarding conversation topics; rather, the participants conversed freely. Figure 2 shows the conversation recording set-up. We used only one microphone for the two speakers.

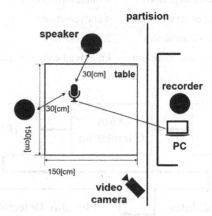

Fig. 2. Conversation recording set-up

After recording, we created a transcript database from the video recording data. Morphological analysis was performed on the transcript text database using "MeCab," which is a Japanese language text morphological analyzer engine.

3 Recognition Error Characteristics for Daily Conversation

To propose a solution to speech recognition errors in daily conversation, we analyzed the speech features resulting from ambiguity in the utterances presented in Sect. 2. Two features are analyzed below.

3.1 Extraction Rates of Fundamental Frequency (F0)

Experiment Conditions. For each conversation, the recorded speech was output as a result of speech recognition using the "Microsoft Azure Speech-to-Text" speech recognition tool. Next, the transcribed text and the speech recognition result were compared, the speech waveforms of the parts where the transcribed text and the speech recognition result produced different results were checked, and the speech waveforms corresponding to the parts that were misrecognized were identified. This is defined as the misrecognition word period.

The fundamental frequency values (F0) in each such speech segment was extracted. The extraction process is described in Fig. 3. The extraction parameters were as follows: sampling frequency = 44100 Hz; window length = 40 ms; frame shift = 10 ms.

Table 1. Details of the conversations dataset

Number of Speakers	6 speakers
Male/Female	4 males, 2 females
Conversation periods	3 min/conversation
Number of conversations	4 conversations
Number of sentences	237 sentences
Conversation condition	Free dyadic conversation

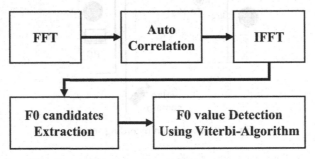

Fig. 3. Process of fundamental frequency extraction

For each word period, the value shown in Eq. (1) was defined as the pitch extraction rate; the pitch extraction rate between correctly and incorrectly recognized words was compared. The correctly recognized words were randomly selected so that the number of words was equal to the number of misrecognized words. However, if the extracted pitch frequency was 400 Hz or higher, it was considered as not extracted.

$$F0 \text{ extraction rate} = Number \text{ of frames successfully extracted}$$
$$for \text{ } F0/total \text{ number of frames in the word period} \quad (1)$$

F0 Extraction Rates for Each Conversation. From the four conversations shown in Table 1, we randomly pick up 10–15 correctly recognized words and approximately the same number of misrecognized words, and calculate the pitch extraction rate for each word using Eq. (1). The average and standard deviation values of the F0 extraction rate calculated for each conversation are shown in Table 2. In three of the four conversations, the average F0 acquisition rate for correctly recognized words exceeded that of incorrectly recognized words.

Table 2. Average (Ave.) and standard deviation (S.D.) values of F0 extraction rates for each conversation

Conversation		1	2	3	4
Correct Recognition Results	Ave.	0.644023	0.752935	0.576165	0.687681
	S.D.	0.232543	0.275534	0.17131	0.127164
Misrecognition Results	Ave.	0.60904	0.589967	0.675621	0.583152
	S.D.	0.224186	0.187089	0.281469	0.367544

Discussion. Vowels /i/ and /u/ are silent when adjacent to certain consonants, and it has been reported that the voicelessness of vowel is accentuated when the speed of articulation is increased[7]. The occurrence of this voicelessness is often observed to be the cause of misrecognition of some words. An example is shown below. The word on the left side was misrecognized for the word on the right side. The /u/ in italicized characters was voiceless, resulting in misrecognition for the word on the right side.

ho u ko *ku ka* i → ho u ka i
i n si n ga *ku* → i n si n ga

In addition to vowels, there are several words with silent nasal sounds at the end of the word.

o o su ga ke *n* → o su da ke

3.2 Number of Words for Each Utterance

Experiment Conditions. The Table 2 shows the conversations dataset content. In each of the seven conversations between an elderly and a young person recorded with the specifications described in Sect. 2. The transcribed sentences were divided into 44 conversations by grouping together the parts of the conversations that discussed the same topic. For each topic, the number of words in the transcriptions and the number of words in the speech recognition results were counted and compared. MeCab, introduced in Sect. 2, was used for morphological analysis (Table 3).

Number of Content and Function Words in Recognition Results Sentences. Figure 4 shows the number of words in the transcription and recognition results for each topic. The vertical axis represents the number of content word and the horizontal axis represents the number of function word. When the conversation was divided per topic, there was a considerable difference in the number of words when a topic was conversed for a long time and the number of words when conversation on a topic did not continue for a long time before transitioning to another. Therefore, the number of function and content

Table 3. Details of the conversation dataset

Number of speakers	6 elderly speakers, 7 young speakers
Age	Elderly adults: 62–82 years old Young persons: 21–23 years old
Number of conversations	14 conversations (7 conversations each)
Conversation periods	3 min/conversation
Conversation condition	Free dyadic conversation

words was normalized by assuming that all conversations on each topic lasted for one minute. It can be seen that both function and content words tend to have a fewer when speech recognition error occurs.

On the other hand, the original transcriptions tend to have more functional and content words than the recognition result sentences. In particular, for content words, only the transcribed sentences have more than 150 words uttered per minute.

Discussion. When several words are spoken continuously, some syllables may be uttered for a very short time or may be silent. When unspoken syllables are present at the boundaries of multiple words, the multiple words are often grouped together and misrecognized as a single word. Hence, the recognition result is likely to have fewer words. Table 4 shows examples of where the number of words in the recognition result is smaller than that in the transcription result.

Table 4. Example of recognition results with reduced word count in the speech recognition text compared to the transcribed text

Transcription text	Recognition result
Chi ga u + ko o ki	Hi ko o ki
Ma e + ni + ko ji ma	Ma e ko ji ma

Reference [7] found that the silence of vowels depends on the speech rate, and that the faster the speech rate, the more accentuated is the silence. Similarly, the missing syllables owing to unclear utterances as described earlier may also depend on the speech rate. Therefore, we examined the mora of misrecognized and correctly recognized words in one conversation selected from the conversations in Table 2.

The mora values of several words are shown in Fig. 5. In the case of correct recognition words, the average of mora (Ave. 0.11) is more than that of misrecognition words (Ave: 0.08).The results indicate that a recognition errors is more likely to occur where the mora is shorter, i.e., where the speech velocity is greater. Also the standard deviation of the correct recognition words (S.D. 0.02) are less than that of misrecognition words (S.D. 0.06). The mora values of all misrecognition words are not short. Sometimes the misrecognition words which mora values are quite long are found. That means mora values of misrecognition words are not stable.

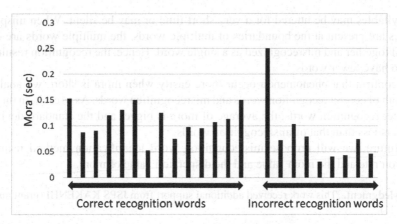

Fig. 4. Comparison of mora length between correct recognition words and misrecognition words

The reason why the number of words is smaller in the speech recognition result sentences containing misrecognition than in the correct transcription sentences is largely due to the ambiguity of the utterance, as described in Sect. 3.2. But it is also due to linguistic features. Words consisting of a small number of syllables, including fillers, frequently appear in daily conversation. For example, the fillers /a/ and /e/ and the final particles /ne/ and /ya/ constitute a word with one syllable. In the process of recognition, these are regarded as words consisting of multiple syllables, so the number of words is reduced more in the recognition result. Table 5 shows an example of a word that is recognized as a single word by concatenating multiple words.

Table 5. Example of recognition errors with several words combined into one word

Transcription text	Recognition result
Na tsu ba + ya + si	Na tsu ba ya si

4   Conclusion

This paper discusses the speech utterances characteristics that are prone to speech recognition errors to identify speech recognition errors caused by ambiguity in daily conversation. In particularly, we focused on F0 and mora and analyzed how these factors differ between correctly and incorrectly recognized speech. As a result of F0 extraction rate analysis, in three of the four conversations, the average F0 extraction rate for correctly recognized words exceeded that of incorrectly recognized words. This result suggests the vowel voicelessness occurs in daily conversation frequently, and that is the cause of misrecognition.

Also, it could be seen that number of both function and content words tend to be fewer when speech recognition error occurs. When several words are spoken continuously, some syllables may be uttered for a very short time or may be silent. When unspoken syllables are present at the boundaries of multiple words, the multiple words are often grouped together and misrecognized as a single word. Hence, the recognition result was likely to have fewer words.

To confirm that phenomenon occur more easily when mora is short, we analyzed mora both of correct recognition words and misrecognition words. As a result, in the case of correct recognition words, the average of mora is bigger and the standard deviation of mora is less than that of misrecognition words.

In future, we will propose misrecognition word identification method using F0 extraction rate and the mora value and the dispersion value of mora.

Acknowledgment. This work received additional support from JSPS KAKENHI (grant number 22K04626).

References

1. Kim, T., Chang, A., Holland, L., Pentland, A.S.: Meeting mediator: enhancing group collaboration using sociometric feedback. In: Proceedings of the 2008 ACM Conference on Computer Supported Cooperative Work, pp. 457–466 (2008)
2. Otsuka, K., Itoh, J., Munnemori, J.: Communication support system for enabling group management of community units. Procedia Comput. Sci. **60**(1), 900–907 (2015)
3. Devlin, J., Chang, M.-W., Lee, K., Toutanova, K.: BERT: pre-training of deep bidirectional transformers for language understanding. In: Proceedings of the 2019 Conference of the North American Chapter of the Association for Computational Linguistics (NAACL): Human Language Technologies, vol. 1, pp. 4171–4186 (2019)
4. Xie, Z., et al.: Data noising as smoothing in neural network language model. In: Conference Paper at ICLR (2017)
5. Asao, Y., Kloetzer, J., Mizuno, J., Saiki, D., Kadowaki, K., Torisawa, K.: Understanding user utterances in a dialog system for caregiving. In: Proceedings of the 12th Language Resources and Evaluation Conference, LREC 2020, pp. 653–661 (2020)
6. Ko, T., Peddinti, V., Povey, D., Khudanpur, S.: Audio augmentation for speech recognition. In: Proceedings of Interspeech 2015, pp 3586–3589 (2015)
7. Fujimoto, M.: Effects of consonantal environment and speech rate on vowel devoicing. In: Proceedings of the Phonetic Society, pp.1–13 (2012)

BLEU Skies for Endangered Language Revitalization: Lemko Rusyn and Ukrainian Neural AI Translation Accuracy Soars

Petro Orynycz[✉] [iD]

Orynycz.com, Edgewater, MD 21037, USA
p@orynycz.com

Abstract. Accelerating global language loss, associated with elevated incidence of illicit substance use, type 2 diabetes, binge drinking, and assault, as well as sixfold higher youth suicide rates, poses a mounting challenge for minority, Indigenous, refugee, colonized, and immigrant communities. In environments where intergenerational transmission is often disrupted, artificial intelligence neural machine translation systems have the potential to revitalize heritage languages and empower new speakers by allowing them to understand and be understood via instantaneous translation. Yet, artificial intelligence solutions pose problems, such as prohibitive cost and output quality issues. A solution is to couple neural engines to classical, rule-based ones, which empower engineers to purge loanwords and neutralize interference from dominant languages. This work describes an overhaul of the engine deployed at LemkoTran.com to enable translation into and out of Lemko, a severely endangered, minority lect of Ukrainian genetic classificability indigenous to borderlands between Poland and Slovakia (where it is also referred to as Rusyn). Dictionary-based translation modules were fitted with morphologically and syntactically informed noun, verb, and adjective generators fueled by 877 lemmata together with 708 glossary entries, and the entire system was riveted by 9,518 automatic, codification-referencing, must-pass quality-control tests. The fruits of this labor are a 23% improvement since last publication in translation quality into English and 35% increase in quality translating from English into Lemko, providing translations that outperform every Google Translate service by every metric, and score 396% higher than Google's Ukrainian service when translating into Lemko.

Keywords: Lemko · Neural Machine Translation · Language Revitalization

1 Introduction

1.1 The Problem

Languages are being lost at a rate of at least one per calendar quarter, with such loss set to triple by 2062, and increase fivefold by 2100, affecting over 1,500 speaker communities [1, pp. 163 and 169]. Such outcomes are associated with elevated incidence of illicit

H. Degen and S. Ntoa (Eds.): HCII 2023, LNAI 14051, pp. 135–149, 2023.
https://doi.org/10.1007/978-3-031-35894-4_10

substance use [2, p. 179], type 2 diabetes [3], binge drinking, and assault [4], as well as sixfold higher youth suicide rates when fewer than of half of community members have language knowledge [5].

A recent study in the United States found that Indigenous language use has positive effects on health, regardless of proficiency level [6]. An experiment on speakers in Poland has found that use of Lemko moderates emotional, behavioral, and depressive symptoms stemming from cognitive availability of trauma [7].

Artificial intelligence machine translation might be of service in spreading the afore-mentioned protective effects to heritage speakers by revitalizing dying and Sleeping languages [8, p. 577]. For example, new speakers might produce correct text instanta-neously and enjoy reading comprehension using automatic machine translation devices as an aid until full, independent fluency is achieved.

1.2 System Under Study

Language. Lemko is a definitively to severely endangered [9, pp. 177–178] East Slavic lect of southwestern Ukrainian genetic classificability [10, p. 52; 11, p. 39] indigenous to borderlands between the Republic of Poland and Slovak Republic; some have referred to it as Rusyn [11, p. 39; 12].

Eastern Boundaries. A unique isogloss differentiating Lemko to the East is fixed parox-ytonic (penultimate syllable) stress, a feature shared with Polish and Eastern Slovak dialects [10, pp. 161–162 and 972–973; 11, p. 50; 13, pp. 70–73], making its extent in Eastern Slovakia at least to the Laborec River, with a transitional zone extending there-after [13, p. 70; 11, p. 50]. Meanwhile in Poland, the historical extent of Lemko reaches at least the Osławica or Wisłok rivers, with a transitional zone beyond them [11, p. 50].

Western Boundaries. The historical western boundaries of Lemko are the Poprad and Dunajec rivers [14, p. 459].

Locale. Ancestral villages of native speakers whose interviews comprise the corpus are found within the current administrative borders of today's Lessor Poland Province, whose capital is Cracow (Table 1).

Table 1. Ancestral villages of native speakers interviewed in corpus material.

Lemko name	Transliteration	Polish name	County Seat	Commune Seat
Ізбы	Izbŷ	Izby	Gorlice	Uście Gorlickie
Ґладышів	Gladŷšiv	Gładyszów	Gorlice	Uście Gorlickie
Чорне	Čorne	Czarne	Gorlice	Sękowa
Долге	Dolhe	Długie	Gorlice	Sękowa
Білцарьова	Bilcar′ova	Binczarowa	Nowy Sącz	Grybów
Фльоринка	Fl′orynka	Florynka	Nowy Sącz	Grybów
Чырна	Čŷrna	Czyrna	Nowy Sącz	Krynica-Zdrój

2 State of the Art

Last year, the world's first quality evaluation results were published for machine translations into Lemko: BLEU 6.28, which was nearly triple that of Google Translate's Ukrainian service[1] (BLEU 2.17) [15, p. 570]. The year before, my colleagues and I had published and presented the world's first results for Lemko to English machine translation: BLEU 14.57 [16].

The engine has been deployed and made freely available at the universal resource locator https://www.LemkoTran.com, where a transliteration engine has been in service since the autumn of 2017. The translation engine was first alluded to in print by Drs. Scherrer and Rabus in the Cambridge University Press journal *Natural Language Engineering* in 2019 [17].

3 Materials and Methods

3.1 Materials

The experiment was performed on a bilingual corpus comprising Lemko Cyrillic transcripts and English translations of interviews with survivors and children of forced resettlements from ancestral lands in Poland. The transcripts and their translations[2] were aligned across 3,267 segments, with Microsoft Word providing a Lemko source word count of 68,944 and an English target word count of 81,188.

Sources of truth included the dictionaries of Jarosław Horoszczak [18], Petro Pyrtej [19], Ihor Duda [20], and Janusz Rieger [21], as well as the grammars of Henryk Fontański and Mirosława Chomiak [22] and Petro Pyrtej [23].

3.2 Methods

Engine Upgrades. For this experiment, the engine deployed at LemkoTran.com was fitted with newly built generators informed by part of speech, grammatical case, and number for the purpose of producing grammatically and syntactically appropriate translations for 1,585 dictionary entries, about half of which do not inflect in Polish or Lemko, allowing for simple substitution.

Quality Assurance Tests. Quality was ensured by 9,518 tests cross-referenced when feasible with the Lemko codifications, grammars, and dictionaries listed above under *Materials*. The tests themselves assert that the system translates given utterances in the desired manner (Table 2).

---

[1] Disclosure: I work as a paid Ukrainian, Polish, and Russian translation quality control specialist for the Google Translate project. My client's headquarters are in San Francisco, California.

[2] I was hired to produce the transcripts and translate them by the John and Helen Timo Foundation of Wilmington, Delaware, who then donated the work products to my scientific research and development endeavors.

Table 2. System vocabulary.

Description	Quantity
Noun stem	414
Verb stem	296
Adjective stem	167
Pronoun, personal	87
Pronoun, other	178
Numeral	86
Other dictionary entries	357
Total	1,585

Rule-Based Machine Translation (RMBT). Text was given a Lemko or Polish look and feel by replacing character sequences, and especially inflectional endings (Table 3).

Table 3. Example character sequence replacements.

Polish Sequence	Lemko Sequence	Position
ować	uwaty	Final
iami	iamy	Final
ają	ajut	Final
ze	zo	Initial
pod	pid	Initial

Translation Quality Scoring. Translation quality was measured per industry standard metrics using the default settings of the SACREBLEU tool invented at Amazon Research by Matt Post [24]. For the sake of comparability, Polish was rendered in Lemko Cyrillic in the same way as the last experiment [15, p. 573].

Bilingual Evaluation Understudy (BLEU). This *n*-gram-based metric has enjoyed wide currency for decades. It was developed in the United States at the IBM T. J. Watson Research Center with support from the Defense Advanced Research Projects Agency (DARPA) and monitoring by the United States Space and Naval Warfare Systems Command (SPAWAR) [25].

Translation Edit Rate (TER). This metric reflects the number of edits necessary for output to semantically approach a correct translation, aiming to be more tolerant of phrasal shifts than BLEU and other *n*-gram-based metrics. It is determined by dividing a calculation of edit distance between a hypothesis and a reference by average reference wordcount. Its development in the United States was also supported by DARPA [26].

Character n-gram F-score (chrF). This European metric been shown to correlate very well with human judgments and even outperform both BLEU and TER [27].

4 Results and Discussion

The experimental system, LemkoTran.com, outperformed every Google Translate service by every metric. English to Lemko translation BLEU quality scores improved 35% in comparison with the last published results [15], producing results four times better than Google Translate's next-best offering, its Ukrainian service. Meanwhile, Lemko to English translation quality improved by 23% since the last published results [16], achieving BLEU scores 16% higher than the best obtained by Google Translate, which automatically recognized Lemko as Ukrainian 76% of the time, as Russian 16% of the time, and as Belarusian 6% of the time.

4.1 English to Lemko Translation Quality

Scores. The engine deployed at LemkoTran.com bested Google Translate by every metric when translating from English into Lemko. The next-highest scoring system in the experiment was either the output of Google Translate's Ukrainian service (using the BLEU or CHRF metrics) or that of its Polish service (using the TER metric).

BLEU. The translation quality of the system deployed at LemkoTran.com as measured by the most widespread BLEU metric rose to 8.48, a 35% improvement on results last published in 2022 [15], and now quadruple Google Translate's highest score (Fig. 1).

CHRF. The LemkoTran.com engine achieved the best English to Lemko character *n*-gram f-score (CHRF 37.30), which is 37% higher than the next best, Google Translate's Ukrainian service. Meanwhile, Google Translate's Russian service scored higher than its Polish and Belarusian counterparts when measured against the Lemko corpus by this metric (Fig. 2).

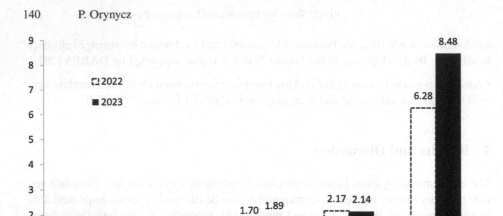

Fig. 1. English to Lemko translation quality as measured by Bilingual Evaluation Understudy (BLEU) score, Google Cloud Neural Machine Translation (NMT) services versus LemkoTran. com. The higher, the better.

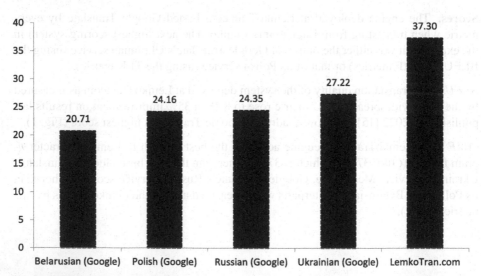

Fig. 2. English to Lemko translation quality as measured by character *n*-gram F-score (CHRF) score, Google Cloud Neural Machine Translation (NMT) versus the experimental system Lem koTran.com. The higher, the better.

TER. The LemkoTran.com engine achieved the best English to Lemko Translation Edit Rate (TER), scoring 81.33. Google Translate's Polish service scored second best, followed closely by its Ukrainian one (Fig. 3).

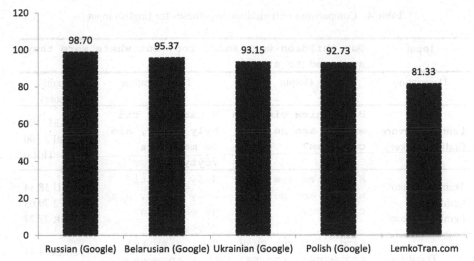

Fig. 3. English to Lemko Translation Edit Rate (TER), Google Cloud Neural Machine Translation (NMT) versus LemkoTran.com. The lower, the better.

Samples. Output from the translation systems when fed English is given below (Tables 4 and 5).

4.2 Lemko to English Translation

Scores. For every metric, the engine deployed at LemkoTran.com outperformed Google Translate, for which translation as if from Standard Ukrainian was always second best, followed by it automatically detecting the source language, then translating as if from Belarusian, and then Polish, with Russian always coming in last place. Google Translate recognized Lemko as Ukrainian 76% of the time, as Russian 16% of the time, as Belarusian 6% of the time, and as sundry languages using Cyrillic alphabets (e.g. Mongolian) the rest of the time.

BLEU. LemkoTran.com scored BLEU 17.95 when translating into English, a 23% improvement on last published results of BLEU 14.57, and 16% higher than Google Translate's Ukrainian service's score of BLEU 15.43 (Fig. 4).

chrF. The engine deployed at LemkoTran.com achieved a character *n*-gram f-score (CHRF) of 45.89 when translating into English, which was 5% better than the score of Google Translate's Ukrainian service (Fig. 5).

Table 4. Comparisons of translation hypotheses for English input.

Input	Our children were smart too. But where were they supposed to study?		
Description	Output	Transliteration	Quality Scores
Lemko reference (native speaker)	В нас діти тіж были мудры, але де мали ся вчыти?	V nas dity tiž bŷly mudrŷ, ale de maly sja včŷty?	BLEU 100 CHRF2 100 TER 0
Translation into Lemko by LemkoTran.com	Нашы діти тіж были мудры. але де мали ся вчыти?	Našŷ dity tiž bŷly mudrŷ. ale de maly sja včŷty?	BLEU 58.34 CHRF2 79.03 TER 27.27
Translation into Ukrainian	Наші діти теж були розумними. Але де вони мали вчитися?	Naši dity tež buly rozumnymy. Ale de vony maly včytysja?	BLEU 4.41 CHRF2 25.80 TER 72.73
Translation into Russian	Наши дети тоже были умными. Но где им было учиться?	Naši deti tože byli umnymi. No gde im bylo učit'sja?	BLEU 3.71 CHRF2 16.95 TER 90.91
Translation into Polish	Наше дзеці теж били мондре. Але гдзе мелі се учиць?	Naše dzjeci tež byly mondre. Alje gdzje mjeli sje učyc'?	BLEU 3.12 CHRF2 13.84 TER 100
Translation into Belarusian	Разумныя былі і нашы дзеці. Але дзе яны павінны былі вучыцца?	Razumnyja byli i našy dzeci. Ale dze jany pavinny byli vučycca?	BLEU 3.09 CHRF2 12.83 TER 100

The "Google Translate (control)" label spans the Ukrainian, Russian, Polish, and Belarusian rows.

Table 5. Comparisons of translation hypotheses for English input.

Input	And generally speaking, Lemkos in Poland don't have a leader, so to speak, who would say something.		
Description	Product	Transliteration	Quality Scores
Lemko reference (native speaker)	А воґулі Лемкы в Польщы не мают такого, же так повім, такого лідера, котрий бы штоси повіл.	A voguli Lemkŷ v Pol'ščŷ ne majut takoho, že tak povim, takoho lidera, kotryj bŷ štosy povil.	BLEU 100 CHRF2 100 TER 0
Translation into Lemko by Lem-koTran.com	І генеральні Лемкы в Польщы не мают лидера, же так повім, котрий бы штоси повіл.	I heneral'ni Lemkŷ v Pol'ščŷ ne majut lydera, že tak povim, ko-tryj bŷ štosy povil.	BLEU 55.58 CHRF2 65.32 TER 29.41
Google Translate (control) — Translation into Polish	І ґенеральнє Лемковє в Польсце не майон лідера, же так повєм, ктури би цось поведзял.	I general'nje Lemkovje v Pol'sce nie majon lidera, že tak povjem, ktury by cos' povjedzjal.	BLEU 9.26 CHRF2 29.29 TER 82.35
Translation into Ukrainian	І взагалі, лемки в Польщі не мають лідера, так би мовити, який би щось сказав.	I vzahali, lemky v Pol'shchi ne mayut' lidera, tak by movyty, yakyj by shchos' skazav.	BLEU 5.15 CHRF2 26.56 TER 82.35
Translation into Russian	И вообще, у лемков в Польше нет, так сказать, лидера, который бы что-то сказал.	I voobšče, u lem-kov v Pol'še net, tak skazat', lid-era, kotoryj by čto-to skazal.	BLEU 2.96 CHRF2 25.87 TER 88.24
Translation into Belarusian	І ўвогуле лэмкі ў Польшчы ня маюць лідэра, так бы мовіць, які б нешта сказаў.	I ŭvohule lèmki ŭ Pol'ščy nja ma-juc' lidèra, tak by movic', jaki b nešta skazaŭ.	BLEU 2.72 CHRF2 18.05 TER 94.12

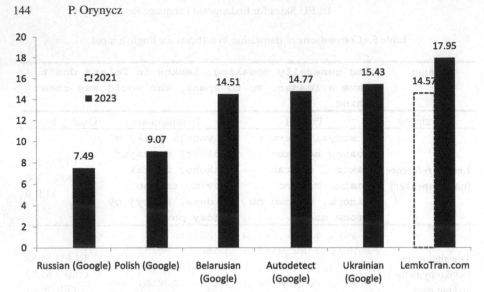

Fig. 4. Lemko to English translation quality as measured by Bilingual Evaluation Understudy (BLEU) score, Google Cloud Neural Machine Translation (NMT) services versus the experimental system LemkoTran.com. The higher, the better.

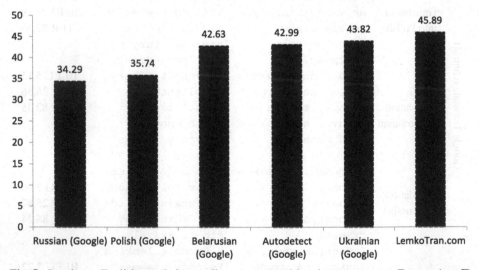

Fig. 5. Lemko to English translation quality as measured by character n-gram F-score (CHRF) score, Google Cloud Neural Machine Translation (GNMT) versus the experimental system LemkoTran.com. The higher, the better.

TER. LemkoTran.com scored a Translation Edit Rate (TER) of 70.38 translating into English, which was 7% better than the score of Google Translate's Ukrainian service (Fig. 6).

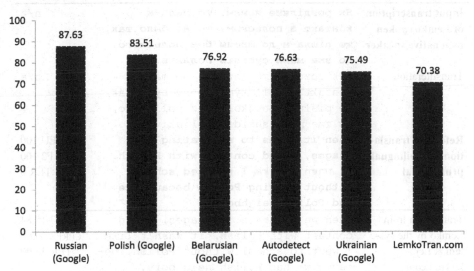

Fig. 6. Lemko to English Translation Edit Rate (TER), Google Cloud Neural Machine Translation (GNMT) versus the experimental system LemkoTran.com. The lower, the better.

Samples. Output from the translation systems when fed English is given below (Table 6).

Table 6. Comparisons of translation hypotheses for Lemko input.

Description	Product	Quality Scores
Input transcription of Lemko spoken by a native speaker	Як розділяме языкы, то мала-м контакт з польскым, то не было так, же пішла-м до школы без польского, бо зме мали сусідів Поляків.	n/a
Transliteration	Jak rozdiljame jazŷkŷ, to mala-m kontakt z pol'skŷm, to ne bŷlo tak, že pišla-m do školŷ bez pol'skoho, bo zme maly susidiv Poljakiv.	n/a
Reference translation by a bilingual professional	When it comes to separating languages, I had contact with Polish. It wasn't like I started school without knowing Polish because we had Polish neighbors.	BLEU 100 CHRF2 100 TER 0
Translation from Lemko by the system at LemkoTran.com	When we separate languages, I had contact with Polish, it wasn't like I went to school without Polish, because we had Polish neighbors.	BLEU 45.84 CHRF2 69.60 TER 32.00
from Ukrainian (autodetected with 92% confidence)	As we divide the languages, then I had contact with Polish, then it was not like that, and I went to school without Polish, because I had Poles as neighbors.	BLEU 15.87 CHRF2 54.38 TER 72.00
from Belarusian	As we separate the languages, then I had little contact with Polish, then it was not like that, but I went to school without Polish, because we had few Polish neighbors.	BLEU 11.76 CHRF2 58.92 TER 68.00
from Russian	As we spread languages, then there was little contact with Polish, then it wasn't like that, but I went to school without Polish, for the snakes were sucid in Polyakiv.	BLEU 6.87 CHRF2 42.66 TER 92.00
from Polish	As I spread the language, I have little contact with the Polish language, it wasn't like that I went to school without Polish, because I will change my little Polish language.	BLEU 5.02 CHRF2 45.35 TER 84.00

Google Translate (control)

5 Conclusion

Coupling morphologically and syntactically informed generators to neural engines can improve machine translation quality by at least a third, while also having the side benefit of empowering engineers to purge loanwords and counteract other dominant-language interference, as well as ensure compliance with standards, such as codifications of minority languages. Quality-score glass ceilings imposed by the imperfections inherent to artificial intelligence models can also be shattered through sound engineering. For Lemko, as well as fellow low-resource, Indigenous minority languages, the sky is now the limit for translation quality, as well as revitalization revolutions just over the horizon.

Acknowledgements. I would like to thank Dr. Ming Qian of Charles River Analytics for the inspiration to conduct this experiment, Michael Decerbo of Raytheon BBN Technologies and Dr. James Joshua Pennington for their insightful remarks, as well as Dr. Yves Scherrer of the University of Helsinki for his interest in the project and ideas.

References

1. Bromham, L., et al.: Global predictors of language endangerment and the future of linguistic diversity. Nat. Ecol. Evol. **6**, 163–173 (2022). https://doi.org/10.1038/s41559-021-01604-y
2. Gonzalez, M., Aronson, B., Kellar, S., Walls, M., Greenfield, B.: Language as a facilitator of cultural connection. ab-Original **1**(2), 176–194 (2017). https://doi.org/10.5325/aboriginal.1.2.0176
3. Oster, R., Grier, A., Lightning, R., Mayan, M., Toth, E.: Cultural continuity, traditional Indigenous language, and diabetes in Alberta First Nations: a mixed methods study. Int. J. Equity Health **13**, 92 (2014). https://doi.org/10.1186/s12939-014-0092-4
4. Culture, Heritage and Leisure: Speaking Aboriginal and Torres Strait Islander Languages. In: 4725.0 - Aboriginal and Torres Strait Islander Wellbeing: A focus on children and youth. Australian Bureau of Statistics (2011). https://www.abs.gov.au/ausstats/abs@.nsf/Latestproducts/1E6BE19175C1F8C3CA257A0600229ADC
5. Hallett, D., Chandler, M., Lalonde, C.: Aboriginal language knowledge and youth suicide. Cogn. Dev. **22**(3), 392–399 (2007). https://doi.org/10.1016/j.cogdev.2007.02.001
6. Whalen, D., Lewis, M., Gillson, S., McBeath, B., Alexander, B., Nyhan, K.: Health effects of Indigenous language use and revitalization: a realist review. Int. J. Equity Health **21**, 169 (2022). https://doi.org/10.1186/s12939-022-01782-6
7. Skrodzka, M., Hansen, K., Olko, J., Bilewicz, M.: The twofold role of a minority language in historical trauma: the case of Lemko minority in Poland. J. Lang. Soc. Psychol. **39**(4), 551–566 (2020). https://doi.org/10.1177/0261927X20932629
8. Zhang, S., Frey, B., Bansal, M.: ChrEn: Cherokee-English machine translation for endangered language revitalization. In: Proceedings of the 2020 Conference on Empirical Methods in Natural Language Processing (EMNLP), pp. 577–595. Association for Computational Linguistics (2020, Online). https://doi.org/10.18653/v1/2020.emnlp-main.43
9. Duć-Fajfer, O.: Literatura a proces rozwoju i rewitalizacja tożsamości językowej na przykładzie literatury łemkowskiej (in Polish), 1st edn. In: Olko, J., Wicherkiewicz, T., Borges, R. (eds.) Integral Strategies for Language Revitalization, pp. 175–200. Faculty of "Artes Liberales", University of Warsaw, Warsaw (2016). https://culturalcontinuity.al.uw.edu.pl/resource/integral-strategies-for-language-revitalization/

10. Shevelov, G.: A historical phonology of the Ukrainian language (Ukrainian translation). Vaku-lenko, S., Danylenko, A. (trans.), Ushkalov, L. (ed.). Naukove vydavnyctvo "AKTA", Kharkiv (2002, original work published 1979). http://irbis-nbuv.gov.ua/ulib/item/UKR0001641

11. Rieger, J.: Stanovysko i zrižnycjuvanja "rusynskŷx" dialektiv v Karpatax (in Rusyn), 2nd edn. In: Magosci, P. (ed.) Najnowsze dzieje języków słowiańskich. Rusyn′skŷj jazŷk, pp. 39–66. Uniwersytet Opolski — Instytut Filologii Polskiej, Opole (2007). https://www.unipo.sk/cjknm/hlavne-sekcie/urjk/vedecko-vyskumna-cinnost/publikacie/26405/

12. Vaňko, J.: Klasifikacija i holovnŷ znakŷ Karpat′skŷx Rusyn′skŷx dialektiv (in Rusyn), 2nd edn. In: Magosci, P. (ed.) Najnowsze dzieje języków słowiańskich. Rusyn′skŷj jazŷk, pp. 67–84. Uniwersytet Opolski — Instytut Filologii Polskiej, Opole (2007). https://www.unipo.sk/cjknm/hlavne-sekcie/urjk/vedecko-vyskumna-cinnost/publikacie/26405/

13. Vaňko, J.: The Rusyn language in Slovakia: between a rock and a hard place. Int. J. Sociol. Lang. **2007**(183), 75–96 (2007). https://doi.org/10.1515/IJSL.2007.005

14. Sopolyha, M.: Do pytan′ etničnoï identyfikaciï ta sučasnyx etničnyx procesiv ukraïnciv Prjašivščyny (in Ukrainian). In: Skrypnyk, H. (ed.) Ukraïnci-rusyny: etnol′inhvistyčni ta etnokul′turni procesy v istoryčnomu rozvytku, pp. 454–487. National Academy of Sciences of Ukraine, National Association of Ukrainian Studies, Rylsky Institute of Art Studies, Folklore and Ethnology, Kyiv (2013). http://irbis-nbuv.gov.ua/ulib/item/UKR0001502

15. Orynycz, P.: Say it right: AI neural machine translation empowers new speakers to revitalize Lemko. In: Degen, H., Ntoa, S. (eds.) Artificial Intelligence in HCI, HCII 2022. Lecture Notes in Computer Science, vol. 13336, pp. 567–580. Springer, Cham (2022). https://doi.org/10.1007/978-3-031-05643-7_37

16. Orynycz, P., Dobry, T., Jackson, A., Litzenberg, K.: Yes I Speak… AI neural machine translation in multi-lingual training. In: Proceedings of the Interservice/Industry Training, Simulation, and Education Conference (I/ITSEC) 2021, Paper no. 21176. National Training and Simulation Association, Orlando (2021). https://www.xcdsystem.com/iitsec/proceedings/index.cfm?Year=2021&AbID=96953&CID=862

17. Scherrer, Y., Rabus, A.: Neural morphosyntactic tagging for Rusyn. In: Mitkov, R., Tait, J., Boguraev, B. (eds.) Natural Language Engineering, vol. 25, no. 5, pp. 633–650. Cambridge University Press, Cambridge (2019). https://doi.org/10.1017/S1351324919000287

18. Horoszczak, J.: Słownik łemkowsko-polski, polsko-łemkowski (in Polish). Rutenika, Warsaw (2004)

19. Pyrtej, P.: Korotkyj slovnyk lemkivs′kyx hovirok (in Ukrainian). Siversiya MV, Ivano-Frankivsk (2004)

20. Duda, I.: Lemkivs′kyj slovnyk (in Ukrainian). Aston, Ternopil (2011)

21. Rieger, J.: Słownictwo i nazewnictwo łemkowskie (in Polish). Wydawnictwo naukowe Semper, Warsaw (1995)

22. Fontański, H., Chomiak, M.: Gramatyka języka łemkowskiego (in Polish). Wydawnictwo Naukowe "Śląsk", Katowice (2000)

23. Pyrtej, P.: Dialekt łemkowski. Fonetyka i morfologia (in Polish). In: Hojsak, W. (ed.). Zjednoczenie Łemków, Gorlice (2013)

24. Post, M.: A call for clarity in reporting BLEU scores. In: Proceedings of the 3rd Conference on Machine Translation (WMT), vol. 1, pp. 186–191. Association for Computational Linguistics, Brussels (2018).https://doi.org/10.48550/arXiv.1804.08771

25. Papineni, K., Roukos, S., Ward, T., Wei-Jing, Z.: BLEU: a method for automatic evaluation of machine translation. In: Proceedings of the 40th Annual Meeting of the Association for Computational Linguistics, ACL 2002, pp. 311–318. Association for Computational Linguistics, Philadelphia (2002). https://doi.org/10.3115/1073083.1073135

26. Snover, M., Dorr, B., Schwartz, R., Micciulla, L., Makhoul, J.: A study of translation edit rate with targeted human annotation. In: Proceedings of the 7th Conference of the Association for Machine Translation in the Americas: Technical Papers, pp. 223–231. Association for Machine Translation in the Americas, Cambridge (2006). https://aclanthology.org/2006.amta-papers.25
27. Popović, M.: CHRF: character n-gram F-score for automatic MT evaluation. In: Proceedings of the 10th Workshop on Statistical Machine Translation, pp. 392–395. Association for Computational Linguistics, Lisbon (2015). https://doi.org/10.18653/v1/W15-3049

Translators as Information Seekers: Strategies and Novel Techniques

Ming Qian[1](✉) and Huaqing Wu[2]

[1] Charles River Analytics, Cambridge, MA, USA
mqian@cra.com
[2] ATA-Certified Translator, Foshan, China
huaqing@wutrans.com

Abstract. Translators search for information to resolve various types of uncertainties they face such as confirming the source of original texts, gaining proper understanding, and verifying whether the selected keywords are spelled correctly, commonly used, or matched properly between source and target languages. Under the constraints of tighter time schedules and stricter cost-effectiveness requirements imposed by the machine translation (MT) plus human post-editing (PE) business model, translators strive to achieve the goals of information seeking with enhanced efficiency and accuracy. This study investigates four information seeking strategies: (1) top-ranked results or featured snippets returned by large-scale web search engines; (2) abductive reasoning based on search result counts returned by large-scale web search engines; (3) direct answers provided by ChatGPT—a long-form question-answering conversational AI; (4) A novel conversational search engine (Perplexity.ai) combining OpenAI's GPT language modeling technology and a large Internet search engine—Microsoft Bing. Human users should focus on forming effective human queries to develop an effective collaboration between human and large-scale web search engines, long-form question-answering conversational AI systems, and conversational search engine. While top-ranked search results and count-based abductive reasoning are effective strategies, emerging technologies such as long-form question-answering conversational AI and conversational search engine provide accurate and comprehensive answers to specific queries, and additional data and resources such as reference links and related questions.

Keywords: Search Strategy · Information Seeking · ChatGPT · Abductive Reasoning · Human Heuristics · Large Language Model · Conversational AI · Long-form Question-answering · Human-centered AI · Human-machine Teaming · Human-machine Collaboration · Search Engine · Answer Engine · Conversational Search Engine · AI-chat

1 Introduction

In the practice of translation, the source language is the language being translated from, while the target language is the language being translated into. According to translation industry practice, a translator's mother tongue is preferably the target language

H. Degen and S. Ntoa (Eds.): HCII 2023, LNAI 14051, pp. 150–166, 2023.
https://doi.org/10.1007/978-3-031-35894-4_11

because translating into a language requires more linguistic and cultural competency than writing original text in that language. However, in recent years, a growing number of translators have served the role of translating into a target language that is not their native language while their native tongue is the source language. Since understanding is the basis of translation, a deeper understanding of the source text is an obvious benefit of such arrangements. On the other hand, the inherent disadvantages of being a non-native speaker of the target language can be offset by information seeking skills leveraging large-scale web search engines (e.g. Google search) and novel long-form question-answering conversational AI.

Using the Chinese-to-English language pair as an example: Chinese is one of the most difficult languages to learn. Translators whose native language is Chinese have an advantage in understanding the original Chinese text. On the other hand, in contrast to native English speaker translators, they rely more on web search engines and AI technologies to fill knowledge gaps, maintain accuracy, and seek verification.

In an ideal situation, translators should invest an indefinite amount of time and effort to investigate throughout their efforts, ensuring the highest quality of the output. Yet with the advancement of technology, machine translation (MT) plus human post-editing (PE) has been gaining dominance as a business model due to lower costs and higher efficiency. Human translators in this model often take on the role of post-editors and their job is to identify and correct errors in the MT pre-translated texts to produce final target texts. Consequently, translators face the challenges of tighter time schedules and stricter cost-effectiveness requirements. Consequently, strategies of information seeking [1] have become very important because translators want to identify the related information and resolve the uncertainty with enhanced efficiency and accuracy.

This study aims to analyze three types of information seeking approaches:

1. Retrieve knowledge based on top-ranked results and featured snippets returned by a large-scale web search engine (e.g., Google search).
2. Guesstimate the answer by arbitrating among alternative answers based on the number of counts of returned results by customized keyword search using a large-scale web search engine (e.g., Google search).
3. Use a long-form question-answering conversational AI systems such as ChatGPT.
4. A novel conversational search engine (Perplexity.ai) combining OpenAI's GPT language modeling technology and a large Internet search engine—Microsoft Bing.

We evaluate and compare pros and cons of each strategy using real-world Chinese-to-English translation examples.

2 Information Seeking Strategies and Examples

2.1 The Objectives of Information Seeking

In translation work, translators perform information seeking to resolve various types of uncertainties: quickly confirm the source of original source texts; gain proper understanding, or verify whether the selected keywords are spelled correctly, commonly used, or matched properly between source and target languages. These keywords include:

- Heading or sentence segment—identifying the source of the original text may reveal the entire original texts or related material that may serve as a key for better understanding.
- Names of people and organizations—quickly confirming spelling, word order, and background information. Techniques can even be used to assist typesetting, using "" combined with * to search and verify illegible names or signatures.
- Names of businesses, chemical ingredients, products, and scientific names—e.g., quickly verify whether the term suggested by the dictionary or machine translation is correct.
- Terminology—e.g., judging whether it is commonly used.
- Phrase or text span—e.g., judging whether it is commonly used.

2.2 Strategy 1: Top-Ranked Entries and Featured Snippets Returned by Search Engines Based on Bottom-Up Search Strategy

In general, there are two types of web search approaches [2, 3]: top-down versus bottom-up. A top-down strategy means that users start with a general search and then narrow down the search by following the content returned by the general search, and this process continues until users find the specific knowledge they are looking for. A bottom-up strategy follows an analytic style of searching in which specific keywords are identified first (based on various factors such as a translator's knowledge, judgment, and confidence level), and used as search terms in a web search engine (e.g., Google search). Then, the search engine's results are examined systematically and pursued until the desired information is found, or the uncertainty can be reduced to acceptable levels. As the MTPE business model has been gaining momentum, translators have been facing challenges of tighter time schedules and stricter cost-effectiveness requirement, and consequently they usually adopt the bottom-up approach.

Common Google search operators [4] are often used by translators to combine related search terms: all these keywords; exact word/phrase (""); any of these words (OR); none of these words (-); limit the search to one site or domain (site:); query the definition of a term (define:); only display a specific file type for search results (filetype:); …

Web search engines build searchable databases by crawling and pulling content from a huge number of webpages [5]. Accordingly, search algorithms are used to match web links with the search query and rank relevant results based on multiple factors: relevance, backlinks, freshness, a page's response speed, …

In many instances, users can find correct answers by investigating the top-ranked results returned by the web search engine. Even better, sometimes featured snippets can provide the best solutions towards a specific search request at the very top of the search results—a 'featured snippet box' is a relatively recent capability introduced by Google to present one or more direct answers in the box without having to visit any website [6].

2.3 Strategy 2: Guesstimate Among Alternative Answers Based on the Number of Results Returned by Customized Keyword Search Using a Large-Scale Web Search Engine

In many other instances, the large web search engine does not provide featured snippet, or it is hard to make a judgment—within a reasonable time constraint—based on reading a few top-ranked search results. Under such circumstances and under the pressure of time constraint and cost-effectiveness requirements, translators use abductive reasoning by arbitrating among alternative solutions through counting the number of results returned by a large-scale web search engine.

Such an approach is questionable because it has been widely reported that even though a web search engine such as Google lists a large number of search results on the first page (from a few hundred thousand to several millions), in reality it has only found about several hundred results [7]. Even though it could serve as a good indicator on how common something is, it could lead to false sense of reality because many other factors could falsely boost the counts (e.g. some web pages might have been mirrored many times so that the counts are falsely boosted). This issue can usually be solved by using a combination of search operators, such as combining "" (exact search) and – (putting a minus sign in front of a word you want to leave out) based on common sense or knowledge.

2.4 Strategy 3: New Search Experience Enabled by Long-Form Question and Answer Conversational AI (ChatGPT)

Transformer-based deep learning language model, such as GPT-3 and ChatGPT [5], can take an input sentence and auto-generate detailed follow-up text. Consequently, instead of clicking on links returned by a search engine (e.g., Google), human users can query a large language model (LLM) chatbot, such as ChatGPT, using conversational format.

Unlike Google search engine, ChatGPT is not a web browser, so it can't crawl the internet to collect and rank information one is searching for. But ChatGPT is able to share knowledge with human users in a conversational manner and provide arguments and opinions in a nuanced way that Google cannot really provide. For translators, ChatGPT can serve as a source of knowledge and it can provide the relevant knowledge a rather short time that would take much longer to conclude via web search.

Even though the ultimate source of truth might be reached thorough a web search, users have to traverse multiple links sequentially. The large web search platform (e.g. Google) makes it so anybody can skim the surface endlessly but only the most determined and wise users can push on and trace down the final result. But often users could be distracted into wrong paths that end up without solution. What it lacks is the capability to dive deeply and accurately, and reap the reward of discovery directly [9]. For this exact reason, search engine tech giant such as Google are worried about the threat imposed by ChatGPT towards the future of the search engine business [10].

2.5 Strategy 4: Conversational Search Engine Combining Large Language Model and Large-Scale Web Search Engines

Novel conversational search engines (e.g. perplexity.ai [11]) combines the power of GPT models [5] and a large-scale web search engine (e.g. Microsoft Bing). Consequently, they can provide both answers and highly relevant references from Internet. One obvious benefit, compared with a ChatGPT, is to provide source of the solution. Consequently, users can retrieve additional data and resources.

3   Information Seeking Examples

Three examples were excerpted from multiple blog posts from ATA-CLD (Chinese Language Division of American Translators' Association) blogs (https://www.ata-divisions.org/CLD/) where translators described their information seeking heuristics to solve real-life translation-related examples [12, 13]. Three strategies described in the previous section were applied on the examples and below their pros and cons are evaluated.

3.1   Example 1: Medical Term (Medical Record)

Example 1 (Table 1) was excerpted from a medical record translation. After looking at the machine translated result, the translator had doubts on whether the Chinese term '呼吸' should be translated as "respiration" or "respiration rate" and whether the unit of respiration rate should be 'beats/min' or 'breaths/min'.

Table 2 shows the Google search results based on the search term '"heart rate" 'per minute'" and '"breath rate" 'per minute'". A featured snippet returned by the Google search engine successfully points us to the correct information: 'respiration rate' and 'breaths/min' are the right terms.

Table 3 shows the ChatGPT approach in which users can ask a specific question instead of giving a list of keywords. The ChatGPT provided answers are both accurate and comprehensive.

Table 4 shows the perplexity.ai approach in which users can ask a specific question and obtain accurate and comprehensive answers. In addition, this approach provides reference sources, related questions, and allows the user to ask follow-up questions.

Strategy 1 (top-ranked search results & feature snippets) and 3 (ChatGPT) work well on this example. Direct and accurate explanations were provided by both Google's feature snippet and ChatGPT's answers. Strategy 4 works the best because it provides not only direct and accurate solution and answer, but also sources of references, related questions, and allows users to ask follow-up questions.

3.2   Example 2: Technology Terms (Patent Claim)

Example 2 (Table 5) was excerpted from the claims section of a patent translation. By looking at the machine translated result, the translator found two 'suspicious' words and text spans that need to be investigated further:

(1) Should the Chinese term '驱动单元' be translated to "driving unit" or "drive unit"?
    While both alternative phrases are plausible in the opinion of the translator, one of

Table 1. Example one was excerpted from a medical record translation example.

Original source text (in Chinese)	...入院查体: 体温37.2 °C, 心率120次/分, 呼吸20 次/分, 血压100/70 mmHg.
Machine translation results (in English)	... Admission examination: body temperature 37.2 °C, heart rate 120 beats/min, **respiration** 20 **beats/min**, blood pressure 100/70 mmHg
Specific questions or keywords under investigation	- Should the Chinese term '呼吸' be translated to **"respiration"** or **"respiration rate"**? Should the **unit** of respiration be **"beats/min"** or **"breaths**/min"?

Table 2. Featured snippets provided by Google searches lead us to the right knowledge.

them could be a conventional choice in the specific technical domain. A search is needed to determine which phrase should be selected.

(2) Based on previous knowledge of the translator, when translating patent claims, the Chinese term "用于" is generally not translated as "be used to", but customarily translated as "be configured to". A search is needed to confirm the translator's judgment.

Since this example focuses on commonly used terms and their combination, strategy 2 (count-based abductive reasoning) seems to be the natural choice. An exact Google search using "驱动单元 driving unit" and "驱动单元 drive unit" come back with 9 and 191 results respectively (Table 6). An exact Google search using "driving unit is configured to drive" and "drive unit is configured to drive" come back with 3,630 and 9,120 results respectively (Table 7). A Google search using "'drive unit' optical lens" and "'driving unit' optical lens" come back with 905,000 and 88,600 results. Based on

Table 3. ChatGPT provides accurate knowledge by answering a user's question directly.

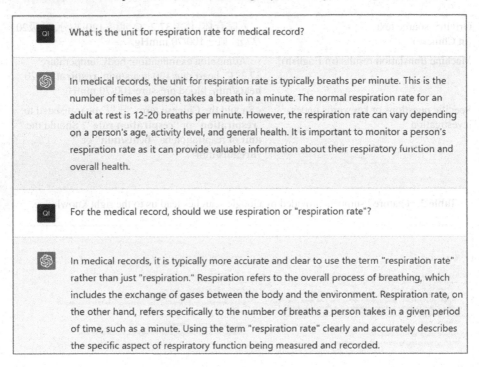

Q| What is the unit for respiration rate for medical record?

In medical records, the unit for respiration rate is typically breaths per minute. This is the number of times a person takes a breath in a minute. The normal respiration rate for an adult at rest is 12-20 breaths per minute. However, the respiration rate can vary depending on a person's age, activity level, and general health. It is important to monitor a person's respiration rate as it can provide valuable information about their respiratory function and overall health.

Q| For the medical record, should we use respiration or "respiration rate"?

In medical records, it is typically more accurate and clear to use the term "respiration rate" rather than just "respiration." Respiration refers to the overall process of breathing, which includes the exchange of gases between the body and the environment. Respiration rate, on the other hand, refers specifically to the number of breaths a person takes in a given period of time, such as a minute. Using the term "respiration rate" clearly and accurately describes the specific aspect of respiratory function being measured and recorded.

Table 4. Perplexity.ai conversational search engine provides accurate knowledge, reference sources, related questions, and allows the user to ask follow-up questions.

this series of search results, a translator following a count heuristic would prefer to go with "the drive unit" instead of "the driving unit".

Now to confirm the translator's belief on "be configured to" versus "be used to", we search Google patents (https://patents.google.com/) because the translator's

Table 5. Example two was excerpted from the claims section of a patent translation

Original source text (in Chinese)	… 所述驱动单元用于驱动所述图像传感器单元（1）在垂直于所述光学镜头（5）光轴的方向运动。
Machine translation results (in English)	… the driving unit is used to drive the image sensor unit (1) to move in the direction perpendicular to the optical axis of the optical lens (5).
Specific questions or keywords under investigation	- Should the Chinese term '驱动单元' be translated to "**driving unit**" or "**drive unit**"? What are the semantic differences? - When translating patent claims, the Chinese term "用于" is generally not translated as "**be used to**", but customarily translated as "**be configured to**".

belief/knowledge is unique to the patent domain. In addition, we also run the same searches listed in Table 6, 7, and 8 through Google patents. Here, the count-based abductive reasoning fails because the number of returned results by "drive unit" and "driving unit", "be configured" and "be used to" are not significantly different from each other (Table 9). Therefore, the effectiveness of the count-based abductive reasoning approach is questionable because the results returned by general Google search and Google patent search give us different count ratios between two alternatives.

On the other hand, ChatGPT based results provide good answers on the differences between 'drive unit' and 'driving unit' and between "be configured to" and "be used to" (Table 10 and 11). Perplexity.ai based results provide not only good answers but also reference sources, related questions, and allows the user to ask follow-up questions (Table 12).

Table 6. An exact Google search using "驱动单元 driving unit" and "驱动单元 drive unit".

Table 7. An exact Google search using "driving unit is configured to drive" and "drive unit is configured to drive".

Table 8. A Google search using "'driving unit' optical lens" and "'drive unit' optical lens".

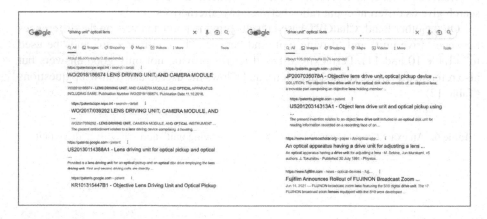

Strategy 1 (top-ranked search results & feature snippets) does not work well for this example because the reasons for commonly used patterns are not provided by top ranked search results and no snippet was provided.

Strategy 2 was very frequently used as an abductive reasoning approach by experienced translators. However, as we observed in this example, sometimes this heuristic cannot lead us to a definite answer.

Strategy 3 provides the proper knowledge to address this example. Strategy 4 works the best because it provides not only direct and accurate solution and answer, but also sources of references, related questions, and allows users to ask follow-up questions.

Table 9. Google patent (https://patents.google.com/) versus general Google search results on related keywords.

Keywords and text spans	# of results by searching google patents	# of results by searching general google
"drive unit is configured to drive"	109,404	27,000
"drive unit is used to drive"	115,340	49,600
"驱动单元 driving unit"	42	9
"驱动单元 drive unit"	35	172
"driving unit" optical lens	136,181	91,000
"drive unit" optical lens	136,018	841,000
"drive unit is configured to drive" site: sony.com	853	0
"drive unit is used to drive" site: sony.com	861	0
"driving unit" optical lens site: sony.com	3,439	1
"drive unit" optical lens site: sony.com	4,307	101

Table 10. ChatGPT provided knowledge on the difference between 'drive unit' and 'driving unit'.

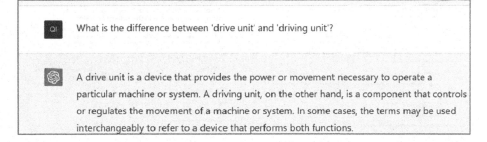

> **QI** What is the difference between 'drive unit' and 'driving unit'?
>
> A drive unit is a device that provides the power or movement necessary to operate a particular machine or system. A driving unit, on the other hand, is a component that controls or regulates the movement of a machine or system. In some cases, the terms may be used interchangeably to refer to a device that performs both functions.

3.3   Example 3: Ambiguous Source Expression (Social Media Blog Post)

Example 3 (Table 13) was excerpted from a social media blog post. Since the source language expression can have two different semantic interpretations (Table 13): (1) By 2025, the Internet economy will increase Africa's GDP by 10%. (2) By 2025, the contribution of the Internet economy will account for 10% of Africa's GDP. Therefore, information seeking is needed to find further background evidence.

The source of the statement, as guessed by the translator, could be a report published by an international research institute. Therefore, we can start with a Google search for the whole sentence in source language (Table 14). The top ranked web link says that

Table 11. ChatGPT provided knowledge on the difference between "be configured to" and "be used to" in the patent context.

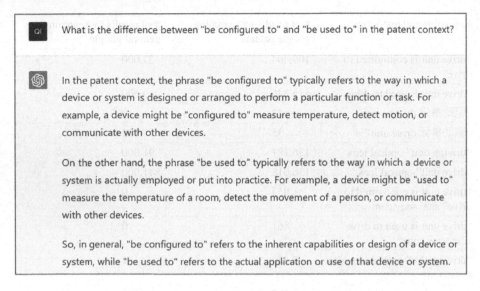

Table 12. Perplexity.ai provided knowledge on the difference between "be configured to" and "be used to" in the patent context. It also provided reference sources, related questions, and allows the user to ask follow-up questions.

"Africa's internet economy will be worth $180 billion by 2025." And the second ranked web link says that "a joint study by IFC and Google predicted that by 2025, the African Internet economy is expected to reach 5.2% of the African continent's gross domestic product (GDP) and bring nearly 180 billion US dollars to its economy, equivalent to 1.18 trillion yuan in revenue." These results do not seem to confirm either "increase Africa's GDP by 10%" or "account for 10% of Africa's GDP".

Table 13. Example three was excerpted from a social media (Weibo) blog post.

Original Source Text (in Chinese)	… 2025年, 互联网将驱动非洲**GDP10%**的增长。
Machine Translation Results (in English)	… In 2025, the Internet will drive the growth of Africa's GDP by 10%
Identified text segment (hypotheses and alternatives)	- 'In 2025' is wrong; should be 'by 2025' (no search needed; the correct is based on grammar knowledge) - The description in the original Chinese text "驱动非洲**GDP10%**的增长" is a bit vague. By 2025, will **the Internet economy will increase Africa's GDP by 10%**, or will **the contribution of the Internet economy will account for 10% of Africa's GDP**?

Table 14. Google search results for the whole sentence in source language (accessed on December 29th, 2022).

Next, we search the combination of three important information segments: "by 2025", "Africa's GDP", and "10 percent". The top ranked weblink (Table 15) leads us to the right background information (Table 16).

Strategy 1 (top-ranked search results & feature snippets) works well for this example after attempting different keyword phrase combinations. Due to the success of Strategy 1, Strategy 2 becomes unnecessary because it is inferior to a solution that can provide the accurate facts.

Strategy 3 (ChatGPT) is not a good solution for this example (Table 17 and 18) because ChatGPT is not good at providing fact-based knowledge.

Table 15. Google search results using a combination of keyword phrases (accessed on December 29th, 2022).

Table 16. The content of the original background knowledge found through Google search.

Strategy 4 (Perplexity.ai search) provided the right source once the right question was asked because the approach combines the capabilities of OpenAI's GPT-3 and a large scale search engine (Microsoft BING). Compared with strategy 1, instead of attempting different keyword phrases combinations, strategy 4 attempted different questions (Table 19). The reasoning process and results of strategy 1 and 4 are very similar because they both rely on the same human queries and a search engine.

Table 17. ChatGPT is not good at providing fact-based knowledge (social media blog post question and answering example 1).

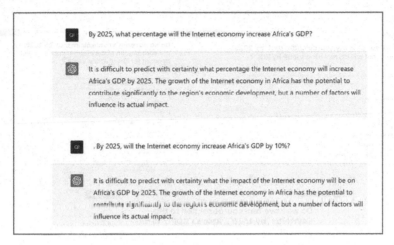

Table 18. ChatGPT is not good at providing fact-based knowledge (social media blog post question and answering example 2).

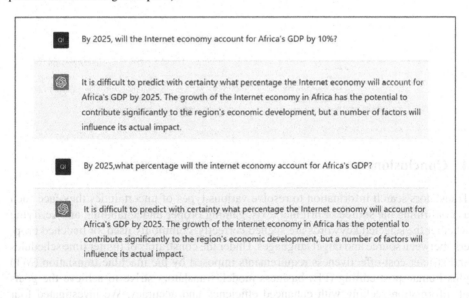

Table 19. Perplexity.ai provided the right source once the right question was asked because the approach combines the capabilities of OpenAI's GPT-3 and a large scale search engine (Microsoft BING).

4   Conclusion

Translators search information to resolve various types of uncertainties they face such as confirming the source of original texts, gaining proper understanding, and verifying whether the selected keywords are spelled correctly, commonly used, or matched properly between source and target languages. Under the constraints of tighter time schedules and stricter cost-effectiveness requirements imposed by the machine translation (MT) plus human post-editing (PE) business model, translators strive to achieve the goals of information seeking with enhanced efficiency and accuracy. We investigated four information seeking strategies using several real-life information seeking problems: 1. top-ranked results and featured snippets returned by large-scale web search engines; 2. abductive reasoning based on search result counts returned by large-scale web search engines; 3. direct answers provided by ChatGPT—a long-form question-answering conversational AI. 4. Solutions provided by perplexity.ai—a conversational search engine combining OpenAI's GPT language model technology and Microsoft Bing.

Top-ranked search results sometimes contain the accurate solution, but they also could lead to misleading or useless websites that take users' time and effort to be sorted out. Using different search operators can lead users to different answers. This is helpful because it could lead the user to the right answer. But it also leads to abundant answers requiring further investigation that can overwhelm users. A 'featured snippet box' is a relatively recent capability introduced by Google to present the correct answer in the box directly so that the user does not have to visit any website. Google's automated algorithms determine whether a page would make a good featured snippet to highlight for a specific search request. Feature snippets frequently provide accurate answers, but they are only provided on some search requests.

Experienced translators adopt a strategy of selective abduction by forming effective keyword search requests based on domain knowledge and then using the counts of returned search results as collected evidence to justify alternative hypotheses. The benefit of this approach is that it is fast and relatively effective most of the time. The downside is that it could lead to misjudgment sometimes and the counts of search results returned by the search website could be falsified information.

Direct answers provided by novel long-form question-answering conversational AI systems such as ChatGPT can provide amazingly accurate and insightful answers towards well-described queries. Similar to featured snippets, direct answers are provided. Since ChatGPT relies on a large language model trained on a huge corpus, it performs well on general-purpose knowledge and reasoning, but it is not good at fact-based knowledge if the knowledge does not exist in the training corpus. Therefore, human users can ask ChatGPT questions about unfamiliar topic and receive results that are vastly superior compared to results returned by search engines. Even if ChatGPT gives inaccurate answers—we should assume that it is unreliable), it usually provides a succinct introduction to a topic/question and points you to the right direction in terms of what to look for.

Direct answers provided by novel conversational search engine such as perplexity.ai can provide amazingly accurate and insightful answers towards well-described queries. Since the conversational search engine combines the benefits of large language models and large scale search engine, it performs well on general-purpose knowledge and reasoning, and fact-based knowledge. It also provides reference sources, related questions, and allows the user to ask follow-up questions.

Human users should focus on forming effective human queries to develop an effective collaboration between humans, web search tools, long-form question-answering conversational AI systems, and conversational search engines. While it is ideal to obtain direct answers primarily through the conversational search engine, long-form question-answering conversational AI, and search engine featured snippet box, top-ranked search results and count-based selective abduction are also useful strategies for information seeking.

References

1. https://en.wikipedia.org/wiki/Information_seeking. Accessed 2 Dec 2022
2. Marchionini, G.: Information Seeking in Electronic Environments, vol. 9. Cambridge University Press (1997)

3. Navarro-Prieto, R., Scaife, M., Rogers, Y.: Cognitive strategies in web searching. In: Proceedings of the 5th Conference on Human Factors & the Web, pp. 43–56, July 1999
4. Common Google search Operators. https://www.google.com/advanced_search. Accessed 17 Dec 2022
5. Hardwick, J.: How do search engines work. https://ahrefs.com/blog/how-do-search-engines-work/#:~:text=Search%20engines%20work%20by%20crawling,if%20you're%20doing%20SEO. Accessed 24 Dec 2022
6. How Google's featured snippets work. https://support.google.com/websearch/answer/935 1707?hl=en. Accessed 24 Dec 2022
7. Justin O'Hara, 2021, Google's "millions of search results" are not being served in the later pages search results. https://serpapi.com/blog/googles-millions-of-search-results-are-not-being-served-in-the-later-pages-search-results/. Accessed 26 Dec 2022
8. https://beta.openai.com/. Accessed 16 Dec 2022
9. Magnet, P.: ChatGPT Will be the Next Google, not for Searchers, but for Seekers (2022). https://medium.com/geekculture/chatgpt-will-be-the-next-google-not-for-searchers-but-for-seekers-c4a485707537. Accessed 27 Dec 2022
10. A New Chat Bot Is a 'Code Red' for Google's Search Business, New York Times
11. Perplxity.ai. Accessed 29 Jan 2023
12. Wu, H.(M.): How to Semi-Automate Google search to Aid Translation, Part 1 (2022). https://www.ata-divisions.org/CLD/how-to-semi-automate-google-search-to-aid-translation/. Accessed 28 Dec 2022
13. Wu, H.(M.): How to Semi-Automate Google search to Aid Translation, Part 2 (2022). https://www.ata-divisions.org/CLD/how-to-semi-automate-google-search-to-aid-translation-2/. Accessed 28 Dec 2022

Comparing Sentiment Analysis and Emotion Analysis of Algorithms vs. People

Samuel Romine⬤, Joshua Jensen(✉) ⬤, and Robert Ball⬤

Weber State University, 3848 Harrison Blvd, Ogden, UT 84408, USA
samuelromine@mail.weber.edu, {joshuajensen1,roberball}@weber.edu

Abstract. Sentiment analysis and emotion analysis have seen continued growth within recent years. Due to this growth, it is important to question the methodology used in previous studies to validate new and novel approaches to these subjects. In this paper we show that the use of secondary sentiment is a valid replacement for primary source sentiment in cases where obtaining primary sentiment might not be available. In other words, state-of-the-art sentiment analysis is approximately as good as crowdsourcing sentiment analysis from humans. However, when applying the same concept with emotion analysis we find that state-of-the-art emotion analysis is far inferior to crowdsourcing emotion from humans.

Keywords: Natural Language Processing · Sentiment Analysis · Emotion Analysis

1 Background

Sentiment analysis and emotion analysis can have a direct impact on people's lives. Understanding sentiment and emotion in text enables businesses to understand how people feel about their products, services, or brand. This information can be used to improve customer satisfaction, identify potential problems, and make data-driven decisions. Additionally, sentiment analysis and emotion analysis can be used in industries such as marketing, customer service, and public relations to track the effectiveness of campaigns, measure customer satisfaction, and identify trends in customer feedback. Furthermore, it also can be used to help detect and predict potential crisis or negative situations in real-time. Overall, sentiment analysis and emotion analysis can provide valuable insights that can help organizations make better business decisions and improve customer relationships.

As sentiment analysis and emotion analysis are becoming more relevant in mainstream society and are being used to drive direct business decisions in many different industries such as healthcare, education, the financial sector, politics and more. As the adoption increases, it is necessary to compare the accuracy of the traditional practices of generating them. Sentiment analysis determines whether a given text is positive, neutral, or negative.

For example, a person might read a review online and decide that overall the review provides a positive sentiment. While emotion analysis assigns an emotion, such as sad,

H. Degen and S. Ntoa (Eds.): HCII 2023, LNAI 14051, pp. 167–178, 2023.
https://doi.org/10.1007/978-3-031-35894-4_12

happy, etc. This additional level helps in the application of decision data enabling more informed business decisions by those using these algorithms. From a business perspective, it is better to know that users are frustrated and surprised, than simply a negative sentiment. A particular challenge faced by those using sentiment and emotional analysis tools is the source of the sentiment/emotion. There exist several methods for determining sentiment and emotion programmatically, such as lexicon algorithms that compare negative words and positive words from a lexicon (a type of look up table) to the textual dataset. Sentiment/emotion can also be determined by crowdsourcing, which uses other people besides the author to decide the sentiment or emotion, or manual tagging – a form of crowdsourcing – done by the researchers or practitioners directly. However, each of these methods involve applying secondary sentiment and emotion to a given piece of text rather than determining sentiment or emotion from the author directly.

It is generally preferable to get sentiment directly from the original author because it is considered to be more reliable, authentic, provides more context, granularity, and is done in real-time. The reason that authors are rarely asked to annotate their own text for sentiment or emotion is that it is often impossible or impractical to do so. For example, it is impractical to ask millions of strangers to annotate their text from social media. Over 800 million tweets from Twitter are sent daily [1]. It is impractical to contact every author of every tweet and ask them what the primary sentiment and emotion of their tweet is. Likewise, reviews are left on products on sites all over the internet at a massive scale. It is impractical to ask the authors of all those reviews for their sentiment and emotion of the review.

Based on the impracticality of sourcing sentiment and emotion directly from the original authors, this paper answers the following question: Does the source of secondary sentiment and emotion (e.g., lexicon algorithms, crowdsourcing, etc.) have an impact on the accuracy of determining the sentiment and emotion of the original author? In other words, sentiment analysis and emotion analysis is routinely done primarily through lexicon algorithms; how well do lexicon algorithms compare to other methods?

1.1 History of Sentiment Analysis

Sentiment analysis has roots stemming from ancient Greece, but it began taking off in the late 1930s and early 1940s as governments across the world wanted to know their population's opinion on joining the second world war [2]. Sentiment analysis has continued to grow; from 2005 to 2016 sentiment analysis experienced a 50 times growth when compared to the previous ten years [3]. Today sentiment analysis is being used in a variety of technologies, including personal shopping website review systems like Amazon and eBay, search engines, medical record processing, and stock market predictions [4, 5]. Companies and governments routinely gather text from different sources, such as social media, and automatically generate sentiment from massive text datasets that would be impossible to examine quickly manually. Some examples of popular sentiment lexicon algorithms are VADER and AFINN, which are used extensively in industry and research [7, 8].

2 Data Gathering

To begin testing our hypothesis, we first needed to gather a corpus of first-person annotated text. To do so, we chose to conduct a series of surveys using a popular surveying
tool hosted by Amazon Web Services (AWS) known as Mechanical Turk[1] (MTurk).
MTurk has been used for a variety of applications, including sentiment analysis, photographic recognition, and general surveying [9, 10]. We acknowledge that use of MTurk
has had a certain level of controversy in previous years regarding the performance of its
Workers[2], however a number of studies have been done that show MTurk can and does
produce meaningful data for research use [11, 12].

2.1 First Survey

To create our emotion-invoking prompts, we utilized the basic emotional theory created
by Ekman to help tailor each of the surveyor's responses to a specific emotion [13]. From
this, we derived 6 emotions: Anger, Disgust, Fear, Happiness, Sadness, and Surprise.
Each of these emotions were used as a given prompt for our first survey. Each question
was divided into two parts: A prompted written segment, and a sentiment evaluation
segment. Each participant was compensated for participating in this survey.

Emotional Survey

Once again, if you do not feel comfortable writing about a certain emotion, feel free to skip that emotion and move onto the next one.
Please write at least two sentences for each response. You can write about anything you would like, as long as it relates to the current emotion. There are no wrong answers.
You must fill out at least 3 of the 6 emotions for your response to be approved.

Happy

Please write about a time you felt happy, without using the word: "happy"

Please enter your response here...

On a scale of 1-7 (1 being "overall negative" and 7 being "overall positive") please rate what you just wrote about the word "happy"

Fig. 1. This figure shows one of the six questions within the first survey distributed by MTurk

For the written segment, the following prompt was given once for each emotion
(For a total of 6 questions): "Please write about a time you felt ___ without using the
word ___", as seen in Fig. 1. Along with the emotion prompt, we also requested that the
participant not use the associated emotion word to help increase the vocabular diversity
from response to response. We did not want hundreds of responses that read "One time I
felt happy was when...", "One time I felt sad was when...", etc. This was not a hard-set
rule, a participant's responses would generally not reject for this reason, but overall it
did help to reduce repetitive style responses.

The second segment can also be seen at the bottom of Fig. 1. The Workers were
asked to rate the sentiment of what they personally wrote from the matching prompt on

---

[1] https://www.mturk.com/

[2] MTurk's own term for the individuals participating in responding to surveys.

a Likert scale [14]. The scale ranged from 1 to 7, where 1 was "overall negative" and 7 was "overall positive".

Results

In total, we had the first survey distributed a total of 200 times, resulting in 200 responses. There were only 3 requirements for a participant to have their response accepted:

1. Answer a minimum of 3 of the 6 prompts.
2. Reponses must be at least one sentence in length. (No one word answers)
3. Responses must be written in English.

We ended up receiving 1106 pieces of text from our survey.

2.2 Second Survey

After the completion of the first survey, we proceeded to perform sentiment analysis and compare various sentiment sources. During this process we also created the second survey to replicate crowd-source sentiment analysis. We randomly selected 222 responses from our original 1106 responses and used them to create this second survey. As seen in Fig. 2, the participants were randomly presented with 1 of the 222 pieces of text and then asked 2 questions about the text. First, they were asked to rate what they thought the overall sentiment was for the piece of text on the same 1 to 7 scale as was used in the first survey which generated the text. Second, they were asked to select a single emotion that best matched the text in the prompt. Once again, the surveyors were compensated for their responses.

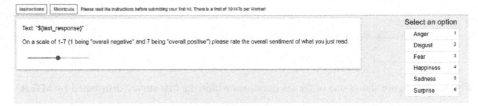

Fig. 2. This figure shows the complete layout of the second survey distributed on MTurk

We requested each of the 222 pieces of text to be analyzed 20 times each. However, due to a glitch on MTurk's side, 2 pieces of text each ended up with one additional review, resulting in a total of 4442 responses instead of 4440. We decided to keep these two responses as their presence would only increase the sentiment/emotion accuracy of their related texts.

2.3 Third Survey

The third survey was nearly identical to the second survey. However, we decided not to use MTurk and instead utilized the research team to do the survey. We wanted to examine the difference between a crowdsourced approach where the participants cared about the project instead of the mixed quality we experienced in the MTurk survey pool. Each member of the research team was asked to perform the same task that the participants did on the second survey. We were all given an excel sheet that contained the 222 pieces of text, then individually we rated every piece of text with what we thought the matching sentiment/emotion the original author assigned the text with. We used the same Likert scale for sentiment.

3   Text Pre-processing

Before sentiment analysis could be performed, our 1106 responses from the first survey needed to be pre-processed and cleaned. All the text processing was performed with the popular python package NLTK[3,4] [15]. NLTK is used heavily within sentiment analysis as it provides a diverse set of tools for performing various tasks for preparing and processing text for various purposes [16]. In our case specifically, we utilized NLTK's stop-words, lemmatization, and then fed the results into scikit-learn's[5] CountVectorizer to create a bag-of-words.

First, we needed to remove stop-words from our 1106 pieces of text. Words such as "and", "the", "for", "or", and "what" are extremely common words within the English language. However, this is detrimental for machine learning algorithms, as these words may appear in nearly every response within our data, hindering our selected machine learning models' ability to correctly identify patterns between the words and the matching sentiment/emotion. NLTK has a pre-built corpus containing a large dataset of common stop-words within the English language which we utilized, we also added some additional words to their list of stop-words. These words were found commonly within our dataset. Their presence had the potential to create false correlations within the machine learning algorithms.

```
'time',            'feel',             'felt',             'one',
'day', 'feeling', 'got', 'something', 'get', 'really', 'made',
'would', 'might', ' make', 'first', 'feelings', 'know', 'could',
'without', 'things', 'away', 'saw', 'went', 'think', 'see', 'go',
'back', 'came', 'left', 'way', 'much', 'going', 'state', 'told',
'deep', 'makes', 'many', 'often', 'rate', 'ago', 'get-
ting', 'even', 'make', 'long', 'take', 'found', 'response', 'lot',
'us', 'days', 'day', 'also', 'another', 'every', 'water', 'heard',
'strong', 'well', 'ever', 'upset', 'close', 'seeing', 'took',
'times', 'since', 'leave', 'past', 'give', 'today', 'increased',
'specific', 'able', 'words', 'place', 'still', 'gives', 'yes'
```

Once the stop-words were removed, we still needed to further reduce the complexity of our dataset. Within the English language words can have a multitude of prefixes, suffixes, and any number of combinations between these two. A word like "amaze" can be

---

[3] Natural Language Tool-Kit.

[4] https://www.nltk.org/

[5] https://scikit-learn.org/

expanded into "amaz-ing", "amaz-ing-ly", "un-amaz-ing", "un-amaz-ing-ly", etc. Each of these words stem from "amaze", however some maintain a similar meaning to the original such as "amazingly", but others like "unamazed" have a different meaning than the original. We preformed POS-tagging (Part of Speech) and lemmatization to reduce the lexical complexity of our dataset. Each word within a given sentence was computationally tagged with its matching POS such as, noun, proper-noun, verb, adjective, etc. then the lemmatizer was fed this information, along with the word, to determine if the word could be reduced back to its root.

Finally, we needed to convert our dataset into data usable by various machine learning algorithms. Scikit-learn also has a large variety of tools revolving around NLP (Natural Language Processing), including CountVectorizor. This function allowed us to convert our now cleaned responses into a 2D array. In this new dataset, each response is a row, where every word is represented by a column, that contains a count of the occurrences of that word within the given response/row. This data structure is commonly referred to as a "bag-of-words." This allows machine learning algorithms to process the text and identify patterns between words and sentiment/emotion.

4 Sentiment Analysis

Now that we had clean data and text within primary source sentiment, we needed to create alternative sentiment sources for basing the machine learning algorithms on. Of the 1106 responses, 222 were randomly selected as test data, and the remaining 884 were used as training data. Each of the 3 sentiment sources, along with the original sentiment, had their sentiment polarized (negative sentiments became 0, and neutral/positives became 1). These sentiment scores were then fed into 4 machine learning algorithms as the training data, where the sentiment type in question was considered the "correct" answer, resulting in a total of 16 unique models (4 sentiment sources X 4 algorithms). Then, each of these models were fed the 222 test responses and were asked to predict a sentiment score for each one. These predictions were compared to the author's original sentiment and had their overall accuracies recorded. We also decided to create an ensemble algorithm from each sentiment category. The four models relating to a given sentiment source had their predictions combined per response to see if the conjoined models would perform better than any singular model alone.

4.1 Sentiment Sources

First, we used NLTK's built in sentiment analyzer, VADER [6]. VADER is a lexical approach to sentiment analysis. VADER contains roughly 7,500 pre-annotated words on a scale ranging from -4 to 4 relating to the matching sentiment score. Each word within a piece of text is processed with its matching score, then returns an overall score between -1 and 1 to match the more traditional range used for sentiment analysis. VADER was applied to all 1106 pieces of text. However, the participants were limited to a categorical scale from 1 to 7. In response to this, we scaled the scores from the 1–7 to a matching -1 to 1.

The second source of sentiment we used was another lexical approach known as AFINN [17]. AFINN operates similarly to VADER, but AFINN has a smaller corpus size, about 2,500 words in total. AFINN also operates on an alternative sentiment range of -5 to 5. We chose to use two lexical approaches because VADER and AFINN are commonly used together so we saw value in testing both [18, 19].

Finally, we had the primary researcher Samuel Romine annotate all 1106 pieces of text with a sentiment score on the scale of 1 to 7. There are examples of previous works where the research team applied their own sentiment to their own data for testing, so we attempted to replicate this as well [20]. These scorings were used as a sentiment source for machine learning purposes. Later, the 222 pieces of text were taken from this set and combined with the rest of the research team's responses for both sentiment and emotion predictions.

4.2 Algorithms

Of the four algorithms we chose, the first was Naïve Bayes. Naïve Bayes is a commonly used algorithm for sentiment analysis [21]. Naïve Bayes operates on the premise that each observation, or text response in our case, is independent from one another. It then uses the frequency of attributes, (e.g., words), to predict what the expected outcome, or sentiment, will be.

Next, we selected logistic regression for predicting sentiment [22]. Logistic regression attempts to find correlations between the counts of the word's vs the sentiment score. If a given word occurs more often with responses rated as "positive" or 1, logistic regression will try to formulate a relation between that word and the given score.

After logistic regression, we chose KNN (K-nearest neighbor) [23]. KNN was chosen because the algorithm is designed to find distances in the nth dimension between responses, then create clusters based on these distances. The test data is then graphed into this nth dimension and is placed into a given cluster relating to a positive or negative sentiment score.

The last algorithm we chose to use was a random forest [24]. Random forests are also popular choices for sentiment analysis as they do well with classification problems. Random forests operate by creating groups of observations, or responses, that are as distinct as possible from each other, but the responses within a given group are as similar as possible. These groups are created repeatedly until all features, or words, within the data have been exhausted. New responses are then fed into this system and placed into the best matching group and uses this to determine its sentiment prediction.

Also, we decided to create our own ensemble algorithm based on the sentiment source and the models created by each of the algorithms previously discussed. We wanted to see if these models working together would outperform each of them working individually. We grouped the models by their sentiment source, (I.E. The Naïve Bayes model, the logistic regression model, the KNN model, and the random forest model that were all trained on the VADER sentiment) and combined their answers. For a given response in the test set, each model gave a prediction of either 0 or 1, for negative or positive sentiment, these predictions were combined based on a majority vote for the predicted sentiment. Ties in prediction were treated as a positive sentiment.

4.3 Results

Figure 3 shows the results from each of the 20 models that were created. This chart shows the models grouped by their source of sentiment. From a visual inspection alone, there is very little variation within each group, and from group to group. Each of the models based on the secondary sentiment performed adequately when compared back to the matching model trained on the surveyor sentiment. To be sure of this observation however, we conducted a series of tests to measure statistical significance.

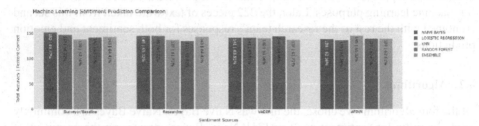

Fig. 3. Results from the 20 models based on secondary sentiment.

For a given algorithm, each of the secondary sentiment-based models were compared individually to their matching surveyor/baseline counterpart to see if the alternative sentiment sources produced any meaningful significance. We used a two-tailed t-test to evaluate this. Each of these models created their predictions independently of one another, and all the results maintained similar variances. Two-tailed was selected instead of one-tailed because we were only concerned if a given model's predictions were better/worse than the baseline, not the estimated difference within population means. Also, everything was performed using a 95% confidence interval. Overall, no model when compared to their respective baseline managed to produce statistical significance.

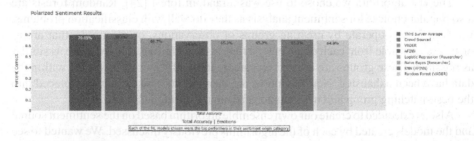

Fig. 4. This chart shows the results of various sentiment prediction methods.

After finding no statistical significance between each of the models and their sentiment sources, we decided to expand our exploration to other common approaches to see if we could identify some method that would outperform the models. We took the top performing model from each of the four algorithms and compared them to the results from the second and third survey, along with VADER and AFINN's predictions without machine learning applied. Overall, the top performer was the crowd sourced sentiment from the second survey, correctly identifying the sentiment for 157 of the 222 responses in the test set. As the top performer, another round of t-tests were run, using crowd-sourced as the "baseline" to see if any of other predictors were statistically significant. No statistical significance was found.

The results found in Figs. 3 and 4 provide substantial evidence that the source of sentiment does not have any major impact on the prediction accuracy of various machine learning algorithms. From this, we conclude utilizing secondary sentiment in place of the primary source is appropriate and does not invalidate the results of novel approaches in situations where it is not possible to gather the original sentiment.

5 Emotion Analysis

From the data we had gathered across our three surveys, we did not just have a corpus for sentiment analysis, we had also created a useful dataset for emotion analysis as well. From this, we performed a brief exploration into emotion analysis and the contrast of machine prediction vs human beings. We utilized the first survey's emotion prompts to create a relation between a given response and an emotion. For example, all responses for the "happy" prompt, were tagged as the emotion happy. This process was repeated for all 6 emotions. From there we were able to create emotion predictions and had a baseline to compare against.

5.1 Emotion Sources

Surprisingly, we struggled to find tools for emotion analysis. When compared to the variety of options within sentiment analysis from machine learning to lexical, to black-box online predictors, there a very few options available for emotion analysis. Ultimately, we used two lexical approaches, T2E[6,7] and LeXmo[8] for the machine portion. As for the human-based emotion predictions, we used the results from the crowd-sourced survey and the results from the research team. Because of this, we used the same 222 responses used previously, rather than generating a new set.

T2E and LeXmo operate in similar fashions but do have a distinction worth noting. Namely, T2E does not support the emotion "disgust". This does create a certain disparity between the results of the two algorithms, however we were only able to work with the outputs that are provided. It is also important to mention that both predictors return multi-variate answers. Rather than returning a single predicted emotion, both T2E and LeXmo provide a score for each emotion ranging from 0 to 1, relating to the strength/presence of the given emotion. This introduces a problem, as our data is not multivariate; each response has only a single matching emotion. To combat this, we chose to use the highest scoring emotion from LeXmo and T2E respectively as their singular emotion prediction. For example, if T2E gave returned a happiness score of 0.3, a fear score of 0.4, and 0 for all other emotions, we said that T2E predicted the emotion "fear".

---

[6] Text2Emotion.

[7] https://pypi.org/project/text2emotion/

[8] https://github.com/dinbav/LeXmo.

As for the other emotion sources, the process was simple. The committee members had already recorded their emotion predictions within the third survey. The crowd-sourced prediction was selected based on the most popular emotion. For a given response, the 20, or 21 in the case of 2, responses were totaled and the most predicted emotion was used as the overall prediction of the crowd-sourced results. No ties were found in the crowd-sourced data. Ties were not possible in the other sources.

5.2 Results

Figure 5 shows the results of the emotion analysis. Unlike the sentiment analysis results, there is a large disparity between machine predictions and human predictors. More interestingly however, there is a disparity found within the human predictors as well. The four committee members can be considered as subject matter experts in the field of sentiment/emotion analysis, whereas the crowd-sourced results were from the general public. The crowd-sourced did manage to outperform both machine predictors but was dwarfed by the accuracy of the research team. We acknowledge that this is a limited example, and that further research will be necessary to solidify this claim, but we do believe the results provide beginning evidence that non-human emotion analysis methods are inferior to the layman, let alone subject matter experts.

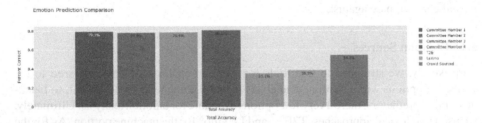

Fig. 5. This chart shows the results of various emotion prediction methods.

6 Conclusions

In this paper we have created substantial evidence to answer our initial question: Does the source of secondary sentiment and emotion have an impact on the accuracy of determining the sentiment and emotion of the original author? In the case of sentiment, we conclude that no, the source of sentiment does not have an impact on the accuracy of determining said sentiment. There are a multitude of algorithms that can be used, and a larger, more robust dataset could be acquired, but within the limitations of this study, there is enough evidence to answer the sentiment portion of this question.

As for emotion analysis, we answer this question with a bit more caution. We conclude that there is enough evidence to say that there is a measurable difference between lexical-based emotion prediction and alternatives such as crowd-sourced or subject matter experts.

References

1. Yaqub, M. "How Many Tweets per Day 2022 (New Data)." Last referenced October 2022. https://www.renolon.com/number-of-tweets-per-day/
2. Stagner, R.: The cross-out technique as a method in public opinion analysis. J. Soc. Psychol. **11**(1), 79–90 (1940)
3. Mäntylä, M.V., Graziotin, D., Kuutila, M.: The evolution of sentiment analysis—A review of research topics, venues, and top cited papers. Comput. Sci. Rev. **27**, 16–32 (2018)
4. Pagolu, V.S., Reddy, K.N., Panda, G., Majhi, B.: Sentiment analysis of Twitter data for predicting stock market movements. In: 2016 International Conference on Signal Processing, Communication, Power And Embedded System (SCOPES), pp. 1345–1350. IEEE (2016)
5. Nandal, N., Tanwar, R., Pruthi, J.: Machine learning based aspect level sentiment analysis for Amazon products. Spat. Inf. Res. **28**(5), 601–607 (2020). https://doi.org/10.1007/s41324-020-00320-2
6. Hutto, C., Gilbert, E.: Vader: A parsimonious rule-based model for sentiment analysis of social media text. Proc. Int. AAAI Conf. Web Soc. Media **8**(1), 216–225 (2014)
7. Chandler, J., Rosenzweig, C., Moss, A.J., Robinson, J., Litman, L.: Online panels in social science research. Expanding sampling methods beyond Mechanical Turk. Behav. Res. Methods **51**(5), 2022–2038 (2019). https://doi.org/10.3758/s13428-019-01273-7
8. Ekman, P.: Are there basic emotions? Psychol. Rev. **99**(3), 550–553 (1992). https://doi.org/10.1037/0033-295X.99.3.550
9. Saryazdi, R., Bannon, J., Rodrigues, A., Klammer, C., Chambers, C.G.: Picture perfect: A stimulus set of 225 pairs of matched clipart and photographic images normed by Mechanical Turk and laboratory participants. Behav. Res. Methods **50**(6), 2498–2510 (2018). https://doi.org/10.3758/s13428-018-1028-5
10. Wang, H., Can, D., Kazemzadeh, A., Bar, F., Narayanan, S.: A system for real-time twitter sentiment analysis of 2012 us presidential election cycle. In: Proceedings of the ACL 2012 System Demonstrations, pp. 115–120 (2012)
11. Burnham, M.J., Le, Y.K., Piedmont, R.L.: Who is Mturk? Personal characteristics and sample consistency of these online workers. Ment. Health Relig. Cult. **21**(9–10), 934–944 (2018)
12. Rouse, S.V.: Reliability of MTurk data from masters and workers. J. Indiv. Diff. (2019)
13. Ekman, P.: Are there basic emotions? (1992)
14. Joshi, A., Kale, S., Chandel, S., Pal, D.K.: Likert scale: Explored and explained. Br. J. Appl. Sci. Technol. **7**(4), 396 (2015)
15. Loper, E., Bird, S.: Nltk: The natural language toolkit. arXiv, 2002, preprint cs/0205028
16. Bonta, V., Janardhan, N.K.N.: A comprehensive study on lexicon based approaches for sentiment analysis. Asian J. Comput. Sci. Technol. **8**(S2), 1–6 (2019)
17. Nielsen, F.Å.: afinn project (2017)
18. RamyaSri, V.I.S., Niharika, C., Maneesh, K., Ismail, M.: Sentiment analysis of patients' opinions in healthcare using lexicon-based method. Int. J. Eng. Adv. Technol. **9**(1), 6977–6981 (2019)
19. Alam, S., Shovon, S.D., Joy, N.H.: Machine learning and lexical semantic-based sentiment analysis for determining the impacts of the COVID-19 Vaccine. In: 2021 IEEE International Conference on Signal Processing, Information, Communication & Systems (SPICSCON), pp. 60–65. IEEE (2021)
20. Hu, M., Liu, B.: Mining and summarizing customer reviews. In: Proceedings of the Tenth ACM SIGKDD International Conference on Knowledge Discovery and Data Mining, pp. 168–177 (2004)
21. Parveen, H., Pandey, S.: Sentiment analysis on Twitter Data-set using Naive Bayes algorithm. In: 2016 2nd International Conference on Applied and Theoretical Computing and Communication Technology, (iCATccT), pp. 416–419. IEEE (2016)

22. Speelman, D.: "Logistic regression." Corpus methods for semantics: Quantitative studies in polysemy and synonymy, **43**, 487–533 (2014)
23. Chomboon, K., Chujai, P., Teerarassamee, P., Kerdprasop, K., Kerdprasop, N.: An empirical study of distance metrics for k-nearest neighbor algorithm. In: Proceedings of the 3rd International Conference on Industrial Application Engineering, vol. 2 (2015)
24. Gupte, A., Joshi, S., Gadgul, P., Kadam, A., Gupte, A.: Comparative study of classification algorithms used in sentiment analysis. Int. J. Comput. Sci. Inf. Technol. **5**(5), 6261–6264 (2014)

Tell Me, What Are You Most Afraid Of? Exploring the Effects of Agent Representation on Information Disclosure in Human-Chatbot Interaction

Anna Stock, Stephan Schlögl[(✉)] [iD], and Aleksander Groth [iD]

Department of Management, Communication and IT, MCI — The Entrepreneurial
School, Innsbruck, Austria
stephan.schloegl@mci.edu
https://www.mci.edu

Abstract. Self-disclosure counts as a key factor influencing successful health treatment, particularly when it comes to building a functioning patient-therapist-connection. To this end, the use of chatbots may be considered a promising puzzle piece that helps foster respective information provision. Several studies have shown that people disclose more information when they are interacting with a chatbot than when they are interacting with another human being. If and how the chatbot is embodied, however, seems to play an important role influencing the extent to which information is disclosed. Here, research shows that people disclose less if the chatbot is embodied with a human avatar in comparison to a chatbot without embodiment. Still, there is only little information available as to whether it is the embodiment with a human face that inhibits disclosure, or whether any type of face will reduce the amount of shared information. The study presented in this paper thus aims to investigate how the type of chatbot embodiment influences self-disclosure in human-chatbot-interaction. We conducted a quasi-experimental study in which $n = 178$ participants were asked to interact with one of three settings of a chatbot app. In each setting, the humanness of the chatbot embodiment was different (i.e., human vs. robot vs. disembodied). A subsequent discourse analysis explored difference in the breadth and depth of self-disclosure. Results show that non-human embodiment seems to have little effect on self-disclosure. Yet, our data also shows, that, contradicting to previous work, human embodiment may have a positive effect on the breadth and depth of self-disclosure.

Keywords: Health Chatbots · Agent Visualization · Anthropomorphism · Information Disclosure · Self-Disclosure

1 Introduction and Related Work

The increasing propagation of voice based conversational assistants such as Apple's *Siri*, Google's *Assistant*, Microsoft's *Cortana* and Amazon's *Alexa*, has

© The Author(s), under exclusive license to Springer Nature Switzerland AG 2023
H. Degen and S. Ntoa (Eds.): HCII 2023, LNAI 14051, pp. 179–191, 2023.
https://doi.org/10.1007/978-3-031-35894-4_13

also led to an increase in chatbot use. Ever since in 2016 Facebook decided to allow for artificial bots to be integrated into its messaging platform, the number of available text-based chatbots has been growing significantly [1], so that in 2018, already more than 300,000 chatbots were actively interacting with users via Facebook Messenger[1].

1.1 Chatbot Visual Appearance and Classification

Chatbots can, but do not have to have a visual appearance (often called agent or avatar representations[2]). Visualization options range from static and interactive virtual to physically completely embodied agents [14]. These differences in presentation also offer the possibility to integrate various non-verbal features, which may influence how users perceive chatbots [4] and consequently interact with them.

Beyond their appearance, chatbots can be classified in different ways. Work by Adamopoulou and Moussiades [1], based on Nimavat & Champaneria [40], for example, proposes a classification according to seven key aspects. These include: (1) the subject area in which a chatbot must be able to 'converse' (i.e., overarching or topic-specific); (2) the type of service a chatbot provides (i.e., offer company, provide a specific service, or allow for a connection to another human and/or chatbot); (3) the goal of the interaction (provide information, have a conversation, fulfil a task); (4) the way the answers have to be generated; (5) the level of required human intervention; (6) the licensing (open source vs. commercial); and (7) the communication channel (text, language, images or a combination thereof).

1.2 Chatbots in Health Care and Therapy

While there is a general increase in chatbot use, it is particularly the health domain that has seen strong uptakes throughout recent years. Particularly with respect to mental health, experts put great hope in conversational technology [12]. In fact, chatbots have already shown promising results in several studies both clinical [27,42] and non-clinical [15]. Measurable success was particularly evident in the support of people in relation to psycho-education and adherence. That is, chatbots are deemed effective in helping people help themselves by offering assistance to access relevant information and therapy material [18,50]. While health apps can help with meditation (e.g., *Headspace*[3], *Calm*[4]), recov-

---

[1] Online: https://venturebeat.com/2018/05/01/facebook-messenger-passes-300000-bots/ [accessed: February 10th 2023].

[2] Note: strictly speaking the visual representation of a chatbot should be called 'agent' since it is controlled by an algorithm whereas a human-controlled visual appearance should be referred to as 'avatar' [16].

[3] Online: https://www.headspace.com/ [accessed: February 10th 2023].

[4] Online: https://www.calm.com/ [accessed: February 10th 2023].

ery from addiction (e.g., *Recovery Record*[5]) or depression (e.g., *Talkspace*[6]), the more advanced chatbot systems may further engage in simple conversations and thus even offer basic therapy [12].

Although chatbot conversations may not replace therapy sessions, proponents argue that they can provide support and have a supplementary and relieving effect on mental health [12]. Following the rules of cognitive behavioral therapy, successful examples include *Woebot*[7] [36], *Wysa*[8] [25] or *Tess*[9]. It is particularly the 'around-the-clock availability' and the low entry threshold of these conversational tools that helps to reach people who are often reluctant to seek help from therapy – whether due to cost or due to social stigma [32,50].

1.3   Information Disclosure

To clarify treatment of psychological and physical illnesses, disclosure plays a major role. Griffin describes disclosure as *"the voluntary sharing of personal history, preferences, attitudes, feelings, values, secrets, etc., with another person"* [22, p. 114], whereas Cozby summarizes it as *"any information about oneself that a person A verbally communicates to a person B"* [11, p. 73]. Finally, Pickard & Roster refer to it as *"the truthful, sincere, and intentional communication of private information about oneself or others that makes oneself or others more vulnerable"* [44, p. 2].

Social Penetration Theory (SPT) describes the development of interpersonal relationships, where an initially superficial relationship becomes increasingly intimate [3]. In SPT, disclosure is described as consisting of two dimensions, i.e. breadth and depth of disclosure. Depth describes the degree of intimacy in a relationship and the degree to which a particular area of life is discussed. Breadth describes the range of areas of a person's life that are talked about. To this end, it is possible for a person to be very open in one area, while not talking about another area. The higher the degree of intimacy, the more areas can be disclosed at the same time [22].

Disclosure usually happens when the expected benefits outweigh the expected risks [2]. Here Omarzu's Disclosure Decision Model [43] describes the path to disclosure as a multi-step decision process: (1) evaluate whether a social benefit may be achieved (e.g., social affirmation, intimacy, relief in case of distress or despair, social control, etc.); (2) evaluate whether disclosure is a plausible means of achieving this goal; and (3) assess the potential risk of disclosure (e.g., potential rejection, weakening of one's own autonomy and personal integrity, embarrassment, etc.).

In health contexts, the challenge is usually to achieve the highest possible degree of disclosure. The underlying motivation may be to obtain important

---

[5] Online: https://www.recoveryrecord.eu/ [accessed: February 10th 2023].

[6] Online: https://www.betterhelp.com/ [accessed: February 10th 2023].

[7] Online: https://woebothealth.com/ [accessed: February 10th 2023].

[8] Online: https://www.wysa.io/ [accessed: February 10th 2023].

[9] Online: https://www.x2ai.com/individuals [accessed: February 10th 2023].

information [32] or to benefit from the positive effects that disclosure produces in interactions. Ho and colleagues summarize these positive effects found in previous studies into three categeues: the improvement of short-term emotional experience (stress, anxiety, reduction), which can ultimately lead to long-term mental health improvement, the improvement of relationship quality through the promotion of closeness and intimacy, and the improvement of the psychological condition by promoting self-esteem and affirmation [24].

Building on previous research in decision making related to information disclosure Greene developed the Disclosure Decision-making Model, which focuses on disclosure in the health context – in this case, particularly on how people deal with the disclosure of information after a disease diagnosis or in the course of medical treatment [20]. Empirical analyses found that the efficacy of information disclose is particularly important. If an individual assumes that the response to the disclosure is helpful and that the disclosure therefore effective, the willingness to disclose increases significantly [21].

Several studies comparing different conversational settings furthermore found, that people are willing to disclose more about themselves when interacting with a chatbot or other form of conversational agent than when talking to a human [31,32,45]. To this end, chatbots may be considered media agents which are capable of social interaction [17].

1.4   Chatbots as Social Actors

According to the CASA-Framework (i.e., *Computers Are Social Actors*) and its underlying media equation, chatbots should trigger natural responses similar to those triggered by human interlocutors [39]. Here anthropomorphism may help in the establishment and maintenance of human-chatbot relationships [8], enhance the perceived social presence of the chatbot [5], and have a positive effect on customer satisfaction [51]. Of particular importance in this regard are the form in which the chatbot is presented (i.e., the visual cues) and the degree of human resemblance with which this is done. That is, while anthropomorphism in the representation favors trust in chatbots [13] and increases its social presence [48], people seem to disclose more to chatbots when they are represented in a less anthropomorphic way [7]. The level of disclosure typically decreases when a chatbot with a human face is presented [31,44]. This suggests that people feel less social risk when disclosing information to a non-human like entity.

Another negative effect of anthropomorphism is shown in the so-called 'Uncanny Valley' effect [38], which describes the reaction of humans to anthropomorphic entities. Accordingly, if an entity is almost, but not quite human-/lifelike, the human response to it abruptly changes from empathy to rejection. Despite these negative effects of human-like appearance, research has also shown that faces may encourage disclosure as they foster social connection [28] – even, if they are not human [46].

Considering both positive and negative effects of anthropomorphic visual cues, Pickard & Roster [44] thus argue that disclosure to a chatbot may be highest when it is presented with a face that humans can connect with, but at the same time does not have such a strong human resemblance that it would risk causing feelings of eeriness. Our work aimed to investigate this assumption.

2   Theoretical Framework and Hypothesis Development

Following the definition by Gambino et al. [17] we may assume for chatbots to fulfill the criteria to be considered media agents. Consequently, we may further assume that humans show similar social reactions towards chatbots as they do towards humans.

Various studies have furthermore shown that anthropomorphism, i.e., the degree to which a chatbot is perceived to exhibit human characteristics, has a significant influence on the strength of certain reactions. Anthropomorphism can, for example, promote the establishment and maintenance of long-term human-chatbot relationships [8], increase the perceived social presence of a chatbot [5], and have a positive effect on customer satisfaction [51].

The chatbot's representation (i.c., its visual cues) and its degree of human resemblance are of particular importance here. That is, while anthropomorphism in the representation favors trust in a chatbot [13] and increases its social presence [48], the effect in other areas can be negative. For example, people disclose more to a chatbot when it is presented in a less realistic way [7]. And in general, the level of disclosure typically decreases when a chatbot is presented with a human face [31,44]. This suggests that people would feel to be subject to the same social risk when conversing with a chatbot as they feel when disclosing in a conversation with a human, especially if the chatbot is presented with a human-like face.

On the other hand, the visual representation of a face can also encourage disclosure. That is, people can build a social connection to a face [28], even if it is not human [46]. This social connection in turn encourages disclosure [3], unless its representation taps into Mori's 'Uncanny Valey' [37]. Here, an imperfect almost human-like representation starts to trigger feelings of eeriness [35]. Several studies have shown that the uncanny valley effect also occurs in human-chatbot interaction (cf., [10,34,49]).

Considering the positive effect of faces on the one hand and the potential negative effect of the uncanny valley on the other hand, Pickard & Roster [44] thus argue that a chatbot may work most effective when it offers a face that is not too human-like. From this, we derive the following hypothesis:

H1: The degree of people's information disclosure is higher when questions are asked by a "non-embodied" (i.e. not visually represented) chatbot or a chatbot that has only some human-like appearance than by a chatbot whose representation shows a high degree of human resemblance.

In order to test this hypothesis we designed a study in which participants were asked to interact with one of three chatbots and answer a number of questions.

3   Methodology

Our goal was to evaluate the effect the visual representation of chatbots has on people's information disclosure behavior. To do so, we used a survey-setup in which participants were asked to interact with one of three chatbot designs in order to answer personal questions. We then evaluated people's responses in light of the chatbot design they were interacting with. The following three designs were used (cf. Fig. 1):

1. High human resemblance based on a slightly stylized photo of a woman (i.e., human-like)
2. Low human resemblance depicted by a robot pictorial (i.e., robot-like)
3. Without any form of 'embodiment' (i.e, none-embodied)

Fig. 1. Chatbot designs to investigate the effect of visual representation on information disclosure. The left image shows high human resemblance, the image in the middles low human resemblance, and the image on the right no form of embodimnent

Chatbots were available online and optimized to be accessible through either PC or mobile devices. The language and expression as well as the typeface which was used to display the dialog were standardized and the same for all the three chatbot designs. Slightly delayed response times aimed to increase the perceived social presence of the chatbots [19]. We used both open and closed questions, all of which required some form of personal disclosure. Closed questions were inspired by Lind et al. [31] and it was expected that people would be honest when reporting on negative things about themselves [29]. Open questions were taken from Pickard & Roster [44], who also investigated depth and breadth of information disclosure in different interview settings. Simiarly, we used the 'Objective Information Disclosure' (OID) scale to measure the depth and the number of words [26, 27] to evaluate the breath of the disclosure in these questions.

With respect to the type of information that was requested, questions were classified as *demographic, perceptive* and *informative* (cf. Sect. 4.1). Demographic questions were collecting demographic information and used to investigate group differences between participants' answers to the other questions. Perceptive questions focused on the perceived level of human-likeness attached to our three chatbot designs, and informative questions explored participants' information disclosure behaviour. All questions were reviewed and approved by the school's Research Ethics Committee in terms of ethical considerations regarding research with human participation. Also, none of the questions were compulsory so that participants could decide for themselves whether they felt comfortable providing an answer or not.

4   Instruments

4.1   Questions

The following questions were asked by the chatbot during the interaction with a participant:

- Demographic Questions:
  1. *How old are you?* [< 18 | 18–35 | > 35]
  2. *Where do you live?* [Austria | Germany | Italy | Switzerland | Other]
  3. *What is your occupation?* [Student | Employed/Self-employed | Unemployed | Homemaker | Other]
  4. *What is your gender?* [Male | Female | Diverse | Do not want to say]
- Perceptive Questions:
  1. *The picture looks human-like:* [I totally disagree | I disagree | neutral | I agree | I totally agree]
  2. *The picture looks realistic:* [I totally disagree | I disagree | neutral | I agree | I totally agree]
  3. *The picture looks cartoon-like:* [I totally disagree | I disagree | neutral | I agree | I totally agree]
- Informative Questions:
  1. *How often do you read a newspaper (both printed and online)?* [never | less than once a week | once a week | several times during the week | daily]
  2. *What is it that you like to do with your closest friends or family?* [...]
  3. *Which of the following describes your money saving habits best:* [I don't save money – I usually spend more than I have | I don't save money – I usually spend as much as I have | I save what is left at the end of the month – no regular saving plan | We save the income of one family member – the rest we spend | I spend my regular income and save additional, irregular income | I save regularly every month]
  4. *What is it that you dislike the most about your look?* [...]
  5. *How often during the last 12 months have you in a bus or public place offered your seat to a stranger?* [never during the last 12 months | once during the last 12 months | two to three times during the last 12 months | once per month | once per week | more than once per week | I don't know]
  6. *How often during the last 12 months have you given money to a homeless person?* [never during the last 12 months | once during the last 12 months | two to three times during the last 12 months | once per month | once per week | more than once per week | I don't know]
  7. *What are you most scared of?* [...]
  8. *Think about a person that you love. Why do you love this person?* [...]

4.2   OID Analysis Scheme

The following evaluation scheme was used to analyze participants' responses to the chatbot: *The response to the question contains...* [1 = Not at all, 5 = A great deal]:

– *shame.*
– *concrete details.*
– *an answer to the question asked.*
– *embarrassing information.*
– *sensitive information.*
– *information that violates social norms.*
– *information that increases the person's risk for harm or negative consequences.*
– *an admission of the person's imperfection.*
– *an admission of guilt.*
– *an admission of failure on the person's part.*
– *negative emotions.*
– *positive emotions.*

5   Results

The link to the chatbot-driven survey was distributed via social networks, mainly focusing on people under the age of 35 living in the DACH region (i.e. Germany, Austria, Switzerland, North of Italy). Data from respondents who were under the age of 18 was excluded from the analysis and consequently deleted straight away. Answers from $n = 178$ people aged 18 or above were collected and evaluated (113 female, 62 male, 1 diverse, 2 did not want to say). Of these, 158 were in the 18–35 age group and 20 were over 35 years old. Participants were randomly assigned to one of the three chatbot designs. This yielded data from 60 interactions with the human-like chatbot (human), 66 interactions with the robot-like chatbot (robot) and 52 interactions with the non-embodied chatbot (no embodiment).

Similar to Nowak & Rauh [41], we used three question items to evaluate the human-like appearance of the chabtbots (cf., Sect. 4.1). As expected, the data shows that the photo of the stylized women was perceived as being significantly more anthropomorphic ($M = 3.25, SD = 0.86$) than the robot pictorial ($M = 1.40, SD = 0.60$); $t(177) = -26.03, p < 0.001, r = 0.890$.

Investigating differences in information disclosure, the data shows that participants state to have more often offered a seat to a stranger (informative question 5; cf. Sect. 4.1) when the question was asked by the human-like chatbot representation than by the one without embodiment; $Mann - Whitney\ U = 315, p = 0.006, r = 0.341$. Further exploring the depth of participant answers we used Pickard & Roster's [44] answer analysis scheme to calculate an average OID scale (cf. Sect. 4.2) for each of of the open questions (i.e., informative question 2, 4, 7 and 8; cf. Sect. 4.1). The data shows more depth in answers to the human-like chatbot compared to the robot-like chatbot with respect to the questions about people's greatest fear (informative question 7; cf. Sect. 4.1); $t(118) = 3.17, p = 0.002, r = 0.280$. A comparison between the human-like chatbot and the none-embodied chatbot showed a similar although less significant difference; $t(103) = 2.14, p = 0.035, r = 0.206$. Other than this, the data does not point to any differences concerning the depth of participants' answers.

Looking at the breath of provided answers we compared the number of words participants wrote. Also here, it was the question about people's greatest fear (informative question 7; cf. Sect. 4.1) where the data shows a significant difference in answering behaviour. That is, the human-like chatbot representation triggered more words in participants' answers than the robot-like representation $(t_{Welsch}(78.38) = 2.31, p = 0.024, r = 0.252)$ or the none-embodied representation $(t_{Welsch}(93.56) = 2.15, p = 0.034, r = 0.217)$.

Looking at the answer behavior, it can further be seen that the robot-like chatbot representation produced the highest number of missing or elusive answers to questions. That is, 15.15% of participants interacting with the robot-like chatbot left at least one question empty or did not really answer it, compared to 11.54% of participants interacting with the none-embodied chatbot and 10.00% of participants interacting with the human-like chatbot.

6   Discussion of Results and Their Limitations

Our investigation evaluated the extent to which the human resemblance of chatbots influences information disclosure. The collected data was subjected to a discourse analysis. It was expected that disclosure would be highest with little human resemblance, compared to high human resemblance and none-embodiment. Analysis results, however, suggest the contrary. That is, the analysis on breadth and depth of disclosure indicates that disclosure to a chatbot with high human resemblance is higher than to a chatbot with less human resemblance or without embodiment. The latter, in particular, contradicts previous work by Pickard & Roster [44], Joinson [26], and Lind et al. [31]. Reasons for this may be found in our research design. Most studies on disclosure in chatbot settings work with monitored experiments in which participants communicate with a system via spoken language. Our study, however, focused on text-based interaction.

A study by Hill et al. for example found that people communicate with chatbots in written form differently than they communicate in spoken language [23]. At the same time, the setting, in which the respondents answered the questions (i.e., in private and without supervision) may have had an effect. For example, a study by Li et al. [30] found that people in the private sphere are more willing to disclose. It is therefore possible that our participants were generally more open to disclosure and that accordingly fewer differences triggered by chatbot representations were found.

Furthermore, in contrast to other studies on the subject (e.g., [6,27,31,33, 44]), the human-like representation in our study was static. The lack of animation may have alleviated a potential uncanny valley effect and increased the acceptance of the more anthropomorphic representation.

Finally, a more frequent use of emoticons with our embodied (i.e., human-like and robot-like) chatbots does suggest that both representations received a higher degree of liking than the non-embodiment representation. Altman & Taylor's [3] social penetration theory assumes that relationships become deeper and more intimate over time and that disclosure occurs after a personal 'cost-benefit analysis'. Our study was not designed to produce any benefit for participants so one may argue that they had little reasons to disclose information. A long-term study design thus may have produced a more diverse answering behaviour.

7   Conclusion and Future Outlook

We have reported on the results of a chatbot-driven survey which investigated people's information disclosure behaviour with respect to different types of chatbot representation. Results have shown that, contrary to previous work, our human-like representation was not affected by the uncanny valley and able to trigger responses with a higher level of breath and depth – at least when it come to people reporting on their greatest fear.

These results, however, are subject to a number of limitations. First, they are based on rather small samples sizes of approx. 60 people per survey setting. Second, we furthermore assumed that the interaction with the different chatbots is significantly influenced by the social reactions their representations trigger in participants – be it in relation to the uncanny valley effect, sympathy or the establishment of a social connection. Since no data was collected that could provide clear information on what triggered responses, manipulations could have had a different effect. Finally, the evaluation of disclosure via the OID scale assumes that participants adhere to the same social norms and have similar feelings in relation to the disclosure of information. It disregards the fact that people, depending on their life experience or value system, may regard the sensitivity of information differently and therefore choose different levels of disclosure [44].

To tackle some of these limitations, future work, should use a greater sample size and focus on long-term studies of human-chatbot interaction so as to investigate how social penetration over time effects information disclosure. It furthermore should use post-survey questionnaires to record emotional attitudes of participants towards the different chatbot representations. And finally, with respect to chatbot representation, we recommend exploring the effect of chatbot gender stereotypes (e.g., [9]) or the influence of various ethnic representations (e.g., [47]).

References

1. Adamopoulou, E., Moussiades, L.: Chatbots: History, technology, and applications. Mach. Learn. Appl. **2**, 100006 (2020)
2. Afifi, T., Steuber, K.: The revelation risk model (RRM): Factors that predict the revelation of secrets and the strategies used to reveal them. Commun. Monogr. **76**(2), 144–176 (2009). https://doi.org/10.1080/03637750902828412

3. Altman, I., Taylor, D.A.: Social Penetration: The Development of Interpersonal Relationships. Rinehart & Winston, Holt (1973)
4. Appel, J., von der Pütten, A., Krämer, N.C., Gratch, J.: Does humanity matter? analyzing the importance of social cues and perceived agency of a computer system for the emergence of social reactions during human-computer interaction. Adv. Hum. Comput. Interact. **2012** (2012)
5. Araujo, T.: Living up to the chatbot hype: The influence of anthropomorphic design cues and communicative agency framing on conversational agent and company perceptions. Comput. Hum. Behav. **85**, 183–189 (2018). https://doi.org/10.1016/j.chb.2018.03.051
6. Astrid, M., Krämer, N.C., Gratch, J., Kang, S.H.: "It doesn't matter what you are!" explaining social effects of agents and avatars. Comput. Hum. Behav. **26**(6), 1641–1650 (2010)
7. Bailenson, J.N., Yee, N., Merget, D., Schroeder, R.: The effect of behavioral realism and form realism of real-time avatar faces on verbal disclosure, nonverbal disclosure, emotion recognition, and copresence in dyadic interaction. Presence· Teleoper. Virt. Environ. 15(4), 359 372 (2000)
8. Bickmore, T.W., Picard, R.W.: Establishing and maintaining long-term human-computer relationships. ACM Trans. Comput. Hum. Interact. **12**(2), 293–327 (2005)
9. Chaves, A.P., Gerosa, M.A.: How should my chatbot interact? a survey on social characteristics in human-chatbot interaction design. Int. J. Hum. Comput. Interact. **37**(8), 729–758 (2021)
10. Ciechanowski, L., Przegalinska, A., Magnuski, M., Gloor, P.: In the shades of the uncanny valley: An experimental study of human-chatbot interaction. Future Gen. Comput. Syst. **92**, 539–548 (2019)
11. Cozby, P.C.: Self-disclosure: A literature review. Psychol. Bull. **79**(2), 73 (1973)
12. D'Alfonso, S.: Ai in mental health. Curr. Opin. Psychol. **36**, 112–117 (2020)
13. De Visser, E.J., et al.: Almost human: Anthropomorphism increases trust resilience in cognitive agents. J. Exp. Psychol. Appl. **22**(3), 331 (2016)
14. Diederich, S., Brendel, A.B., Kolbe, L.M.: On conversational agents in information systems research: Analyzing the past to guide future work. In: Proceedings of WI, pp. 1550–1564. AIS (2019)
15. Fitzpatrick, K.K., Darcy, A., Vierhile, M.: Delivering cognitive behavior therapy to young adults with symptoms of depression and anxiety using a fully automated conversational agent (woebot): a randomized controlled trial. JMIR Mental Health **4**(2), e7785 (2017)
16. Fox, J., Ahn, S.J., Janssen, J.H., Yeykelis, L., Segovia, K.Y., Bailenson, J.N.: Avatars versus agents: A meta-analysis quantifying the effect of agency on social influence. Hum. Comput. Interact. **30**(5), 401–432 (2015)
17. Gambino, A., Fox, J., Ratan, R.A.: Building a stronger casa: Extending the computers are social actors paradigm. Hum. Mach. Commun. **1**, 71–85 (2020)
18. Gardiner, P.M., et al.: Engaging women with an embodied conversational agent to deliver mindfulness and lifestyle recommendations: A feasibility randomized control trial. Patient Educ. Counsel. **100**(9), 1720–1729 (2017)
19. Gnewuch, U., Morana, S., Adam, M.T., Maedche, A.: Faster is not always better: Understanding the effect of dynamic response delays in human-chatbot interaction. In: Frank, U. (ed.). 26th European Conference on Information Systems: Beyond Digitization-Facets of Socio-Technical Change, ECIS 2018, Portsmouth, UK, 23–28 June, 2018, p. 143975 (2018)

20. Greene, K.: An integrated model of health disclosure decision-making. In: Uncertainty, Information Management, and Disclosure Decisions, pp. 242–269. Routledge (2015)
21. Greene, K., Magsamen-Conrad, K., Venetis, M.K., Checton, M.G., Bagdasarov, Z., Banerjee, S.C.: Assessing health diagnosis disclosure decisions in relationships: Testing the disclosure decision-making model. Health Commun. **27**(4), 356–368 (2012)
22. Griffin, E.A.: A First Look at Communication Theory. McGraw-Hill (2003)
23. Hill, J., Ford, W.R., Farreras, I.G.: Real conversations with artificial intelligence: A comparison between human-human online conversations and human-chatbot conversations. Comput. Hum. Behav. **49**, 245–250 (2015)
24. Ho, A., Hancock, J., Miner, A.S.: Psychological, relational, and emotional effects of self-disclosure after conversations with a chatbot. J. Commun. **68**(4), 712–733 (2018)
25. Inkster, B., Sarda, S., Subramanian, V., et al.: An empathy-driven, conversational artificial intelligence agent (WYSA) for digital mental well-being: Real-world data evaluation mixed-methods study. JMIR mHealth uHealth **6**(11), e12106 (2018)
26. Joinson, A.N.: Knowing me, knowing you: Reciprocal self-disclosure in internet-based surveys. Cyber Psychol. Behav. **4**(5), 587–591 (2001)
27. Kang, S.H., Gratch, J.: Virtual humans elicit socially anxious interactants' verbal self-disclosure. Comput. Anim. Virt. Worlds **21**(3–4), 473–482 (2010)
28. Knapp, M.L., Hall, J.A., Horgan, T.G.: Nonverbal Communication in Human Interaction. Cengage Learning (2013)
29. Kreuter, F., Presser, S., Tourangeau, R.: Social desirability bias in CATI, IVR, and web surveysthe effects of mode and question sensitivity. Publ. Opin. Quart. **72**(5), 847–865 (2008)
30. Li, Z., Rau, P.L.P., Huang, D.: Self-disclosure to an IoT conversational agent: Effects of space and user context on users' willingness to self-disclose personal information. Appl. Sci. **9**(9), 1887 (2019)
31. Lind, L.H., Schober, M.F., Conrad, F.G., Reichert, H.: Why do survey respondents disclose more when computers ask the questions? Publ. Opin. Quart. **77**(4), 888–935 (2013)
32. Lucas, G.M., Gratch, J., King, A., Morency, L.P.: It's only a computer: Virtual humans increase willingness to disclose. Comput. Hum. Behav. **37**, 94–100 (2014). https://doi.org/10.1016/j.chb.2014.04.043
33. Lucas, G.M., et al.: Reporting mental health symptoms: Breaking down barriers to care with virtual human interviewers. Front. Robot. AI **4**, 51 (2017)
34. MacDorman, K.F., Green, R.D., Ho, C.C., Koch, C.T.: Too real for comfort? Uncanny responses to computer generated faces. Comput. Hum. Behav. **25**(3), 695–710 (2009)
35. MacDorman, K.F., Ishiguro, H.: The uncanny advantage of using androids in cognitive and social science research. Interact. Stud. **7**(3), 297–337 (2006)
36. Monnier, D.: Woebot: A continuation of and an end to psychotherapy? Psychotherapies **40**(2), 71–78 (2020)
37. Mori, M.: The uncanny valley: The original essay by masahiro mori. IEEE Spectrum (1970)
38. Mori, M., MacDorman, K.F., Kageki, N.: The uncanny valley [from the field]. IEEE Robot. Automat. Magaz. **19**(2), 98–100 (2012)
39. Nass, C., Moon, Y., Green, N.: Are machines gender neutral? Gender-stereotypic responses to computers with voices. J. Appl. Soc. Psychol. **27**(10), 864–876 (1997)

40. Nimavat, K., Champaneria, T.: Chatbots: An overview types, architecture, tools and future possibilities. Int. J. Sci. Res. Dev. **5**(7), 1019–1024 (2017)
41. Nowak, K.L., Rauh, C.: The influence of the avatar on online perceptions of anthropomorphism, androgyny, credibility, homophily, and attraction. J. Comput. Mediat. Commun. **11**(1), 153–178 (2005)
42. Oh, J., Jang, S., Kim, H., Kim, J.J.: Efficacy of mobile app-based interactive cognitive behavioral therapy using a chatbot for panic disorder. Int. J. Med. Inf. **140**, 104171 (2020)
43. Omarzu, J.: A disclosure decision model: Determining how and when individuals will self-disclose. Personal. Soc. Psychol. Rev. **4**(2), 174–185 (2000)
44. Pickard, M.D., Roster, C.A.: Using computer automated systems to conduct personal interviews: Does the mere presence of a human face inhibit disclosure? Comput. Hum. Behav. **105**, 106197 (2020)
45. Pickard, M.D., Roster, C.A., Chen, Y.: Revealing sensitive information in personal interviews: Is self-disclosure easier with humans or avatars and under what conditions? Comput. Hum. Behav. **65**, 23–30 (2016). https://doi.org/10.1016/j.chb.2016.08.004
46. Rosenthal-von der Pütten, A.M., Krämer, N.C., Hoffmann, L., Sobieraj, S., Eimler, S.C.: An experimental study on emotional reactions towards a robot. Int. J. Soc. Robot. **5**(1), 17–34 (2013). https://doi.org/10.1007/s12369-012-0173-8
47. Ruane, E., Birhane, A., Ventresque, A.: Conversational AI: Social and ethical considerations. In: AICS, pp. 104–115 (2019)
48. Sah, Y.J., Peng, W.: Effects of visual and linguistic anthropomorphic cues on social perception, self-awareness, and information disclosure in a health website. Comput. Hum. Behav. **45**, 392–401 (2015)
49. Thaler, M., Schlögl, S., Groth, A.: Agent vs. avatar: Comparing embodied conversational agents concerning characteristics of the uncanny valley. In: 2020 IEEE International Conference on Human-Machine Systems (ICHMS), pp. 1–6. IEEE (2020)
50. Vaidyam, A.N., Wisniewski, H., Halamka, J.D., Kashavan, M.S., Torous, J.B.: Chatbots and conversational agents in mental health: a review of the psychiatric landscape. Canadian J. Psychiat. **64**(7), 456–464 (2019)
51. Verhagen, T., Van Nes, J., Feldberg, F., Van Dolen, W.: Virtual customer service agents: Using social presence and personalization to shape online service encounters. J. Comput. Mediat. Commun. **19**(3), 529–545 (2014)

Human Decision-Making and Machine Assistance in Subtitle Translation Through the Lens of Viewer Experience

Sijin Xian(✉) (iD)

Translaxian LLC, Silver Spring, MD 20906, USA
projects@xiansijin.com

Abstract. Subtitle translation, which entails a unique blend of language skills and technical know-how, has benefited from the productivity boost enabled by various forms of technology, such as machine translation, automatic reading speed calculation, waveform display, and shot change detection. While these tools provide helpful assistance, the success of audiovisual translation projects is predicated upon the human linguist that interacts with the subtitling interface. By documenting the working and decision-making process of the author, an experienced English-to-Chinese subtitler and quality controller (QCer) of streaming and entertainment content, this paper explores what the machine can and cannot yet do for us in audiovisual translation, highlights the importance of empathy and judgment in creating top-notch viewer experience, and informs potential directions for future machine development in aid of human expertise.

Keywords: Audiovisual Translation · Viewer Experience · Technology Humanization · Multimodality · User Centricity · User Experience Design

1 Introduction

Thanks to technological advancements, entertainment and streaming content such as movies, drama series, unscripted reality shows, and documentaries can be localized and subtitled with accelerated productivity. The efficiency boost has been made possible in two ways. The first is the integration of the various components of audiovisual translation workflow into one tool or interface. Long gone were the days when "subtitlers needed a desktop computer, an external video player in which to play the VHS tapes with the material to be translated, and a television monitor to watch the audiovisual productions" [1]. The second is a suite of machine assistance capabilities that remove unnecessary labor and tedium on the subtitler's part. Even with heavyhanded edits, working with machine-translated output saves time and keystrokes compared to typing every word from scratch. Automatic reading speed calculation alerts the linguist when the subtitle exceeds the suggested length for the display time without requiring manual calculation. Waveform display enables precise identification of audio timeframes, avoiding reaction delay from auditory perception to manual marking. Shot change detection removes the need to examine a video frame by frame.

© The Author(s), under exclusive license to Springer Nature Switzerland AG 2023
H. Degen and S. Ntoa (Eds.): HCII 2023, LNAI 14051, pp. 192–204, 2023.
https://doi.org/10.1007/978-3-031-35894-4_14

Against the backdrop of technological efficiency, how are human subtitlers interacting with the machine? Where are we in terms of building a professional translation world where the machine does what it does best while human expertise shines in the arena of its incomparable mastery? What potential new use cases could we explore for future technological developments? As a professional English-Chinese translator who has worked in the streaming content localization field since 2018 both as a subtitle translator and quality controller (QCer), the author investigates these questions by documenting her reflections on and observations of the thoughtful and deliberate considerations needed to accommodate audio, visual, and storytelling elements. By presenting the pitfalls and best practices through the lens of viewer experience, the author highlights the beautiful minuet between human decision-making and machine assistance.

The viewer experience angle is meant to provide a unifying focal point for the intricate balance a subtitle translator needs to strike when attempting to accommodate reading speed, shot changes, and linguistic particularities while preserving readability and honoring creative intent. This perspective is also in line with the focus on cognitive and empirical research identified by Chaume [2] as one of the four methodological turns in the discipline of audiovisual translation, where "the interest is geared not only towards the translator's mental processes…but also, and mainly, on the audience's response to audiovisual translation."

Furthermore, this perspective is optimal for highlighting the most valuable asset of human expertise in audiovisual translation: empathy and judgment. Empathy puts the translator in the shoes—or in the context of audiovisual translation, seats—of the viewers they serve. This awareness requires the translator, who is bilingual and bicultural themselves, to be actively cognizant of what it is like to navigate an audiovisual asset as someone unfamiliar with the source language and culture. Judgment is especially salient when different priorities are in conflict, and an informed choice needs to be made to sort out the least of multiple evils. These two essential skills are the central thread that runs through the human expertise that we will explore later.

This paper is organized by the four cornerstones of viewer experience: accurate translation, scriptwriting mindset, effortless reading, and equivalent experience. These are derived from the four sets of unique characteristics of audiovisual translation compared to traditional text-based translation: the heavy presence of idiomatic expressions, slang terms, and cultural references; the essential components of plot, lines, and characters; the limited display time and continuous play of subtitles; and the artistry of direction, audience reaction, and creative intent. Each section covers the role of machine assistance in terms of benefits and challenges, best practices to achieve optimal viewer experience, and potential directions for future machine advancements.

2 First Cornerstone: Accurate Translation

Accurate translation is the first cornerstone of the audiovisual viewer experience. All other considerations are reduced to pointlessness when plot lines and intended messages are skewed to the point of impeding authentic storytelling. The adoption of machine translation in audiovisual translation has been slower compared to traditional text-based translation projects [3], and it was fairly recent when one of the author's clients incorporated pre-translated subtitles into the workflow. It needs to be highlighted that the use of machine translation in the professional world—contrary to those who turn to the likes of Google Translate to sidestep hiring a trained linguist—comes with the awareness that it is a productivity enhancement tool with inaccurate output and that it is the human expert's job to catch and fix the errors.

Achieving accuracy requires impeccable execution on three fronts: processing the source text, internalizing the message, and producing the end rendition. This process faces two notable challenges in audiovisual translation. First, the script or audio transcription of audiovisual content is only one-third of the "source text." Translating the source text alone in isolation from the audiovisual elements is a doomed attempt. Second, the abundance of idiomatic expressions, slang terms, and cultural references puts exceedingly high demands on the linguist's source language mastery to understand and convey the essence of the message.

2.1 Three-Dimensional Context

In translation, we say context is king. In audiovisual translation, we have three: the audio elements (such as tone, tempo, delivery of the speech, and background audio cues), the visual elements (such as on-screen information for storylines, facial expressions, and gestures), and the transcribed source text. For example, the same line of text, "I should report this to the boss," may need to be rendered differently based on the actor's delivery. If "I" is the focal point of this statement, then what should be conveyed is "I should be the one who reports this to the boss," not "I have the obligation to report this to the boss."

Similarly, the source text's translation is also affected by the on-screen visual cues. In one QC instance, two sequential lines both read "Hello?" in English. The character says the first "Hello?" to check if the person on the phone can still hear her, and the linguist assumes the second "Hello?" to be a repeated follow-up query. However, the latter utterance takes place a few seconds later, when the character gets up to scan the house upon hearing a strange sound. In Chinese, these should be rendered differently, and the oversight is a telltale sign that the linguist did not watch the movie closely.

The two examples above show the contextual variations within standard language usage: emphasis matters; a word has more than one meaning. Apart from these scenarios, there are cases where the standard dictionary definition and everyday usage differ. In another movie the author QCed, three women are being chased by some thugs, and one of the women makes it into a safe room first. The two other women arrive later, knocking on the door and requesting to be let in. The woman in the room asks, out of caution, "Are you alone?" to ensure the dangerous men are not around. The machine translation treated "alone" as one solitary person. However, from the context, we know the speaker is asking, "Are there just the two of you?" Again, the rendition would be different in Chinese, and this contextually jarring output was not corrected by the linguist. A similar case would be the phrase "a couple of." While its standard meaning is two, it is used in informal contexts to mean two or three. Simply having the source text available is not enough to produce an accurate translation.

As highlighted in the above examples, machine translation, besides its usual issues and challenges [4], encounters the critical issue that source text is not the whole context in audiovisual translation. Furthermore, the author's QC experience has shown that when the machine translation output is grammatically correct yet contextually unfitting, it is not always detected by linguists if they are not watching the video with a keen eye and taking in the three-dimensional context themselves. In other words, audiovisual translators must not think of their job as simply checking the source text against the machine output. In future technological developments, while linguists are trained on the importance of grasping the entirety of the context, machines might be trained on the fronts of integrated audio, visual, and text-level comprehension. There could also be a flagging mechanism for contextual or usage uncertainty to alert linguists that additional confirmation is needed.

2.2 Tricky Translations

Machine translation tends to run into trouble regarding idioms [5], slang terms [6], and cultural references [7], and human expertise is essential to correcting these errors. In this realm of human-machine interaction, three issues are particularly salient in the author's QC experience: mistranslations hiding in plain sight, hidden messages uncaptured, and unidiomatic or unnatural renditions. The culprits behind these issues are usually a lack of mindful engagement with the context, inadequate language mastery causing difficulty understanding nuances, and getting swayed by source text phrasing. Below are some examples for each category.

Glaring errors can escape detection when the translator goes on autopilot. Knee-jerk reaction as such happens when the linguist has a go-to rendition or understanding of a phrase or expression when they first learned the source language and never paused to ponder other meanings. As a result, when the machine translation output is also based on the dominant interpretation, the mistake ends up flying under the radar. For example, the primary usage of "I don't know," meaning "I do not have the knowledge or information," can be so ingrained in translators that they fail to entertain the possibility of it having a second usage. However, frequently in everyday speech, "I don't know" is used to signal uncertainty, hesitation, or disagreement.

Similarly, when someone says "I don't blame you" in response to the other person's rant, this phrase has nothing to do with assigning blame and is instead an expression of sympathy and understanding. When the machine translates "I don't blame you" word for word, the linguist must have the contextual awareness and sensitivity to uncover the right message. In other words, translators need an inner alarm system for jarring renditions that prompts them to perform due diligence.

Difficulty understanding linguistic or cultural nuances leaves hidden messages uncaptured. In a notable QC instance, a translator rendered the expression "playing for the other team" literally in the sense of sports team allegiance—which is also something machine translation would do—instead of the intended reference to one's sexuality. The author has also seen the expression "good morning to you, too" rendered as a morning greeting instead of a sarcastic tease implying the other person did not greet them properly. Humor and sarcasm are typical tripwires in audiovisual translation and require an intimate understanding of the source language and culture, which further shows that in a workflow that intends to utilize machine translation to save time and increase productivity, higher priority must be placed on cultivating a talent pool that supplies highly qualified translators to make up the machine's shortcomings.

The third issue is unnatural translation. Being bilingual means constantly picking up new vocabulary, expressions, and linguistic nuances from both directions. This could lead to mixing up languages, forgetting words, or losing some sensibilities of what sounds natural and idiomatic. One of the challenges in translation is being able to think as if one only knew one language so that their rendition is not "polluted" by the patterns and habits of the other. Stiff, awkward, unidiomatic translations happen when the translator— and the machine—performs word-for-word conversion instead of holistic and artful translation, which necessitates an abstract extraction of the message, tone, and intent before conveying them naturally into another language.

The future of audiovisual translation is a "teamwork makes the dream work" scenario for human-machine interaction. In order to produce the sophisticated and creative localization critical to a delightful viewing experience, investment in translators of the highest caliber must be in tandem with machine-enabled productivity boost to keep tricky errors at bay. Future machine training might consider a targeted effort on collecting quality translation memories for frequently occurring slang terms, idiomatic expressions, and cultural references and provide multiple options for translators to select from based on the context.

3 Second Cornerstone: Scriptwriting Mindset

Though different from dubbing, which places a heavy emphasis on matching the mouth shapes and movements of the on-screen actors, a subtitle is nevertheless viewed as the replacement of the spoken line heard in the original language and requires a high level of character embodiment. To this end, the translated subtitles must match the audible utterances while conforming to the world-building and plot lines. Therefore, it is essential for subtitlers to have a scriptwriting mindset and understand that the translations are lines for the actors to say aloud as if they were acting in another language. This section focuses on the importance of creative recasting and subtitle flow in bringing subtitles to life.

3.1 Creative Recasting

Recasting is a natural process in translation, as different languages have different grammatical and syntactical construction rules. In subtitle translation, however, a different recasting is required to match the audio with the on-screen context and avoid potential spoilers. For instance, to translate "I'll let you play with your friends if you do your homework first" into Chinese, the order is switched to "if you do your homework first, I'll let you play with your friends," as it is customary to put the if-clause at the beginning of a sentence.

Let us imagine, however, this is a scene from a movie, where the child looks excited upon hearing the first half of the sentence at the prospect of a fun time with friends. Then, when the mother raises the condition of doing homework, he shows a slightly disappointed look. In this case, as demonstrated in the visual demonstration below, the usual recasting would fail as a subtitle because the translation delivers the information in a different order that's jarring for the storyline.

Conventional text translation strategy:
English: I'll let you play with your friends if you do your homework first.
Chinese: 如果你先把作业做了，我就让你跟小伙伴玩

Movie translation (incorrect):
If you do your homework first, [kid looks excited]
[Mom continues] I'll let you play with your friends. [kid looks disappointed]

A dilemma like this calls for a different translation approach: we need to rethink the source text so that we do not need to move the segments around in translation. In this case, a good solution is to circumvent the if-clause issue so that our translation reads, "I'll let you play with your friends, but you need to do your homework first." This way, the viewers can receive the information in the proper, harmonious order.

Movie translation (correct):
Subtitle 1: 你可以去跟小伙伴玩
Subtitle 2: 但是你要先把作业做了
I'll let you play with your friends, [kid looks excited]
[Mom continues] but you need to do your homework first. [kid looks disappointed]

Here is another example. A sentence such as "I want to live in a world where the grass is green, the roses are red, and the sky is blue with you" would be rendered into Chinese as "I want to with you live in a green-grass, red-rose, and blue-sky world." If this is a line from a movie, where images of green grass, red roses, and blue sky are shown on screen as the character speaks, and before "with you" is uttered, there is a deliberate pause before "with you," it intends to deliver a crescendo of romantic sentiments. However, the typical recasting would create a chaotic viewing experience where the subtitle does not match the on-screen sequence, and when the pivotal "with you" is spoken, the subtitle would show "world."

Conventional text translation strategy:
English: I want to live in a world where the grass is green, the roses are red, and the sky is blue with you.

Chinese: 我想和你生活在一个绿草如茵、玫瑰红艳、天空蔚蓝的世界里

Movie translation (incorrect):

I want to with you live in a [showing green grass] green-grass [showing red roses], red-rose [showing blue sky], blue-sky [impactful pause, eye contact] world.

Thus, human expertise is required to rewrite the sentence so the translation would read, "In my ideal world, there is green grass, red roses, blue sky, and you," which unfolds the same way as the original.

Movie translation (correct):
Subtitle 1: 在我梦想的世界里
Subtitle 2: 有绿绿的青草
Subtitle 3: 红艳的玫瑰
Subtitle 4: 蔚蓝的天空
Subtitle 5: 还有你
In my ideal word, [showing green grass] there is green grass, [showing red roses] red roses, [showing blue sky] blue sky, [impactful pause, eye contact] and you.

The previous segment on the three-dimensional context of audiovisual translation demonstrates the challenge for the machine to produce accurate translations due to the lack of contextual input from the audio and visual elements. The above examples add another layer of difficulty by cautioning against switching subtitle orders arbitrarily, a common and innocuous practice for text-based translation that might create confusion in an audiovisual viewing experience. The deep understanding of the context and a high level of sensitivity to the nuances of language can be hard for machines to replicate.

3.2 Subtitle Flow

Another unique characteristic of subtitle translation is that a whole sentence can be broken into multiple subtitle instances due to audio's delivery tempo (as seen in the example above) or shot changes. Different languages have different considerations for line breaking and how a sentence flows from one subtitle box to another. Focusing only on segment-to-segment equivalent horizontally (from source to target) cause incoherence in the vertical direction, which is how the content flows from the viewer's perspective.

For example, in the Netflix show *Wednesday* (Season 1, Episode 6: "Quid Pro Woe," 40:50), the original English line reads, "Now you know what's at stake. Everything you vowed to protect, no less." As this utterance is broken into two subtitles to accommodate the shot change, the Chinese subtitle translation reads:

Subtitle 1: 你知道这其中的利害关系
Subtitle 2: 你发誓要保护的一切

Subtitle 1 English back translation: You understand the situation of vital interests.
Subtitle 2 English back translation: Everything you vowed to protect.

Subtitle 1 English original: Now you know what's at stake.
Subtitle 2 English original: Everything you vowed to protect, no less.

Subtitle 2 English original: ⎡Everything⎤ you vowed to protect, no less.

As seen above, the Chinese translation lacks coherence because "everything" is not a "situation," whereas in the English original, "everything" is precisely "what" is at stake. While the author cannot ascertain whether this incoherence is caused by machine error or human oversight, putting the whole sentence in versus putting in two segments does make a different in machine translation, too. Using DeepL as an example:

Full input: You understand what's at stake: everything you vowed to protect.
DeepL: 你明白什么是危险的：你发誓要保护的一切。
Back translation: You understand what's dangerous: everything you vowed to protect.

Input 1: You understand what's at stake.
DeepL: 你明白这其中的利害关系。
Back translation 1: You understand the situation of vital interests in this.

Input 2: Everything you vowed to protect.
DeepL: 你发誓要保护的一切。
Back translation 2: Everything you vowed to protect.

While the translation "what's dangerous," as opposed to "what's in danger," is not the most accurate, the example shows that segmentation affects machine translation output. Similarly, suppose the original English line is "I am embarrassed…for you." The machine can competently translate "I am embarrassed for you," but in this particular instance, the sentence needs to be broken into two parts to deliver the desired effect. Because the syntax would be different in Chinese, it needs human intervention to render it properly. The same applies to "I think the door is unlocked" versus "The door is unlocked…I think." The machine can render the first utterance correctly, but when "The door is unlocked" and "I think" are treated as two lines, the output will not establish the ideal subtitle flow.

Therefore, for better output, the machine needs to learn to move beyond segments to ensure coherence. It must be highlighted that this kind of segmented tunnel vision is not unique to machine translation. In the author's QC experience, linguists also make the mistake of focusing on the horizontal translation, seeing if their translation on the right matches the source text on the left, not paying attention to if the translation flows vertically from one subtitle event to the next. It is therefore advisable to "proofwatch"— as opposed to proofread—one's subtitle work before submission so that one can see if the translated lines match the audiovisual elements and flow naturally. It might be helpful for quality control purposes only to enable project submission after the finished work has been watched from beginning to end with the subtitles.

4 Third Cornerstone: Effortless Reading

Subpar subtitle translation can not only lack accuracy or scriptwriting flair but also be exhausting to read. One study shows even the fact that whether subtitles are syntactically or non-syntactically segmented can affect the viewer's cognitive load [8]. To deliver a first-rate viewing experience, one must ensure concise subtitle translation. When the writing is efficient, clear, and devoid of unnecessary distractions, the viewer can have a better experience. Another factor that can add to the viewing effort is the movement of on-screen visuals accompanied by the subtitles. In this regard, shot change is an essential concept in the audiovisual field. This part will discuss concise writing and attention to shot changes as strategies for effortless reading.

4.1 Concise Writing

Every line of subtitles, whose display time is dictated by the audio length, comes with an expiration date in a matter of seconds, making concision a key element in audiovisual translation to reduce cognitive load. To this end, reading speed standards are established to set the parameters of how many characters should be in a subtitle, given the time constraint. Machine assistance comes in handy by automatically alerting linguists when the subtitle is too long for preset limits without the need for manual counting. However, reading speed should only be a preliminary baseline or reference, not a gold standard as a cut-off point.

The first reason is that languages expand or contract in relation to each other. Szarkowska and Geber-Morón [9] found that"faster subtitles with unreduced text were preferred in the case of English videos, and slower subtitles with text edited down in Hungarian videos." For English-into-Chinese translation, the text typically shrinks in character space, which is why many redundant and wordy Chinese translations that are overwhelming or unpleasant to read never trigger machine warnings. For example, in the Netflix show *Love Is Blind* (Season 2, Episode 14: "After the Altar: The Future Looks Bright," 19:11), a mother-in-law says to a young couple, "We said 'better or worse.' This is worse." This was intended to encourage them to support each other as they were going through a rough patch. The Chinese translation doesn't seem significantly longer than the English original in terms of character space:

> English: We said "better or worse." This is worse.
> Chinese: 说好无论好坏都要互相扶持 这就是不好的时候

However, upon scrutiny, the Chinese translation was a result of explanatory expansion because the translator unpacked the idea of this pithy utterance into: "You said you would support each other for better or worse, and this is one of the worse times." This is a fair translation that conveys the meaning without violating any reading speed limit. However, as the aforementioned three-dimensional nature of audiovisual translation suggests, the subtitle does not exist in a vacuum. When the viewer watches the show, it is the balance of what they are reading, watching, and listening that brings viewing satisfaction, yet there is a perceptible gap in syllable density (eight for English versus 20 for Chinese) in this example, which creates disharmony.

An advisable strategy would be to rephrase to convey the intent and circumvent the inevitable expansion created by following the original wording. For example, this could be rendered as, "既然结了婚，就要共渡难关"(Since this is a marriage, you should get through this hard time together). The new rendition clearly states the intended message and cuts down the syllable count almost by half, creating a more unified reading experience. This demonstrates that when the target language gets more wiggle room for the characters-per-second limitation, it is all the more important for the translators not to think of the machine as the ultimate overlord to please—the final yardstick should always be the viewer experience. Linguists need to understand that passing a mechanical reading speed check does not mean the subtitle is good to go and that there should always be a conscious effort to tighten up and optimize the writing.

Moreover, a subtitle can be short and strenuous to read all at once if it is syntactically complex or contains unfamiliar phrasing. In languages like Chinese, where sentences are punctuated, but words are not spaced in between, characters can stick together and make a sentence difficult to parse upon first glance, necessitating rephrasing or more reading time. When the machine registers the reading speed, it is a simple calculation that relies only on the character amount and display time. Given the chasm between an objective measurement versus a subjective reading experience, the linguist must watch the audiovisual asset with their subtitle translation to gauge the reading experience instead of relying on a number.

Therefore, efficient writing and sound judgment are essential to concise subtitling. In future technological developments, it can be worthwhile to consider more sophisticated metrics for reading speed calculation so that it is not simply based on cold, hard numbers such as characters per second. Instead, it should incorporate nuanced and complex considerations of syntax and readability analysis from a viewer's perspective.

4.2 Shot Changes

An audiovisual file is a combination of various continuous shots spliced together. The "stitch," or the transition point, is a shot change. An eye movement tracking study found that "participants had significantly more gaze shifts between subtitles and image in the case of subtitles displayed over shot changes compared to those which did not cross any cuts" [10]. While it cannot always be achieved—an utterance can cross multiple shot changes quickly and could not be broken into mini segments—it is good practice to contain a subtitle event within a shot change so that the viewer's gaze is not disrupted.

In this regard, automatic shot change detection is a helpful tool. However, false shot changes can sometimes be detected, such as when there is a sudden shift of lighting in a continuous shot, such as in a scene at a dance club with flashing disco balls. In these cases, human discernment is necessary to override machine detection.

During QC, the author frequently encounters instances where the machine indicates where the shot change is, but the linguist fails to split the subtitle event accordingly, even when it is grammatically and syntactically appropriate. For this issue, it would be helpful for future interfaces to detect shot changes and automatically create subtitle boxes around them upon determining that the spoken audio fits in the subtitle box as a standalone unit grammatically. For example, consider a scenario where a woman is speaking on the stage, saying, "With advanced technology in renewable energy, we can create a better and more beautiful world," with a shot change to the audience's reaction during this utterance. It will be desirable to for the machine to detect whether the shot change falls on a comma (or a period in other cases)—namely a proper spot to split the subtitles—and automatically generate two subtitle boxes around the shot change.

5   Fourth Cornerstone: Equivalent Experience

In subtitle translation, we should strive not to subject our audience to a second-rate experience because they cannot understand the original language. Thus, it is essential to design subtitles in a way that provides an equivalent experience to what a native-speaking viewer would have without the subtitles as much as possible. This includes ensuring that subtitles reflect the rhythm, pace, and emotion of the spoken dialogue. It is also important to pay attention to details such as audio length, syllable density (as demonstrated in the "for better or worse" example), and parallelism or repetition in the dialogue. This section focuses on two aspects of equivalent experience. First, strategic subtitle segmentation ensures the viewers of our subtitle translation can watch the story as it unfolds rather than being spoiled significantly ahead of time. Second, an audiovisual product is the combination and culmination of the creative intent of all creators involved, which must be honored by the subtitle translator.

5.1   Subtitle Segmentation

If the audio utterance is water flowing down a faucet, then a subtitle box is a container to hold the water. In the author's QC experience, some subtitlers tend to focus on how much water one box can hold, only creating another subtitle event when the space runs out. This mindset is inconducive to creating an equivalent experience. Imagine a general giving a powerful speech, "Comrades, we must fight back with all our might." While delivering, he takes significant pauses between phrases. Putting out the whole sentence spoils the line for the audience because the emotion of the viewers is supposed to rise as the speech unfolds. Instead of seeing this as one sentence that can be fit into one subtitle box, the right approach is to watch the flow of the water.

Comrades, [long pause] we must fight back, [long pause] with all our might!

Subtitle 1: Comrades,

Subtitle 2: we must fight back,

Subtitle 3: with all our might!

Similarly, suppose someone is looking for Jason while shouting out his name. Then upon opening the door, something shocking is revealed, and the character says, "What are you doing?" The effect will be very different if the whole line is in one subtitle as "Jason! What are you doing?" One aspect of segmentation is facilitated by audio waveform detection, as we can clearly see how the water is flowing. For future technological developments, options can be explored about detecting dialogue audio and conducting syntax analysis so that the subtitle boxes can be automatically created according to the waveform.

Another consideration to time subtitle events even better is rethinking the way it is displayed. In the Chinese stand-up comedy competition show *Rock & Roast* (脱口秀大会),, a Karaoke-like subtitle display is used to avoid showing the punchline before the joke is completed. This innovative practice addresses a long-standing issue in subtitling, where one invariably reads ahead of the audio. Furthermore, imagine a movie scene where someone is speaking before an unexpected explosion or accident. This element of surprise, to the annoyance of the viewer, is usually foreshadowed by a dash in the subtitle. The ability to synch up a key and revealing subtitle with the audio is worth exploring as a new addition to the subtitling toolkit.

5.2 Creative Intent

From scriptwriting to direction and from camerawork to acting, filmmakers are intentional with their creative decisions. The translator needs to have an appreciative eye for these thoughtful intricacies and convey them to the viewers through deliberate decision-making. For example, if the character has a catchphrase, it needs to be rendered consistently for it to be memorable. If something is intentionally cryptic, the translation also needs to be vague. Timing decisions also need to be made by observing the camerawork, such as zoom-ins. Recreating humor is another aspect where human creativity shines, as the translator needs to reinvent wordplay while staying relevant to the plot line. Ultimately, human perception and intentionality are indispensable to successful subtitling, and modern subtitling tools must be placed in capable hands.

6 Conclusion

Audiovisual translation makes an intriguing arena to observe human-machine interaction because it combines the creative aspect of translation with the use of technological tools. This paper draws from the author's experience as a subtitler and QCer and discusses common issues and best practices through the lens of the four cornerstones of a pleasurable viewer experience. It documents the author's thought process and interaction with the subtitling interface in order to achieve accurate translation, scriptwriting mindset, effortless reading, and equivalent experience.

There are a lot of potential areas future technical advancements can explore in audiovisual translation. Continued research in these areas will lead to a more enjoyable subtitling experience for the audience. One possibility is to train the machine to understand both the source text and the situational context for the utterance. Machine translation can also be improved to take into account the prevalence of idiomatic expressions, slang terms, and cultural references in streaming and entertainment content. There is also potential in advanced rhetorical relationship and syntax analysis capabilities to ensure better subtitle segmentation and flow. In addition, there could be more advanced metrics than reading speed alone, such as readability scores and cognitive load assessment. Another innovative approach could be synching the punchline or key revelation with the audio, so that the subtitles are seamlessly integrated into the audiovisual experience.

Ultimately, the priority of audiovisual translation is to serve the story, and we need linguists who have the eye to appreciate creative intent and storytelling to craft a beautiful experience. The more advanced the subtitling machine becomes, the more essential it is to put the machine in the hands of top-notch linguists who can skillfully utilize machine assistance while practicing audience empathy and strategic judgment.

References

1. Díaz-Cintas, J., Massidda, S.: Technological advances in audiovisual translation. In: O'hagan, M. (ed.) The Routledge Handbook of Translation and Technology, pp. 255–270. Roudge, London (2019)
2. Chaume, F.: An overview of audiovisual translation: four methodological turns in a mature discipline. J. Audiovis. Transl. 1(1), 40–63 (2018). https://doi.org/10.47476/jat.v1i1.43
3. Bywood, L., Georgakopoulou, P., Etchegoyhen, T.: Embracing the threat: Machine translation as a solution for subtitling. Perspectives 25(3), 492–508 (2017). https://doi.org/10.1080/090 7676X.2017.1291695
4. Okpor, M.: Machine translation approaches: Issues and challenges. Int. J. Comput. Sci. J. 11(5), 2 (2014)
5. Shao, Y., Sennrich, R., Webber, B., Fancellu, F.: Evaluating machine translation performance on Chinese idioms with a blacklist method. In: Proceedings of the Eleventh International Conference on Language Resources and Evaluation, pp. 31–38. European Language Resources Association, Miyazaki (2018)
6. Lin, B., Xu, F., Zhu, K., Hwang, S.: Mining cross-cultural differences and similarities in social media. In: Proceedings of the 56th Annual Meeting of the Association for Computational Linguistics, vol. 1, pp. 709–719. Association for Computational Linguistics, Melbourne (2018). https://doi.org/10.18653/v1/P18-1066
7. Tekwa, K., Jiexiu, J.L.: Neural machine translation systems and Chinese *wuxia* movies: moving into uncharted territory. In: Jiao, D., Li, D., Meng, L., Peng, Y. (eds.) Understanding and Translating Chinese Martial Arts, pp. 71–89. New Frontiers in Translation Studies. Springer, Singapore (2023). https://doi.org/10.1007/978-981-19-8425-9_5
8. Gerber-Morón, O., Szarkowska, A., Woll, B.: The impact of text segmentation on subtitle reading. J. Eye Movem. Res. 11(4), 2 (2018). https://doi.org/10.16910/11.4.2
9. Szarkowska, A., Geber-Morón, O.: Viewers can keep up with fast subtitles: Evidence from eye movements. PLoS ONE 13(6), e0199331 (2018). https://doi.org/10.1371/journal.pone. 0199331
10. Krejtz, I., Szarkowska, A., Krejtz, K.: The effects of shot changes on eye movements in subtitling. J. Eye Movem. Res. 6(5), 3, 1–12 (2013). https://doi.org/10.16910/jemr.6.5.3

Human-AI Collaboration

Human Satisfaction in Ad Hoc Human-Agent Teams

Sami Abuhaimed$^{(\boxtimes)}$ and Sandip Sen

Tandy's School of Computer Science, The University of Tulsa, Tulsa, USA
saa8061@utulsa.edu

Abstract. With recent progress in connectivity and the transition into knowledge economies, mixed human and agent teams will become increasingly commonplace in both our personal and professional spheres. Hence, further examination of factors that affect human satisfaction in these types of teams can inform the design and use of effective human-agent teams. In particular, we are interested in virtual and ad-hoc team scenarios where a human is paired with an agent, and both need to assess and adapt to the capabilities of the partner to maximize team performance. We designed, implemented, and experimented with an environment in which virtual human-agent teams repeatedly collaborate to complete heterogeneous task sets. We investigate the role humans and autonomous agents play, as task allocators, on human satisfaction of virtual and adhoc human-agent repeated teamwork. We evaluated the satisfaction of human participants, recruited from the Amazon Mechanical Turk platform, using survey questions focusing on different aspects of team collaboration, including the process, allocation strategy, team performance, and agent partner. We find that participants are more satisfied (a) with the process when they allocate and (b) with the team outcome when the agent is allocating. We analyze and identify the factors that contributed to this result. This work contributes to our understanding of how to allocate tasks in virtual and ad hoc human-agent to improve team effectiveness.

Keywords: Human-agent Interaction · User Satisfaction · Task Allocation

1 Introduction

Teams of humans and agents are becoming more commonplace in which human and agent team members play different roles on the team. As human-agent teams are increasingly recognized as a routine and functionally critical important component of our societies, researchers have been studying the interactions and dynamics within these teams to understand and improve on their design [4,15]. Many of these environments configure agents with supporting roles for humans within the team [11], and have been studied in robotic and simulation settings [18].

© The Author(s), under exclusive license to Springer Nature Switzerland AG 2023
H. Degen and S. Ntoa (Eds.): HCII 2023, LNAI 14051, pp. 207–219, 2023.
https://doi.org/10.1007/978-3-031-35894-4_15

We are studying environments where humans start to collaborate with agents in a new environment with no prior interaction experience with the agent. The agent also does not have prior knowledge of the abilities and preferences of its human partners. Such collaborations correspond to *ad hoc teams*: *An ad hoc team setting is one in which teammates must work together to achieve a common goal, but without any prior agreement on how to work together* [3].

We believe that continued engagement in a team and the use of agent partners by humans will depend on, among other factors, *how satisfied the human is* with how the team operates, the distribution of workload in the team, the behavior of her agent partner, and the performance of the team. Hence, our research focuses on better understanding human satisfaction in new collaborations among humans and agents, and in particular in ad hoc human-agent teams.

In this paper, we consider ad hoc teams that are trying to accomplish a set of diverse task types. We also assume that the same human-agent pair will repeat this process of teamwork a few times. A few repetitions are common in ad hoc situations and allow for studying human satisfaction in the initial stages of collaboration, which might dictate if they will continue to collaborate with the agent. The success of such ad hoc human-agent teams in completing assigned team tasks, therefore, will critically depend on effective adaptability in the task allocation process. Confounding the situation is the fact that task allocation will affect not only team performance, but also satisfaction of different facets of teamwork, such as the interaction process, nature of teammate and outcome of collaboration. An unsatisfied human may quit the ad hoc team if unhappy with either the process or the outcome of tasks allocations received. To better understand the effect of task allocations on human satisfaction with ad hoc human-agent teamwork, in this paper we evaluate the effect of human vs agent allocator on human satisfaction with various aspects of teamwork. Some of the related questions that we study in this paper are:

- Are humans' satisfaction in the human-agent team influenced by who is allocating the tasks?
- Is a human's satisfaction in their agent teammate predicated on or correlated with their satisfaction with the collaboration process or team outcome?
- Are humans more satisfied when they are allocated task types they prefer? How much human satisfaction in human-agent teams is due to the nature of the tasks they do?

2 Related Work

Human-agent teams have been studied in different domains such as space robotics [4] and decision-making [1]. The focus is on agents who play supportive roles for human teammates [11], and are studied in robotic and simulation settings [18].

We focus on an adhoc environment, whereas studies, such as [4,15], incorporate training or interaction sessions with the agent and environment prior to the study. We are also interested in agents that are autonomous; DeChurch and

Larson view an autonomous agent as a "team member fulfilling a distinct role in the team and making a unique contribution" [12].

Task allocation has been extensively studied in multi-agent teams [14]. In agent teams, the focus is on designing efficient mechanisms for agents to distribute tasks within their society. Task allocation is also studied in the literature on human teams and organizations. The task allocation mechanism, which includes capability identification, role specification, and task planning, is considered an important component of teamwork [13]. For any organization to achieve its goals, Puranam points out that it needs to solve four universal problems, including task allocation [16]. In human teams, the focus is on understanding the characteristics of human teams to design the best possible task allocation mechanism

The study of task allocation with combined human and agent team members is promising. The few existing work in this area does not empirically investigate the area, focused on industrial settings, configures the agent in supporting roles, and it is not clear whether human participants received training prior to experiments, making the scenario not ad hoc.

Human satisfaction is recognized as a major component of team effectiveness in team models [5]. Team member satisfaction has positive effects on team dimensions, such as performance [9]. [20] studied the influence of different factors, such as team familiarity, on member satisfaction in virtual human teams. Furthermore, most recognized human team frameworks, such as Input-Process-Output (IPO) model, examine teamwork through different dimensions, which include members, the process in which they interact, and teamwork outcome [13]. Other researchers in different domains have measured team member satisfaction with a similar outlook [6,17]. One may be more satisfied with the team members than with the interaction protocol or outcome of teamwork. It is worth mentioning that most human-agent team studies overlook or do not fully recognize these distinctions when measuring human perceptions. Furthermore, to the best of our knowledge, there is little investigation of team member satisfaction in the human-agent team literature. [15] studies human satisfaction, among other factors, with only teamwork outcome in a negotiation domain.

Therefore, we study general human satisfaction, in a collaborative setting, with adhoc human-agent team; we further examine satisfaction levels with teamwork outcome, interaction protocol, and the autonomous agent teammate, in relation to task allocation protocols.

3   Research Hypotheses

We investigate human satisfaction in ad hoc human-agent teams. We examine satisfaction levels with different team dimensions including team outcome, interaction protocol, allocation strategy, and agent teammate. We are particularly interested in how human members in human-agent teams are influenced by protocols in which the role of task allocator is performed by either the human (Human Allocator Protocol) or an agent (Agent Allocator Protocol). Task allocation is an important component of teamwork, and we expect it to influence human perceptions of the team. In particular, we expect that general satisfaction, which typically encapsulates satisfaction with the agent, interaction protocol, and team outcome, will be different between teams assigned to human or agent allocators. When the agent is assigned an allocator role, the human may feel less sense of control in the team's decision-making process and thus less satisfied generally.

Hypothesis 1a (H1a): *There is a difference in human general satisfaction in teams that interact through Human- and Agent- Allocator Protocols.*

Hypothesis 1b (H1b): *Human teammates will have higher overall satisfaction in teams that interact through Human rather Agent Allocator Protocols*

We expect the allocations strategies used by different humans to vary. Even the same individual may not be consistent in how she allocates tasks or estimates the relative expertise of team members over multiple interactions [10]. In particular, there are no guarantees of optimality given available information and stated task requirements. The allocation strategy used by an agent, however, can be fixed and based on optimal allocation for the estimated expertise of the team member and the requirements for the tasks at hand [19]. Thus, we expect the agent allocation strategy to do well and that should be reflected in the humans' satisfaction with team outcome. Hence, we expect humans to be more satisfied with team outcome when the agent allocates rather than the human.

Hypothesis 2 (H2): *Humans' satisfaction with Team outcome, namely performance, will be higher when Agent, rather than human, allocates tasks to the team.*

The task allocation mechanism in the ad hoc human-agent teams we study share many components but differs in the designation of allocator role between situations where the human or the agent teammate is allocating tasks. As agents' capabilities increase, they are designated to new roles within human-agent teams. Humans may not be accustomed to the agent playing an increasing role, i.e., task allocator, in the team, and may not trust the agent to adequately assign tasks, as this is an ad hoc interaction without reputation information. Thus, we expect humans to view agent teammates with allocator roles within the team less favorably.

Hypothesis 3 (H3): *Human teammates will exhibit less satisfaction with Agent, rather than human, Allocator Protocol.*

Humans may perceive the interaction protocol differently if they, rather than the agent, are making the decisions for the allocation process. Even though the agent teammate is effectively fulfilling the responsibilities of the role, the human teammates may be unclear and wondering about the rationale behind the task assignments, e.g., why cannot they be assigned other task types that they might enjoy doing more or think they are better at even if their performance is relatively worse. We expect some hesitancy among humans toward the interaction protocol that assigns the task allocator role to the agent teammate.

Hypothesis 4 (H4): *Human teammates will exhibit more satisfaction with their own allocation strategy outcome than agent's strategy.*
Hypothesis 5a (H5a): *Humans' overall satisfaction will be positively associated with allocated tasks likeability.*
Hypothesis 5b (H5b): *Humans will be more satisfied with agent teammate when it assigns them tasks they like.*

4   Methodology

We empirically investigated the hypotheses by conducting between-subject experiments with human subjects recruited on the Amazon Mechanical Turk platform. We developed an environment in which both humans and agents can collaborate to share and complete tasks. We designed two task-sharing protocols that differ primarily on who is responsible for allocating tasks to the team members. Now we describe the domain, protocols, and agent task allocation strategy.

4.1   Experimentation Domain Characteristics and Description

For systematic experimentation to evaluate the above hypotheses, we needed a domain that encapsulates the following characteristics:

- The team tasks used should be such that there would be significant variation in the level of expertise in the general population. Larger variability would allow more space for team adaptation and human satisfaction with teamwork. We should also have the latitude to easily and believably configure varying agent capability distribution over the task types.
- The domain should allow an agent to be perceived as autonomous and plays a distinct peer role in the team.
- The domain should not require significant prior knowledge or training for the human participant and should be accessible to non-experts for effectively operating in an ad hoc team setting.
- There should be flexibility in sharing team information, including task allocations and completions, with team members. The environment should be configurable between perfect and imperfect information scenarios as required by the research question being investigated.

We developed Collaborative Human-Agent TaskBoard (CHATboard), an environment that facilitates human-agent, as well as human-human, team coordination. CHATboard contains a graphical interface that supports human-agent team coordination to complete a set of tasks (see Fig. 1). CHATboard allows for displaying the task sets to be completed, supports multiple allocation protocols, communication between team members for expressing confidence levels, displaying allocations and performance by team members on assigned tasks, etc.

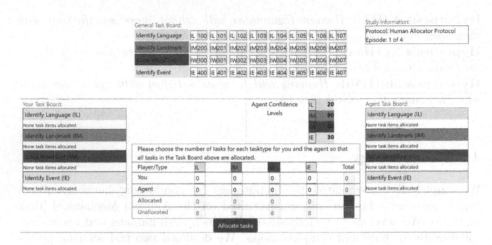

Fig. 1. CHATboard showing allocation phase of Human Allocation Protocol.

The framework utilizes the concept of tasks posted on blackboards, often used in coordination within human teams, to facilitate a human team member perceiving an agent as a distinct team member. Blackboards have also been used effectively in agent teams as a common repository for information sharing between agents [8]. We incorporate three task boards in our task sharing frame: one shared board, which includes the set of team tasks organized by type, and two other boards, respectively, for the tasks assigned to the human and the agent team member. These task boards facilitate coordination and act as easily navigable repositories for team information, allowing team members to share and view information through these boards.

We define a set of n team members N: $\{p_1, p_2,...,p_n\}$, a set of m task types M: $\{y_1, y_2,...,y_m\}$, a set of r tasks, T_{jr}:$\{t_{j1}, t_{j2},...,t_{jr}\}$, for each task type y_j. Team member i can share their confidence levels $p_i(y_j)$ over task types y_j. The set C_i:$\{p_i(y_1),p_i(y_2),.....,p_i(y_m)\}$ represent confidence levels for different task types for team player, p_i. The team members will interact over E episodes, where episode numbers range from $1...E$. $A_{i,e}$ denotes the set of tasks allocated to player i in episode e and we assume that all available tasks are exhaustively allocated, i.e., $\bigcup_i A_{i,e} = \bigcup_j T_{jr}$. The performance of player p_i for a task t_{jk} in episode e is referred to as $o_{ijke} \in \{0,1\}$. We define the performance of p_i on task type y_j in episode e as $\mu_{i,y_j,e} = \sum_{t_{jk} \in A_{i,e}} o_{ijke}$.

4.2 Interaction Protocols

Protocols are processes that organize human-agent teamwork; they provide mechanisms for engagement, and act as a foundational component of effective teamwork. Two interaction protocols have been designed to guide task allocation process in an ad hoc environment. The Human Allocator Protocol assigns the task allocator role to the human teammate, and is illustrated as follows:

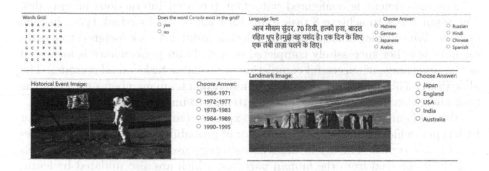

Fig. 2. Examples of different task types.

1. *The protocol asks agent teammate for their task type preferences.*
2. *The protocol passes the agent's preferences or confidence levels to the human. The following steps are repeated for N episodes*
   Episode starts:
3. *The protocol asks Human to provide task allocations for the team.*
4. *Tasks are assigned to the team.*
5. *The protocol receives human and agent task performance measures and computes statistics.*
6. *The protocol displays team overall team performance as well as individual team member performances for the episode on their respective task boards.*
   Eepisode ends
   Go to step 3

The Agent Allocator Protocol is the flip side and assigns the task allocator to the agent. In both protocols, team members repeatedly interact through episodes, which encapsulates different components: Task Allocation, Task Completion, and Taskwork results. Though these protocols provide a framework for team interaction and task allocation, they do not dictate the allocation strategy of team members. The task allocators are free to devise their own allocation strategies.

4.3   Experimental Setup

We designed a set of experiments to evaluate the relative effects of the two protocols on human satisfaction. We now describe the experimental configurations. We conduct experiments with teams composing of two members: human and agent, N: $\{p_a, p_h\}$. We use four different task types, M: $\{y_1, y_2, y_4, y_4\}$: the chosen task types are *Identify Language, Solve WordGrid, Identify Landmark*, and *Identify Event* (examples of these task types are available in Fig. 2). We created 32 task item instances for each of the four task types.

The experiment is configured with four repeated interactions or episodes. The team needs to achieve 8 task items for each of the four task types in each episode. We consider boolean task completion results: A task assigned to a team member is either successfully completed or not. Team performance is measured as the percentage of successful completion of available tasks on all episodes. The allocator can observe the performance of individual team members and adapt the task allocation between episodes in an attempt to improve team performance.

We configure the agent with variable expertise (confidence level) for different task types, which is represented as a vector of probabilities for successful completion of task types[1]. The agent allocation strategy uses its own confidence levels and those received from the human partners, which are also updated by learning from experiences over the episodes. We encoded a linear programming-based task allocation strategy (the strategy is outside the scope of this paper).

We use a between-subject experimental design, since our environment is ad hoc and subjects need to be exposed to a condition only once. We deploy two conditions on Amazon Mechanical Turk; one for the Agent Allocator protocol and the other is for the Human Allocator protocol. Both conditions follow same set of rules but differ on the allocation role.

We recruited 130 participants, 65 for each condition, as is recommended for a medium-sized effect [2], from Amazon Mechanical Turk. After participants agree to the Informed Consent Form, they read a description of the study and then start the first episode. Each episode contains three phases : taskwork allocation, taskwork completion, and taskwork results. Once participants complete all four episodes, they are asked to complete a survey that includes their satisfaction with various aspects of teamwork and their likeability of task types. We incorporate random comprehension attention checks to ensure result fidelity [7]. Participants receive a bonus payment based on team performance.

4.4   Satisfaction and Task Likeability Measurements

We measure general satisfaction through an aggregate score of the human's satisfaction with teamwork outcome, interaction protocol, allocation strategy, and in their partner agent. We adapt the satisfaction survey proposed by [6] and [17] with five questions: one for the interaction protocol, two for the outcome, and one for the agent partner. The survey follows a 5-point Likert scale setting administered at the end of the study. The following are the questions incorporated into the survey.

Task Allocation Protocol: *"I feel satisfied with the procedures/protocol used in the team's task allocation."*

---

[1] Agent expertise is simulated by flipping a coin with success probability of P_t, the confidence level.

Tasks: *"I feel satisfied with the tasks allocated to me and team members."*
Agent teammate: *"I enjoyed working with my agent teammate."*
Team Outcome: *"I feel satisfied with how our team performed."*

Participant's task likeability is measured at the end of the experiment through a survey item: *"Please rate how much you liked each task type."* Participants are asked to rate their likeability of each task type on 10-point Likert scale. For each participant, we compute a weighted likeability over all allocated tasks.

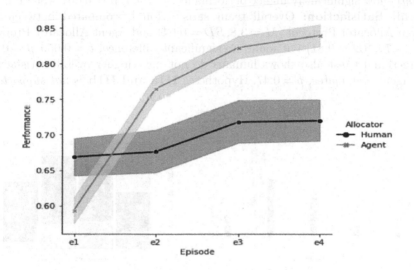

Fig. 3. Team Performance over episodes.

Table 1. Satisfaction survey measure outcomes.

Satisfaction with	Human Allocator		Agent Allocator		t-value	p-value
	Mean	SD	Mean	SD		
Team Outcome	3.51	0.90	**3.86**	0.95	2.18	**0.031**
Agent Teammate	3.53	0.98	3.66	0.88	0.74	0.45
Allocated Tasks	4.05	0.77	3.98	0.90	0.41	0.67
Task Allocation Protocol	**4.10**	0.66	3.8	0.90	2.20	**0.029**
Overall Satisfaction	3.8	0.64	3.79	0.81	0.059	0.95

5   Results

A total of 130 participants, 65 for each protocol, took part in the study. Team performance is different between Agent and Human Allocator Protocols. In addition, human participants express different levels of satisfaction for different aspects of teamwork. Figure 4 illustrates how humans view each dimension within the Human Allocator Protocol. For example, human satisfaction with Team Outcome is different than their satisfaction with the Protocol.

We perform Welch Two Sample t-tests to compare performance and satisfaction measurements between Human and Agent Allocator protocols, presented in Table 1. We now present some highlights from these tests:

Team Performance: The teams using Agent Allocator Protocol (M = 0.75, SD = 0.04) compared to ones using Human Allocator Protocol (M = 0.69, SD = 0.09) show significantly higher performance, t = 4.4, p < 0.001 (See Fig. 3).

Overall Satisfaction: Overall team satisfaction is compared between the Human Allocator Protocol ($M = 3.8, SD = 0.64$) and Agent Allocator Protocol ($M = 3.79, SD = 0.81$) but found no significant difference, $t = 0.059, p = 0.95$. A directional t-test also shows humans do not have higher overall satisfaction than agent teammates, $p = 0.47$. Hypotheses **H1a and H1b** *is not supported*.

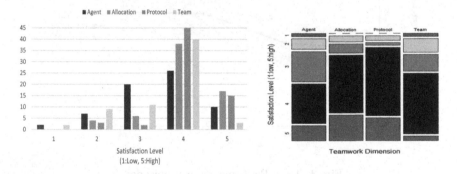

Fig. 4. Variation of human satisfaction over teamwork dimensions (Human Allocator Protocol): (left) histogram of human satisfaction at each satisfaction levels; (right) variation in satisfaction levels for each teamwork dimension.

Team Outcome: We compared human satisfaction with Team Outcome when the human ($M = 3.51, SD = 0.90$) and agent ($M = 3.86, SD = 0.95$) are allocating. We found a significant difference for human satisfaction with Team outcome: $t = 2.18, p = 0.031$. Participants are more satisfied with the Team outcome when they are in the Agent Allocator Protocol condition rather than the Human one. Hypothesis **H2** *is supported*.

Allocation Protocol: We compared human satisfaction with the Allocation Protocol in the Human ($M = 4.10, SD = 0.66$) and Agent ($M = 3.8, SD = 0.90$) Protocols, and found a significant difference: $t = 2.20, p = 0.029$. Participants are more satisfied with the process of the Human Allocator Protocol than the Agent Allocator one. Hypothesis **H3** *is supported*.

Allocated Tasks: We compared human satisfaction with Team Outcome when the human ($M = 4.05, SD = 0.77$) and agent ($M = 3.98, SD = 0.90$) are allocating. We found no signification difference for human satisfaction with Allocated Tasks, $t = 0.41, p = 0.67$. Hypothesis **H4** *is not supported*.

Task Likeability: We examined the relation between weighted allocated task likeability and satisfaction dimensions using the Spearman Correlation Test. In Human Allocator Protocol, weighted likeability is positively correlated with Protocol, Allocation Strategy, Agent Teammate, and overall satisfaction, $r_{protocol} = 0.28, p_{protocol} = 0.001, r_{allocation} = 0.28, p_{allocation} = 0.01, r_{agent} = 0.22, p_{agent} = 0.03$, and $r_{overall} = 0.29, p_{overall} = 0.01$. The association with Team Outcome is statistically insignificant, $r = 0.07, p = 0.28$. In the Agent Protocol, weighed likeability is positively correlated with Protocol, Allocation Strategy, Team Outcome, Agent Teammate, and overall satisfaction, $r_{protocol} = 0.30, p_{protocol} = 0.01, r_{allocation} = 0.33, p_{allocation} = 0.003, r_{team} = 0.23, p_{team} = 0.03, r_{agent} = 0.40, p_{agent} = 0.004$, and $r_{overall} = 0.37, p_{overall} = 0.001$. When the human is allocating, human satisfaction is weakly associated with allocated tasks' likeability, whereas when the agent is allocating, we observe a positive and moderate correlation between human satisfaction and task likeability. In both protocols, there is a positive correlation between overall satisfaction and task likeability. Table 2 shows these results. Hypotheses **H5a** and **H5b** *are supported*.

Table 2. Spearman Correlations between Weighted Likeability and Satisfaction.

Satisfaction in	Allocator	
	Human	Agent
Protocol	r = 0.28, p = 0.001	r = 30, p = 0.01
Allocation	r = 0.28, p = 0.01	r = 0.33, p = 0.003
Team Outcome	r = 0.07, p = 0.28	r = 0.23, p = 0.03
Agent Teammate	r = 0.22, p = 0.03	r = 0.40, p = 0.0004
Overall	r = 0.29, p = 0.01	r = 0.37, p = 0.001

6 Discussion and Future Work

We investigate different tasks allocation mechanisms and their influence on human satisfaction within ad hoc human-agent teams. We present CHATBoard, which is a new ad hoc human-agent team collaboration framework. We develop two allocation protocols that are differentiated by allocator role: Human and Agent Allocator Protocols. We use CHATBoard to conduct user study to compare the two protocols through satisfaction and performance measurements.

In contrast to other human-agent teamwork literature, we view human satisfaction in human-agent teams as a multifaceted entity: it involves satisfaction with team members, process, and team outcome. This treatment of satisfaction is inspired by the literature on human satisfaction in human teams. We note that although there is no significant statistical difference in overall human satisfaction between Agent and Human Allocator protocols, there are statistical differences when we evaluate human satisfaction with different aspects of teamwork.

Moreover, humans are more satisfied with Team Outcome when an agent, rather than the human, is assigned an allocator role. This is possibly due to better team performance because the agent is more effective in adapting to the capabilities within the team. Humans are also less satisfied with Allocation Protocol in which the agent plays allocator role. This is likely due to human feeling of less control over the allocation decisions or the agent's lack of explanation capability to justify allocated tasks. They may also not trust the agent to adequately assign tasks, as this is an ad hoc interaction without reputation information.

The significant takeaway is that we found an interesting dichotomy in which humans are more satisfied with the Allocation Protocol when they are allocating but are more satisfied with Team Outcome when the agent is assigned the allocator role. It raises the following question: How can we design task allocation mechanisms for adhoc human-agent teams to increase human satisfaction in both the protocol and the team outcome? We plan to investigate research pathways to address this question, including the use of shared allocation protocols and the use of explanations by the agent for allocated tasks. We also plan to evaluate the effect of different agent expertise distributions and how the dynamics of human-agent teams change when the team consists of more than two members.

References

1. Anderson, A., Kleinberg, J., Mullainathan, S.: Assessing human error against a benchmark of perfection. ACM Trans. Knowl. Discov. Data (TKDD) **11**(4), 1–25 (2017)
2. Brinkman, W.P.: Design of a questionnaire instrument. In: Handbook of Mobile Technology Research Methods, pp. 31–57. Nova Publishers (2009)
3. Genter, K., Agmon, N., Stone, P.: Role-based ad hoc teamwork. In: Proceedings of the Plan, Activity, and Intent Recognition Workshop at the Twenty-Fifth Conference on Artificial Intelligence (PAIR-11) (2011)
4. Gervits, F., Thurston, D., Thielstrom, R., Fong, T., Pham, Q., Scheutz, M.: Toward genuine robot teammates: Improving human-robot team performance using robot shared mental models. In: AAMAS, pp. 429–437 (2020)
5. Gladstein, D.L.: Groups in context: A model of task group effectiveness. Administrative Science Quarterly, pp. 499–517 (1984)
6. Green, S.G., Taber, T.D.: The effects of three social decision schemes on decision group process. Organ. Behav. Hum. Perform. **25**(1) (1980)
7. Hauser, D., Paolacci, G., Chandler, J.: Common concerns with mturk as a participant pool: Evidence and solutions (2019)
8. Hayes-Roth, B.: A blackboard architecture for control. Artif. Intell. **26**(3), 251–321 (1985)
9. Hertel, G., Geister, S., Konradt, U.: Managing virtual teams: A review of current empirical research. Hum. Resour. Manag. Rev. **15**(1), 69–95 (2005)
10. Kahneman, D.: Thinking, Fast and Slow. Macmillan (2011)

11. Lai, V., Tan, C.: On human predictions with explanations and predictions of machine learning models: A case study on deception detection. In: Proceedings of the Conference on Fairness, Accountability, and Transparency, pp. 29–38 (2019)
12. Larson, L., DeChurch, L.A.: Leading teams in the digital age: Four perspectives on technology and what they mean for leading teams. Leadersh. Quart. **31**(1), 101377 (2020)
13. Mathieu, J.E., Hollenbeck, J.R., van Knippenberg, D., Ilgen, D.R.: A century of work teams in the journal of applied psychology. J. Appl. Psychol. **102**(3), 452 (2017)
14. Mosteo, A.R., Montano, L.: A survey of multi-robot task allocation. Instituto de Investigacin en Ingenierła de Aragn (I3A), Tech. Rep. (2010)
15. Prajod, P., Al Owayyed, M., Rietveld, T., van der Steeg, J.J., Broekens, J.: The effect of virtual agent warmth on human-agent negotiation. In: Proceedings of the 18th International Conference on Autonomous Agents and MultiAgent Systems, pp. 71–76 (2019)
16. Puranam, P., Alexy, O., Reitzig, M.: What's "new" about new forms of organizing? Acad. Manag. Rev. **09**(2), 162–180 (2014)
17. Reinig, B.A.: Toward an understanding of satisfaction with the process and outcomes of teamwork. J. Manag. Inf. Syst. **19**(4), 65–83 (2003)
18. Rosenfeld, A., Agmon, N., Maksimov, O., Kraus, S.: Intelligent agent supporting human-multi-robot team collaboration. Artif. Intell. **252**, 211–231 (2017)
19. Shoham, Y., Leyton-Brown, K.: Multiagent Systems: Algorithmic, Game-Theoretic, and Logical Foundations. Cambridge University Press (2008)
20. Stark, E.M., Bierly, P.E., III.: An analysis of predictors of team satisfaction in product development teams with differing levels of virtualness. R&d Management **39**(5), 461–472 (2009)

Composite Emotion Recognition and Feedback of Social Assistive Robot for Elderly People

Yegang Du[1]([✉]), Kaiyuan Zhang[2], and Gabriele Trovato[3]

[1] Future Robotics Organization, Waseda University, Tokyo, Japan
`yg.du@aoni.waseda.jp`
[2] School of Creative Science and Engineering, Waseda University, Tokyo, Japan
[3] Innovative Global Program, Shibaura Institute of Technology, Tokyo, Japan

Abstract. As the world's population ages, the issue of medical care and daily care for the elderly population is becoming more and more critical. While there are many efforts to ensure the physical health of older adults, there is a lack of effective solutions to the psychological problems caused by the lack of companionship. To solve this problem, we built a social robot with an emotion recognition and feedback model. The emotion recognition module achieves composite emotion recognition by integrating voice emotion recognition, semantic emotion recognition and topic emotion recognition. The audio data and corresponding text data are mined using CNN and LSTM algorithms, and the emotional information they contain can be further refined. Meanwhile, the emotion feedback module provides the appropriate emotion feedback based on the recognised emotions. The emotional feedback is achieved by generating the appropriate robot facial expressions. The proposed emotion recognition and feedback model is validated by the corresponding database respectively. In addition, the real-world implementation validation and real scenario application of the model are also discussed in the paper.

Keywords: Emotion Recognition · Elderly Care · Social Robotic · Emotion Feedback

1 Introduction

In recent years, the growth of the elderly population has brought the issue of medical and daily care to the forefront. As a result, advancements in the Internet of Things (IoT) and Artificial Intelligence (AI) have led to the creation of various home medical assistance applications for the elderly. These applications aim to monitor the physical well-being of the elderly through the use of sensors and smart homes [7,8]. However, despite their efforts to improve the physical health of the elderly, the emotional and psychological needs of this demographic are often left unfulfilled. And these needs have been clearly identified and analysed by scholars as early as the 1990s [12]. In recent years, social robots that integrate multiple technologies have been seen as an effective solution to this challenge [4,9].

H. Degen and S. Ntoa (Eds.): HCII 2023, LNAI 14051, pp. 220–231, 2023.
https://doi.org/10.1007/978-3-031-35894-4_16

Many researchers have come up with their own solutions for emotion recognition and feedback in robots. Aronsson argues that the introduction of emotional technologies into the care equation can lead to new relationships and ways of interacting [3]. Castillo et al. proposed a framework that can recognise emotions by studying physiological signals, facial expression and voice. Emotion regulation is enabled by tuning music, colour and light to the specific needs of the elderly [5]. Khosla et al. reported on the design and field trial of Matilda, a human-like assistive communication robot in Australian residential and community care settings [13]. Facial expression and voice analysis were used to identify and measure the emotional state of the participants during the interaction between elderly participants and the social robot Misa [6]. An empathic robot Ryan was created using a multimodal emotion recognition algorithm and a multimodal emotion expression system. Using different input modalities for emotion, i.e. facial expression and speech sentiment, the empathic Ryan detected the emotional state of the user and uses an affective dialogue manager to generate a response [1]. These studies provide compelling evidence of the potential for emotional technologies to revolutionize the care of the elderly. Through the integration of emotion recognition and feedback, robots have the potential to provide not only physical assistance, but also emotional support and companionship, thus improving the quality of life for the elderly population.

However, the above studies still suffer from several shortcomings in practical application scenarios. Firstly, some studies require the use of multiple sensor combinations, and deploying these complex sensor networks indoors would require extensive installation and commissioning. Second, emotion recognition systems based on facial expression recognition often rely on one or more cameras. These indoor cameras pose a significant privacy risk to the user. In addition, due to the relatively high real-time processing requirements, the computational process of emotion recognition and feedback can only be performed on the robot, making it difficult to apply algorithms that rely on server computing power in practice.

To address the above issues, a new solution has been proposed: the development of a social assistance robot for the elderly named DarumaTO. Figure 1 illustrates the design of this innovative solution. The robot is designed with emotional interaction as a key component, with the aim of alleviating the loneliness and isolation commonly experienced by the elderly population. The robot is not equipped with a camera as shown in the Figure. Emotion recognition is performed by analysing speech data only, which avoids privacy issues and reduces the amount of data to be processed, allowing the algorithm to run on robots with relatively low computing power. The speech data was decomposed into audio data and textual data, and the voice emotion, semantic emotion and topic emotion embedded in them were analysed using convolutional neural networks (CNN) and long-short term memory (LSTM) algorithms respectively. The algorithm is first trained offline on an existing database and then deployed to the robot, reducing computation time while maintaining model performance. In addition, the robot's emotional feedback is achieved by dynamically generating appropriate robot facial expressions on the display.

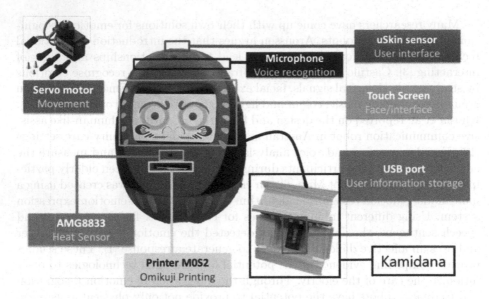

Fig. 1. The DarumaTO social assistive robot for elderly perple.

By incorporating emotional intelligence into the design of DarumaTO, the robot is able to provide not only physical assistance, but also companionship and emotional support to the elderly. The emotion recognition and feedback model introduced by this paper minimises the difficulty of operation for older users, while presenting the robot's feedback emotions in the most intuitive way. With its focus on emotional interaction, DarumaTO has the potential to revolutionize the way we provide care and support to the elderly.

2   DarumaTO Social Robot

The design of DarumaTO is specifically intended to evoke a sense of familiarity and comfort among Japanese elderly individuals, who may recognize the cultural significance of the Daruma doll. The robot is equipped with various sensors and actuators, allowing it to collect data from the environment and make decisions on the most effective way to interact with the user. In this sense, DarumaTO operates as a form of an IoT system. This enables the robot to respond to the needs and preferences of the user in real-time, providing a highly personalized and interactive experience. The design of DarumaTO highlights the importance of cultural awareness and sensitivity in the development of social robots for the elderly. By incorporating cultural elements into the design, these robots can provide elderly individuals with a sense of comfort and familiarity, and enhance the quality of the caregiving experience.

As shown in the Fig. 1, the Jetson Nano is responsible for managing the various inputs from the sensors and executing the algorithms that drive the

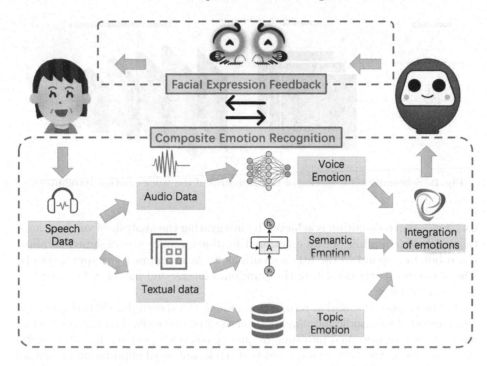

Fig. 2. Overall architecture of composite emotion recognition and feedback model.

robot's behavior. The sensors include a heat sensor, touch sensor, and microphone, which provide the robot with real-time information about the environment and the user's physical and emotional state. The touch screen interface allows the elderly to interact directly with the robot, providing a simple and intuitive means of communication. Additionally, the robot is equipped with two servo motors that control its Yaw and Pitch movements, allowing it to move in response to the user's actions and gestures. The printer feature enables DarumaTO to provide users with Omikuji (Japanese fortune-telling), advice, and reminders, adding a fun and engaging element to the overall experience. Finally, the external cabling to the Kamidana allows DarumaTO to read and transfer personal information, providing the robot with a more complete understanding of the user's preferences and needs.

3 Design of Composite Emotion Recognition

DarumaTO is able to communicate with people with simple dialogue as well as the facial expressions. Because of the privacy issue, DarumaTO does not equip with a camera. And this poses a challenge to its emotional interaction with older people. Different from the widely used recognition of user's emotion through visual information, this paper proposes a fused emotion recognition model through speech data. Under the premise of using only speech data, the

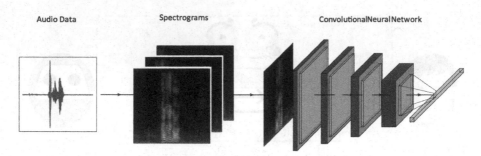

Fig. 3. Schematic visualization of the structure of the voice emotion recognition.

user's emotion recognition is achieved by integrating the analysis of voice, semantic and topic. In addition, an emotional feedback model was designed to allow the robot to respond to the user's emotions by facial expressions appropriately. The above two parts constitute the emotional interaction model of DarumaTO, as shown in Fig. 2.

In the composite emotion recognition model, the speech data is first recorded and converted into audio data and textual data respectively. And the time-series audio data is transformed into time-frequency resolved spectrograms after audio decomposition. The tokenization and text irrelevant word elimination of textual data needs to be conducted before further analysis.

3.1 Voice Emotion

In order to recognize and respond to emotional cues in the voice, DarumaTO employs advanced signal processing techniques that analyze various acoustic parameters of speech. These parameters are known to reflect physiological changes that occur in the speech production system during emotional states, such as changes in respiration, vocal fold frequency, and articulation [11]. The voice emotional detection model in DarumaTO categorizes a sample of audio data into one of several emotional classes, such as joy, anger, or sadness. This is achieved through the analysis of the parameters of the acoustic waveform, including fundamental frequency, jitter, pitch, speech rate, speech pauses, syllable rates, intensity, energy, and relative energy in different frequency bands. The use of these parameters allows DarumaTO to accurately detect and respond to the emotional state of the user, providing a more engaging and personalized experience. By combining speech analysis with other modalities, DarumaTO provides a comprehensive solution for emotional recognition and feedback in social robots.

In practice, the voice emotion detection is based on the signal decomposition of time-series audio wave signals into time-frequency resolved spectrograms. Then, the spectrograms generated above are passed through a CNN with partially frozen weights, which allows for transfer learning in parts of the network. Some of these weights were frozen because the Japanese language database was too small to train the model. We first pre-trained the model using other language databases, and later used the Japanese database for transfer learning. Note that the new Japanese variant is currently based on the OGVC [2], MULTEXT-J [14], and KEIO-ESD [15]. And the emotion labels are placed at the output of the network, as shown in Fig. 3.

When we want to use the model to recognise emotion, the model expects clear audio input from the end user's speech. The input data should be in wave format and last for several seconds to provide a reasonable basis for estimation. The data must be sampled at a minimum of 16kHz sampling frequency and 16 bit depth (i.e. 256 kbit/s bit rate). The model works with speech samples as short as one second. However, detection will be more reliable if longer samples are provided.

3.2 Semantic Emotion

ang_01 今回は見逃すけど二度目はないからな
ang_02 甘ったれるなよ
ang_03 何度思い返しても忌々しい

Fig. 4. Examples of semantic emotion dataset.

The so-called semantic model is to judge emotion by analysing the meaning of the linguistic information in the conversation, using the method as the Recurrent Neural Network (RNN) in the popular NLP deep learning. The sound signal received from the microphone is converted into text that can be used for semantic analysis, which can be simply understood as "dictation". To create the training set for the model, a 600-character text dataset was created with the labels "angry", "happy", "neutral" and "sad" to generally cover the emotions and attitudes of human conversations in life, as shown in Fig. 4. However, after experimental validation, we found that this database was too small to train the proposed model, so we created the necessary Japanese database by translating an English database [16].

Language is a communication tool, which is essentially a system of signs. Semantic is the information meaning expressed by language, which can be the form of the objective world or subjective thoughts and feelings. And we assume the dialogue is sequence of words that contains the consciousness and emotions of the speaker. In this paper, LSTM network is used for semantic emotion recognition because of its ability to process sequential data. The textual data is converted into word vector available to the neural network after word embedding by word2vec. The LSTM network is constructed as shown in Fig. 5 and trained by the dataset we made.

For our training data set, most of the training samples are composed of one or two long and short sentences, which is very suitable for the characteristics of the

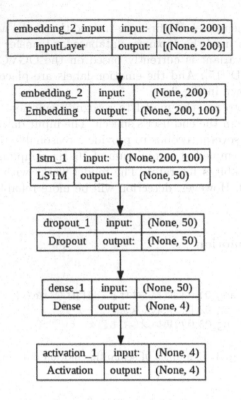

Fig. 5. The structure of LSTM for semantic emotion recognition.

LSTM model and can well capture the information and interaction relationship of word combination in sentences. Therefore, the core algorithm of the model uses the LSTM algorithm to fit the data set.

3.3 Topic Emotion

The proposed topic analysis method in DarumaTO is a novel approach to speech recognition that captures keywords and emotions in daily conversations. The method involves the creation of a set of topic keywords that reflect the emotions frequently expressed in recent years. These keywords, such as "COVID-19," "headache," "stress," and "birthday," play an important role in determining the emotional direction of conversations and avoiding misjudgments due to data noise. Therefore, we constructed a database of topics and mapped the topics in the database to emotion tags, as shown in Fig. 6.

The topic analysis method enhances DarumaTO's ability to analyze and understand speech, as it allows for error correction and judgment in ambiguous situations. This approach represents a significant improvement over existing speech recognition systems, as it emulates the human ability to understand statements and emotional nuances in conversation.

cat_begood	begood	goodheart	virtues
cat_blessing	blessing	beatitude	
cat_cat	cat		
cat_children	children	sons	offspring
cat_church	church		
cat_climate	climate	warming	
cat_death	death		
cat_disabled	disabled	impaired	
cat_divorce	divorce		

Fig. 6. Examples of topic dataset.

3.4 Integration

Afterwards, the emotion labels identified by the three approaches are mapped to the same emotional space, which in turn generates a composite emotion vector. Thus, the emotions of the elderly can be recognized by means of dialogues with the DarumaTO.

$$\widehat{Y} = \frac{1}{N}\sum_{i=1}^{N}\omega_i y_i \tag{1}$$

As shown in the Eq. 1, the results of each sentiment recognition model were mapped to the same dimensional space and a different result vector y was obtained separately. Correspondingly, the results of each model will have a confidence factor ω, which we use as a weight for their results. After a simple weighted average calculation, the final fusion result $\widehat{Y}$ can be obtained. In this paper, N is equal to 3, but offers the possibility of incorporating a wider range of emotion recognition models at a later stage.

4 Emotion Feedback with Facial Expression

The research shows that the facial display of a robot has a significant influence on the user experience of human-computer interaction [10]. And the screen mounted on top of the robot makes it possible to display a wide range of facial expressions. We therefore chose to use facial expressions as a channel for emotional feedback from the robot. DarumaTO's facial expressions consist of the eyes, eyebrows, nose, and beard. These organs are programmed to produce a certain degree of deformation and displacement to create different types of facial expressions.

Emotional feedback is not simply the reproduction of emotions or the feedback of opposing emotions to suppress negative emotions. Some people want to vent their feelings when they are angry or sad, or get empathy and understanding from others, so as to release the negative emotions in their hearts. Of course, when most people are faced with negative emotions, they can reconcile negative energy by receiving positive emotions, so as to achieve the function of comfort. Therefore, in this paper, we establish emotional feedback rules in such a way that older adults always receive positive emotional facilitation, as shown in Table 1.

Table 1. Human emotion and corresponding facial expression feedback.

Human Emotion	DarumaTO's Reaction
Angry	Fear
	Shocked
	Angry
Joy	Smiling
	Laughing
Neutral	Smiling
	Neutral
	Laughing
Sad	Smiling
	Sad
	Crying

5   Experiments and Analysis

In this section, we separately validate the sentiment recognition models proposed in this paper. As topic-based emotion recognition is performed by means of keyword retrieval, its performance is not discussed in this section.

5.1   Voice Emotion

The results in Fig. 7 indicate that the performance of the DarumaTO's voice emotion detection system was tested on each independent validation set, and the performance was evaluated using various metrics. In total, nine emotions were identified. Compared to a baseline zeroR classifier, the weighted average recall (WAR) of the system improved slightly from 0.26 to 0.30, while the unweighted average recall increased from 0.11 to 0.27. The weighted F1-score also improved from 0.10 to 0.30.

5.2   Semantic Emotion

As mentioned earlier, we trained the model by translating the English database due to the insufficient size of the Japanese database. However, this approach does have some limitations. One such limitation is the potential bias in Google Translate's understanding of English to Japanese translations, which can lead to significant cultural differences in the dataset. To overcome this issue, the authors used the English translation dataset as the training data and the original Japanese speech text dataset as the test data to verify the model's ability to understand and analyze real Japanese cultural contexts and dialogue situations.

Despite these limitations, the preprocessing of the dataset and the algorithmic model remained unchanged, and the previously mentioned method was still used. After 100 times of complete learning and training of the whole data set, we

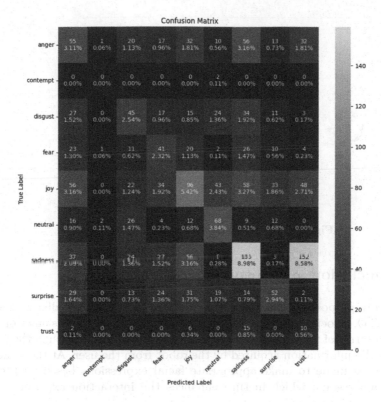

Fig. 7. Confusion matrix for the performance of voice emotion recognition in Japanese variant.

obtained the accuracy curve and loss function curve respectively on the training set and verification set. The accuracy of the new model was found to be 74% on the test dataset, as shown in Fig. 8. The loss was 0.52 and 0.69 on the training and validation sets, respectively (Fig. 9).

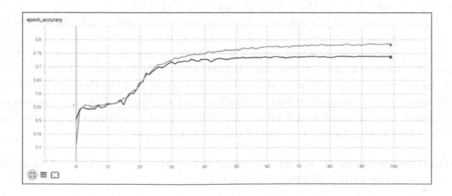

Fig. 8. Accuracy of semantic emotion recognition model.

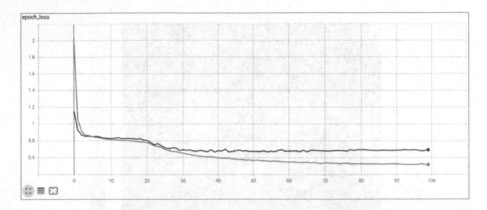

Fig. 9. Loss of semantic emotion recognition model.

6   Conclusion and Future Work

This study proposes a composite emotion recognition and feedback model for DarumaTO, a social robot for elderly users. The model performs emotion recognition in terms of voice, semantics and subject matter only through the analysis of the audio information acquired by the robot from the user. At the same time, the robot is made to make appropriate facial expressions based on the fused recognition results, which in turn enhances the interaction experience of the robot.

Although acceptable performance was achieved in the semantic emotion recognition section, the experimental results were poor in the voice emotion recognition. As the model was pre-trained in the English speech database and then transferred to the Japanese speech database, it was difficult to obtain good training results with the small amount of data in the Japanese speech database. This reflects the fact that there are significant differences in pronunciation styles between languages and that audio features cannot be transferred between languages, especially when there is an unequal level of data.

In the future, we will implement the emotion recognition and feedback model proposed in this paper into DarumaTO and hand it over to the elderly in nursing homes for evaluation. We will verify the validity of the model proposed in this paper by means of group comparison experiments. The DarumaTO with immobile facial expressions will be used as the control group and the DarumaTO fitted with an emotion recognition and feedback model will be used as the experimental group. Questionnaires and interviews will be used to obtain the satisfaction of the elderly with the two groups of robots respectively.

Acknowledgements. This work was supported by Ministry of Internal Affairs and Communications (MIC) of Japan (Grant no. JPJ000595).

References

1. Abdollahi, H., Mahoor, M., Zandie, R., Sewierski, J., Qualls, S.: Artificial emotional intelligence in socially assistive robots for older adults: A pilot study. IEEE Trans. Affect. Comput. (2022)
2. Arimoto, Y., Kawatsu, H., Ohno, S., Iida, H.: Naturalistic emotional speech collection paradigm with online game and its psychological and acoustical assessment. Acoust. Sci. Technol. **33**(6), 359–369 (2012)
3. Aronsson, A.S.: Social robots in elder care the turn toward emotional machines in contemporary japan. Japan. Rev. Cult. Anthropol. **21**(1), 421–455 (2020)
4. Broekens, J., Heerink, M., Rosendal, H., et al.: Assistive social robots in elderly care: A review. Gerontechnology **8**(2), 94–103 (2009)
5. Castillo, J.C., Fernández-Caballero, A., Castro-González, Á., Salichs, M.A., López, M.T.: A framework for recognizing and regulating emotions in the elderly. In: Pecchia, L., Chen, L.L., Nugent, C., Bravo, J. (eds.) IWAAL 2014. LNCS, vol. 8868, pp. 320–327. Springer, Cham (2014). https://doi.org/10.1007/978-3-319-13105-4 16
6. Demaeght, A., Miclau, C., Hartmann, J., Markwardt, J., Korn, O.: Multimodal emotion analysis of robotic assistance in elderly care. In: Proceedings of the 15th International Conference on Pervasive Technologies Related to Assistive Environments, pp. 230–236 (2022)
7. Du, Y., Lim, Y., Tan, Y.: A novel human activity recognition and prediction in smart home based on interaction. Sensors **19**(20), 4474 (2019)
8. Du, Y., Lim, Y., Tan, Y.: Rf-arp: Rfid-based activity recognition and prediction in smart home. In: 2019 IEEE 25th International Conference on Parallel and Distributed Systems (ICPADS), pp. 618–624. IEEE (2019)
9. Getson, C., Nejat, G.: Socially assistive robots helping older adults through the pandemic and life after covid-19. Robotics **10**(3), 106 (2021)
10. Hashimoto, T., Hitramatsu, S., Tsuji, T., Kobayashi, H.: Development of the face robot Saya for rich facial expressions. In: 2006 SICE-ICASE International Joint Conference, pp. 5423–5428. IEEE (2006)
11. Johnstone, T., Scherer, K.R.: Vocal communication of emotion. Handb. Emotions **2**, 220–235 (2000)
12. Kasser, V.G., Ryan, R.M.: The relation of psychological needs for autonomy and relatedness to vitality, well-being, and mortality in a nursing home 1. J. Appl. Soc. Psychol. **29**(5), 935–954 (1999)
13. Khosla, R., Chu, M.T., Nguyen, K.: Enhancing emotional well being of elderly using assistive social robots in Australia. In: 2013 International Conference on Biometrics and Kansei Engineering, pp. 41–46. IEEE (2013)
14. Kitazawa, S.: "Prosody and speech processing" Japanese multext prosodic corpus (multext-j) (2010)
15. Mori, S., Moriyama, T., Ozawa, S.: Emotional speech synthesis using subspace constraints in prosody. In: 2006 IEEE International Conference on Multimedia and Expo, pp. 1093–1096. IEEE (2006)
16. Mower, E., Matarić, M.J., Narayanan, S.: A framework for automatic human emotion classification using emotion profiles. IEEE Trans. Audio Speech Lang. Process. **19**(5), 1057–1070 (2010)

My Actions Speak Louder Than Your Words: When User Behavior Predicts Their Beliefs About Agents' Attributes

Nikolos Gurney(✉) , David V. Pynadath , and Ning Wang

Institute for Creative Technologies, Viterbi School of Engineering, Computer Science Department, University of Southern California, Los Angeles, CA, USA
{gurney,pynadath,nwang}@ict.usc.edu

Abstract. An implicit expectation of asking users to rate agents, such as an AI decision-aid, is that they will use only relevant information—ask them about an agent's benevolence, and they should consider whether or not it was kind. Behavioral science, however, suggests that people sometimes use irrelevant information. We identify an instance of this phenomenon, where users who experience better outcomes in a human-agent interaction systematically rated the agent as having better abilities, being more benevolent, and exhibiting greater integrity in a post hoc assessment than users who experienced worse outcomes—which were the result of their own behavior—with the same agent. Our analyses suggest the need for augmentation of models so they account for such biased perceptions as well as mechanisms so that agents can detect and even actively work to correct this and similar biases of users.

Keywords: Agent factors · Trait attribution · Cognitive bias · Agent-user interactions

1 Introduction

Perceived trustworthiness of an AI agent (we simplify this to *agent*) is frequently referenced as an important determinant of successful human-agent interactions (e.g. [4,11,27]). A widely cited explanation for how humans think about trustworthiness posits that people consider three factors, or traits, of a person (or agent) when they evaluate trustworthiness: ability, benevolence, and integrity [18]. It is common practice for intelligent agent researchers to adapt a psychometric inventory of this three-factor model of trustworthiness for assessing users'

Part of the effort behind this work was sponsored by the Defense Advanced Research Projects Agency (DARPA) under contract number W911NF2010011. The work was or is also sponsored by the U.S. Army Research Laboratory (ARL) under contract number W911NF-14-D-0005. The content of the information does not necessarily reflect the position or the policy of the U.S. Government or the Defense Advanced Research Projects Agency, and no official endorsements should be inferred.

H. Degen and S. Ntoa (Eds.): HCII 2023, LNAI 14051, pp. 232–248, 2023.
https://doi.org/10.1007/978-3-031-35894-4_17

perceived trustworthiness of agents [17]. In theory, administering the inventory prior to an interaction allows researchers to assess the role of anticipated agent trustworthiness in users' behavior, while post hoc administration allows researchers to assess whether particular elements of an interaction, perhaps an experimental manipulation, impacted users' opinions of the agent.

In practice, however, people frequently misuse information when they form judgments and make decisions [6,15]. For example, a person who is momentarily happy (sad), perhaps from reminiscing about a positive (negative) event from their recent past, is likely to rate their life satisfaction as higher (lower) than if you asked them when they were in a neutral state [24]. Regardless of the saliency of information, the normative approach is to always use it the same way. That is, the negative life event and the related emotions (the information) should always be factored into the assessment the same way—in most instances, because such information is highly subjective and often irrelevant, this means not integrating it at all.

A person taking a normative approach to human-agent trust might form perceptions of the agent's ability, benevolence, and integrity based solely on its behavior, particularly the degree to which its behavior was consistent with that of someone who had those qualities. If people followed such a "rational" approach, we would expect their perceptions of the agent to depend entirely on its behavior and how said behavior impacted outcomes, not on their own subsequent decisions or feelings about those decisions regardless of the agent's input. To illustrate a *non-normative approach*, imagine two graduate students writing literature reviews for a course on intelligent agents. The students are matched in every imaginable way, e.g. aptitude, intellect, motivation, etc., and both have access to the same intelligent, although fallible, literature-review agent. One student happens to appropriately follow the agent's correct advice and ignore its incorrect advice on relevant papers. The other student, who received the exact same advice from the agent, failed to make the right choices, purely by chance. Their respective success in navigating the literature is reflected in the grades that they receive, with the former student receiving a higher grade than the latter. A normative prediction would be that the grades received do not affect the students' perception of the agent, as the agent's advice to the students was identical. However, one can easily imagine that if both students rate the agent's traits after they are told their grades that the former student will rate the agent's traits more positively than the latter will, despite the agent providing them with the same input on their assignments and there being no meaningful difference between the students.

More generally, we expect that people's perceptions of the agent's ability, benevolence, and integrity will be biased by the outcomes of the overall interaction, even when stochasticity and their own decisions affect those outcomes. In particular, the same agent exhibiting the same behavior will be rated more positively on these measures by people who experience more positive outcomes, all else being equal. It is important to note that such a difference in ratings would appear even when people followed a Bayesian prescription *if* the positive outcomes were attributable to better performance by the agent. To distinguish between the biased and unbiased perceptions, we must therefore ensure that the agent's behavior (including mistakes made, the language used, etc.) is either identical across participants or else control for these differences in our analysis.

We report analyses testing this research question using data that were collected in two prior human-agent interaction studies, one of trust calibration [27] and another of compliance [9,19]. Each data set represents interactions with a simulated robot that provided users with safety recommendations during a search-based task. After completing a mission, i.e., searching a fixed number of locations, study participants (users) responded to a battery of questions about their interactions with the agent, including a modified version of the trust inventory reported in [17]. We show that a higher percentage of correct choices during the task was correlated with more positive ratings of the agent's traits, all else being equal. That is, after controlling for treatment conditions and the total number of times that a participant complied with the robot's recommendations, participants' percentage of correct compliance choices was still a meaningful instrument for predicting how they viewed the robot's ability, benevolence, and integrity ratings.

We suggest that this points to the users' own private information, e.g. an affective state related to the experiment, coloring their evaluations of their AI teammate. Such behavior is well studied in humans and commonly known as the *fundamental attribution error* [21]. This cognitive bias occurs when people over-weight dispositional features of the person and underweight situational factors when forming judgments. The results of our analyses are important for multiple reasons, but minimally because:

- Agents can benefit from accurate models of the beliefs the people maintain about them [7,8] and this result may prove beneficial to such models.
- It highlights a possible bias in the way that people think about agents that developers can potentially correct.
- It suggests factors to be included in existing models of cognition that do not currently consider how such seemingly irrelevant personal information is used by people when they anthropomorphize an agent (e.g. [3,20]).

2 Data

Both experiments relied on adaptations of an online human-agent interaction simulation testbed from [28]. The testbed was designed to study how giving an AI the ability to verbally explain its recommendations impacted participants' trust. This was accomplished by pairing participants with an intelligent robot during a simulated reconnaissance mission. Each mission was comprised of a series of potentially dangerous locations for the team to clear. Entering a dangerous location without the appropriate protective equipment always resulted in death, but the protective equipment also always neutralized a threat. The robot entered each location before the participant and then recommended whether

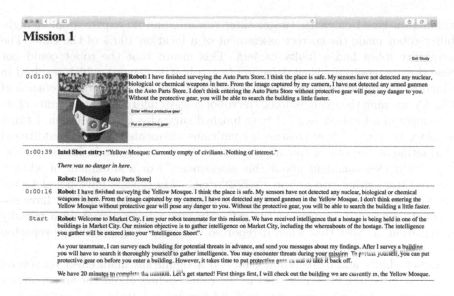

Fig. 1. Screenshot from HRI testbed

or not the participant needed to put on protective gear. It based these recommendations on readings from three sensors—a camera, microphone, and nuclear, biological, and chemical (NBC) sensor—which were potentially faulty. The participants were then free to follow or ignore the robot's recommendation, with the outcome depending on their decision. During the second study, the robot also learned about the accuracy of its sensors using machine learning and then communicated to the study participant any updates that it made to its decision algorithm. Finally, the incentive structure was designed to motivate participants to clear locations quickly and without dying. Figure 1 is a screenshot of the interface taken early in one such mission.

Importantly, the robot's sensor readings in both studies were scripted to generate a fixed sequence of correct/incorrect readings and recommendations. Thus, participants who experienced different outcomes did so only because of differences in their own decisions to follow or ignore the robot's recommendations.

2.1 Study 1 Task and Treatment Conditions

Participants in study 1 worked with one of eight different versions of the robot (a 2 × 4 design) to complete three separate missions, each of which had eight locations to clear (see [27] for a complete explanation). Each participant worked with the same robot version for all three missions. All of the robots used a Partially Observable Markov Decision Process (POMDP) [13] to form beliefs and select recommendations based on their sensor readings. The different robots, thus behaviors, were generated by crossing two ability levels, high and low, with four different types of explanations: confidence-level explanation, observation explanation based on either two or three sensors, and no explanation. A high-ability robot made the correct assessment of a location 100% of the time. The low-ability robot had a faulty camera. This meant that the robot could not sense threats requiring visual detection (e.g. a hostile person), which resulted in it incorrectly reporting such locations as being safe for an overall accuracy of 80%. Concerning the explanations, the robot always informed participants of its assessment of a location (e.g., "I have finished surveying the opium den. I think the place is safe."). Three treatment conditions augmented this with additional information at the end of the message: the robot's confidence in its assessment (e.g. "I am 78% confident about this assessment.") or a statement of what it observed from either two or three sensors (e.g. "My sensors have not detected any NBC weapons in here. From the image captured by my camera, I have not detected any armed gunmen in the cafe. My microphone picked up a friendly conversation."). Note that when it reported sensor readings, it always reported the same type and number of readings for a participant.

Robot ability and explanation type had a significant main effect on several measured outcomes, including trust in the robot, beliefs about the transparency of its communications, compliance with its recommendations, and participants' fraction of correct decisions. Participants that worked with the high-ability robot were more positive in their ratings, but interestingly, they did not necessarily perform better given its ability. Also of note is the impact of explanations: in the case of the low-ability robot, better explanations were correlated with better decision-making by participants. More complete analyses and explanations are available in [27].

2.2 Study 2 Task and Treatment Conditions

Participants in study 2 worked with one of three robots during a single mission comprised of 45 locations [9,19]. The robots of study 2 differed from those of study 1 in that they used model-free reinforcement learning (RL) [14,25] instead of POMDPs. The resulting dynamics in their behavior induced additional richness in their assessment explanations. The simplest robot offered no explanation of its assessment, which yielded messages similar to the base messages of study 1. The medium-sophistication robot added an explanation of its decision process (e.g. "I think the place is dangerous. My NBC sensors have detected traces of dangerous chemicals."). The most sophisticated explanation conveyed the robot's decision and learning processes (e.g. "It seems that my estimate of the Unemployment Office was incorrect. I've updated the parameters of my model based on this result. I will give the same recommendation if my sensors pick up the same readings in the future."). There was not an ability manipulation in study 2.

The robot generated its decision and learning explanations based on self-generated decision-tree representations of its current RL policy. The robot used the path through the tree to explain its decision process and any changes to the tree during the most recent update of its policy to explain what it had learned [19]. When the robot provided both a decision and a learning explanation, participant compliance was significantly higher than when it provided only the decision or no explanation at all. Moreover, this effect appeared to be driven by the decision to follow the robot's advice to *not* equip the protective gear. In the case of making correct decisions, the participants in the decision and learning explanations group again did significantly better than the other two groups. More complete analyses and explanations are available in [19].

2.3 Measures

The main dependent variables of interest are the average responses to the three modified sub-measures for ability, benevolence, and integrity from the Mayer and Davis trust inventory. We are not interested here in predicting how mission outcomes impacted "trust" ratings as measured, holistically, by the Mayer and Davis scale items. Rather, we are interested in participants' perceptions of the individual traits that are measured by the scale and if these are predicted by their individual mission outcomes, all else being equal.

The original scale was developed to measure trust in managers, which is reflected in the items (e.g. "Top management is very capable of performing its job."). Some items required only editing any references to management to refer to the robot instead. Others, however, were altogether irrelevant. The final measures used in the experiments are reproduced below with a "*" indicating reverse coding of a variable.

In addition to the ability questions of the original Mayer and Davis inventory, the robot ability measure included items related to its specific instruments (camera, microphone, and NBC sensor).

1. The robot is capable of performing its tasks.
2. I feel confident about the robot's capability.
3. The robot has specialized capabilities that can increase our performance.
4. The robot is well qualified for this job.
5. The robot's capable of making sound decisions based on its sensor readings.
6. The robot's NBC (nuclear, biological, and chemical weapon) sensor is capable of making accurate readings.
7. The robot's microphone is capable of making accurate readings.
8. The robot's camera is capable of making accurate readings.
9. I feel confident about the robot's NBC sensor's sensing capability.
10. I feel confident about the robot's camera's sensing capability.
11. I feel confident about the robot's microphone's sensing capability.
12. I feel confident about the robot's sensors.
13. The robot is aware of its own limitations.

The five benevolence items, again slightly modified from the original scale to better fit the human-agent interaction domain (versus management), are:

1. The robot is concerned about my welfare.
2. I feel that my needs and desires are important to the robot.

3. The robot would not knowingly do anything to hurt me.
4. The robot looks out for what is important to me.
5. The robot understands my goals in the mission.

One item, "Top management will go out of its way to help me" was removed and replaced by item (5) because the robot's propensity to help participants was fixed, i.e., it could not go out of its way.

Similarly, the integrity scale was trimmed from six to three items, but without replacement. Two removed items dealt with irrelevant topics (justice and fairness) and the third implied that the robot would share its plans, which it did not. The three items are:

1. The robot's actions and behaviors are not very consistent.*
2. I like the robot's values.
3. Sound principles seem to guide the robot's behavior.

Participants were asked to "Please rate the extent to which you agree with the following statement" for each item in the inventory. The 7-point scale ranged from *Strongly Disagree* to *Strongly Agree*. The measures for each sub-item are computed by mapping the scale responses to values from 1–7, 1 representing strongly disagree and 7 strongly agree, and averaging across the inventory items.

Participants in study 1 completed this inventory three times, once after each mission, thus we compute a composite score by averaging across all three measurements. Study 2 participants completed the inventory only once, so no composite was necessary.

Our independent variables include controls for the treatment conditions, which we delineated above and are addressed in the aforementioned citations. The two predictor variables of interest are the percentage of times that a participant followed the robot's recommendation and the percentage of times that they made the correct decision. In the three high-ability conditions of study 1, perfect compliance and perfect decision-making coincide because the robot never errs. In the other three treatment conditions of study 1 and all the conditions of study 2, the robot made mistakes, thus perfect compliance did not equate to perfect decision-making.

3   Analyses

We rely on regression modeling to test our hypothesized relationship between participants' performance and their eventual responses to the inventory items. The control model is:

$$Y_i = \beta_0 + \beta_{\text{Treat}} X_{i1} + \epsilon_i \tag{1}$$

And the hypothesized model is:

$$Y_i = \beta_0 + \beta_{\text{CP}} X_{i\text{CP}} + \beta_{\text{FP}} X_{i\text{FP}} + \beta_{\text{Treat}} X_{i1} + \epsilon_i \tag{2}$$

Y is the measure of a given trait, that is, ability, benevolence, or integrity. β_0 is the intercept and captures a control condition for the given experiment. These are the Constant values in the regression tables. β_{CP} is the variable of interest, correct percentage of choices. β_{FP} controls for the percentage of times that a participant followed the robot's advice. β_{Treat} captures the treatment conditions of the experiments, i.e., they account for what experimental condition that a participant experienced. We do not include the treatment condition fitted values in the tables for brevity's sake, as we are only interested in how a participant's choices during the mission(s) were correlated with their later ratings of the agent. The regression model, in effect, allows us to isolate the impact of the experimental conditions from the impact of a participant's own choices on their eventual ratings of the robot.

We report the fitted values of the regression models in a separate table for each study. As noted, we do not report values for the treatment conditions, which are discussed in the original papers; however, their presence in the models is indicated by "Controls" and a "Yes." Unfortunately, in Study 1, only a subset

Table 1. Study 1 Regression Models

| | Dependent variable: | | | | | |
| | Ability | | Benevolence | | Integrity | |
	(1)	(2)	(3)	(4)	(5)	(6)
CP		0.122		3.016*		1.913*
		(1.453)		(1.262)		(0.894)
FP		1.889		−1.024		−0.254
		(1.360)		(1.127)		(0.798)
Constant	5.871***	4.344***	4.557***	2.741***	4.466***	3.036***
	(0.144)	(0.677)	(0.227)	(0.621)	(0.161)	(0.440)
Controls	Yes	Yes	Yes	Yes	Yes	Yes
Obs	78	78	199	199	109	199
R^2	0.031	0.132	0.052	0.099	0.209	0.257
Adj. R^2	0.005	0.085	0.032	0.070	0.193	0.233
RSE	0.777	0.745	1.355	1.328	0.965	0.941
–	(df = 75)	(df = 73)	(df = 194)	(df = 192)	(df = 194)	(df = 192)
F Stat.	1.203	2.780*	2.654*	3.498**	12.837***	11.044***
–	(df = 2; 75)	(df = 4; 73)	(df = 4; 194)	(df = 6; 192)	(df = 4; 194)	(df = 6; 192)

Note: *p<0.05; **p<0.01; ***p<0.001

Each column in the table represents a different regression model. (1), (3), and (5) are the control models in which the dependent variable of interest, noted above the column numbers, is predicted only by the treatment conditions of the experiment (the "Controls," which are addressed in the original research). The other columns report the hypothesized models in which the correct choice percentage, CP, controlling for compliance, FP, predicts the trait ratings. The Constant β parameter for each model is the average participant response to the given inventory in the basic experimental condition. The primary coefficient of interest, β_{CP}, represents the change in the $\beta_{Constant}$ when going from 0% to 100% correct decisions. The mean correct choices were 20.632 and 29.436 for studies 1 and 2, respectively. These are roughly what one would expect from the average participant captured by the Constant. Thus, adding the β_{CP} to this would be incorrect. Instead, adding β_{CP}/n, where n is the number of choices in the given study, yields the effect of the average person making one more correct choice (or one fewer when subtracted).

of participants provided complete responses to the Ability measure leaving the related models underpowered (models (1) and (2) of Table 1). The coefficients for two continuous variables, β_{CP} and β_{FP}, should be interpreted as the expected percentage change in the dependent variable, all else being equal, if the predicted variable (a rating for Ability, Benevolence, or Integrity) were to go from zero to one.

Interpretation of the β_{CP} values is not entirely straightforward. Recall that in the ordinary least squares regression model a β value represents a one-unit change in the variable. Because our independent variables are percentages, a one-unit change would represent going from no correct choices to all correct choices. The regression model, however, represents a hypothetical average participant and the mean correct choices were 20.632 and 29.436 for studies 1 and 2, respectively. Thus, to understand how getting one additional choice correct would hypothetically impact a benevolence rating, we can divide the β_{CP} value by the total number of choices and add or subtract this from the average benevolence rating to see how a 1 choice difference would, hypothetically, change the benevolence score. In study 1, the average increase in rated benevolence for each additional correct choice was $3.016/24 = 0.126$, and in study 2, $4.522/45 = 0.100$, all else being equal. With these explanations of the fitted values in mind, interpreting the models becomes much more meaningful.[1]

In the case of both sets of study data, we reject the null hypothesis that there is no correlation between the correct choice percentage and ratings of an agent's benevolence (see the fourth column and first row of Tables 1 and 2). The more

Table 2. Study 2 Regression Models

	Dependent variable:					
	Ability		Benevolence		Integrity	
	(1)	(2)	(3)	(4)	(5)	(6)
CP		3.034*		4.522**		−0.707
		(1.377)		(1.640)		(1.605)
FP		−2.884*		−5.211***		1.130 (1.481)
		(1.271)		(1.513)		
Constant	5.117***	5.159***	5.135***	5.800***	4.333***	4.021***
	(0.116)	(0.268)	(0.143)	(0.320)	(0.134)	(0.313)
Controls	Yes	Yes	Yes	Yes	Yes	Yes
Obs	159	159	159	159	159	159
R^2	0.150	0.177	0.025	0.114	0.012	0.023
Adj. R^2	0.139	0.156	0.013	0.091	−0.0002	−0.003
RSE	0.861	0.852	1.058	1.015	0.992	0.993
–	(df = 156)	(df = 154)	(df = 156)	(df = 154)	(df = 156)	(df = 154)
F Stat.	13.737***	8.297***	2.005	4.966***	0.986	0.899
–	(df = 2; 156)	(df = 4; 154)	(df = 2; 156)	(df = 4; 154)	(df = 2; 156)	(df = 4; 154)

Note: *p<0.05; **p<0.01; ***p<0.001

---

[1] CP and FP are, obviously, correlated, however, controlling for the variance that they mutually explain via an interaction term was not warranted. Doing so for both study 1 and study 2 did not result in better model fits, so we stick to the simpler models in which they only individually explain variance.

Table 3. Benevolence Model Comparisons

Statistic	Study 1	Study 2
	Control (3) Vs. CP (4)	Control (3) Vs. CP (4)
Sum of Sq	17.532	15.963
F	4.968	7.755
$Pr(>F)$	0.008	<0.001

Results of ANOVAs comparing the treatment only and hypothesized models.

correct choices that participants made, the higher they rated the robot's benevolence. Keep in mind that these models are controlling for any differences in what the robot actually did or said. Moreover, F tests from ANOVAs comparing the treatment only and hypothesized models support acceptance of the hypothesized models (see Table 3). This finding supports the idea that participants were using, arguably irrelevant, personal information when evaluating the robot's benevolence. When we control for the fraction of times that a participant followed the robot and the experimental treatment condition they received, the only experiential differences, then any remaining variance in the model explained by CP must be an artifact of the participants. To reiterate our position, if participants were only using the normatively correct information (the robot's recommendations, whether those recommendations were correct, and the harm created by bad recommendations), then the percentage of correct choices that a participant made should not factor into their evaluation of the robot. When it does, then it points to participants using extemporaneous information—we argue their own affective state, or how they feel about the interaction and outcome.

As noted, the Ability measure was only completed by a fraction of the participants in Study 1, leaving these models underpowered. Study 1 included six treatment conditions. There are simply too few responses (78 in total that completed the measure) in each condition to have statistical power, nevertheless, we included the models for completeness. The data from Study 2 do suggest, however, that we can reject the null hypothesis that there is no correlation between the correct choice percentage and ratings of the agent's ability (columns (1) and (2) of Table 2). Note, however, that the richer model, Table 2 column (2), did not explain a significantly higher amount of variance than the control model in column (1). Table 4 presents the F test from an ANOVA comparing these two models. We interpret this as weak support for our hypothesis that people are using personal information when evaluating the robot's ability. This may be attributable to the task setting and somewhat limited interactions with the robot. Whereas benevolence is a dispositional trait of the robot, ability is situational. It is feasible that participants were somewhat more reserved if they thought the robot would be better (or worse) if another setting, thus were less extreme in their evaluations.

Table 4. Study 2 Ability Model Comparison

Statistic	Control (1) Vs. CP (2)
Sum of Sq	3.747
F	2.580
$Pr(>F)$	0.079

Results of an ANOVA comparing the treatment and hypothesized models for Study 2.

The data from Study 1 suggest that we can reject the null hypothesis that there is no correlation between the correct choice percentage and the ratings of the agent's integrity; however, the Study 2 data do not support this conclusion (columns (5) and (6) of Tables 1 and 2). Additionally, an F test from an ANOVA reported in Table 5 revealed that the model which controls for correct choice percentage, Table 1 column (6), explains a significantly greater amount of variance than the control model, column (5). The integrity sub-scale, as we mentioned, was significantly trimmed due to many items in the scale lacking relevance for our setting. In retrospect, it is not surprising that these results were not significant as having fewer items in the measure will result in a more chaotic variance structure (i.e. make it less friendly to prediction).

Table 5. Study 1 Integrity Model Comparison

Statistic	Control (1) Vs. CP (2)
Sum of Sq	10.817
F	6.108
$Pr(>F)$	0.003

Results of an ANOVA comparing the treatment and hypothesized models for Study 1.

4   Discussion

Psychologists have long studied how people ascribe individual factors, from knowledge (ability) to personality traits (benevolence and integrity), to others. Generally, those others are humans. Occasionally, they are animals, plants, and even inanimate objects. In these instances, we say that the person is anthropomorphizing the object, or in other words, they are implying that the object has human-like traits. Increasingly, people interact with intelligent agents imbued with capabilities that reflect the factors we see in other humans, such as the robots of the above experiments which were capable of explaining their decision-making processes in human-interpretable terms. Thus, it is somewhat unsurprising when people start ascribing those factors to such agents, just as they do with pets, etc.

When a person anthropomorphizes an agent, they attribute human-like mental states to the agent which can lead them to react differently to its behavior [3]. Researchers and developers that work in the HCI, HRI, and similar spaces explicitly try to curate such anthropomorphic responses [2, 29], whether through clever design (e.g. having an agent use gestures that match its speech [22]) or actual implementation of human-like traits (e.g. incorporating personality traits into an agent that mimic those of a human [1]). There is some evidence, albeit conflicted, that the personality traits designed into an agent may color how a person interprets said agent's behavior. For example, some people may or may not prefer that an agent's degree of extroversion matches their own [1, 12, 26]. It is also worth noting that anthropomorphism is not necessarily a mindful process, meaning that the simple presence of cues that suggest human-like traits can result in the mindless anthropomorphism of an agent [16]. It is even possible that the simple act of asking people whether or not an agent acted in a benevolent fashion triggers them to anthropomorphize it, as it is well documented that the way in which we ask such questions can in part determine responses [23].

In psychology, the study of how a person gathers and uses information in causal judgments is known as *attribution theory* [5], a process that is closely tied to the tendency to anthropomorphize non-human objects. Psychologists generally divide attributions into dispositional, in which the cause of the behavior is assigned to the agent, and situational, in which the cause of behavior is assigned to events or other external factors. One of the earliest experimental investigations of attribution asked study participants to watch an animation in which shapes moved around on the screen and describe what they observed [10]. The famous result of the experiment is that participants spontaneously attributed traits to the shapes solely on the short animation. The attributed traits included both dispositional traits, such as one shape being a bully, and situational, such as one shape being afraid of a particular event (but not having a generalized trait of fearfulness). The reconnaissance mission data demonstrate instances of both types of attribution: the agent's ability being situational and its degree of benevolence and integrity dispositional. Absent from the literature on anthropomorphizing agents and attribution theory, however, is the artifact observed in the reconnaissance mission data: individual's choices coloring their attribution of traits to other agents.

The observed effect appears to be a close cousin of a well-studied phenomenon in social psychology: the fundamental attribution error, or the tendency of people to overweight dispositional factors, like personality traits, and underweight situational factors when judging others' behavior and the associated outcomes [21]. In interpersonal interactions, this often looks like blaming a poor outcome on a person, particularly because of some aspect of who they are, rather than contextual features that were more likely the causal factors. Unfortunately, the data that we analyzed do not support the identification of the precise cognitive process that is driving the error that we observed. A few possible explanations include: using information about one's affective state (a person feels good or bad and then projects that onto the assessment), explanation-seeking behavior (a person needs to explain a phenomenon and it is more comfortable to blame the robot than themselves), or switching between causal and counterfactual reasoning based on outcomes, to name a few. In other words, situational factors, e.g. a person's affective state, can also influence personality trait judgments. In cases of repeated interactions with an agent, this sets up the potential for a perverse cycle where the accuracy of people's beliefs related to the factors engineered into an agent is contingent on and reinforced by their subjective experiences. There is extensive literature on the fundamental attribution error, including work on how to reduce or eliminate the bias. We believe that extending the existing literature into the human-agent systems arena is important for future work.

4.1   Limitations

This research has three main limitations: 1) it considers ratings of only a narrow set of attributes, 2) it looks at data from only a single experimental paradigm, and 3) it does not consider the full spectrum of judgments made during trait attributions. Obviously, both humans and agents have a broad range of factors that define who they are. Some of these factors are situational, such as ability. If any of the authors were judged on their ability to play American football, for example, the reality is that we are poor players to such a degree that, even if a fellow teammate were judging us after winning the Super Bowl, they would almost certainly still say that we are terrible. Conversely, if one of us were asked to rate another on their research skills, the outcome of a recent journal or conference submission may very well color that assessment. On the other hand, certain ratings of some dispositional traits, such as integrity or benevolence, may be impacted by outcomes in domains where the factor under consideration does not matter. To illustrate, rather than rating research skills, perhaps one author rates the likeability of a coauthor after a paper rejection. Our results suggest that this rating would be lower, all else being equal, than if we just received an acceptance.

This all, of course, is contingent on the result generalizing outside of the research paradigm that we examined. Although our intuition is that it will, we do not have data to support that intuition. Like any correlational result, it is entirely possible that the observed effect is an artifact of the particular experimental interactions and settings. Thus, additional research is needed to generalize the effect that we observe across different agent factors and settings.

Finally, there are at least three different judgments a person must make when attributing agent factors as they did in the data we analyzed: is the attribute situationally relevant, whether the agent does in fact possess the attribute, and if so, to what degree. Each individual judgment comes with an opportunity to appropriately, or not, use information. Our interpretation of the result is that study participants misused their own, private information, e.g., their affective state related to mission performance, when making a judgment about the degree to which the agent possessed each trait. The first judgment, situational relevance, was largely unnecessary as the questions were designed to either be or imply relevance. The second judgment, about the actual presence of the factors, was obviated as well by the questions: they were conveyed in a way that assumed that the agent, at least to some degree, had the attributes. Thus, the data that we analyzed did not allow us to study, precisely, when the flawed judgment was occurring.

Another, we believe minor limitation, to interpreting our results is the narrowness of the integrity scale. As pointed out, the studies that donated the data only asked participants a portion of the questions in the integrity sub-scale. This was due to the original questions not having relevance to the HRI setting of the experiments. Obviously, changing domains already undermines the scale and warrants revalidation (arguably, new inventories need to be developed for human-agent interactions). Decreasing the number of questions in the inventory further exasperates this problem.

5   Conclusions and Future Work

We document instances of people providing ratings of agents that, rather than only considering information about the agent, reflect their experiences from a task in which they worked with the agent. For example, participants that did better in the task, all else being equal, tended to rate the benevolence of the agent higher. An implicit expectation of asking users to rate agents is that they will use only relevant information. These results point to people not following this normative expectation and using unrelated information in their evaluations. The traits in question, ability, benevolence, and integrity, are widely accepted as important components of trustworthiness. Thus, our findings suggest that the perceived trustworthiness of an agent, which is argued to impact compliance [9,27], may be influenced by irrelevant information.

The data that we analyzed were not collected for this purpose; rather, they were collected to study how different degrees of explainability impact compliance. The measures were included out of a matter of practice; that is, their presence was not hypothesis-driven. Thus, the first step in future work is to undertake hypothesis-driven research in which experimental manipulation is used to study the correlation between attribute ratings and interaction outcomes. This includes using empirically validated measures for a broader range of traits in different empirical settings as well as formulating clearly stated hypotheses. One simple prediction is that positive (negative) interactions will lead to higher (lower) ratings of positive traits and lower (higher) ratings of negative traits. A related research question is: does the relevance of the trait to the interaction co-vary with the ratings? The prediction is that a highly important trait will receive more extreme ratings based on outcomes than a less relevant one.

Once these initial research questions are answered, the critical next step is exploring the cognitive processes driving the phenomenon. As noted, there are multiple plausible explanations, such as user affect, explanation-seeking behavior, and switching between causal and counterfactual reasoning based on outcomes—in all likelihood, it is some combination of these and other reasoning processes. Taking a controlled, experimental approach will allow us to understand how much variance each explanation may account for. We believe that the resulting insights will contribute to the development of more robust user models for deployment in agents.

To illustrate, consider the hypothesis that a person uses personal information about their own affective state when rating the agent's traits. This hypothesis factors down into two sub-predictions: first, there is the prediction that participants experience an affective response to the mission outcome, specifically, that they have a negative (positive) emotional response to doing poorly (well). Second, the contingent prediction, is that participants misuse this private information about their own affective state when rating the agent. Rather than allowing for performance and affect to vary naturally, we could fix performance such that all participants achieve similar results and induce different affective states, either related to the mission or not, and then collect assessments of the agent. This simple design would allow us to validate the misuse of affective information prediction as well as test the role of setting relevancy. Knowing how participants may (mis)use information about their own affective state may allow developers to anticipate and avoid the error.

Another example of an aspect of the phenomenon that the data do not support exploring is whether priming participants about the eventual rating will alter how they view the interaction. To illustrate, telling participants before an interaction that they will eventually rate an agent's benevolence may change what information they ultimately use—it might even debias their responses such that they do not use irrelevant information, like their own affective state. Such debiasing experiments, once the variance in ratings is explained, are important steps toward curating predictable, appropriate interactions with intelligent agents.

The perceived trustworthiness of AI agents is often cited as a determinant of successful human-agent interactions. Ideally, such perceptions would be based entirely on the features and behavior of the agent—not extemporaneous information. We believe that the effect documented herein, that a human's perception of an agent can change based on their own private information such as a feeling or emotion, points to an important aspect of human-agent interaction that should be more thoroughly studied.

References

1. Cafaro, A., Vilhjálmsson, H.H., Bickmore, T.: First impressions in human-agent virtual encounters. ACM Trans. Comput. Hum. Interact. (TOCHI) **23**(4), 1–40 (2016)
2. De Visser, E.J., et al.: Almost human: anthropomorphism increases trust resilience in cognitive agents. J. Exp. Psychol. Appl. **22**(3), 331 (2016)
3. Epley, N., Waytz, A., Cacioppo, J.T.: On seeing human: a three-factor theory of anthropomorphism. Psychol. Rev. **114**(4), 864 (2007)
4. Ferrario, A., Loi, M., Viganò, E.: In AI we trust incrementally: a multi-layer model of trust to analyze human-artificial intelligence interactions. Philos. Technol. **33**(3), 523–539 (2020)

5. Fiske, S.T., Taylor, S.E.: Social Cognition. Mcgraw-Hill Book Company, New York (1991)
6. Gigerenzer, G., Gaissmaier, W.: Heuristic decision making. Annu. Rev. Psychol. **62**, 451–482 (2011)
7. Gurney, N., Marsella, S., Ustun, V., Pynadath, D.V.: Operationalizing theories of theory of mind: a survey. In: Gurney, N., Sukthankar, G. (eds.) Computational Theory of Mind for Human-Machine Teams. AAAI-FSS 2021. Lecture Notes in Computer Science, vol. 13775. Springer, Cham (2022). https://doi.org/10.1007/978-3-031-21671-8_1
8. Gurney, N., Pynadath, D.V.: Robots with theory of mind for humans: a survey. In: 2022 31st IEEE International Conference on Robot and Human Interactive Communication (RO-MAN), pp. 993–1000. IEEE (2022)
9. Gurney, N., Pynadath, D.V., Wang, N.: Measuring and predicting human trust in recommendations from an AI teammate. In: Degen, H., Ntoa, S. (eds.) Artificial Intelligence in HCI. HCII 2022. Lecture Notes in Computer Science, vol. 13336. Springer, Cham (2022). https://doi.org/10.1007/978-3-031-05643-7_2
10. Heider, F., Simmel, M.: An experimental study of apparent behavior. Am. J. Psychol. **57**(2), 243–259 (1944)
11. Huang, H.Y., Bashir, M.: Personal influences on dynamic trust formation in human-agent interaction. In: Proceedings of the 5th International Conference on Human Agent Interaction, pp. 233–243 (2017)
12. Isbister, K., Nass, C.: Consistency of personality in interactive characters: verbal cues, non-verbal cues, and user characteristics. Int. J. Hum. Comput. Stud. **53**(2), 251–267 (2000)
13. Kaelbling, L.P., Littman, M.L., Cassandra, A.R.: Planning and acting in partially observable stochastic domains. Artif. Intell. **101**, 99–134 (1998)
14. Kaelbling, L.P., Littman, M.L., Moore, A.W.: Reinforcement learning: a survey. J. Artif. Intell. Res. **4**, 237–285 (1996)
15. Kahneman, D., Slovic, S.P., Slovic, P., Tversky, A.: Judgment Under Uncertainty: Heuristics and Biases. Cambridge University Press, Cambridge (1982)
16. Kim, Y., Sundar, S.S.: Anthropomorphism of computers: is it mindful or mindless? Comput. Hum. Behav. **28**(1), 241–250 (2012)
17. Mayer, R.C., Davis, J.H.: The effect of the performance appraisal system on trust for management: a field quasi-experiment. J. Appl. Psychol. **84**(1), 123 (1999)
18. Mayer, R.C., Davis, J.H., Schoorman, F.D.: An integrative model of organizational trust. Acad. Manage. Rev. **20**(3), 709–734 (1995)
19. Pynadath, D.V., Gurney, N., Wang, N.: Explainable reinforcement learning in human-robot teams: the impact of decision-tree explanations on transparency. In: 2022 31st IEEE International Conference on Robot and Human Interactive Communication (RO-MAN), pp. 749–756. IEEE (2022)
20. Reeves, B., Nass, C.: The Media Equation: How People Treat Computers, Television, and new Media Like Real People. Cambridge, UK, vol. 10, pp. 236605 (1996)
21. Ross, L.: The intuitive psychologist and his shortcomings: distortions in the attribution process. In: Advances in experimental social psychology, vol. 10, pp. 173–220. Elsevier (1977)
22. Salem, M., Eyssel, F., Rohlfing, K., Kopp, S., Joublin, F.: To err is human (-like): effects of robot gesture on perceived anthropomorphism and likability. Int. J. Soc. Robot. **5**(3), 313–323 (2013)
23. Schwarz, N.: Self-reports: how the questions shape the answers. Am. Psychol. **54**(2), 93 (1999)

24. Schwarz, N., Clore, G.L.: Mood, misattribution, and judgments of well-being: informative and directive functions of affective states. J. Pers. Soc. Psychol. **45**(3), 513 (1983)
25. Sutton, R.S., Barto, A.G.: Reinforcement Learning: An Introduction. MIT press, Cambridge (2018)
26. Tapus, A., Ţăpuş, C., Matarić, M.J.: User-robot personality matching and assistive robot behavior adaptation for post-stroke rehabilitation therapy. Intell. Serv. Rob. **1**(2), 169–183 (2008)
27. Wang, N., Pynadath, D.V., Hill, S.G.: Trust calibration within a human-robot team: comparing automatically generated explanations. In: 2016 11th ACM/IEEE International Conference on Human-Robot Interaction (HRI), pp. 109–116. IEEE (2016)
28. Wang, N., Pynadath, D.V., Hill, S.G., Ground, A.P.: Building trust in a human-robot team with automatically generated explanations. In: Proceedings of the Interservice/Industry Training, Simulation and Education Conference (I/ITSEC). vol. 15315, pp. 1–12 (2015)
29. Złotowski, J., Proudfoot, D., Yogeeswaran, K., Bartneck, C.: Anthropomorphism: opportunities and challenges in human-robot interaction. Int. J. Soc. Rob. **7**(3), 347–360 (2015)

Collaborative Appropriation of AI in the Context of Interacting with AI

Thomas Herrmann(✉) (iD)

Institut Für Arbeitswissenschaft, Ruhr-University Bochum, Bochum, Germany
Thomas.Herrmann@ruhr-uni-bochum.de

Abstract. In the context of maintaining technical equipment, AI is used to detect possible problems. Human specialists check whether a real problem is addressed, and, in this case, try to solve it. Furthermore, they go on trying to translate the problem notification into an improvement of other software components into which the AI system is embedded. Thus, every AI result is not only the cause of immediate action but is also a trigger within the process of continuous appropriation of the technical infrastructure that includes AI. The whole socio-technical system is a subject of AI-related improvement as a collaborative task that requires continuous advancement of human competences and skills. This has to be supported by a type of explainable AI by which the process of understanding the reasons driving AI output is not a task for a single end-user but rather the result of combining different specialists' viewpoints and competences.

Keywords: human-centered artificial intelligence · organizational practices · socio-technical design · rule extraction · appropriation · keeping the organization in the loop

1 Introduction

Human-centered artificial intelligence or HCAI (Shneiderman, 2022) asserts that humans and AI together deliver better results than either alone. It aims to foster and develop human competencies and capabilities as well as improving AI solutions (Dellermann et al., 2019).

HCAI deals with developing modes of interaction (Herrmann, 2022) that support human involvement such as assisting humans in exploring and adaptation of AI systems (Schmidt, 2020). Further approaches support the refinement of AI results (Cai et al., 2019), vetoing results (Rakova et al., 2021), or intervening into AI-controlled processes (Schmidt & Herrmann, 2017). Shneiderman's (2022) view of HCAI argues for a tool perspective on AI. By contrast, other points of view see AI systems as autonomous agents or teammates with which collaboration should become possible (Baird & Maruping, 2021). These approaches assume a symmetrical relationship between humans and AI.

Human-AI Teaming (Dubey et al., 2020) or human autonomy teaming (O'Neill et al., 2022) are approaches in which a combination of human and artificial intelligence is applied to complex goals with each site (human or AI) continuously improving by mutual

H. Degen and S. Ntoa (Eds.): HCII 2023, LNAI 14051, pp. 249–260, 2023.
https://doi.org/10.1007/978-3-031-35894-4_18

learning. Both sites have phases of highly interdependent activities varying according to the distinct roles they occupy within the team. To function within such a teaming constellation, AI components not only need knowledge about the handling of certain tasks but also about how to cooperate including abilities for communication, coordination and understanding organizational context (Pacaux-Lemoine & Flemisch, 2019).

A main issue that influences the efficiency and effectiveness of this kind of teams is trust calibration. For the human site this is about the judgement regarding the degree to which one can rely on each other to achieve the team's goals – even under conditions of uncertainty. If trust is inappropriately high, there is an increased risk that malfunctioning will not be detected; if it is too low, more effort than necessary is invested in the supervising and awareness of automated processes and in assessing the quality of results (Okamura & Yamada, 2020). A crucial concept of HCAI and a key for trust calibration is the interpretability of AI processes and of results by explainable AI (XAI) (Chromik & Butz, 2021) or by interaction modes for exploration (Herrmann, 2022; Schmidt & Herrmann, 2017). So far, explainability is mainly considered as a matter of interaction between AI and an end-user; the potential of achieving interpretability of AI by collaboration between human experts is widely neglected.

We suggest that a future AI will be able to support both perspectives – using and adapting AI as a tool or collaborating with AI as a teammate – and that AI also will support switching flexibly and immediately between both modes. Which of the modes will be practiced under which condition depends on the process of appropriation that will be instantiated by the users and the organizations where AI is employed. Appropriation (Pipek, 2005) includes tailoring but is not limited to it since it also covers discussing the technology as well as negotiating the way of using and tailoring it. Appropriation also includes going beyond the intentions of the designers and the rules of the organization that had been initially associated with the artifact being introduced (Pipek, 2005, p. 30). We suggest adding that appropriation systematically includes an ongoing process of learning about the artefact and its context, and that appropriating one type of technology also supports the appropriation of other types that are included in the same context of technical infrastructure.

Both perspectives (tool vs. teammate) emphasize the interaction between humans and computers. They hardly look at the socio-technical aspect including organizational practices of the collaboration between people in the context of AI usage. However, collaboration between people and their organizational practices (Herrmann & Pfeiffer, 2022) are crucial for drawing benefits from AI. Herrmann and Pfeiffer (2022, 2023) suggest that keeping the human in the loop has to be interwoven with keeping the organization in the loop as presented in Fig. 1.

On the human side, activities such as awareness, evaluation of the situation, planning and acting (Jiang et al., 2022) as well as reflection (Prilla & Herrmann, 2018) are relevant from the perspective of human cognition. On the organizational site, management activities are a starting point for developing organizational practices (Herrmann & Pfeiffer, 2022) to make sure that:

- The original tasks, such as plant maintenance, treating patients etc. are appropriately aligned with AI usage.

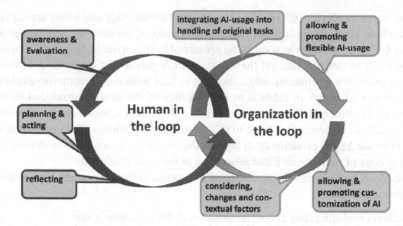

Fig. 1. Keeping the Organization in the Loop

- This usage can be conducted flexibly so that users are allowed to reject or modify AI outcome when going on with the original task.
- Not only is it possible to customize the AI systems or to initiate customization, employees are also encouraged and made competent to do so.
- Changes in the context of AI usage, such as new laws or new technical possibilities, are continuously checked and considered.

With respect to keeping the organization in the loop, we ask what kind of collaboration as part of organizational practices between humans can or should take place in the context of using AI to promote the aims of HCAI? We try to give preliminary answers to this question using a case study in which the customer service of a pump manufacturer uses ML algorithms to detect anomalies. This detection supports predictive maintenance (Zonta et al., 2020) that helps avoid malfunctions before they take place. These anomalies cannot easily be identified by human data analysts and are therefore a typical subject for employing machine learning. Based on our analysis of this case, we propose HCAI features that support the collaboration between humans in the context of employing AI. In what follows we describe the analyzed case, our method and the findings that lead to a discussion and final conclusions.

2   The Case

The case examined relates to the customer service of a pump manufacturer. Pumps are installed and taken into operation by the manufacturer at the customer's site. The pump manufacturer has established a systematic process management. One central process covers the activities and decisions between the request for an offer and the final installation of the delivered technology at the customer's site. This process precedes the activities of the customer service and makes sure that consistency and completeness of all necessary information is achieved by employing software-supported form-filling. This formalized information exchange contrasts with the more agile communication and information sharing within projects set up to realize innovation.

The customer service (CS) processes are central to our study since they are supported by a machine learning application that supports tasks of monitoring and data analysis (M&A). CS processes start as soon as the sensors of the pump technology at the customer site are ready to deliver data. At the beginning, CS gets a first impression of the data and the customer's equipment, and a meeting is held with the customer to explain the characteristics of M&A in relation to the specifics of the newly introduced technical equipment. In principle, the customers can use the M&A component by themselves. Alternatively, a customer can decide to rely on the manufacturer's CS team. A main task of CS is to use M&A proactively to consult the customer, to avoid breakdowns and to trigger actions of maintenance and adaptation at the customer's site.

The M&A tool mirrors the operation of the pumps at the customers' sites and offers the following features:

- It delivers real-time data about the situation at the customer's site.
- It provides statistics, aggregates data, and creates graphs to help interpret the data.
- It includes a rule-based component that delivers notifications if thresholds are violated that indicate a malfunctioning or an upcoming breakdown. These rules are based on experience with previous malfunctioning.
- It employs a ML-system for outlier detection. This can point to problems that are not detected by the other components because outliers reflect phenomena that are not yet well understood. It helps to identify problems that were previously unknown. This can be especially important in cases where deviations from regular functioning can lead to cascades that cause a major breakdown. The outlier detection is based on unsupervised machine learning.

To use M&A professionally, the CS team includes two types of competencies: the technical specialists such as electricians and mechatronic engineers, and the data analysts. They support each other to translate insights derived from M&A into activities to support the customer. Furthermore, the features of M&A are subject of continuous improvement. Therefore, the CS team collaborates with a developer team. The data analysts are in the intersection of both teams as represented in Fig. 2. To support the ongoing development of M&A, weekly meetings take place.

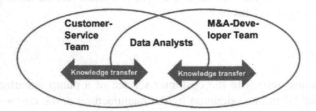

Fig. 2. Data analysts at the intersection

Overall, the CS team becomes active by the following triggers:

1. The customer reports problems.

2. Indicators delivered by the M&A-component:
   a. Insights gained by analyzing data using appropriately prepared plots (charts, etc.) so that trends can be identified that deviate from the usual operating patterns.
   b. Warnings that are triggered by rules if certain thresholds are violated.
   c. Machine-learning based detection of anomalies that are hard to detect for the CS team.

In all the three cases (a – c), possible malfunctioning becomes manifest as a result of data analysis. Subsequently, human decision-makers must determine what needs to be done, possibly in consultation with the customer (see Fig. 3). In addition, these triggers also initiate consideration of whether the M&A component should be adjusted or improved.

3   Method

The methodological approach involves mainly the analysis of workflows by the means of group discussion. The goal of the workflow analysis was to evaluate the prerequisites for successful human-centered use of AI and to expand the various ways of employing AI. In particular, the socio-technical consideration of the interaction of people, technology and organization was in the foreground (Herrmann et al., 2021). The workshops were run as socio-technical walkthroughs (STWT) (Herrmann et al., 2007) where the sequences of activities were step-by-step analyzed and challenges or possibilities for improvement were considered. The STWT-workshops use guiding questions that are applied throughout the meeting. Answers to questions are immediately documented by modifying the process diagrams that are continuously visible. This documentation is complimented by text notes. Thus, the answers of the participants are immediately evaluated by transforming them to elements of a process model. Consequently, data gathering and its evaluation are widely integrated (Jahnke et al., 2008). If necessary, incomplete clarity about the processes and lacking information was compensated by additional interviews to complete the process models, for instance to achieve a better understanding of problems or possibilities of improvement.

To analyze the relevant collaboration processes we conducted three workshops:

- The first and second included nine participants (salesforce, customer service, MAP-developer team, data analysts, scientists). They considered the process between incoming orders and the installation of pumps. Furthermore, the subsequent process of providing services for the installed equipment at the customers' sites was discussed. Overall, it became clear that the process is understood in detail and supported by technical components.
- The third workshop focused on collaboration between customer service and other departments, in particular with the MAP-developer team (13 participants). The objectives of the workshop were to survey the nature and occasions for collaboration between customer service and AI development, as well as to explore possible optimization of the work processes and the respective work results. To prepare the workshop, the diagram in Fig. 3 was drafted based on the results of the first two workshops to inspire participants to systematically think through all possible feedback routes.

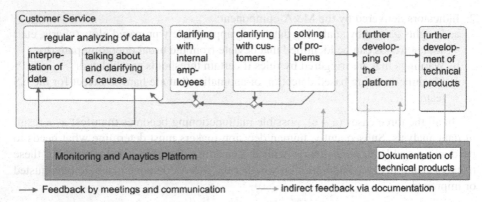

Fig. 3. Possibilities of Collaboration and Feedback

4   Findings

The analysis of the processes and of the CS team's work revealed that an intensive exchange of information is necessary. This is accomplished mainly by software-based form filling. However, in certain situations, especially if innovations have to be brought into reality, more agile and informal types of information exchanging are adequate.

4.1   Problems and Proposals

A number of problems became apparent:

- If the salesforce team talks with the customer, the succeeding information flow to the CS team is not managed in an agile mode. Textual information might be documented without seeking a dialogue with the CS team. When documenting a talk, the salesforce team cannot exactly anticipate which information might be needed by the CS team.
- Fully sharing information beyond what is absolutely necessary is not really rewarded.
- Cross-departmental feedback processes are only initiated in the case of new introductions of methods or technology, or if serious problems occur.
- There is a lack of mutual understanding of the activities and objectives of the various departments, which could serve as the basis for assessing the need for an informal exchange.

   In view of these problems, solutions were proposed:

- On the communicative level, both interdisciplinary (cross-departmental) cooperation and exchange opportunities are emphasized as a necessity for effective task processing.
- It was recommended that the new insights gained should be documented in a transparent and comprehensible manner.
- On the communicative level, in addition to regular coordination rounds, direct, spontaneous discussions were also emphasized as particularly effective. This measure would go beyond the fixed structure of regular meetings.

- To compensate for knowledge deficits, bilateral in-depth discussions within one's own team are preferred.
- For the data analysts, among others, customer meetings are particularly important, in which a joint review and discussion of the collected data takes place. In addition, input from customers and field staff is generally necessary.

4.2 The Customer Service Team

The work of the CS team can be seen in the light of these problems and proposals for improvement. At the time of data gathering, the CS team had just integrated the support provided by data analysts and the AI for outlier detection. However, it was felt that the expanded analysis options provided by AI will not result in any essential change in the processes of how the CS team supports the customer.

The interaction between the technicians in the CS team and the data analysts can be outlined as follows based on our data. The technicians on the CS team use the evaluations that the data analysts (DA) prepare to identify problems, find causes, and propose solutions. The DA team additionally asks what can be learned from the data, going beyond how to understand current problems and find solutions for them. It is about uncovering or predicting problems in advance that the customer does not know about yet. Figure 3 shows that the first step is to analyze the data and clarify the situation internally within the CS team. In addition, a clarification is carried out with the customer, which supports the internal clarifying processes. From this "problem solving," additional experience can be gained that can be added to the clarifying process.

Within customer service, there are individual regulations governing responsibilities for processing customers' inquiries and automated alarms. For example, individual employees can be assigned to specific pumps or specific customers. However, these responsibilities are handled in an agile and flexible manner. This flexibility is necessary, for example, if a customer needs ad hoc support; then every employee must be able to respond to the request and call in specialists if necessary. The company also reacts flexibly to outlier detection. The detection of an outlier always results in follow-up activities and the need for discussions. The exchange of experience, reciprocal support, and the clarification of task assignments take place directly either in the open-plan office or via MS Teams.

The original intention was that customers would largely service themselves using the M&A Platform. However, customers were reluctant. This is due on the one hand to the low level of digitization at the customers' sites and on the other hand to their limited experience of the added value of the self-service solutions. As a result, customers have a greater need for personal consulting, especially in case of specific problems with installations. Consequently, more and more customers develop a sustaining appreciation of end-to-end support from the CS team ranging from the monitoring of the pumps to spare parts delivery.

4.3 Further Development of the M&A-Platform

The problems identified with the customer, as well as frequent queries or requests, are also regularly reported to the developer team by CS in order to find out how these problems can be better mitigated. To this end, existing features of the M&A platform are improved or new ones added based on experience. The AI component for outlier detection can also be optimized in this process.

The iterative development process is strongly based on an intensive exchange of experience and the collaboratively developed integration of new technical possibilities and identified requirements. This is supported by regular internal team meetings as well as cross-team exchange formats.

In most cases, further development is not about time-critical challenges. Further development can be aimed at new types of charts, aggregations of data or the expansion of the rule-base on the basis of which warnings for possible malfunctions are derived. Outlier detection can be viewed as a trigger that initiates the development of new rules or their adaptation on a case-by-case basis. The teams (CS and developers) first decide if the outliers really represent anomalies. If yes, they try to understand the background of the anomaly and adjust the rule base based on this understanding.

If a further development of the M&A platform is successfully implemented, it is discussed whether and how the measures taken can be generalized and transferred to other plants. A decision must then be made, for example, if the measures relate to a specific pump, as to whether this is a special case or whether new ways of data evaluation can also be transferred to other pumps.

In general, such transfers of measures are difficult because pumps are not readily comparable to one another once installed. This is all the more true for plants as a whole. In addition, there are hardly any meta-evaluations that consider several pumps together.

Overall, the further development of the M&A platform is agile and experience-driven. It must be adapted to the respective situation and current needs.

5   Discussion and Conclusion

The analyzed case reveals how organizational practices can promote HCAI and the capabilities of the CS team. There are some characteristics that highly influence the type of ongoing collaboration within these organizational practices:

1. Integrating AI usage into an infrastructure of tools, such as visualizing data, provides a larger context for the CS team and more autonomy in judging a situation.
2. Based on outlier detection by ML, the CS team is authorized to collaboratively reflect with the developer team on whether new thresholds or new rules that reproduce the ML-results can be found.
3. The eventually established organizational practice is that data analysts inform the customer about critical ML-based outlier detection and take control of the task to explain the AI results, their background, and their consequences to the customer. This limits the implementation of the original plan for the customer to work with the AI-assisted M&A component itself.
4. New features or measures to improve the M&A platform cannot necessarily be transformed from one element of technical equipment to others.
5. The technical experts of the CS team gradually adopt the capabilities of the data analysts.

6. Multiple communication channels could be established to share how AI results, in concert with other tools, can serve as a basis for feedback to others of the company and to the advancement of its products, or for the performance of the CS team.

Consequently, we suggest that AI usage in environments where technical problems have to be solved or technical equipment has to be maintained are of a special nature. It is not mainly the pattern, for instance, that an AI chatbot receives a question or data is submitted to it and the resulting answer can be accepted, rejected or be a basis for a refinement dialogue. In the technical context, AI is used to detect possible problems. On the human side, specialists check whether a real problem is addressed, and, in this case, try to solve the problem. However, this is not the end of dealing with this AI-based problem detection. By contrast, the specialists try to translate the result – here the detected outliers – into an improvement of other software components into which the AI system is embedded or is at least related to. In the considered case, the data analysts try to specify rules that mirror the outlier detection. Consequently, every AI result is not only the cause of immediate action but also a trigger within the process of continuous improvement. Apparently, developing new rules, or features, is more than XAI. It is about appropriation as a way of understanding and interpreting the systems background for the purpose of adapting the system, here by proposing new rules. Interaction with the rule-based component demonstrates how human contribution is still involved.

This ongoing improvement refers to the technical infrastructure –supporting a team – as a whole. Not only AI, but AI and its context are improved: in the case studied, a misleading outlier detection or a false negative – where an outlier should have been detected, but was not – indicate the need for improvement. Additionally, and most important, the whole socio-technical system is a subject of AI-triggered improvement, since changes of the technical infrastructure affect processes of communication and coordination (with the customer as well as within the company). Consequently, the usage of AI as a trigger for socio-technical improvement necessarily is a collaborative task where various human actors and roles – and their capabilities and responsibilities – are involved. Thus, understanding the reasons behind an AI output is not only the task of a single end-user but is a result of combining different viewpoints and competences – here of the technical experts on the CS team, the data analysts, and the developers of the M&A system. The same applies for the task of deriving new rules from the outlier detection, integrating them into a rule-based system for predictive warnings, testing it etc. In addition, this kind of appropriation of AI-related technical contributes to the continuous development of the competencies of the teams involved. A subtle balancing between various features has to be arranged that integrates visibility and interpretability, promoting direct personal communication, and advancing information exchange (Herrmann et al., 2021). Furthermore, the information exchange that is triggered by continuous improvement can be relevant for the whole company where AI is employed: as outlined in Fig. 3, the development of the technical products themselves can also benefit from the advancement of the M&A-platform.

The collaborative appropriation of AI can be supported by technical features that are integrated into the AI application itself:

● The tasks of developing new rules based on an outlier detection requires a type of XAI (Gilpin et al., 2019) that supports this task. Rule extraction is already an established topic of AI design (Barbado et al., 2022; Hailesilassie, 2016). In the context of this study it has to be emphasized that a kind of rule extraction is needed that additionally considers the set of rules that has been already developed, either by human or based on ML.

- Future AI should support the described collaboration processes by actively informing people and knowing who has to be informed and how. Approaches of deriving recommendation for process handling (Kubrak et al., 2021) could be used for this purpose, if they can be specified in a way that takes agility into account.
- Facilitating the collaboration can also be considered as a managerial task for deciding who should be informed and when. An agile balancing between information overflow and extensive information exchange is needed that is based on context awareness. Concepts can be applied that have been developed to take over tasks of facilitation (Briggs et al., 2010).

In summary, the described case is a striking example of how keeping the human in-the loop and keeping the organization inthe loop have to be integrated (see Fig. 1). Within the organizational practices that have been developed, AI is more a subject of appropriation and less a teammate. However, both modes have a certain relevance and advantage. Future research might focus on the question of how a smooth transition between both modes could be achieved. Overall, the described case is an example for a design that integrates possibilities its own evolution in accordance with the concept of sociotechnical meta-design (Fischer & Herrmann, 2015).

Acknowledgement. This work was supported by Felix Thewes within the Humaine project (Human Centered AI Network), funded (02L19C200) by the German Federal Ministry of Education and Research (BMBF).

References

Baird, A., Maruping, L.M.: The next generation of research on is use: a theoretical framework of delegation to and from agentic is artifacts. MIS Quart **45**(1) (2021)

Barbado, A., Corcho, Ó., Benjamins, R.: Rule extraction in unsupervised anomaly detection for model explainability: application to OneClass SVM. Expert Syst. Appl. **189**, 116100 (2022). https://doi.org/10.1016/j.eswa.2021.116100

Briggs, R.O., Kolfschoten, G.L., de Vreede, G.-J., Albrecht, C. C., Lukosch, S. G.: Facilitator in a box: Computer assisted collaboration engineering and process support systems for rapid development of collaborative applications for high-value tasks. System Sciences (HICSS). In: 2010 43rd Hawaii International Conference On, pp. 1–10 (2010). http://www.computer.org/csdl/proceedings/hicss/2010/3869/00/01-13-05.pdf

Cai, C.J., et al.: Human-centered tools for coping with imperfect algorithms during medical decision-making. In: Proceedings of the 2019 CHI Conference on Human Factors in Computing Systems, pp. 1–14 (2019)

Chromik, M., Butz, A.: Human-XAI Interaction: A Review and Design Principles for Explanation User Interfaces. In: IFIP Conference on Human-Computer Interaction, pp. 619–640 (2021)

Dellermann, D., Calma, A., Lipusch, N., Weber, T., Weigel, S., Ebel, P.: The future of human-AI collaboration: A taxonomy of design knowledge for hybrid intelligence systems. In: Proceedings of the 52nd Hawaii International Conference on System Sciences (HICSS) (2019)

Dubey, A., Abhinav, K., Jain, S., Arora, V., Puttaveerana, A.: HACO: A Framework for Developing Human-AI Teaming. In: Proceedings of the 13th Innovations in Software Engineering Conference on Formerly Known as India Software Engineering Conference, pp. 1–9 (2020). https://doi.org/10.1145/3385032.3385044

Fischer, G., Herrmann, T.: Meta-design: Transforming and enriching the design and use of sociotechnical systems. In: Wulf, V., Schmidt, K., Randall, D. (eds.) Designing Socially Embedded Technologies in the Real-World. CSCW, pp. 79–109. Springer, London (2015). https://doi.org/10.1007/978-1-4471-6720-4_6

Gilpin, L.H., Bau, D., Yuan, B.Z., Bajwa, A., Specter, M., Kagal, L.: Explaining Explanations: An Overview of Interpretability of Machine Learning (2019). (arXiv:1806.00069). arXiv. http://arxiv.org/abs/1806.00069

Hailesilassie, T.: Rule Extraction Algorithm for Deep Neural Networks: A Review. **14**(7) (2016)

Herrmann, T.: Promoting Human Competences by Appropriate Modes of Interaction for Human-Centered-AI. In H. Degen & S. Ntoa (Eds.), Artificial Intelligence in HCI (Vol. 13336, pp. 35–50). Springer International Publishing (2022). https://doi.org/10.1007/978-3-031-05643-7_3

Herrmann, T., Jahnke, I., Nolte, A.: A problem-based approach to the advancement of heuristics for socio-technical evaluation. Behav. Inform. Technol. **1–23**,(2021). https://doi.org/10.1080/0144929X.2021.1972157

Herrmann, T., Loser, K.-U., Jahnke, I.: Socio-technical Walkthrough (STWT): A means for Knowledge Integration. The Learning Organization. Int. J. Knowl. Organization. Learn. Manage. **14**(5), 450–464 (2007)

Herrmann, T., Pfeiffer, S.: Keeping the organization in the loop: A socio-technical extension of human-centered artificial intelligence. (2022). https://doi.org/10.1007/s00146-022-01391-5

Herrmann, T., Pfeiffer, S: Keeping the Organization in the Loop as a General Concept for Human-Centered AI: The Example of Medical Imaging. In: Proceedings of the 56th Hawaii International Conference on System Sciences (HICSS), pp. 5272–5281 (2023)

Jahnke, I., Herrmann, T., Prilla, M.: Modellierung statt Interviews? Eine neue qualitative Erhebungsmethode. In M. Herczeg & M. C. Kindsmüller (Eds.). In: Proceedings of Mensch und Computer (2008)

Jiang, J., Karran, A.J., Coursaris, C.K., Léger, P.-M., Beringer, J.: A situation awareness perspective on human-ai interaction: tensions and opportunities. Int. J. Human-Comput. Interact. **1–18**,(2022). https://doi.org/10.1080/10447318.2022.2093863

Kubrak, K., Milani, F., Nolte, A., Dumas, M.: Prescriptive Process Monitoring: Quo Vadis? (2021) (arXiv:2112.01769). arXiv. http://arxiv.org/abs/2112.01769

Okamura, K., Yamada, S.: Adaptive trust calibration for human-AI collaboration. PLoS ONE **15**(2), e0229132 (2020). https://doi.org/10.1371/journal.pone.0229132

O'Neill, T., McNeese, N., Barron, A., Schelble, B.: Human-autonomy teaming: a review and analysis of the empirical literature. Human Factors: J. Human Factors Ergonom. Society **64**(5), 904–938 (2022). https://doi.org/10.1177/0018720820960865

Pacaux-Lemoine, M.-P., Flemisch, F.: Layers of shared and cooperative control, assistance, and automation. Cogn. Technol. Work **21**(4), 579–591 (2018). https://doi.org/10.1007/s10111-018-0537-4

Pipek, V.: From Tailoring to Appropriation Support: Negotiating Groupware Usage Faculty of Science. Department of Information Processing Science (ACTA UNIVERSITATIS OULUENSIS A 430), University of Oulu, Oulu, Finland (2005)

Prilla, M., Herrmann, T.: Challenges for Socio-technical Design in Health Care: Lessons Learned From Designing Reflection Support. In: Designing Healthcare That Works. A Socio-technical Approach, pp. 149–166. Academic Press (Elsevier) (2018)

Rakova, B., Yang, J., Cramer, H., Chowdhury, R.: Where responsible AI meets reality: Practitioner perspectives on enablers for shifting organizational practices. Proc. ACM Human-Comput. Interact. **5**(CSCW1), 1–23 (2021)

Schmidt, A.: Interactive human centered artificial intelligence: a definition and research challenges. Proc. Int. Conf. Adv. Visual Interfaces **1–4**,(2020). https://doi.org/10.1145/3399715.3400873

Schmidt, A., Herrmann, T.: Intervention user interfaces: a new interaction paradigm for automated systems. Interactions **24**(5), 40–45 (2017)

Shneiderman, B.: Human-Centered AI. Oxford University Press (2022)

Zonta, T., da Costa, C.A., da Rosa Righi, R., de Lima, M.J., da Trindade, E.S., Li, G.P.: Predictive maintenance in the Industry 4.0: a systematic literature review. Comput. Indust. Eng. **150**, 106889 (2020). https://doi.org/10.1016/j.cie.2020.106889

Understanding User Experience with AI-Assisted Writing Service

Gayoung Kim, Jiyeon Kim, and Hyun K. Kim$^{(\boxtimes)}$

Department of Artificial Intelligence Application, School of Information Convergence,
Kwangwoon University, Seoul 01897, Korea
hyunkkim@kw.ac.kr

Abstract. With the recent development of artificial intelligence (AI) technology, services such as automatic writing evaluation (AWE) and AI-assisted writing have been developed. AWE is often used in education to correct grammar. Unlike AWE, AI-assisted writing is a service that generates content for users. Currently, being a new field, research on AI-assisted writing is insufficient compared to studies on AWE. This study derives user experience factors of AI-assisted writing through a literature review and checks the difference in experience according to the writing case and creativity level. Seven user experience factors were derived through literature research, and the factors were evaluated for "Rytr," an assisted writing service. Thirty-six subjects participated in an online survey. Four prototypes were designed and provided according to the writing case (e-mail, story plot) and creativity level (high, low) of text generation, and a two-way ANOVA was conducted based on survey data. A significant difference was found for each creativity level and writing case. Users obtained more creative writing results when writing a story plot and thought positively about the assisted writing service. In the AI-assisted writing service, the users experienced increased trust and satisfaction when writing a story plot. This study can help design functions based on various types of writing, considering user experience in developing AI-assisted writing services in the future.

Keywords: Ethical and trustworthy AI · Human-Centered AI · AI-assistant Service · AI-assisted Writing · User Experience

1 Introduction

Demand for artificial intelligence (AI) is increasing, as it can improve work efficiency using minimal human resources [1]. AI is applied in various fields, such as computer vision, prediction, semantic analysis, and natural language processing [2], and has expanded to creative activities such as painting, music, and writing. Among them, writing has developed towards analyzing the causal relationship of input sentences and proceeding with additional writing using the learned handwriting of the writer. AI-based writing systems are in the limelight. Moreover, in some cases, AI has been registered as co-author of full-length novels along with novelists.

H. Degen and S. Ntoa (Eds.): HCII 2023, LNAI 14051, pp. 261–272, 2023.
https://doi.org/10.1007/978-3-031-35894-4_19

Writing activities using AI can be classified into automated writing evaluation (AWE) and AI-assisted writing systems. AWE uses natural language processing and machine learning algorithms to generate writing-related evaluation scores and feedback [3]. AWE, mainly used in the field of education, has the advantage of grading essays and saving time. Previous studies on AWE investigated learning effects and attitudes of learners. AWE systems such as Grammark and Grammarly have improved learners' writing abilities [4, 5]. Learners positively perceive accurate and easy-to-understand feedback systems, which affect users' continued use [6]. A study using structural equation modeling on the intention to continue using AWE revealed the significant effects of satisfaction, usefulness, ease of use, and self-efficacy on the continuation intention to use AWE. [7].

AI-assisted writing has emerged with the expansion of AI technology into the creative field. In AI-assisted writing, the AI generates content for users. Novelists can focus on high-level tasks such as topic setting and conception, and using AI, they can perform writing as a simple task, enabling efficient writing. "Rytr," "Jasper," and "Wordtune" are representative AI-based services that help users with their writing activities. Users can write more efficiently through the detailed functions provided by each service, but the performance is not perfect and can only be used for specific writing topics.

Most user experience studies in AI-based writing activities have focused on AWE while ignoring AI-assisted writing. Apart from proofreading, as AI-assisted writing can write new text and learn the written text, additional research on the resulting user experience is needed. This study analyzed user experience according to the writing case and creativity level of AI-assisted writing systems. Our analysis centered on the following three research questions.

RQ1: How is the overall user experience structured in AI-assisted writing?

RQ2: Do user experiences differ depending on the creativity level of AI-assisted writing?

RQ3: Do user experiences differ depending on the writing case in AI-assisted writing?

The rest of this paper is organized as follows. Section 2 reviews previous studies on user experience with AI-based assistive tools. Section 3 presents the research method detailing the subjects, constructed questionnaires, and experimental design. In Sect. 4, data analysis and results are summarized, and finally, in Sects. 5 and 6, the summary, conclusion, and limitations of this study are presented.

2   Literature Review

2.1   AI-Assisted Writing Service

An AI-assisted writing service is a tool that helps users write, using natural language generation systems that automatically generate verbal and nonverbal texts using natural language processing technology [8]. AI-assisted writing is mainly used to assist people with writing difficulties, such as language-impaired readers or adults with dyslexia [9, 10]. The LaMPost system addresses the various needs of dyslexic patients by providing functions such as Suggest Possible Changes and Rewrite My Selection [10]. A commercial AI-assisted writing service helps users refine their ideas or write in their desired tone [11]. Rytr is a leading commercial writing tool that supports various languages and provides several writing options to generate copywriting phrases. In this study, various types of texts were obtained using the use case and creativity level function of Rytr, from which the user experience was evaluated.

2.2 AI-Assisted Service User Experience

Since research on user experience related to AI writing services is limited, user experience factors related to AI-assisted service were derived by a literature review of AI-assisted service and AI collaboration [9, 10, 12, 16, 18]. We identified seven factors: competence, reciprocity, benevolence, self-efficacy, controllability, trust, and satisfaction.

Competence, reciprocity, and benevolence affect trust in AI assistants [12]. Competence indicates the degree to which a technology performs or the degree to which a system provides necessary functions [13]. Users are more likely to act on the advice and recommendations provided if they find the technology helpful [14]. Reciprocity refers to the degree to which a user develops a symbiotic relationship with technology. When an agent provides services to a user cooperatively, the user forms a mutual relationship with the agent [15]. Benevolence is the degree to which a user perceives technology to help and act in their best interests, which is achieved with trust and continuous use of technology [13]. Self-efficacy refers to the extent to which users believe in their ability to perform in a particular situation or task. It evaluates confidence in the performance of AWE and the composition of AI-assisted services [7, 9, 16]. Participants with high self-efficacy could trust, adhere, and use the system more than those with low self-efficacy [17]. Controllability refers to the degree to which users can control an AI system. It has been evaluated in Duet Draw, a drawing-related AI-assisted tool and writing AI-assisted service [9, 18]. Users wanted to fix the text/drawing when the AI behaved unexpectedly. In a previous study, users wanted to directly correct results provided by a highly accurate automated system [19]. Satisfaction and trust have a positive effect each other. If a chatbot offers reliable information, it can increase user satisfaction [20]. In addition, increasing satisfaction can increase trust, creating positive user perception [21].

Based on user experiences, this study investigated whether users correctly understand and use the functions provided by AI-assisted writing services and whether they affect trust or satisfaction with the service.

3   Methods

3.1 Participants

Thirty-six subjects (22 males and 14 females; average age 23.7 ± 2.27) participated in this study. The subjects were aware of AI even if they had no direct experience using AI-assisted services. Ten participants (28%) responded having experience using AI-assisted tools. Of these, four had experience using AI-assisted tools that help diagnose diseases, and the remaining had experience using AI-assisted services related to writing, composition, medical care, and coding.

3.2 Prototype

In this study, "Rytr," an AI-assisted writing service based on GPT-3, was used. As shown in Fig. 1, Rytr provides five options to implement various sentences. With Rytr, the user can (1) select the desired language using the *Select Language* function and (2) select the tone of the text using the *Select tone* function. In addition, (3) provides various writing types through the *Choose use case* function, and (4) helps to adjust the number of results using the *Number of variants*. Finally, (5) helps the user increase the creativity of text generated based on the value entered in the *Creativity level* function. The higher the creativity level, the more creative the generated texts are compared to the user's input value, and vice versa.

Fig. 1. Copywriting automation tool "Rytr."

This study investigated the differences in user experience according to writing case and creativity level. The most used e-mail and story plot categories were considered for the writing case. The creativity level sets the conditions to derive the most appropriate result values that Low and High can compare.

Therefore, as shown in Fig. 2, prototypes were designed for four conditions. Type A and B indicate low and high creativity levels when writing an e-mail; Type C and D indicate low and high creativity levels when writing a story plot.

Two different scenarios were provided for each writing case, with three different results for each scenario. The same type of writing provides different results with the same user input. When writing an e-mail, a scenario was designed in which a grade-related e-mail is sent to a professor and a meeting schedule is adjusted. In the story plot, scenarios related to Science Fiction and crying characters were selected.

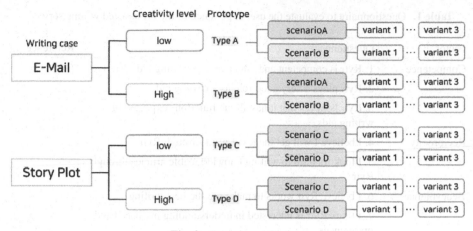

Fig. 2. Experiment Design

3.3 Procedures

Experiments were conducted in the Within-Subject Design(WSD) method using prototypes under four conditions according to the writing case (e-mail, story plot) and creativity level (high, low). First, the subjects were informed about the experiment and the
"Rytr" program. Next, for each of the four prototypes, an online survey was conducted
using 20 questions after checking the results for two scenarios, as shown in Fig. 2; this
was performed under all conditions. Based on the survey data, a two-way ANOVA was
conducted using R studio to analyze significant differences in the seven user experience
factors depending on the writing case and creativity level.

3.4 Measures

The questionnaire consisted of 20 questions, given in Table 1, on the AI-based writing
service's competence, reciprocity, benevolence, self-efficacy, controllability, trust, and
satisfaction on a 5-point Likert scale (1 = strongly disagree – 5 = strongly agree).

For solving the first research question, items on competence, reciprocity, and benevolence were constructed from previous research [12] related to AI user experience.
Although AI-based assistive tools were investigated in [12], they differ from the present
study in that they are services that directly interact with users; therefore, the context was
modified to suit the purpose of this study. Similarly, controllability items were extracted
from [22] and modified. For self-efficacy, questions from Computer Self-efficacy [23]
were borrowed and modified to fit AI-assisted service.

Table 1. Questionnaire to evaluate the user experience of the AI-assisted writing service.

Factor	Questionnaire	Reference
Competence	1. Rytr is competent and effective as a writing aid	[12]
	2. Rytr plays a very good role as a writing aid	
	3. Rytr believes that it has all the functions expected of writing aids	
Reciprocity	4. I believe I will get the text I want through Rytr	
	5. I look forward to writing knowledgeable articles through Rytr	
Benevolence	6. I believe Rytr works to make me the best writing	
	7. I think Rytr is interested in understanding my needs and preferences	
	8. I believe Rytr will do its best to help me with my writing	
Controllability	9. I can control Rytr to write in the direction I want	[22]
	10. I am free to write any text using Rytr	
Self-efficacy	11. I am confident of completing the writing using Rytr	[23]
	12. I believe in my ability to complete writing using Rytr	
	13. I understood how to complete the writing using Rytr	
Trust	14. Rytr can solve difficulties in writing	[24]
	15. Rytr's writing results are in line with my expectations	
	16. I trust the writing results provided by Rytr	
Satisfaction	17. I am generally satisfied with Rytr	[25]
	18. It's fun to use Rytr	
	19. Rytr's writing skills are excellent	
	20. Rytr feels necessary for writing	

4   Results

A two-way ANOVA of the user experience factors revealed that the writing case and creativity level condition derived statistically significant differences for factors other than self-efficacy. However, there was no significant difference in the interaction between writing case and creativity level, as given in Table 2.

Table 2. User experience analysis results according to creativity level when writing e-mail and story plots.

Factor	Writing Case		Creativity Level		Writing Case*Creativity Level	
	F	p	F	p	F	p
Competence	8.665	$< 0.01^{**}$	11.502	$< 0.001^{***}$	0.409	0.523
Reciprocity	13.777	$< 0.001^{***}$	9.824	$< 0.01^{**}$	0.435	0.510
Benevolence	5.484	$< 0.05^{**}$	8.772	$< 0.01^{**}$	0.119	0.731
Controllability	6.561	$< 0.05^{**}$	5.625	$< 0.05^{**}$	0.009	0.924
Self-efficacy	0.6859	0.409	1.039	0.31	0.037	0.849
Trust	5.44	$< 0.05^{**}$	3.14	0.078	0.001	0.975
Satisfaction	10.863	$< 0.001^{***}$	2.146	0.145	0.134	0.715

4.1 User Experience According to Creativity Level

When writing e-mails and story plots, factors except trust, satisfaction, and self-efficacy showed statistically significant differences according to high and low creativity levels (F-value and p-value values are shown in Table 2). Competence, reciprocity, benevolence, and controllability had high values when the creativity level was high, as shown in Fig. 3. Therefore, Prototype B received the highest score when writing an e-mail, and Prototype D received the highest score when writing a story plot.

4.2 User Experience According to Writing Case

Different user experiences were found in e-mails and story plots in terms of writing type. Unlike the creativity level condition, significant differences were derived for all factors except self-efficacy (F-value and p-value are given in Table 2). Competence, reciprocity, benevolence, controllability, trust, and satisfaction received high scores when writing a story plot. Therefore, Prototypes C and D, corresponding to the story plot, obtained high results.

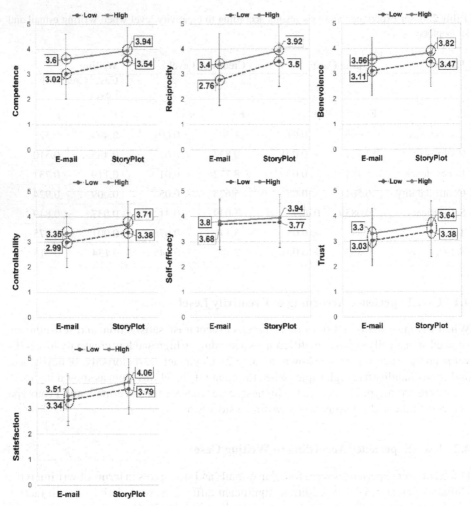

Fig. 3. AI-assisted service user experience box plot results based on creativity level when writing an e-mail and a story plot. (Circles indicate no statistically significant difference).

5   Discussions

5.1   Significant Findings

When writing novels creatively, users feel optimistic about using AI-assisted writing services when they obtain increasingly useful writing results. When the subjects used prototype D (writing case: story plot, creativity level: high), the highest values of user experience factors were derived. Thus, when writing a novel, the users assumed that the writing was satisfactory or the necessary system functions were sufficient for a variety of rich writing results. In addition, users find the assisted writing service helpful and want to continue using them. Moreover, they expect AI to produce good writing results. Therefore, when writing a novel creatively, users get more useful writing results, and accordingly, they think positively about continuing to use the service. Competence, reciprocity, and benevolence affect trust according to a previous study on AI trust [12]. Competence, reciprocity, benevolence, controllability, and trust obtained the highest values under the same conditions, consistent with the results of previous studies.

The User's self-efficacy is not affected by the creativity level of the AI-assisted writing service content but shows a positive trend in the overall writing situation. Unlike other user experience factors, self-efficacy did not show significant differences according to writing type and creativity level conditions. Self-efficacy is the ability to perform in a specific situation or task and is mainly used when evaluating AI-assisted writing services of AWE and e-mail writing. In AWE, self-efficacy indicates increased confidence in one's writing skills when studying a foreign language [7]. In addition, AI-assisted writing service has been evaluated for self-efficacy in terms of writing for those having difficulties in creative writing [9]. In this study, it was difficult to obtain meaningful results like in previous studies because the evaluation of user experience in AI-assisted writing services was conducted with the public. However, looking at the overall self-efficacy evaluation results, the average was 3.7 ($\pm$ 0.86), indicating that there is a high expectation on one's writing ability when using an AI-assisted writing service.

The user feels more trust and satisfaction when writing a story plot using an AI-assisted writing service. AI writing assistants primarily aim to embody ideas and help with creative writing. When writing an e-mail, users' credibility can be obtained only when accurate content is written rather than just providing concepts for content. However, the prototypes had poor grammar owing to limitations, lowering the satisfaction than that achieved when writing novels. When reading compositions about novels, the focus is mainly on whether the context naturally connects rather than focusing on grammar. Therefore, the reliability and satisfaction for novel writing were high.

We confirmed that the different writing services provided by "Rytr" were recognized differently by actual users, by verifying that the user's experience with the AI-assisted writing service varied depending on the writing type and creativity level of e-mail or story plot writing. However, "Rytr" did not provide perfect writing results owing to the limitations of the AI system's performance. Therefore, when writing e-mails with low satisfaction, the AI generates text and provides an additional AWE service for grammar correction to complement the reliability and satisfaction aspects. Moreover, when writing a story plot, higher satisfaction and trust can be obtained by emphasizing the creativity level function, which allows for writing rich content.

5.2 Limitations

There is a possibility of carryover and order effects by WSD because all subjects participated in the experiment in the same order due to the nature of the online survey. In addition, subjects might lack an understanding of the service or have an insincere attitude because they responded by looking at the picture of the result without directly using the service. Finally, in this study, the evaluation of the specialized user experience for the AI-assisted writing service was not properly conducted. Moreover, because prior research on AI-based writing assistance tools has not been actively conducted, this research referred to other AI-assisted services in addition to existing research. In addition, the applicability of the indicators used in previous studies to this service was not sufficiently verified.

6 Conclusions

This study analyzed whether user experiences vary depending on the type of writing and the degree of creativity in AI-assisted writing. Based on previous studies on AI-assisted service, seven user experience factors were derived for evaluation: competence, reciprocity, benevolence, self-efficiency, controllability, trust, and satisfaction. Prototype D (writing case: story plot, creativity level: High) showed high values for all user experience factors. Competence, reciprocity, benevolence, and controllability were high when the creativity level was high. For the story plot in the writing case, competence, reciprocity, benevolence, and controllability were higher than that in the e-mail case. There was no significant difference between satisfaction and trust depending on the creativity level, but there was a significant difference depending on the situation for the writing case, and a high value was derived from the story plot. Therefore, when users derive richer writing results for novels through AI-assisted writing, they have a positive perception of AI-assisted writing services.

This study is meaningful as early research on the analysis of user experience of AI-assisted writing services. In addition, when developing an AI-assisted writing service in the future, it will be helpful to design functions based on user experience for each writing type.

Acknowledgement. This work was supported by the National Research Foundation of Korea (NRF) grant funded by the Korea government (MSIT) (No. NRF-2021R1F1A1063155). And this research was also supported by the MSIT(Ministry of Science and ICT), Korea, under the ICAN(ICT Challenge and Advanced Network of HRD) program (IITP-2022-RS-2022–00156215) supervised by the IITP(Institute of Information & Communications Technology Planning & Evaluation).

References

1. Nof, S.Y.: Automation: What it means to us around the world. In: Springer handbook of automation (pp. 13–52). Springer, Berlin, Heidelberg (2009). https://doi.org/10.1007/978-3-540-78831-7_3
2. Shinde, P.P., Shah, S.: A review of machine learning and deep learning applications. In: 2018 Fourth International Conference on Computing Communication Control and Automation (ICCUBEA) (pp. 1–6). IEEE (2018, August)
3. Wilson, J., Roscoe, R.D.: Automated writing evaluation and feedback: multiple metrics of efficacy. J. Educ. Comput. Res. **58**(1), 87–125 (2020)
4. Parra G,L., Calero, S.X.: Automated writing evaluation tools in the improvement of the writing skill. Int. J. Instruct. **12**(2), 209–226 (2019)
5. Wang, Y.J., Shang, H.F., Briody, P.: Exploring the impact of using automated writing evaluation in English as a foreign language university students' writing. Comput. Assist. Lang. Learn. **26**(3), 234–257 (2013)

6. Roscoe, R.D., Wilson, J., Johnson, A.C., Mayra, C.R.: Presentation, expectations, and experience: Sources of student perceptions of automated writing evaluation. Comput. Hum. Behav. **70**, 207–221 (2017)
7. Li, R.: Modeling the continuance intention to use automated writing evaluation among Chinese EFL learners. SAGE Open **11**(4), 21582440211060784 (2021)
8. Reiter, E., Dale, R.: Building Natural Language Generation Systems. Cambridge University Press (2000)
9. Goodman, S.M., Buehler, E., Clary, P., Coenen, A., Donsbach, A., Horne, T.N., Morris, M. R.: LaMPost: Design and Evaluation of an AI-assisted Email Writing Prototype for Adults with Dyslexia. In: Proceedings of the 24th International ACM SIGACCESS Conference on Computers and Accessibility, pp. 1–18 (2022, October)
10. Max, A.: Writing for language-impaired readers. In: Gelbukh, A. (ed.) CICLing 2006. LNCS, vol. 3878, pp. 567–570. Springer, Heidelberg (2006). https://doi.org/10.1007/11671299_59
11. Zhao, X.: Leveraging artificial intelligence (AI) technology for English writing: Introducing wordtune as a digital writing assistant for EFL writers. RELC J. 00336882221094089 (2022)
12. Gulati, S., Sousa, S., Lamas, D.: Modelling trust in human-like technologies. In: Proceedings of the 9th Indian Conference on Human Computer Interaction, pp. 1–10 (2018, December)
13. Harrison McKnight, D., Carter, M., Thatcher, J.B., Clay, P.F.: Trust in a specific technology: an investigation of its components and measures. ACM Trans. Manage. Inform. Syst. (TMIS) **2**(2), 12 (2011)
14. Sousa, S., Lamas, D., Dias, P.: A Model for Human-Computer Trust: Contributions Towards Leveraging User Engagement. In: Zaphiris, P., Ioannou, A. (eds.) Learning and Collaboration Technologies. Designing and Developing Novel Learning Experiences: First International Conference, LCT 2014, Held as Part of HCI International 2014, Heraklion, Crete, Greece, June 22-27, 2014, Proceedings, Part I, pp. 128–137. Springer International Publishing, Cham (2014). https://doi.org/10.1007/978-3-319-07482-5_13
15. Li, J., Dong, S., Chiou, E.K., Xu, J.: Reciprocity and its neurological correlates in human-agent cooperation. IEEE Trans. Human-Mach. Syst. **50**(5), 384–394 (2020)
16. Louie, R., Coenen, A., Huang, C.Z., Terry, M., Cai, C.J.: Novice-AI music co-creation via AI-steering tools for deep generative models. In: Proceedings of the 2020 CHI Conference on Human Factors in Computing Systems, pp. 1–13 (2020, April)
17. Madhavan, P., Phillips, R.R.: Effects of computer self-efficacy and system reliability on user interaction with decision support systems. Comput. Hum. Behav. **26**(2), 199–204 (2010)
18. Oh, C., Song, J., Choi, J., Kim, S., Lee, S., Suh, B.: I lead, you help but only with enough details: Understanding user experience of co-creation with artificial intelligence. In: Proceedings of the 2018 CHI Conference on Human Factors in Computing Systems, pp. 1–13 (2018, April)
19. Roy, Q., Zhang, F., Vogel, D.: Automation accuracy is good, but high controllability may be better. In: Proceedings of the 2019 CHI Conference on Human Factors in Computing Systems, pp. 1–8 (2019, May)
20. Ashfaq, M., Yun, J., Yu, S., Loureiro, S.M.C.: I, Chatbot: modeling the determinants of users' satisfaction and continuance intention of AI-powered service agents. Telematics Inform. **54**, 101473 (2020)
21. Shin, D.: The effects of explainability and causability on perception, trust, and acceptance: Implications for explainable AI. Int. J. Hum Comput Stud. **146**, 102551 (2021)
22. Purwanto, P., Kuswandi, K., Fatmah, F.: Interactive applications with artificial intelligence: the role of trust among digital assistant users. Форсайт, **14**(2 (eng)), 64–75 (2020)
23. Deng, X., Doll, W., Truong, D.: Computer self-efficacy in an ongoing use context. Behav. Inform. Technol. **23**(6), 395–412 (2004)

24. Everard, A., Galletta, D.F.: How presentation flaws affect perceived site quality, trust, and intention to purchase from an online store. J. Manag. Inf. Syst. **22**(3), 56–95 (2005)
25. Gao, M., Kortum, P., Oswald, F.: Psychometric evaluation of the use (usefulness, satisfaction, and ease of use) questionnaire for reliability and validity. In: Proceedings of the Human Factors and Ergonomics Society Annual Meeting (Vol. 62, No. 1, pp. 1414–1418). Sage CA: Los Angeles, CA: SAGE Publications (2018, September)

A Methodology for Personalized Dialogues Between Social Robots and Users Based on Social Media

Teresa Onorati[1]([✉]) [iD], Álvaro Castro-González[2] [iD], Paloma Díaz[1] [iD],
and Enrique Fernández-Rodicio[2] [iD]

[1] Computer Science Department, University Carlos III of Madrid, Getafe, Spain
{tonorati,pdp}@inf.uc3m.es
[2] Systems Engineering and Automation Department, University Carlos III of
Madrid, Getafe, Spain
{acgonzal,enrifern}@ing.uc3m.es

Abstract. Social robots are devoted to interacting and communicating with humans. Traditionally, the interaction capabilities of social robots are limited because the dialogues they can maintain are perceived as predictable, repetitive, and unnatural. This can lead the user to lose interest in the robot. If we want to bet on a successful and long coexistence of humans and robots, it is necessary to provide robots with more varied speeches that can be easily adapted to the users' needs. In this contribution, we propose a methodology that uses social media mining techniques to find topics that might interest a user. Then, using machine learning techniques, we create the robot's verbal communication. This methodology, implemented in our social robot Mini, uses three types of deep learning models for natural language processing: a summarization model, a long-form query-answer model, and a generative model. We rely on pre-trained models that have been integrated into Mini, allowing our robot to maintain conversations about different topics that change dynamically.

Keywords: social robots · human-robot interaction · social media mining · Natural Language Processing

1 Introduction

Traditionally, robots have been applied to environments where human-robot communication was irrelevant to achieving their tasks, such as vehicle assembly lines. Nowadays, social robots are reaching environments where they coexist with people, share the same space, and interact actively. In these environments, social robots aim at establishing fruitful, long-term relationships with people who coexist with them. To this end, these robots must be equipped with systems that allow fluid communication between them and those with whom they interact. Currently, most robots interact with people predictably and repetitively, following predefined rules. These predefined interactions can make the user bored and

H. Degen and S. Ntoa (Eds.): HCII 2023, LNAI 14051, pp. 273–284, 2023.
https://doi.org/10.1007/978-3-031-35894-4_20

lose interest after some time. To avoid this limitation, the so-called dialogue systems try to achieve a natural human-robot interaction, i.e., as close as possible to that which would be established between two people.

In this paper, we propose a methodology to endow robots with more varied and personalized dialogues, considering the changing needs of the users. In this methodology, we combine social media mining and deep learning techniques to define the verbal communication of the robot in a dynamic way taking advantage of the content published on social networks.

The widespread use among the population of social networks represents an important source of updated information about a wide range of topics. Considering the user's domain of interest, we search for related information on social networks to define the dialogue topics. However, the data shared in social networks is usually unstructured and heterogeneous and, consequently, hard to collect and analyze. For this reason, the first step is a preprocessing phase to store, filter, and organize the data collected from social networks in structures that facilitate their analysis. Then, in the second phase, we extract the relevant data, such as links to a more detailed topic description. With this relevant information, we rely on state-of-the-art deep learning models for Natural Language Processing (NLP) to generate a dialogue about a specific topic. These models will allow robots to take the initiative in the dialogue, talking about the topic of interest and responding appropriately to questions posed by the user. These models will be used whenever new content relevant to the user is posted on social networks. When new content matches the user's interests, the robot will initiate a conversation about a new topic. Consequently, we end up with a dialogue where the robot offers new conversations about novel topics in the user's domain of interest. This domain of interest can be defined by several factors that influence the interaction between the robot and the human; for example, the user interests (e.g., sports or local news), the user profile (including information such as his/her age), the configuration of the robot (e.g., its language), and the characteristics of the environment (e.g., its location). These factors will be considered when searching social media.

With this methodology, we try to contribute to solving some important problems in human-robot interaction. For instance, using our approach, the robot can take the initiative to start a coherent conversation about matters that the user likes while avoiding others; it could answer questions using data obtained from social networks; and our method considers new content published in social networks to talk about different topics. This guarantees the use of updated information to change the robot discourse, reducing the likelihood of boring the user.

The rest of the paper is structured as follows. The next section, Sect. 2, reviews other approaches for generating human-robot dialogues and how social media has been applied to robotics. After, in Sect. 3, we present our methodology and describe the four steps. Section 4 describes a particular use case where we have applied our methodology to a social robot interacting with a user. Finally, Sect. 5 summarizes the contributions of our methodology, its benefits, and also its limitations. Also, future directions are mentioned in the last section.

2   Related Works

In order to establish the expected links with people, social robots must be equipped with systems that allow fluid communication between them and the people with whom they interact. These systems are the so-called dialogue systems that try to achieve a natural human-robot interaction, i.e., an interaction as close as possible to that which would be established between two people. To this end, these systems consider multimodal communication using different channels, such as voice, touch, or gestures. In this section, we focus on dialogue systems that consider verbal communication. The generation of non-verbal communication in robots is out of the scope of this contribution.

Over the last two decades, researchers have worked intensively on modeling and managing dialogues from various approaches. Early systems defined dialogues as a set of "information gaps" that had to be filled through interaction. These gaps corresponded to information that had to be provided by a user, such as a person's name and age. In this line, Wessel et al. proposed using ontologies to parse user sentences and fill in these information gaps [28]. Other approach to dialogue modeling is represented by the state-based dialogue systems. In these systems, dialogues are considered finite state machines [22]. In plan-based systems, the robot and other actors must collaborate to complete some task or achieve some goal by interacting [5,27]. Probabilistic dialogue systems predict the state of the dialogue and the actions to be taken [14,34]. A few years ago, Milhorat et al. presented the Erica android dialogue manager [18], which uses probabilistic techniques to react to events detected by the robot and decide between answering a question or generating an assertion. In this same line, Kiefer et al. presented VOnDA, a rule-based dialogue manager with a statistical model responsible for selecting the best rule to apply in given situations [10]. Another type of system is an agent-based system where several software agents are coordinated, each one is in charge of different tasks during the interaction [11]. In all these works, the interaction possibilities are predefined at development time, and the topics of conversation are limited.

The latest systems to appear are end-to-end systems. These systems allow greater adaptability thanks to the learning performed by neural networks from a set of initial documents [6,8,13,15,24,30]. Advanced end-to-end systems, such as Google Duplex [12], are intended for automated calling systems and feature highly advanced verbal communication capabilities. They are based on deep neural networks and can carry out conversations in a very natural way for a very specific task (booking a table or making an appointment for a hairdresser); for example, Xu et al. presented an end-to-end dialogue manager for medical diagnosis [31]. However, these systems have to be intensively trained on specific scenarios and cannot carry out more generic conversations or outside that domain. Furthermore, these systems are not easily applicable to human-robot dialogue as they require (i) huge amounts of data, (ii) long training times, (iii) high computational capabilities, and (iv) such data are often proprietary and, therefore, not easily accessible to everyone.

Recently, large NLP models have generated great expectations in the NLP community, such as the irruption of Chat-GPT [21]. These optimized language models for dialogue provide very realistic conversations. However, its application to human-robot interaction (HRI) has just begun. In this work, we proposed to use some of these models to generate verbal communication during a human-robot dialogue. Particularly, we propose combining data obtained through social media mining techniques with NLP models to generate dynamic, non-repetitive dialogue in the user's domain of interest.

Some researchers have already started to use social media in social robotics. The first case was in the Facebots project [17], where real robots posted messages on Facebook to improve human-robot interaction in the long run. In the work of Takagi et al., [26], in 2011, they used Twitter to communicate with the robot. In 2014, [16] Ma et al. presented a study where participants could interact with a robot vacuum cleaner and a surveillance robot through different social media platforms. In a paper presented in 2019, Zeller et al. proposed using social media as a new mechanism for collecting data on the acceptance and sociability of robots [33]. Going back to 2011, Cramer and Büttner used a rabbit robot and the location, current and past, of its human friends via the social network Foursquare to launch provocative messages (e.g., Henriette and Sebastian are at Bagel Street Café, I imagine you weren't invited) [7]. In these works, the information people shared on social media platforms had been used as an additional communication channel or to launch simple pre-structured messages.

However, the content posted on social media represents a relevant source of information for many applications. One example is the management of emergency situations, where operators can find useful data about a crisis posted by citizens on social networks [19,20]. In this way, citizens have begun to actively produce and exchange information about events and circumstances around them, participating in the phenomenon that Westlund defined as citizen journalism [29].

Mining social media to extract relevant knowledge for building new applications raises several challenges [32]. First of all, despite the enormous volume of data generated, most individual posts do not contain relevant information. This is known as the Big Data Paradox and represents the need to analyze the collected data as a whole to extract knowledge from the aggregation. Secondly, social media do not have control over the quality of the shared messages, which can lead to noisy data, like fake news. Identifying these situations could be a tricky task that requires focusing not only on the content but also on the author's profile. In literature, several solutions have been proposed to deal with these challenges. Bakar et al. have proposed a process to clean and prepare social media data to be analyzed based on classic NLP techniques [1], and Kauter et al. have defined several modules for parsing texts and recognizing well-known elements [9], like the named entity (e.g., people, organizations or places).

In this paper, we propose to filter the most valuable information from social media to generate rich human-robot conversations and to this scope, we are going to define a four-step methodology taking into account also the pointed out limitations.

3   Our Methodology for Human-Robot Dialogue Generation

To improve human-robot communication, in this paper, we propose a four-step methodology that generates personalized dialogues about a topic of interest based on data extracted from social networks. These platforms offer several advantages, including the possibility of informing quickly about the last events and creating a sense of community where everybody can share opinions, thoughts, and feelings. There are also disadvantages, like the growing generation of unstructured and heterogeneous data that makes it difficult to filter out the most relevant information about a specific subject, distinguish between real and fake news or apply NLP techniques to analyze messages not grammatically well-formed.

To avoid these issues, the proposed methodology focuses on a list of official news accounts that we have selected to cover different domains, for example, politics, sports, and economics. The accounts in the list can be personalized depending on the user's interests. Figure 1 shows the four steps of the process: *link extraction*, *content extraction*, *dialogue prompt*, and *dialogue generation*.

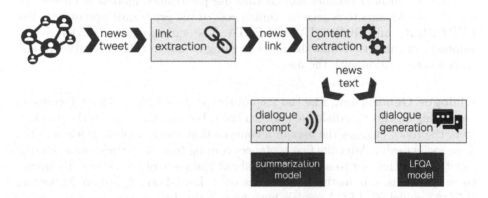

Fig. 1. Human-Robot Dialogue generation methodology.

Link Extraction. The first step of the methodology consists of monitoring the most recent messages posted by a list of media accounts defined based on the user's interests to guarantee the customization of the dialogue between the robot and the user. In particular, we are interested in messages containing links to articles hosted on trusted websites to extract and collect them automatically. In this way, we can access up-to-date information from trusted sources and limit the impact of fake news on dialogue generation.

Content Extraction. The second step receives the links previously identified from the official news account, accesses them and analyzes the web pages to extract the full body text of the article. It is worth noting that each website organizes the content by building its own structural layer. To deal with this issue, it is necessary to analyze each media to understand how its articles are structured and then build an ad-hoc parser to filter out any advertisements or irrelevant information that could affect the quality of the extracted text. The result of this step is a clean text prepared to be used as input for the following two steps.

Dialogue Prompt. The third step defines how the robot takes the initiative and starts the dialogue with the user. Finding a message that can capture the person's attention is crucial to establish the basis for building an interesting exchange of opinions and facts. In our methodology, the robot's initial message is about the latest news published in one of the media accounts selected based on the user's preferences, as explained in the first step. In particular, we run a deep learning summarization model over the text extracted from the news article. This model aims at building a shorter version of a long text, maintaining the most relevant information. Depending on the training, the characteristics of the text, and the language, these models can give different results. Examples are the encoder-decoder models that use pre-trained models as encoder or decoder checkpoints to reduce the timing cost of the pre-training phase [23], like BERT2BERT and ROBERTA2ROBERTA. The summarization model gives a summary of the article that the robot is going to use to take the initiative and start a conversation with the user.

Dialogue Generation. The last step of the proposed methodology focuses on generating an effective dialogue between the robot and the user. In the previous step, the robot engages the user in a conversation about a news article selected from social media. After the first sentences coming from the article summary, the robot invites the user to ask questions about the topic of the article. To answer these questions, our methodology relies on a Long-Form Question Answering (LFQA) model [4]. LFQA models have been trained to answer a question using a large store of documents that cover multiple topics. The answer is built as multiple sentences generated using an encoder-decoder model. In our methodology, the input to the LFQA model is a tuple formed by the question asked by the user and the context corresponding to the clean text obtained from the Content Extraction step. The model outputs the answer based on the information provided in the context.

4   Use Case

This section presents a running example where the robot Mini (see Fig. 2) interacts with a user. Mini is a desktop social robot developed by the Robotics Lab at Carlos III University of Madrid [25]. This robot is intended for interacting with seniors and assisting them in daily activities providing companionship, entertainment, and cognitive stimulation. Mini is equipped with microphones and an automatic speech-recognition engine that translates the user's utterance into text. Also, the robot has speakers and a text-to-speech engine that synthesizes the robot's utterances. The non-verbal expressions of the robot are automatically generated by a module designed to generate the illusion that the robot is alive [3].

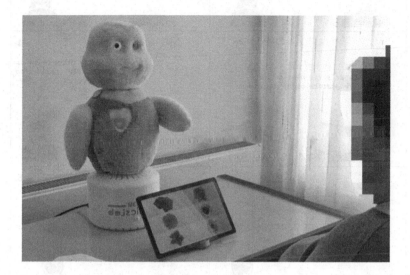

Fig. 2. The robot Mini interacting with a user.

In this use case, the user is interested in Spanish news, so Mini follows the social media accounts of the most important national newspapers and magazines. Figure 3 shows the storyboard of the interaction between Mini and a user. When one of these media publishes a tweet (Fig. 3.1), the robot receives it and searches for the link to the full article in the newspaper website. In this example, the received tweet translated to English said: "Queen Sofia traveled this Friday to the town of Fraga in Huesca to inaugurate a shelter for seasonal workers or people in a situation of social exclusion. https://t.co/5jMjFAnoQI".

Then, the robot extracts the link to the news, collects the full body text, and filters out the elements that are not part of the news (such as advertisements, publication date, or not printable characters). The remaining text is then fed into the summarization model. In this case, we have used the Spanish BERT2BERT model fine-tuned on the dataset MLSUM available in Hugging Face[1]. MLSUM is a large-scale multiLingual summarization dataset from online newspapers in five languages. The robot uses this model's output to briefly inform the user about the news (Fig. 3.2).

---

[1] https://huggingface.co/mrm8488/bert2bert_shared-spanish-finetuned-summarization.

Fig. 3. Use case example of the proposed methodology presented in six cartoons

If the user wants to know more about that news, (s)he can ask questions (Fig. 3.3). Then, Mini uses an LFQA model to generate the answer to that question. In this case, we have opted for the model LFQA BART-based Seq2Seq [4], a model trained with question/answer pairs from three Reddit[2] forums in English. Considering that our user is interacting with the robot in Spanish, we need to add an additional step to the process: translating the inputs of the LFQA model from Spanish into English and, conversely, the output of the model needs to be translated from English into Spanish. To this end, we rely on the GPT3-based model called Davinci [2] using the prompt "Translate this into [language]: [text to be translated]". Thus, the original filtered body text of the news and the question, both in Spanish, are input to the Davinci model. The Davinci output, i.e. the body text and the question in English, is fed into the LFQA model. Its outcome is then translated back into Spanish through Davinci obtaining the utterance the robot synthesizes for answering the user's question (Fig. 3.4).

---

[2] https://www.reddit.com/.

This question-answer dialogue can continue (Fig. 3.5) until the user decides that it is enough (Fig. 3.6).

5 Conclusions and Future Works

Human-robot interaction has been traditionally limited by predefined dialogues that usually lead to boring interactions after a certain time. Here, we propose a methodology to generate human-robot dialogues that, using the information published in social media, are customized to the user and change over time. The customization is based on defining the set of social media sources that each user is interested in. These sources will provide the topics our robot Mini will talk about with the user. Thanks to the nature of social media, the robot is aware of the breaking news when they are published and the topics of the conversations are updated frequently. The conversation is generated thanks to state of the art NLP models.

The use of NLP models opens new possibilities in human-technology interaction. In this paper, we have shown how three different types of models can benefit the natural interaction between a user and a robot communicating autonomously. In particular, we have used a summarization model to arouse the user's interest in breaking news and engage him/her in the interaction. Then, an LFQA model is used to clarify any doubts the user may have regarding the breaking news. Finally, a generative model is used to translate text when required.

The proposed methodology has been applied to our robot Mini. We have shown a use case where Mini chats with a user about a particular topic using the pipeline with the three NLP models.

The work presented in this paper has raised several limitations to consider. Human-robot interaction is very sensitive to excessive delays. Considering that the NLP models need time to process their inputs and generate the corresponding outputs, this could lead to unwanted delays that might hinder the interaction. This problem can be mitigated using conversational fillers when the robot needs extra time. For example, if the robot needs time to generate the answer to a question, the robot can say *"mmmm let me think about that"*.

Moreover, large deep learning models, like the ones we proposed in our methodology, consume resources (CPU and memory). Sometimes, the limited resources available onboard the robot are not enough. In these situations, we might consider using external servers with higher computational power while we watch carefully the additional delays caused by the latency in the communications.

Finally, we have to be aware of the actual limitations of the NLP models too. Although the results of the most advanced language models are impressive [21], they have some limitations related to the quality of their output. Every now and then, the output of these models is a text that is not true or the content might not be appropriate for the user. Also, they can produce texts that are grammatically awkward or, simply, they cannot find an answer to a question and the output does not match the question. These limitations are currently under research and they might affect how the user perceives the interaction with the robot.

We expect that our methodology can be applied in many areas where social robots and people need to communicate. For example, it would be relevant for scenarios where social robots interact with seniors, especially those that feel isolated and alone. In these scenarios, seniors, many times, are willing to talk to someone, but it is not always possible. Using our methodology, social robots could help mitigate their feelings and improve their quality of life.

Acknowledgements. This work has been supported by the Madrid Government (Comunidad de Madrid-Spain) under the Multiannual Agreement with UC3M ("Fostering Young Doctors Research", SMM4HRI-CM-UC3M), and in the context of the V PRICIT (Research and Technological Innovation Regional Programme). This work has been partially supported by the projects sense2MakeSense, funded by the Spanish State Agency of Research (PID2019-109388GB-I00), and IntCare-CM, funded by the regional government of the Community of Madrid.

References

1. Bakar, A.A., Othman, Z.A., Shuib, N.L.M.: Building a new taxonomy for data discretization techniques. In: 2009 2nd Conference on Data Mining and Optimization, pp. 132–140. IEEE (2009)
2. Bavarian, M., Jiang, A., Jun, H., Pondé, H.: New gpt-3 capabilities: Edit & insert (2022). https://openai.com/blog/gpt-3-edit-insert/
3. Bertó Giménez, A., Fernández-Rodicio, E., Castro-González, A., Salichs, M.A.: Do you want to make your robot warmer? make it more reactive! IEEE Transactions on Cognitive and Developmental Systems, pp. 1–1 (2022). https://doi.org/10.1109/TCDS.2022.3222038
4. Blagojevic, V.: Long-form qa beyond eli5: an updated dataset and approach (2022). towardsdatascience.com/long-form-qa-beyond-eli5-an-updated-dataset-and-approach-319cb841aabb
5. Bohus, D., Rudnicky, A.I.: The RavenClaw dialog management framework: architecture and systems. Comput. Speech Lang. **23**(3), 332–361 (2009)
6. Budzianowski, P., Casanueva, I., Tseng, B.H., Gasic, M.: Towards end-to-end multi-domain dialogue modelling. Technical Report CUED/F-INFENG/TR.706 (2018)
7. Cramer, H., Büttner, S.: Things that tweet, check-in and are befriended.: two explorations on robotics & social media. In: Proceedings of the 6th International Conference On Human-robot Interaction - HRI '11. p. 125. ACM Press (2011). https://doi.org/10.1145/1957656.1957693, http://portal.acm.org/citation.cfm?doid=1957656.1957693
8. Cuayáhuitl, H., Yu, S., Williamson, A., Carse, J.: Deep reinforcement learning for multi-domain dialogue systems. arXiv preprint arXiv:1611.08675 (2016)
9. Van de Kauter, M., Coorman, G., Lefever, E., Desmet, B., Macken, L., Hoste, V.: LeTs preprocess: the multilingual LT3 linguistic preprocessing toolkit. Comput. Ling. Netherlands J. **3**, 103–120 (2013)
10. Kiefer, B., Welker, A., Biwer, C.: VOnDA: A framework for ontology-based dialogue management. arXiv:1910.00340 [cs] (2019-10-01). http://arxiv.org/abs/1910.00340

11. Lee, C., Jung, S., Kim, S., Lee, G.G.: Example-based dialog modeling for practical multi-domain dialog system. Speech Communication **51**(5), 466–484 (2009-05). https://doi.org/10.1016/j.specom.2009.01.008, https://linkinghub.elsevier.com/retrieve/pii/S0167639309000107
12. Leviathan, Y., Matias, Y.: Google duplex: An AI system for accomplishing real-world tasks over the phone (2018-05-08).https://ai.googleblog.com/2018/05/duplex-ai-system-for-natural-conversation.html
13. Li, X., Chen, Y.N., Li, L., Gao, J., Celikyilmaz, A.: End-to-end task-completion neural dialogue systems. arXiv preprint arXiv:1703.01008 (2017)
14. Lison, P.: A hybrid approach to dialogue management based on probabilistic rules. Comput. Speech Lang. **34**(1), 232–255 (2015-11). https://doi.org/10.1016/j.csl.2015.01.001, https://linkinghub.elsevier.com/retrieve/pii/S0885230815000029
15. Liu, B., Lane, I.: An end-to-end trainable neural network model with belief tracking for task-oriented dialog. arXiv preprint arXiv:1708.05956 (2017)
16. Ma, X., Yang, X., Zhao, S., Fu, C.W., Lan, Z., Pu, Y.: Using social media platforms for human-robot interaction in domestic environment. Int. J. Human-Computer. Interact. **30**(8), 627 042 (2014-08-03). https://doi.org/10.1080/10447318.2014.907011, http://www.tandfonline.com/doi/abs/10.1080/10447318.2014.907011
17. Mavridis, N., Petychakis, M., Tsamakos, A., Toulis, P., Emami, S., Kazmi, W., Datta, C., BenAbdelkader, C., Tanoto, A.: FaceBots: steps towards enhanced long-term human-robot interaction by utilizing and publishing online social information. Paladyn, J. Behav. Robot. **1**(3), 169–178 (2010)
18. Milhorat, P., Lala, D., Inoue, K., Zhao, T., Ishida, M., Takanashi, K., Nakamura, S., Kawahara, T.: A conversational dialogue manager for the humanoid robot ERICA. In: Eskenazi, M., Devillers, L., Mariani, J. (eds.) Advanced Social Interaction with Agents. LNEE, vol. 510, pp. 119–131. Springer, Cham (2019). https://doi.org/10.1007/978-3-319-92108-2_14
19. Onorati, T., Díaz, P.: Giving meaning to tweets in emergency situations: a semantic approach for filtering and visualizing social data. Springerplus **5**(1), 1–17 (2016). https://doi.org/10.1186/s40064-016-3384-x
20. Onorati, T., Díaz, P., Carrion, B.: From social networks to emergency operation centers: a semantic visualization approach. Futur. Gener. Comput. Syst. **95**, 829–840 (2019)
21. OpenAI: Chatgpt: Optimizing language models for dialogue (2022). https://openai.com/blog/chatgpt/
22. Peltason, J., Wrede, B.: Pamini: A framework for assembling mixed-initiative human-robot interaction from generic interaction patterns. In: Proceedings of the SIGDIAL 2010 Conference, pp. 229–232. Association for Computational Linguistics (2010-09), https://www.aclweb.org/anthology/W10-4341
23. Rothe, S., Narayan, S., Severyn, A.: Leveraging pre-trained checkpoints for sequence generation tasks. Trans. Assoc. Comput. Linguist. **8**, 264–280 (2020)
24. Saha, T., Saha, S., Bhattacharyya, P.: Towards sentiment aided dialogue policy learning for multi-intent conversations using hierarchical reinforcement learning. PLOS ONE **15**(7), e0235367 (2020-07-02). https://doi.org/10.1371/journal.pone.0235367, https://dx.plos.org/10.1371/journal.pone.0235367
25. Salichs, M.A., et al.: Mini: A new social robot for the elderly. International J. Social Robot. **12**(6), 1231–1249 (2020-12). https://doi.org/10.1007/s12369-020-00687-0, http://link.springer.com/10.1007/s12369-020-00687-0
26. Takagi, K., Rzepka, R., Araki, K.: Just keep tweeting, dear: web-mining methods for helping a social robot understand user needs. In: 2011 AAAI Spring Symposium Series (2011)

27. Wahde, M.: A dialogue manager for task-oriented agents based on dialogue building-blocks and generic cognitive processing. In: 2019 IEEE International Symposium on INnovations in Intelligent SysTems and Applications (INISTA), pp. 1–8. IEEE (2019-07). https://doi.org/10.1109/INISTA.2019.8778354, https://ieeexplore.ieee.org/document/8778354/

28. Wessel, M., Acharya, G., Carpenter, J., Yin, M.: An ontology-based dialogue management system for virtual personal assistants — SRI international. In: International Workshop on Spoken Dialogue Systems Technology, p. 12 (2017), https://www.sri.com/work/publications/ontology-based-dialogue-management-system-virtual-personal-assistants

29. Westlund, O.: Mobile news. Digital J. 1(1), 6–26 (2013). https://doi.org/10.1080/21670811.2012.740273, https://doi.org/10.1080/21670811.2012.740273

30. Xu, H., Peng, H., Xie, H., Cambria, E., Zhou, L., Zheng, W.: End-to-end latent-variable task-oriented dialogue system with exact log-likelihood optimization. World Wide Web 23(3), 1989–2002 (2020-05). https://doi.org/10.1007/s11280-019-00688-8, http://link.springer.com/10.1007/s11280-019-00688-8

31. Xu, L., Zhou, Q., Gong, K., Liang, X., Tang, J., Lin, L.: End-to-end knowledge-routed relational dialogue system for automatic diagnosis. Proceedings of the AAAI Conference on Artificial Intelligence 33, 7346–7353 (2019-07-17). https://doi.org/10.1609/aaai.v33i01.33017346, https://wvvw.aaai.org/ojs/index.php/AAAI/article/view/4722

32. Zafarani, R., Abbasi, M.A., Liu, H.: Social media mining: an introduction. Cambridge University Press (2014)

33. Zeller, F., Smith, D.H., Au Duong, J., Mager, A.: Social media in human–robot interaction. Int. J. Social Robot.(2019-07-03). https://doi.org/10.1007/s12369-019-00573-4, http://link.springer.com/10.1007/s12369-019-00573-4

34. Zhao, T.: Reinforest: Multi-domain dialogue management using hierarchical policies and knowledge ontology (2016)

EEG-Based Machine Learning Models
for Emotion Recognition in HRI

Mariacarla Staffa[1](✉) and Lorenzo D'Errico[2]

[1] Università degli Studi di Napoli Parthenope, Naples, Italy
mariacarla.staffa@uniparthenope.it
[2] Università degli Studi di Napoli Federico II, Naples, Italy
lorenzo.derrico@unina.it

Abstract. This work attempts to provide a measure of the human affective state employing the analysis of electroencephalographic (EEG) activity to accurately identify the psychological state of the human during the interaction with a humanoid robot. Here, it's presented the implementation and validation of different optimized classifiers such as Support Vector Machine, Decision Tree and Deep Neural Networks for estimating human affective state using the humanoid robot Pepper, equipped with two opposite personality configurations (positive and negative) to observe if and how a particular robot personality can affect the users' affective response during the interaction. Affective state was estimated from physiological signals extracted from EEG relying on the two dimensional valence-arousal representation of emotions. The results show how feature selection improves the classification of the affective state of the individual as well as a fine process of hyperparameters optimization. Finally, a proof of the positive effect of a positive attitude of the robot in the interaction between human and robot, in terms of lower levels of negative emotion (such as Stress) recorded, is given.

Keywords: EEG-based emotion Recognition in SAR · Classifiers Optimization

1 Introduction

In order to increase the degree of acceptability of robotic devices from human users, a lot of effort is being made in the last decade to humanize both the robot shape [20] and functioning. It has been shown that in SAR the study of the emotional states of humans facilitates human-robot mutual affective understanding and, in turn, allows an empathetic interaction enhancing legibility and acceptability of robots [21]. Additionally, endowing robots with this high level cognitive capability can also permit better engagement of the interlocutor in complex social interaction [6, 19]. Typical approaches are able to assess humans' affective responses from the observation of overt behavior. However, there are cases in which the overt observable behaviors could not match with the internal states (e.g., people with diseases compromising normal emotional responses). In such cases, having an objective measure of the users' state from 'inside' is of paramount importance. This work aims to demonstrate the effectiveness of EEG measurements in determining the emotional state in experimental subjects during the

H. Degen and S. Ntoa (Eds.): HCII 2023, LNAI 14051, pp. 285–297, 2023.
https://doi.org/10.1007/978-3-031-35894-4_21

interaction with a robot. In particular, we investigate the correlation between the parameters of valence and arousal and the emotional state of users in correspondence with a particular personality profile of the robot, namely *positive* and *negative*, designed to induce greater positive responses (positive engagament) and lower negative responces (such as stress) during the interaction. This hypothesis arises from the observation of the congruity between the physiological brain response relating to the state of positive mental engagement, which can be assimilated to a positive emotional state, and the information extracted from the parameters of valence and arousal in relation to the brain activity of alpha and beta bands of the frontal areas of the brain [10]. Machine learning and deep learning algorithms are used for data classification, such as Support Vector Machine (SVM), Decision Tree (DT) and Deep Neural Network (DNN). From the application of a careful process of features selection and hyperparameters optimization a considerable presence of noise is highlighted within the data, it is therefore observed how the removal of the latter can strongly affect the improvement of the predictive quality of the models proposed. The paper is structured as follows: in Sect.2 background notions of valence and arousal are given as well as a description of the classifiers used; in Sect.3 a step by step description of the experimental setup, the recording procedure and the creation of the dataset is explained and the general workflow is given; Sect.4 investigates the results obtained and finally, in Sect.5 conclusions are presented along with a discussion on possible future works.

2   Materials and Methods

2.1   Valence and Arousal

In the EEG frequency domain, the frontal asymmetry feature detects valence and arousal values. The valence and arousal values are calculated from the difference, in terms of signal, in the α (8-13 Hz) and β (13-30 Hz) frequency bands received between the brain's left and right frontal hemispheres. This is called EEG asymmetry [12]. The power of the α-band is related to the relaxed state of mind [23]: an increase in the power of the α-band in the right hemisphere can occur when viewing negative stimuli [23]. In contrast, a decrease in the power of the frontal α-band can be observed when someone is exposed to high-arousal stimuli [16]. The β-band is associated with the sensory-motor system; an increase in the power of this band has been found when someone is exposed to positive stimuli [13]. Furthermore, an increase in the power of the frontal β-band is observed during the visualization of high excitation stimuli [12]. From numerous studies, one can deduce a shift towards right frontal activity when exposed to negative stimuli or stressful conditions [10]. So the more significant activity of the right frontal hemisphere is associated with a negative valence, and the more significant activity of the left frontal hemisphere is associated with a positive valence. Furthermore, a high β frequency and low α frequency of the frontal hemisphere of the brain characterize high arousal [15]. The features of frontal EEG asymmetry are measured by the ratio between the α and β bands to determine valence and excitation according to the formula presented in [1] to compute the four characteristics for frontal valence (Eq. 1 to Eq. 4) and arousal (Eq. 5 to Eq. 8). Where α_{F7}, α_{F8}, β_{F7}, and β_{F8} are the α and β power bands measured on channels AF7 and AF8 (See Fig. 1, yellow marked). Since the recording procedure channel order output, differently from [1], channels F7 (the phisically closest to AF7) and F8 (the fiscally closest to AF8) have been used instead of AF7 and AF8 (See Fig. 1, red rounded).

$$v_1 = \frac{\alpha_{F8}}{\beta_{F8}} - \frac{\alpha_{F7}}{\beta_{F7}} \tag{1}$$

$$v_2 = ln(\alpha_{F7}) - ln(\alpha_{F8}) \tag{2}$$

$$v_3 = \frac{\beta_{F7}}{\alpha_{F7}} - \frac{\beta_{F8}}{\alpha_{F8}} \tag{3}$$

$$v_4 = \alpha_{F8} - \alpha_{F7} \tag{4}$$

$$\alpha_1 = \frac{\alpha_{F7} + \alpha_{F8}}{\beta_{F7} + \beta_{F8}} \tag{5}$$

$$\alpha_2 = -(ln(\alpha_{F7}) + ln(\alpha_{F8})) \tag{6}$$

$$\alpha_3 = log_2(\frac{\beta_{F7} + \beta_{F8}}{\alpha_{F7} + \alpha_{F8}}) \tag{7}$$

$$\alpha_4 = \frac{\beta_{F7} + \beta_{F8}}{\alpha_{F7} + \alpha_{F8}} \tag{8}$$

2.2 Classifiers

For classification purposes several models have been used: SVM with different kernels (all tested in this work) such as linear, polynomial, rbf and sigmoidal; Decision Tree and Deep Neural Network. All these classifiers have shown excellent results in stress and emotion classification using EEG signals. Authors in [2] use SVM to discriminate different stress levels through EEG signals with an accuracy of 94.79%. Authors in [8] use and compare K-nearest neighbors (KNN) and SVM to classify a person's stress levels before and after the examination, by achieving 90% accuracy in binary classification for stress and relaxation. A similar study was conducted by [5]. Stress symptoms have also been used in the literature to prevent depression. Authors in [11] use DNN to predict the user's feeling of stress through listening to music. They showed that music could not only provide a psychological treatment effect but also improve the person's ability to concentrate. Authors in [14] classify stress using the EEG signal from movie clips that induce (or not) stress. They compared MLP and Long short-term memory (LSTM) to classify stress, and the maximum accuracy was achieved at 93% by the LSTM. The study in [22] performs an emotion recognition using only the FP1 and FP2 channels of the frontal EEG signal by obtaining the highest accuracy of 76% with the Gradient boosting DT also comparing the results with classifiers such as RF, SVM and KNN.

3 Experiment

3.1 Partecipants

Tests were performed in a study with limited external acustic noise. A sample of 10 students was enrolled in the experiments: 7 males and 3 females with ages ranging from 20 to 26.

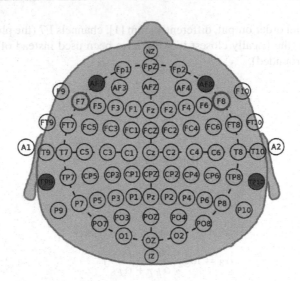

Fig. 1. AF7-AF8 (yellow marked) and F7-F8 (red rounded) electrode locations in the International 10-20 system.

3.2 Stimuli

We designed an experimental study where a humanoid Pepper robot was used to interact with subjects through a simple dialogue while showing to different personalities:

– *positive* aiming at creating a positive relationship with the users that, in the context of therapeutic and cognitive interventions, can help in facilitating the success of the interaction [7] also profiting of the robot embodiment condition [20];
– *negative* that, even if in some condition has been shown to affect adherence to treatments in assistive scenarios [19], as a side effect can induce a negative emotion in the subjects (such as stress) by negatively impacting on the users' willingness to interact with robots.

The robot's behavior personalities have been designed by modeling eyes LED color, head and body movements, voice and dialogue according to the works of [3,4,9]. Conversely from the majority of existing elicitation and evaluation of emotion interpretation systems in HRI, which use a baseline such as for example a resting state or a neutral condition or stimuli that users view (e.g., looking at images, watching videos containing certain emotions) [18] without the presence of a robot, we foster the concept that for a better detection of user's affect states during HRI, the systems should be trained and validated during HRI. This is because it has been observed that the affective response in HRI is primarily related to the presence of the robot itself, independently from the interaction modality [17]. Meaning that if we aim at observing diverse affective responses during the use of the robot as elicited by the robot's diverse personality, we should avoid a baseline where the robot is not accounted for.

3.3 Acquisition Device

EEG signals were gathered by the Emotiv *EPOC+* headset, a non-invasive 14-channels (AF3, AF4, F3, F4, FC5, FC6, F7, F8, T7, T8, P7, P8, O1, O2 wrt to International 10-20 system) helmet characterized by lightweight, easy donning, and wireless connection. Then, the EEG headset was set up on the participant's head and EEG data acquisition started when the robot introduced itself. In Fig. 2 a subject interacts with the robot with negative Fig. 2(a) and positive Fig. 2(b) personality.

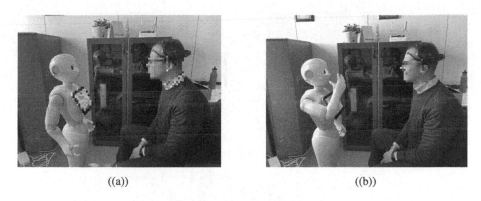

((a))   ((b))

Fig. 2. HRI testing phase with (a) negative and (b) positive personality Pepper.

Each test (interaction with the *positive* and *negative* robot) had both the same duration of 10 min. The order of the tests was random.

3.4 Dataset

The set of data collected by the experimental subjects is composed of 2048 record (balanced) for each of the 10 experimental subjects, for a total of 20480 entries. The data, in its original form, consists of vectors of 148 floating point features and classified according to two possible classes (negative, positive). For each single experimental subject the data collected are equally balanced between the two classes. As for the labelling procedure, the value 0 it's been associated with samples collected during the interaction with the negative robot and 1 with those acquired during the interaction with the positive robot.

3.5 Feature Extraction

Feature extraction is been performed using all 14 electrodes supplied with the helmet. For the noise removal a Butterworth filter, in the high-pass version, with cutoff frequency at 0.16 Hz was used while a IIR filter was applied to remove the DC Offset. Then, a band-pass filter is applied to each channel for splitting the signal into the following 5 frequency bands: σ (0 Hz–0.14 Hz), θ (4 Hz–8 Hz), α (8 Hz–14 Hz), β (14 Hz–30 Hz), and γ (30 Hz–40 Hz). Thus, 70 distinct signals are obtained, 5 for each of the 14 channels of the helmet (see Fig. 3).

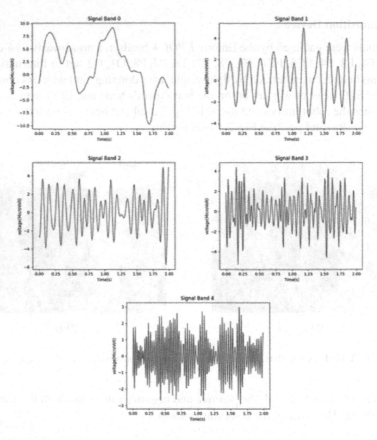

Fig. 3. Channel F3-Subject 0 examples of signal for each band of frequency.

Each of the 70 signals is broken down into time windows of 1 s with an overlap of 80% and a periodigram function is applied to each window obtained to calculate the power spectral density moving from the time to the frequency domain (see Fig. 4). Therefore, each time-window of the signal is converted into the relative power distribution on the frequency axis, from which the statistical information of mean and standard deviation is extracted and this procedure is repeated for each of the 5 bands and for each of the 14 channels: a total amount of 140 features are thus obtained. Since the state of tension/stress/effort belongs to the human emotional spectrum, we added to the features vector the 8 features (valence characteristics from v1-v4 and the excitation characteristics from a1-a4) presented in [1] used to determine the valence and arousal levels. So in conclusion, each record is characterized by 148 features.

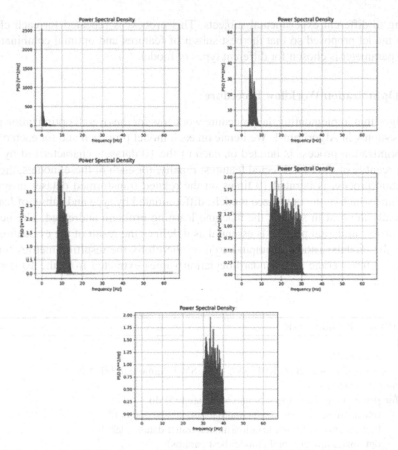

Fig. 4. Spectral density distribution for the 5 bands for Channel F3-Subject 0 on 1s time window.

3.6 Feature Selection

Univariate feature selection (i.e. the selection of the best features based on univariate statistical tests) has been used as technique to perform feature selection. It can be seen as a pre-processing stage for an estimator. *SelectPercentile* from python library Scikit-learn has been chosen to implement feature selection. Feature selection was executed as function of the percentile variable in the range [10, 100] with steps of amplitude 5. Each subset thus obtained is subsequently used for training and evaluation of the predictive models chosen by performing an hyper-parameters optimization. The hyper-parameter optimization process consists in creating a set of possible hyper-parameter configurations, initialize models based on these configurations, and evaluate their quality by training and testing the input dataset. Hence, a cross validation is performed to calculate the average accuracy scores obtained from the models to determine the optimal configuration. The outputs are the configuration that achieved the best rating. Subsequently, models are evaluated by cross-validation splitting each dataset in subset relating to different experimental subjects. This process is repeated for each classification model proposed so that the best subset of features and optimal combination of hyper-parameter is chosen for different types of model.

3.7 Optimization Workflow Procedure

The algorithm implementing the procedure workflow for the overall optimization procedure is shonw in Algorithm 1. We iterate on each model proposed and for each of them the optimization process is iterated on each of the 10 datasets characterized by a certain percentile of the best selected features. Finally, for each of these models, the cross validation process is iterated 10 times on the related transformed dataset in order to determine which of the optimized models, differentiated by type and subset of features, is globally the best in solving the machine learning problem addressed. The iteration of the cross validation process is essential as it defines the result of the evaluation metrics of the models with high output variance; therefore, the resulting metrics for each model are the average and standard deviation values extracted from the 10 iterations performed.

Algorithm 1. Pseudo-Code

```
start
test iteration = 10
models = (SVC Linear, SVC RBF, SVC Poly, SVC Sigmoidal, DT, NN)
for model in models do
    for percentile in range(min=5, max=100, step=5) do
        transf dataset = feature selection(dataset, labels, percentile)
        best params = HP optimization(model, transf dataset, labels)
        optimized model = build model(best params)
        for iteration in range(test iteration) do
            metrics = cross validation(optimized model, transf dataset, labels)
            save(metrics)
        end for
    end for
end for
generate plots and tables
end
```

---

4   Results Analysis

To evaluate the accuracy of the proposed classifiers, we deployed the classical statistical evaluation methodology. Thus, the results of the classification can fall into one of these 4 classes:

1. True Positive (TP), when the hypothesis of a high-stress level is confirmed;
2. False Positive (FP), when the hypothesis of a low-stress level is confirmed;

3. False Positive (FP), when the hypothesis of a high-stress level is wrong;
4. False Negative (FN), when the hypothesis of a low-stress level is wrong.

We then computed the statistical variables allowing a quantitative analysis of the model: TP rate (Eq. 9), FP rate (Eq. 10), Precision (Eq. 11), Recall (Eq. 12), and F-measure (Eq. 13) giving rise to the confusion matrix shown in Fig. 5 - for the best model trained.

$$TP_{rate} = \frac{TP}{TP + FN} \tag{9}$$

$$FP_{rate} = \frac{FP}{(FP + TN)} \tag{10}$$

$$Precision = \frac{TP}{TP + FP} \tag{11}$$

$$Recall = \frac{TP}{TP + FN} \tag{12}$$

$$F - measure = \frac{FP}{FP + TN} \tag{13}$$

TP, TN, and FP are the numbers of correctly predicted true positives and true negatives, whereas FP and FN are the numbers of incorrect predicted false positives and false negatives, respectively. The degree to which the measured value of a quantity corresponds to its true value is known as *accuracy* (ACC). The *sensitivity* (SN) of a test refers to its ability to detect true positives. Finally, the ability of a test to detect true negatives is measured by its *specificity* (SP).

The best overall accuracy is obtained from the NN model (see Table 1) with 736 neurons, dropout value of $0, 6$, Sigmoid as activation function and Adam as optimezer. It's possible to distinguish the performance for the two classes 0 (negative) and 1 (positive):

– Case 0 (negative): Precion scores vary among the models: SVC models got the worst performances reaching 0.79 only for the POLY kernel while TREE and NN got better performances, especially NN models; Recall scores are quite the same for all models, SVC and NN outperfom TREE model; NN models still outperfom other models in f1-score reaching 0.96 for the best parametrization while the SVC got worst scores except the POLY kernel one;
– Case 1 (positive): same Precision score is obtained for all NN and TREE models, but in general it's quite the same for all the models; Recall scores are all around 0.98 for NN and TREE models while it drops for the others where the POLY SVC turns out to outperform the others; same about the f1-score for NN and TREE models while SVC's got worst performances except the POLY one.

Grouping by model, instead:

– SVC: shows a higher Precision on positive over negative signals while Recall scores are higher for the negative cases and finally the f1-score turns out a better performances for quite all models working on positive signals;

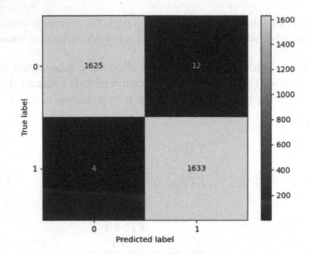

Fig. 5. Confusion matrix for the best model trained, DNN.

- TREE: excluding the Recall values that are similar for all the models, Precision and f1-score values demonstrate better performances on positive signals;
- NN: same as TREE models, Recall scores are slightly higher for negative signals but very similar among them, while Precision and f1-score values show better performances for positive signals.

All TREE and NN models got high values of accuracy, NN slightly outperform the TREE. So, in conclusion, NN models got the best performances among all the tested ones showing a better Precision and f1-score for the positive signals.

Table 1. Table results for 0 "negative" and 1 "Stress" cases, where: K states for "KERNEL", C for "CRITERION", a_o for "ACTIVATION_OUTPUT"=, SIG for "SIGMOID", SFT for "SOFT-MAX", A for "ADAM", AX for "ADAMAX", n_n for "n_neurons" and d for "dropout".

model	Precision 0	Precision 1	Recall 0	Recall 1	f1-score 0	f1-score 1	Accuracy
LIN_SVC(C=1, K=LINEAR)	0.46	1.00	0.99	0.75	0.63	0.86	0.79
RBF_SVC(C=1, K=RBF, GAMMA=0.7)	0.19	0.99	1.0	0.08	0.32	0.15	0.24
POLY_SVC(C=1, K=POLY, DEGREE=3)	0.79	0.98	0.90	0.95	0.84	0.96	0.94
SVC(C=1)	0.37	1.00	1.0	0.63	0.54	0.77	0.69
TREE(m.d=3, C=ENTROPY)	0.90	0.99	0.97	0.98	0.93	0.98	0.98
TREE(m.d=6, C=ENTROPY)	0.85	0.99	0.98	0.96	0.91	0.98	0.96
TREE(m.d=9, C=ENTROPY)	0.90	0.99	0.96	0.98	0.93	0.98	0.97
TREE(m.d=12, C=ENTROPY)	0.84	0.99	0.96	0.96	0.89	0.97	0.96
NN(a_o=SIG, opt=A, n_n=736, d=0.6)	0.93	1.00	0.99	0.98	0.96	0.99	0.9862
NN(a_o=SOFT, opt=A, n_n=232, d=0.6)	0.89	1.00	0.99	0.97	0.94	0.99	0.9764
NN(a_o=SIG, opt=AX, n_n=736, d=0.6)	0.92	1.00	0.99	0.98	0.96	0.99	0.9840
NN(a_o=SOFT, opt=AX, n_n =720, d=0.6)	0.92	1.00	0.99	0.98	0.95	0.99	0.9823

5   Conclusions and Discussion

The results show a correlation between the extracted (and subsequently selected) features and the emotional state of the subject in the two experimental tests. The importance of the contribution provided by the features selection process in optimizing the predictive efficiency thanks to the removal of the noise carried by the inessential features has been demonstrated. The results of the "feature selection" show a strong correlation between the state of mental effort and the characteristics of "valence" (v1, v2, v3, v4) and a lower correlation, but still above the average, with the variables of "arousal" (a1, a2, a3, a4). Therefore, these parameters of "valence" and "arousal" appear to be incisive in determining the state of mental commitment and undoubtedly deserve further study on their application in solving the machine learning problem addressed in this work. For future purposes, a first highly incisive improvement factor concerns the use of higher quality professional instrumentation, a helmet equipped with a greater number of electrodes, with preferably non fragile fastenings of the same and a stable assembly structure on the subject's head. It is also equally essential to make sure you use electrodes with a high capacity to maintain a moist state by retaining the saline solution for as long as possible. In order to make the classification capacity of predictive models as independent as possible from the characteristic physiological responses of single subjects, a greater number of experimental subjects is needed, for example 100 or more. Furthermore, it should be ensured that each subject carries out a task suited to their respective interests, or at least avoid associating tasks that are not very stimulating and interesting given the aptitudes of the experimental subject under examination. It would also be important to carry out a preliminary estimate of the subject's basic emotional state using a specific self-completed questionnaire, taking care to exclude from the test those subjects who show a strong perennial emotional state (depression, anxiety, etc.) potentially capable of strongly polluting the data. A final improvement factor concerns the execution of the experiments in a controlled environment that minimizes the presence of external distraction factors capable of disturbing the emotional state of the subject. The experiment was performed with the sole use of the EEG helmet, the possible integration of the measurement of other vital parameters (pressure, heart rate, respiration, eye movement, etc.), whether for direct classification purposes or as a tool support for the rejection of any "polluted" data, by crossing the data from the various sensors it allows to acquire greater awareness of the emotional state of the subject and to identify any "contradictory" emotional states. Therefore, even if it does not have the purpose of generating data for classification, this technique would allow to increase the noise cleaning from the EEG data used for the construction of the model training dataset.

Acknowledgement. The work was also supported by the Italian Ministry of University and Research—MIUR, within the PRIN2022 research project "RESTART - Robot Enhanced Social abilities based on Theory of mind for Acceptance of Robot in assistive Treatments" (Prot. 2022WCMNTT), approved by the MIUR with D.D. no. 861.

References

1. Al-Nafjan, A., Hosny, M., Al-Wabil, A., Al-Ohali, Y.: Classification of human emotions from electroencephalogram (eeg) signal using deep neural network. Int. J. Adv. Comput. Sci. Applicat. **8**(9) (2017)
2. Shargie, F.A., Tang, T.B., Badruddin, N., Kiguchi, M.: Towards multilevel mental stress assessment using svm with ecoc: an eeg approach. Medical Biol. Eng. Comput. **56**(1), 125–136 (2018)
3. Caccavale, R., Leone, E., Lucignano, L., Rossi, S., Staffa, M., Finzi, A.: Attentional regulations in a situated human-robot dialogue. In RO-MAN, pp. 844–849. IEEE (2014)
4. Coulson, M.: Attributing emotion to static body postures: Recognition accuracy, confusions, and viewpoint dependence. J. Nonverbal Behav. **28**, 117–139 (2004)
5. Rajendran, V.G., Jayalalitha, S., Adalarasu, K., Usha, G.: Analysis and classification of stress among students using eeg as biomarker. ECS Trans. **107**(1), 1857 (2022)
6. Iengo, S., Origlia, A., Staffa, M., Finzi, A.: Attentional and emotional regulation in human-robot interaction. In RO-MAN, pp. 1135–1140. IEEE (2012)
7. Jani, B.D., Blane, D.N., Mercer, S.W.: The role of empathy in therapy and the physician-patient relationship. Complem. Med. Res. **19**(5), 252–257 (2012)
8. Khosrowabadi, R., Quek, C., Ang, K.K., Tung, S.W., Heijnen, M.: A brain-computer interface for classifying eeg correlates of chronic mental stress. In: The 2011 International Joint Conference on Neural Networks, pp. 757–762 (2011)
9. Kleinsmith, A., Bianchi-Berthouze, N.: Affective body expression perception and recognition: A survey. IEEE Trans. Affect. Comput. **4**, 15–33 (2013)
10. Lewis, R.S., Weekes, N.Y., Wang, T.H.: The effect of a naturalistic stressor on frontal eeg asymmetry, stress, and health. Biol. Psychol. **75**(3), 239–247 (2007)
11. Liao, C.-Y., Chen, R.-C., Tai, S.-K.: Emotion stress detection using eeg signal and deep learning technologies. In: 2018 IEEE International Conference on Applied System Invention (ICASI), pp. 90–93 (2018)
12. Menon, S., Geethanjali, B., Guhan Seshadri, N.P., Muthumeenakshi, S., Nair, S.: Evaluating the induced emotions on physiological response. In: Nandi, A.K., Sujatha, N., Menaka, R., Alex, J.S.R. (eds.) Computational Signal Processing and Analysis. LNEE, vol. 490, pp. 211–220. Springer, Singapore (2018). https://doi.org/10.1007/978-981-10-8354-9_19
13. Mühl, C., Allison, B., Nijholt, A., Chanel, G.: A survey of affective brain computer interfaces: principles, state-of-the-art, and challenges. Brain-Comput. Interfaces **1**(2), 66–84 (2014)
14. Nishtha, P., Devanjali, R., Goldie, G., Ponnurangam, K., Mesay, S.: Stress classification using brain signals based on lstm network. Comput. Intell. Neurosci., Article ID 7607592, 13 pages (2022)
15. Ramirez, R., Vamvakousis, Z.: Detecting emotion from EEG signals using the emotive Epoc device. In: Zanzotto, F.M., Tsumoto, S., Taatgen, N., Yao, Y. (eds.) BI 2012. LNCS (LNAI), vol. 7670, pp. 175–184. Springer, Heidelberg (2012). https://doi.org/10.1007/978-3-642-35139-6_17
16. Reuderink, B., Mühl, C., Poel, M.: Valence, arousal and dominance in the eeg during game play. Int. J. Auton. Adapt. Commun. Syst. **6**(1), 45–62 (2013)
17. Sanghvi, J., Castellano, G., Leite, I., Pereira, A., McOwan, P.W., Paiva, A.: Automatic analysis of affective postures and body motion to detect engagement with a game companion. In Proceedings of the 6th International Conference on Human-Robot Interaction, pp. 305–312. Association for Computing Machinery, NY, USA (2011)
18. Shao, M., Dos Reis Alves, S.F., Ismail, O., Zhang, X., Nejat, G., Benhabib, B.: You are doing great! only one rep left: An affect-aware social robot for exercising. In: 2019 IEEE International Conference on Systems, Man and Cybernetics (SMC), pp. 3811–3817 (2019)

19. Rossi, S., Santangelo, G., Staffa, M., Varrasi, S., Conti, D., Di Nuovo, A.: Psychometric evaluation supported by a social robot: Personality factors and technology acceptance, pp. 802–807 (2018)
20. Staffa, M., Rossi, S.: Recommender Interfaces: the more human-like, the more humans like. In: Agah, A., Cabibihan, J.-J., Howard, A.M., Salichs, M.A., He, H. (eds.) ICSR 2016. LNCS (LNAI), vol. 9979, pp. 200–210. Springer, Cham (2016). https://doi.org/10.1007/978-3-319-47437-3_20
21. van der Veer, G.C., del Carmen, M., Melguizo, P.: Mental Models, pp. 52–80. L. Erlbaum Associates Inc., USA (2002)
22. Wu, S., Xu, X., Shu, L., Hu, B.: Estimation of valence of emotion using two frontal eeg channels. In: Hu, X., et al., (eds.) BIBM, pp. 1127–1130. IEEE Computer Society (2017)
23. Zhao, G., Zhang, Y., Ge, Y.: Frontal eeg asymmetry and middle line power difference in discrete emotions. Front. Behav. Neurosci. **12** (2018)

We Want AI to Help Us

An Explorative Study Regarding How AI Could Assist Operators in the Main Control Room of Nuclear Power Plants

Ruochen Wang[✉], Fei Song, Jun Ma, and Shuhui Zhang

Shanghai Nuclear Engineering Research and Design Institute, Shanghai, China
{wangruochen,songfei,majun,zhangshuhui}@snerdi.com.cn

Abstract. Artificial intelligence is regarded as a very promising tool in nuclear power plants. While recent research has made progress in utilizing AI to improve digital systems' performances in nuclear power plants, less research focuses on connecting AI and reactor operators and understanding how operators want AI to assist them in their work. Such understanding is important because it is the prerequisite for good usability and positive user experience. We address this research gap by conducting an exploratory interview and letting reactor operators' opinions be voiced out. Through thematic analysis, we derived insights on operators' understanding of AI, the pain points of their work, and how they expect AI to assist them in their work. We identified three assistive roles that operators want AI to be in nuclear power plants to mitigate their work pressure and discussed the reasons behind their choices. Finally, we discussed the limitations of our research and provide possible future research directions.

Keywords: Artificial Intelligence · Reactor Operator · Human-Centered AI

1 Introduction

The human factor has long been considered a crucial factor that affects the safe operation of nuclear power plants (NPPs) [1–3]. To reduce human error, the design of computerized devices for reactor operators in the main control room (MCR) has a focus on mitigating work stress and helping operators do their jobs effectively and efficiently [1]. Many nuclear power plants are now experiencing a digital revolution and more advanced digital technologies have been adopted to improve the operational performance of NPPs [4]. Among those technologies, artificial intelligence (AI) has unique advantages in reducing operators' workload because AI could imitate and augment human natural ability (e.g. speaking, watching, and hearing, etc.) and is capable of helping operators finish their tasks in a complex work environment [5]. Because of its great potential, recent research has been considering utilizing and designing AI in assisting reactor operators in their work [6].

However, it is not easy to employ AI in NPPs. On the one hand, AI is kind of like a black box and as an untransparent technology, it raised people's concerns regarding its safety, explainability, transparency, and ethical issues [7]. Particularly, NPPs have more strict standards concerning safety, explainability, and transparency when adopting new technologies. Hence, people working in NPPs are more conservative in using AI in their workplace because they do not know AI very well. On the other hand, relevant research focuses more on utilizing AI to improve digital systems' performances in NPPs, e.g. to make fault detection even more precise, rather than bridging the gap between AI and the reactor operators [6]. Focusing on utilizing AI to improve digital systems' performance is not enough, as it is equally important to connect AI and its users. The separation between the technology and its users could cause poor usability of the technology, affect its functionality, and make it less productive for users [8].

Connecting AI and reactor operators has been less explored in HCI. To the best of our knowledge, we still lack knowledge of what operators expect from AI in terms of assisting them in NPPs. We acclaim that understanding operators' expectations for AI is very important because such understanding plays a prerequisite role in designing AI for operators in NPPs and ensuring good usability and positive user experience.

To address this gap, we engaged in an exploratory interview, with the aim of understanding what reactor operators expect AI to assist them in their work and elucidating why they have such expectations towards AI. Inspired by user-centered approach [9] and human-centered AI approach [10], the interview questions were deliberately developed to connect AI and reactor operators. 14 participants who have at least 10 years of work experience in the MCR of NPPs were invited to our research. We explored their understanding of AI, their perspectives of reactors' work pressure and how AI could assist them in their work. The interview responses were transcribed and analyzed through thematic analysis [11]. The results showed our participants' positive and negative perceptions of AI and the reasons behind their opinions. The results also revealed details of reactor operators' work pressure and identified three assistive roles that operators wanted AI to be in NPPs to mitigate their work pressure.

This paper contributes to and extends current research in applying AI in the context of NPPs with a focus on connecting AI and reactor operators and has three main contributions: 1) connecting AI and reactor operators to explore reactor operators' perception of AI; 2) presenting operators' opinions on how AI could be used to reduce their workload; 3) elucidating the reasons why reactors have such expectations on AI.

2 Related Work

2.1 Working as a Reactor Operator

Working as a rector operator in nuclear power plants is not easy. Instead, it can be an extremely stressful job as the work environment is complex, dynamic, and demanding [12]. The reactor operators must maintain high awareness to monitor, control, and regulate the systems in the main control room [13–15]. Oftentimes, they are expected to make decisions and take action in a very limited time when an unexpected emergency happens. Even though advanced digital instrumental and control (I&C) systems have been widely applied in nuclear power plants, operators are required to monitor the system information collected from nearly 1000 monitors via 16 screens and one wide display panel [16, 17]. Moreover, reactor operators have to face new challenges brought by new digital technologies such as cybersecurity issues, digital information errors and being lost in too many screens [12]. Human error happens more easily while individuals are under great pressure [18, 19], which can have negative impacts on the operation of NPPs.

Apart from pressure, another feature that affects the operation of NPPs is teamwork [12, 17]. Working with a complex and difficult sociotechnical system like nuclear power plant requires close cooperation and mature teamwork. Typically, an operating team in MCR consists of one reactor operator (RO), one assistant reactor operator (ARO) and a shift supervisor (SS) [20, 21]. The RO is responsible for the safe-related systems whereas the ARO focuses on monitoring the non-safe related system. Both RO and ARO shall report to SS. The SS coordinates the cooperation between RO and ARO, makes commands, and handles emergency conditions. If the operating team does not function well when an emergency happens, then the command from SS will not be executed properly by RO and ARO, which will worsen the emergency in NPPs. In this paper, we use this understanding of working as a rector operator to theoretically ground our research work and to discuss how AI could assist operators in their work and mitigate their work pressure.

2.2   The User-Centered Design Approach in NPPs

Designing systems in NPPs has long been designer-centered rather than user-centered. This is because of the high standard requirements for safety in NPPs. The design of safety-critical systems in NPPs usually puts more consideration into meeting safety-related requirement rather than user experience and usability. However, ignorance of designing systems from users' perspectives can lead to bad design of systems and poor performance of the systems, resulting in stress, human errors and even nuclear accidents [22, 23]. After the Three Mile Island accident, a user-centered design approach was recommended in the design of systems in NPPs and human-related factors such as cognitive and physiological characteristics should be considered in systems design [24].

User-centered design (UCD) approach originates from Donald Norman's co-authored book where he recognized the needs and interests of end-users and puts an emphasis on the usability of the design [9]. According to UCD, the design of the system should facilitate the task for the users and help users learn how to use the system with minimum effort [25]. UCD is not just a design method, but also a design philosophy, that is, sufficient consideration should be given to the end users' opinions to ensure they could use the system as intended. In this paper, our approach to connecting AI and operators in NPPs is inspired by the theory of UCD and we investigated operators' opinions about how they want AI to be designed for them.

2.3   AI in NPPs

In general terms, AI is concerned with getting computers or machines to do tasks that would require human intelligence. John McCarthy, the first to coin the term artificial intelligence, defines AI as "the science and engineering of making intelligent machines, especially intelligent computer programs." [5]. A more elaborate definition characterizes AI as "a system's ability to interpret external data correctly, to learn from such data, and

to use those learnings to achieve specific goals and tasks through flexible adaptation."
[26]. From this definition, we can see that AI-based systems acquire their intelligence
by learning from data. Using deep learning methods such as deep convolutional neural
network (CNN) to process data, AI has developed much humanoid intelligence such
as perception (e.g., computer vision [27], speech recognition [28]), natural language
processing [29], reasoning [30], decision making [31], motion and manipulation [32],
and social intelligence [33], etc.

Due to AI's great performance in developing human-like intelligence, researchers
and engineers have attempted to apply AI in the nuclear engineering field. AI has been
adopted to process nuclear data for detection and prediction [34], monitor the safety
operation [35], achieve autonomous control of power plant's safety systems [36], conduct
fault detection [37], improve the performance of alarm processing system (APS) [38],
and support operators' decision-making process [39], etc. While state-of-art research
makes progress in utilizing AI to improve the operational performance in NPPs, this
paper has a focus on connecting AI and reactor operators and discussing the relationship
between AI and operators in depth from the perspective of human-centered AI.

Human-centered AI (HCAI) is an approach that focuses more on amplifying human
ability rather than eroding or replacing human agency [10]. According to the theory
of HCAI, human knowledge cannot totally be replaced by data and machine learning
algorithms because AI is not inherently motivated by curiosity, desire, or common sense
and therefore cannot learn things proactively like a human. Also, AI can be disrespectful,
vulgar and even evil since AI lack morality and could not understand hidden biases [10].
Hence, there is a call for humans to take the control of AI and be able to interpret the
outcomes that AI generates. AI should be explainable, transparent, and accountable so
that humans could understand what is happening inside the AI systems and regulate AI
when necessary.

3   Methodology and Methods

Since this is exploratory research, and we strived to let operators speak out their opinion
regarding what AI can do for them, we adopted interviews as our research method. By
doing so, we could gain knowledge and insights directly from the end users [40]. This
choice is in accordance with our user-centered design and human-centered AI approach.

3.1   Data Gathering and Data Analysis

Elaborating upon related work, we developed a group of semi-structured interview questions under three themes: understanding of AI; pain points of operator's work; what AI
can do for operators. Table 1 provides our interview questions. 14 experienced interviewees were invited to our study. They are either reactor operators who work in the
main control room in NPPs for more than 10 years or designers who design the information systems in MCR in NPPs for more than 10 years as well. All participants were
recruited in China. We believe a hybrid group of interviewees could provide us with
abundant knowledge and discuss questions from multi perspectives based on their rich

work experience and thus our research question could be answered. By asking the interviewees the first group of questions, we aimed to 1) understand their knowledge about AI and their opinion towards AI; 2) deepen their understanding of AI through mutual communication.

Table 1. Interview Questions.

Themes	Questions	Sources that inspire us to develop this question
Understanding of AI	1. Can you give me your definition of AI?	[5, 26]
	2. Do you think AI can replace human jobs? Why?	[10]
	3. Do you trust AI's work? Why?	[10]
	4. Do you want AI to be your colleagues or assistants?	[10]
Pain points of operators' work	5. Do you think being an operator in MCR is stressful in their daily work?	[13–15]
	6. Where do you think the stress comes from?	[12–16]
	7. Do you think current digital technologies in MCR are helpful? If not, why?	[16, 17]
What AI could do for operators?	8. If you are offered an AI system, what do you want it to do to reduce your workload?	[6]

By asking them the second group of questions, we aimed to 1) understand operators' work in detail, 2) more importantly, to help interviewees recall the work condition of the operators and to lay a good foundation to ask the third group of questions. The aim of the third group of questions is to connect AI and operators' work and let interviewees speak out their opinions about how AI could assist operators in MCR.

Before the formative interview, we conducted a pilot study to see whether the interview questions were sufficient to answer our research question and whether the interviewees could clearly understand our interview questions. Due to the explorative nature of this research, we conducted a semi-structured interview. For example, during our interview, we were not only listening carefully and taking notes but also observing our interviewees. If they needed clarification about using a proper word to describe their opinion, we would give them some prompts to elicit meaningful answers. When they became silent, we would rephrase the interview questions to make sure that they could understand what we were asking.

We employed the thematic analysis method to conduct data analysis because it is widely used in qualitative research and it can help us to discern the common themes from our participants' statements to answer our research question [11, 41]. The interviews were transcribed and coded through a combination of inductive and deductive manner: the former could simplify the connection between our empirical findings to notions in previous literature; the latter could help to identify newly constructed codes from the interviewees' statements. The first author led the analysis and the constructed codes and themes were frequently discussed and polished with the other authors.

4 Results

Overall, the participants showed interest in using AI to assist reactor operators' daily work in MCR in NPPs. They perceived AI as a promising technology in the next digital revolution in the MCR. Whereas no one had opposition to using AI in MCR, all participants showed their worry about using AI because they did not completely trust AI. Furthermore, all participants wanted AI to be an assistant and provide them with processed information, but they should be the ones who make decisions. They did not think AI was capable of being a colleague or an expert. As for the usage of AI in MCR, 12 participants preferred AI to help them process large amount of information and then provide them with possible solutions to reduce their workload and save time. As one of the participants said: *"There are so many indicators on the wide display panel and screens. When an abnormal condition occurs, there are so many alarm indicators beaming simultaneously. It is time-consuming for us to track down the original problem from so many indicators. I hope AI could tackle this problem"* (P6). 7 participants mentioned that they hoped that AI could provide them with the appropriate procedures when an emergency happens because clear instructions was demanded under that situation, which could increase their work efficiency. 5 participants were talking about using AI to help them predict the abnormal conditions in NPPs. Next, we report our findings for each group interview question through constructed themes.

4.1 Understanding of AI

Untransparent Intelligence. When asked to describe AI using their own language, 11 participants mentioned AI is a sort of intelligence that is able to learn from data. However, all of them admitted that they were not clear how AI gained such a learning ability. They had a vague idea about machine leaning algorithms, and they could list some scenarios where machine learning algorithms has made our life more convincement (e.g., recommendation systems, facial recognition systems). But they did not dive into how machine learning algorithms could make recommendation or achieve recognition. 10 participants perceived machine learning algorithms as complex and hard to learn. Hence, we can infer that our participants could relate AI to data and algorithm, but the underlying mechanism of AI is still a black box to them.

Doubt about AI. All participants admitted that they could not completely trust AI and let AI take over their job in a complex work environment like NPPs. The finding is well captured by two quotes from P1 and P3 – "*I could not trust AI. I have read on the news* *that self-driving cars caused serious accidents. The car system is much simpler than the nuclear power plants' system. I cannot imagine if the whole plant system is controlled by AI and then AI makes mistakes. Then there will be a disaster"* (P1). *"I do not understand how AI works. I mean, if AI gives me a suggestion, I have no evidence to prove it is right or wrong. That can be fatal in a safety critical industry, where you must one hundred per cent make sure you know how the result is generated"* (P3). Lacking explainability, transparency and interpretability hinders AI being widely applied in a safety critical nuclear power plants.

Assistant Rather than Co-worker. All participants preferred AI to be a personal digital assistant than co-working with AI. They expected that AI could help them deal with tremendous information, draw insights, and provide solutions. That is, AI should work *for* them rather than work *with* them. They did not regard AI as an equal role as their colleagues in work context because they were not convinced that AI could fully replace human's job based on AI's recent ability. All participants asserted that AI could be asked to do some easy and repetitive work while creative work is not the domain for AI. One participant well explained the reason for this assertion: *"In my opinion, AI learns from the past. If AI encounters new problems that never happened before, then from where could AI learn to solve them?"* (P5). In addition, one participant mentioned that AI lack morality and could not deal with ethical issues like human and due to this reason, AI could not become a real co-worker forever. 5 participants, however, believed that AI can be even more powerful in the future and in that case, they believed that AI acquires the ability and morality to co-work with them.

4.2 Pain Points of Operator's Work

Drown in Information. 12 participants mentioned a dilemma: although digital technologies have been applied in MCR in NPPs, it brings a new problem: when an anomaly occurs, the operators have to deal with a large amount of information displayed on the screens to track down the origin of the anomaly. This is because the digital technologies currently deployed in NPPs only present operational information rather than extrapolate knowledge or insights from information. Extracting knowledge from displayed information is still manually done by operators, which can be very time-consuming. The situation can be even worse when an emergency happens: many alarm indicators beam together, and the operators have to react in very limited time. *"[..] that requires you to have a strong heart. You have to react quickly to find the origin of the problem from so many informative cues"* (P12). Even though, all participants declared that digital technologies were very helpful, and the efficiency of their work was largely improved than before.

Complex Procedures. 7 participants talked about the complex procedures that operators had to follow during the operation, and they thought those procedures also made operators feel anxious. The complex procedures mainly include two parts: the first part is about teamwork. Operators should follow the rules for teamwork, and they must be clear about their own duty and understand to whom they should report or ask for help as well. The second part is about the required procedures they must follow when checking the situation of the plants, fixing the anomalies, and writing daily reports, etc. The two parts of the procedures are usually winded up together. When emergency happens, following the procedures can be a big challenge: *"We have to recall the procedure and follow the procedures step by step even though we are stressed out. Otherwise, more mistakes will be made due to human error. Operators have exams regularly to make sure that they remember the right procedures"* (P9). However, it is not easy to remember all the steps when operators are under pressure in emergency.

4.3   What AI Can Do for Operators?

Information Processing Assistant.   13 participants mentioned that they want AI to be an assistant to help them process the large amounts of data collected by the sensors. Among them, 5 participants expected that AI should be able to deal with alarming-related data to prioritize alarming events and filter unimportant events. Besides, 4 participants hoped AI could find the origin of anomalies from tremendous information and then locate the origin in a very short time. 4 participants wanted AI to visualize operational information so that they could read the information directly. Most participants believed that AI acquired the ability to extrapolate insights from tremendous information and that is why they thought AI could be capable of being an information processing assistant. Another reason for choosing AI as information processing assistant is that the operators wanted AI to help them save time in dealing with so much information displayed in MCR.

Smart Reminder.   7 participants wanted AI to play a role like a reminder to remind them of the right steps so that they could not make mistakes. One participant mentioned that human error was somehow inevitable and that was why a reminder was needed, as he said:" *[..] it is impossible to completely avoid human error. If...If there could be an AI reminder telling me what to do next and reminding me if I did wrong. That would be much better"* (P9). Moreover, operators believed that they could be more focused on their tasks as their cognitive workload could be reduced if AI could remind them of the next steps. This is well captured by one quote from the participant: *"[...] if AI could guide me, I could be more focused on dealing with problems. I don't have to recall what I should do next."* (P9).

Predictor.   5 participants hoped that AI could make predictions about the abnormal conditions before the systems alarm. This is because reactors do not want abnormal conditions to occur. Once an abnormal condition happens, reactors not only have to fix the problems but also are required to take responsibilities for those abnormal conditions. If the abnormal conditions cause the shutdown in NPPs and even economical losses, the operators' salary will be affected. Hence, a predictor that could help to avoid abnormal conditions in NPPs are demanded by operators. This finding is illustrated by one participant's quote: *"I hope AI could tell us, for example, the radiation dose is on the way beyond the high limit and thus we could take action in advance and control the situation. Otherwise, we have to take the responsibilities for the economical losses"* (P11).

5 Discussion

In this section, we first reflect on the operators' choices on how AI could be utilized to assist them in their work. We also reflect on the core reasons to justify the operators' choices based on their disclosure. We connect our empirical findings to the relevant literature and ground why our research work is meaningful. Furthermore, we discuss the methodological considerations that facilitate our research which we hope could benefit future research. Finally, the limitation of our work and possible future direction to advance it are also surfaced.

It is interesting that all participants do not want AI to take over their job. Instead, they want AI to be an assistive role and they still want to take control. This finding strengthens Shneiderman's assertion that AI should amplify human's ability rather than erode human agency [10]. An AI system can be an information processing assistant, a smart reminder or a predictor, but the operators should keep their rights to make the decision and take action. This is less discussed in previous literature because previous research focuses more on how to use AI to solve technical nuclear-related issues such as detecting operative problems [34], and monitoring the safety operation [35], etc., rather than considering the demand of operators. Furthermore, the research also reveals the core reason for operators' preference for using AI as an assistive tool is that they do not trust AI completely. Although the participants perceive AI as a powerful tool, they still do not understand how AI works. Such ambiguousness in AI's underlying mechanism leads to their worries about losing control of the operation and then causing severe accidents. Hence, improving the interpretability and explainability of AI systems is much more important in the context of NPPs so that AI can be accepted widely by operators. This finding substantiates the conclusion of the systematic review by [6], who argue the black-box issues of AI will hinder the popularity of AI in NPPs in the long run.

As for the usage of AI technologies in NPPs, we identified three assistive roles that operators wanted AI to be in their work. First, operators wanted to use AI as a information processing assistant to help them relieve the stress caused by information overload. Second, operators wanted to use AI as a smart reminder to reduce the memory load of complex operation-related procedures. Third, our research finding also reveals a fact that operators are more willing to take action ahead of abnormal conditions or accidents in NPPs, which motivates them to have AI as a predictor. Compared to prior research work in applying AI in nuclear engineering [34–39], our work makes operators' expectations for AI more explicit and identifies the reasons behind their expectations. We believe that the three assistive roles could serve as a source of inspiration while designing AI systems for reactor operators in the future. Furthermore, we want to call for a more empathetic understanding of the operators in NPPs in the future. Operators are usually required to adjust themselves to the system. An empathetic understanding could help designers of the systems set aside their assumptions of the operators and gain insights into their work context and their demands, which could be helpful to design AI systems with good user experience for operators.

In regard to methodological reflection, involving nuclear professional operators and designers in our research helps to generate fruitful research outcomes. Based on the knowledge acquired from the participants, it was possible for us to reveal the operators' demands and worries regarding utilizing AI in assisting them and the core reasons why they have such understanding. Secondly, we found the HCAI approach very useful and insightful when driving our research work. The approach leads us to the less concerned areas, i.e., the operators' perspective on the usage of AI, and helps us identify the three assistive roles that operators want AI to be in their work. Most importantly, this approach evokes our empathy with the operators and thus we could gain a deep understanding of the operators and their choices.

A limitation of our work relates to the generalizability of our findings because this is explorative and qualitative research. We can argue that our research findings are non-particular as they are empirically grounded in the account of professional nuclear reactor operators and designers, who have been working in this field for more than 10 years. However, we cannot claim generalizability as explorative and qualitative research work could achieve [42]. Moreover, the single nationality of operators also impacts the generalizability of our research work. Future research work will be, if possible, conducting similar research in different countries and letting the operators of different backgrounds speak outs their opinions. Based on that, we could have comparative research, towards elucidating generalizability issues in different countries and diverse backgrounds of operators.

The other limitation of our research work stems from the study setup. During the discussion, we realized that it would be better if we had provided our participants with some AI-based tools or software and let them play with those tools before we had the interview so that they could have a direct and concrete understanding of advanced AI technologies. In this way, the operators could relate particular AI technologies (e.g. speech recognition, computer vision, etc.) to certain demands and therefore more concrete ideas with regard to how AI could assist their work could be generated. A relevant future work would be investigating which AI technologies could be utilized and developed to serve as an information processing assistant, a smart reminder or a predictor.

6 Conclusion

This paper contributes to connecting AI and reactor operators in the context of MCR in NPPs and providing a thorough understanding of what operators expect from AI to assist them in their work.

As we presented in this paper, our participants perceive AI as a promising tool to assist them as an information processing assistant, a smart reminder, or a predictor. However, our participants also expressed their worry about AI as AI lacks interpretability and transparency and therefore they could not let AI completely take over their job. This paper strengthens the fact that AI has its unique advantages in assisting operators in NPPs as its ability to process tremendous information and make predictions. This paper also indicates viewing AI from the perspective of reactor operators could help to shed light on less discussed research areas. It is our hope that our research findings could inspire future design and research in the domain of using AI to assist reactor operators in their work.

Acknowledgement. This study is supported by Science and Technology Commission of Shanghai Municipality (No. 20QB1403100).

References

1. Hamer, R., Waterson, P., Jun, G.T.: Human factors and nuclear safety since 1970 – A critical review of the past, present and future. Saf. Sci. **133**, 105021 (2021). https://doi.org/10.1016/j.ssci.2020.105021
2. Moray, N.P., Huey, B.M.: Human factors research and nuclear safety. National Academies Press (1988)
3. Swaton, E., Neboyan, V., Lederman, L.: Human factors in the operation of nuclear power plants. IAEA Bull. **29**, 27–30 (1987)
4. Zhang, L., Shi, J., Chen, W.: Revolution of nuclear power plant design through digital technology. In: International Atomic Energy Agency (IAEA) (2015)
5. McCarthy, J.: What is artificial intelligence? (2007)
6. Lu, C., et al.: Nuclear power plants with artificial intelligence in industry 4.0 era: Top-level design and current applications—A systemic review. IEEE Access **8**, 194315–194332 (2020). https://doi.org/10.1109/ACCESS.2020.3032529
7. Adadi, A., Berrada, M.: Peeking inside the black-box: a survey on explainable artificial intelligence (XAI). IEEE Access. **6**, 52138–52160 (2018). https://doi.org/10.1109/ACCESS.2018.2870052
8. Goodwin, N.C.: Functionality and usability. Commun. ACM **30**, 229–233 (1987). https://doi.org/10.1145/214748.214758
9. Norman, D.: User centered system design. New Perspect. Hum.-Comput. Interact. (1986)
10. Shneiderman, B.: Human-centered AI. Oxford University Press (2022)
11. Braun, V., Clarke, V.: Using thematic analysis in psychology. Qual. Res. Psychol. **3**, 77–101 (2006). https://doi.org/10.1191/1478088706qp063oa
12. Medema, H., Savchenko, K., Boring, R., Ulrich, T.: Defining mutual awareness: Results of reactor operator surveys on the emergence of digital technology in main control rooms. In: Advances in Human Error, Reliability, Resilience, and Performance: Proceedings of the AHFE 2018 International Conference on Human Error, Reliability, Resilience, and Performance, 21–25 July 2018, Loews Sapphire Falls Resort at Universal Studios, Orlando, Florida, USA, vol. 9, pp. 58–67. Springer (2019). https://doi.org/10.1007/978-3-319-94391-6_6
13. Gertman, D.I., Haney, L.N., Jenkins, J.P., Blackman, H.S.: Operational decisionmaking and action selection under psychological stress in nuclear power plants. EG and G Idaho Inc, Idaho Falls (USA) (1985)
14. Kontogiannis, T.: Stress and operator decision making in coping with emergencies. Int. J. Hum.-Comput. Stud. **45**, 75–104 (1996). https://doi.org/10.1006/ijhc.1996.0043
15. Park, J., Kim, J., Jung, W.: Comparing the complexity of procedural steps with the operators' performance observed under stressful conditions. Reliab. Eng. Syst. Saf. **83**, 79–91 (2004). https://doi.org/10.1016/j.ress.2003.09.001
16. Chuang, C.F., Chou, H.P.: Investigation on the design of human-system interface for advanced nuclear plant control room (2006)
17. Lin, C.J., Hsieh, T.-L., Tsai, P.-J., Yang, C.-W., Yenn, T.-C.: Development of a team workload assessment technique for the main control room of advanced nuclear power plants. Hum. Factors Ergon. Manuf. Serv. Ind. **21**, 397–411 (2011). https://doi.org/10.1002/hfm.20247
18. Preischl, W., Hellmich, M.: Human error probabilities from operational experience of German nuclear power plants. Reliab. Eng. Syst. Saf. **109**, 150–159 (2013). https://doi.org/10.1016/j.ress.2012.08.004
19. Sheridan, T.B.: Human error in nuclear power plants. Technol. Rev. **82**, 22–33 (1980)
20. O'hara, J.M., Higgins, J.C., Persensky, J.J., Lewis, P.M., Bongarra, J.P.: Human factors engineering program review model. Brookhaven National Lab Upton NY (2004)

21. Plott, C., Engh, T., Barnes, V.E.: Technical basis for regulatory guidance for assessing exemption requests from the nuclear power plant licensed operator staffing requirements specified in 10 CFR 50.54 (m). Division of Systems Analysis and Regulatory Effectiveness, Office of Nuclear (2004)
22. Kuang, C., Fabricant, R.: User friendly: How the hidden rules of design are changing the way we live, work & play. Random House (2019)
23. Rouse, W.B., Rouse, S.H.: Human information seeking and design of information systems. Inf. Process. Manag. **20**, 129–138 (1984). https://doi.org/10.1016/0306-4573(84)90044-X
24. Carvalho, P.V., Gomes, J.O., Borges, M.R.: Human centered design for nuclear power plant control room modernization. In: CEUR Proceedings 4th Workshop HCP Human Centered Processes, pp. 10–11 (2011)
25. Abras, C., Maloney-Krichmar, D., Preece, J., Bainbridge, W.: Encyclopedia of human-computer interaction. Thousand Oaks Sage Publ. **37**, 445–456 (2004)
26. Buchanan, B.G.: A (very) brief history of artificial intelligence. Ai Mag. **26**, 53 (2005)
27. Voulodimos, A., Doulamis, N., Doulamis, A., Protopapadakis, E.: Deep learning for computer vision: A brief review. Comput. Intell. Neurosci. 2018 (2018). https://doi.org/10.1155/2018/7068349
28. Gaikwad, S.K., Gawali, B.W., Yannawar, P.: A review on speech recognition technique. Int. J. Comput. Appl. **10**, 16–24 (2010). https://doi.org/10.5120/1462-1976
29. Nadkarni, P.M., Ohno-Machado, L., Chapman, W.W.: Natural language processing: an introduction. J. Am. Med. Inform. Assoc. **18**, 544–551 (2011). https://doi.org/10.1136/amiajnl-2011-000464
30. Harika, J., Baleeshwar, P., Navya, K., Shanmugasundaram, H.: A review on artificial intelligence with deep human reasoning. In: 2022 International Conference on Applied Artificial Intelligence and Computing (ICAAIC), pp. 81–84. IEEE (2022)
31. Duan, Y., Edwards, J.S., Dwivedi, Y.K.: Artificial intelligence for decision making in the era of Big Data–evolution, challenges and research agenda. Int. J. Inf. Manag. **48**, 63–71 (2019). https://doi.org/10.1016/j.ijinfomgt.2019.01.021
32. Rajan, K., Saffiotti, A.: Towards a science of integrated AI and Robotics. Elsevier (2017)
33. Herzig, A., Lorini, E., Pearce, D.: Social intelligence. Springer (2019)
34. Alamaniotis, M., Tsoukalas, L.H.: Neuro-SVM anticipatory system for online monitoring of radiation and abrupt change detection. Int. J. Monit. Surveill. Technol. Res. IJMSTR. **1**, 40–53 (2013). https://doi.org/10.4018/ijmstr.2013040103
35. McCoy, K., Alamaniotis, M., Jevremovic, T.: A conceptual model for integrative monitoring of nuclear power plants operational activities based on historical nuclear incidents and accidents. Int. J. Monit. Surveill. Technol. Res. IJMSTR. **1**, 69–81 (2013). https://doi.org/10.4018/ijmstr.2013010105
36. Lee, D., Kim, J.: Autonomous algorithm for safety systems of the nuclear power plant by using the deep learning. In: Advances in Human Factors in Energy: Oil, Gas, Nuclear and Electric Power Industries: Proceedings of the AHFE 2017 International Conference on Human Factors in Energy: Oil, Gas, Nuclear and Electric Power Industries, July 17–21, 2017, The Westin Bonaventure Hotel, Los Angeles, California, USA, vol. 8, pp. 72–82. Springer (2018). https://doi.org/10.1007/978-3-319-60204-2_8
37. Saeed, H.A., Wang, H., Peng, M., Hussain, A., Nawaz, A.: Online fault monitoring based on deep neural network & sliding window technique. Prog. Nucl. Energy. **121**, 103236 (2020). https://doi.org/10.1016/j.pnucene.2019.103236
38. Quan, Y., Yang, X.: A method for alarming water level of boiler drum on nuclear power plant based on BP neural network. In: 2014 10th International Conference on Natural Computation (ICNC), pp. 83–87. IEEE (2014)

39. Hanna, B., Son, T.C., Dinh, N.: An artificial intelligence-guided decision support system for the nuclear power plant management. In: Proceedings of the 18th International Topical Meeting on Nuclear Reactor Thermal Hydraulics (NURETH 2019) (2019)
40. Lazar, J., Feng, J.H., Hochheiser, H.: Research methods in human-computer interaction. Morgan Kaufmann (2017)
41. Saldaña, J.: The coding manual for qualitative researchers. Coding Man. Qual. Res. 1–440 (2021)
42. Bhattacherjee, A.: Social science research: Principles, methods, and practices (2012)

The Design of Transparency Communication for Human-Multirobot Teams

Ning Wang[1,2], David V. Pynadath[1,2(✉)] ⓘ, and Nikolos Gurney[1] ⓘ

[1] Institute for Creative Technologies, University of Southern California,
Los Angeles, USA
{nwang,pynadath,gurney}@ict.usc.edu

[2] Department of Computer Science, University of Southern California,
Los Angeles, USA

Abstract. Successful human-machine teaming often hinges on the ability of eXplainable Artificial Intelligence (XAI) to make an agent's reasoning transparent to human teammates. Doing so requires that the agent navigate a tradeoff between revealing its reasoning to those teammates without overwhelming them with too much information. This challenge is amplified when a person is teamed with multiple agents. This amplification is not simply linear, due to the increase from 1 to N agents' worth of reasoning content, but also due to the interdependency among the agents' reasoning that must be made transparent as well. In this work, we examine the challenges in conveying this interdependency to people teaming with multiple agents. We also propose alternate domain-independent strategies for a team of simulated robots to generate messages about their reasoning to be conveyed to a human teammate. We illustrate these strategies through their implementation in a search-and-rescue simulation testbed.

Keywords: Robots · Avatars and Virtual Humans · Human-Robot Interaction · Explainable Artificial Intelligence

1 Introduction

Artificial intelligence (AI) is central to the future of work [13]. Since 2020, the U.S. National Science Foundation has invested over $100 million to establish AI Research Institutes to advance six research frontiers in AI, including "Human-AI Interaction and Collaboration" [14]. Understanding the decisions and rationale of autonomous AIs is key to the success of the man-machine team. The complexity and the "black-box" nature of AI algorithms often create a barrier for establishing such understanding. Additionally, many human-AI tasks, such as search and rescue, involve the use of a team of autonomous AIs, including Unmanned Aerial/Ground/Underwater Vehicles (UAV/UGV/UUVs). While autonomous AIs have the potential to enhance human-AI team efficiency and reduce the

H. Degen and S. Ntoa (Eds.): HCII 2023, LNAI 14051, pp. 311–321, 2023.
https://doi.org/10.1007/978-3-031-35894-4_23

human operator's mental workload, such benefits can only be achieved if the AIs are completely reliable, a requirement that is less than realistic given the inherent uncertainty of the real-world environments the AIs operate in [21,22]. Human supervision is thus necessary to allow for the management of unexpected events and to ensure progress toward mission goals [27].

The vision of one human commanding multiple AI-powered AIs creates significant challenges for the human to maintain situational awareness for effective and efficient decision-making. Prior studies have consistently shown that human-machine team performance rarely increases and, in fact, often decreases with an increasing number of AIs for the human to supervise [5,7,24]. These challenges are further complicated by variables such as the degree of autonomy of the AIs, the AI team composition, task complexity, and human factors such as trust [4].

Research on human-AI teaming has suggested the promise of automatically generated transparency communication provided by an AI, such as explanations of its objectives, rationale, and expected outcome, in improving a team of one human and one AI [17,26]. Translating these benefits to a human teaming with multiple AIs (such as a team of autonomous robots) may alleviate the degradation of human-machine team performance as the number of AIs increases, but additional challenges arise and must be addressed. For a team of robots, the transparency communication may expand from an individual robot's objectives, rationale, and expected outcome, to such information for the team. The challenge lies in explaining not only the AI algorithms in decision-making for individual robots, but also the algorithms for multi-robot coordination and decision-making. The increase in the number of robots within a team will inevitably result in the increase in the number of communications to the human supervisor. Such an increase may ultimately overwhelm the human supervisor, resulting in hindrances to human decision-making without realizing the benefit that transparency communication intends to achieve. Thus, there need to be mechanisms to coordinate and select communication, so that the important messages (e.g., "I am going to ignore the injured person in this building, because the injury is minor.") can stand out from the rest.

To address these challenges, we developed a human-multirobot teaming online testbed and explanation generation of AI algorithms used in multirobot decision-making, and experimented with different designs of the individual and team communications for the robots. The testbed implements scenarios set in search-and-rescue missions, where a human operator supervises a team of n robots (n is the number of robots in the team we can vary in the testbed) to search for injured persons and recover valuable assets (e.g., important documents) in an urban area (e.g., simulated as a 11×11 grid). While the team communicates its findings, the human supervisor decides how to dispatch members of a (simulated) human rescue team to certain locations. In the testbed, an individual robot's decision is modeled using Partially Observable Markov Decision Problems (POMDPs), while the coordination planning of the team, using Decentralized POMDPs (DEC-POMDPs) [15]. We developed algorithms to automatically generate explanations for individual robots to communicate their decisions (e.g., "Robot00 will move to the animal feed store"), observations (e.g., "Robot01's microphone detected a call for help in the blue mosque."), beliefs (e.g., "Robot00's camera detected a victim in the animal feed store. It's 98% confident about this assessment."), etc.

For communication at the team level, there are a wealth of options on what aspects of team decisions and behaviors to communicate, considering the complexity of algorithms such as DEC-POMDPs. As a starting point, we developed algorithms that focus on generating explanations that support human decision-making (e.g., alternatives to the proposed plan), and explanations of emergent team behaviors that could be of interest to a human operator (e.g., behaviors suggest a "divide-and-conquer" strategy, or seemingly inefficient behaviors of robots "double-checking" on each other). We experimented with a number of heuristics-based methods to selectively communicate the explanations to satisfy the constraints of human cognitive load, which has been identified as a critical factor in human supervision of a robot team [8].

2 Empirical Testbed

To illustrate and evaluate alternate approaches to such explanations, we started with an existing evaluation testbed and reconnaissance scenario that was previous used to assess the impact of explanations on people teamed with a single simulated robot [25]. In this scenario, the team must explore a series of buildings, each potentially containing a threat: either a gunman or a nuclear, biological, or chemical (NBC) weapon. In the original single-robot setting, the robot would enter each building first, determine whether or not the human teammate should don protective gear before entering, and then report its findings. The human teammate would then decide whether or not to follow the robot's guidance before entering the building. When the human teammate failed to equip the protective gear when needed, a time penalty was imposed in the testbed to simulate the cost of injury or dying. Donning and doffing the protective gear were associated with a smaller time cost. The mission continued until the human teammate entered all of the buildings, with success achieved if the mission completes within a time limit.

Extending this single-agent testbed to a multi-robot setting requires some small, but crucial, variations. Most importantly, each individual robot is free to choose what building to explore next, meaning that at any point in time, the robot team is scanning multiple buildings. Because there is only a single person teamed with the robots, they can enter only one of the buildings that the robots have finished scanning. Thus, the person no longer has to follow a single robot in a lockstep fashion, but now has an additional choice to make as to which building to enter next. The original testbed used a fixed sequence of 45 buildings; we expand it here to an 11×11 grid of 121 buildings that the human and robots can explore in any order.

In the original single-robot testbed, the robot was equipped with three sensors: a camera for detecting gunmen, an NBC sensor, and a microphone capable of classifying any overheard speech (e.g., friendly vs. suspicious conversations). In the multi-robot setting, we restrict each robot to have only one of the three possible sensors. Thus, while the robots have incentive to spread out to scan as many buildings as quickly as possible, they also have incentive to re-scan buildings that may have been previously scanned by robots with different sensors.

Complicating the scanning decision (and eventual recommendation) was the fact that the original single robot's sensors were potentially unreliable, yielding either false positives or false negatives on occasion (to stimulate potential trust breakdowns). We carry that unreliability over to the multi-robot setting, so that there is an additional incentive to re-scan a building, simply to increase the confidence of the overall assessment through additional observations. We also add an additional wrinkle through varying reliability across the team. In other words, one robot may be equipped with an NBC sensor that has a higher probability of error than another's.

The robot team faces the same task as the original single robot: assess the potential threat in each building and recommend the appropriate gear for their human teammate to wear when entering it. However, because the robots are simultaneously scanning multiple buildings, they may have to communicate multiple assessments and recommendations. In addition, because the robots may re-scan a building, they may have to communicate revised assessments and recommendations for buildings, which did not occur in the original single-robot testbed.

The human teammate can enter only one building at a time, while the robot team be assessing multiple buildings at a time. To assist in the person's decision, the team is also tasked with recommending which building to enter next, based on its assessment of the risks across the buildings scanned so far. The decision-making framework that we use for our robots must therefore be able to not only plan the movement for the robots, but also for the human.

3   Team Decision-Making

In the original testbed, the single robot made its decisions using a Partially Observable Markov Decision Process (POMDP) [12]. A POMDP is a tuple $\langle S, A, P, \Omega, O, R \rangle$ with the following components:

- S: the state of the world
- A: the robot's possible action choices
- P: the transition probability function, capturing the effects of the robot's action choices on the state of the world
- Ω: the robot's possible observations
- O: the observation probability function, capturing the likelihood of the robot's observations given the true state of the world and its chosen action
- R: the reward function, capturing how good or bad the current state of the world

One straightforward generalization of this formulation to a multi-robot team is to give each robot its own POMDP. The original robot was modeled within

PsychSim [19], which supports such a formulation. Furthermore, like interactive POMDPs (I-POMDPs) [10] and Partially Observable Stochastic Games (POSGs) [11], PsychSim allows the agents to recursively model each other— e.g., each robot models the others as having their own POMDP, with some uncertainty about the values for R and their current beliefs. Such a general representation can capture deviations in priorities across the team, allowing for robots to differ in terms of their commitment to team objectives. It also allows for robots to be uncertain about what their teammates have observed and, subsequently, what they currently believe about the state of the world.

In this investigation, we do not explore this very general case, but rather assume a fully collaborative robot team. More precisely, we assume that all of the robots share the same reward function, R, meaning that they are all identically committed to the same objectives. We make an additional assumption that the robots communicate all of their observations instantaneously and use the same belief-update mechanism. As a result, they (and we) can assume that they all share the same beliefs about the state of the world. This shared reward function, R, and common knowledge about the state, S, reduces the problem to be a Decentralized POMDP (DEC-POMDP) [15].

Although these assumptions of pure collaboration and common knowledge might be considered strong, the remaining decision problem is still complex from a computational perspective, let alone from a human understanding one. In fact, the problem of computing an optimal policy for a DEC-POMDP is NEXP-Complete, meaning that there is no polynomial-time solution [2]. In contrast, solving a POMDP (i.e., the single-robot case) is only PSPACE-Complete [16]. In fact, if we apply the PsychSim decision-making algorithms used in the single-robot case to the multi-robot case without making any adaptation to the additional dimensions of complexity, even a team as small as three robots cannot make decisions in real time.

We have addressed this computational scalability concern via Monte Carlo simulation, as in a similar application within I-POMDPs [9]. However, such an approach does not address the challenge of communicating the robot team's increasingly complex decision-making to its human teammate. In the single-robot case, one can exploit the piecewise-linear nature of POMDPs and reinforcement learning to build a decision-tree representation of the robot's policy of behavior [18]. In the multi-robot DEC-POMDP case, the robots' policies have a much complex structure, due to their dependence on the possible belief states and expected behavior of other robots, which depend, in turn, on the possible belief states and expected behavior of other robots, which depend, in turn, ad infinitum in the worst case. One common representation of a DEC-POMDP policy is a *policy tree*, which branches on the sequence of observations received by the robot, arriving at actions at the leaves (e.g., [23]). Policy trees are general enough to capture any possible DEC-POMDP behavior, at the cost of accounting for all possible observation sequences that a robot could receive over the entire course of execution. An alternative policy representation uses finite-state controllers [3], which are more compact than policy trees, but which can still be opaque to a human observer if the robot cannot convey what the "states" of its controller mean.

Even if more human-understandable policy representations were found for DEC-POMDPs, the multi-robot challenge is not simply in conveying the behavior of each robot individually: there is the additional challenge of conveying the *joint* behavior of the robots that is the result of their coordination. For example, if a human team were scouting out the same grid of buildings, they might adopt a "divide-and-conquer" strategy and spread out. Alternatively, they may decide that the unreliability of their sensors justifies repeated scanning of the same buildings to double-check on the assessments made so far. For the robot team, even if their optimal policies cause them to adhere to either one of these strategies, there is nothing in the policy representation that would lead to such an abstract characterization as "divide-and-conquer".

Similarly, the common knowledge that the robots maintain about their cumulative sensor readings and assessments would feed into a recommendation that would maximize the expected reward received when followed by their human teammate. However, from the human's perspective, the provenance of the robots' resulting assessments and recommendations is obscured by the complexity of this expected-reward calculation. For example, the robots must look multiple steps into the future, considering the possible actions of its teammates (both robot and human) and the possible sensor readings that might be received. This Bayesian aggregation might functionally be equivalent to a weighted voting scheme, but there is a large gap between the mechanics of the robots' reasoning and human-understandable terms regarding group decision-making.

4   Team Explanation

While the full details of the robots' reasoning may be required to achieve perfect transparency, it is most likely that trying to convey all of them to a human teammate will only exacerbate the already-present issue of cognitive load [8]. The robots should instead communicate only the most salient details. The following communication goals were identified in an analysis of human teams operating in a real-world domain similar to our virtual testbed, with that analysis explicitly aimed toward identifying communication necessary for human-robot teaming [1]:

- Request assistance
- Describe event and activities
- Report degree of hazard
- Receive commands
- Coordinate cross-team activities
- Public warnings

In this work, we address the goals to *Describe event and activities* and *Report degree of hazard* as the most relevant. The goals to *Request assistance*, *Receive commands*, and *Coordinate cross-team activities* would become more relevant if we enrich the interaction between the human and the robot team. In particular, it would require bidirectional communication, which we leave to future refinements of the testbed. The goal to provide *Public warnings* is not relevant, given the lack of any public-facing interaction in the simulation.

Although individual robots could communicate with the human supervisor, we centralize such communication decisions within a separate agent, following examples in the literature such as RoboLeader [6] and similar agent advisors [20]. In this section, we present a variety of candidate mechanisms for such an agent to automatically generate explanations that target the communication goals to *Report degree of hazard* and *Describe event and activities*. In the context of our team formulation, the former relates to the team's recommendation of which building for the person to go to and with what gear (Sect. 4.1). The latter relates to achieving situational awareness of what the robots are doing, both individually and as a team (Sect. 4.2).

4.1   Automatic Explanation of Joint Assessment

The DEC-POMDP formulation of the robot team's decision-making computes an expected reward for all of their possible action choices. The communication goal to *Report degree of hazard* pertain to those action choices that directly impact the human teammate, i.e., recommendations of which building for them to enter next and what gear to put on when doing so. The simplest choice for the robots to make in this regard is to *not* report a degree of hazard, i.e., to simply provide the recommendation with no elaboration. Such a communication policy would minimize the person's cognitive load, but it also provides little in the way of transparency. In the single-robot version of this domain, not providing *any* explanation had a clear negative impact on trust and team performance [26].

In the single-robot domain, we explored two alternate explanation mechanisms that would translate to the multi-robot case as well. In the first, the robot presented its sensor readings (i.e., "My microphone picked up a suspicious conversation."), which led to improved trust and team performance over the no-explanation case. In the multi-robot case, this would expand into the sensor readings provided all of the robots. Enumerating all of the sensor readings is unlikely to scale well; even the enumeration of the sensor readings for a single robot was often skimmed too quickly by participants. An alternative would be to aggregate the sensor readings (e.g., "4 out of 5 robots with microphones picked up a suspicious conversation.").

The second single-agent explanation provided only a confidence rating (in terms of a probability of correctness), with no enumeration of the actual sensor readings. Despite containing much less information (or perhaps *because* of that compactness), this explanation condition also demonstrated improved trust and team performance. This explanation mechanism would also translate without any change in complexity to the multi-robot case, as the decision-theoretic DEC-POMDP mechanism would arrive at a probability of threats in the robot team's beliefs, just as the analogous POMDP mechanism did in the single-robot case.

Translating the single-robot explanation mechanisms would occur on a per-building basis, but in the multi-robot scenario, the robots would be providing a recommendation based on simultaneous assessments of multiple buildings. So while the individual sensor readings and confidence values would most likely help the human teammate understand the recommendations of gear for a particular building, they may not help in understanding which building to enter next. In that regard, the robot team will need to provide comparative explanations across different building choices.

One possible communication policy is for the team to provide a ranked list of all of the building locations (annotated by the gear recommended for each one). The Monte Carlo sampling method allows us to approximate the expected reward over all candidate actions, which we can then use to generate such a ranking. Note that such a ranking is not possible if the robots have computed only an optimal policy a priori and no longer have access to the value function informing that policy. Given the value function, the communication agent could also augment the ranked list with the actual expected rewards, conveying how much better each building is than the ones below it in the rankings. This additional information could lead to a more informed choice by the human teammate. It would also provide more transparency into the team's reasoning by exposing the alternatives under consideration and their eventual evaluation. On the other hand, this additional numeric information runs the risk of overly increasing their cognitive load, leading to a decrease in understanding and performance.

In the single-robot case, the team progressed through the buildings in a fixed sequence. In the multi-robot case, the person is free to choose which building to enter next. To make its recommendation, the robot team considers not only the immediate gain/loss from the building entered next, but possible sequences of subsequent building exploration. For example, the robot team might not always recommend the building that it is currently most confident about if it anticipates receiving another robot sensor reading in the near future. To increase the transparency about the lookahead in its reasoning, the robot team could recommend not just the next building to enter, but a *sequence* of buildings to enter. Again, this provides an opportunity to measure the tradeoff between transparency and cognitive load. The impact of cognitive load is amplified, because presenting a sequence could stimulate a completely different decision problem for the human teammate. In other words, if the communication agent recommends only the next immediate building, a person might think about only the next immediate building, but if the agent presents a sequence, that might cause the person to no longer think about the choice as a local decision.

4.2   Automatic Explanation of Team Activities

In the single-agent case, there is no real decision-making about the sequence of buildings to visit, so the goal to *Describe event and activities* was not relevant. Thus, there was need to explain anything about what the robot was currently doing. In the multi-robot case, this goal is very relevant, as there is a large challenge in conveying what the robots are doing. The simplest description is to enumerate where each robot is going (e.g., "Robot00 will move to the animal feed store. Robot01 will move to the. . . "). As the number of robots increases, this is likely to overwhelm the human teammate, if not cause their eyes to completely glaze over.

An alternative explanation would aggregate the robot behaviors, with geographic regions being one possible discretization. For example, the communication agent could summarize the team's behavior by saying: "23 robots are scanning the southeast sector". A coarser discretization (i.e., larger, but fewer, sectors) would lead to a less informative, but more compact message. Systematically varying this discretization provides an opportunity empirically quantify the impact of this tradeoff.

It is possible that a human teammate might not care about what the robots are doing unless there is something "unusual" about their choices. In other words, clear and easy decisions may not need explanation. The expected-reward calculation offers one means to identify "difficult" choices that might need explanation. In particular, if the difference between the action recommended by the team and the second-best action is less than some threshold, then the communication agent can augment its recommendation with this alternative choice and a breakdown of the expected-reward difference. Increasing this threshold will increase the number of alternatives exposed to the human teammate, increasing both transparency and cognitive load. Systematically varying threshold provides a mechanism for quantifying this tradeoff, in a way that can provide insight into how salience to the robot team (i.e., expected reward) translates into salience to the human teammate (i.e., trust and performance).

5   Conclusion

The testbed and explanation algorithms described here constitute a plausible setting for gathering data on people react to different levels of detail in those explanations. As a next step, we plan to conduct human-subject studies to understand how such variations in communication impact task load, trust, and human-multirobot team performance. These will provide quantitative insight into the tradeoff between volume of communication and cognitive load. We expect there to be many individual differences exhibited by our participants, meaning that it is very unlikely that there is a strictly dominant form of explanation. Instead, we hope that the data gathered will help inform an adaptive explanation mechanism that can dynamically change its communication content based on the particular preferences and capabilities of its current human teammate.

As mentioned in Sect. 4, we left some previously identified communication goals unaddressed in this investigation. Expanding our experimental scenario to allow for bidirectional communication and a generally richer interaction would allow us to explore three of those communication goals: *Request assistance*, *Receive commands*, and *Coordinate cross-team activities*. Varying the robots' approach to these goals would provide a means to empirically evaluate different supervisory control models, such as management by consent (require human approval before AI takes any action) and management by exception (AI performs action unless overruled by human). Layering these variations on top of our current dimensions of manipulation will allow us to explore the interaction among these goals within a common experimental framework. We thus view the testbed and algorithms presented here as a valuable foundation for systematic exploration and quantification of the impact of automatically generated explanations on human supervision of a robot team.

Acknowledgments. This work was sponsored by the U.S. Army Research Laboratory (ARL) under contract number W911NF-14-D-0005 and the Defense Advanced Research Projects Agency (DARPA) under contract number W911NF2010011. Statements and opinions expressed do not necessarily reflect the position or the policy of the United States Government or the Defense Advanced Research Projects Agency, and no official endorsements should be inferred.

References

1. Adams, J.A.: Human-robot interaction design: Understanding user needs and requirements. In: Proceedings of the Human Factors and Ergonomics Society Annual Meeting, pp. 447–451 (2005)
2. Bernstein, D.S., Givan, R., Immerman, N., Zilberstein, S.: The complexity of decentralized control of Markov decision processes. Math. Oper. Res. **27**(4), 819–840 (2002)
3. Bernstein, D.S., Hansen, E.A., Zilberstein, S.: Bounded policy iteration for decentralized POMDPs. In: Proceedings of the International Joint Conference on Artificial Intelligence, pp. 52–57 (2005)
4. Chen, J.Y., Barnes, M.J., Harper-Sciarini, M.: Supervisory control of multiple robots: Human-performance issues and user-interface design. IEEE Trans. Syst. Man Cybernet. Part C (Appli. Rev.) **41**(4), 435–454 (2010)
5. Chen, J.Y., Barnes, M.J., Kenny, C.: Effects of unreliable automation and individual differences on supervisory control of multiple ground robots. In: Proceedings of the International Conference on Human-Robot Interaction, pp. 371–378 (2011)
6. Chen, J.Y., Barnes, M.J., Qu, Z.: RoboLeader: An agent for supervisory control of multiple robots. In: Proceedings of the International Conference on Human-Robot Interaction, pp. 81–82 (2010)
7. Chien, S.Y., Lewis, M., Mehrotra, S., Sycara, K.: Imperfect automation in scheduling operator attention on control of multi-robots. In: Proceedings of the Human Factors and Ergonomics Society Annual Meeting, pp. 1169–1173 (2013)
8. Cummings, M.L., Bruni, S., Mercier, S., Mitchell, P.: Automation architecture for single operator, multiple UAV command and control. Tech. rep, Massachusetts Institute Of Technology (2007)
9. Doshi, P., Gmytrasiewicz, P.J.: Monte Carlo sampling methods for approximating interactive POMDPs. J. Artifi. Intell. Res. **34**, 297–337 (2009)
10. Gmytrasiewicz, P.J., Doshi, P.: Interactive POMDPs: properties and preliminary results. In: Proceedings of the International Joint Conference on Autonomous Agents and Multiagent Systems, vol. 3, pp. 1374–1375 (2004)
11. Hansen, E.A., Bernstein, D.S., Zilberstein, S.: Dynamic programming for partially observable stochastic games. In: AAAI, vol. 4, pp. 709–715 (2004)
12. Kaelbling, L.P., Littman, M.L., Cassandra, A.R.: Planning and acting in partially observable stochastic domains. Artif. Intell. **101**(1–2), 99–134 (1998)

13. McKinsey: A future that works: Automation, employment, and productivity. Tech. rep., McKinsey Global Institute (2017)
14. NSF: National artificial intelligence (AI) research institutes: Accelerating research, transforming society, and growing the American workforce. Tech. rep., National Science Foundation (2020)
15. Oliehoek, F.A., Amato, C.: A concise introduction to decentralized POMDPs. Springer (2016). https://doi.org/10.1007/978-3-319-28929-8
16. Papadimitriou, C.H., Tsitsiklis, J.N.: The complexity of Markov decision processes. Math. Oper. Res. **12**(3), 441–450 (1987)
17. Pynadath, David V.., Barnes, Michael J.., Wang, Ning, Chen, Jessie Y. C..: Transparency communication for machine learning in human-automation interaction. In: Zhou, Jianlong, Chen, Fang (eds.) Human and Machine Learning. HIS, pp. 75–90. Springer, Cham (2018). https://doi.org/10.1007/978-3-319-90403-0_5
18. Pynadath, D.V., Gurney, N., Wang, N.: Explainable reinforcement learning in human-robot teams: The impact of decision-tree explanations on transparency. In: IEEE International Conference on Robot and Human Interactive Communication (2022)
19. Pynadath, D.V., Marsella, S.C.: PsychSim: Modeling theory of mind with decision-theoretic agents. In: Proceedings of the International Joint Conference on Artificial Intelligence, pp. 1181–1186 (2005)
20. Rosenfeld, A., Agmon, N., Maksimov, O., Kraus, S.: Intelligent agent supporting human-multi-robot team collaboration. Artif. Intell. **252**, 211–231 (2017)
21. Rovira, E., McGarry, K., Parasuraman, R.: Effects of unreliable automation on decision making in command and control. In: Proceedings of the Human Factors and Ergonomics Society Annual Meeting, vol. 46, pp. 428–432 (2002)
22. Sarter, N.B., Schroeder, B.: Supporting decision making and action selection under time pressure and uncertainty: The case of in-flight icing. Hum. Factors **43**(4), 573–583 (2001)
23. Szer, D., Charpillet, F., Zilberstein, S.: MAA*: A heuristic search algorithm for solving decentralized POMDPs. In: Proceedings of the Conference on Uncertainty in Artificial Intelligence (2005)
24. Velagapudi, P., Scerri, P.: Scaling human-robot systems. In: Proceedings of the ACM CHI Conference on Human Factors in Computing Systems (2009)
25. Wang, N., Pynadath, D.V., Hill, S.G.: Building trust in a human-robot team with automatically generated explanations. In: Proceedings of the Interservice/Industry Training, Simulation and Education Conference, vol. 15315, pp. 1–12 (2015)
26. Wang, N., Pynadath, D.V., Hill, S.G.: The impact of POMDP-generated explanations on trust and performance in human-robot teams. In: Proceedings of the International Joint Conference on Autonomous Agents and Multi-Agent Systems, pp. 997–1005 (2016)
27. Zigoris, P., Siu, J., Wang, O., Hayes, A.T.: Balancing automated behavior and human control in multi-agent systems: A case study in RoboFlag. In: Proceedings of the American Control Conference, vol. 1, pp. 667–671 (2003)

User Transparency of Artificial Intelligence and Digital Twins in Production – Research on Lead Applications and the Transfer to Industry

Carsten Wittenberg[✉], Sabine Boos, Felix Harst, Carsten Lanquillon,
Morris Ohrnberger, Nicholas Schloer, Fabian Schoch, and Nicolaj C. Stache

Center for Industrial Artificial Intelligence (iAI), Heilbronn University, Max-Planck-Str. 39,
74081 Heilbronn, Germany
`carsten.wittenberg@hs-heilbronn.de`

Abstract. The use of artificial intelligence (AI) methods in automated production is currently still very challenging. Adapted AI solutions are too difficult to transfer to other use cases, the setup and operation of AI approaches require in-depth technical know-how, and their results are often difficult and incompletely comprehensible by humans. In addition, data treasures are sometimes available in companies, but there is a lack of tools to evaluate them. In an interdisciplinary project funded by the Carl-Zeiss-Foundation, these problems are addressed by research, and possible solutions are shown based on industrial lead applications. In addition to the lead applications and the promised industrial cooperation, the "Center for industrial AI" will be established as a permanent structure at Heilbronn University to ensure a sustainable transfer of results.

Keywords: Artificial Intelligence · Predictive Maintenance · Predictive Quality · Anomaly detection · process parameter optimization · Explainable AI · Human-Computer Interaction · Mixed Reality

1 Introduction

At the latest with the proclamation of the fourth industrial revolution about ten years ago, the trend to comprehensively digitalize industrial automated production is unstoppable [1–3]. In industrial automated production, digitization primarily means a focus on the acquisition and evaluation of data, which is already collected through the networking of individual subsystems by means of programmable logic controllers and fieldbus systems and analyzed in the field or in cloud systems. While terms such as big data (= originally a very large amount of data) initially appeared, it was soon recognized that it is not so much the pure amount of data, but the usability of the data (= smart data) that is much more relevant.

© The Author(s), under exclusive license to Springer Nature Switzerland AG 2023
H. Degen and S. Ntoa (Eds.): HCII 2023, LNAI 14051, pp. 322–332, 2023.
https://doi.org/10.1007/978-3-031-35894-4_24

Parallel to the developments in the context of Industry 4.0, new and better AI processes have been developed and are being used in various domains, favored by technological advances in hardware. Popular examples are speech recognition and translation tools.

However, there is also a variety of possible applications of AI in industrial production, based on digital networking through the introduction of Industry 4.0. Software-defined-manufacturing (SDM) [4–6] can be mentioned as a current trend. In this research project, the detection of anomalies in data sets for the timely implementation of possible maintenance operations (topic "predictive maintenance") as well as the optimization of process parameters to increase and ensure product quality (topic "predictive quality") are considered.

In contrast to many popular AI applications, humans are still responsible for production processes in an industrial context. Transparency of the AI's decisions is therefore indispensable to make the AI's results explainable. Therefore, a special focus in this research project is also on the interaction between the human and the automated production plant optimized by means of AI.

2 Goal of the Research Project

The research project funded by the Carl Zeiss Foundation started in the first half of 2022. As already mentioned in the introduction, this research project focuses on the topics of "predictive maintenance" by detecting anomalies as well as "predictive quality" by optimizing the associated process parameters. For the implementation, lead applications from industry as well as a model factory of Heilbronn University [7, 8] are used.

A special feature of industrial production, in contrast to the consumer market, is that solutions are usually developed specifically for a single area of application (e.g., a production plant). Commonly, transferability to other plants is not addressed. Furthermore, at the beginning of a project it is often unclear which and how much data can be used or is needed. Therefore, the following research questions have been formulated in this research project:

- How can the use of AI processes in production be made as simple as possible - ideally in such a way that no AI expert is required to set it up?
- How can the flexibility of AI methods be increased so that they can be applied to a wide range of problems, using the smallest possible amount of training data?
- How can the decision-making of AI procedures be made comprehensible to a human (keyword: explainable AI)?
- How can a toolbox be developed to evaluate existing production data in such a way that new correlations - e.g., causes of errors in production or optimal production parameter sets - can be found?
- How can plants be parameterized in such a way that production is particularly resource-efficient?

3 Predictive Maintenance Through Anomaly Detection

One challenge in industrial production is the avoidance of downtimes or temporary stops in production. Predictive maintenance based on detected anomalies in production data is one possibility to avoid or at least reduce downtimes. Due to the increase in computing power of IT systems enabling the broad implementation of deep learning (DL) models, there is a steady growth of new methods and models for the field of anomaly detection. Thus, there is a rapidly growing number of use cases, and, at the same time, new anomaly detection methods derived from DL methods. Applying DL methods to anomaly detection use cases and creating the right boundary conditions is not always easy. The major challenges in industrial applications include data accessibility, lack of anomalous data and validation capabilities especially in industrial plants, interpretation of anomalies, basic research that is still not widespread, lack of experts, lack of explainability, and more.

1. Data accessibility: The data needed for anomaly detection often already exists - in industrial plants, for example, where dozens to hundreds of sensors are installed, hundreds of data points are generated every second. The problem, however, is to make the data usable. There is the major challenge of building the right infrastructure to store the data and to make it accessible to the anomaly detection algorithm in real time, especially if it is not embedded in the system. With the efforts to implement the ideas of Industry 4.0, these problems could be reduced in the future and the availability of data could be greatly increased.

2. Validation of data: The nature of anomalies is that they occur very infrequently. Therefore, the acquisition of a sufficient amount of data sets containing anomalies takes a comparatively long time. This can lead to the fact that the test of the system cannot be carried out sufficiently and, thus, the validity is not sufficiently ensured. Especially in the industrial environment, in new plants, there is only little or even no erroneous data, which makes validation considerably more difficult. The sufficient existence of data within the plant or within similar plants or by way of a multiple use of sub-processes, is a prerequisite for the collection of data from which reliable models can be created. This long-term acquisition of data forms part of the aforementioned challenge to accessibility and acquisition of data.

3. Interpretation of data: The interpretation of anomalies becomes very important especially when, for example, an industrial plant may be shut down only in case of critical faults, since an otherwise too frequent shutdown (e.g., due to anomalies that do not pose a hazard) can disrupt productivity enormously. One of the biggest challenges in anomaly detection is the correct definition of the threshold above or below which an anomaly is detected, since most of the time - as in the point mentioned before - there is a lack of anomalous data to set the algorithm. In the end, only the reliability of the AI methods and the reliability of the data used from production will be able to ensure user confidence in the technology. Unnecessary false alarms must be avoided.

4. Anomaly detection: Usually, classification approaches are not used in anomaly detection because the data are very unevenly distributed among classes. For this reason, other approaches are used that attempt to create a model that reflects the normal state. This means that the model is trained only with normal data and not with anomalous data. With the trained model it is then possible to analyze deviations of the current state from the normal state. In the simplest case, a threshold value is defined above or below which a deviation from the normal state is recognized as an anomaly. There are different approaches from statistics and machine learning to build such models. Popular approaches from statistics include kernel density estimation, extreme value

theory, Mahalanobis distance, and SARIMA. In contrast to DL approaches, statistical approaches provide sufficient explanatory power of the model and require much less data to train. The disadvantage of these approaches is the low complexity of the model, which can quickly reach its limits. DL models, on the other hand, can represent very complex processes. The most frequently used DL approaches include autoencoders, LSTMs and transformer models. The relatively new transformer models such as the recently released chatbot ChatGPT from OpenAI deliver impressive results in natural language processing (NLP) tasks due to their attention mechanism. So-called attention heads allow transformer models to better focus on relevant previous and future values allowing them to better learn context than, for example, LSTMs [9]. What works well for NLP can also be applied to time series prediction, where the context of surrounding time points also plays an important role [10].

4   Predictive Quality by Optimizing Process Parameters Using Deep Reinforcement Learning

Parameterizing plants in an optimal way is a complex task. Depending on the number of dependencies and the number of influencing factors, e.g., for plants with several hundred parameters, conventional approaches cannot consider the number of possible combinations. By using deep reinforcement learning it should be possible to continuously find the optimal parameters, even under dynamically changing influencing factors.

The use of current state-of-the-art deep reinforcement learning (DRL) algorithms for the control of industrial plants and systems is investigated based on leading applications. The advantages as well as the difficulties of this method with respect to industrial applications will be evaluated.

4.1   Deep Reinforcement Learning

Deep reinforcement learning is a subcategory of machine learning in which an algorithm learns independently to solve a task in a given environment and to optimize it. Two core concepts are used: the agent and the environment (see Fig. 1). The agent learns to interact with the environment in such a way that it solves a task in the best possible way.

The environment represents the environment with which the agent can interact through predefined actions. The environment can be a simulation, for example, but also the real world that surrounds us. At a time t, the agent receives a state s_t from the environment, which contains information about the environment. Based on the state, the agent executes an action a_t that affects the environment. The environment, in turn, outputs a next state s_{t+1} and a reward R_t (cf. Fig. 1). The reward is determined by a function of the environment depending on s_t and s_{t+1} and serves as feedback to the agent about how good the chosen action a_t was. This creates a feedback loop through which the agent learns to "get better" by trying to maximize the reward.

The agent is the learning entity, which is implemented in DRL by a neural network (NN). The property of NN to approximate any Borel-measurable function [9] is used in this process to learn an ideal strategy to solve the task through gradient-based optimization. The function that is approximated in the case of DRL is called the policy. The

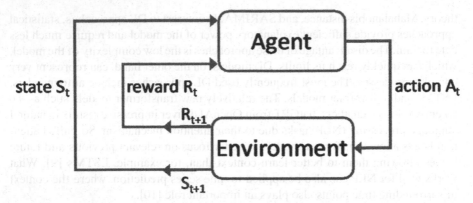

Fig. 1. Core concept of reinforcement learning [11]

optimal policy function is a mapping between the states and the actions that lead to the highest possible reward. An alternative approach is to learn a state-value function or an action-value (Q)-function. In so-called actor-critic methods, both methods are combined.

In this study, the soft actor-critic (SAC) algorithm [11] is used. Compared to other DRL algorithms, it shows a consistently high performance and is robust to the choice of hyperparameters, which has, among other things, the advantage that the method can be transferred to other problems without much effort. The SAC algorithm is one of the state-of-the-art algorithms in the field of (robot) control with continuous action space.

In the objective function, an entropy term is added to ensure that the agent not only optimizes its behavior with respect to the obtained reward, but also keeps the action choice as random as possible by a high entropy. A parameter, which is dynamically adjusted by the model itself during training, is used in the objective function to weight how much entropy should be included.

This gives the agent the incentive to explore more and, at the same time, to neglect actions that lead to low rewards. Exploration means gaining new experience so that the agent has the opportunity to find even better solutions. Other DRL algorithms resort to separate exploration methods, such as epsilon-greedy or noise vectors. By optimizing with respect to entropy, SAC does not require an additional exploration method. Moreover, multimodal probabilities for similar optimal actions can be learned. This enables the agent to learn redundant solution possibilities, which contributes to more robust solution finding.

The availability of a sufficient amount of data of sufficient quality is a major hurdle for many machine learning applications in the industrial domain. Therefore, it is important to use methods that are sample- or data-efficient. Unlike supervised learning problems where a large data set is acquired upfront, deep reinforcement learning often requires a new data set to be recorded for each iteration (optimization) of the policy. Depending on the environment, this can be an expensive proposition. Especially at the beginning of the training, the action selection is random, which makes online learning on a real system risky. The random actions could destroy the plant or endanger people in the environment. Therefore, training often relies on a simulation, which can be implemented by a digital twin, for example. The better the real application is represented by the digital image, the better a model can be trained with it. Simulation also has the great advantage that the simulation time can be virtually accelerated by taking advantage of the resources available today. As a result, data can be generated faster and the DRL model can be trained faster.

Using off-policy algorithms such as the SAC algorithm also increases data efficiency because the data recorded during training can be stored in a buffer and the model can be trained using batches from the buffer and, thus, reusing data. This is made possible by indirect learning of the policy, through feedback from the learned Q-value function. The Q-value function, unlike the policy function, can be trained using recorded state transitions.

4.2 Offline Reinforcement Learning

Another field of interest for industrial applications that is being investigated is the topic of offline reinforcement learning. Here, an agent learns - instead of interacting online with an environment - the optimal solution strategy based on previously recorded data. This data can, for example, be recorded in advance from the operation of a plant equipped with sensors. Afterwards, a DRL agent can be trained with this data. Many companies already have such data, so this method is perfect for optimizing such plants. However, offline DRL causes some difficulties. For example, the effects of actions that move the environment too far away from the recorded data cannot be validated because there is no data for these regions in the recorded data set. The goal of the research project is to implement different offline DRL methods and evaluate their application using an example task.

5 Explainable AI, Digital Twin and Augmented Reality

Innovative production systems must enable the use of AI to reach new horizons in production. For this, it is essential to create trust in the decisions. Ideally, acceptance can be built up through explainable and transparent AI decisions. Explainability must be built up as simply as possible. This is achieved by holographically and interactively presenting decisions. Mixed reality is an extended form of augmented reality (AR). In contrast to AR applications, mixed reality allows to grasp holographic objects and to interact with them in other ways. Figure 4 shows innovative approaches made possible by this technology. Among other things, holographic objects can be projected digitally and then manipulated.

Explainable AI describes the decision-making of artificial intelligences [11]. To achieve this and to increase the acceptance of decisions, digital twins can be used. For this purpose, the data of the real plant is visualized in the mixed reality environment. The modeling of the twin is the mapping of the properties, methods, behaviors and other characteristics of the physical object in the virtual space [18].

5.1 Explainability

The use of machine learning models is ubiquitous, and complex tasks lead to an increasing interest in optimizing the models not only on metrics such as accuracy, but also on criteria such as safety, avoiding discrimination e.g. in the area of human resources. In addition, deep learning models are being used in increasingly responsible tasks, such as prescribing medication to a patient or investing in stocks in finance. This requires that decisions can be tracked so that erroneous decisions and serious consequences that depend on them can be detected and prevented [14]. One problem with deep neural networks is that they are trained by end-to-end learning. End-to-end learning refers to the fact that only the input and output are relevant when training. For the most part, the representation of the data in the model itself provides no recognizable context for humans. This has the disadvantage of providing little transparency and interpretability, making the model a black box [11].

For trust to be built with such models and for them to be integrated into responsible tasks, interpretability is crucial. Interpretability can, on the one hand, help to improve the model by identifying deficiencies and providing visual hints for solution approaches. On the other hand, models that have already been tested gain wider acceptance by users through explainability. The visualization of the basis for decision-making can also show correlations of the data that are not yet known, so that new conclusions can be drawn.

Grad Cam

One way to interpret convolutional neural networks (CNN) is the grad cam method. In this method, the gradient flow related to a concept, e.g. a category, up to a layer of the CNN is used to create a localization map over the regions in the image that are most important for the prediction (Fig. 2).

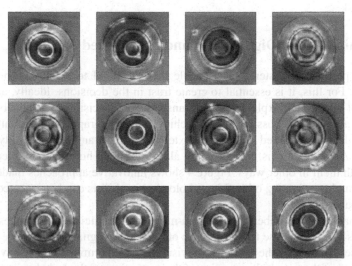

Fig. 2. As an example, an overlay localization map over input images to classify production defects. (Input images from [12])

Attention Maps

Attention maps in so-called vision transformer (ViT) architectures [16] are an architecture-specific way to visualize model decisions. Transformer models, in contrast to conventional architectures, work with attention mechanisms. This could be formulated like this: The attention mechanism is a non-parametric model that has the ability to dynamically adjust parameters to the data during runtime [17] (Fig. 3).

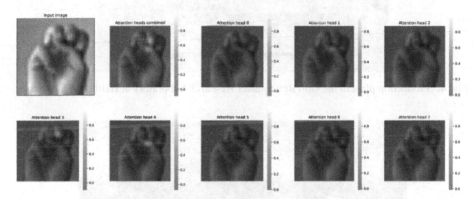

Fig. 3. Visualization of attention maps using the example of hand gestures

Digital Twin

In the design of the digital twin, there are still many challenges in terms of technologies and tools that need to be solved. Current research focuses on macro-level frameworks, processes, and know-how rather than specific technologies. Furthermore, modeling the digital twin is an extremely complicated process that requires time-consuming orientation and fine-tuning [19]. Once this process is complete, this work can also be used to simulate processes. This in turn allows for easy training of artificial intelligences. This can save time and money during the development process. Figure 5 shows the current state of the digital twin, which is being built in the Unity Game Engine. Figure 4 shows the real system at Heilbronn University.

Mixed Reality

Mixed reality is an extension of augmented reality. In contrast to augmented reality, not only are holographic objects displayed, but it is also possible to interact with these objects. Different types of input are supported. The application for interacting with the production plant in the Otto Rettenmaier Research Laboratory relies on gestures, eye tracking and voice commands. For the implementation, the Unity Game Engine is used. This game engine provides functions for simulating physical models (like the digital

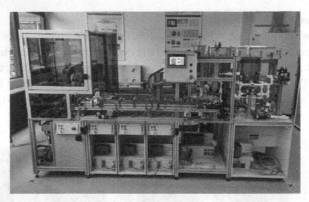

Fig. 4. Production plant in the Otto Rettenmaier Research Laboratory at Heilbronn University

Fig. 5. Digital twin of the production plant in the Otto Rettenmaier Research Laboratory at Heilbronn University

twin) and interaction (for the mixed reality interface). The approach of mixed reality will be used to make the visual comprehensibility of the complex system as well as the AI decisions more vivid to the user and to allow the user to experience the technology (Fig. 6).

The communication between the real plant and the digital twin or the mixed reality glasses is realized via OPC UA. To prevent unintentional changes of variables, an initial command must first be sent that the digital twin is allowed to connect to the real plant. In addition, various parameters are protected from manipulation by the protocol.

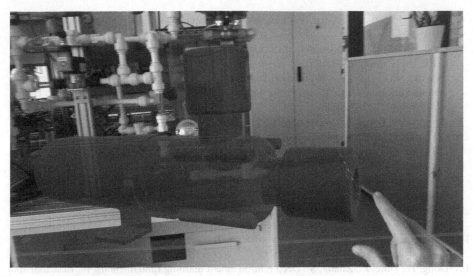

Fig. 6. Mixed reality interaction with the digital twin of a pump (original on the system in the background).

6 Outlook

After the start of the project, work is currently being done on the selection and collection of data for the use of the AI methods. In parallel, the digital twin of the model factory is becoming more and more concrete, so that the data deviation between the simulation by means of the digital twin and the process values in the real plant can also be used here to detect anomalies and for process optimization.

In a further step, in accordance with the user-centered development process, suitable forms of interaction, also using Mixed Reality, will be adapted to the user and, if necessary, newly developed, which can present the explainability, comprehensibility and transparency of the results from the AI of both anomaly detection and process optimization to the relevant user group.

Acknowledgements. The authors would like to thank the Carl Zeiss Foundation for funding the Center for industrial AI and the accompanying support for our research.

Carl Zeiss
Stiftung

References

1. Kolberg, D., Zühlke, D.: Lean Automation enabled by Industry 4.0 Technologies. IFAC-PapersOnLine **48**(3), 1870–1875 (2015)
2. Lasi, H., Fettke, P., Kemper, H.-G., Feld, T., Hoffmann, M.: Industrie 4.0. Wirtschaftsinformatik **56**(4), 261–264 (2014). https://doi.org/10.1007/s11576-014-0424-4
3. Wittenberg, C.: Challenges for the human-machine interaction in times of digitization. CPS & IIoT, and artificial intelligence in production systems. IFAC-PapersOnLine **55**(29), 114–119 (2022). https://doi.org/10.1016/j.ifacol.2022.10.241,ISSN2405-8963

4. Monostori L., et al.: Cyber-physical systems in manufacturing. CIRP Ann., **65**(2), 621–641 (2016)
5. Lane, T., Dirk, S.: Software-defined cloud manufacturing for industry 4.0 In: Procedia CIRP, vol. 52, pp. 12–17 (2016)
6. Nayak, N.G., Dürr, F., Rothermel, K.: Software-defined environment for reconfigurable manufacturing systems, In: 2015 5th International Conference on the Internet of Things (IOT), pp. 122–129 (2015)
7. Rempel, W., Bauer, B., Wittenberg, C.: Der Einsatz von Augmented Reality in der Industrie 4.0 am Beispiel einer Modellfabrik. In: Bauer, B., Wittenberg, C. (eds.) Tagungsband AALE 2019, pp. 395–401. VDE-Verlag, Berlin (2019)
8. Wittenberg, C., Bauer, B., Stache, N.: A smart factory in a laboratory size for developing and testing innovative human-machine interaction concepts. In: Ahram, T., Falcão, C. (eds.) AHFE 2019. AISC, vol. 972, pp. 160–166. Springer, Cham (2020). https://doi.org/10.1007/978-3-030-19135-1_16
9. Vaswani, A.: Attention is All You Need, arXiv:1706.03762. (2017)
10. Grigsby, J., Wang, Z., Qi, Y.: Long-Range Transformers for Dynamic Spatiotemporal Forecast-ing, arXiv:2109.12218. (2021)
11. Dong, H., Ding, Z., Zhang, S.: Deep reinforcement learning fundamentals. In: Research and Application. Springer, Singapore (2020). https://doi.org/10.1007/978-981-15-4095-0
12. https://www.kaggle.com/datasets/ravirajsinh45/real-life-industrial-dataset-of-casting-pro duct,eingesehenam22.12.2022,
13. Haarnoja, T., et al.: Soft actor-critic algorithms and applications. arXiv preprint arXiv:1812.05905, (2018)
14. https://datascience.eu/de/maschinelles-lernen/interpretierbarkeit-beim-maschinellen-lernen/
15. Selvaraju, R., Cogswell, M., Das, A., Vedantam, R., Parikh, D., Batra, D.: Grad-CAM: Visual Explanations from Deep Networks via Gradient-based Localization. arXiv preprint arXiv: 1610.02391v4, (2019)
16. Dosovitskiy, A., et al.: An Image is Worth 16x16 Words: Transformers for Image Recognition at Scale. arXiv preprint arXiv:2010.11929, (2020)
17. Zai, B.: Deep reinforcement learning in action. Manning (2020)
18. Tao, F., Xiao, B., Qi, Q., Cheng, J., Ji, P.: Digital twin modeling. J. Manuf. Syst. **64**, 372–389 (2022)
19. Singh, M., Fuenmayor, E., Hinchy, E.P., Qiao, Y., Murray, N., Devine, D.: Digital twin: origin to future. Appli. Syst. Innovat. **4**(2), 36 (2021)

Artificial Intelligence
for Decision-Support and Perception
Analysis

Redundancy in Multi-source Information and Its Impact on Uncertainty

Thom Hawkins[1]([✉]) [iD], Justine Rawal[2] [iD], and Adrienne Raglin[2] [iD]

[1] US Army Project Manager Mission Command, Aberdeen Proving Ground, Atlanta, MD 21005, Georgia
jeffrey.t.hawkins10.civ@army.mil, thom.hawkins@gmail.com
[2] DEVCOM Army Research Laboratory, Adelphi, MD 20783, USA

Abstract. This paper explores the relationship between the uncertainty of information (UoI) and information entropy as applied to multiple-source data fusion (MSDF). Many MSDF methods maximize system-wide entropy by minimizing source-data redundancy. However, the potential for uncertainty in the system provides a role for redundancy to confirm or validate the sensory inputs. While the relationship between uncertainty and entropy is neither wholly dependent nor independent, it is sufficiently complex to require modeling for each MSDF system. A one-dimensional model of redundancy versus entropy will not suffice when considering the UoI. The concept of UoI includes identifying the category associated with uncertainty. Thus, considering the redundancy within one category in relation to multiple categories may further reduce overall uncertainty. This paper proposes using utility functions, as well as a two-dimensional model with certainty on the x-axis and entropy on the y-axis, as tools for optimizing redundancy to benefit certainty and entropy maximally.

Keywords: Uncertainty of Information · Information Entropy · Information Redundancy · Shannon Entropy · Multi-source Information · Information Uncertainty · Data Fusion

1 Introduction

This paper discusses the concepts of Shannon entropy and uncertainty of information (UoI) and their application to multi-source data fusion (MSDF) and information processing. Though most research considers these frameworks separately, they are not wholly independent and could benefit from further study of their interaction. Information entropy can and has been optimized for data fusion [1–3]; however, this process tends to eliminate redundancy that could reduce the uncertainty of information. Therefore, the data fusion process must integrate the concept of UoI.

2 Discussion

2.1 Shannon Entropy at the Sensor and Sensor System Levels

In the book-length version [4] of his seminal paper [5] on communication theory, Claude Shannon introduced what became known as "Shannon entropy." Shannon borrowed the concept from thermodynamics, where entropy measures a system's possible states of atoms or molecules [6]. In Shannon information theory, "bits" replace atoms, each with two possible outcomes (0 and 1), representing a single unit of entropy. Beyond Shannon's initial conception, the bit is replaced with a measurable datum, which could be several values, whether quantitative or qualitative (for example, see Fig. 1). Entropy is measured as a percentage of possible complexity. In Fig. 1, each sensor has 100 percent entropy because all the listed state values are still possible. Sensor 1 no longer reads a cool color as they narrow, and the entropy drops to sixty percent—only three of five values are now possible. That drop in redundancy is information gain. Knowing which values the sensor does not read gives us information about which values it could be.

Sensor 1
red
orange
yellow
green
blue

Sensor 2
red
blue
violet

Fig. 1. Entropy at sensor and sensor system levels

If we know that when Sensor 2 reads 'red,' Sensor 1 also reads 'red,' then redundancy exists. By definition [5], redundancy is the complement to entropy. For example, if entropy is sixty percent, redundancy is forty percent. That a reader can recognize a word even with missing letters (because some letters often appear together in groups of two or three) demonstrates redundancy in language. The identity of a single hidden character on its own could have one of 26 alternatives, but in the context of a word, the letters on either side provide information about the missing letter. The less frequent the letter, the more information it provides. An 's' or a 't' provide little information when revealed in a hidden message, given the commonality of both letters in English [7]. Because they are relatively frequent, the probability that a random letter is an 's' or a 't' is much higher.[1]

In contrast, a character with high entropy could be many different letters. More information gain means greater redundancy and less entropy. This echoes earlier work

---

[1] In the game show *Wheel of Fortune*, contestants spin a wheel to assign a dollar value to each of the letters revealed in a concealed message. If they name a letter that is not in the message, they lose their turn. Because of this, they are incentivized to reveal many redundant letters for short-term gain as opposed to revealing high-entropy letters that would make the overall message clearer.

by Zipf [8] on the frequency of letters in language. Entropy, therefore, can be seen as a measure of uncertainty in the variable.

Returning to Fig. 1, if a sensor's signal is predictable, its entropy is low and will have little value as an input to a sensor system or within a prediction algorithm.[2] There are degrees of variability, and for the economy of an algorithm, a variable with low entropy may be treated as a constant (e.g., an obstructed camera lens). Considering a sensor in isolation, entropy and uncertainty are the same. The entropy measures the degree of variability—Sensor 1 can return any five of the listed states. Entropy is lost when data is received that may narrow the probability matrix for future data based on a Bayesian profile.

Entropy will refer to the probability matrix across all sensors after integrating a second sensor as a holistic system. Note that the system contains some redundancy— namely, measurement of 'red' and 'blue' states occur in both Sensor 1 and Sensor 2 (assuming same-target measurement). Uncertainty may still refer to the potential variability, but UoI discussed subsequently refers to the system's reliability in conveying the measured state or states.

We can apply Shannon's framework at the systems level; for example, when the sensors feeding a system overlap. Here, the entropy is from the unique contributions of each sensor (i.e., what Dubois et al. [14] refer to as "information items"[3]). One sensor can be redundant or have low entropy concerning the cumulative input of both sensors. However, while entropy and uncertainty can be synonymous at the individual sensor level, entropy and uncertainty diverge at the systems level and could even be working in conflict. Two sensors measuring the same signal, while presumably redundant, could increase the reliability of the information in two ways. First, it could provide a corroborating signal (e.g., both Sensors 1 and 2 detect the presence of blue in the sample). Also, it may reveal the uncertainty of both sensors by providing a conflicting signal (e.g., Sensor 1 detects the presence of blue while Sensor 2 does not). Optimizing data fusion requires balancing the number of inputs with the gain in output, such as in best subsets regression; however, we must also consider the potential stabilizing effect of redundancy on uncertainty.

2.2 The Concept of Uncertainty of Information and Identifying Categories

The UoI[4] provides both a qualitative and a quantitative way to communicate uncertainty. The UoI concept has two major variables; the first represents the data source, which can include devices, networks, visualization applications, text, imagery, and video, as

---

[2] Bayesian priors may be established in a "possibility matrix" based on previous input. If Sensor 1 has sensed 'red' nine out of ten times in the past, then the likelihood that the next reading will be 'red' is ninety percent. [9–13].

[3] "An information item is understood as a statement, possibly tainted with uncertainty, forwarded by some source, and describing what the current state of affairs is" [14].

[4] Fassinut-Mombot & Choquel [2, 15], based on an earlier paper by De Luca & Termini [16] discuss uncertainty with respect to entropy as that inherent in a probability distribution. For UoI, certainty is more akin to reliability.

well as human, software, and physical agents (see [17] for definitions).[5] The second represents the type or description of the uncertainty. These category descriptors follow the taxonomy presented in Gershon's work on the imperfect nature of information [18]. For UoI, inaccurate, questionable, incomplete, corrupt, disjoint, imperfect, inconsistent, and inappropriate have been selected (see [19] for definitions).[6] Thus, the UoI concept allows the type or category of uncertainty associated with the quantitative value of uncertainty to be communicated to the "receiver" (human or non-human). The intent is to provide greater context to the uncertainty. The UoI represents a total value across a set of data sources and descriptors or as a matrix of data sources and descriptors. Figures 2a and 2b show Shannon's original general communication system [4, 5], with the introduction of noise in the signal transport and a communication system within the framework of Gershon [18], which shows the widespread effects of uncertainty across the system.

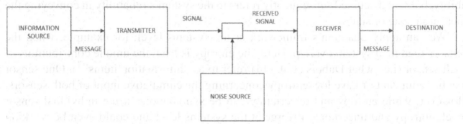

a. Shannon's depiction of a general communication system [4][5]

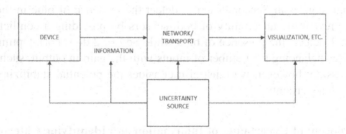

b. General communication system with Gershon's framework [18]

Fig. 2. a. Shannon's depiction of a general communication system [4, 5], b. General communication system with Gershon's framework [18]

One potential benefit of UoI is identifying where and what information reduces entropy. For this case, the total UoI can decrease by using information from another

---

[5] Shannon [4], in his employment with Bell Labs, was primarily interested in error correction of the transport mechanism (network) and did not account for these other factors of uncertainty.

[6] More broadly, these descriptors can be binned as: "(i) aleatoric uncertainty (random effects, signal noise, etc.) and (ii) epistemic uncertainty (incomplete knowledge regarding a complex system, etc.)." [9]

source or descriptor with less individual UoI value or associated with a different type of UoI.

A second potential benefit of UoI is identifying how to achieve greater information gain. For this case, the matrix of UoIs allows the use of combinations of information from different sources or descriptors with lower individual UoIs. We can express this by the equation below, where $H(S)$ is across all sources and descriptors, and $H(A,S)$ is across individual sources and descriptors.

$$H(S) = -\sum_{i=1}^{N} P_i log_2 P_i$$

$$Information\ Gain(A, S) = H(S) - \sum_{j=1}^{v} \frac{|S_j|}{|S|} H(S_j) = H(S) - H(A, S)$$

Because the UoI concept has qualitative and quantitative components, it can also bridge the redundancy relationship. The uncertainty associated with each information item can be assigned by an agent to the (Gershon) descriptor category. This agent can have set rules or computational models that identify the uncertainty across multiple data sources where redundancy exists. This UoI agent can then provide a trigger when there is redundancy and determine whether maintaining the redundancy reduces the overall uncertainty across the information.

Fig. 3. Sensor configuration for use case

For example, in a paper by Zhu et al. [20] on a novel reconnaissance method that relies on the propagation of Wi-Fi signals, the researchers found that a Wi-Fi sniffer device detects movement near a Wi-Fi transmitter. Because Wi-Fi emits beyond the walls of a building, a spy could identify an individual's whereabouts and movement inside the building based on modulations of the Wi-Fi signal created by the target blocking and/or reflecting the signal as they move. By analyzing the strength of the Wi-Fi signal, it is possible to infer movement by a person in that space. We can set a simple rule for assigning UoI for inaccurate information related to the ability to detect motion based on these signals. In the configuration in Fig. 3, two sensors labeled A and B are in the room on the left, and one sensor labeled C is in the room on the right. Here we have a use case for discussing UoI, entropy, and redundancy. Table 1 shows a sample of the Wi-Fi signals for each sensor. The UoI values are assigned based on their difference from the mean Wi-Fi strength. Focusing on the first ten values for Sensor A, UoI values of 0.8 are assigned, indicating significant uncertainty in the individual's location relative to the sensor.

In contrast, using Sensor B's data, the assignment of 0.2 UoI values indicates an absence of significant uncertainty. Therefore, the UoI can trigger the use of Sensor B for the motion detection task. Having redundant sensors allows the overall system to reduce the overall entropy or maintain lower entropy with the aid of the UoI if there are two motion sensors in one location. Using the uncertainty value and descriptive category of the uncertainty can notify the system of more efficient use of the data from the set of sensors.

Table 1. Sample Wi-Fi signal for example use case

Sensor A Wi-Fi Strength	UoI for Sensor A	Sensor B Wi-Fi Strength	UoI for Sensor B	Sensor C Wi-Fi Strength	UoI for Sensor C
0	0.8	0.252808	0.3	0.071	0.50
0	0.8	0.365265	0.2	0.066719	0.50
0	0.8	0.463272	0.0	0.060204	0.50
0	0.8	0.451642	0.0	0.053152	0.50
0	0.8	0.421572	0.0	0.048288	0.50
0.016479	0.8	0.374307	0.2	0.043551	0.50
0	0.8	0.367711	0.2	0.041997	0.50
0	0.8	0.335514	0.3	0.036633	0.50
0	0.8	0.30725	0.3	0.040779	0.50
0	0.8	0.2657	0.3	0.039784	0.50

2.3 The Value of Redundancy in Uncertain Information

The central problem in MSDF is optimizing the input volume with the gain in output [10]; for example, using best subsets regression. Redundancy at the systems level for MSDF is multiple sensors providing the same information (i.e., multiple sources can derive the same information from different data). Entropy for MSDF, abstracted from the sensor level, is the ability to derive unique information from sensor data. A single sensor could convey information using multiple media (for example, audio and video or object detection and motion). A combination of data from multiple sensors may derive emergent information.

MSDF redundancy can reduce UoI, whether from duplication of a device to validate the data stream or, given a discrepancy, to identify that a sensor may not provide the expected data (e.g., "unreliable, drifting, or malfunctioning sensors" [21] or less-than-complete redundancy). Redundancy on a sensor-system level may help by validating individual sensors with high entropy. In contrast, sensors with low entropy require less redundancy on the systems level because of the low number of potential states for the sensor. We cannot assume a linear relationship between redundancy and certainty at the sensor or sensor-system level.

2.4 A Two-Dimensional Model of Redundancy and Entropy

Fassinut-Mombot & Choquel [15] present a model that identifies the maximum entropy for each sensor (that is, given any available priors and the maximum number of possible different outputs from that sensor). Their model then fuses the data by applying conditional entropy for these distributions. It identifies the resulting model with the lowest conditional entropy—where Y tells you the least about X. The challenge with this model is that it assumes reliable sensor data[7], though the values may be difficult to predict in advance. Like Shannon's original work that concentrated on data transport, modeling MSDF on the entropy of data at the sensor level alone may not yield the optimal results when extrapolating to the sensor system from data to information.

The entropy of a combination of sensors is their joint entropy (see Fig. 4)—$H(X,Y)$—which can calculate the conditional entropy of a single sensor given the input from the complementary sensor:

$H(X|Y) = H(X,Y) - H(Y)$, where

$$0 \leq H(X|Y) \leq H(X)$$

If $H(X|Y)$ is equal to 0, then if we know the value of Y, we also know the value of X. If $H(X|Y)$ is equal to $H(X)$, then, if we know the value of Y, the value of X is still unknown (i.e., X and Y are independent). The intersection of $H(X|Y)$ and $H(Y|X)$ is $I(X;Y)$, the mutual information or bilateral redundancy of X and Y.

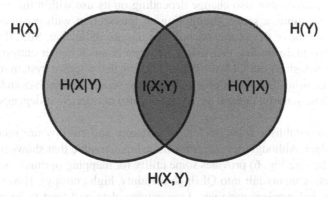

Fig. 4. Conditional entropy and mutual information

Figure 5 shows the notional utility functions for uncertainty and entropy. The y-axis represents entropy from $H(X|Y) = 0$, complete redundancy, to $H(X|Y) = H(X)$, complete independence. Even with no defined standards for the measurement of UoI, Raglin et al. [22] have used a percentage index similar to Shannon's measurement of entropy [5]. From the perspective of economizing data sources, independence is preferred. Each step toward increasing independence increases the utility of the sensor system. Certainty, however,

---

[7] As noted by Dubois et al. [14], "the presence of incomplete, unreliable and inconsistent information leads to uncertainty, and the necessity of coping with it.".

benefits from the confirming effects of redundancy, increasing utility. To maximize the utility for both, we must identify the point where the curves overlap that has the highest utility. These curves are merely explanatory and require calculation for a specific sensor system.

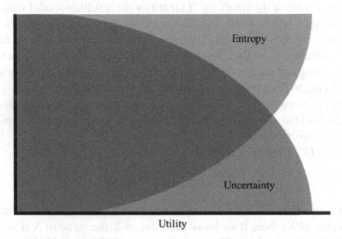

Fig. 5. Notional utility diagram of uncertainty versus entropy

A signal's entropy can also change depending on its use within the context of the outcome. For example, a sensor monitoring an intersection with predictable activity cycles based on time of day or day of the week may be redundant. Still, if the intent is to identify individual vehicles, that sensor will have a much higher entropy as various vehicles pass through its field. Marlin et al. [23] note that a sensor system may perform various tasks requiring different configurations of the sensors themselves and the weights attributed to those sensors. Indeed, the entropy is also not static—it depends on the task performed.

As we have established, the vectors of certainty and entropy are related but not wholly dependent. Although not independent, using a graphic that shows these vectors as perpendicular (see Fig. 6) provides some utility for mapping optimal combinations.

Ideally, sensor inputs fall into QI (high certainty, high entropy). However, x and y are not strictly independent variables. Low entropy data will tend to be more certain (QIV) simply because the low rate of variability, once validated, establishes a Bayesian precedent for future prediction.[8] High entropy data will tend to be less certain (QII) because the probability distribution is less influenced by Bayesian priors. Therefore, most sensor inputs will cluster around a line that bisects Qs II and IV ($y = -x$). This gravity line creates a trough that requires energy (effort) to move from Qs II and IV to QI.

---

[8] As noted previously, a low entropy sensor may even be replaced with a constant—eliminating the need for that sensor feed—when simplifying for data fusion.

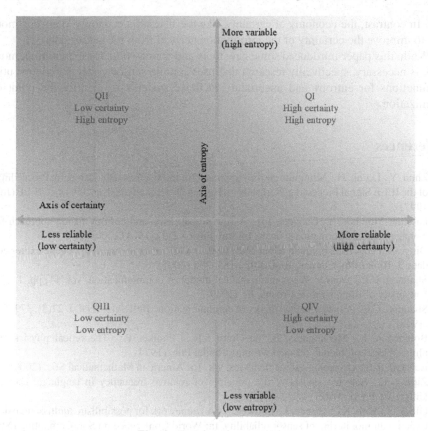

Fig. 6. Certainty versus entropy

A QI sensor input will have naturally high entropy, but the certainty results from complementary inputs that are only incidentally redundant. For example, sensor x measures value X while sensor y measures value Y; however, certain states of value X only occur coincidentally with certain states of value Y. The key is for the measured inputs to be complementary but not colinear.

3 Conclusion and Future Work

In *Human behavior and the principle of least effort: An introduction to human ecology* [24], Zipf defines a dichotomy of economies. A speaker may convey a message with minimal words resulting in use of vague words that contain multiple or conflicting meanings without qualifiers. Meanwhile, the listener wants more words, aiming toward the precision required to understand the message. These two competing economies drive the size of a language's vocabulary.

Source redundancy has similar economies driving the number and complexity of sensors. The economy of entropy optimizes for the fewest sensors to provide the most data. In contrast, the economy of certainty, like the listener's economy, demands more data to improve the certainty of the information derived from the sensor data.

While this paper introduced some new tools and frameworks for exploration, more work is necessary, specifically research that uses sample sensor systems to define utility functions for entropy and uncertainty in those systems to identify the point of optimization.

References

1. Zhou, Y., Leung, H.: Minimum entropy approach for multisensor data fusion. In: Proceedings of the IEEE Signal Processing Workshop on Higher-Order Statistics, pp. 336–339. IEEE (July 1997)
2. Fassinut-Mombot, B., Choquel, J.B.: A new probabilistic and entropy fusion approach for management of information sources. Inform. Fusion **5**(1), 35–47 (2004)
3. Ding, C., Peng, H.: Minimum redundancy feature selection from microarray gene expression data. J. Bioinform. Comput. Biol. **3**(02), 185–205 (2005)
4. Shannon, C.E., Weaver, W.: A mathematical model of communication, vol. 11, pp. 11–20. University of Illinois Press, Urbana, IL (1949)
5. Shannon, C.E.: A mathematical theory of communication. Bell Syst. Tech. J. **27**(3), 379–423 (1948)
6. Boltzmann, L., McGuinness, B., de Groot S.R., Foulkes P.: Theoretical physics and philosophical problems: selected writings. Reidel Pub. (1974)
7. Lewand, R.E.: Cryptological mathematics, vol. 16. American Mathematical Soc. (2000)
8. Zipf, G.K.: Selected studies of the principle of relative frequency in language. Harvard University Press (1932)
9. Glock, S., Voth, K., Schaede, J., Lohweg, V.: A framework for possibilistic multi-source data fusion with monitoring of sensor reliability. In: World Conference on Soft Computing (May 2011)
10. Holst, C.A., Lohweg, V.: A redundancy metric set within possibility theory for multi-sensor systems. Sensors **21**(7), 2508 (2021)
11. Wang, Y., Liu, Y.: Bayesian entropy network for fusion of different types of information. Reliab. Eng. Syst. Saf. **195**, 106747 (2020)
12. Lohweg, V., Voth, K., Glock, S.: A possibilistic framework for sensor fusion with monitoring of sensor reliability. Sensor Fusion-Foundation and Applications, intechopen. com, 191–226 (2011)
13. Mohammad-Djafari, A.: . Probabilistic methods for data fusion. In: Maximum Entropy and Bayesian Methods: Boise, Idaho, USA, 1997 Proceedings of the 17th International Workshop on Maximum Entropy and Bayesian Methods of Statistical Analysis, pp. 57–69. Springer Netherlands (1998)
14. Dubois, D., Liu, W., Ma, J., Prade, H.: The basic principles of uncertain information fusion. An organised review of merging rules in different representation frameworks. Informat. Fusion **32**, 12–39 (2016)
15. Fassinut-Mombot, B., Choquel, J.B.: An entropy method for multisource data fusion. In: Proceedings of the Third International Conference on Information Fusion, vol. 2, pp. THC5–17. IEEE (July 2000)
16. De Luca, A., Termini, S.: A definition of a nonprobabilistic entropy in the setting of fuzzy sets theory. In: Readings in Fuzzy Sets for Intelligent Systems, pp. 197–202. Morgan Kaufmann (1993)

17. Lott, D. A., Raglin, A., Metu, S.: On the use of operations research for decision making with uncertainty for IoT devices in battlefield situations: simulations and outcomes. In: Virtual, Augmented, and Mixed Reality (XR) Technology for Multi-Domain Operations, vol. 11426, pp. 31–44. SPIE (April 2020)
18. Gershon, N.: Visualization of an imperfect world. IEEE Comput. Graphics Appl. 18(4), 43–45 (1998)
19. Lott, D. A., Raglin, A., Metu, S.: On the use of operations research for decision making with uncertainty for IoT devices in battlefield situations. In: 2019 IEEE 5th International Conference on Collaboration and Internet Computing (CIC), pp. 266–297. IEEE (December 2019)
20. Zhu, Y., et al.: Et tu alexa? when commodity Wi-Fi devices turn into adversarial motion sensors (2018). arXiv preprintarXiv:1810.10109
21. Holst, C.A., Lohweg, V.: Designing possibilistic information fusion—The importance of associativity, consistency, and redundancy. Metrology 2(2), 180–215 (2022)
22. B.Raglin, A., et al.: Enhanced tactical inferencing (ETI): an initial assessment. In: Artificial Intelligence and Machine Learning for Multi-Domain Operations Applications IV, vol. 12113, pp. 648–652. SPIE (June 2022)
23. Marlin, B. M., et al.: On uncertainty and robustness in large-scale intelligent data fusion systems. In: 2020 IEEE Second International Conference on Cognitive Machine Intelligence (CogMI), pp. 82–91. IEEE (October 2020)
24. Zipf, G.K.: Human behavior and the principle of least effort: An introduction to human ecology. Ravenio Books (2016)

Experimental Validation of a Multi-objective Planning Decision Support System for Ship Routing Under Time Stress

Matthew Macesker[1]([⊠]), Krishna R. Pattipati[1], David Sidoti[2], Adam Bienkowski[1], Lingyi Zhang[1], David L. Kleinman[1], Mollie McGuire[3], Steven Uziel[3], Senjuti Basu Roy[4], and Francesco Primerano[4]

[1] University of Connecticut, Storrs, CT 06269, USA
{matthew.macesker,krishna.pattipati,adam.bienkowski,
lingyi.zhang}@uconn.edu
[2] U.S Naval Research Laboratory, Monterey, CA 93943, USA
david.sidoti@nrlmry.navy.mil
[3] Naval Postgraduate School, Monterey, CA 93943, USA
{mrmcguir,steven.uziel}@nps.edu
[4] New Jersey Institute of Technology, Newark, NJ 07102, USA
{senjutib,fap24}@njit.edu

Abstract. Integration of sophisticated planning algorithms into Naval operations requires the systematic design of decision-support systems (DSS) that improve the understanding of AI-suggested courses of action (CoAs) by humans without overwhelming their cognitive processes. A successful interface would permit operators to fully understand the context of the problem so that they can select a computer-generated CoA that best matches their preferences. In this paper, the authors investigated such a system for routing ships using two sequential human-in-the-loop experiments, one which evaluated the impact of various forms of graphical decision support on decision-making and the cognitive load, and another in which time pressure was manipulated. The results showed that a mix between tabular and graphical information reduced the cognitive load, given adequate time to make a decision. Participant responses were used to build models of human decision rules to integrate into the DSS, revealing that humans heavily weighted certain contextual attributes that were indirectly integrated into the planning algorithm through the cost structure. A novel technique for representing decisions as a distribution of common heuristic trade-offs among Pareto solutions found that the context of each scenario dictated the choice of the heuristic. The results of these experiments guided the design of a follow-up experiment on multi-ship routing that is currently in pilot testing.

Keywords: Decision Support Systems · Ship Routing · TMPLAR · Collaborative AI · Human-in-the-loop Experiment · Pareto-optimal · Association Rule Mining

Supported by ONR under grants N00014-18-1-2838 and N00014–21-1–2187.

1 Introduction

Collaborative artificial intelligence (AI) systems manage uncertainty better than humans or AI alone by distributing intuitive and deliberative processing [1] between humans and AI, and by letting human operators focus on the most pressing issues during time-sensitive tasks. This collaboration is particularly relevant in mission planning, where AI can serve as a powerful tool to augment the decision-making capabilities of human planners by generating options that are beyond the capacity of an individual expert. Integration of AI in these error-intolerant domains, however, depends on how much a human can understand and trust the outputs of an AI algorithm without significant mental strain [2]. The success of collaborative AI rests partly on the development of a human-computer interface, referred to herein as a decision-support system (DSS), that succeeds in presenting the salient details of each AI-generated course of action (CoA) without overwhelming the operators, thereby increasing their confidence in decisions while reducing the time-to-decision (TTD).

The successful design of a DSS that minimizes information loss between a rational machine and an experienced human is of critical importance to the US Navy. The Department of Defense's AI strategy emphasizes the ability of AI to improve human decision-making and reduce the likelihood of lapses in judgement that have led to unintentional harm (e.g., with the Patriot missile system in the Iraq war). Humans are still required in-the-loop, however, to keep AI accountable in complex stochastic domains so that they continue to follow the commander's intent [3]. Although an emphasis on the fallibility of human reasoning may evoke a preference towards purely "rational" decision-making in the spirit of prospect decision theory [1], there are some mission contexts where difficult-to-quantify human expertise is helpful in improving performance. Specifically, in route-planning for ships, a multitude of solutions, which are equally appealing, can be quickly pruned by a planner by applying experience and instinct-based preferences. According to heuristic decision theory [4], human instinct has significant value that can improve the performance of an AI system via the distinct and unique evaluation of contextual information that differs from conventional modelling.

The focus of our recent efforts has been to apply these principles of human-computer interaction (HCI) and decision theory to improve the utilization and accuracy of a route planning tool, previously developed by the co-authors [5], and that is currently in the process of being put into operational use by the US Navy. Our algorithm, Tool for Multi-objective Planning and Asset Routing (TMPLAR), provides a set of solutions to the ship routing problem given the mission parameters. Produced using a set of potential forecast realizations of meteorological and oceanographic (METOC) conditions [6], each CoA (route) generated by TMPLAR is Pareto optimal over the specified set of objectives (e.g., total fuel and distance travelled). The goal of the human operator is to choose a solution from this Pareto front for implementation.

The process of guiding humans to choose a solution from an often-large Pareto-front has been investigated earlier, often under the rubric of multi-criteria decision-making. For instance, Cuate and Schütze [7] demonstrated a software tool that could help a decision maker (DM) explore a Pareto-front based on the objective function values when no preferences are present, and Hartikainen et al. [8] proposed an interactive method to continuously produce new solutions based on the preferences articulated at a previous iteration. Outside of software engineering, Wang and Rangaiah [9] listed several ranking, weighting, and elimination-based strategies to support a DM in winnowing their choices, and then listed how each strategy may bias the chosen solution.

These methods, however, are mostly inappropriate for our use case. Firstly, the CoAs produced by TMPLAR are highly complex due to the intricacies of dynamic ship routing context (e.g., mission, environment, asset status, obstacles), and as such it is infeasible to generate new solutions from old ones based on preference elicitation. Secondly, given the hands-on experience of Naval operators, there may be other features that are salient in a DM's mental model that are not currently viewed as objectives for optimization (e.g., bathymetry, routes not close to the shore, straightness of a route). Finally, and most relevant to this article, we intend to learn the preferences of operators indirectly from their route selections, so we must present the entire set of solutions to reduce any chance of bias. The results may then be used to "personalize" the results of TMPLAR by applying inverse or preference-based reinforcement learning [10, 11].

To collect data on human preferences, we designed a tunable DSS to allow each user to make informed judgments on TMPLAR-produced CoAs without overwhelming them. To validate this platform, we ran multiple human-in-the-loop experiments where subjects used the DSS platform to choose among CoAs across several mission scenarios. The first experiment focused primarily on determining what features were necessary in a DSS, while the second experiment focused on how effective it remains under time stress. We analyzed the data collected to gain insight on two related issues: the need to design an interface that improves the ability of operators to accurately choose among AI-generated routes, and the desire to tune our algorithm so that it better matches the thought processes used by the navigators.

The rest of the paper is organized as follows. Section 2 provides background on AI-assisted Naval routing and discusses the design of the DSS. Sections 3 and 4 describe the design and implementation of the two sequential experiments. Section 5 analyzes the experimental results, followed by a discussion of the limitations and future research directions of this work in Sect. 6. Finally, Sect. 7 provides a summary.

2   Design of a Decision-Support System for Ship Routing

2.1   Recent Advancements in AI-Assisted Naval Planning

Humans are notoriously poor at trading-off multiple conflicting objectives, especially if the task is dynamic and has inherent uncertainty [12]. Consequently, human-AI collaborative decision support tools are needed to optimize routes by evaluating and recommending multiple CoAs for consideration by a Naval planner. To support such mixed-initiative planning, the tool(s) must either aid the DM to create CoAs and evaluate his or her own plan against optimized ones, or combine both human expectation of the forecast, geographic hazards, and possible uncertainty with the automated algorithm output for hybrid human-machine consensus on what routes to consider. TMPLAR is the decision support system created to address this problem.

The canonical problem addressed by TMPLAR is the following: given a graph (e.g., a grid map with a source, a destination and waypoints), find the set of routes with Pareto efficient costs, where "cost" may be evaluated with respect to a variety of objectives (e.g., reduce fuel, time, and/or distance, fulfill training requirements, and/or prolong ship's life expectancy). This problem falls under the rubric of a multi-objective shortest path problem under uncertainty with time windows, power plant configuration, speed, and bearing as control variables. Complexity, dynamicity, and uncertainty in the routing problem stem from time-varying stochastic and nonconvex costs at nodes and along arcs in the network, time windows of arrival and departure at each node due to training needs, weather, and uncertainty due to environmental impacts on ship's capabilities, etc. The complexity of the problem space and contextual constraints render the majority of provably optimal multi-objective approaches inappropriate, thus necessitating the approximate dynamic programming-based multi-objective ship routing approach of TMPLAR. The environmental uncertainty associated with the node and arc costs is both spatially and temporally-dependent, the evolution of which is similar to the timescale of the ship's transit. Thus, a primary innovation of TMPLAR is that it emulates real world concepts of operation of a Navy ship navigator. For example, if it were known *a priori* that uncertainty associated with a set of arcs/nodes, lying between the source and destination, will be reduced or eliminated by the time an asset traverses to that region, TMPLAR may indeed send the asset straight toward the "risky" region with the understanding that there may be a reduction in prediction uncertainty before the ship arrives at the area in question, thus allowing for a more informed routing decision at a later time. Algorithmic details on TMPLAR may be found in [5].

2.2 DSS Design Principles

The successful design of a HCI involves translating the parameters used by the machine into a format suitable for human decision-making. To this end, we aimed to design a DSS that minimized the cognitive load endured by the participants [13]. Cognitive load, a measure of the strain of a task on an individual's working memory [14], has been correlated with degraded analytical performance on complex tasks involving the use of uncertain information, and high cognitive loads can cause a user's preferences to vary. Even after TMPLAR removes the need to consider suboptimal routes, there is a high intrinsic cognitive load [15] on the DM, induced by the need to consider numerous contextual factors that may vary in salience during a mission. Such factors include METOC parameters (e.g. true wind, relative wind, wave height, swell height, air temperature), their distribution over the forecast realizations, the actual speed and position of the ship across a route's waypoints, and the objective function values of fuel and distance. Thus, our task was to design a user interface (UI) that reduced the extraneous load of the task so that users could best express their preferences and make accurate and timely decisions.

The cognitive load of a complex analytical task can be somewhat alleviated with the use of graphical aids [16], although the fidelity of the decision data could be lost with the abstraction. Therefore, in our design, we hypothesized that more decision support in the form of graphical aids would result in reduced cognitive load and thus better decisions. Validation of this hypothesis would be conducted by comparing the performances of participants assigned to separate experimental groups, each of whom would be assigned to use a UI with a certain "level" of decision support to select routes in a fixed set of scenarios synthesized based on actual use cases of TMPLAR.

The design of our experiment bears some similarities to several previous studies within the Naval domains. Morrison *et al.* [17] explored the analysis of a tactical DSS based on a modular design; a design paradigm which we also adopted due to both the ease of swapping out modules with different decision aids and the simplified analysis of click and eye-tracking data when each region of interest (RoI) is clearly delineated. Grasso *et al.* [18] designed an interface that accentuated the risk stemming from METOC forecasts on mission planning, which is necessary to properly evaluate the outputs of TMPLAR. A comparison across different DSSs was also performed in [19], but while they were able to utilize an objective measure of success (number of errors) for the analysis of variance, we lack a similar means of measuring performance due to the emphasis on individual heuristics used in decision-making. One manner of ranking non-dominated solutions is to measure each solution's distance to a "Utopian", but infeasible, solution comprising the best objective function value in each dimension, although this discounts the importance of other feature data which may be significant in human decision making; we later explore the use of this data for modelling decision rules in Sect. 5.3. Instead, our analysis of each DSS's efficacy is based on estimates of the effective cognitive load, garnered through a set of measurements including the TTD [15] and pupil dilation [20, 21]; increased levels of both attributes are correlated with a higher mental effort.

2.3 Levels of Decision Support

We designed our DSS by augmenting a baseline used by the current navigators, *viz.* Selecting CoAs from a tabular view of options using a single-screen terminal. On top of this baseline, we would add graphical elements intended to provide a better "at-a-glance" understanding of the uncertainty associated with each route and how the routes compared to each other. The DSS design was limited to a single screen of Full HD resolution (1920x1080). As such, to maintain readability at a distance, the table size had to be reduced and/or modified as additional modules of graphical information were added to the DSS. The UI's color scheme was primarily limited to grayscale for better pupillometry measurements, although unique colors were allowed in several key areas to help users distinguish among CoAs. Each interface was refined in an iterative fashion via internal prototypes, discussions with subject matter experts, and feedback from pilot tests conducted with student volunteers at the Naval Postgraduate School (NPS).

In the first experiment, we evaluated three different DSS designs, divided into discrete "levels" based on how many graphs and features were added to better improve usability and readability. At the lowest level was "DSS Level 0" or DSS0 (See Fig. 1). It consisted of only an interactive map in the top two quadrants and a simple spreadsheet consisting of summary statistics of each route at the bottom of the screen. This table (and all those in the other DSSs) could be sorted by any column in an ascending or descending order by left-clicking on the table header, and a secondary sort could be implemented by right-clicking a second column. Selecting any of the colored "route" labels on the chart would toggle a display of that CoA on the map for visual analysis. Selecting the "Show Grid" button overlaid the map with the grid used internally in TMPLAR with each arc colored relative to its estimated fuel cost. When a participant decides on a route, he/she would click the "Select Route" button on the row corresponding to the preferred COA and, after a confirmation screen which assessed their confidence, would automatically proceed to the next scenario until completion.

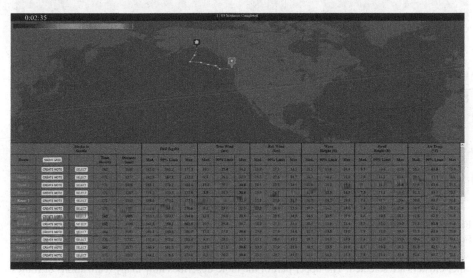

Fig. 1. DSS0: The UI is divided from top to bottom into two RoIs, the map and the route table. Each row on the table is a CoA, and the median, max and 90th percentile for fuel and METOC values are listed. Currently, routes 1 and 5 are selected for display on the map.

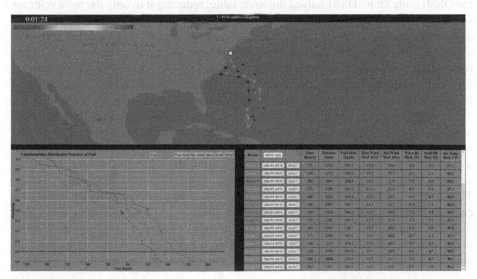

Fig. 2. DSS1: From top to bottom, left to right, the RoI on this UI are the map, CCDF, and the route table. The table only displays median values; distribution data can be found by selecting a route and viewing the CCDF. Tabs above the CCDF switch among the displayed parameters.

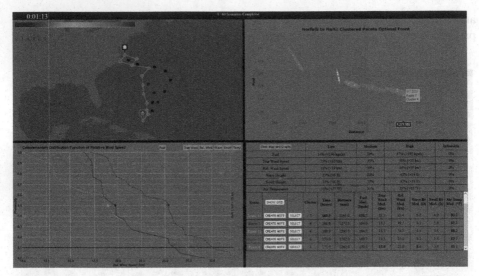

Fig. 3. DSS3: From top to bottom, left to right, the RoI on this UI are the map, clustered Pareto Front, CCDF, and augmented route table. Selecting a cluster adds every route it contains to the table. Highlighting a route for display on the map/CCDF "locks" it so it does not disappear when other clusters are selected. The upper part of the table describes how many realizations of routes within each cluster have high or low values for each parameter.

Subsequent DSS levels added more graphical features, making room by simplifying the DSS0 route table. DSS1 halved the route table, reducing it to only the most relevant summary statistics, and replaced the distribution data with a complementary cumulative distribution function (CCDF) plot that displayed the risk of each selected route for a given feature (objective function, weather parameters, bearing) across all weather realizations. Labels indicating the median value and the 90th percentile were displayed for rapid visualization of risk, and a line marking the ship operating limits was presented for features that affected the ship safety, such as the wind speed and wave height (Fig. 2). The next level that was considered, DSS2, added a non-clustered Pareto chart from which to select CoAs, but was removed from testing after subject matter experts opined that it would not be a significant step in decision support. The third level, DSS3, which *was* used in the experiment, included a Pareto-front that clustered similar CoAs. By selecting a cluster, the participant would add all of its constituents to the table at once. This design was intended to reduce clutter by allowing participants to focus only on certain interesting regions in the solution space. Once a cluster was selected, they could then "hold" routes for comparison with those in other clusters. In addition, each route in the table provided an estimate of the chance of failure (e.g. exceeding a safe limit for the wind speed or wave height) for the CoAs currently under consideration. (Fig. 3).

3 Experimental Design for the Evaluation of DSS Levels

3.1 Scorecard Routes and Difficulty Levels

To maintain the Naval relevance of our experiment, we algorithmically generated a set of fictional scenarios based on a set of standard Naval missions commonly used for evaluation, called "scorecard routes," and actual historical weather data. In the first experiment, four start-end pairs, denoted $r \in R$ were chosen from the scorecard routes and are listed in Table 1. Twenty-four different weather realizations, each denoted as $q \in Q$, were available to provide the METOC uncertainty associated with route generation. Thus, for any start-end pair r and a given (assumed) weather realization q, TMPLAR produced a unique set of Pareto-optimal routes P_{qr}, which were then evaluated against the other $Q \backslash \{q\}$ realizations (i.e., all realizations except q) to produce the distribution of parameters viewable on the CCDF and a table representing a route's risk. In total, this process yielded 96 unique scenarios, from which we selected 60 scenarios for use in the experiment.

It was difficult to objectively evaluate the difficulty of each scenario, a function of average intrinsic cognitive load, without extensive pilot testing; this would have significantly depleted the pool of participants available for the final experiment. Therefore, we intuited that the difficulty of each scenario could be estimated based on the number of options and the complexity of the uncertain information that the participant was expected to process. Our solution was to rank each scenario's difficulty as "Easy," "Medium," or "Hard" using a metric based on the objective function values of fuel ($\{x_{qr}[i] : i \in P_{qr}\}$) and distance ($\{y_{qr}[i] : i \in P_{qr}\}$). Note that while the fuel varied significantly across weather realizations Q in the set of Pareto-optimal solutions, the distance stayed the same for a given start-end pair and route for an assumed weather realization. The scoring procedure is as follows:

1. Compute a value for fuel ($\bar{x}_{qr}$) and distance ($\bar{y}_{qr}$) for a route, given a start-end pair r and an assumed realization q, , by normalizing the fuel ($\{x_{qr}[i] : i \in P_{qr}\}$) and distances ($\{y_{qr}[i] : i \in P_{qr}\}$) across the Pareto set of solutions P_{qr}:

$$\bar{x}_{qr} = \sum_{i \in P_{qr}} \frac{\max\limits_{q' \in Q} x_{q'r}[i] - \min\limits_{q' \in Q} x_{q'r}[i]}{\operatorname*{median}\limits_{q' \in Q} x_{q'r}[i]} \text{ and } \bar{y}_{qr} = \sum_{i \in P_{qr}} y_{qr}[i]$$

2. Determine the difficulty score for each scenario by normalizing each $\bar{x}_{qr}$ and $\bar{y}_{qr}$ over the realizations, $q' \in Q$, and then summing the normalized values of fuel and distance so that $z_{qr} \in [0, 2]$:

$$z_{qr} = \frac{\bar{x}_{qr} - \min\limits_{q' \in Q} \bar{x}_{q'r}}{\max\limits_{q' \in Q} \bar{x}_{q'r} - \min\limits_{q' \in Q} \bar{x}_{q'r}} + \frac{\bar{y}_{qr} - \min\limits_{q' \in Q} \bar{y}_{q'r}}{\max\limits_{q' \in Q} \bar{y}_{q'r} - \min\limits_{q' \in Q} \bar{y}_{q'r}}$$

3. For each start-end pair r, divide the scenarios generated into three bins of Easy, Medium, and Hard using the computed scores such that there is an equal number of scenarios at each difficulty level (see Table 1).

The distribution of scenario difficulties across scorecard routes is represented in Table 1. The complexity of each scenario was further controlled by removing realizations from the distribution of each CoA that produced fuel values which were outside of one, two, or three standard deviations of the average fuel for Easy, Medium, and Hard scenarios, respectively. After this process was completed, we randomly chose 60 scenarios, evenly divided between the three difficulties, for use in the experiment (See numbers in parentheses in Table 1), plus an additional five "Easy" scenarios for use in participant training. During the experiment, each participant would then proceed through the scenarios in a random order, experiencing 20 scenarios of each difficulty level.

Table 1. Number of scenarios in each scorecard group after applying the scoring metric described above. In parenthesis are the number of scenarios randomly selected from each group for use in the experiment

		Source and Destination			
		Gibraltar to Norfolk	Norfolk to Haiti	Alaska to Seattle	Alaska to San Diego
Difficulty	Easy	10 (6)	2 (2)	13 (7)	7 (5)
	Medium	8 (6)	11 (7)	7 (4)	6 (3)
	Hard	6 (2)	11 (7)	4 (4)	11 (7)

3.2 Participants

Several rounds of pilot testing were performed at NPS to validate the experimental procedures and the software's robustness [22]. In both the pilot tests and the final experiment, participants were volunteers selected from the NPS student body. They were not compensated. Data was made anonymous by having the experiment proctor at NPS assign each participant a randomized numeric ID for access to the experiment portal, such that no identifiable information was available to the remote team at UConn performing the data analysis. Out of a planned 60 participants, only 39 participants completed all 60 scenarios before COVID-19 caused large-scale closures in March 2020.

3.3 Procedure

In order to evaluate what kinds of graphical summary information are needed to make rapid and accurate choices with high levels of confidence, we implemented a 3 (DSS level) by 3 (scenario difficulty) factorial design, where DSS was manipulated between subject (extrinsic cognitive load) and difficulty level was manipulated within subjects (intrinsic cognitive load). Each participant was randomly assigned to one of the three groups that was each provided a single DSS interface (Level 0, 1 or 3) to use in completing the same 60 scenarios, divided into one of three difficulty levels, as described above. We did not provide DMs with any specific instructions on which objective (fuel or distance) was more valued to avoid biasing their decision-making. Ideally, the DMs would express their preferences implicitly through their patterns of CoA selection, and we could then categorize the DMs by their style of decision-making conditioned on various factors, including the scenario context, their assigned DSS, and how informed they were of the situation via the DSS level.

A brief manual describing the function of their assigned DSS was provided to each participant, and the experimental proctor was available to answer questions during the first five training scenarios. After completing each scenario, participants were asked to rate how confident they were of having picked the best route from the options provided on a 7-point Likert scale, which ranged from 1 for "No Confidence" in their decision to 7 for "Very Confident." After completing all 60 experimental scenarios, participants were presented with a completion screen and then asked to complete a paper survey that asked them to evaluate the efficiency of the software and provide qualitative feedback. Eye tracking data, including fixation tracking and pupillometry, was collected using a Gazepoint GP3HD eye tracker. Four participants had issues that prevented eye tracking data from being collected; however, click tracking was available for all participants because it was implemented in the custom-written DSS software.

4 Follow-Up Experiment Involving Time Pressure

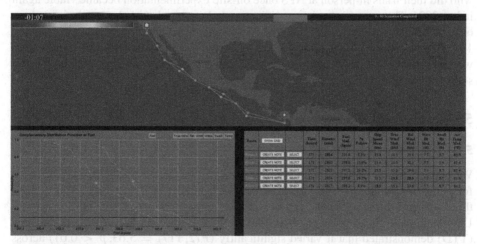

Fig. 4. Modified DSS1 used in the second experiment displaying an "Easy" scenario. Note the similarity to Fig. 1; however, two additional columns were added to the third RoI (table), and the time remaining in the scenario is represented using a countdown bar and a numerical display

One limitation of the initial experiment was that there was no time limit for making the route selection decision. Since time pressure has a significant effect on cognitive load when dealing with probabilistic information [23], we conducted a follow-up experiment to gauge the effect of time stress on route selection decisions. Due to the constraints of the COVID-19 pandemic, the follow-up experiment used an online and asynchronous interface in mid-2021 where the level of decision support in the factorial design was replaced with the time pressure at four different levels per scenario (45, 60, 90 and 120 s), one assigned to each user. Eye-tracking data was not collected due to the online nature of the experiment.

Based on the responses to the original experiment (based on TTD and pupillometry; see Results section), DSS1 was chosen as the interface for the experiment with time limits. Some adjustments were made to the experiment, however, to address common suggestions from the previous experiment's survey. The table was adjusted to include the average ship speed and the likelihood of route failure (Fig. 4). The experience of tedium reflected in the survey responses was addressed by adding four additional artificial start-end pairs into the scenario generation process to add variety. When they signed up, participants were randomly assigned a user ID which was used as a unique login for a web page that then brought them to the DSS with the time limit they were assigned to. After completion of all 65 scenarios, again comprising five Easy training scenarios followed by 20 each of Easy, Medium, and Hard scenarios in a random order, participants were directed to an online survey page to answer questions on whether the DSS was efficient, how they felt about their decisions and the time limit, and if they had any additional suggestions.

Of approximately 100 participants who had signed up for remote experimentation, only 12 completed all 60 scenarios. Data is also available for 10 additional participants who did their trials in-person at NPS once on-site experimentation became viable again in late 2021. This inconsistency in participation led to a highly imbalanced design, where only 2 participants were recorded in the 45 s group, 6 for 60 s, 9 for 90 s, and 5 for the 120 s group. Although we acknowledge the statistical limitations of this experiment, we still found value in its analysis for evaluating patterns in decision-making and in selecting time limits for our future experiment designs.

5   Results and Discussion

5.1   Which DSS is Better?

We applied a bevy of statistical tests to the data collected during the first experiment, focusing on how measures of cognitive load varied under the three DSS levels and the three scenario difficulty levels, and to what extent each module of the DSS was used. Univariate analysis of variance (ANOVA) applied to the measure of time-to-decision (TTD) demonstrated that it varied significantly ($F(2, 117) = 5.63, p < 0.01$) across the experimental groups, as the average TTD was found to be significantly higher using DSS3 than DSS0 ($p < 0.05$) or DSS1 ($p < 0.01$). Median scenario times are illustrated in Table 2; although DSS1 has the lowest average times, they are not significantly different from those of DSS0 ($p = 0.28$). Pupil diameter also significantly changed among DSS levels ($F(2, 103358) = 6192.69, p < 0.01$), greatly expanding from DSS1 to DSS0

($p < 0.01$) and then to DSS 3 ($p < 0.01$). As confidence did not vary significantly among experimental groups ($F(2, 36) = 0.46, p = 0.64$) and there was no interaction between scenario difficulty and DSS level ($p = 0.52$), we concluded that DSS1 required the least cognitive load under all circumstances. For this reason, we selected DSS1 for implementation in our follow-up experiments with TMPLAR.

Table 2. Median TTD (in seconds) across all users for each DSS

		DSS Level			
		DSS0	DSS1	DSS3	Overall
Difficulty	Easy	22	16	26	22
	Medium	25	20	35	27
	Hard	34	22	46	33
	Overall	27	19	33	31

In addition to the results favoring DSS1, we found that subjects interacted with the data table and map at a much higher frequency than the other visual aids. Modeling the fixations and clicks as a percentage of time per scenario, averaging across participants in each group, and then applying ANOVA and post-hoc tests confirmed that the use of route table was significantly higher than that of the other decision aids across all DSS levels. It is evident that participants preferred the tabular information as a primary source of route information. Tables 3 and 4 summarize these results for click and eye-tracking data, respectively. Further analysis of this data may be found in [22].

Table 3. Percentage frequency of clicks within each module per experimental group

		Module			
		Map	Route Table	CDF	Pareto Front
DSS Level	DSS0	0.4%	99.6%	N/A	N/A
	DSS1	10%	83%	7%	N/A
	DSS3	0.02%	55%	1%	44%

5.2 Time Pressure Findings

Despite the restrictions imposed by the online nature of this experiment, we analyzed the effect of time limits on DSS interaction and cognitive load to gain insights into how to design our next experiment. As each participant in this experiment was using the same DSS, we conducted a univariate ANOVA comparing the utilization of the interface under different time limits and found that neither the average click percentage

Table 4. Percentage frequency of eye fixations within each module per experimental group

		Module			
		Map	Route Table	CDF	Pareto Front
DSS Level	DSS0	23%	77%	N/A	N/A
	DSS1	19%	66%	15%	N/A
	DSS3	11%	51%	10%	28%

for the map ($p = 0.75$), CDF ($p = 0.98$), nor the table ($p = 0.55$) differed significantly among the experimental groups. Patterns of use did, however, vary between the two experiments; utilization of the CCDF risk plots increased significantly in the second experiment ($p < 0.01$), with a corresponding decrease in relative interactions with the route table ($p < 0.01$). The average percentage of interactions with the map also increased, but not to a statistically significant level ($p = 0.16$). We attribute the increased use of risk plots with improvements to the participant training documentation between the experiments. The post-hoc survey revealed that participants found the DSS to be generally efficient, rating it an average score of 4.8/7, and 75% of respondents agreed that it helped them choose the optimal routes.

Table 5. Median TTD (in seconds) across all users for each time limit

		Time Limit				
		45 s	60 s	90 s	120 s	Overall
Difficulty	Easy	31	28	43	61	**45**
	Medium	28	26	36	56	**37**
	Hard	32	27	37	53	**39**
	Overall	**30**	**27**	**39**	**59**	**39**

Although we lacked pupil measurements for most participants, we still could estimate the cognitive load through the TTD and confidence data. A significant relationship was found between time limit and TTD per scenario ($F(3, 1154) = 85.45, p < 0.01$) (Table 5). Pairwise post-hoc analysis with Tukey's honestly significant difference procedure indicated that the group with the 120 s limit had significantly different mean TTD from every other group ($p < 0.01$) and that the 60 s and 90 s groups also differed significantly ($p < 0.01$). The 45 s group stands out by having the only mean TTD that is within 40% of the time limit; although the results may be skewed by the lack of participants, this indicates that the pressure of having only 45 s stressed participants to the point that they would take longer to make a decision even if it would not improve the end result. This hypothesis is supported by the ANOVA performed between the time limit and confidence ($F(3, 1154) = 31.98, p < 0.001$), demonstrating a relationship between the time limit and confidence that is almost linear. The 45 s group had a mean confidence of 3.7 that was significantly ($p < 0.01$) lower than every other group, and the 120 s group had a similarly significant ($p < 0.01$) high mean confidence of 5.7. Neither the 60 s nor 90 s group differed from each other ($p = 0.35$), but they differed from the other two groups with their average confidence of 4.7. These results indicate a significant cognitive load brought on by time pressure that is likely perceived as such by individuals while making routing decisions under time stress.

No significant relationship was found between scenario difficulty and TTD ($p = 0.128$) or confidence ($p = 0.890$). It is noted, however, that, unlike in the first experiment, the average TTD of the Easy scenarios was slightly larger than those of the Medium or Hard scenarios. The introduction of additional scorecard routes of much longer distances is a likely explanation for this incongruity, as it becomes difficult to consider objective function information over many waypoints.

5.3 Indirect Inference of Human Preferences

Initially, we assumed that each participant would choose routes as determined by their preferences. Clusters of individuals with differing preferences towards fuel over distance were expected to form, with some variation depending on experience and scenario context. Strikingly, we found that not only 70% of DMs tended to pick the same CoA in each scenario on average, but that the criteria by which they selected the CoAs did not form a consistent fuel/distance preference weight vector across different scenarios. Instead, patterns of decision-making only began to emerge when we grouped all the participants together and started categorizing decisions by context.

Given that TMPLAR has the potential to produce larger sets of Pareto-optimal routes as the number of objectives increase, it is critical to "filter" the CoAs so as not to overwhelm the operator. This filter can be learned by relating the scenario contexts and observed interactions. Here, we explored two avenues for filtering the COAs; one based on the optimization criteria used in TMPLAR and the other based on context parameters (features) that enter indirectly into the algorithm via the cost structure.

Rule Mining
With respect to the distribution of feasible non-dominated CoAs unique to each scenario, we sought to determine which subsets of features were most closely associated with user selections beyond the Pareto-optimal trade-offs. Association rule mining, an analysis procedure often affiliated with determining opportunities for cross-selling in online shopping [24], gives ways to quantify common associations between rows in a database and produces a set of rules that govern these interactions. In our context, we can view DMs as "shoppers" needing to choose between CoAs which are unique "carts" of parameters, each of which is roughly discretized by how high or low they are compared to those from alternative options. We expect that in the process of making the trade-offs necessary to select a route, the participants would apply common "if-then" heuristics which related the parameters to each other; otherwise known as association rules. The relevance of each rule is evaluated using its support, the percentage of subsets in the data that contain all the parameters listed in the rule, and its lift, a measure of the probabilistic dependence between the antecedent and consequent of the rule.

The "arulesViz" package in R [25] was used to apply the Apriori algorithm to help us explore possible association rules within our dataset of user decisions. To apply the algorithm, we first discretized the dataset by normalizing each feature using its maximum and minimum values per scenario and then binning the data into 2 levels based on whether they exceed the mean. Then, we applied the algorithm using a minimum support of 0.2 to determine the most prominent rules (sorted by lift) across all participants, given the lack of individual differentiation demonstrated previously. The only rules having a support above this value had lower lift and only related high fuel with low distance and vice versa; obvious and uninteresting, considering the Pareto-optimal nature of the objectives. In contrast, the set of top rules at 20% support, considered across all difficulties and DSS groups (Fig. 5), indicates that high values of certain METOC values, especially wind speed, and the normalized bearing (a measure of the "straightness" of a route) play a significant role in decision-making relative to fuel or distance.

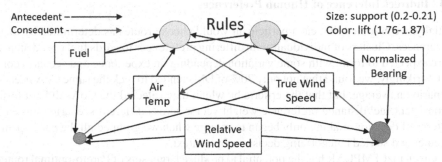

Fig. 5. Graph connecting the top 4 rules computed across all users and scenarios. Each circle represents a rule, comprised of the antecedent features pointing into the circle and the consequent feature pointed towards with a blue arrow. The size and color of each circle represent the relative support and lift of each rule, respectively.

This indicates a partial disconnect between the objective functions used by TMPLAR and the mental models applied by DMs. Weather parameters and the visual cues provided by the map were more strongly correlated with the decisions than the Pareto-optimal objective function trade-off. These results indicate that several of these features should be included as additional objectives for optimization in TMPLAR rather than only being weighed indirectly through the cost structure. Based on this observation, TMPLAR has been enhanced to handle as many as 15 objectives. Adding more parameters as objectives, however, increases the number of viable CoAs and complicates multi-criteria decision-making. In the next section, we attempted to categorize how participants made different Pareto-optimal trade-offs within each scenario context so that, in the future, we can apply these results for faster decision-making in higher-dimensional spaces.

User Preferences as Pareto Solutions

We can view the selection of a CoA as making a trade-off between fuel or distance, depending upon the scenario context. As the selection of the Utopian point is impossible, often decision-makers will try to select a solution that tries to balance these conflicting objectives in a way not dissimilar to a competitive game. To examine this hypothesis, we evaluated the similarity between human preferences and game theoretic equilibrium strategies. These include the compromise solution, the Nash solution, the Kalai-Smorodinsky solution, and the disagreement points for each objective (see Fig. 6) [26]. As the solutions chosen rarely differed among users, we aimed to model what kinds of common trade-offs were occurring, such that, in a future iteration of the DSS, we could remove or deemphasize groups of CoAs that are redundant or irrelevant to the scenario, in essence performing a "smarter" version of DSS3's clustering.

In a given scenario (i.e., fixed start-end pair r and assumed realization q) with more than six routes, the fuel cost $x_{qr}[i]$ and distance $y_{qr}[i]$ for each CoA $i \in P_{qr}$ was normalized between 0 and 1 using the minimum and maximum of the respective objective function values for that scenario. Each CoA was then converted to a vector of five scores using each one of the five metrics below that represent how close or how far each choice is relative to the "ideal" Pareto solution for each criterion:

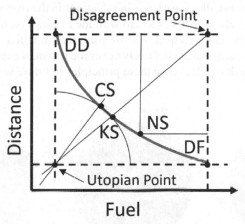

Fig. 6. Example placement of indicated solution types on a normalized continuous Pareto Front (DD: Disagreement point for distance; DF: Disagreement point for fuel; CS: Compromise Solution; NS: Nash solution; KS: Kalai-Smorodinsky solution).

- Compromise Solution (CS) is closest to the Utopian point:
$$\min_i \sqrt{\left(1 - x_{qr}[i]\right)^2 + \left(1 - y_{qr}[i]\right)^2}$$
- Nash Solution (NS) maximizes the area of the region bounded by the Pareto-front and the disagreement point: $\max_i\left[\left(1 - x_{qr}[i]\right)\left(1 - y_{qr}[i]\right)\right]$
- Kalai-Smorodinsky (KS) is the closest solution to the 45-degree line connecting the disagreement point to the Utopian point: $\min_i \left|\frac{y_{qr}[i] - x_{qr}[i]}{\sqrt{2}}\right|$
- Disagreement Point for Fuel (DF) is the solution that minimizes fuel and maximizes distance: $\min_i x_{qr}[i]$

- Disagreement Point for Distance (DD) is the solution that minimizes distance and maximizes fuel: $\min_i y_{qr}[i]$

Each score in the vector is normalized between 0 and 1 based on the respective range of values for each solution. For a given scenario context, the score vectors corresponding to all the participant choices from the experiment are summed to estimate the proportion of selected Pareto solution types. Figure 7 below indicates that there is considerable dissimilarity between each start-end pair. For example, the selections made in scenarios involving the Gibraltar to Norfolk scorecard route primarily reside near the disagreement point for fuel, indicating that fuel is preferred among all participants for a given route. Alaska to San Diego has a more even distribution of selections, but in contrast the similar Alaska to Seattle demonstrates a higher preference towards distance-based decisions. Guantanamo to Gibraltar is an example of a scenario where the majority of decisions were similar to the Nash solution, indicating a preference towards even trade-off. Considering both experiments, the consistency in selections in the shared scorecard routes is significant. Thus, we believe that, combined with the readings on important parameters from the rule mining, we can selectively choose solutions for initial presentation to a DM based on the scenario context that effectively cover the gamut of expected trade-offs. We intend to synthesize a design based on these principles in future versions of TMPLAR.

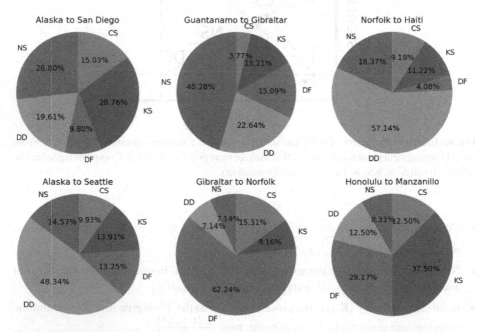

Fig. 7. Example distributions of Pareto decisions based on user selections from both experiments. Both "true" scorecard routes used in both experiments and the new start-end pairs added to the second experiment are represented

6 Limitations and Future Work

One aspect of the experiment's implementation that is likely to have affected results is the experience and motivation of each participant. Our scenarios assumed some knowledge of Naval routing, but according to post-hoc surveys only 43% of participants had previous maritime routing experience, despite the vast majority hailing from the US Navy or the Marine Corps. Several individuals with known subject matter experience were asked to do pilot testing of the experiment because we felt their insight was more valuable during the design phase, thereby preventing their involvement in the data collection phase. In addition, survey responses to both experiments indicated that a subject's attention likely waned during the course of 60 scenarios, affecting the expression of preferences. Even after the addition of four new scorecard routes in the time limit experiment, we feel that it may still have been considered tedious due to the abysmally low online completion rate. Without the ability to compensate participants, we have to rely on their honest interest in the task.

After the set of trials involving time limits, we decided to proceed with a follow-up experiment which addressed some of the aforementioned limitations and extended the design of the DSS for improved operational relevance. To encourage the integration of TMPLAR with CONFIDENT, an algorithm which quickly determines where and when ships may come within an unsafe distance from each other [27, 28], we designed an experiment that tasked participants to route multiple ships simultaneously using a modified DSS1. This DSS includes both a "local" view for analyzing the CoAs available for each ship and a "global" view to help address inter-ship routing conflicts. In addition, the difficulty of a scenario is no longer quantified by the distribution of weather parameters (which is still a major factor in the selection), but also by the introduction of one or more "context changes" that can be experienced within a scenario. Each context change, drawn from operationally-relevant settings, such as ship status affecting travel speed or the sudden appearance of a storm system or NO-GO zones, causes an additional phase of replanning to adjust the previously selected routes, which encourages participants to make decisions that are robust against risk.

This experiment will satisfy multiple objectives informed by the last set of experiments. Varying both the number of ships and the number of context changes provides an intuitive means for us to adjust the intrinsic cognitive load and better ascertain whether the new views on the DSS are helpful in managing complexity. To ensure each participant finished in a reasonable amount of time, we added a time limit to each scenario that was generous enough not to induce excessive time stress; based on the time stress experiment, we estimated that about 60 s per ship is an adequate time for a decision and that each planning period with context changes averaged to a realistic five-minute limit per scenario. This increased complexity will likely cause the average TTD of each scenario to increase, so we now only ask each participant to complete only 18 scenarios instead of the previous 60; however, this gives us the ability to produce scenarios that are more interesting and less tedious, helped by manually augmenting each with textual descriptions of the context changes. In pilot testing, respondents reacted favorably to the new scenarios, treating each with the same interest they would in a real-world situation. Positive feedback collected from pilot test participants and subject matter experts encouraged us to begin collecting data with this design, which is currently ongoing at NPS as of this writing.

7 Conclusion

In this paper, we detailed the design and results of two sequential experiments involving the design and validation of a novel human-computer interface for improved utilization of an optimal route planning algorithm, TMPLAR. A modular testing platform was developed from the ground up to determine what mix of tabular and graphical information is ideal for Naval planners. Volunteers were asked to use this interface and apply their insights to select CoAs in various scenarios with uncertain weather information. Eye-tracking and click data, chosen routes, and post-hoc survey responses provided measures of participant's route selection behavior; a medium level of decision support was found to reduce the measures of cognitive load without loss in decision confidence.

We took our initial conclusions from this experiment to launch a follow-up that explored the impact of time pressure on decision-making. Although the amount of data collected was reduced due to external circumstances, we did receive feedback on the DSS and time pressure that was useful in designing the next iteration of the experiment. After completion, decision data from both experiments was used to explore the modelling of user's preferences to improve the suggestions provided by TMPLAR. Application of the Apriori algorithm for association rule mining found that participants favored straighter routes that reduced the possibility of dangerous weather conditions, and our method for building a distribution of Pareto solutions for each scenario type demonstrated that users often tended to prefer a certain type of objective trade-off depending on the scenario context. We will continue our work by applying these insights to improve TMPLAR and validate the DSS with future experiments at NPS.

References

1. Kahneman, D.: Thinking, Fast and Slow. Farrar, Straus and Giroux, New York (2013)
2. van den Bosch, K., Brokhorst, A.: Human-AI cooperation to benefit military decision making. In: Proceedings of the STO IST Panel IST-160 Specialists' Meeting. Bordeaux, France (2018)
3. US Department of Defense: Summary of the 2018 Department of Defense Artificial Intelligence Strategy (2019)
4. Gigerenzer, G., Gaissmaier, W.: Heuristic decision making. Annu. Rev. Psychol. **62**, 451–482 (2011)
5. Sidoti, D., et al.: A multiobjective path-planning algorithm with time windows for asset routing in a dynamic weather-impacted environment. IEEE Trans. Syst. Man Cybern Syst. **47**, 3256–3271 (2017)
6. Chu, P.C., Miller, S.E., Hansen, J.A.: Fuel-saving ship route using the Navy's ensemble meteorological and oceanic forecasts. J. Def. Model. Simul. **12**, 41–56 (2015)
7. Cuate, O., Schütze, O.: pareto explorer for finding the knee for many objective optimization problems. Mathematics **8**, 1651 (2020)
8. Hartikainen, M., Miettinen, K., Wiecek, M.M.: PAINT: pareto front interpolation for nonlinear multiobjective optimization. Comput. Optim. Appl. **52**, 845–867 (2012)

9. Wang, Z., Rangaiah, G.P.: Application and analysis of methods for selecting an optimal solution from the pareto-optimal front obtained by multiobjective optimization. Ind. Eng. Chem. Res. **56**, 560–574 (2017)

10. Wirth, C., Akrour, R., Neumann, G., Fürnkranz, J.: A survey of preference-based reinforcement learning methods. J. Mach. Learn. Res. **18**, 1–46 (2017)

11. Zhifei, S., Meng Joo, E.: A survey of inverse reinforcement learning techniques. Int. J. Intell. Comput. Cybern. **5**, 293–311 (2012)

12. Simon, H.A.: Rational choice and the structure of the environment. Psychol. Rev. **63**, 129–138 (1956)

13. Oviatt, S.: Human-centered design meets cognitive load theory: designing interfaces that help people think. In: Proceedings of the 14th ACM International Conference on Multimedia, pp. 871–880 (2006)

14. van Merriënboer, J.J.G., Sweller, J.: Cognitive load theory and complex learning: recent developments and future directions. Educ. Psychol. Rev. **17**, 147–177 (2005)

15. Paas, F., Tuovinen, J.E., Tabbers, H., Van Gerven, P.W.M.: Cognitive load measurement as a means to advance cognitive load theory. Educ. Psychol. **38**, 63–71 (2003)

16. Allen, P.M., Edwards, J.A., Snyder, F.J., Makinson, K.A., Hamby, D.M.: The effect of cognitive load on decision making with graphically displayed uncertainty information: effect of cognitive load on decision making. Risk Anal. **34**, 1495–1505 (2014)

17. Morrison, J.G., Kelly, D., Marshall, S., Moore, R.: Eye-tracking in tactical decision-making environments. In: Presented at the Third International Command and Control Research and Technology Symposium, National Defense University (1997)

18. Grasso, R., Cococcioni, M., Mourre, B., Chiggiato, J., Rixen, M.: A maritime decision support system to assess risk in the presence of environmental uncertainties: the REP10 experiment. Ocean Dyn. **62**(3), 469–493 (2012). https://doi.org/10.1007/s10236-011-0512-6

19. Lafond, D., Vallières, B.R., Vachon, F., Tremblay, S.: Comparing naval decision support technologies using decision models, process tracing and error analysis. Proc. Human Fact. Ergon. Soc. Ann. Meet. **61**, 1178–1182 (2017)

20. Krejtz, K., Duchowski, A.T., Niedzielska, A., Biele, C., Krejtz, I.: Eye tracking cognitive load using pupil diameter and microsaccades with fixed gaze. PLoS ONE **13** (2018)

21. Coyne, J.T., Baldwin, C., Cole, A., Sibley, C., Roberts, D.M.: Applying real time physiological measures of cognitive load to improve training. In: Schmorrow, D.D., Estabrooke, I.V., Grootjen, M. (eds.) FAC 2009. LNCS (LNAI), vol. 5638, pp. 469–478. Springer, Heidelberg (2009). https://doi.org/10.1007/978-3-642-02812-0_55

22. Uziel, S.J.: AI-Augmented Decision Support Systems: Application in Maritime Decision Making Under Conditions of METOC Uncertainty, (2020)

23. Ordóñez, L., Benson, L.: Decisions under time pressure: how time constraint affects risky decision making. Organ. Behav. Hum. Decis. Process. **71**, 121–141 (1997)

24. Zhao, Q., Bhowmick, S.S.: Association Rule Mining: A Survey. Nanyang Technological University, Singapore (2003)

25. Hahsler, M., Chelluboina, S., Hornik, K., Buchta, C.: The arules R-package ecosystem: analyzing interesting patterns from large transaction data sets. J. Mach. Learn. Res. **12**, 2021–2025 (2011)

26. Santín, I., Pedret, C., Vilanova, R.: Control and Decision Strategies in Wastewater Treatment Plants for Operation Improvement. Springer, Cham (2017). https://doi.org/10.1007/978-3-319-46367-4

27. Mcmenemy, D., Avvari, G.V., Sidoti, D., Bienkowski, A., Pattipati, K.R.: A decision support system for managing the water space. IEEE Access. **7**, 2856–2869 (2019)

28. Bienkowski, A., Sidoti, D., Pattipati, K.R.: Interference identification for time-varying polyhedra. IEEE Access **9**, 138647–138657 (2021)

Modeling Users' Localized Preferences
for More Effective News Recommendation

Payam Pourashraf[(✉)] and Bamshad Mobasher

DePaul university, Chicago, IL, USA
ppourash@depaul.edu, mobasher@cs.depaul.edu

Abstract. During the past two decades, Local newspapers have been experiencing major declines in readership due to the proliferation of national and global online news sources. Local media companies, whose predominant business model is subscription-based, need to increase user engagement to provide added value for local subscribers. Personalization and recommender systems are one way for these news companies to accomplish this goal. However, using standard modeling approaches that focus on users' global preferences is not appropriate in this context because the local preferences of users exhibit some specific characteristics which do not necessarily match their long-term or broader preferences in the news. Our research explores a localized session-based recommendation approach, using recommendations based on local news articles and articles pertaining to the different local news categories. Experiments performed on a news dataset from a local newspaper show that these local models, particularly related to certain categories of items, do indeed provide more accuracy and effectiveness for personalization which, in turn, may lead to more user engagement with local news content.

Keywords: News recommender system · User engagement · Local news

1 Introduction

The goal of personalization is to create a fulfilling interaction experience for an end-user by tailoring that experience to the user's preferences and goals. Personalization has been used effectively by a variety of businesses and organizations to enhance customer engagement and increase customer retention and loyalty.

To create an effective personalized experience, the system requires knowledge of past user preferences and interactions to generate its tailored and targeted content. Thus, the ongoing interaction between users and the system enables the mechanisms that maintain customer relationships for an extended period.

In recent years, the importance of driving user engagement through personalization has become apparent for local news outlets. American local news has been drastically losing readers and business due to ineffective user engagement as well as the proliferation of large national or international online news outfits that take market share away from local papers. Studies have shown the internet has become a major source of news due to its constant availability, and about nine in ten adults in the US read news online [19]. However, an essential issue in online news is the lack of attention to newsworthiness [20], especially when readers' local concerns are not taken into account.

Now, local newspapers are trying to switch to subscription-based models that try to create added value by focusing on engaging and essential local news stories not covered by larger non-local outlets. Personalization and recommender systems are potential tools for local newspapers to increase their customer advocacy and build loyalty. The goal of the recommender system is to improve user experience and user engagement by prompting appropriate news articles to newsreaders. Intelligent personalized applications such as recommender systems have become essential online tools in many domains, such as e-commerce, music and video streaming, online news, and social media marketing. These systems help alleviate information overload and assist users in decision-making by tailoring their recommendations users' preferences. One of the key emerging application domains is the recommendation of online news.

Personalized news applications tend to use machine learning models that prioritize news items based on topics in global user preferences across all news categories and geographical locations, as well as based on the popularity and recency of news items. However, the focus on long-term high-level preferences may, in fact, result in taking attention away from local stories that help provide the distinguishing added value for local newspapers.

For example, a local newsreader may not generally be a sports fan, and hence sports-related features may not play a major role in generating personalized content for that user. However, the user, like many other local readers, might have an intense interest in the local high school team. Similarly, local readers may be interested in reading about local crime, even though for most users, this may not be part of their global news preferences. In such situations, global user preferences cannot be used to generate recommendations for users interested in local news content. At the same time, purely localized models will not be able to represent the users' broader interests that are needed to generate recommendations on more general topics such as national politics, entertainment news, etc. Ideally, the recommender system must combine global preferences with localized models for specific content categories in order to provide useful recommendations at all levels and to help increase user engagement on content where there is intense local interest among readers.

In this research, we explore a session-based modeling approach to personalized recommendation by focusing on different topic categories both at the local as well as global preference levels. We perform an offline empirical evaluation of different scenarios based on recorded past data rather than online experiments on a live system such as a news app. These experiments aim to inform the design of a hybrid recommendation framework that will allow local news outlets to provide added value and enhance user experience at the local level. Local news companies are shifting to digital subscription-based models because system effectiveness can translate to user satisfaction; personalized local news apps can then lead to reader advocacy and reader retention. We believe more focus on users' local interests would lead to a better recommender system to boost reader retention.

Thus the main Research Questions (RQ) of this work are as follows:

RQ1 - How do localized recommendation models perform in regard to system accuracy compared to standard models that focus on users' global preferences for news?

RQ2 - What is the effect of leveraging different local news categories on the overall quality of news recommendations?

RQ3 - Can automatic clustering be used to identify localized preference patterns of users in order to effectively automate the process of building localized recommendation models?

We answer these research questions through a series of experiments based on a local news dataset from the city of Syracuse, building on our preliminary work [16]. We hypothesized that considering the context on the item side, which in this case is locality, would increase news recommender system accuracy for certain categories of local news. Our experiments will show that considering a localized model is indeed helpful in improving the effectiveness of personalization along all of the considered evaluation metrics. We further show that the approach of focusing on subcategories will allow the system to identify those local news categories where localized recommendations are most useful. Finally, our experiments with clustering suggest that the process of developing localized models can effectively be automated without the necessity to manually identify user and item groups with specific preference characteristics.

There are three ways that user experience is commonly evaluated in recommender systems, according to [9]: (i) by carrying out user studies where the subjects are given certain questionnaires during different stages of recommendations, (ii) by combining the study on longitudinally logged data with the questionnaire-based user study (iii) by addressing other evaluation measures, such as combining accuracy and beyond-accuracy measures in certain ways. We used the third approach to evaluate our work.

This paper is organized as follows: Sect. 2 reviews related works. In Sect. 3, we discuss our dataset, and baseline methods metrics we used for our empirical experiments. In Sect. 4, we present details of the experimental evaluation and discuss our findings. The paper ends with conclusions and future work in Sect. 5.

2   Related Work

Throughout the past decade, well-known news agencies such as The New York Times, Washington Post, and BBC have created personalized news feeds for their subscribers based on their profile or the content information of the articles read by the users. Increasingly these online systems use personalization to cater to users' interests and drive user engagement [4,18,22]. Research in news recommendation has explored a variety of methods such as Content-Based Filtering

[2], Collaborative Filtering [3], Hybrid approaches [3], Deep Learning [17,21] and Graph-based models [24].

These recommender systems have been trying to increase user engagement by filtering large article spaces and by assisting users in finding articles relevant to their interests through customization or personalization. [7].

Recently, session-based recommendation algorithms in the news domain have been shown to be effective in recommending news items, in part because of the importance of factors such as recency and freshness in the news domain [6]. The goal is to consider the latest user session in session-based approaches and neglect or discount long-term user preferences [6]. In [21], the authors have proposed a deep learning meta-architecture named Chameleon on session-based news recommendations, which focuses solely on short-term users' preferences. The architecture includes a convolutional neural network for extracting textual features and a Long Short-Term Memory (LSTM) layer to model the sequence of clicked items in ongoing user sessions.

Some efforts have recently considered both long-term and short-term user preferences in the recommendation system [10,23,25]. In [24], authors applied random walks with restart strategy and different time windows on heterogeneous graph networks to capture both users' long-term and short-term preferences. They applied their approach onto different news datasets and showed the efficiency of their approach.

In addition to these systems, there has also been research conducted around applying context to recommender systems in order to generate better recommendations. Context factors may include the time a user reads an article, the general location of the user, or the specific order of articles read by a user. An example is music recommendation systems that use different contexts, situations, and musical preferences of users to create a more accurate recommendation algorithm [8]. In the domain of news recommendation, the Chinese news recommender system CROWN [26], for example, uses contextual user data such as time and location to increase the accuracy of recommendations and enhance user engagement. This real-time news recommender system uses contextual information, such as time, day of the week, the user's device, and a combination of different algorithms to account for the changes to user preferences during the day.

While there have been many experiments with recommender systems in a broader news context, we found a research gap in using recommender systems for local news outlets in order to increase their reader retention rates.

We also wanted to explore using locality as an item-based context since previous research mostly focused on user-based context. However, locality in general does not necessarily lead to effective recommendation, even for local news sources. Readers of local news sources are interested in both local news as well content in broader non-local context. Furthermore, some local news categories require specific models for recommendation due unique characteristics of these news categories and how users interact with them.

3   Experimental Methodology

Our approach involves considering local preferences in creating session-based news recommendation models that hopefully translate to increased user engagement. To conduct our empirical study, we collected and processed the data from a local news source. We designed our experiments based on the data to compare the localized models with standardized models and identify the effects of different news categories on overall recommendations.

3.1   Dataset

The data from this research is roughly ten years of subscriber and user-interactions data from Syracuse News[1], a local newspaper in Syracuse, New York. The dataset has different content, behavioral, contextual, and session information. We organized this data using two categories of tags, one based on the articles' main types and one based on the URL information. The main categories that we used were news, sports, and life & culture. Based on the URL, the second category is more specific and sorts the article into one of the subcategories. We've selected 4 months of all available user sessions for our experiments: December 1st, 2018 to March 31st, 2019. We elected to only focus on 4 months of data to account for the fact that this is a session-based model that would not need to be trained long-term. In a pre-processing step, we set a tag based on locality. Using a semi-automatic system, we used keywords that would define an article as global (i.e., US Government, Celebrity news, Lottery...) or local (i.e., Restaurants, Local sports teams, Local crime, Weather reports, State news, etc.). For example, the article titled "US government quietly spends millions to guard confederate cemeteries." was tagged as non-local, with "US Government" being the keywords used.

In contrast, the article titled "On this date: Binghamton 'evacuated' in nation's largest civil defense drill in 1957" was tagged as local since Binghamton is a New York county. For our dataset, we used Syracuse's city, so local news would include any articles that discussed New York state, New York counties, or cities of New York, in addition to global articles. Figure 1 shows how a Syracuse news source includes local and national news stories. The news source contains the top news categories and the list of various specific subcategories that the stories fall under.

While many articles were categorized based on their headline, we manually read through a select number of articles to assign a tag accurately. The data was organized into sessions with a length of 1 day and sorted by their timestamp. Sessions with only one interaction were excluded since they are not helpful in our session-based recommender systems study. The results and statistics of the pre-processed datasets are shown in Fig. 2 and Tables 1 and 2. In the first table, we can see we have 2826 non-local articles and 8145 local articles.

---

[1] https://www.syracuse.com.

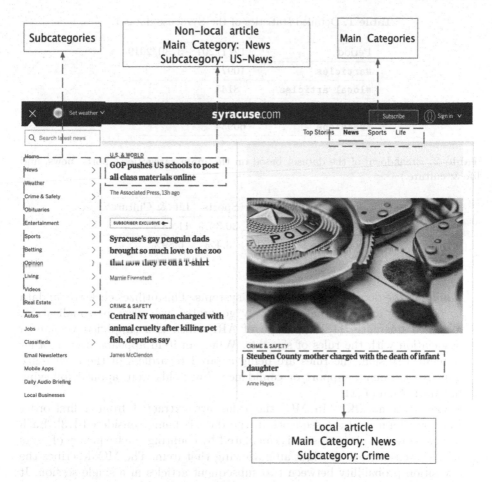

Fig. 1. An example homepage of Syracuse news and two example news articles on it.

3.2 Baseline Methods and Evaluation Metrics

We employed the following baseline techniques for our experiments using the implementation from [11]: Association Rules (AR) [1,12], first-order Markov Chains (MC) [13], Sequential Rules (SR) [11], and Session-based KNN (SKNN) [5]. We did not use the hybrid approach because the only content information we had from articles was the headline and URL. We had minimal contextual information surrounding the users, only looking at their location and time stamps. The deep learning approach needs a larger data set, so we neglect to report the results of that approach. We elected to use the so-mentioned simple baseline methods because they have mostly outperformed the more complicated approaches [11].

- **Association Rules (AR):** AR was based on the methodology proposed by [1] and discussed in [12], which was the first application of association rule

Table 1. Detailed statistics of the Syracuse dataset.

Period	12/1/2018–3/30/2019
#articles	10971
#local articles	8145
#non-local articles	2826
#sessions	60934

Table 2. Breakdown of the dataset based on the main categories (sports, news, and life & culture.)

Locality	News	Sports	Life & Culture
Local Articles	34.02%	30.35%	11.43%
Non-local Articles	13.92%	3.4%	6.89%

mining in the domain of recommender systems. This utilizes clickstream data to formulate a model that effectively generates web news personalization. We used reference [11] adaptation of AR, which is a simplified version of association with the rules of size two. When an item appears after another item in a session, the rules are being created regardless of the occurrence gap. No minimum support or confidence thresholds were applied following our utilization of [11].

– **Markov Chains (MC):** In MC, the rules are extracted from a first-order Markov Chain, and the sequence in the data is being considered [13]. Each item's score in a given session is calculated by counting the frequency of users who viewed other items right after viewing that item. The MC describes the transition probability between two subsequent articles in a single session. It calculates how often a reader views a specific article after viewing another one.

– **Sequential Rules (SR):** SR is similar to AR and MC. It considers the items' order, but unlike MC, with a minimum of one step distance between the two items. The rule is then getting a weight associated with the item-gap inverse (one over the number of steps between the two items). From the currently viewed item in one session, we set the maximum number of clicks to step back to 10. Another important hyper-parameter was the decay function, which measures the distance between two clicks set to a linear function [11].

– **Session-based KNN (SKNN):** SKNN compares the entire current session with the training data's past sessions to determine the recommended items. Rather than considering only the last event in the current session, as in ItemKNN, the SKNN method compares the entire current session with the training data's neighboring sessions. After trying several values for k, we decided to use k = 20 because it suited our experiment the best. For the session similarity measure, we used cosine similarity, which was used to find the k most similar past sessions for any given session [5].

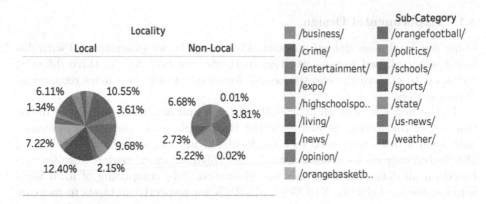

Fig. 2. Distribution of the Syracuse dataset based on the sub categories (sports, news, and life & culture)

There are two main evaluation methods: objective measures, such as accuracy and diversity, and subjective measures, such as reader satisfaction. This study focused on objective measures since we were using offline experiments and did not have access to the users. To measure quality factors such as accuracy, we have selected a set of metrics such as Hit Rate (HR), NDCG, and Mean Reciprocal Rank (MRR) [14, 15].

- HR@K: Among the top K items (articles in our experiments) HR finds the rate of times in which relevant items are retrieved [15, 27].
- NDCG@K: is a standard ranking metric that uses the graded relevance to rank each item (which commonly, an article is viewed as either relevant or not relevant by the other ranking metrics) [15, 27].
- MRR@K: is a ranking metric that takes the average of the reciprocal ranks of the top K results for a sample of recommendation lists. MRR considers the rank of the item [15, 27].

4   Experimental Results and Analysis

In this section, we present our experiments to address the research questions. As noted earlier, the primary goal of these experiments is to determine the degree to which models trained on certain local news categories outperform recommendation models based on general and global user preferences. In this context, we also want to identify scenarios in which broader models based on both local and non-local preferences are more appropriate to provide the most effective recommendations. Our ultimate goal from this study is to gain insights into the best way to design hybrid news recommenders (combining both localized and general models) for local news outlets.

4.1 Experimental Design

Using our local news dataset (presented in Sect. 3.1), we experimented with different session-based recommendation methods (see Sect. 3.2) in three different scenarios to explore the effectiveness of localized models in a news recommendation system.

In the first scenario, all articles (both local and non-local) were used in the training of the models as well as in the testing phase. In the second scenario, only local articles were used to learn localized models, and these models were also tested only on local news data. In the third scenario, models were learned based on all data, but were only tested on test data comprising of local news articles. We used HR@K, NDCG@k, MRR@K for respective datasets to measure the system's performance in each scenario.

For training and testing splits, we used one single train-test split. The data was split in such a way that the sessions of all four months except those of the last ten days of the entire dataset were placed in the training set. We used the articles from the last ten days for testing. We report the results of applying this evaluation scheme using the Syracuse dataset. Sessions with only one interaction were excluded as we could not use them for the next-lick prediction.

In the initial experiment, we compared the performance of our baseline session-based recommender systems in the above three scenarios. It should be noted that our aim here is not to identify the best algorithm for making news recommendations. Instead our goal as to address RQ1, i.e., to determine how much more effective the recommendations would be when the algorithm focuses on local news. We compared the local and general models using several different algorithms to show that the results were not algorithm-specific.

To address RQ2, we designed an experiment to determine the impact of "hyper-local" models where models were trained and/or tested on specific news categories and subcategories both at the local and the global levels. With these experiments, we hope to find effective models to recommend different local article categories. We also wanted to distinguish local news categories where these localized models are beneficial and those categories where the broader and global preference models are more appropriate.

So, in the next set of experiments, we implemented nine different scenarios to find the effectiveness of training models on all vs. training on local articles in various news categories. We chose the categories of sports, life & culture, and news since they have the largest amount of articles compared to other categories. We created three scenarios with each of these categories to test the model effectiveness when trained on all articles (local and non-local) compared to when it's trained on just local articles (in different categories). The first scenario trained on all articles and tested on local sports articles, the second trained on all articles and tested on all sports, and the third trained on local articles and tested on local sports articles. We ran these three scenarios following the same protocol as the first experiment, using performance metrics such as HR@K, MRR@K, and NDCG@K. We also replicated these experimental scenarios in all three categories mentioned above.

RQ3 was addressed in the last research phase. It evaluated the feasibility of automatically capturing granular user preference patterns in various news categories. Clustering algorithms (unsupervised learning) were used to categorize similar articles and users with respect to their interaction history rather than relying on manually selecting users and articles. We aimed to evaluate the degree to which automatic clustering can capture the localized preference patterns of the users that we observed when using manual categorization.

The K-Means clustering algorithm was applied to group items based on the item-user interaction matrix, where the items represent articles and the users represent readers. Each article is defined as a feature vector, the length of which was the number of users (readers). The item-user matrix entry was assigned to 1 if the reader read the article and 0 otherwise. The K-Means clustering algorithm recognizes patterns among the articles and readers by grouping items with similar user interaction patterns into K clusters. The clustering of articles into several groups was performed with cluster numbers ranging from 2 to 10.

The transaction data were divided into two sections based on time. The earlier transactions were used for generating recommendations, and the later ones were applied for evaluating the results (see Sect. 3.1 for more details). Two models were built for each cluster C: the general model and the localized model. The training of the general models was on all user-item interactions involving all items (not just those in cluster C). Then the general models were tested on user transactions after filtering out items not belonging to C. On the other hand, the training of localized models was on user transactions after filtering out items not belonging to C and testing the model on filtered transactions as in the general model.

Similar to our previous experiments, the standard evaluation metrics HR@K, NDCG@K, and MRR@K were used to test the performance of general and localized models. We followed the same experimental protocol as our previous studies: dividing the transactions data into two training and testing sets based on time and deleting sessions with only one interaction.

4.2   Main Results and Discussion

In this section, we present the main results from our empirical evaluation and discuss their ramifications in addressing the three aforementioned research questions.

Impact of Recommendation Algorithms on the Accuracy of Localized Models. The results of our first experiment are depicted in Table 3. These results show that, in general, recommendation models that are trained on local news articles tend to be more accurate when recommending local articles than recommenders that were trained on both local and non-local articles.

Also, looking at the results across different recommendation algorithms, the session-based KNN model (SKNN) generally performed better than the other methods with respect to all three metrics. More importantly, the overall finding of the effectiveness of localized models is not affected by the choice of the

Table 3. Results on the test set of Syracuse Local and All datasets.

Method	Training Set	Testing Set	HR@10	HR@20	MRR@10	MRR@20	NDCG@10	NDCG@20
SKNN	All	All	0.4368	0.5460	0.1288	0.1366	0.2566	0.2852
	Local	Local	**0.4940**	**0.5938**	**0.1446**	**0.1514**	**0.2926**	**0.3183**
	All	Local	0.4584	0.5653	0.1378	0.1452	0.273	0.3008
MARKOV	All	All	0.3276	0.3918	0.16096	0.1655	0.2295	0.2463
	Local	Local	**0.361**	**0.4441**	**0.1845**	**0.1904**	**0.2547**	**0.2764**
	All	Local	0.3396	0.4109	0.1700	0.175	0.2393	0.25796
AR	All	All	0.4304	0.5117	0.2069	0.2128	0.2997	0.3213
	Local	Local	**0.4631**	**0.5486**	**0.2198**	**0.2266**	**0.31930**	**0.3437**
	All	Local	0.456	0.5391	0.2147	0.22	0.3184	0.3382
SR	All	All	0.3918	0.471	0.1732	0.17892	0.259	0.2798
	Local	Local	**0.4156**	**0.5011**	**0.2090**	**0.2151**	**0.2969**	**0.3193**
	All	Local	0.4133	0.4916	0.1873	0.1929	0.2766	0.2972

algorithm. For these reasons, in subsequent experiments, we only used SKNN to compare the performance of different models in the context of different scenarios.

Table 4. Results for different scenarios on various news categories using SKNN method.

Training Set	Testing Set	HR@20	MRR@20	NDCG@20
All	All	0.5460	0.1366	0.2852
Local	Local	**0.593**	**0.1514**	**0.3183**
All	Local	0.5653	0.1452	0.3008
All	All Sports	0.5410	0.1334	0.2862
Local	Local Sports	**0.5583**	**0.1397**	**0.2930**
All	Local Sports	0.5329	0.1327	0.2839
All	All Life&Culture	0.5797	0.1906	0.3478
Local	Local Life&Culture	**0.6557**	0.1885	**0.3919**
All	Local Life&Culture	0.6393	**0.2125**	0.3865
All	All News	0.6460	0.1729	0.3553
Local	Local News	**0.75**	**0.2015**	**0.4240**
All	Local News	0.6979	0.1912	0.3909

Impact of Variances in User Preferences Across Local News Categories. With the second set of experiments (shown in Table 4), we found that, when recommending local articles, training on local articles yielded better personalization than training with all articles. This effect was observed across all of the scenarios involving local news categories. These findings support the conjecture that users' local news preferences may differ from their general preferences

Table 5. Results on various news subcategories.

Training Set	Testing Set	News/Crime	News/Politics	News/news
Local	Local	0.25	0.1	0.127
Local	Local News	**0.46**	0.238	0.173
All	All	0	0.189474	0.152
All	All News	0	**0.340**	**0.214**
		Sport/sports	Sport/Orange basketball	Sport/highschool sports
Local	Local	0.095	0.596	0.32704
Local	Local Sports	**0.1607**	**0.7622**	**0.3798**
All	All	0.117	0	0
All	All Sports	0.155	0	0

on news topics. For example, users may not be interested in general news articles related to the life & culture category. However, specific local art and culture events are often the subject of intense interest on the part of local readers. Such articles may be recommended using localized recommendation models but may be omitted from recommendation lists otherwise.

We also observe a difference in the degree of improvement in recommendation effectiveness across categories. For example, there is a greater advantage in using localized models for the Local News Category than there is for the other two categories. In fact, it may be possible that the more general models trained on all news articles perform better than localized models in the case of some news categories. This indicates that simply training based on local news is not enough. The overall system must be calibrated carefully to take advantage of those localized models where there is a significant difference in user preferences between local news items and general news items.

The localization effect mentioned above is even more evident when a more granular categorization of local news articles is used. In order to find specific characteristics of users' local preferences, we decided to explore the main categories by breaking them down into subcategories. Referring to the 3.1 section, the article subcategories are based on URL information. For example, the URL of the article, which is titled "A closer look at Chevy's 2020 silverado hd pickup that will debut in February," is: "https://www.syracuse.com/auto/2018/12/new_silverado_in_february_2019.html". Based on this, the extracted subcategory is "/auto/" which is the first subdirectory of the URL. The main categories and subcategories are not mutually exclusive sets. For example, News and Life & Culture are in two separate main categories but share the same /auto/ subcategory.

In each scenario, the main categories are broken down to probe how the top subcategories perform, which is shown in Table 5). The performance using HitRate@20 shows significant variance across different subcategories depending on training sets (local vs. all). For example, in the subcategory of News/Politics, we can observe a higher performance when the model is trained on all articles.

Table 6. Results for different scenarios on news clusters using SKNN method.

Training Set	Testing Set	HR@20	MRR@20	NDCG@20
All	Cluster 1	0.854	0.304	0.600
Cluster 1	Cluster 1	**0.86**	**0.31**	**0.614**
All	Cluster 2	0.536	0.114	0.255
Cluster 2	Cluster 2	**0.639**	**0.172**	**0.36**
All	Cluster 3	0.261	0.04	0.1077
Cluster 3	Cluster 3	**0.39**	**0.09**	**0.20**

This is an example of the situation where localized models would be less effective than global models. In this case, the effect is likely due to the fact that among local readers, their news preferences related to politics center more around non-local and national issues.

Using Clustering to Automate the Development of Localized Models. To address RQ3, we explored the use of clustering algorithms to uncover the underlying patterns in the user preference data automatically. We applied a clustering algorithm (in this case, the K-Means clustering algorithm) to the item-user interaction matrix and identified distinct clusters of items. We explored varying numbers of clusters, but for our experiments, we chose a clustering based on k = 3 as it provided to an optimum distinction between item categories and subcategories across the clusters while minimizing the degree of bifurcation for individual categories.

The clustering results with three item clusters are depicted in Fig. 3a and Fig. 3b. As can be observed, Clusters 1 and 2 primarily consisted of local news articles, with a strong focus on local sports such as Orange basketball and Orange football (sports teams of Syracuse University) and crime news in the Syracuse area and the state of New York. In contrast, the last cluster showed a mixed pattern of articles across various article genres and news categories. An example of the top article regarding reader count visits is "Peter Girardi of C-NS is Empire 8, St. John Fisher athlete of the year" for cluster 1, "Rumble at the golden corral: Syracuse police haul two away" for cluster 2, and "Town of clay to save about $16,000 a year with solar energy project" for cluster 3.

Using these clusters to build localized models, we found that training recommendation models on clusters 1 and 2 improved the recommendation efficacy when recommending local news articles. In contrast, as expected, the last cluster did not yield as good a performance, as it lacked a clear focus on specific local news categories (see Table 6 for more details). Our results demonstrate the potential of clustering algorithms for recognizing patterns and relationships in large-scale news datasets, highlighting the significance of considering user preferences and local news categories when developing localized models.

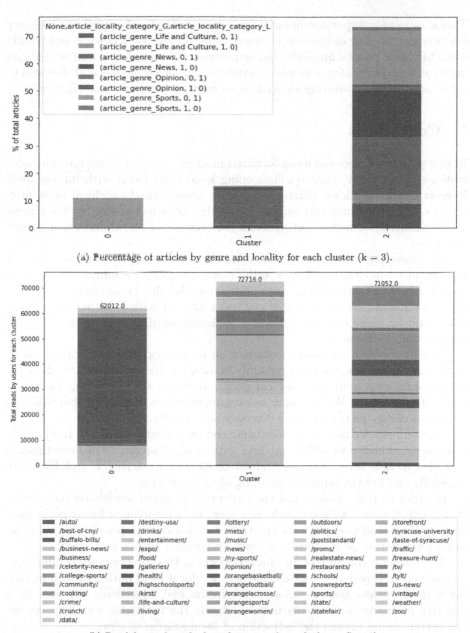

(a) Percentage of articles by genre and locality for each cluster (k = 3).

(b) Breakdown of articles by subcategory for each cluster (k = 3).

Fig. 3. Analysis of news clusters.

Overall, our findings suggest that it is possible to use cluster analysis as a way to generate effective localized models for the recommendation automatically.

380   P. Pourashraf and B. Mobasher

This is especially important in large-scale news datasets where reliable category information, or clear distinction between local and non-local news, is not readily available. Our results highlight the importance of considering the underlying patterns and user preferences when developing localized models and the need to select appropriate clustering algorithms to capture these patterns effectively.

5 Conclusions

In this paper, we proposed using localized models in session-based recommender systems, particularly when recommending local news items with intense local interest and a significant difference between users' global and local news preferences. These findings can inform the design of a more effective local news recommender system that distinguishes between certain local and general news categories.

We conducted extensive offline experiments on a local news dataset showing how localized models based on specific news categories performed better than models based on users' general news preferences. We did a case study that shows there is a distinction between the way users interact with local news vs. global news, and for some categories, there is a significant difference in users' global and local preferences.

Moving forward, we plan to conduct additional experiments with datasets from other local news sources, possibly combining these datasets to allow for experiments with more granular category structures while reducing the possibility of over-fitting. We also plan to explore the effect of model localization on beyond-accuracy metrics such as diversity and novelty.

Furthermore, we plan to explore using content features extracted from article headlines and bodies as additional data sources for clustering. This investigation will also include leveraging pre-trained models such as BERT and GloVe to hopefully capture the semantic meaning of news articles.

In order to truly understand the impact of localized models on recommendation effectiveness, we must perform a user study involving a live experimental system. We intend to explore the creation of such a system, possibly as an extension of an existing online local news site, to conduct such a user study.

The ultimate goal of this and future efforts in this direction are to find ways to more effectively derive user engagement for local news outlets, which in turn helps these outlets generate more subscription and advertising revenue. Such effective recommender systems may be among the tools that can help reverse the current trend toward the extinction of local sources of news.

References

1. Agrawal, R., Srikant, R., et al.: Fast algorithms for mining association rules. In: Proceedings of 20th International Conferenc Very Large Data Bases, VLDB, vol. 1215, pp. 487–499. Citeseer (1994)

2. Capelle, M., Frasincar, F., Moerland, M., Hogenboom, F.: Semantics-based news recommendation, pp. 1–9 (2012)
3. Das, A.S., Datar, M., Garg, A., Rajaram, S.: Google news personalization: scalable online collaborative filtering, pp. 271–280 (2007)
4. Graff, R.: How the Washington post used data and natural language processing to get people to read more news. Knight Lab (2015)
5. Jannach, D., Ludewig, M.: When recurrent neural networks meet the neighborhood for session-based recommendation, pp. 306–310 (2017)
6. Jannach, D., Mobasher, B., Berkovsky, S.: Research directions in session-based and sequential recommendation. User Model. User-Adapt. Interact. **30**(4), 609–616 (2020). https://doi.org/10.1007/s11257-020-09274-4
7. Jawaheer, G., Weller, P., Kostkova, P.: Modeling user preferences in recommender systems: a classification framework for explicit and implicit user feedback. ACM Trans. Interact. Intell. Syst. (TiiS) **4**(2), 1–26 (2014)
8. Kaminskas, M., Ricci, F.: Contextual music information retrieval and recommendation: state of the art and challenges. Comput. Sci. Rev. **6**(2–3), 80 119 (2012)
9. Konstan, J.A., Riedl, J.: Recommender systems. from algorithms to user experience. User Model. User Adapt. Interact. **22**(1), 101–123 (2012)
10. Liu, Q., Zeng, Y., Mokhosi, R., Zhang, H.: Stamp: short-term attention/memory priority model for session-based recommendation, pp. 1831–1839 (2018)
11. Ludewig, M., Jannach, D.: Evaluation of session-based recommendation algorithms. User Model. User-Adapt. Interact. **28**(4–5), 331–390 (2018)
12. Mobasher, B., Dai, H., Luo, T., Nakagawa, M.: Effective personalization based on association rule discovery from web usage data, pp. 9–15 (2001)
13. Norris, J.R., Norris, J.R.: Markov Chains, 2nd edn. Cambridge University Press, Cambridge (1998)
14. Özgöbek, Ö., Gulla, J.A., Erdur, R.C.: A survey on challenges and methods in news recommendation, pp. 278–285 (2014)
15. Parra, D., Sahebi, S.: Recommender systems: sources of knowledge and evaluation metrics, pp. 149–175 (2013)
16. Pourashraf, P., Mobasher, B.: Using recommender systems to help revitalize local news. In: Adjunct Proceedings of the 30th ACM Conference on User Modeling, Adaptation and Personalization, pp. 80–84 (2022)
17. Qin, J.: Research progress of news recommendation methods. arXiv preprint arXiv:2012.02360 (2020)
18. Raza, S., Ding, C.: A survey on news recommender system-dealing with timeliness, dynamic user interest and content quality, and effects of recommendation on news readers. arXiv preprint arXiv:2009.04964 (2020)
19. Raza, S., Ding, C.: News recommender system: a review of recent progress, challenges, and opportunities. Artif. Intell. Rev. **55**(1), 749–800 (2021). https://doi.org/10.1007/s10462-021-10043-x
20. Shoemaker, P.J.: News and newsworthiness: a commentary (2006)
21. de Souza Pereira Moreira, G.: Chameleon: a deep learning meta-architecture for news recommender systems, pp. 578–583 (2018)
22. Spangher, A.: Building the next new york times recommendation engine. The New York Times (2015)
23. Sun, K., Qian, T., Chen, T., Liang, Y., Nguyen, Q.V.H., Yin, H.: Where to go next: modeling long-and short-term user preferences for point-of-interest recommendation, vol. 34, no. 01, pp. 214–221 (2020)

24. Symeonidis, P., Kirjackaja, L., Zanker, M.: Session-aware news recommendations using random walks on time-evolving heterogeneous information networks. User Model. User-Adapt. Interact. **30**(4), 727–755 (2020). https://doi.org/10.1007/s11257-020-09261-9
25. Villatel, K., Smirnova, E., Mary, J., Preux, P.: Recurrent neural networks for long and short-term sequential recommendation. arXiv preprint arXiv:1807.09142 (2018)
26. Wang, S., Zou, B., Li, C., Zhao, K., Liu, Q., Chen, H.: Crown: a context-aware recommender for web news, pp. 1420–1423 (2015)
27. Wu, C., Wu, F., Huang, Y., Xie, X.: Personalized news recommendation: a survey. arXiv preprint arXiv:2106.08934 (2021)

What Color is Your Swan? Uncertainty of Information Across Data

Adrienne Raglin(✉), Allison Newcomb, and Lisa Scott

Army Research Laboratory, 2800 Powder Mill Road, Adelphi, MD 20863, USA
adrienne.raglin2.civ@army.mil

Abstract. In 2007, Taleb coined the term "Black Swan" to describe those events that are extremely rare but unpredictable. However, if as Taleb states it is "our blindness with respect to randomness particularly large deviations" that is the issue, then how do we continue to understand these potential deviations and how do we adapt when they occur? Researchers continue to explore the area of uncertainty, how it is quantified, represented, and communicated. This paper is inspired by the concept of uncertainty and the association with the swans' color as a means of expressing the uncertainty. In addition, this paper will discuss the concept of uncertainty of information, utilizing a taxonomy based on Gershon's nature of imperfect information with a value. Firstly, we will explore existing associations made to different swan colors. Secondly, we will discuss how this concept can be modified relevant to uncertainty of information, and the challenges this idea presents such as risk and trust. Thirdly, we will explore applying a modified version of "uncertainty of information swan color" to a specific application.

Keywords: Uncertainty of Information · Black Swan · Data

1 Introduction

As choices and decisions are made, there is an underlying belief that what I know is reliable, with no or limited uncertainty. This uncertainty is usually presented as a probability. The definition of a probability is the measure of the likelihood of an event occurring. It can also be defined as how likely it is that a proposition (a statement that expresses a judgement) is true. Moreover, the uncertainty is the condition of being uncertain, not able to be relied on, not known or definite. Thus, probability is considered "a concept that allows predictions to be made in the face of uncertainty."

Given these subtly different definitions, is there a different way to consider uncertainty? Would it be more beneficial to have more than a mathematical value, particularly when identifying choices and making decisions? What about the remaining portion that is not known? This led to an investigation of the intersection of uncertainty and ideas posed by Black Swan logic.

The idea of the Black Swan logic Taleb [1] states "makes what you don't know far more relevant that what you do know." This idea is magnified by the unexpected nature, particularly when the impact is significant and damaging. Thus, a Black Swan is "an

© The Author(s), under exclusive license to Springer Nature Switzerland AG 2023
H. Degen and S. Ntoa (Eds.): HCII 2023, LNAI 14051, pp. 383–388, 2023.
https://doi.org/10.1007/978-3-031-35894-4_28

outlier because nothing in the past can convincingly point to its possibility, carrying an extreme impact, something that can be rationally explained after it occurs." A Grey Swan is a "very significant event whose occurrence may be predicted beforehand, but its probability is small." [2] A grey swan could be positive or negative altering the way a system would operate. A White Swan is defined as "something almost certain to happen" [3]. A Green Swan has been defined as "risks we humans create for ourselves." [4].

The concept of Uncertainty of Information [5] is related to the notion that uncertainty is not generic. There are multiple causes that generate uncertainty. Moreover, there are aspects of uncertainty that can have greater or lesser importance given the event, the data, the person, as well as other various factors. In the UoI concept, two factors were identified; the data source and a descriptor to associate the type of uncertainty from that data source. The descriptor was inspired by Gershon's work on the imperfect nature of information [6]. Thus, the UoI taxonomy includes corrupt, incomplete, inconsistent, questionable, inappropriate, and inaccurate. The descriptors are defined as follows:

- Corrupt – data and information with any errors
- Incomplete – data and information that is missing or inaccessible
- Inconsistent – data and information not aligned with previous known data
- Complicated – data and information that is difficult to understand
- Imperfect – data and information is perceived incorrectly
- Inappropriate – data and information that useful
- Questionable – data and information that is unreliable
- Imprecise – data and information that lacks detail, exactness or accuracy
- Disjoint – data and information that lacks cohesion or organization

The data sources were broad categories that represent the different types of data that can influence a decision or a choice. The data source categories include human, agents, algorithms, devices, visualization applications, networks, and information that can be text, audio, video, or images. The focus of the UoI concept is to include the categories associated with the uncertainty and not just a numerical value.

The computational model for UoI is a weighted sum of values. However, the idea of a matrix which shows the contribution of uncertainty by category is the presentation that may be the most meaningful. By knowing which category per data source the greatest uncertainty is found, could help adjust the choice or the decision. For example, having a series of matrices for each data source identify uncertainty.

An alternate use can be predictive in nature, where shifting uncertainty across categories, or decreases or increases within a category can be identified. This alternative could stem from simulations that explore uncertainty across and within a category and the impact on the choice and decision, opening potential windows of opportunity, exposing black, grey, white, or green swan events.

2 Use Case

In this concept paper, we use cyber operations as an application for treatment of swan colors and related uncertainty. Our interest is defensive cyber operations (DCO), but it should be noted that in some cases, defensive actions could necessarily employ offensive cyber operations (OCO) as a natural part of the cyber kill chain. This section will discuss a cyber event that could be considered a black swan and suggest data sources and descriptors that could be included in the UoI computational model. Improved decision making is one of the benefits of having quantitative measures as they relate to uncertainty in cyber. The ubiquity of the Internet and modern society's reliance on it cannot be overemphasized. Most tasks that span diverse environments rely heavily on communications and information, both of which are inextricably linked to the cyber domain.

Information overload is a component of Gershon's taxonomy of imperfect information. This concept paper is a first step in defining a framework to support human interaction and understanding of information across multiple domains as it relates to cyber operations. From there, we can identify the structures necessary for automation of these concepts to support machine speed cyberspace operations.

Taleb postulates that increased connectivity leads to nonlinearity in a wide variety of systems. The size, distributed nature and complexity of the Internet, with its varying configurations of heterogeneous equipment, operating systems and application software, and the vast array of users' purposes and needs contribute to the Internet being possibly the most critical inorganic non-linear system to date.

Consider the famous Morris Worm as an example of how connectivity and nonlinearity in relation to Taleb's black swan theory. As a reminder, according to Taleb, the three criteria for a black swan event are 1) the observer is surprised, 2) there is a major effect, either positive or negative, and 3) in hindsight, the event can be rationalized.

In November 1988, a computer science student at Cornell University wrote a self-replicating, self-propagating program, or worm. The worm's author, Robert Tappan Morris, intended to test the size of the ARPAnet, which is the predecessor of the Internet [7, 8]. The worm targeted specific versions of two operating systems and was not coded for destruction. Due to its unexpected behavior, the worm consumed computing resources to the point that machines' performance slowed to a crawl. As denial of service (DoS) attack, its impact was measured in dollars due to lost in productivity. There were an estimated 60,000 machines on the ARPAnet in 1988, and roughly 10% of those devices were infected with the worm. Losses due to the worm were estimated at $98 million [9]. On a positive note, some claim this event was the "big bang of cyber security" [10].

The Morris Worm infection meets Taleb's criteria in this manner:

1. Morris was surprised by the rate of speed and spread of the worm's infection.
2. Computer Emergency Response Taskforce (CERT) was formed.
3. It was only a question of when, not if, the lack of security measures on the ARPAnet would be exploited.

The code Morris wrote behaved differently than he intended. Instead of creating a single copy of itself, the worm replicated itself until the computer essentially ran out of resources. It also propagated at an unexpected rate. Using the UoI taxonomy and example matrix, we could say the data source is *algorithms* and the descriptor is *complexity*, as Morris did not understand the complexity of the data. In this case, his own source code. The *network* and *devices* are other data sources to consider. How did the *incomplete* nature of data for those sources contribute to the worm's total consumption of computing resources? Had Morris been aware of each computing device's memory and physical storage limitations, he might have included code to delete copies of the worm to prevent resource depletion.

As an example, we can designate values to indicate high, medium or low impact when physical storage availability approaches some limit. The values used here are arbitrary and only intended to demonstrate the concept.

We also use high, medium, and low to indicate the criticality of the network's health or functionality in relation to a given operation.

The success of the task relies heavily on the network. The devices and applications are sources of information. The health of the network is dependent upon the devices. We can portray impact to the task in terms of the importance of network health, relative to the amount of available physical storage space.

In Table 1 below, the importance of Network Health is label as HIGH, MEDIUM, LOW and the device physical available storage is shown on the Y axis. The values VH (Very High), H (High), Mod (Moderate), Low and VL (Very Low), indicate the impacts of UoI on the operation/mission.

This rendering is at a very high level and the use of subjective terms is intentionally vague at this point. Our aim in this paper is to introduce a conceptual framework that will assist humans with decision-making where disparate data and time scales are constituent components. Knowledge elicitation with subject matter experts is required to shift from the current qualitative terms to quantitative values. Further, the example of *network health* must be more granular for it to be useful.

Table 1. UoI for Incomplete Data

		Available Storage				
		0.2	0.3	0.5	0.75	0.9
Network Health	HIGH	VH	VH	H	Mod	Low
	MEDIUM	H	H	Mod	Mod	Low
	LOW	Mod	L	L	VL	VL

This same scheme could be applied to many aspects of networks, devices and applications. For example, the effects of available bandwidth on software applications, or vice versa, or predicting the impacts of applying software patches to address known vulnerabilities in relation to the criticality of certain devices.

This scheme is also helpful in learning from past events the information that was uncertain due to being incomplete. Knowing now what we didn't know then, we could make more informed judgements about the implications of such an act and more confidently make the assertions presented below. Refer to the Introduction for the characteristics of each swan color.

1. The Morris Worm Infection was a Black Swan Event that was Highly Improbable.
2. Relating the *network health* indicators in Table 1 to a Grey Swan event, we could say that the amount of physical storage has high impact to the network. Thus, one would

want high certainty regarding the accuracy and completeness of information being reported on physical storage.

3. It has been estimated that 30,000 websites worldwide are hacked daily [11]. Those are just website hacks! That number does not account for other types of cyber attacks. Given the frequency of hacks, it follows that we can say with high certainty that an attack will occur and, having decades of cases to analyze, the cause is due to human error. Thus, meeting the criteria for a White Swan event. WannaCry (2017), the most recent worm, exploited vulnerabilities in an operating system that was deemed obsolete in 2014. Humans failed to upgrade the operating system or apply security patches.

3 Conclusion

As we continue exploration in the topic of UoI and its application in other domains, we will investigate methods of representing other events using the swan colors and taxonomy discussed in this paper. Applying the UoI algorithm to include properties from the cyber domain is particularly important as the amount of available information and the reliance of global economies are ever-increasing. Those responsible for providing secured and assured networks would benefit from quantitative assessments that could be used in conjunction with risk assessment methods.

We propose to investigate ways to incorporate these quantitative methods with existing user interfaces to support improved decision-making. Additionally, we will research how to combine these methods with resilience measures and metrics to explore mitigation strategies and higher order effects. The interplay of UoI and time need to be modeled to understand how values shift as steps in the operation unfold. This work might yield new knowledge in task priority algorithm work.

References

1. Taleb, N.N.: The Black Swan: The Impact of the Highly Improbable, vol. 2. Random house, New York (2007)
2. Carrasco, S.-P.: Black Swans Gray Swans and White Swans – A Silicon Valley Insider (2008)
3. Hutchins, G.: Black Swans, Grey Swans, White Swans(2023). https://accendoreliability.com
4. Elkington, J.: Green Swans: The Coming Boom in Regenerative Capitalism. Fast Company Press, Manhattan (2020)
5. Raglin, A., Metu, S., Lott, D.: Challenges of simulating uncertainty of information. In: Stephanidis, C., Antona, M., Ntoa, S. (eds.) HCII 2020. CCIS, vol. 1293, pp. 255–261. Springer, Cham (2020). https://doi.org/10.1007/978-3-030-60700-5_33
6. Gershon, N.: Visualization of an imperfect world. IEEE Comput. Graphics Appl. **18**(4), 43–45 (1998)
7. Boettger, L.: The Morris worm: how it affected computer security and lessons learned by it. SANS Institute White Paper (2000)
8. Seeley, D.: A tour of the worm. In: Proceedings of 1989 Winter USENIX Conference. Usenix Association, San Diego (1989)
9. Jajoo, A.: A study on the morris worm (2021). arXiv preprint arXiv:2112.07647

10. Baker, J.: Why cybersecurity can make you feel lost in space. ZPE white paper (2022). https://zpesystems.com/why-cybersecurity-can-make-you-feel-lost-in-space/. Accessed 03 Mar 2023
11. Bulao, J.: How Many Cyber Attacks Happen Per Day in 2023. techJury blog (2023). https://techjury.net/blog/how-many-cyber-attacks-per-day/#gref. Accessed 03 Mar 2023

AI Enabled Decision Support Framework

Adrienne Raglin and Somiya Metu[✉]

Army Research Laboratory, 2800 Powder Mill Rd., Adelphi, MD 20783, USA
somiya.metu.civ@army.mil

Abstract. In the current Army operation, information plays an instrumental role in the decision-making processes. However, the sheer volume of information coming from heterogenous sources may contribute to higher associated uncertainty in the information. A framework to investigate uncertainty from different sources of information is warranted, specifically to explore the effects of uncertainty on decision making. In this paper, we discuss our ongoing work on developing an AI enabled framework that comprises of different information systems. It serves as a platform for exploring artificial reasoning theories and allows different levels of reasoning across heterogeneous data sources taking uncertainty of information into consideration.

Keywords: uncertainty · decision-making · simulation framework

1 Introduction

In [1], the article discusses key steps for decision making as well as key challenges to this process. For the decision-making process they broke it into seven steps. First, is identifying the decision which includes defining the problem. Second, is gathering information which includes having the facts and data. This step also includes setting the priority of the data based on how valuable or important it is to the decision. Here relevant information for the decision can be explored to identify associated uncertainty. Third, is identifying alternative solutions and the actions that are a part of achieving the solution. Fourth, is establishing the pros and cons of each solution to form recommendations. Here as well associated uncertainties can be captured creating the overall uncertainty for the candidate recommendations. Fifth, is making the difficult final decision with consideration to any risks. Sixth, refers to carrying out the decision. Seven, is given to allow review of the outcomes based on the decision taken. At this step, analysis of the decisions and outcomes linked with uncertainty can also be conducted. The common challenges discussed in this article are grouped into three categories. The first is either having the problem of data overload or data scarcity. The second is when mistakes are made in defining the problem space. The third is how to address the factors that may contribute to negative outcomes due to that fact that no one decision is perfect particularly when there is significant complexity and there are rapid changes to the environments, events, or other components for the problem space.

H. Degen and S. Ntoa (Eds.): HCII 2023, LNAI 14051, pp. 389–394, 2023.
https://doi.org/10.1007/978-3-031-35894-4_29

In [2], the article talks about AI driven decision making. This article separates the ideas of "data-driven" and "AI-driven" decision making. A "data-driven" approach focuses on the data. However, and "AI-driven" approach focuses on processing ability. These ideas are relevant to our research in artificial reasoning. The artificial reasoning research considers that "data holds the insights that can enable better decision making" while "processing is the way to extract those insights and take actions." With these ideas in mind this project focuses on bridging data and processing, specifically utilizing various types of data and reasoning models for processing. This paper presents the framework created to allow experimentation and refinement to the artificial reasoning research focusing on decision making.

2 Enhanced Tactical Inferencing (ETI)

The Enhanced Tactical Inferencing framework has been developed to aid in the process of decision-making. Decision making can be an extremely difficult task requiring relevant and timely data. Moreover, this data requires processing that contributes to making it actionable information. However, the data and in turn the information that is utilized in decision-making may come with an associated uncertainty. Considering this uncertainty in decision-making is crucial to effective decision outcomes. The ETI framework facilitates the consideration of uncertainty in the decision-making process. The framework is designed to ingest multiple heterogeneous data sources, determine associated uncertainties from those data sources, reason based on this information, and eventually provide probable recommendations for decision making. ETI has been developed utilizing Sentry Agents Framework (SAGE) [5]. In the following sub-sections, we briefly talk about SAGE and the various components of ETI that have been implemented in the SAGE platform.

2.1 Sentry Agents Framework (SAGE)

SAGE has been developed by Naval Research Laboratory. It is an open-source software that can be utilized to dynamically construct agents in order to develop an agent-based system. One such system is our ETI framework. An important feature of SAGE is that it allows development and incorporation of custom behaviors for the constructed agents within the platform. In ETI, this feature has been utilized for reasoning purposes motivating agent's behavior. It allows for agents to be dictated by their own unique behaviors. SAGE is extensible thus allowing for integration with external applications/systems. This feature of SAGE has been instrumental as we continue to develop the ETI framework and integrate it with other systems. The section below provides a general description for various types of agents within ETI.

2.2 ETI Agents

The ETI framework comprises of different types of agents that interact with each other. The figure below Fig. 1 depicts the SAGE platform that hosts different types of ETI agents. These agents are briefly described below:

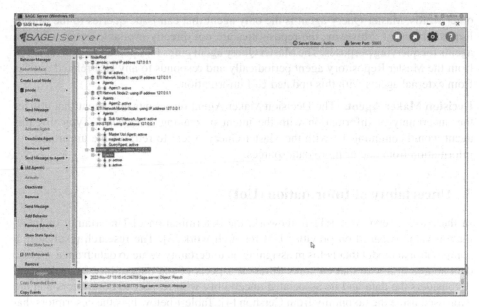

Fig. 1. ETI Agents in SAGE

Data Source Agents. Decision making typically involves information from multiple sources. In order to accommodate this, we created heterogeneous data source agents. These data source agents are representational information sources. They can represent different kinds of information for example Network data, Device data, Visualization data etc. These agents are responsible for parsing and ingesting data in their original format, retrieving important attributes and then transforming it to a format that allows for further accessibility. Subsequently, this processed data is then streamed by the Data Source agents periodically for other interested agents within the ETI framework.

Data Source Subscriber Agent. These Subscriber agents as the name suggests, subscribe to the Data source agents. Every Data source agent has a corresponding Subscriber agent dedicated to listening for messages from the Data source agents. These agents are reactive and only responds when messages arrive from the subscribed Data Source. On message arrival, relevant data is extracted for determination of Uncertainty of Information (UoI) value. This is performed by applying a set of designated rules on the data that comes from the Data source agents. Every Subscriber agent has their own set of unique rules. A high UoI value suggests higher uncertainty with the data and a lower UoI value indicates better credibility for the data. The determined UoI value is then forwarded to a master repository agent described below.

Master Repository Agent and Master Query Agent. The Master Repository agent as the name suggest maintains a repository of the current UoI values that are generated by the various Data source Subscriber agents. In addition, it is also responsible for responding to queries from the Master Query agent. Those queries are processed by utilizing the repository that is stored by the agent. The Master Query agent acts a bridge between the Master Repository agent and any external agent that requests for UoI information. In other words, Master Query agent is the only agent that can issue queries to the Master Repository agent. This way, the repositories are not directly available to any external agents for querying purposes. The Master Query agent pings for updated UoI information from the Master Repository agent periodically and responds to any UoI related queries from external agents with this updated UoI information.

Decision Maker Agent. The Decision Maker Agent represents any agent that utilizes the uncertainty of information with the intent of making a decision. Typically, this agent would communicate with the Master Query Agent to retrieve the uncertainty of information from one or more data sources.

3 Uncertainty of Information (UoI)

In the current version of ETI framework, the determination of Uncertainty of Information value is based on previous UoI research work [3]. The research resulted in a computational model that helps in assigning an uncertainty value to data from a specific data source in a way that captures different aspects of the uncertainty from the data. It considers the data and its associated uncertainty with respect to descriptors that are expressed using the taxonomy from Gershon [4]. Table 1 below lists the descriptors that provides supporting causal reasoning for the categories of uncertainty. UoI uses these terms to form the weighted summation of an overall UoI value.

Table 1. Uncertainty Descriptors

Inconsistent	Uncertainty due to a source that varies or does not stay the same
Corrupt	Uncertainty due to a source containing errors or alterations
Questionable	Uncertainty due to a source that is suspicious or lacks confirmation
Disjoint	Uncertainty due to a source that lacks cohesion or organization
Disjoint	Uncertainty due to a source that is unfinished, fragmented or not complete
Imprecise	Uncertainty due to a source that lacks exactness and accuracy of expression or detail
Complicated	Uncertainty due to a source that is convoluted, cumbersome, or consists of numerous, intricately connected parts

4 Integration of ETI with Tactical Service-Oriented Architecture

In this section, we will discuss the integration of ETI framework with Tactical Service-oriented Architecture (TSoA). TSoA [6] is an information management system that provides a standards-based approach to information sharing between disparate data systems. As we develop our ETI framework, we continue to expand its capabilities by integrating with other external systems thus providing a working platform for conducting reasoning experiments. The picture below depicts the integration of ETI framework with TSoA (Fig. 2).

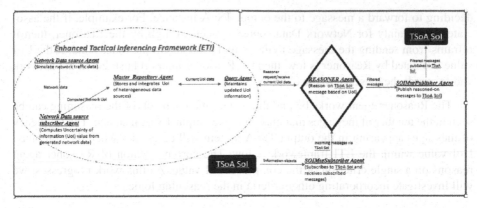

Fig. 2. ETI integration with TSoA

A snapshot of ETI framework with the different types of agents can be seen in the picture above. The current version of the ETI framework is capable of simulating multiple heterogeneous representational data sources. However, in this work, we have chosen to include only one Data source that is the Network Data source. In the sections below, we will describe a mechanism utilizing the ETI framework that helps to reason on messages that comes from TSoA.

ETI: UoI Generation. The UoI generation in ETI is a result of several agents working in tandem to quantify uncertainty for a specific data source. In this work, we make use of a representational network data source. Network traffic is simulated by Network Data source agents. This data is then utilized by the Network Data source Subscriber agent to determine certain attributes like message latency and message loss from the simulated network data. The Subscriber agent uses these attributes and applies a set of rules to compute an Uncertainty of Information value for the Network Data source.

TSoA Subscriber and Publisher Agents. In this reasoning mechanism, two TSoA instances have been employed. The first instance of TSoA serves as a source of information objects that can be utilized for reasoning purposes. The TSoA Subscriber agent facilitates connection with the first TSoA instance. It is responsible for subscribing to specific information object type(s) and ingesting the information objects. The second TSoA instance serves as an output system where the result from reasoning gets published. The Publisher agent servers as an intermediary between the Reasoner agent and the output TSoA system. The Reasoner agent utilizes the Publisher agent to publish the result.

Reasoner Agent. The Reasoner Agent as the name suggests, is responsible for performing reasoning on the data ingested from different components within the reasoning framework. It is responsible for ingesting the information objects from the first TSoA instance via the dedicated TSoA Subscriber agent. In addition, it also requests for updated Uncertainty of Information from the ETI framework periodically. The information from ETI serves as a critical input for reasoning on information objects from TSoA. In this current version of the Reasoner agent, the UoI value is evaluated and is instrumental in deciding to forward a message to the output TSoA instance. For example, if the associated uncertainty for Network Data source is deemed high by the Reasoner, then it refrains from sending the message to the output system. On the other hand, if the UoI value evaluated by Reasoner is low, then the Reasoner infers robustness in the network and forwards the message to the output system.

The Reasoner agent works behind the scenes and the result of the reasoning can be seen in the number of messages that make it to the output TSoA instance. The frequency of messages appearing in the output TSoA system will be greater when the computed UoI value within the ETI framework is low. The current version of Reasoner agent reasons on a single criterion of the computed UoI value. As this work progresses, we will investigate incorporating other criteria in the reasoning logic.

5 Conclusion

This framework is an initial prototype that demonstrates AI enabled experimentation framework. It helps to begin exploration of different aspects of decision making with uncertainty. As we continue to refine and augment this framework, we will be looking into integrating with other information systems for expanding our data sources. We would also be looking into refining our reasoning algorithm within the framework.

References

1. 7 Steps of the Decision Making Process|CSP Global.https://online.csp.edu/resources/article/decision-making-process
2. What AI-Driven Decision Making Looks Like (hbr.org)
3. Lott, D., Raglin, A., Metu, S.: Decision making with uncertainty using the LRM method MATLAB versus Java. In: SPIE Defense + Commercial Sensing (2021)
4. Gershon, N.: Visualization of an imperfect world. IEEE Comput. Graphics Appl. **18**(4), 43–45 (1998)
5. https://usnavalresearchlaboratory.github.io/sageframework/
6. Lenzi, R., et al.: Interconnecting "Tactical Service-Oriented Infrastructures with Federation Services". In: IEEE Military Communications Conference (2013)

A Framework for Contextual Recommendations Using Instance Segmentation

Dimitris Tsiktsiris[1]([✉]), Nikolaos Dimitriou[1], Zisis Kolias[2], Stavri Skourti[2], Paul Girssas[2], Antonios Lalas[1], Konstantinos Votis[1], and Dimitrios Tzovaras[1]

[1] Information Technologies Institute, Centre for Research and Technology-Hellas, Thessaloniki, Greece
{tsiktsiris,nikdim,lalas,kvotis,dimitrios.tzovaras}@iti.gr
[2] arx.net, Thessaloniki, Greece
{zisis,skourtis,paulg}@arx.net

Abstract. Due to the restrictive measures to prevent COVID-19 from spreading, an increasingly large number of viewers are eschewing traditional television programs, resorting to streaming and on-demand platforms. This rapid change in audience preference, combined with the great appeal of streaming services, has constituted a form of "threat" for traditional advertising, causing advertisers and advertising agencies to adapt by participating in content that is, among others, supported by online advertising and streaming platforms. In this work, a novel framework for contextual recommendations using instance segmentation in movies is presented. The proposed service employs deep learning and computer vision algorithms to automatically detect objects in real-time on video streams. The experiments conducted offered satisfactory results regarding both the mAP (mean average precision) for the bounding box and the masks and the continuous decrease of the loss, as well as the correctly detected objects in real time.

Keywords: Contextual Recommendation · Framework · Instance Segmentation · Real-time Object Detection · YOLACT

1 Introduction

An increasingly large number of viewers are eschewing traditional television programs, such as broadcasts and news, and resorting to streaming and on-demand platforms, which have claimed an increasing share of the advertising market and become an integral part of the television industry. In addition, the pandemic contributed to the further development and spread of digital streaming services due to the restrictive COVID-19 measures that translate to more hours watching TV [10,16].

This rapid change in audience preference, combined with the great appeal of streaming services, has constituted a form of "threat" for traditional advertising.

H. Degen and S. Ntoa (Eds.): HCII 2023, LNAI 14051, pp. 395–408, 2023.
https://doi.org/10.1007/978-3-031-35894-4_30

As a result, advertisers and advertising agencies have now adapted by participating in content that is, among others, supported by online advertising but
also on streaming platforms. These services are a dynamic medium that offers
advertising companies the opportunity to reach their audience in the context of
entertainment and in an environment that does not distract the end-user/viewer.

In the most recent literature, among many approaches proposed for targeting
video content [17] and video popularity prediction [18], there are also several ways
in which an advertisement can be displayed to the viewer. The most frequent
and immediate solution is to interrupt the program, even for about five seconds,
so that the advertised product can be shown briefly. However, even solutions like
these can often tire the viewer if they are frequent or last longer.

For this purpose, the approach presented in this paper proposes a more indirect and less invasive way of displaying advertisements: by recognising objects
displayed in the movie in real time. The proposed framework is based on the logic
that the viewer will be more positively inclined to items shown in the movie.
However, to successfully reach the consumer audience in the context of an advertising campaign, the advertised product should be related to some extent to the
content of the film being shown. For this reason, it is necessary to sample the
objects of interest during the movie.

The remainder of this paper is organized as follows. In Sect. 2 an overview
of similar approaches for contextual recommendations from the most recent bibliography is presented. Section 3 analyses the use case scenario that this work
aims to solve, as well as the methodology followed, while Sect. 4 presents the
experimental results of the implemented approach. Finally, in Sect. 5 a summary
of the implemented work is offered.

2   Related Work

In the most recent bibliography, there are some similar approaches that implement deep Neural Networks (NNs) for designing appropriate models to offer
contextual recommendations in videos. Motion segmentation is a common technique for improving object detection and scene understanding especially if the
scene has intense camera movement or contains multiple objects that are moving
rigidly and independently in 3D space. In some early works on segmentation the
authors used trajectories for motion segmentation. Dimitriou and Delopoulos
proposed a method that can be applied to streaming content based on Ranking
of Locally sampled Subspaces (RLS). It is an effective method for motion segmentation in various video processing applications by adopting the affine camera
model [2]. The proposed model evaluates a large number of 4-subsets of each trajectory's neighbourhood and then applies FastMap [4] on K for dimensionality
reduction. Moreover, the authors apply a spectral clustering algorithm [12] and
conclude by evaluating their proposed method, which showed promising results.
Finally, as a follow-up to their previous research, they present a method for temporally dividing a video shot into successive and overlapping windows and then
performing motion segmentation on each window [3].

In the Deep Learning (DL) era other methods have gained a lot of popularity. Zhang et al. [19] proposed an end-to-end architecture for displaying similar clothing to the viewer of the film. The authors implemented deep Convolutional Neural Networks (CNNs), such as Faster Region-based CNNs (RCNNs), Single Shot Detectors (SSDs), AlexNet, etc., for image feature extraction. The first step in the proposed approach consisted of detecting the human body in the image, while the second one was carrying out the body's pose estimation based on the previous information extracted. The following steps included the implementation of face recognition models on the film's protagonists and feature extraction from the clothes they wore in the film. The end solution offered satisfactory results, but had a significant weakness in execution time due to the increased algorithmic complexity.

Another technique by Vrochidis et al. [17] proposes a fusion of video content analysis and early viewership for predicting video popularity. The video content analysis features a Linear Regression model that utilizes pose estimation data along with emotion and audio data [18].

Another similar approach by Luo et al. [11] proposed the extraction of similar features using a CNN. The authors implemented networks based on YOLOv2, SSD and Region-based Fully CNN (R-FCN) extended using Recurrent NNs (RNNs) to account for prior states. By using Yes-Net the authors extracted local image features using a CNN and combined them with features from all the other frames using RNNs. The experimental results of this study reported a 3.71% improvement in ad clicks compared to other traditional methods.

Li et al. [7] developed DeepLink, a system used for detecting clothing from movies and connecting them to online stores by implementing CNN models. More specifically, the proposed work combines body position, body posture detection, facial recognition, and clothing detection data, as well as data from clothing ads from various online stores. However, the pilot tests of the system did not include any video testing, so no conclusions can be drawn regarding its performance in real-life scenarios.

While the aforementioned approaches manage to efficiently solve the problem of contextual advertising through object detection in pixels, some features of their architecture, such as attitude estimation but also the computational complexity of RNNs, significantly increase the execution time. This is not desirable in the case of an online streaming service since there are cases of processing movies that sometimes exceed 60 min and 100,000 frames in total.

3   Methodology

Analyzing movie content is a time-consuming and iterative process due to the huge amount of data that needs to be processed. For this reason, it is imperative to create a service that will undertake the automatic detection of objects in image sequences using Deep Learning (DL) and Computer Vision (CV) algorithms. To accomplish this There are several design constrains that need to be fulfilled. The service has to be fast; faster than real-time in order to be able to cope with

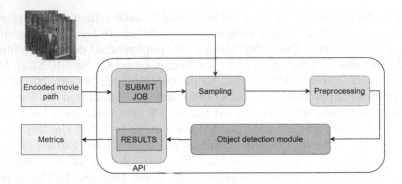

Fig. 1. System architecture.

the extreme video volumes. Furthermore, a modular architecture with a flexible Application Programming Interface (API) is required for interfacing with video archiving platforms. Finally, it should be able to run on an hardware abstraction layer that will adapt and utilize the underlying hardware resources for acceleration (if present). This abstraction will assist the deployment on virtual machines and cloud infrastructure.

In Fig. 1 the proposed service is described, presenting its core: the decoding, sampling, and preprocessing units. In addition, at the core of the visual analysis is the object detection module, while at a higher level is the Application Programming Interface (API) for the external service interface.

More specifically, our use case scenario can be described with the following steps:

- **Stage 1:** The API accepts a call to the endpoint to create a new process. This call contains the full path to the movie file.
- **Stage 2:** The movie frames are serialized and forwarded to the sampling unit by the decoding unit.
- **Stage 3:** During the frame sampling, the film characteristics (frames per second, width and height of frames, etc.) and detections from previous timestamps are taken into account, in order to intelligently select the frames of greatest interest. This particular technique speeds up the localization process and lowers the processing time without affecting the accuracy of the localization.
- **Stage 4:** The object detection module accepts a frame as input and calls ML-based models for the task of object detection. The objects are saved in the process cache.
- **Stage 5:** The object list is updated in the API and the call to the corresponding endpoint returns the objects detected.

In addition, to successfully reach the consumer audience in the context of an advertising campaign, the advertised product should be related to some extent to the content of the film being projected. For this reason, it is necessary to

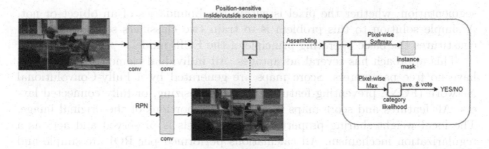

Fig. 2. General architecture of the Fully-Convolutional Instance-Aware Semantic Segmentation (FCIS) network using the ResNet model. The last fully-convolutional layer is not used and as a result feature maps with 2048 channels are developed. An additional convolutional 1 × 1 layer is added to reduce the channel dimension to 1024.

sample the objects of interest during the movie. An extensive list of such items is described in Table 1, which was later used as a guide for detection in our proposed framework.

When choosing the appropriate algorithm, special emphasis was placed on the accuracy of the model – mAP (mean average precision) in relation to the processing time (throughput) in frames per second (FPS). The tests were done with the FCIS [7], Mask-RCNN [6], RetinaMask [5], PA-Net [9], MS-RCNN [14] and YOLACT [1] models, which are presented in detail in the following subsections.

3.1 Fully-Convolutional Instance-Aware Semantic Segmentation (FCIS)

In the FCIS model, for each specific Region of Interest (ROI), the pixel-wise score maps are produced by the assembly operation within the ROI. For each pixel in each specific ROI, two tasks are performed: (a) detection, whether the pixel belongs to an object bounding box at a relative position or not; and (b)

Table 1. List of objects to be detected.

Category	Object
Vehicles	Bicycle, car, motorcycle, airplane, bus, train, truck, boat
Objects	Backpack, umbrella, handbag, tie, suitcase, frisbee, ski equipment, football, kite, glove, surfing board, tennis racket, bottle, wineglass, cup, fork, knife, bowl
Fruit	Banana, apple, sandwich, orange, broccoli, carrot
Food	Hot dog, pizza, donut, cake
Furniture	Chair, sofa, flowerpot, bed, table, WC
Electronic Devices	Television, laptop, mouse, remote, keyboard, cellphone
Devices	Sink, fridge, oven, stove, microwave, toaster
Interior Space	Book, watch, vase, scissors, air dryer, toothbrush

segmentation, whether the pixel is within the boundaries of an object or not. A simple solution to this problem is to train two classifiers separately, which constitutes the basic operating principle of the FCIS model.

This approach has several advantages. All individual elements of each ROI have no free parameters. Score maps are generated by a Fully-Convolutional Network (FCN), preventing feature distortion, resizing, or fully connected layers. All features and score maps respect the proportions of the original image. The local weight sharing property of FCN models is preserved and acts as a regularization mechanism. All calculations performed per ROI are simple and fast, thus reducing the computational cost for each ROI.

Figure 2 presents the FCIS architecture, using the ResNet model [6]. The last fully connected layer is not used, but instead only the previous convolution layers are used. The result is feature maps with 2048 channels. Additionally, a 1×1 convolution layer is added to reduce the dimension to 1024.

3.2   Mask-Region-Based Convolutional Neural Network (Mask-RCNN)

This method is an extension of Faster-RCNN [5] by adding an additional branch for the prediction of segmentation masks in each ROI, alongside the branch of classification and bounding box regression. The overall process is shown in Fig. 3. The mask branch is a small FCN network applied to each ROI for predicting a pixel-to-pixel segmentation mask. Mask-RCNN is easier to implement and train than Faster-RCNN, facilitating a wide range of architectural designs. Additionally, the mask branch adds only a very small computational overhead, allowing for fast system design and rapid experimentation.

The concept of Mask-RCNN is relatively simple. Faster-RCNN gives two outputs for each candidate object: a class label and a bounding box offset. Mask-RCNN then adds a third branch that will output the object mask. Mask-RCNN also adopts the same two-stage process as Faster-RCNN, with exactly the same initial stage, which is a Region Proposition Network (RPN). At the second level, along with class and box offset prediction. One stage Mask-RCNN also outputs a binary mask for each ROI, unlike other systems where classification is based on mask predictions. In general, one stage object detectors are faster but not as accurate as their two-stage equivalents.

Basically, Mask-RCNN is an extension of Faster-RCNN. However, the correct implementation of the mask branch is very important to achieving good results. Furthermore, Faster-RCNN is not built for pixel-to-pixel alignment between input and output nodes of the network. This is why the RoIAlign layer was included, which maintains accurate positions, to increase mask accuracy by 10% to as much as 50%. RoIAlign manages to improve the accuracy due to the RoI pooling and the interpolation that performs on mask boundaries.

3.3   RetinaMask

RetinaMask is considered an extension of single-shot detectors (RetinaNet [9], SSD [14]), on one hand, due to the addition of instance mask prediction during

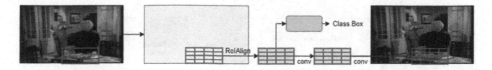

Fig. 3. General architecture of the Mask-Region-based Convolutional Neural Network (Mask-RCNN) network. The mask branch is a small FCN network deployed in every region of interest (ROI).

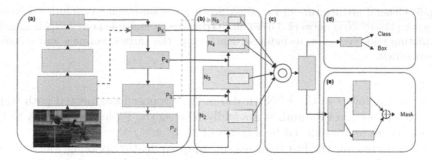

Fig. 4. General architecture of the Path Aggregation Network (PA-Net) network. Subfigures show the following modules: (a) FPN network, (b) bottom-up path enhancement, (c) adaptive feature pooling, (d) box branching, and (e) fully-connected data fusion.

training and, on the other hand, to the adaptive loss that helps to improve the robustness of the network. The name "RetinaMask" arises from the need to separate it from the other approaches by adding an extra task for prediction, as mentioned above.

This particular network can be used in a variety of embedded systems that use single-shot detectors, as the structure of the detector during testing remains the same. This particular approach offers a solution to the problem of choosing between two-stage detectors and single-shot detectors. Before this approach, two-stage detectors offered better results than single-shot detectors. However, in the case of low-power embedded systems, the cost of resampling leads to hardware degradation with the CPU. On the other hand, with single-shot detectors, this particular problem can be avoided, which makes them easier to use in similar applications.

3.4 Path Aggregation Network (PA-Net)

Figure 4 shows a graphical representation of the PA-Net network architecture. First, an augmented bottom-up path was created (Fig. 4(b)), leading to a reduction of the information path and enhancement of the feature pyramid. As shown in the diagram, the FPN network is followed by defining that the layers that will give feature masks of the same size will be in the same layer of the network. At the same time, the ResNet network is used, and the layers P_2, P_3, P_4, and

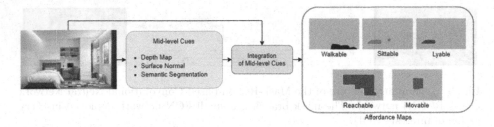

Fig. 5. General architecture of the Mask Scoring Region-based Convolutional Neural Network (MS-RCNN) network. Given an RGB image, a multiple layer CNN is used for calculating mid-level cues, including a depth map, the surface normals and semantic segmentation.

P_5 define the layers of the FPN's features.The proposed augmented path starts from the lowest level P_2 until it gradually reaches the P_5 level. From P_2 to P_5, the size is gradually reduced by a factor of 2.

Then, to recover the lost information, adaptive feature pooling was designed (Fig. 4(c)). It is a simple building block used to sum the attributes from each level, avoiding randomly assigned results. As a result, cleaner paths are produced. The new feature masks are represented by layers N_2, N_3, N_4, and N_5.The N_2 layer is simply the P_2 layer without any preprocessing.

Finally, to capture the different results of each proposal, the mask prediction process was improved by adding small fully-connected layers, which complement the properties of the original FCN network. By fusing the data from both proposals, the diversity is increased and better quality masks are produced (Fig. 4(e)). The first two building blocks in Fig. 4 ((a) and (b)) are common to both detection and instance segmentation, offering better performance for both tasks.

3.5 Mask Scoring Region-based Convolutional Neural Network (MS-RCNN)

Figure 5 shows a general description of the operation of the MS-RCNN network. More specifically, given an RGB image, a multi-level CNN [14] is used to calculate mid-level cues, including a depth map, surface normals, and semantic segmentation of general categories of surfaces (e.g., walls, floors, furniture). The CNN also contributes to combining these mid-level cues in a form of feedforward to predict the five affordance maps for each of the types: (a) walkable: any horizontal surface the same height as the plane with free vertical space not occupied by another object;(b) sittable: any horizontal surface below a certain height (relative to the person's height) that has free space and allows the person to sit on it; (c) lyable: any horizontal surface on which a person can sit but is also long enough to lie down on; (d) reachable: any object or surface in the space that is within the person's reachable height so that the person can stand next to it and grasp it; and (e) movable: any object that can be easily moved by hand and has sufficient free space around it to allow for it to be moved.

More specifically, initially the depth map of the image is used. Next, the three multi-level CNNs respectively produce three mid-level cues (depth map, surface normal, and semantic segmentation) as outputs, which are then fed as inputs to another CNN to predict N affordance maps for each of the N types. The final model estimate is analyzed for reasoning about important geometric properties of the room, such as the identification of surfaces, their orientation, the height of objects, etc.

3.6 You only Look at Coefficients (YOLACT)

YOLACT is a framework that can be used to correctly identify all objects in instance segmentation problems. In this framework, the segmentation is performed in parallel with two separate tasks: (a) creating the appropriate vocabulary for the original masks of the entire image; and (b) predicting a set of linear combinations of the coefficients per object (instance). The full-image instance segmentation of these two substeps is then produced as follows: for each object, the features are linearly combined using the corresponding predicted coefficients, and then the object is cropped from the image using a predicted bounding box. In this way, the network learns how to detect the masks of each object on its own, in cases where visually, spatially, and semantically similar objects appear differently in the training data. Furthermore, since the number of mask prototypes is independent of the number of categories (e.g., there may be more categories than prototypes), YOLACT learns a distributed representation in which each object is partitioned with a combination of prototypes that are divided into different categories. This distributed representation can lead to an interesting ascending behavior of the prototypes: some prototypes divide the image into segments; some detect objects; some detect the contours of objects; etc.

This approach also offers several advantages. First off, it's fast. Thanks to its parallel structure and its particularly lightweight build process, YOLACT adds only minimal computational overhead, making it easy to reach 30 FPS, even when RetinaNet-101 is used (the process for the mask branch takes a total of 5 ms). Furthermore, since the masks fully utilize the image space without quality loss, the masks in YOLACT have significantly better quality than other methods. Finally, prototypes and mask coefficients can be added to almost any object detector.

3.7 Model Selection

Among all the aforementioned models, YOLACT was found to offer the best tradeoff between accuracy and performance, achieving a maximum processing speed of 43 FPS. This corresponds to a latency of 23 ms per frame, which is considered adequate, and for this reason, YOLACT was chosen in our implementation.

Implementation. For the implementation of the YOLACT detector, a combination of ResNet-101 [6] with FPN was used as the core network, while the basic image size was set to 550×550 pixels. The decision to use FPN was made since it is significantly lighter and faster than RetinaNet. Additionally, in order to maintain per-image evaluation time consistency, the aspect ratio is not maintained.

As in RetinaNet, in FPN, an appropriate modification was made to produce P_6 and P_7 levels as successive 3×3 convolution layers with a step equal to 2, starting from the P_5 level and placing 3 anchors with aspect ratios $[1, \frac{1}{2}, 2]$ in each. The anchors of level P_3 correspond to an area equal to 24 pixels² and each subsequent layer has twice the scale of the previous one (ending up at scales [24, 48, 96, 192, 384]). For the implementation of each prediction head connected to each P_i level, there is a 3×3 convolution layer common to all three branches, and then each branch has its own 3×3 convolution layer available in parallel. The training of the box regressors and the coding of the coordinates were done in a similar way to that followed in an SSD network. For the prediction, the softmax cross entropy with c positive labels and the background level equal to 1 was used, using the OHEM method [15] to select the training data in a ratio of 3:1 negative to positive. In this way, focal loss is not used, as is the case in RetinaNet, as it is not a viable option.

With the specific design choices, it was observed that the proposed model outperforms an SSD network using ResNet-101 for the same image size. The second reason why YOLACT was chosen is due to the fact that the masks are spatially interdependent. This means that pixels that are close to each other are very likely to be part of the same object. However, while a convolutional layer can exploit this interdependence, a fully connected layer cannot. This is therefore a problem as single-layer object detectors produce class coefficients and box coefficients for each anchor as the output of a fully connected layer. On the other hand, two-layer approaches, such as Mask-RCNN, solve this particular problem by using a localization step, which preserves the spatial interdependence of features while allowing the mask to be the output of a convolutional layer. However, this particular procedure assumes that a significant part of the

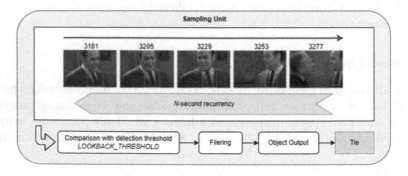

Fig. 6. Overall architecture and execution flow of the sampling unit.

model will have to wait until the first-level RPN proposes the candidates for the constraint, causing a significant time delay.

To solve the time delay problem, YOLACT's model splits the process into two subtasks that run in parallel, using fully connected layers (which are useful for producing semantic vectors) and convolutional layers (which are useful for producing spatially interdependent masks) to produce mask coefficients and original masks, respectively. Then, since both the coefficients and mask prototypes can be computed independently, the computational overhead is caused by the assembly step, which can be implemented as the product of a single matrix. In this way, spatial interdependence is preserved while at the same time offering a single-level and fast model.

Sampling. The object detection task constitutes the basis for extracting the information required for targeted advertising. In the previous the final selection of the machine learning model which extracts the data per frame was carried out. This chapter analyzes the post-processing of this data to filter and optimize the results.

The sampling unit takes into account the detection frame, the object class, and the confidence score of the network while combining information related to the current frame of the processing and the frames per second of the movie. For each detected object, the search algorithm is recursively performed in previous frames, corresponding to a time interval of N seconds. As long as the object is found at least as many times as T (buffer threshold), the interval N (buffer seconds) and the constant T are configurable from the configuration file of the service. The architecture of the sampling unit along with an execution flow are illustrated in Fig. 6.

4   Experimental Results

4.1   Quantitative Data

In this section, the quantitative and qualitative results of the system implementation are offered in detail. The GPU used is an NVIDIA GTX 1080 Ti with 8 gigabytes of video RAM. The proposed YOLACT model was trained on the MS-COCO dataset [8] with the PyTorch framework [13], and the SGD optimizer with variable learning rate was used.

In Fig. 7 the training metrics for 168,000 iterations are presented. It can be observed that at the end of the training the mAP for the bounding box and the mask amounts to 29.73% and 27.64%, respectively, while the loss continues to decrease gradually.

4.2   Qualitative Data

Figure 8 depicts some indicative experimental results from the processing of a classic Greek movie. Detected objects are marked in boxes, along with their

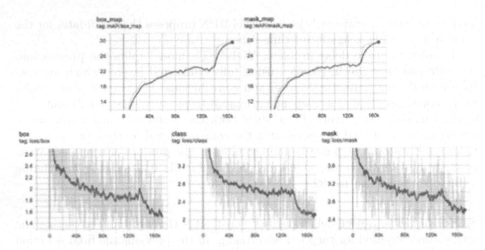

Fig. 7. Training metrics - box/mask mAP and box/mask/class losses.

Fig. 8. Experimental results along with the corresponding confidence score during a movie streaming. The objects detected are: (a) the tie; (b) the chair; (c) the bicycle and (d) the handbag.

description and a number indicating the algorithm's confidence score. The colors are different and unique for each class. The processing of the movies was completed in about 15 min in a Docker environment, using an Intel dual-core i5 processor without graphics card acceleration.

5   Conclusions

In this work, a novel framework for offering contextual recommendations in movies using instance segmentation was presented. For choosing the appropriate algorithm, special emphasis was placed on the accuracy of the model – mAP in relation to the processing time (throughput) in FPS. The tests were carried out by examining several approaches; however, the YOLACT model offered the best tradeoff between accuracy and performance, achieving a maximum processing speed of 43 FPS, which corresponds to a latency of 23 ms per frame that is considered acceptable. The proposed YOLACT model was trained on the MS-COCO dataset with the PyTorch framework, and the SGD optimizer with a variable learning was used. For the implementation of the YOLACT detector, a combination of ResNet-101 and FPN was used as the core network, while the basic image size was set to 550 × 550 pixels. The detected objects were marked in boxes along with their description and a number indicating the algorithm's confidence score. The processing of the movies was completed in about 15 min in a Docker environment, using an Intel dual-core i5 processor without graphics card acceleration. The experiments conducted offered satisfactory results regarding both the mAP of the bounding box and the masks and the continuous decrease of the loss, as well as the correctly detected objects in real time. In the future, the proposed framework will be further developed using an extended list of objects to be detected. Additional steps will be considered to improve the accuracy of the model by exploiting attention-based methods, as well.

Funding Information. This work is supported by the cine.gr project, co-financed by the European Regional Development Fund of the European Union and Greek national funds through the Operational Program Competitiveness, Entrepreneurship and Innovation, under the call RESEARCH - CREATE - INNOVATE (project code: T2EDK-3569).

References

1. Bolya, D., Zhou, C., Xiao, F., Lee, Y.J.: Yolact: real-time instance segmentation. In: Proceedings of the IEEE/CVF International Conference on Computer Vision (ICCV) (2019)
2. Dimitriou, N., Delopoulos, A.: Improved motion segmentation using locally sampled subspaces. In: 2012 19th IEEE International Conference on Image Processing, pp. 309–312. IEEE (2012)
3. Dimitriou, N., Delopoulos, A.: Motion-based segmentation of objects using overlapping temporal windows. Image Vision Comput. **31**(9), 593–602 (2013)
4. Faloutsos, C., Lin, K.I.: Fastmap: a fast algorithm for indexing, data-mining and visualization of traditional and multimedia datasets. In: Proceedings of the 1995 ACM SIGMOD International Conference on Management of Data, pp. 163–174 (1995)
5. Fu, C.Y., Shvets, M., Berg, A.C.: Retinamask: learning to predict masks improves state-of-the-art single-shot detection for free. arXiv preprint arXiv:1901.03353 (2019)

6. He, K., Gkioxari, G., Dollár, P., Girshick, R.: Mask r-cnn. In: Proceedings of the IEEE International Conference on Computer Vision, pp. 2961–2969 (2017)
7. Li, Y., Qi, H., Dai, J., Ji, X., Wei, Y.: Fully convolutional instance-aware semantic segmentation. In: Proceedings of the IEEE Conference on Computer Vision and Pattern Recognition, pp. 2359–2367 (2017)
8. Lin, T.-Y., et al.: Microsoft COCO: common objects in context. In: Fleet, D., Pajdla, T., Schiele, B., Tuytelaars, T. (eds.) ECCV 2014. LNCS, vol. 8693, pp. 740–755. Springer, Cham (2014). https://doi.org/10.1007/978-3-319-10602-1_48
9. Liu, S., Qi, L., Qin, H., Shi, J., Jia, J.: Path aggregation network for instance segmentation. In: Proceedings of the IEEE Conference on Computer Vision and Pattern Recognition, pp. 8759–8768 (2018)
10. Lozic, J.: Financial analysis of netflix platform at the time of covid 19 pandemic. In: Economic and Social Development: Book of Proceedings, pp. 78–86 (2021)
11. Luo, C., Peng, Y., Zhu, T., Li, L.: An optimization framework of video advertising: using deep learning algorithm based on global image information. Cluster Comput. 22(4), 8939–8951 (2019)
12. Ng, A., Jordan, M., Weiss, Y.: On spectral clustering: analysis and an algorithm. Adv. Neural Inf. Process. Syst. 14 (2001)
13. Paszke, A., et al.: Pytorch: an imperative style, high-performance deep learning library. Adv. Neural Inf. Process. Syst. 32 (2019)
14. Roy, A., Todorovic, S.: A multi-scale CNN for affordance segmentation in RGB images. In: Leibe, B., Matas, J., Sebe, N., Welling, M. (eds.) ECCV 2016. LNCS, vol. 9908, pp. 186–201. Springer, Cham (2016). https://doi.org/10.1007/978-3-319-46493-0_12
15. Shrivastava, A., Gupta, A., Girshick, R.: Training region-based object detectors with online hard example mining. In: Proceedings of the IEEE Conference on Computer Vision and Pattern Recognition, pp. 761–769 (2016)
16. Vlassis, A.: Global online platforms, covid-19, and culture: the global pandemic, an accelerator towards which direction? Media Cult. Soc. 43(5), 957–969 (2021)
17. Vrochidis, A., Dimitriou, N., Krinidis, S., Panagiotidis, S., Parcharidis, S., Tzovaras, D.: A multi-modal audience analysis system for predicting popularity of online videos. In: Iliadis, L., Macintyre, J., Jayne, C., Pimenidis, E. (eds.) EANN 2021. PINNS, vol. 3, pp. 465–476. Springer, Cham (2021). https://doi.org/10.1007/978-3-030-80568-5_38
18. Vrochidis, A., Dimitriou, N., Krinidis, S., Panagiotidis, S., Parcharidis, S., Tzovaras, D.: Video popularity prediction through fusing early viewership with video content. In: Vincze, M., Patten, T., Christensen, H.I., Nalpantidis, L., Liu, M. (eds.) ICVS 2021. LNCS, vol. 12899, pp. 159–168. Springer, Cham (2021). https://doi.org/10.1007/978-3-030-87156-7_13
19. Zhang, H., Ji, Y., Huang, W., Liu, L.: Sitcom-star-based clothing retrieval for video advertising: a deep learning framework. Neural Comput. Appl. 31(11), 7361–7380 (2019)

Development of a Domain Specific Sentiment Lexicon (DSSL) for Evaluating the Quality of Experience (QoE) of Cloud Gaming

Tao Wen[1], Siqi Li[2（✉）] 🆔, Hongyan Yan[1], and Xiangang Qin[2] 🆔

[1] Department of User and Market, China Mobile Research Institute, Beijing 100053, China
wentao@chinamobile.com
[2] Beijing University of Posts and Telecommunications, Beijing 100876, China
wentao@chinamobile.com, veryL333@163.com

Abstract. Domain-specific reviews created by the user on cloud gaming platforms offer valuable and cost effective information of high ecological validity. While the user generated content (UGC) has been used widely across many fields successfully in evaluating user experience and satisfaction, it has received proportionally less attention in the field of measuring the quality of experience (QoE) of cloud gaming. Besides, it remains an open question how well the UGC can be applied to measure the QoE of cloud gaming. In view of the poor performance of general purpose emotion lexicons (GPEL) in the modeling user experience of a specific product, this paper proposed a method of measuring the QoE of cloud gaming grounded on a Domain Specific Sentiment Lexicon (DSSL). This DSSL provides a structural distribution of the sentiment on 62 indicators. Its high criterion validity and discriminative power demonstrated the potential of transforming DSSL into a psychometric scale of QoE of cloud gaming.

Keywords: Cloud gaming · Quality of Experience (QoE) · Domain Specific Sentiment Lexicon · User Generated Content

1 Introduction

User-generated content (UGC) comes from regular people who voluntarily contribute data, information, or media that then appears before others in a useful or entertaining way, usually on the Web—for example, restaurant ratings, wikis, and videos. The use of such content has seen rapid growth in recent years, in part because it's fairly inexpensive to obtain (users normally supply it for no charge) [1]. Besides, the text in the contents contains rich emotional information, which also reflects the quality of the experience (QoE) of the product or service to a certain extent. And compared with traditional survey methods, UGC texts have the advantages of easy collection, low financial cost, high ecological validity, low sampling error, etc. [2]. As a result, researchers have done a lot of valuable research on how UGC is used to analyze the experience of products and services.

H. Degen and S. Ntoa (Eds.): HCII 2023, LNAI 14051, pp. 409–418, 2023.
https://doi.org/10.1007/978-3-031-35894-4_31

Emotional analysis of the text is an important research direction to explore how to apply UGC text to the evaluation of QoE. It aims to classify existing emotions in text into one (or more) of a set of pre-defined categories. To recognize emotions, this classification task typically relies on emotion lexicons or makes use of an existing machine learning classifier [3].

Emotion analysis of text requires careful modeling of text since words are associated with different emotions in different contexts with varying levels of magnitude, making the identification of words for document representation more challenging. And a lexicon containing these emotional words is called an emotional lexicon. The existing general purpose emotion lexicons (GPELs) include WordNet-Affect (WNA), EmoSenticNet (ESN), the NRC word-emotion lexicon, etc. While these lexicons perform poorly in modeling specific product user experiences, for example, "Glee" might normally connote joy, but would need to be assumed neutral in the context of a document corpus talking about the television series with the same name [4]. So, it is important to develop the domain specific sentiment lexicon (DSSL).

A lexicon in the automotive field based on the UGC of the automotive vertical website used a word2vec deep learning model to conduct emotional analysis on the UGC, built a set of evaluation items using automotive product expertise, and finally determined the weight of the evaluation items by using the analytic hierarchy process and the frequency and proportion of words corresponding to the evaluation index [5]. Another study extracted keywords from the text of comments on 75 sample mobile phones, calculated the Kansei tendency on the keywords by using the lexical similarity, and then extracted the features of the products. Finally, the BP neural network was used to predict the Kansei parameters of the products with the product features as inputs, and a good prediction effect was obtained [6]. These are all valid explorations for QoE evaluation using a domain specific sentiment lexicon.

In recent years, the development and pervasiveness of 5G networks have reduced the obstacles to bandwidth and network delay for cloud-based mobile services. Cloud gaming technology can theoretically provide users with a high-quality gaming experience on any terminal [7]. It is challenging to deploy network and computing power according to the dynamic network environment where cloud gaming players are located to provide reliable and stable QoE [8]. Reliable measurement is the premise for evaluating the QoE of cloud gaming (CGQoE) [9].

In view of the above problems, this study develops a domain specific sentiment lexicon for evaluating the quality of experience of cloud gaming. The main technical routes are as follows:

1. Extract feature words and statistics frequency, using CountVectorizer and transfer.fit_transform in sklearn.feature_extraction.text in Python, and vectorize each comment text using the feature words and frequencies.
2. Create a DSSL with feature words selected by the expertise of CGQoE.
3. Get the QoE evaluation data based on DSSL with the approach of Emotion Distribution Learning (EDL), which maps the emotion information contained in the cloud gaming-related text UGC into the emotion distribution represented by multiple emotion feature words.
4. Analyze the criterion validity of QoE evaluation data.

5. Filter and correct the dataset of comment texts based on the DSSL.
6. Analyze the lexicon's discriminative power in differentiating the QoE of eight cloud gaming services.

The contributions of this study include:

1. Create a DSSL of CGQoE based on the emotional information in the UGC texts of cloud gaming and the existing expertise in the field of CGQoE.
2. Evaluate the QoE of comment text based on the DSSL and EDL approaches.
3. Analyze the potential of transforming DSSL into a psychometric scale of CGQoE based on criterion validity and discriminative power.

2 Related Work

2.1 Approach of Evaluating the CGQoE

The purpose of this study is to develop a DSSL from UGC texts, thereby evaluating the CGQoE. So, it is critical to obtain the emotional words included in the DSSL and verify the validity of the DSSL.

Inspired by the idea of questionnaire survey method with psychometric properties, each measurement item corresponds to a semantically unique evaluation index. Therefore, to achieve the purpose of this study, it is very critical to use the multiple emotional feature words extracted from UGC to structurally evaluate the QoE contained in each UGC text and measure the validity of the evaluation results.

In the classic single-label text emotion distribution approach, each piece of text information can only be represented by a single emotion tag [10], which is insufficient for analyzing the CGQoE via several structured items in the current study. The Emotion Distribution Learning (EDL) method can map one or more sentences or paragraphs of user-generated content to a distribution of numerous emotion tags or feature words. In this study, the EDL approach was used to characterize the cloud gaming QoE in UGC.

Some studies have shown that the emotional information in a sentence can be characterized by the emotional words contained therein [11], which provides the possibility of label emotion distribution based on the emotional feature words. The goal is to map emotional information in a text into a vector space comprised of many emotional feature words, with each distribution labeling containing information about emotional intensity. Some researchers have discovered that the EDL approach based on six emotion feature words (joy, fear, anger, surprise, happiness, and disgust) outperforms other approaches in terms of the prediction performance of emotion and the prediction effect of single emotion feature words in the SemVal training set [3]. Since the separate emotion lexicon does not reflect the significance between emotion words, other scholars proposed the concept of an emotion wheel to strengthen the emotion distribution marking. The results demonstrate that this strategy outperforms other emotion distribution marking systems [10] in an emotion recognition test using seven Chinese and English text emotion datasets.

2.2 EDL Approach Based on the DSSL, Semantic Similarity, and Word Frequency

EDL's purpose in this study is to quantitatively evaluate the QoE of each UGC based on the created DSSL across multiple dimensions., that is, to map the emotional information in the UGC texts to the distribution of emotions d_i shown by several emotional feature words, so as to get the QoE evaluation result [10].

$$d_i = \left\{ d_i^j \right\}_{j-1}^{C} \tag{1}$$

d_i^j refers to the extent to which that text t_i in UGC can be represented by the emotional feature word j. This study examines two approaches of EDL:

- Based on the frequency of feature words in UGC texts.
- Based on the semantic similarity between feature words and UGC texts.

The EDL approaches proposed in this study include the following steps:

4. Use jieba.cut in Python to cut UGC text in Chinese and extract feature words.
5. Use the CountVectorizer in sklearn.feature_extraction.text counts the frequency of feature words after word segmentation
6. Use transfer fit_ Transform converts each text into a vector represented by a plurality of feature words (the number is 2 or more to meet the requirements of structural degree)
7. Based on the expertise of CGQoE, simplify the feature word base to make a word base that only contains QoE-related feature words
8. Use the sentiments in snowNLP to rate the emotion of each comment text
9. Use the sentiments in snowNLP to rate the emotion of each feature word extracted from the UGC
10. Characterization of emotion distribution:
   - When the frequency approach is used, d_i^j is represented by the product of the frequency of the feature word j appearing in the text t_i and the emotion score of the feature word j, and finally all d_i^j forms an emotion distribution d_f of frequency approach.
   - In the similarity approach, use the similarity in simtext to calculate the semantic similarity between the feature word j and the UGC text t_i, that is, use the sentiments in snowNLP to rate the emotion of each comment text. s_i^j is represented by the product of the semantic similarity between the feature word j and the text t_i, and finally, all s_i^j form an emotion distribution d_s of frequency approach. The results of two EDL approaches are tested in the experimental part.

3 Experiment

3.1 Dataset About Cloud Gaming

The first step is to achieve this study's goal is to create a dataset due to a lack of a standard comment text dataset from UGC about CGQoE:

11. In the first step, crawl 147,386 pieces of comment texts and their corresponding 5-point Likert scale scores from four cloud game platforms. Comment texts are the dataset for EDL in this study, and the score on the 5-point Likert scale provided by the user is also gathered as a criterion for evaluating the reliability.
12. In the second step, clean the data by removing non-Chinese characters such as numbers, emoticons, English and garbled codes, etc., by the purpose of this study; Remove duplicate water army data, which means multiple users posting the same comment, and remove the information in the comment that has less than 7 characters (at least two feature words are included to make it easier to use multidimensional emotional words for structured text emotion distribution), leaving 123,678 pieces of comment texts.
13. The third step is to use snowNLP to score the emotion of the comment texts.
14. The fourth step is to classify the positive or negative emotion for each UGC text based on the emotion score, greater than 0.5 for positive emotion and less than 0.5 for negative emotion.
15. The fifth step is to classify the positive or negative emotion for each UGC text based on the scale score, greater than 3 for positive emotion and less than 3 for negative emotion.
16. The sixth step is to take the emotional classification result of the user's scale score in the fifth step as the criterion and remove the data that the classification result is inconsistent with the text emotional classification result in the fourth step, leaving 83644 pieces of text information.

After removing the text with inconsistent sentiment classification, the Pearson correlation coefficient between the snowNLP-based text emotion score and the user's scale score went from 0.46 to 0.91. This shows that the distribution of the emotional information in the text comments dataset can be completely matched by the distribution of the user's scale scores.

3.2 Creation of Cloud Gaming QoE DSSL

UGC text was segmented using the Jieba.cut tool and 2412 feature words were generated. Based on the expertise of CGQoE, the feature words unrelated to cloud gaming QoE are removed, and a DSSL of cloud gaming QoE including 62 feature words is created.

In this DSSL, 22 words were positive and 40 were negative (based on the emotion score) (Table 1).

3.3 Filtration of Dataset Based on the CGQoE DSSL

When the frequency approach was first used for emotion distribution labeling, it was revealed that the correlation between labeling results and text emotion scores was just

Table 1. The DSSL of CGQoE

Negative feature words				Positive feature words	
Word	Score	Word	Score	Word	Score
进不去 (can't get in)	0.21	重进 (re-entry)	0.20	特快 (very fast)	0.75
闪退 (flashback)	0.13	太慢 (very slow)	0.21	极速 (extreme speed)	0.76
延迟 (delay)	0.21	模糊 (vague)	0.04	清清楚楚 (clearly)	0.67
重启 (reboot)	0.09	繁忙 (busy)	0.21	不卡 (not stuck)	0.91
崩溃 (collapse)	0.31	很糊 (very confused)	0.28	流畅 (fluent)	0.94
重连 (reconnect)	0.34	太糊 (too pasty)	0.33	清晰 (clarity)	0.80
死慢 (too slow)	0.18	好慢 (so slow)	0.18	较快 (faster)	0.72
不快 (not fast)	0.32	很久 (inactive)	0.18	不慢 (not slow)	0.66
特慢 (extra slow)	0.12	迟钝 (retarded)	0.43	精美 (exquisite)	0.75
缓慢 (slow)	0.18	断断续续 (intermittent)	0.22	细腻 (finesse)	0.81
很慢 (very slow)	0.24	断开 (disconnection)	0.35	顺畅 (smooth)	0.81
极慢 (extremely slow)	0.16	打不开 (can't open)	0.23	连续 (continuous)	0.74
卡死 (stuck)	0.15	忙碌 (bustling)	0.21	通畅 (unobstructed)	0.75
太卡 (too stuck)	0.25	马赛克 (mosaic)	0.12	蛮快 (pretty fast)	0.66
黑屏 (black screen)	0.36	不动 (no movement)	0.30	畅快 (unblocked)	0.83
卡顿 (stopped)	0.22	崩过 (crash through)	0.31	很快 (soon)	0.88
网卡 (stuck network)	0.27	慢死 (greatly slow)	0.18	快速 (clipping)	0.68
卡住 (it is stuck)	0.20	落后 (lagging behind)	0.32	稳定 (stable)	0.72
卡得 (stuck to)	0.22			真快 (it is fast)	0.72
卡成 (stuck into)	0.22			精致 (refined)	0.85
花屏 (blurred screen)	0.08			快捷 (fast)	0.66
重登 (reboard)	0.21			清楚 (clear)	0.53

0.002, which was not statistically significant. After analyzing the text content, it was determined that the discrepancy between the emotion distribution labeling of UGC text using cloud gaming QoE-related feature words and the emotion score of UGC text is because feature words unrelated to the CGQoE contained in UGC text by users, such as "fun," "enjoyable," and so on, are not used for emotion distribution labeling, and this study focuses only on QoE due to network quality of service (QoS). This is partly because the original UGC content has more rich, multidimensional, and adequate unstructured information, which is not enough to focus on the content related to the CGQoE that this study is about. Techniques and approaches for improving content validity must be explored when applying them to the structured measurement of a particular domain.

Consequently, the dataset is continually filtered with a focus on the study topic of QoE variation due to QoS. The dataset, which contained 83,644 items in total, was filtered using 62 feature words from the lexicon. Cases of data that did not contain any of the feature words were eliminated, leaving a total of 9,193 items in the new dataset.

3.4 Emotion Distribution Learning of UGC Based on DSSL

Based on the new dataset (9,193 items), comment texts are labeled with a structured emotion distribution. In the frequency approach, the emotion distribution score of each text is generated by multiplying the frequency of the feature word in the text by the emotion score of the feature word. The average correlation coefficient between the emotion distribution labeling results from the frequency approach and the emotion score of the text is 0.60.

In the similarity approach, the emotion distribution score of each text is generated by multiplying the semantic similarity between the 62 feature words in the CGQoE lexicon and each comment text by the emotion score of each comment text. The average correlation coefficient between the emotion distribution labeling results from the similarity approach and the emotion score of the text is 0.87.

In general, the results of both the frequency approach and the similarity approach for labeling emotion distribution were associated with high scores for emotion in UGC comment texts.

The frequency and similarity approaches for labeling emotion distribution were highly correlated with emotion scores in UGC comment texts.

The findings of the manual evaluation revealed that snowNLP wrongly evaluated the emotion of certain vocabulary feature words. There were cases where positive QoE words were incorrectly identified as negative or conversely, such as stuck (rated 0.50 by snowNLP as neutral emotion while it should be negative) and clearly (rated as 0.33 by snowNLP as a negative emotion, which should be positive emotion). Therefore, a manual modification was undertaken using the average synonym score as the approach. As a result of the modification, the recognition rate of textual emotion tendency increased to 88.92%.

3.5 Correction of Dataset Based on DSSL Labeling Results

Continue to explore the causes of the disparity between the emotion tendency of the scale score and the emotion score based on the results of emotion distribution labeling using the frequency approach. 1009 data points out of 9,193 were determined to have a consistency value of 0, indicating inconsistent emotional tendencies. Through manual evaluation, the causes of inconsistent emotional tendencies were analyzed, and the following results were obtained, as shown in Table 2.

- The 1st reason: The use of negative words, such as "no," "won't," and "rarely," to modify the feature words results in opposite emotional tendencies. Therefore, it is required to determine if a negative word comes before or follows the feature word.
- The 2nd reason: Because the feature words in the comment, such as "continuous avatar frame" and "used for a long time," are not used for describing the CGQoE, such comment text does not need to be modified; it may be deleted directly.
- The 3rd reason: Since the feature word evaluates other situations to highlight the recent cloud game experience, such as "my network does not play other cards" and "I don't get stuck because your network is stuck," such comments do not need to be modified, so they are deleted directly.

Table 2. Reasons for the inconsistent emotional tendency

	Reasons	Cases
1	Negative words appear in the text	213
2	Inappropriate meaning of feature words in text	61
3	Feature words are only used for example, not for experience	413
4	The text mentions the disadvantages, but the score is high	311
5	The text itself is logically confusing	11
Total		1009

- The 4th reason: This is often because the user mentions the disadvantages in the comment but considers the overall cloud gaming experience superior, resulting in a higher scale score, such as "I'm stuck, stuck at 99%, yet this game is still rather pleasant; recommended." In this statement, the user cites "stuck" as the worst part of the cloud game, although the scale score remains at 5. In such cases, the scale score must be modified to reflect the emotional trend of the comment texts about CGQoE.
- The 5th reason: Because the comment itself is logically confused, such text comments are deleted immediately.

3.6 Result

After the above analysis process, a new dataset (6,692 items) was obtained after manual correction. In the similarity approach, the criterion validity of cloud gaming DSSL improved from (r = 0.87, p < .01) to (r = 0.88, p < .01), significantly correlated with users' rating scores. And in the frequency approach, the criterion validity of DSSL-based cloud gaming QoE improved from (r = 0.60, p < .01) to (r = 0.65, p < .01), significantly correlated with users' rating scores. The recognition rate of textual emotion tendency increased to 95.98%. It indicated that DSSL has good criterion validity.

To analyze the discriminative power of cloud gaming DSSL in differentiating the QoE of eight cloud gaming services, the sentiment score of each cloud gaming was calculated (Table 3). The sentiment scores grounded on DSSL of the eight cloud gaming services were consistent with that grounded on the sentiment of the whole sentence of review and rating scores. This result indicates that DSSL has comparable discriminative power with the sentiment grounded on the whole sentence of review and rating scores.

Table 3. Sentiment scores and rank of sentiment scores by different methods

	Sentiment Scores			Rank of Sentiment Scores		
	Sentence	DSSL	Rating Score	Sentence	DSSL	Rating Score
Yowa	−0.66	−0.61	−0.66	1	3	1
Tencent	−0.64	−0.64	−0.64	2	2	2
Netease	−0.57	−0.76	−0.57	3	1	3
Miigu	−0.48	−0.49	−0.47	4	5	5
Gelaiyun	−0.47	−0.47	−0.52	5	6	4
Tianyi	−.040	−0.51	−0.40	6	4	6
Caiji	−0.15	−0.24	−0.15	7	7	7
Mogu	0.44	0.18	0.44	8	8	8

4   Discussion and Future Work

This study attempts to develop a domain specific sentiment lexicon from UGC texts with abundant emotional information for evaluating the CGQoE, based on two EDL methods: the similarity approach and the frequency approach. It demonstrated the potential of transforming DSSL into a psychometric scale of QoE in cloud gaming, considering its high criterion validity and discriminative power. Compared with the single item rating score and sentiment score of a review, DSSL provides a structural distribution of the sentiment on 62 indicators. This study thus leaves room for future studies to develop a scale with 62 indicators and examine the factor structure using psychometric methods.

Acknowledgements. This paper is funded by Beijing University of Posts and Telecommunications-China Mobile Research Institute Joint Innovation Center.

References

1. Krumm, J., Davies, N., Narayanaswami, C.: User-generated content. IEEE Perv. Comput. **7**(4), 10–11 (2008). https://doi.org/10.1109/MPRV.2008.85
2. Lin, C., Hu, J., Kong, X.: A survey of models and evaluation approaches of user quality of experience (QoE). Chin. J. Comput. **35**(01), 1–15 (2012). (in Chinese)
3. Zhang, Y., Fu, J., She, D., Zhang, Y., Wang, S., Yang, J.: Text emotion distribution learning via multi-task convolutional neural network. In: Proceedings of the Twenty-Seventh International Joint Conference on Artificial Intelligence, Stockholm, Sweden, pp. 4595–4601 (2018). https://doi.org/10.24963/ijcai.2018/639
4. Bandhakavi, A., Wiratunga, N., Padmanabhan, D., Massie, S.: Lexicon based feature extraction for emotion text classification. Pattern Recogn. Lett. **93**, 133–142 (2017). https://doi.org/10.1016/j.patrec.2016.12.009
5. Qiu, Z.: Research on user experience evaluation of automotive products based on large-scale text mining. Master, Tianjin University (2018). (in Chinese). https://doi.org/10.27356/d.cnki.gtjdu.2018.000730

6. Liu, B., Chen, Y.: Parametric evaluation method of product image based on review text.Packa. Eng. **43**(12), 142–148 (2022). (in Chinese). https://doi.org/10.19554/j.cnki.1001-3563.2022. 12.016

7. Slivar, I., Skorin-Kapov, L., Suznjevic, M.: Cloud gaming QoE models for deriving video encoding adaptation strategies. In: Proceedings of the 7th International Conference on Multimedia Systems, New York, NY, USA, pp. 1–12 (2016). https://doi.org/10.1145/2910017.291 0602

8. Abar, T., Ben Letaifa, A., El Asmi, S.: Chapter five - user behavior-ensemble learning based improving QoE fairness in HTTP adaptive streaming over SDN approach. In: Hurson, A.R. (ed.) Advances in Computers, vol. 123, pp. 245–269. Elsevier (2021). https://doi.org/10.1016/ bs.adcom.2021.01.004

9. Krasula, L., Le Callet, P.: Chapter 4 - emerging science of QoE in multimedia applications: concepts, experimental guidelines, and validation of models. In: Chellappa, R., Theodoridis, S. (eds.) Academic Press Library in Signal Processing, vol. 6, pp. 163–209. Academic Press (2018). https://doi.org/10.1016/B978-0-12-811889-4.00004-X

10. Zeng, X., Hua, X., Liu, P., Zuo, J., Wang, M.: Emotion wheel and lexicon based emotion distribution label enhancement. Chin. J. Comput. **44**(06), 1080–1094 (2021). (in Chinese)

11. Teng, Z., Vo, D.-T., Zhang, Y.: Context-sensitive lexicon features for neural sentiment analysis. In: Proceedings of the 2016 Conference on Empirical Methods in Natural Language Processing, Austin, Texas, pp. 1629–1638 (2016). https://doi.org/10.18653/v1/D16-1169

Is Turn-Shift Distinguishable with Synchrony?

Jieyeon Woo[✉], Liu Yang, Catherine Pelachaud, and Catherine Achard

Institut des Systèmes Intelligents et de Robotique (CNRS -ISIR), Sorbonne
University, Paris, France
{woo,yangl,pelachaud,achard}@isir.upmc.fr

Abstract. During an interaction, interlocutors emit multimodal social
signals to communicate their intent by exchanging speaking turns
smoothly or through interruptions, and adapting to their interacting
partners which is referred to as interpersonal synchrony. We are interested in understanding whether the synchrony of multimodal signals
could help to distinguish different types of turn-shifts. We consider three
types of turn-shifts: smooth turn exchange, interruption and backchannel in this paper. We segmented each turn-shift into three phases: before,
during and after, we calculated the synchrony measures of the three
phases for multimodal signals (facial expression, head pose, and low-
level acoustic features). In this paper, a brief analysis of synchronization
during turn-shifts is presented, we also study the evolution of interpersonal synchrony before, during and after the turn-shifts. We proposed
computational models for the turn-shift classification task only using
synchrony measures. The best performance was obtained with an FNN
model using the three phases' synchrony score of all features (accuracy
of 0.75).

Keywords: Turn-shift · Synchrony · Neural network

1 Introduction

During an interaction, people communicate information via verbal and non-
verbal channels. Verbal communication transfers information through language
containing explicit content. Nonverbal behavior conveys through "body language" including gestures, facial expressions, body movement, and gaze [8].
Intra-synergies are formed within one's own behavior [14].

While the intent is communicated in a direct manner, by emitting multimodal
social signals, people also coordinate and adapt their behavior to that of their
interlocutors [14] in a continuous manner. Being in sync enables a fluid exchange
of information and increases the engagement level [21]. This coordination of

Supported by ANR-JST-CREST TAPAS (ANR-19-JSTS-0001) and IA ANR-DFG-JST
Panorama (ANR-20-IADJ-0008) projects.

H. Degen and S. Ntoa (Eds.): HCII 2023, LNAI 14051, pp. 419–432, 2023.
https://doi.org/10.1007/978-3-031-35894-4_32

behaviors, which may occur unintentionally [40], is also referred to as synchrony and we define it as in [19].

In conversations, speaking turns are exchanged between the interlocutors which is done smoothly or through interruptions. We call this change of turns as turn-shift in this paper. Beattie [3] and Schegloff and Sacks [39] classified turn-shift into three main categories based on simultaneous speech and willingness to yield the floor: smooth switch, interruption, and overlap. Overlap happens at the end of a speaking turn when the listener starts speaking and over-anticipating the end of the current speaker's turn [37]. On the other hand, interruption grabs the floor against the speaker's will when she/he is not finished. Here we also consider the backchannels which are produced by the listener without the intent to grab the speaking turn. Similar to interruption, backchannels always happen during a speaking floor. They may be mistakenly identified as an interruption when conducting real-time analysis of interlocutors' multimodal signals.

We are interested in understanding whether the synchrony of multimodal signals could help to distinguish different turn-shift types along with backchannel via analysis. A predictor (computational model) is built for the classification task using synchrony measures. We focus on dyadic interactions. To our knowledge, we are the first to build a computational model to classify turn-shift types using only synchrony measures.

In this paper, overlap and smooth switch are merged as smooth turn exchange since they are at the end of a turn. Thus, we analyze synchrony measures for the following three turn-shift types: smooth turn exchange, backchannel and interruption.

Related works of turn-shift and synchrony will be introduced in Sect. 2. In Sect. 3, the analyzed corpus and the studied features will be explained. The analysis will be shared in Sect. 4 and our turn-shift type predictors and their results will be presented in Sect. 5. The paper will be concluded with a brief discussion of the possible future applications and extensions of our work.

2 Related Works

Turn-shift during interaction has been an interesting subject of research for a long time. Emanuel A. Schegloff [38] firstly defined conversation sequencing rules. During the course of a conversation, interlocutors dynamically collaborate with each other by yielding and taking the speaking turns based on rules in order to keep the flow of information exchange and maintain the communication [9,15]. The idea of conversation analysis was then proposed by Harvey Sacks [37] which describes its most basic structure as turn-taking.

Various works analyzed turn-taking, to get a better understanding of the coordination taking place during turn-shifts by looking into multimodal features, such as eye-gaze [17,26], respiration [25,27], and head-direction [42]. Linguistic features such as syntactic structure, turn-ending markers, and language model were also investigated [28,29,32]. They highlighted the importance of prosodic feature variation (e.g. fundamental frequency $F0$ and intensity) during turn-shifts [22,30,43]. Interruptions were observed to be often combined with higher voice energy [23, 24, 41]. These differences in the three turn-shift types might lead to an increased or decreased interpersonal synchrony.

To study the interpersonal synchrony of whether the partners are in sync or not, a multitude of methods were introduced.

Pioneer works consists of manual assessments that rely on trained observers. The synchrony perception was done by directly observing the data on a local time scale using behavior coding methods [12, 16]. For larger time scales, judgment methods were employed [6, 12]. The rating was done using a Likert scale [6, 12].

Manual annotation is a laborious and time-consuming task. This tedious workload was relieved by the appearance of automatic measures. The measures capture relevant signals to detect synchrony. One of the most commonly used measures for interpersonal synchrony is the correlation [11, 18, 35] that calculates the synchrony during a same period. Interlocutors' social signals constantly react to those of the other which leads to behavior coordination. When conversing, the perception of the other interacting partner's behavior is delayed by a certain time period (2 to 4 s [13, 31]). Several works consider this time delay by employing the time-lagged cross-correlation [1, 4, 7]. As such behavior signals are shifted in time, but they can also vary in length. Dynamic Time Warping (DTW) [33], which measures the similarity between two temporal sequences while being invariant to speed and length, can address such problems. It is widely used to find common patterns [5]. Some other studies perform spectral analysis to capture the synchrony between signals. The evolution of the relative phase is measured to obtain information related to synchrony stability [34, 36].

For our study, we choose to employ frequently used synchrony measures of correlation (Pearson correlation coefficient), time-lagged cross-correlation, and DTW to study the synchrony of a turn-shift. As explained above, the three measures differ in the way how they measure synchrony. Correlation expresses the linear relation of signals within the same time window. Time-lagged cross-correlation takes into account the time swift between the signals and DTW maps the signals that are shifted in time and differ in length. This leads us to use all three of them.

Prior works analyzed the synchrony of interlocutors' behavior during the entire course of the interaction. They do not specifically look into them during the turn-shift moments.

We want to check if there is a visible link between synchrony and turn-shift which allows synchrony measures to serve as a potential feature for the characterization of turn-shift types. We also intend to verify the usefulness of synchrony measures in classifying the turn-shift types via computational models.

3   Corpus

The NoXi database [10], which contains screen-mediated face-to-face dyadic interactions, was used for this study. The database is made up of 3 parts depending on the recording location (France, Germany, and UK). For our study, we choose to use the French part that contains 21 dyadic interactions performed by 28 participants with a total duration of 7h22.

All turn-shift moments (1403 smooth turn exchanges, 1651 backchannels, and 929 interruptions) were manually annotated following Yang's annotation schema [44].

The turn-shift and backchannel moments were identified on the onset point of the listener's voice activity which we note as t_0. We segmented each moment into three phases:

- **Before:** $t_0 - 6s \sim t_0 - 2s$;
- **During:** $t_0 - 2s \sim t_0 + 2s$;
- **After:** $t_0 + 2s \sim t_0 + 6s$.

We define the three phases of turn-shift (before, during, and after) to refine the detection of different shifts. For each phase, multimodal features were extracted, and the synchrony scores between partners were calculated separately.

For our study, the features employed are the following:

- **Facial features:** AU1, AU2, AU4, AU12, and AU15;
- **Head features:** Head translation and rotation;
- **Acoustic features:** F0 and loudness.

Facial features were obtained using OpenFace [2] and acoustic features were extracted via openSMILE [20].

As the initial head position of the interlocutor may create a bias, instead of using the absolute position we applied the following equation for the head translation, called head motion activity:

$$v_{Head}(i) = \sqrt{(x_i - x_{i-1})^2 + (y_i - y_{i-1})^2 + (z_i - z_{i-1})^2} \qquad (1)$$

where x_i, y_i and z_i are the coordinates of the head position in the image at timestep i.

And for head rotation, we also calculate the head rotation activity:

$$r_{Head}(i) = |x_i - x_{i-1}| + |y_i - y_{i-1}| + |z_i - z_{i-1}| \qquad (2)$$

where x_i, y_i and z_i are the head angles according to the 3 axes at timestep i.

A z-score normalization was applied to all features for them to be invariant to the quantity of behaviors of interlocutors.

4   Analysis

To understand the relationship between synchrony and turn-shift types, we analyzed the presented multimodal signals. The significance of the turn-shift type difference was checked via a two-tailed t-test.

We start our analysis by looking at the interpersonal synchrony scores (correlation, time-lagged cross-correlation, and DTW) during the turn-shift (*during* phase of $t_0 - 2s \sim t_0 + 2s$) for all features.

Significant differences can be seen for several signals of interruption (Int), smooth turn exchange (ST), and backchannel (BC) with t-test ($p < 0.01$) in

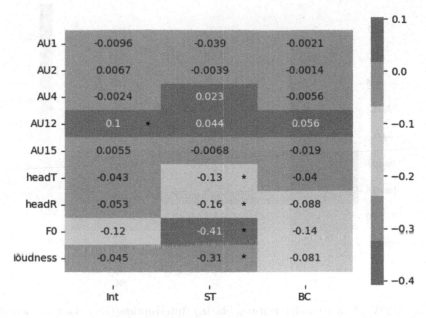

Fig. 1. Correlation of multimodal features *during* Interruption(Int), Backchannel(BC), Smooth turn exchange(ST) (*: $p < 0.01$)

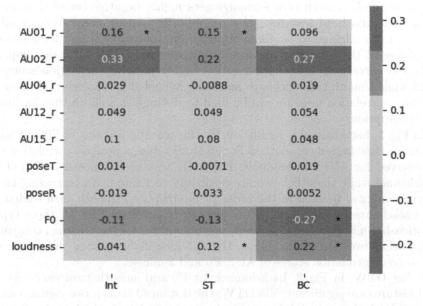

Fig. 2. Time-lagged cross-correlation of multimodal features *during* Interruption(Int), Backchannel(BC), Smooth turn exchange(ST) (*: $p < 0.01$)

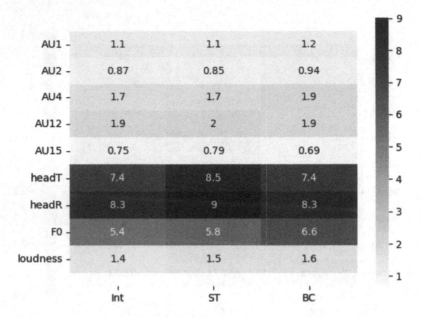

Fig. 3. DTW of multimodal features *during* Interruption(Int), Backchannel(BC), Smooth turn exchange(ST)

Figs. 1, 2, and 3. To detail, with the synchrony score obtained through correlation, in Fig. 1, smooth turn exchange gets higher negative correlation scores for acoustic and head features (showing opposite trends), these features allow smooth turn exchange to be differentiated from interruption and backchannel. The values of the other two are mostly uncorrelated (close to 0) or comparatively less correlated. Interruption gets a higher positive correlation score for AU12 while smooth turn exchange and backchannel shows no relation (close to 0). Thus, correlation measure can be used to distinguish smooth turn exchange and interruption.

In Fig. 2, backchannel is significant for the acoustic features of F0 and loudness using time-lagged correlation. For all three types, a positive correlation can be observed for AU1 and loudness. For AU1, no correlation can be found for backchannel while the other two are positively correlated. An increasing trend of synchrony can be seen in the order of interruption, smooth turn exchange, and backchannel for loudness. F0 is negatively correlated for all three types. A noticeably higher correlation score can be noticed for backchannel compared to the other two. Backchannels can thus be identifiable among the others via time-lagged correlation scores of AU1, F0 and loudness.

Using DTW, in Fig. 3, backchannel for F0 and smooth turn exchange for head features are significant. Via DTW, the distance between two signals can be measured, which can be interpreted to be more synchronized when the distance gets smaller. Here we can note a lower sync during smooth turn exchange via the head translation and rotation compared to interruption and backchannel. In the same manner, a lower sync can be seen for backchannel with F0 compared to the other two. Therefore, DTW can be used to distinguish smooth turn exchange and backchannel.

We can thus identify the three types of smooth turn exchange, interruption, and backchannel using the synchrony measures at the *during* phase of $t_0 - 2s \sim t_0 + 2s$.

The usefulness of synchrony scores has been proved for the task of identifying turn-shift types. However, a clearer way of distinguishing them would be more desirable. To do so, we observe the variation of synchrony scores *before*, *during*, and *after* the turn-shifts.

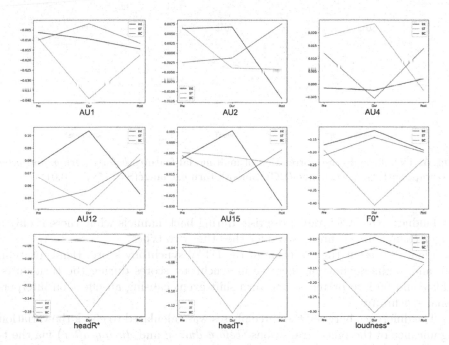

Fig. 4. Correlation of multimodal features *before*, *during*, and *after* Interruption(Int), Backchannel(BC), Smooth turn exchange(ST) (*: $p < 0.01$)

By evaluating the evolution of correlation measures *before*, *during*, and *after* turn-shifts, in Fig. 4, for smooth turn exchange we can find a remarkable sudden increase in negative correlation in the features of F0, loudness, head rotation and translation. For these acoustic and head features, a stable trend or only a slight change in synchrony can be observed for backchannel and interruption.

In the same respect, in Fig. 5 synchrony evolution trends of acoustic features obtained via time-lagged cross-correlation render significant information. The trends of backchannels are easily distinguishable compared to interruption and smooth turn exchange. An increase in inverse correlation can be seen for F0, and

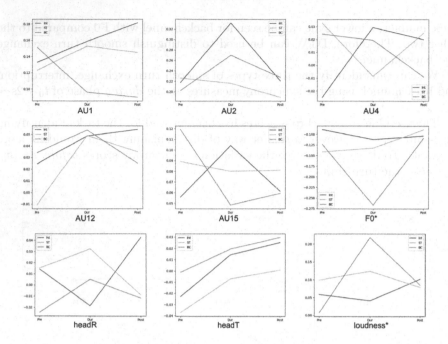

Fig. 5. Time-lagged cross-correlation of multimodal features *before*, *during*, and *after* Interruption(Int), Backchannel(BC), Smooth turn exchange(ST) (*: $p < 0.01$)

for loudness, the synchrony score rises during backchannels while there is only a minor change in synchrony score for the other two types.

Figure 6 present the evolution of the DTW synchrony score. Head rotation, F0, and loudness show an increase in synchrony scores during the turn-shifts. This could be interpreted as the turn-shift event causing an effect on interpersonal synchrony.

The difference between the three phases was calculated to check the variation significance of the phase transitions (*before-during* and *during-after*) via the t-test ($p < 0.01$).

The evolution of synchrony scores of the three phases of *before*, *during*, and *after* provided additional information on distinguishing turn-shift types. As seen above, each turn-shift type has different synchrony evolution trends which have been proven to enable the identification of smooth turn exchange, interruption, and backchannel.

5   Turn-shift Classification Models

With the analysis of the relationship between synchrony and turn-shift types, we want to employ synchrony measures in identifying the different turn-shift types to verify their usefulness. For this, we built computational models only using the

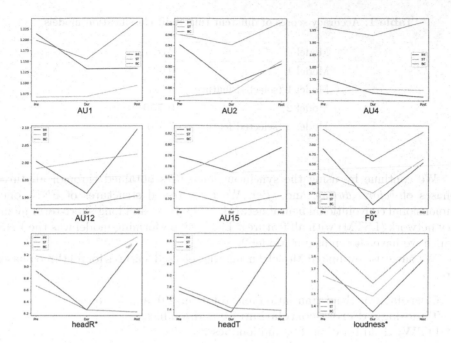

Fig. 6. DTW of multimodal features *before, during,* and *after* Interruption(Int), Backchannel(BC), Smooth turn exchange(ST) (*: $p < 0.01$)

synchrony measures of the three segmented phases in the turn-shift classification task.

We approach this task considering two aspects:

- choice of turn-shift phase(s)
- choice of features

As our Model 1, we start by looking into the synchrony measures of all features *during* turn-shifts. We use a feedforward neural network (FNN) to classify the turn-shift types.

In Sect. 4, we have identified several features by analysis which were significant in differentiating the turn-shift types. We selected these features to check if the same performance could be obtained only by using these features. The selected features for the *during* phase are:

- **Correlation:** AU12 and head translation and rotation;
- **Time-lagged cross-correlation:** AU1, F0, and loudness;
- **DTW:** Head translation and rotation, and F0.

Via Model 1, an accuracy of 0.627, in Table 1, is obtained. With this, we can see that the synchrony measure can be used to identify turn-shift types. Also, the same accuracy of 0.627 is obtained using only the selected features. This supports our analysis that these features indeed are significant in identifying turn-shift types.

Table 1. Accuracy scores of different turn-shift classification models.

Model	Accuracy
Model 1	0.627
Model 1 (selected features)	0.627
Model 2	**0.750**
Model 2 (selected features)	0.650

We continue by using the synchrony measures obtained through all three phases of *before*, *during*, and *after*. We have tested structures of FNN, one-dimensional convolutional neural network (1D CNN), and long short-term memory network (LSTM) with all features. The best-performing model was the FNN which we have chosen as our Model 2.

We have also evaluated Model 2 using the selected features for all three phases are:

- **Correlation:** Head translation and rotation, F0, and loudness;
- **Time-lagged cross-correlation:** F0 and loudness;
- **DTW:** Head rotation, F0, and loudness.

An accuracy score of 0.750 is obtained for Model 2, in Table 1. However, the accuracy decreases to 0.636 when using only the selected features. This can be explained by the fact that the cross-modality information was missed in the analysis, as it is implicit and thus hard to visually capture them.

Model 2 renders a promising accuracy, however, its application is restricted as the future is required. To enable real-time turn-shift identification, we assess Model 2 by varying the moment time range. We studied the 3 time ranges of: $t_0 - 6s \sim t_0 + 2s$, $t_0 - 6s \sim t_0$, and $t_0 - 6s \sim t_0 - 2s$.

Table 2. Accuracy scores of model 2 using all features with different time ranges.

Moment time range	Accuracy
$t_0 - 6s \sim t_0 + 2s$	**0.727**
$t_0 - 6s \sim t_0$	0.478
$t_0 - 6s \sim t_0 - 2s$	0.530

We can remark that a similar accuracy score of 0.727 can be obtained using the moment time range of $t_0 - 6s \sim t_0 + 2s$, in Table 2. This implies that the *after* phase ($t_0 + 2s \sim t_0 + 6s$) does not play a critical role in identifying the turn-shift types, which might be too far from the turn-shift moment to provide useful information. For the identification to work in real-time, the moment time range must be restricted to before the turn-shift moment of t_0. However, the results of $t_0 - 6s \sim t_0$ and $t_0 - 6s \sim t_0 - 2s$ are not acceptable for real-time detection, this indicates that the period just after the turn-shift may carry the most important information to identify the turn-shift type.

Table 3. Accuracy scores of Model 2 using selected features with different time ranges.

Moment time range	Accuracy
$t_0 - 6s \sim t_0 + 2s$	**0.682**
$t_0 - 6s \sim t_0$	0.397
$t_0 - 6s \sim t_0 - 2s$	0.434

As seen above for Model 2, in Table 1, the same result of accuracy score falling (0.682, 0.397, and 0.434 respectively) when using the selected features can be observed in Table 3.

Thus, the best is to use Model 2 with all features with the turn-shift moment time range of $t_0 - 6s \sim t_0 + 2$.

6   Conclusion and Discussion

Several works have been done studying turn-shift types of smooth turn exchange and interruption, backchannels by analyzing multimodal signals. However, the research on turn-shift types and synchrony is still to be done.

Through the analysis of multimodal signals (visual and acoustic features), we investigated the synchrony scores for three phases before, during, and after turn-shift. We were able to find a link between synchrony scores and turn-shift types and backchannel. This relationship was used to build computational models to automatically classify the turn-shift types. The modeling of all features of all three phases showed the most promising result which proved the usefulness of synchrony measures in turn-shift identification task. We also looked into whether the classification could be done in real-time by varying the moment time range. A lower accuracy was obtained compared to that using future information, although it is better than random chance and is a compromise to be considered.

Our turn-shift type identification model can be applied to various purposes. Manual annotation of turn-shifts is a lot of work, this is the problem we need to face every time a new corpus is generated, we are looking forward to integrating this model into automatic annotation systems that can help to detect and annotate different turn-shifts. The identified turn-shifts could also be used to analyze the personality or characteristic of people. We studied the synchrony of the same features of the interlocutors. We would also include cross-modality synchrony measures in the future to improve the performance of our classification model.

References

1. Ashenfelter, K.T., Boker, S.M., Waddell, J.R., Vitanov, N.: Spatiotemporal symmetry and multifractal structure of head movements during dyadic conversation. J. Exp. Psychol. Hum. Percept. Perform. **35**(4), 1072 (2009)
2. Baltrušaitis, T., Robinson, P., Morency, L.P.: Openface: an open source facial behavior analysis toolkit. In: 2016 IEEE Winter Conference on Applications of Computer Vision (WACV), pp. 1–10. IEEE (2016)
3. Beattie, G.W.: Interruption in conversational interaction, and its relation to the sex and status of the interactants (1981)
4. Beňuš, Š, Gravano, A., Hirschberg, J.: Pragmatic aspects of temporal accommodation in turn-taking. J. Pragmat. **43**(12), 3001–3027 (2011)
5. Berndt, D.J., Clifford, J.: Using dynamic time warping to find patterns in time series. In: KDD workshop. vol. 10, pp. 359–370. Seattle, WA, USA: (1994)
6. Bernieri, F.J., Reznick, J.S., Rosenthal, R.: Synchrony, pseudosynchrony, and dissynchrony: measuring the entrainment process in mother-infant interactions. J. Pers. Soc. Psychol. **54**(2), 243 (1988)
7. Boker, S.M., Rotondo, J.L., Xu, M., King, K.: Windowed cross-correlation and peak picking for the analysis of variability in the association between behavioral time series. Psychol. Methods **7**(3), 338 (2002)
8. Burgoon, J.K., Guerrero, L.K., Manusov, V.: Nonverbal signals. The SAGE Handbook of Interpersonal Communication, pp. 239–280 (2011)
9. Burgoon, J.K., Stern, L.A., Dillman, L.: Interpersonal adaptation: Dyadic interaction patterns. Cambridge University Press (1995)
10. Cafaro, A., et al.: The noxi database: multimodal recordings of mediated novice-expert interactions, pp. 350–359 (11 2017)
11. Campbell, N.: Multimodal processing of discourse information; the effect of synchrony. In: 2008 Second International Symposium on Universal Communication, pp. 12–15. IEEE (2008)
12. Cappella, J.N.: Behavioral and judged coordination in adult informal social interactions: Vocal and kinesic indicators. J. Pers. Soc. Psychol. **72**(1), 119 (1997)
13. Chartrand, T.L., Bargh, J.A.: The chameleon effect: the perception-behavior link and social interaction. J. Pers. Soc. Psychol. **76**(6), 893 (1999)
14. Condon, W.S., Ogston, W.D.: Sound film analysis of normal and pathological behavior patterns. J. Nervous Mental Disease (1966)
15. Condon, W.S., Ogston, W.D.: A segmentation of behavior. J. Psychiatr. Res. **5**(3), 221–235 (1967)
16. Condon, W.S., Sander, L.W.: Neonate movement is synchronized with adult speech: interactional participation and language acquisition. Science **183**(4120), 99–101 (1974)
17. De Kok, I., Heylen, D.: Multimodal end-of-turn prediction in multi-party meetings. In: Proceedings of the 2009 International Conference On Multimodal Interfaces, pp. 91–98 (2009)
18. Delaherche, E., Chetouani, M.: Multimodal coordination: exploring relevant features and measures. In: Proceedings of the 2nd International Workshop On Social Signal Processing, pp. 47–52 (2010)
19. Delaherche, E., Chetouani, M., Mahdhaoui, A., Saint-Georges, C., Viaux, S., Cohen, D.: Interpersonal synchrony: a survey of evaluation methods across disciplines. IEEE Trans. Affect. Comput. **3**(3), 349–365 (2012)

20. Eyben, F., Wöllmer, M., Schuller, B.: Opensmile: the munich versatile and fast open-source audio feature extractor. In: Proceedings of the 18th ACM International Conference on Multimedia, pp. 1459–1462 (2010)

21. Fong, T., Nourbakhsh, I., Dautenhahn, K.: A survey of socially interactive robots. Robot. Auton. Syst. **42**(3–4), 143–166 (2003)

22. French, P., Local, J.: Turn-competitive incomings. J. Pragmat. **7**(1), 17–38 (1983)

23. Gravano, A., Hirschberg, J.: A corpus-based study of interruptions in spoken dialogue. In: Thirteenth Annual Conference of the International Speech Communication Association (2012)

24. Hammarberg, B., Fritzell, B., Gaufin, J., Sundberg, J., Wedin, L.: Perceptual and acoustic correlates of abnormal voice qualities. Acta Otolaryngol. **90**(1–6), 441–451 (1980)

25. Heldner, M., Edlund, J.: Pauses, gaps and overlaps in conversations. J. Phon. **38**(4), 555–568 (2010)

26. Ishii, R., Otsuka, K., Kumano, S., Matsuda, M., Yamato, J.: Predicting next speaker and timing from gaze transition patterns in multi-party meetings. In: Proceedings of the 15th ACM on International conference on multimodal interaction, pp. 79–86 (2013)

27. Ishii, R., Otsuka, K., Kumano, S., Yamato, J.: Using respiration to predict who will speak next and when in multiparty meetings. ACM Trans. Interact. Intell. Syst. (TiiS) **6**(2), 1–20 (2016)

28. Ishii, R., Ren, X., Muszynski, M., Morency, L.P.: Multimodal and multitask approach to listener's backchannel prediction: Can prediction of turn-changing and turn-management willingness improve backchannel modeling? In: Proceedings of the 21st ACM International Conference on Intelligent Virtual Agents, pp. 131–138 (2021)

29. Ishimoto, Y., Teraoka, T., Enomoto, M.: End-of-utterance prediction by prosodic features and phrase-dependency structure in spontaneous japanese speech. In: Interspeech, pp. 1681–1685 (2017)

30. Kurtić, E., Brown, G.J., Wells, B.: Resources for turn competition in overlapping talk. Speech Commun. **55**(5), 721–743 (2013)

31. Leander, N.P., Chartrand, T.L., Bargh, J.A.: You give me the chills: embodied reactions to inappropriate amounts of behavioral mimicry. Psychol. Sci. **23**(7), 772–779 (2012)

32. Maier, A., Hough, J., Schlangen, D., et al.: Towards deep end-of-turn prediction for situated spoken dialogue systems (2017)

33. Müller, M.: Dynamic time warping. Information retrieval for music and motion pp. 69–84 (2007)

34. Oullier, O., De Guzman, G.C., Jantzen, K.J., Lagarde, J., Scott Kelso, J.: Social coordination dynamics: measuring human bonding. Soc. Neurosci. **3**(2), 178–192 (2008)

35. Reidsma, D., Nijholt, A., Tschacher, W., Ramseyer, F.: Measuring multimodal synchrony for human-computer interaction. In: 2010 International Conference On Cyberworlds, pp. 67–71. IEEE (2010)

36. Richardson, M.J., Marsh, K.L., Isenhower, R.W., Goodman, J.R., Schmidt, R.C.: Rocking together: dynamics of intentional and unintentional interpersonal coordination. Hum. Mov. Sci. **26**(6), 867–891 (2007)

37. Sacks, H., Schegloff, E.A., Jefferson, G.: A simplest systematics for the organization of turn taking for conversation. In: Studies in the Organization Of Conversational Interaction, pp. 7–55. Elsevier (1978)

38. Schegloff, E.A.: Sequencing in conversational openings 1. Am. Anthropol. **70**(6), 1075–1095 (1968)
39. Schegloff, E.A., Sacks, H.: Opening up closings (1973)
40. Schmidt, R.C., Richardson, M.J.: Dynamics of interpersonal coordination. In: Coordination: Neural, behavioral and social dynamics, pp. 281–308. Springer (2008). https://doi.org/10.1007/978-3-540-74479-5_14
41. Shriberg, E., Stolcke, A., Baron, D.: Observations on overlap: Findings and implications for automatic processing of multi-party conversation. In: Seventh European Conference on Speech Communication and Technology (2001)
42. Skantze, G., Johansson, M., Beskow, J.: Exploring turn-taking cues in multi-party human-robot discussions about objects. In: Proceedings of the 2015 ACM on International Conference On Multimodal Interaction, pp. 67–74 (2015)
43. Truong, K.P.: Classification of cooperative and competitive overlaps in speech using cues from the context, overlapper, and overlappee. In: Interspeech, pp. 1404–1408 (2013)
44. Yang, L., Achard, C., Pelachaud, C.: Annotating interruption in dyadic human interaction. In: Proceedings of the Thirteenth Language Resources and Evaluation Conference, pp. 2292–2297 (2022)

Innovations in AI-Enabled Systems

I-Brow: Hierarchical and Multimodal Transformer Model for Eyebrows Animation Synthesis

Mireille Fares[1,2,4]([✉]), Catherine Pelachaud[1,3,4], and Nicolas Obin[2,4]

[1] ISIR, Paris, France
[2] IRCAM-STMS, Paris, France
[3] CNRS, Paris, France
[4] Sorbonne University, Paris, France
fares@isir.upmc.fr

Abstract. The human face is a key channel of communication in human-human interaction. When communicating, humans spontaneously and continuously display various facial gestures, which convey a large panel of information to the interlocutors. Likewise, appropriate and coherent co-speech facial gestures are essential to render human-like and smooth interactions with social agents. We propose "I-Brow", a model that produces expressive and natural upper facial gestures based on two modalities: text semantics and speech prosody. Our deep learning model is based on Transformers and convolutions. It has a hierarchical two-level encoding property: its input features are encoded, at both word and utterance levels, where an utterance corresponds to an Inter-Pausal Unit (IPU). We conduct subjective and objective evaluations to validate our approach.

Keywords: Eyebrows synthesis · Multimodality · Transformers

1 Introduction

Nonverbal communication is the first form of communication in the lifespan of humans [20]. Before humans evolved their ability to speak and use language, they were able to communicate using their visual body gestures - their non-verbal channels of communication [20]. During speech, a variety of verbal, emotional, and conversational cues are displayed on the speaker's face. Facial gestures are consciously and unconsciously used to adjust speech, accentuate words, or mark speech pauses. [42]. Speakers render their communication expressive by blinking, moving their eyebrows and eyelids, frowning, and nose wrinkling [44].

This work was performed within the Labex SMART (ANR-11-LABX-65) supported by French state funds managed by the ANR within the Investissements d'Avenir programme under reference ANR-11-IDEX-0004-02.

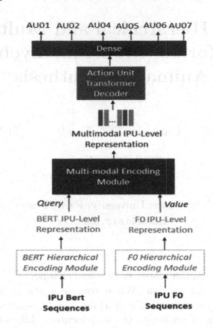

Fig. 1. "I-Brow" overall architecture. The network takes as input sequences of fundamental frequencies that correspond to one Inter-Pausal Unit (IPU) - sequence of continuous stretch of speech in one speaker's channel, delimited by a silence of more than 200ms -, and the corresponding text bert embeddings. With its hierarchical property, it encodes the input features at both word-level, and IPU-level, then generates a multimodal IPU-level representation of the input features. The network then learns to map the resulting representation to upper-facial - eyebrows - gestures.

During speech, Fundamental Frequency (F0) variations are highly correlated with eyebrow motion [5], which are the most relevant and common facial gestures employed during interactions [6]. Eyebrows can be utilized as a back-channel to signal the listener's level of understanding, agreement, or indicate listener's attitude towards what the speaker is saying [5]. Appropriate, expressive and human-like co-speech facial gestures are therefore an essential part of communication. To enable a smooth and engaging interaction with virtual agents, the agents' verbal behavior must be produced in conjunction with appropriate non-verbal communication [30]. In this paper we present "I-Brow" (Fig. 1), a novel approach for upper facial gestures synthesis for Embodied Conversational Agents (ECA). Our model predicts expressive eyebrows and eyelids movements based on audio and text data. Upper facial movements are synthesized based on a hierarchically encoding: information at both, word-level and utterance-level - specifically Inter-Pausal Unit level - are encoded altogether. An Inter-Pausal Unit (IPU) is a continuous stretch of speech in one speaker's channel, delimited by a silence of more than 200ms, with a sequence of words that corresponds to what the speaker is pronouncing. The upper-facial gestures are predicted frame by frame. In contrast to previous works related to facial synthesis

[4,8,9,12,13,17–19,22,26,29,31,37,40,41,43], our work makes use of two modalities to allow for semantic-aware speech-driven continuous upper facial movements. Our contributions can be listed as follows: (1) acoustic and semantic features are mapped into continuous upper-facial gestures per inter-pausal unit, (2) word-level and IPU-level inputs features are encoded hierarchically, to extract important information from both word-level and IPU-level data.

2 Background and Related Work

The development of gesture synthesizing systems for virtual agents has received a lot of attention during the past years.

2.1 Gesture Generation Models

Hofer et al. [17] present a speech driven head motion sequence prediction system based on Hidden Markov Models. Haag et al. [16] propose a technique for speech driven head motion synthesis that uses deep neural networks with stacked bottleneck features, along with an LSTM network. Lu et al. [23] present an approach that predicts head motion based on speech waveforms. Ahuja et al. [1] study the links between spoken language and co-speech gestures. They propose "Adversarial Importance Sampled Learning" (AISLe) which combines adversarial learning with importance sampling. Sadoughi et al. [29] propose a speech-driven system to predict hand and head motion, using a Dynamic Bayesian Network. Their model is constrained by contextual information and these constraints condition the state configuration between speech and gestures. However, their model predicts movements based on only speech. Ferstl et al. [12] use generative adversarial training to map speech to 3D gesture motion. Moreover, Kucherenko et al. [21] propose a speech and text driven gesture generation that maps speech acoustic and semantic gestures into continuous 3D gestures. Yoon et al. [39] present an automatic gesture generation model that uses the multimodal context of speech text, audio, and speaker identity to reliably generate gestures. [14] propose an approach driven by speech to produce body gestures, however their approach uses models trained on single speakers.

2.2 Facial Gestures Synthesis Models

Cao et al. [4] produce expressive facial movement synchronized with the acoustic features of input utterances. Taylor et al. [33] synthesize lower facial movements based on a deep learning approach that employs a sliding window predictor that learns nonlinear mappings from phonemes to mouth motion. Zoric et al. [43] propose a facial gesture generation system for ECAs. Lip motion is generated based on input speech signal. In their work, virtual speakers can read given input text and transform it into the appropriate speech and facial movements. Mariooryad et al. [24] model a facial animation framework based on speech to generate head and eyebrows motion using Dynamic Bayesian Networks.

Ding et al. [8] propose an animation approach that uses HMM: their statistical model maps speech prosody with facial gestures. Song et al. [31] suggest an audio-driven approach based on conditional recurrent generation network, which merges image and audio features into a recurring unit and produce facial animation by time-dependent coupling. Vougioukas et al. [36] generate videos of talking heads based on a person's image, and audio data. They also produce lip movements, that are synchronized with speech, as well as facial expressions like blinks and eyebrow motion. Their approach is based on GAN with three discriminators. Their goal is to generate realistic expressions synchronised with speech. Suwajanakorn et al. [32] propose an approach based on Long Short-Term Memory (LSTM) for synthesizing a video of Obama's speech, they map original audio features to mouth shapes. The model could not perform well in generalizing other identities despite its good accuracy in lip synchronization. Tae-Hyun et al. [26] propose a speech-driven model trained through a large number of videos. Zhou et al. [41] synthesize random facial animation models by breaking the entanglement between audio and video. Chung et al. [18] present a speech-driven model, which integrates an auto-encoder to learn the correspondence between audio features and video data. Generated animation of their talking faces lack continuity. Duarte et al. propose an audio-driven method to synthesize facial videos [9], but the results are ambiguous. Garrido et al. [13] also propose a speech-driven approach that synthesize the speaker's face by moving the mouth shape of the speaker in the dubbing video to the target video. Karras et al. [19] propose a speech-driven real-time 3D facial animation model with low latency through the audio input. [7] also propose a novel approach for synthesizing speech-driven 3D facial animation.

The aforementioned works have focused on producing nonverbal behaviors (facial expression, head movement, gestures in particular) driven namely by speech. However, they have not considered both speech and text semantics for the production of the gestures. Only the work of Kucherenko et al. [21] is driven by speech and text, however they do not synthesize facial gestures.

3   Multimodal Data Features

We consider multiple modalities in our model. The following features were selected to be used for each modality:

Action Units Features - Upper-facial gestures are represented by Action Units (AUs) that are predefined in the Facial Action Coding Systems (FACS) [10]. AUs that represent eyebrows and eyelids movements are AU1 (inner raise eyebrow), AU2 (outer raise eyebrow), AU4 (frown), AU5 (upper lid raiser), AU6 (cheek raiser), and AU7 (lid tightener). Action units are continuous values of intensities ranging from 0 (lowest) to 5 (highest). Continuous AU intensities were quantized to generate a finite range of discrete values. This step was applied to reduce the model size and energy consumption, as recommended by [15].

Audio Features - The audio feature that we are considering in our model is the prosodic feature: the Fundamental Frequency F0. F0 values are continuous values of frequency ranging from 85 180 Hz for the vocal speech of an adult male speakers. The values of an adult female speakers range from 165 255 Hz [3,34]. F0 sequences were similarly quantized as AUs, to generate a finite range of discrete values. **Text features** -Text is a sequence of word. The dataset we have used included BERT embeddings for each word.

4 Training and Testing Dataset

TED (Technology, Entertainment, Design) conferences are conferences where speakers share their main research and expertise with their audience. Each speaker has a unique communicative style, a specific presentation topic, with a main goal to captivate his or her audience. We trained and tested our model on TED dataset [11], containing preprocessed AUs, F0s, and BERT embeddings of shots of 200 TED videos. These shots were filtered such as the speakers' face and head are visible and close to the camera. The average length if these videos is 13 min (minimum length is 1 min, and maximum length is 47 mins). The frame rate is 24 FPS, and the total number of IPUs is 266,000. We shuffled all the IPUs, then split them into: training set (80%), validation set (10%) and test set (10%).

The optimization algorithm that was used for training the model is Adam Optimizer with custom scheduling. The loss function used is the Sparse Categorical Crossentropy loss. Our test set is composed of *Speaker Dependent (SD)* data set, as well as *Speaker Independent (SI)* data set. The *Speaker Dependent (SD)* - the test set we have defined previously. It aims to evaluate to what degree the model can generalize on new IPUs said by the multiple speakers the model has seen during training. On the other hand, *Speaker Independent (SI)* include IPUs said by unseen speakers. It aims to evaluate the degree to which gestures predictions can generalize on unseen speakers.

5 "I-Brow" Model for Speech-driven Upper Facial Gesture Generation

This section describes our proposed approach for generating upper-facial gestures from two modalities: speech acoustics and semantics. We have applied a hierarchical encoding of the input features, such that the encoding encompasses both word-level encoding as well as Inter-Pausal Unit level encoding. The overall architecture of "I-Brow" is depicted in Fig. 1.

To build an optimized IPU-level architecture, we started by implementing an architecture that includes only word-level features. Then, we used the word-level model as a baseline to implement our IPU-level architecture. To decide on the number of tokens to consider in IPUs, we generated the distribution of words in our dataset. We observed that approximately 29, 000 IPUs contain 10 tokens which include words and pauses as well. Thus, we decided to render the size of all IPUs of our training, validation and test sets equal to 10 words. Larger IPUs were truncated, the smaller ones were padded.

The following sections describe the word-level architecture, as well as the different components of the IPU-level architecture.

5.1 Word Level Model Architecture

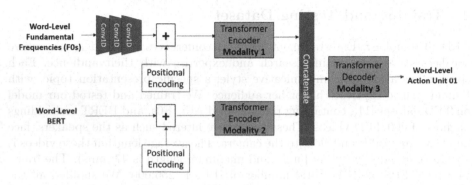

Fig. 2. word-level Network Architecture

As depicted in Fig. 2, the word-level architecture takes as input a sequence of Fundamental Frequencies (F0s) that corresponds to a word unit **W**, as well as the corresponding BERT embedding of the same **W**. The sequences of F0s are first passed through three one dimensional convolutional layers, to produce a representation of F0 contours. These layers include 64 filters, with a kernel size equal to 3. Positional encoding is then applied on the resulting vector, which is then given as input to a Transformer encoder. The Transformer Encoder has 4 encoding layers, with 4 attention heads. It has the same architecture as the one that was first proposed in [35].

On the other hand, positional encoding is applied on BERT embeddings, and the result is fed to another Transformer Encoder that has the same parameters as the previously described one. The outputs of both Transformer Encoders are concatenated, and then fed to a Transformer Decoder, which produces the corresponding word-level action units.

The Transformer Decoder has 4 decoding layers, with 4 attention heads, and has the same architecture as the one in [35]. For simplicity, Fig. 2 only illustrates the whole word-level architecture that predicts one Action Unit. All hyper-parameters of this architecture were chosen empirically.

5.2 IPU-level Model Architecture - "I-Brow"

The IPU-level architecture **"I-Brow"**, illustrated in Fig. 1, takes as input BERT and F0 features that correspond to the 10 words of the IPUs. BERT word embeddings are hierarchically encoded on both word-level and IPU-level. In the same manner, we hierarchically encode F0s on a word-level and IPU-level. BERT and

F0 IPU-level representations are then fed to our Multi-Modal Encoding Module, which produces one representation that encompasses both modalities. This final IPU representation is then fed to the Decoder Module which produces the 6 Action Units: $AU01$, $AU02$, $AU4$, $AU05$, $AU06$ and $AU07$.

Table 1. Details of the model configuration

Model Configuration	
4*T(1) to T(100)	Sequence of Token Representations produced by word level F0 Transformer Encoder
3*P(1) to P(100)	Positional Encoding of each token generated by the 3 layers of CONV1D
3*CONV1D	1 Dimentional Convolutional Layer
3*T(1) to T(768)	Sequence of Token Representations produced by word level BERT Transformer Encoder

The following sections describe each module of the IPU-level architecture. Note that the different acronyms used in the modules are summarized in Table 1.

5.2.1   Encoding Modules

5.2.1.1 F0 Hierarchical Encoding: The first module of our architecture is the F0 Hierarchical Encoding Module. This module produces one final F0 representation for the whole IPU by encoding the fundamental frequencies at the word level as well as at the IPU-level. Figure 3 illustrates the F0 hierarchical encoding architecture with 3 input words, for simplicity. Each word has a corresponding sequence of Fundamental Frequencies. The maximum length of all sequences of F0s is equal to 100 timesteps. First, F0 sequences are passed through 3 one dimensional convolution layers to extract the important features. Positional encoding is then applied on the result, and the output is fed to a Transformer Encoder which produces a sequence of F0 token representation for each word. This Transformer Encoder has the same architecture as the one in the original Transformer encoder [35]. Our encoder contains 4 encoding layers. Afterwards, we add a layer of self-attention which takes as input all F0 token representations that correspond to all words in the IPU. The output of this self attention layer is the final F0 representation for the whole IPU.

5.2.1.2 BERT Hierarchical Encoding: The second module of our architecture is the BERT Hierarchical Encoding Module, and it is illustrated in Fig. 4. This module produces one BERT representation for the 10 words of the IPU. The inputs word-level BERT embeddings are initially represented by a 768 vector each. Afterwards, we add a layer of self-attention which takes as input all BERT token representations that correspond to all words in the IPU. The output of this self attention layer is the final BERT representation for the whole IPU.

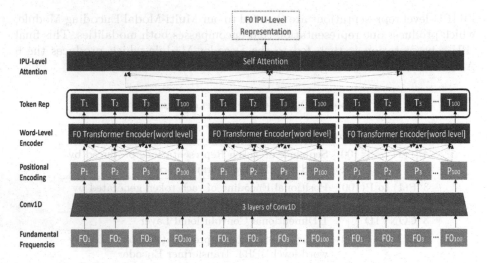

Fig. 3. F0 Hierarchical Encoding Module

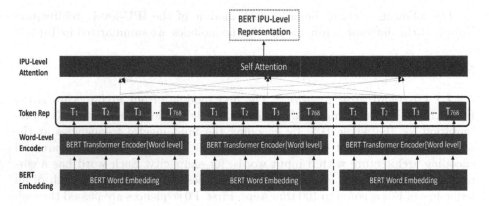

Fig. 4. BERT Hierarchical Encoding Module

5.2.1.3 Multi-Modal Encoding Module: The third module of our architecture is the Multi-Modal Encoding module, which is depicted in Fig. 5: this module takes as input the two IPU-level representations of BERT and F0s, and produces one final representation that encompasses both features. First, both BERT and F0 embeddings are passed to a layer of additive (Bahdanau) attention [2]: we consider the BERT embedding to be the query, and F0 embedding to be the value. The output of the Query-Value attention is then passed to a 1D Global Average Pooling layer. On the other hand, we also add a 1D Global Average Pooling layer to the initial IPU-level BERT embedding (the query). The final multimodal IPU-level representation is the concatenation of the results.

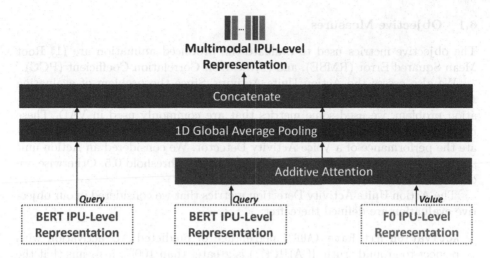

Fig. 5. Multi-modal Encoding Module

5.2.2 Decoding Module. The Decoding Module is depicted in Fig. 1. It takes as input the output of the Multi-Modal Encoding Module, which is the multi-modal IPU-level representation. This representation is fed to 6 different Action Unit Transformer decoders, which are the same ones used in the word-level architecture. The outputs of the decoders are then passed to a Dense layer, which in turn generates the continuous values of the 6 Action Units for all the words of an IPU. For simplicity, Fig. 1 only illustrates a Transformer Decoder for one AU.

5.3 Training and Testing Procedures

We trained and tested our model using the TED dataset. We split the data into 3 sets: training set, validation set and test set. The training set is composed of 80% of the IPUs from the dataset. The remaining IPUs were then split into validation set (10%) and testing set (10%). The optimization algorithm that was used for training is Adam Optimizer, with custom scheduling. After data quantization, we constructed two dictionaries of discrete values corresponding to AU and F0. The loss function used is the Sparse Categorical Crossentropy loss. Our test set is composed of *Speaker Dependent* data, as well as *Speaker Independent* data: the *Speaker Dependent* data include the IPUs said by speakers that the model has seen during training. On the other hand, *Speaker Independent* data correspond to the IPUs said by speakers that the model did not see during training.

6   Evaluation Measures

In this section we describe the objective and subjective measures we used in our experiments.

6.1 Objective Measures

The objective metrics used to evaluate the produced animation are (1) Root Mean Squared Error (RMSE), and (2) Pearson Correlation Coefficient (PCC).

We also assess the Action Units Activity. Since the problem of evaluating Action Units Activity is very similar to Voice Activity Detection (VAD) evaluation problem, we used some metrics that are commonly used in VAD. These metrics were proposed by Freeman et al. [27], and they are widely used to evaluate the performance of a Voice Activity Detector. We considered an Action unit as "Activated" whenever its value is greater than a threshold 0.5. Otherwise, we considered it as "Non-Activated".

The Action Units Activity Detection metrics that we considered in our objective evaluation are defined thereafter:

- `Activation Hit Rate (AHR)`: percentage of predicted AU activation with respect to ground truth. If AHR (%) is greater than 100%, it means that the model is predicting more activation than the amount of activation that is in the ground truth. Otherwise, it means that there are less activation in the prediction than in ground truth.
- `Non-Activation Hit Rate (NHR)`: percentage of predicted non-activity with respect to ground truth. If NHR (%) is greater than 100%, it means that the model is predicting more non-activation than the amount of non-activation that is in the ground truth. Otherwise, it means that there are less non-activation in the prediction than in ground truth.

6.2 Subjective Measures

To investigate human perception of the facial gestures produced by our model, we conduct an experimental study. We make use of Prolific [28], a crowd sourcing website.

6.2.1 Experimental Design. We assess the *naturalness, expressivity, coherence* and *human-likeness* of the virtual agent's generated upper facial gestures. We base our study on the recommendations proposed in [38], by adapting them to facial gesture generation instead of hand gesture generation. More specifically, we asked the following questions: (1) In which video the agent's eyebrows align most with what it is saying ? (2) In which video the agent's eyebrows movements look more natural ? (3) In which video the agent's eyebrows movements are more appropriate ? (4) In which video the agent's eyebrows movements are more expressive ? (5) In which video the agent's eyebrows movements are more synchronized with speech ?

The questions were listed in a random order for each pair of videos. The agent's lower facial gestures were hidden as shown in Fig. 6, to prevent the participants from getting distracted by these gestures.

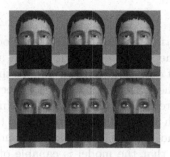

Fig. 6. The lower facial gestures of the Virtual Agents were hidden to prevent participants from getting distracted when evaluating the upper facial gestures

6.2.2 Attention Checks. We add attention check at the beginning of our perceptual evaluation, to filter out inattentive participants. These attention checks include 4 heavily distorted videos (audio and video quality). Participants are asked to report the videos where they experience sound/videos problems. The participants that do not report all 4 videos are excluded automatically from the study.

6.2.3 Experimental Procedure. The perceptual study is done by 30 participants, recruited on Prolific [28]. One requirement to be able to participate to the study is that participants must be fluent in English and above 18 years old. The study is composed of two parts:

1. In the first part, we present 5 sets of pairs of videos. Each pair is composed of two videos of the virtual agent saying a sequence of words that corresponds to one Inter-Pausal Unit. One video uses the *Speaker Dependent* AUs that are produced by our model, and the other one uses the AUs extracted from TED videos which serve as ground truth. For each pair of videos, participants are asked to answer the 6 questions listed in Sect. 6.2.1.
2. The second part of the study is a comparative study in which we present another 5 sets of 3 videos of the agent saying a sequence of words that corresponds to a given inter-pausal unit. The first video uses the AUs from ground truth and is used as a comparison baseline for the participants. They are asked to compare the baseline video with two other videos: one that uses the AUs predicted by our model, and another one that uses the AUs of another IPU. The goal is for the participants to sort the 3 videos by selecting the video that resembles most the ground truth data.

7   Objective Evaluation Results

We present in this section the evaluation we perform on the full architecture and two baselines.

7.1 "I-Brow" Model

We first conduct the experiments on our "**I-Brow**" model driven by both modalities text and speech. The generated metrics which are illustrated in Table 2, reflect the performance of our model with respect to the continuous upper facial gestures data, as well as the Action Unit Activity Detection. The Speaker Dependent RMSE and PCC scores for the different Action Units indicate that the error rate between ground truth and predictions is low, and that AUs 1, 2, 4, and 6 are correlated with the ground truth. The Speaker Dependent Action Unit Activity Detection metrics reflect that the model is capable of detecting the activation of AUs for at least 50% of the time for AU01, AU02, AU04, and AU07. The percentages of predicted non-activity are higher than 100% which means that the model predicted more non-activation than the amount of non-activation in the ground truth.

Table 2. Objective Evaluation Results. Objective evaluation results of objective metrics for (1) I-Brow model tested with SD set, (2) S-Brow baseline model tested with SD set, (3) T-Brow baseline model tested with SD set, and (4) I-Brow model tested with SI set

	I-Brow Model (SD)				S-Brow Baseline Model (SD)				T-Brow Baseline Model (SD)				I-Brow Model (SI)			
	RMSE	PCC	AHR	NAHR	RMSE	PCC	AHR	NAHR	RMSE	PCC	AHR	NAHR	RMSE	PCC	AHR	NAHR
AU01	0.491	0.150	61.538	108.280	0.749	0.002	0.120	134.849	0.766	-0.130	8.062	141.326	0.759	0.150	105.847	97.481
AU02	0.220	0.129	51.632	104.234	0.422	0.000	0.032	108.826	0.512	-0.097	16.279	113.317	0.251	0.100	40.234	103.272
AU04	1.160	0.015	50.666	125.517	1.270	-0.924	0.010	201.467	0.806	0.056	26.524	139.379	0.752	0.008	138.840	87.413
AU05	0.158	-0.058	0.000	100.000	0.372	0.029	0.000	103.053	0.328	-0.023	0.000	105.736	0.097	0.045	0.000	100.000
AU06	0.284	0.112	0.000	111.000	0.637	0.010	0.000	137.541	0.632	-0.115	6.803	117.276	0.727	0.009	0.000	164.630
AU07	0.684	-0.195	56.716	118.954	1.307	-0.994	0.000	223.804	1.077	-0.109	10.860	159.822	0.744	-0.034	70.990	119.880

Metrics were generated for speakers that the model has seen during training (Speaker Dependent), as well as for other speakers that the model did not see during training (Speaker Independent). Speaker Independent results show that the model is capable of generalizing predictions for speakers not seen during training. Figure 7 depicts examples of Speaker Dependent predictions of AUs 1, 4 and 7 over one IPU.

7.2 Baseline Models

In this section, we evaluate the importance of each input modality to our model by individually ablating them, and ending up with 2 different variants of the model.

7.2.1 "S-Brow" Baseline.

The first baseline model "**S-Brow**" is a variant of **I-brow** but with an ablation of the text modality. We repeated the same experiments performed on "**I-Brow**", but this time with only speaker dependent data. Results are shown in Table 2. We can observe that RMSE errors got higher scores while PCC scores are lower. AU Activity Detection scores show that the model is less capable of detecting AU Activity.

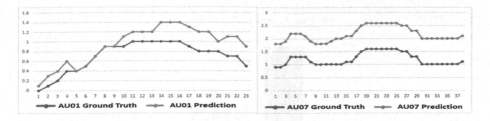

Fig. 7. Full Architecture Speaker Dependent Predictions

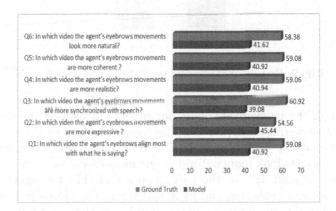

Fig. 8. Results of the first part of the perceptual study

7.2.2 "T-Brow" Baseline. The second baseline model "**T-Brow**" is also a variant of "**I-Brow**" but with an ablation of the speech modality. Same experiments were done after removing the speech modality while keeping the text modality. Results are shown in Table 2. We can notice the worsened performance of the model over the different measures.

8 Perceptual Evaluation Results

We conducted our perceptual study to investigate human perception of the upper facial gestures that are produced by our model. The six evaluation measures that we consider are: agent's *naturalness*, *human-likeness*, *expressiveness*, the *synchronization* of its gestures with speech, as well as the *alignment* of what it is saying with respect to its facial gestures (see Sect. 6.2.1). Note that 6 participants out of 30 did not pass the attention checks, thus we did not consider their participation in our study. Prolific suggested 6 other participants to participate in the experiments and they had successfully passed the attention checks. The results of the first part of the perceptual evaluation are presented in Fig. 8. This part of the evaluation aims to compare the AUs produced by our model, to the AUs of the ground truth. Results show that there was a preference for the ground truth motion facial gestures; however our model did still quite well:

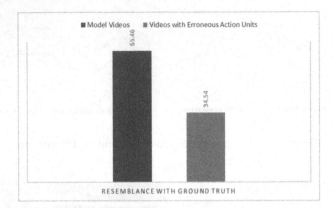

Fig. 9. Results of the second part of the perceptual study

around 40% of the participants chose our model videos over the ground truth videos, when answering each question. This means that our model's Action Units values are close to the ground truth data. 41.62% of the participants find that the eyebrow movements look more natural in our model's videos than in the ground truth videos. Around 41% of the participants find that the agent's eyebrows movements are more coherent and more realistic in the videos produced by our model. Around 41% of the participants found that the agent's eyebrows align more with what it is saying in the videos produced by our model than the ones of ground truth. 39% of participants found that the AUs produced by our model are more synchronized than the ground truth Action Units. The results of the second part of the study are illustrated in Fig. 9. This part aims to compare our model's produced AUs with respect to ground truth, as well as with erroneous AUs (AUs of other IPUs). Results show that participants had a preference towards our model: 65% of participants showed that our model videos resemble more the ground truth videos than the videos where we added the Action Units of other IPUs.

9   Discussion

Objective Evaluation results show that our model is capable of generating speaker dependent upper facial gestures, and is able to predict AUs Activity/Non-Activity. Our model performs better with the two inputs modalities by comparing its performance against the one modality (speech or text) architectures. Speaker Independent results inform us that the model is able to generalize predictions for speakers that it did not see during training. However, results could be improved by training the model on a larger number of TED videos. Subjective Evaluation results show that the videos that were simulated using our prediction model have similar qualities as the ground truth videos simulated on a Virtual Agent. Indeed, 40% of the participants reported that its eyebrows movement looks more natural, coherent, realistic, and aligned with what it is saying compared to the eyebrows movement in the ground truth videos. It means that our model videos look rather similar and resemble the Ground Truth. This conclusion was also validated by the second part of the subjective evaluation.

10   Conclusions and Future Work

This paper explored the use of hierarchy in convolutional and Transformer-based models for upper facial gesture synthesis. We started by proposing a word-level upper facial gesture synthesis model that predicts upper-facial gestures given text and speech inputs with a word-level segmentation. Then, we proposed an architecture that encodes the multimodal inputs and predicts the upper facial gestures for one inter-pausal unit. This architecture hierarchically encodes the input modalities - semantics and speech - at the word-level and IPU-level. The two encodings are then combined through the Multi-Modal Encoding Module which generates a multimodal IPU/utterance representation. This representation is then sent to six Transformer decoders, which in turn predict the six Action Units that correspond to the upper facial muscles. To the best of our knowledge, this is the first data-driven model that generates upper facial gestures based on the speech and text modalities while taking into account word-level and IPU-level features. It is also the first approach that employs Transformers with CNNs for this task, and processes sequences as whole rather than token by token. Through an objective and subjective studies, we further found that a multimodal encoding combining semantic and acoustic features is efficient for upper-facial gesture generation tasks. This paper shows the usefulness of the basic Transformer architecture for upper facial gesture generation. For future work, it would be beneficial to explore the effectiveness of the proposed model when applied to other behavior generation tasks such as head movements. Future work also involves testing the model if it is capable to reproduce behavior expressivity. In this case, we could consider adding the following voice quality features which are useful for expressiveness as the work in [25] suggests: Jitter, Shimmer, Harmonic to Noise Ratio (HNR), and Hammarberg index (Hamml). We also plan to train our model on a bigger training set, to render the model able to better generalize predictions for Speaker Independent data.

References

1. Ahuja, C., Lee, D.W., Ishii, R., Morency, L.P.: No gestures left behind: Learning relationships between spoken language and freeform gestures. In: Proceedings of the 2020 Conference on Empirical Methods in Natural Language Processing: Findings, pp. 1884–1895 (2020)
2. Bahdanau, D., Cho, K., Bengio, Y.: Neural machine translation by jointly learning to align and translate. arXiv preprint arXiv:1409.0473 (2014)
3. Baken, R.J., Orlikoff, R.F.: Clinical measurement of speech and voice. Cengage Learning (2000)

4. Cao, Y., Tien, W.C., Faloutsos, P., Pighin, F.: Expressive speech-driven facial animation. ACM Trans. Graph. (TOG) **24**(4), 1283–1302 (2005)
5. Cavé, C., Guaïtella, I., Bertrand, R., Santi, S., Harlay, F., Espesser, R.: About the relationship between eyebrow movements and fo variations. In: Proceeding of Fourth International Conference on Spoken Language Processing. ICSLP'96. vol. 4, pp. 2175–2178. IEEE (1996)
6. Chovil, N.: Discourse-oriented facial displays in conversation. Res. Lang. Social Interact. **25**(1–4), 163–194 (1991)
7. Cudeiro, D., Bolkart, T., Laidlaw, C., Ranjan, A., Black, M.J.: Capture, learning, and synthesis of 3d speaking styles. In: Proceedings of the IEEE/CVF Conference on Computer Vision and Pattern Recognition, pp. 10101–10111 (2019)
8. Ding, Yu., Pelachaud, C., Artières, T.: Modeling multimodal behaviors from speech prosody. In: Aylett, R., Krenn, B., Pelachaud, C., Shimodaira, H. (eds.) IVA 2013. LNCS (LNAI), vol. 8108, pp. 217–228. Springer, Heidelberg (2013). https://doi. org/10.1007/978-3-642-40415-3_19
9. Duarte, A.C., et al.: Wav2pix: Speech-conditioned face generation using generative adversarial networks. In: ICASSP, pp. 8633–8637 (2019)
10. Ekman, R.: What the face reveals: Basic and applied studies of spontaneous expression using the Facial Action Coding System (FACS). Oxford University Press, USA (1997)
11. Fares, M.: Towards multimodal human-like characteristics and expressive visual prosody in virtual agents. In: Proceedings of the 2020 International Conference on Multimodal Interaction, pp. 743–747 (2020)
12. Ferstl, Y., Neff, M., McDonnell, R.: Adversarial gesture generation with realistic gesture phasing. Compu. Graph. **89**, 117–130 (2020)
13. Garrido, P., et al.: Vdub: Modifying face video of actors for plausible visual alignment to a dubbed audio track. In: Computer graphics forum. vol. 34, pp. 193–204. Wiley Online Library (2015)
14. Ginosar, S., Bar, A., Kohavi, G., Chan, C., Owens, A., Malik, J.: Learning individual styles of conversational gesture. In: Proceedings of the IEEE/CVF Conference on Computer Vision and Pattern Recognition (CVPR) (June 2019)
15. Guo, Y.: A survey on methods and theories of quantized neural networks. arXiv preprint arXiv:1808.04752 (2018)
16. Haag, K., Shimodaira, H.: Bidirectional LSTM networks employing stacked bottleneck features for expressive speech-driven head motion synthesis. In: Traum, D., Swartout, W., Khooshabeh, P., Kopp, S., Scherer, S., Leuski, A. (eds.) IVA 2016. LNCS (LNAI), vol. 10011, pp. 198–207. Springer, Cham (2016). https://doi.org/ 10.1007/978-3-319-47665-0_18
17. Hofer, G., Shimodaira, H.: Automatic head motion prediction from speech data (2007)
18. Jamaludin, A., Chung, J.S., Zisserman, A.: You said that?: synthesising talking faces from audio. Int. J. Comput. Vision **127**(11), 1767–1779 (2019)
19. Karras, T., Aila, T., Laine, S., Herva, A., Lehtinen, J.: Audio-driven facial animation by joint end-to-end learning of pose and emotion. ACM Trans. Graph.(TOG) **36**(4), 1–12 (2017)
20. Knapp, M.L., Hall, J.A., Horgan, T.G.: Nonverbal communication in human interaction. Cengage Learning (2013)
21. Kucherenko, T., et al.: Gesticulator: A framework for semantically-aware speech-driven gesture generation. In: Proceedings of the 2020 International Conference on Multimodal Interaction, pp. 242–250 (2020)

22. Li, X., Zhang, J., Liu, Y.: Speech driven facial animation generation based on gan. Displays **74**, 102260 (2022)
23. Lu, J., Shimodaira, H.: Prediction of head motion from speech waveforms with a canonical-correlation-constrained autoencoder. arXiv preprint arXiv:2002.01869 (2020)
24. Mariooryad, S., Busso, C.: Generating human-like behaviors using joint, speech-driven models for conversational agents. IEEE Trans. Audio Speech Lang. Process. **20**(8), 2329–2340 (2012)
25. Monzo, C., Iriondo, I., Socoró, J.C.: Voice quality modelling for expressive speech synthesis. The Scientific World Journal 2014 (2014)
26. Oh, T.H., Dekel, T., Kim, C., Mosseri, I., Freeman, W.T., Rubinstein, M., Matusik, W.: Speech2face: Learning the face behind a voice. In: Proceedings of the IEEE/CVF Conference On Computer Vision and Pattern Recognition, pp. 7539–7548 (2019)
27. Ong, W.Q., Tan, A.W.C., Vengadasalam, V.V., Tan, C.H., Ooi, T.H.: Real-time robust voice activity detection using the upper envelope weighted entropy measure and the dual-rate adaptive nonlinear filter. Entropy **10**(11), 487 (2017)
28. Palan, S., Schitter, C.: Prolific. ac-a subject pool for online experiments. J. Behav. Experiment. Finance **17**, 22–27 (2018)
29. Sadoughi, N., Busso, C.: Speech-driven animation with meaningful behaviors. Speech Commun. **110**, 90–100 (2019)
30. Salem, M., Rohlfing, K., Kopp, S., Joublin, F.: A friendly gesture: Investigating the effect of multimodal robot behavior in human-robot interaction. In: 2011 Ro-Man, pp. 247–252. IEEE (2011)
31. Song, Y., Zhu, J., Li, D., Wang, X., Qi, H.: Talking face generation by conditional recurrent adversarial network. arXiv preprint arXiv:1804.04786 (2018)
32. Suwajanakorn, S., Seitz, S.M., Kemelmacher-Shlizerman, I.: Synthesizing obama: learning lip sync from audio. ACM Trans. Graph. (ToG) **36**(4), 1–13 (2017)
33. Taylor, S., Kim, T., Yue, Y., Mahler, M., Krahe, J., Rodriguez, A.G., Hodgins, J., Matthews, I.: A deep learning approach for generalized speech animation. ACM Trans. Graph. (TOG) **36**(4), 1–11 (2017)
34. Titze, I.: Principles of Voice Production. Prentice-Hall Inc. (1994)
35. Vaswani, A., et al.: Attention is all you need. arXiv preprint arXiv:1706.03762 (2017)
36. Vougioukas, K., Petridis, S., Pantic, M.: Realistic speech-driven facial animation with gans. Int. J. Comput. Vision, pp. 1–16 (2019)
37. Wan, V., et al.: Photo-realistic expressive text to talking head synthesis. In: INTERSPEECH, pp. 2667–2669 (2013)
38. Wolfert, P., Robinson, N., Belpaeme, T.: A review of evaluation practices of gesture generation in embodied conversational agents. arXiv preprint arXiv:2101.03769 (2021)
39. Yoon, Y., et al.: Speech gesture generation from the trimodal context of text, audio, and speaker identity. ACM Trans. Graph.(TOG) **39**(6), 1–16 (2020)
40. Zhang, Y., Wang, J., Zhang, X.: Conciseness is better: recurrent attention lstm model for document-level sentiment analysis. Neurocomputing **462**, 101–112 (2021)
41. Zhou, H., Liu, Y., Liu, Z., Luo, P., Wang, X.: Talking face generation by adversarially disentangled audio-visual representation. In: Proceedings of the AAAI conference on artificial intelligence. vol. 33, pp. 9299–9306 (2019)
42. Zoric, G., Forchheimer, R., Pandzic, I.S.: On creating multimodal virtual humans-real time speech driven facial gesturing. Multimedia Tools Appl. **54**(1), 165–179 (2011)

43. Zoric, G., Smid, K., Pandzic, I.S.: Automated gesturing for embodied animated agent: Speech-driven and text-driven approaches. J. Multimedia **1**(1)
44. Zoric, G., Smid, K., Pandzic, I.S.: Facial gestures: taxonomy and application of non-verbal, non-emotional facial displays for embodied conversational agents. Conversational Informatics: An Engineering Approach, pp. 161–182 (2007)

YOLO NFPEM: A More Accurate Iris Detector

Xiangyu Ge[1](✉), Chao Yin[2], Qianxiang Zhou[3], Tianqing Zhou[1], Fang Zhang[1],
Zongrui Yang[1], and Bingyuan Fan[1]

[1] Beijing Institute of Computer Application, Beijing, PR China
zhugejiangnan1@163.com
[2] Shanghai United Imaging Healthcare Co., Ltd., Shanghai, PR China
[3] School of Biological Science and Medical Engineering, Beihang University, Beijing, PR China

Abstract. Iris detection remains vital application value in computer vision. Although the considerable advances and successes have been achieved by utilizing deep convolutional neural networks for iris detection, directly locating a small proportion of the iris from the full facial images still confronts considerable challenges. In this study, we proposed the YOLO NFPEM network, which employing the Feature Pyramid Enhancement Module (FPEM) cascaded to enhance and merge the different scale features ($52 \times 52, 26 \times 26, 13 \times 13$) from the PEP7 layer ($52 \times 52$), PEP15 layer ($26 \times 26$) and PEP17 layer ($13 \times 13$) of YOLO Nano network. YOLO NFPEM was train and tested on our presented multi-scale eye dataset (MSED) which contains full and partial facial images, and left/ right eye images. The results shown that YOLO NFPEM with three PEP modules cascaded achieves the best AP for iris of ~ 91.37% higher than YOLO Nano (~83.99%), YOLO Nano with enhanced FPN cascaded and the other YOLO NFPEM architectures, while still reaching a mAP of ~ 84.62%. Furthermore, we found an irreconcilable contradiction, considering the memory consumption and computational cost, neither the enhanced FPN nor FPEM module cascaded can achieve the best performance on both mAP and AP of iris. Testing results also shown that the small-size feature extraction and fusion capabilities of PEP modules cascaded are more powerful than FPN and enhanced FPN.

Keywords: Iris Detection · Small Objects Detection · CNNs

1 Introduction

Iris detection plays an important role in human computer interaction, computer vision application, especially for gaze estimation, AR/VR, and iris authentication. In the field of object detection, objects with smaller physical sizes in the real world or objects occupying areas less than or equal to 32×32 pixels are defined as small objects [1]. Obviously, the iris in the facial image is a representative small object. Due to the iris has a small proportion of pixels in the facial image, in non-cooperative environments, directly detecting iris from the facial images confronts with a great challenge. Iris detection has been an active research area during last few decades. The proposed methods for iris detection include non-learning-based and learning-based methods. The non-learning-based methods generally include the following steps. Firstly, capture eyes from a face image; subsequently, Image format conversion and filtering; finally, obtain the radius and center coordinates of iris by circle fitting. The prerequisite for non-learning-based methods is the known face or eye images with a high resolution, which consumes more computing resources and time, resulting in poor real-time performance.

With the development of deep learning, especially deep convolutional neural networks, which allows learning-based methods to locate iris from the facial images or even the low-resolution images, with a higher accuracy and FPS.

Recently, with leveraging residual projection expansion-projection (PEP) and expansion-projection (EP) macro architectures [2] that comprised of a depth-wise convolution layer, output channels were projected into an output tensor with lower dimensionality, with significant reductions in the architectural and computational complexity while preserving model expressiveness [3]. With the introduction of multi-scale feature extraction, generative adversarial network and unique dedicated networks, small object detection has made a great progress in recent years. Therefore, combining deep neural network and small object detection methods to directly identify iris from facial images can be more efficient and faster.

In this study, under the premise of minimizing the architectural and computational complexity of network, we try to construct a highly efficient deep neural network architectures for iris detection based on the experience and technology of small target detection.

2   Related Works

The essence of locating iris from the facial images is actually small object detection. Therefore, we introduced the recent progress of deep learning applications in small target detection and iris detection.

2.1   Small Object Detection

Small object detection is crucial in many downstream tasks. It remains an active area of research in computer vision and deep learning. Iris and pupil have an extremely small proportion of pixels in the face image, its detection has all the characteristics of small object detection. The main difficulty in small object detection is the extraction of small-size features, which are very fragile and easy to be discarded [4], because small objects usually lack sufficient detailed appearance information, which can be used to distinguish small objects from backgrounds or similar objects [5], and the retained features are too scarce to sustain small objects recognition. Recent impressive progress in small object detection stemmed from modern advances deep learning, especially, with leveraging deep convolutional neural networks and multi-scale fusion, detection accuracy and speed have been greatly enhanced.

Facing the difficulty of feature small scale features extraction, there are plenty of proposed algorithms that can make the performance of small object detection better, as illustrated in Table 1.

Table 1. A taxonomy of small object detection methods.

Type	Methods
Augmentation	By increasing the number of small objects in each image, the number of matched anchors increases, with better detection performance6;
Oversampling	Oversampling the images relatively fewer containing small objects during training is an effortless, effective and straight-forward way to improve performance on small object detection, but result in overfitting67;
Multi-scale feature fusion	A top-down architecture with lateral connections for building high-level semantic feature maps at all scales, with more small size features information retained8 Feature Pyramid Enhancement Module (FPEM) is a cascadable U-shaped module, which can introduce multi-level information to guide the better segmentation9 Extended feature pyramid network (EFPN) is an extra high-resolution pyramid level specialized for small object detection. And, a novel module-feature texture transfer (FTT) was design to super-resolve features and extract credible regional details simultaneously4;
Anchor size and density	Tiling anchors on a wide range of layers to ensure that all scales of object have enough features for detection. Besides, designing anchor scales based on the effective receptive field and a proposed equal proportion interval principle; improving the recall rate of small object by a scale compensation anchor matching strategy, to achieves state-of-the-art detection performance10; By proposing a new anchor densification strategy to make different types of anchors have the same density on the image, to improve the recall rate of small objects11

(*continued*)

Table 1. (*continued*)

Type	Methods
Training strategy	As a novel training scheme, Scale Normalization for Image Pyramids (SNIP), which trains and tests detectors on the same scales of an image pyramid, selectively back-propagates the gradients of object instances of different sizes as a function of the image scale12; Instead of processing every pixel in an image pyramid, SNIPER processes context regions around ground-truth instances (referred to as chips) at the appropriate scale. For background sampling, these context-regions are generated using proposals extracted from a region proposal network trained with a short learning schedule. Hence, the number of chips generated per image during training adaptively changes based on the scene complexity13; Scale Aware Network (SAN) maps the convolutional features from the different scales onto a scale invariant subspace to make CNN-based detection methods more robust to the scale variation, and also construct a unique learning method which considers purely the relationship between channels without the spatial information for the efficient learning of SAN14;
Super-Resolution	Low resolution can jeopardize the detection accuracy. Perceptual Generative Adversarial Networks improve detection performance on small objects by enhancing the representation for small objects to be similar to real large object15
ROI Pooling	To obtain fixed-size feature maps by performing max pooling on inputs of nonuniform sizes1617
Set small target IoU threshold	Considering the idea of using Cascade RCNN to optimize detection of small targets, it is unnecessary to use a strict threshold for small objects
Regression loss	different weighting coefficients of loss function are given according to different target sizes18
Shallow neural networks	Small objects are more likely to be predicted by detectors with a smaller receptive field. The deeper network has a larger receptive field, and it is easy to lose some information about the smaller objects in the coarser layer19
Contextual information	Relations between objects would help object recognition20 By designing novel context anchor to supervise high-level contextual feature learning; using the low-level FPN to combine adequate high-level context semantic feature and low-level feature together, and modeling a context sensitive structure to increase the capacity of prediction network to improve the final accuracy of output.21

Adopt the threshold mechanism, long and short-term memory in recurrent neural network (RNN), meanwhile obtain multi-level feature information. But RNN's training speed is too slow [22, 23]

Based on the above small object detection strategies, many efficient and accurate frameworks were proposed. A discriminative learning and graph-cut framework was presented to exploit the semantic similarity among all predicted objects' candidates to boost the performance of detectors when handling tiny objects [24]. Deconv R-CNN was created to recover small object information by adding a deconvolution layer in the base net-work of Faster R-CNN [11]. By using generative adversarial network to recover the low-resolution images of small objects to high-resolution could achieve better mAP [25]. To address the limitation of small object detection, based on segmenting the original input images into several overlapped patches which are separately fed into an SSD to detect the objects, and merging patches together through two stages, a multi-block SSD mechanism were designed [26]. To deal with the small object detection problem, an end-to-end multi-task generative adversarial network (MTGAN) was proposed [5]. To develop a single architecture that internally lifts representations of small objects to "super-resolved" ones, achieving similar characteristics as large objects and thus more discriminative for detection, a new Perceptual Generative Adversarial Network (Perceptual GAN) model that improves small object detection through narrowing representation difference of small objects from the large ones was built [27]. To improve small object detection in the UAV images, a feature fusion and scaling-based single shot detector (FS-SSD), which is an enhancement based on FSSD, a variety of the original single shot multi-box detector (SSD) was proposed [28]. Aiming at improving the accuracy of small object detection, a more flexible context information integration method was adopted to reconstruct Faster R-CNN [29]. With special focus on the detection of small objects that defined as those under 16×16 pixels, STDnet was presented, which is built on a novel early visual attention mechanism-Region Context Network (RCN) to choose the most promising regions, while discarding the rest of the input image; and, processing only specific areas allows STDnet to keep high resolution feature maps in deeper layers providing low memory overhead and higher frame rates [30].

To enhance the performance of small objects detection, YOLO Nano [3] and YOLO v3 [31] integrated FPN, and achieved a better detection precision and inference time. In addition, Wang proposed Feature Pyramid Enhancement Module (FPEM) and Feature Fusion Module (FFM) to detect text, with a higher FPS without reducing accuracy achieved [32].

2.2 Iris Detection

In non-cooperative environments (illumination variations, long distances, moving subjects, complex background and limited user cooperation), non-learning-based iris detection methods often suffer from poor performance. Recent studies have shown that the deep learning methods could achieve impressive performance on iris detection.

To resolve the problem of reduced recognition rates and enhance accuracy, residual convolutional neural network was widely adopted [33]. Such as Shervin & Amirali constructed an end-to-end R-CNN, which can jointly learn the feature representation and perform recognition [34]. Casian built a well-designed Faster R-CNN with only six layers to locate and classify the eye [35]. As for accomplishing accurate iris segmentation in non-cooperative environments, an Iris R-CNN was proposed, which was derived from

Mask R-CNN, and several novel techniques are proposed to carefully explore the unique characteristics of iris [36].

Based on deep-learning classification models, Hugo & João analyzed the displacements among biologically corresponding patches in pairs of iris images, to discriminate genuine and impostor comparisons [37]. Mateusz adopted deep learning-based iris segmentation models to extract highly irregular iris texture areas in post-mortem iris images [38]. To exploit the inherent correlations between pupil/iris and sclera to boost up the performance of iris segmentation and localization in a unified model, a deep multi-task IrisParseNet was proposed, which applies a Fully Convolutional Encoder-Decoder Attention Network to simultaneously estimate pupil center, iris segmentation mask and iris inner/outer boundary. Abhishek proposed a dual CNN iris segmentation pipeline comprising of an iris bounding boxes detection network and a semantic pixel-wise segmentation network; and, to get compact templates and generate binary iris codes, DeepIrisNet2 was presented [39]. Based on the SegNet architecture, Bilal proposed SIP-SegNet which performed the joint semantic segmentation of ocular traits (sclera, iris and pupil) in unconstrained scenarios with greater accuracy [40]; and, Peter built a deep multi-class eye segmentation, which generalize well to unseen images and to ensure highly accurate segmentation results [41]. PupilNet was developed to detect the pupil by using a CNN classification model with the sliding window technique [42]. Because UNet can perform the classification and localization simultaneously, therefore, UNet was utilized to segment pupil [43]. Based on deep belief network (DBN), He constructed a learning architecture was to further detect potential iris learning representations and make category prediction [44].

3 Methods

In this study, we introduce a novel YOLO N-FPEM, which pursues the low computational complexity and simplified network architecture and promotes iris detection performance by using YOLO Nano as the network backbone and utilizing PEP, EP and FPEM modules.

3.1 Network Backbone

The YOLO family of neural network architectures [44, 45] has an extensive influence on the field of object detection. And, there are plenty of the efficient YOLO-based networks were proposed [3, 46, 47].

YOLO Nano is a highly compact deep convolutional neural network for the object detection task [3], which possesses a model size of~4.0MB and requires 4.57B operations for inference while still achieving a mAP of~69.1% on the VOC 2007 dataset. Compared with the other YOLO family of networks, YOLO Nano network architectures comprised of unique residual projection expansion-projection (PEP) module and expansion-projection (EP) module, which significantly reduce the architectural and computational complexity.

To pursue the reduction in the architecture and computational complexity, and enhance the feature extraction and expression capabilities of network, YOLO Nano was chosen as the backbone for our network.

3.2 Small Size Feature EnhancementSMALL

To improve the accuracy and efficiency of small object detection, both YOLO v3 and YOLO Nano incorporated FPN. While scale-level corresponding detection in FPN alleviates the small object feature extraction, however, feature coupling of various scales still impairs the performance of small objects [4]. And, the backbone of the high efficiency segmentation network must be lightweight, which result in narrow receptive fields and weak representation capabilities [9].

For the arbitrary-shaped text detection, Wang proposed a cascadable U-shaped Feature Pyramid Enhancement Module (FPEM), which includes the up-scale enhancement and the down-scale enhancement. Similar to FPN, in process of the up-scale enhancement, firstly, $2 \times$ linear upsampling of the large receptive field feature layer; subsequently, the upsampled feature is fused with the previous feature layer by elementwise addition; finally, a depth-wise convolution layer is adopted to perform spatial convolutions with a different filter on each of the individual output channels.

As for the downscale enhancement, its calculation process is almost similar to the upscale enhancement, except that the depth-wise convolution layer' stride $= 2$ to perform $2 \times$ down-sampling.

Because FPEM is cascadable, the different scales feature layers are fused more adequately and the receptive fields of features become larger with the increment of cascade. Furthermore, the computational cost of FPEM is very low, its FLOPS is about 1/5 of FPN. Therefore, we attempt to replace FPN module with FEPM module to enhance the performance of small objects detection. The new network framework is named after YOLO N-FPEM, as shown in Fig. 1.

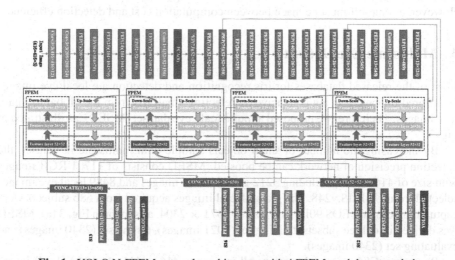

Fig. 1. YOLO N-FPEM network architecture with 4 FPEM modules cascaded.

YOLO N-FPEM predicts boxes at three scales: 52×52, 26×26 and 13×13, which still inherits the three size feature output layers and anchors of YOLO Nano and YOLO V3. The input of the first FPEM is the PEP7 (52×52), PEP15 (26×26) and PEP17 (13

× 13) layers of YOLO Nano. The three different size feature layers of each Down-Scale modules are stitched together respectively by Concatenate layer, then, output to YOLO layer52, 26 and 13 through PEP, EP and Conv1 × 1. The number of S52/S26/S13 layers is adjusted appropriately according to the output channels of Concatenate layer and the number of cascaded FPEM.

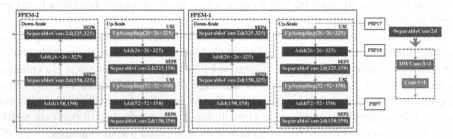

Fig. 2. FEPM architecture and cascade mode. "Add" represents element-wise addition, 2 × upsampling is linear. SeparableConv2d is comprised of a DWConv3 × 3 layer and Conv 1 × 1 layer. DWConv 3 × 3 denotes depth-wise convolution.

The cascade mode between FPEM modules is shown in Fig. 2. The input of each FEPM is the 52 × 52, 26 × 26, and 13 × 13 feature layers of the previous FEPM Down-Scale module.

In theory, the larger the number of cascaded FPEMs, the more comprehensive and abundant the small-size features extracted, and the higher the accuracy of iris detection. However, a trade-off must be made between computation cost and detection efficiency.

4 Multiscale Eye Dataset

Most of the released databases for iris recognition and detection are local eye images or infrared images. It is not conducive to detecting small iris from the global ordinary face images. Therefore, we proposed a multi-scale eye dataset (MSED), as illustrated in Fig. 3.

By increasing the number of small objects sample with multiscale in dataset, the detection precision of network can be boosted. MSED consists of 11701 RGB images with size of 416 × 416, including 3212 global facial images and 8489 local eye images selected from UBIRIS.v248. The global facial images acquired from 686 subjects were captured by Cannon EOS 90D, with size of 3071 × 2304, as shown in Fig. 3 (a). MSED was divided into three subsets: training set (7021 images), testing set (2340 images) and evaluating set (2340 images).

Photoshop CS6 was used to resize all images to 416 × 416. And MATLAB image labeler was selected to perform annotation. We wrote a MATLAB program to convert ".table" files format into VOC ".xml", and a Python program was adopted to convert ".xml" into COCO ".json". MSED has been published on GitHub, please visit the following link: https://github.com/gexiangyu2017/MSED-Multiscale-eye-dataset.git.

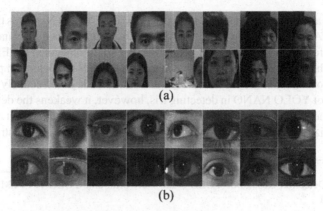

(a)

(b)

Fig. 3. Multiscale eye dataset. (a) is the global facial images, including the full and partial face images; (b) is the local eye images with multiscale from UBIRIS.v2 (Hugo, et al., 2010).

5 Results

As a state-of-the-art network, YOLO Nano has excellent performance in model size and mAP. Therefore, the performance of Yolo Nano on the MSED dataset was used as the baseline. We tested YOLO Nano, YOLO Nano with the different numbers of EFPN modules cascaded (as shown in Fig. 4) and YOLO N-FPEM with the different numbers of FPEM modules cascaded on our dataset MSED. We mainly focus on the performance of these networks in model size, mAP, AP of iris and computational cost.

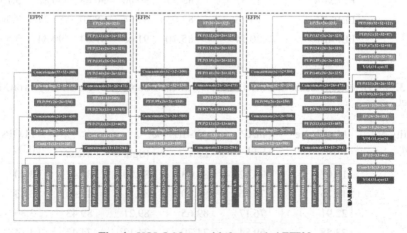

Fig. 4. YOLO Nano with 3 cascaded EFPN.

In some specific applications, there are only high requirements for one or a few parameters of the network, and satisfy computational efficiency. Although dozens of objects are marked in the MSED set, we only focus on the detection performance of left and right iris.

We found an interesting conflict, among all networks, YOLO Nano has the best mAP. However, its AP for iris is lower than mAP. It indicated that YOLO Nano's detection performance for larger size objects is better than for small objects in MSED. We tested the effect of the enhanced FPN and its cascade on YOLO Nano detection performance. And, we discovered that the enhanced FPN and its cascade do effectively improve the performance of YOLO NANO in detecting iris, however, it weakens the detection accuracy of the other larger objects. Furthermore, the more EFPN modules that are cascaded, the network size and the computational cost increase significantly, as illustrated in Table 2.

Table 2. Iris Detection Results of YOLO Nano Networks and YOLO N-FPEM Networks on MSED Test Set

Network	Cascade module and quantity	Model size (MB)	mAP (%)	AP- Iris (%)			FLOPs (G)
				Left	Right	Mean	
YOLO Nano	Baseline	10.92	88.45	83.60	84.38	83.99	2.08
	EFPN-1	18.90	82.96	89.71	89.29	89.50	3.10
	EFPN-2	28.20	82.33	88.87	87.12	88.00	4.50
	EFPN-3	43.27	81.80	87.88	88.75	88.32	9.29
YOLO N-FPEM	FEPM-1	12.44	75.67	79.31	80.52	79.92	2.07
	FEPM-2	14.59	82.66	89.57	88.79	89.18	2.67
	FEPM-3	15.98	84.62	91.04	91.70	91.37	2.90
	FEPM-4	17.37	82.37	90.80	90.83	90.82	3.13
	FEPM-5	18.76	83.91	89.74	88.80	89.27	3.36
	FEPM-6	20.14	85.10	91.63	89.04	90.34	3.59

Table 3. Iris Detection Results of YOLO NFPEM with the Double S52/S26/S13 Layers on MSED Test Set

Quantity of FEPM	Model size (MB)	mAP (%)	AP- Iris (%)			FLOPs (G)
			Left	Right	Mean	
3	18.07	76.52	85.03	85.90	85.47	3.20
4	19.75	75.76	86.80	85.11	85.96	3.43
5	22.91	76.17	89.65	89.21	89.43	3.86
6	23.58	69.84	74.70	74.13	74.42	4.14

Comparing with YOLO Nano and YOLO Nano with enhanced FPN modules cascaded, YOLO N-FPEM with 3 FPEM modules cascaded has the best AP (91.37%) for iris detection; and, FPEM module can effectively improve the ability of network to detect small objects. Moreover, we found that for an image dataset, there is an optimal number of FPEM modules cascaded for small target detection. And, tests results shown that the more modules cascaded, it doesn't mean that the better detection AP.

There is an irreconcilable contradiction between mAP and AP-Iris which is worth of discussion. Whether YOLO Nano networks or YOLO N-FPEM networks, by cascading EFPN or FPEM modules to improve the detection accuracy of small-sized objects meanwhile increasing the network's mAP requires a tradeoff depending on the user's needs. In further, we believe that there must be some strategies that can eliminate this conflict. And, we will spare no efforts to figure it out, to achieve a better mAP and AP-Iris at the same time.

With multiple FPEM modules cascaded, the output channels of Concatenate layer increase significantly. In this case, it's necessary to reduce the channels and avoid loss of feature information, to reduce computation complexity. For YOLO N-FPEM, we leveraged the S52/S26/S13 layer to decrease the output channels of Concatenate layers. Furthermore, we tested the impact of the number of S52/S26/S13 layers on detection accuracy.

As illustrated in Table 3, utilizing the double S52/S26/S13 layers to buffer the feature information loss caused by the sudden shrink in channels of Concatenate layers, we assumed that it helps to enhance detection performance. On the contrary, by analyzing Table 1 and Table 2, the double S52/S26/S13 layers endanger the mAP and AP-Iris of YOLO N-FPEM. Thus, we recommend using the single S52/S26/S13 layer to regulate the output channels and information extraction of Concatenate layers.

6 Conclusion

In this study, a YOLO N-EPEM network for iris detection was proposed. By employing FPEM modules cascaded to extract and fuse small size features, our method achieves a higher detection accuracy for iris. Moreover, cascading FPEM modules is likely to result in a special contradiction between mAP and AP-Iris.

Our experimental results also show that leveraging only one residual projection expansion-projection (PEP) module can effectively deal with the problem of the surge in the output channels of Concatenate layer.

References

1. Tong, K., Wu, Y., Zhou, F.: Recent advances in small object detection based on deep learning: A review. Image Vis. Comput. 97 (2020), https://doi.org/10.1016/j.imavis.2020.103910
2. Sandler, M., Howard, A., Zhu, M., et al.: MobileNetV2: Inverted Residuals and Linear Bottlenecks. In: 2018 IEEE/CVF Conference on Computer Vision and Pattern Recognition, pp. 4510–4520 (2018) https://doi.org/10.1109/CVPR.2018.00474.
3. Wong, A., Famuori, M., Shafiee, M.J., et al.: YOLO Nano: a Highly Compact You Only Look Once Convolutional Neural Network for Object Detection. arXiv:1910.01271
4. Deng, C., Wang, M., Liu, L., et al.: Extended Feature Pyramid Network for Small Object Detection. arXiv: 2003.07021v2
5. Zhang, Y., Bai, Y., Ding, M., Ghanem, B.: Multi-task generative adversarial network for detecting small objects in the wild. Int. J. Comput. Vision 128(6), 1810–1828 (2020). https://doi.org/10.1007/s11263-020-01301-6

6. Kisantal, M., Wojna, Z.,Murawski, J., et al.: Augmentation for small object detection. (2019) arXiv: 1902.07296v1

7. Buda, M., Maki, A., Mazurowski, M.A.: A systematic study of the class imbalance problem in convolutional neural networks. Neural Netw. **106**, 249–259 (2018)

8. Lin, T., Dollár, P., Girshick, R., et al.: Feature Pyramid Networks for Object Detection. 2017 IEEE Conference on Computer Vision and Pattern Recognition (CVPR), pp. 936–944, 2017, https://doi.org/10.1109/CVPR.2017.106.

9. Wang, W., Xie, E., Song, X., et al.: Efficient and Accurate Arbitrary-Shaped Text Detection With Pixel Aggregation Network. In: 2019 IEEE/CVF International Conference on Computer Vision (ICCV), pp. 8439–8448 (2019) https://doi.org/10.1109/ICCV.2019.00853.

10. Zhang, S., Zhu, X., Lei, Z., et al.: S^3FD: single shot scale-invariant face detector. IEEE Int. Conf. Comput. Vis. (ICCV) **2017**, 192–201 (2017). https://doi.org/10.1109/ICCV.2017.30

11. Zhang, W., Wang, S., Thachan, S., Chen, J., Qian, Y.: Deconv R-CNN for Small Object Detection on Remote Sensing Images. In: IGARSS 2018 - 2018 IEEE International Geoscience and Remote Sensing Symposium, 2018, pp. 2483–2486, https://doi.org/10.1109/IGARSS.2018.8517436.

12. Singh, B., Davis, L.S.: An analysis of scale invariance in object detection - SNIP. IEEE/CVF Conf. Comput. Vis. Patt. Recogn. **2018**, 3578–3587 (2018). https://doi.org/10.1109/CVPR.2018.00377

13. Singh, B., Najibi & L.y S. Davis.: SNIPER: Efficient Multi-Scale Training. In: NIPS'18: Proceedings of the 32nd International Conference on Neural Information Processing Systems, Dec. 2018, pp. 9333–9343 (2018)

14. Kim, Y., Kang, B., Kim, D.: "SAN: Learning Relationship between Convolutional Features for Multi-Scale Object Detection", 15th European Conference of Computer Vision, pp. 328–343. Munich, Germany (2018)

15. Wang, X., Shrivastava, A., Gupta, A.: A-fast-RCNN: hard positive generation via adversary for object detection. IEEE Conf. Comput. Vis. Patt. Recogn. (CVPR) **2017**, 3039–3048 (2017). https://doi.org/10.1109/CVPR.2017.324

16. Grel, T.: Region of interest pooling explained. https://deepsense.ai/region-of-interest-pooling-explained/ (2017)

17. Hu, X., Xu, X., Xiao, Y., et al.: SINet: A scale-insensitive convolutional neural network for fast vehicle detection. IEEE Trans. Intell. Transp. Syst. **20**(3), 1010–1019 (2019). https://doi.org/10.1109/TITS.2018.2838132

18. Redmon, J., Divvala, S., Girshick, R., et al.: You only look once: unified, real-time object detection. IEEE Conf. Comput. Vis. Patt. Recogn. (CVPR) **2016**, 779–788 (2016). https://doi.org/10.1109/CVPR.2016.91

19. Soltanolkotabi, M., Javanmard, A., Lee, J.D.: Theoretical insights into the optimization landscape of over-parameterized shallow neural networks. IEEE Trans. Inf. Theor. **65**(2), 742–769 (2019). https://doi.org/10.1109/TIT.2018.2854560

20. Chen, S., Li, Z., Tang, Z.: Relation R-CNN: a graph based relation-aware network for object detection. IEEE Signal Process. Lett. **27**, 1680–1684 (2020). https://doi.org/10.1109/LSP.2020.3025128

21. Tang, X., Du, D.K., He, Z., Liu, J.: PyramidBox: A Context-Assisted Single Shot Face Detector. In: Ferrari, V., Hebert, M., Sminchisescu, C., Weiss, Y. (eds.) ECCV 2018. LNCS, vol. 11213, pp. 812–828. Springer, Cham (2018). https://doi.org/10.1007/978-3-030-01240-3_49

22. Gregor, K., Danihelka, I., Graves, A., et al.: DRAW: A Recurrent Neural Network for Image Generation. In: ICML'15: Proceedings of the 32nd International Conference on International Conference on Machine Learning, vol. 37, pp. 1462–1471 (2015)

23. Sak, H., Senior, A., Beaufays, F.: Long Short-Term Memory Based Recurrent Neural Network Architectures for Large Vocabulary Speech Recognition. Comput. Sci. 338–342, (2014)

24. Xi, Y., Zheng, J., He, X., et al.: Beyond context: exploring semantic similarity for small object detection in crowded scenes. Patt. Recogn. Lett. **137**, 53–60 (2020). https://doi.org/10.1016/j.patrec.2019.03.009
25. Xing, C., Liang, X., Bao, Z.: A Small Object Detection Solution by Using Super- Resolution Recovery. In: 2019 IEEE 7th International Conference on Computer Science and Network Technology (ICCSNT), 2019, pp. 313–316, https://doi.org/10.1109/ICCSNT47585.2019.8962422
26. Li, Y., Dong, H., Li, H., et al.: Multi-block SSD based on small object detection for UAV railway scene surveillance. Chin. J. Aeronaut. **33**(6), 1747–1755 (2020)
27. Li, J., Liang, X., Wei, Y., Xu, T., Feng, J., Yan, S.: Perceptual generative adversarial networks for small object detection. IEEE Conf. Comput. Vis. Patt. Recogn. (CVPR) **2017**, 1951–1959 (2017). https://doi.org/10.1109/CVPR.2017.211
28. Liang, X., Zhang, J., Zhuo, L., et al.: Small object detection in unmanned aerial vehicle images using feature fusion and scaling-based single shot detector with spatial context analysis. IEEE Trans. Circuits Syst. Video Technol. **30**(6), 1758–1770 (2020). https://doi.org/10.1109/TCSVT.2019.2905881
29. Fang, P., Shi, Y.: Small Object Detection Using Context Information Fusion in Faster R-CNN. In: 2018 IEEE 4th International Conference on Computer and Communications (ICCC), 2018, pp. 1537–1540, https://doi.org/10.1109/Comp Comm.2018.8780579
30. Bosquet, B., Mucientes, M., Brea, V.M.: STDnet: Exploiting high resolution feature maps for small object detection. Eng. Appl. Artif. Intell. **91**, (2020) https://doi.org/10.1016/j.engappai.2020.103615
31. Redmon, J., Farhadi, A.: YOLO9000: better, faster, stronger. IEEE Conf. Comput. Vis. Patt. Recogn. (CVPR) **2017**, 6517–6525 (2017). https://doi.org/10.1109/CVPR.2017.690
32. Wang, C., Zhu, Y., Liu, Y., et al.: Joint Iris Segmentation and Localization Using Deep Multi-task Learning Framework (2019) arXiv:1901.11195
33. Lee, Y., Kim, K., Hoang, T., et al.: Deep Residual CNN-based ocular recognition based on rough pupil detection in the images by NIR camera sensor. Sensors **19**(4), 842–872 (2019). https://doi.org/10.3390/s19040842
34. Minaee, S., Abdolrashidi, A.: DeepIris: Iris Recognition Using A Deep Learning Approach (2019) arXiv:1907.09380
35. Miron, C., Pasarica, A., Bozomitu, R.G., et al.: Efficient pupil detection with a convolutional neural network. E-Health Bioeng. Conf. (EHB) **2019**, 1–4 (2019). https://doi.org/10.1109/EHB47216.2019.8969984
36. Feng, C., Sun, Y., Li, X.: Iris R-CNN: Accurate Iris Segmentation in Non-cooperative Environment (2019) arXiv:1903.10140
37. Proença, H., Neves, J.C.: Segmentation-less and non-holistic deep-learning frameworks for iris recognition. IEEE/CVF Conf. Comput. Vis. Patt. Recogn. Workshops (CVPRW) **2019**, 2296–2305 (2019). https://doi.org/10.1109/CVPRW.2019.00283
38. Trokielewicz, M., Czajka, A., Maciejewicz, P.: Post-mortem Iris Recognition with Deep-Learning-based Image Segmentation. Vol. 94, Feb. 2020, https://doi.org/10.1016/j.imavis.2019.103866
39. Gangwar, A., Joshi, A., Joshi, P., et al.: DeepIrisNet2: Learning Deep-IrisCodes from Scratch for Segmentation-Robust Visible Wavelength and Near Infrared Iris Recognition (2019) arXiv:1902.05390
40. Hassan, B., Ahmed, R., Hassan, T., et al.: SIP-SegNet: A Deep Convolutional Encoder-Decoder Network for Joint Semantic Segmentation and Extraction of Sclera, Iris and Pupil based on Periocular Region Suppression (2020) arXiv:2003.00825
41. Rot, P., Emeršič, Ž, Struc, V., Peer, P.: Deep multi-class eye segmentation for ocular biometrics. IEEE Int. Work Conf. Bioinspired Intell. (IWOBI) **2018**, 1–8 (2018). https://doi.org/10.1109/IWOBI.2018.8464133

42. Wolfgang, F., Thiago, S., Gjergji, K., et al.: PupilNet: Convolutional Neural Networks for Robust Pupil Detection (2020) arXiv:1601.04902

43. Han, S.Y., Kim, Y., Lee, S.H., Cho, N.I.: Pupil Center Detection Based on the UNet for the User Interaction in VR and AR Environments. In: 2019 IEEE Conference on Virtual Reality and 3D User Interfaces (VR), 2019, pp. 958–959, https://doi.org/10.1109/VR.2019.8798027

44. He, F., Han, Y., Wang, H., et al.: Deep learning architecture for iris recognition based on optimal Gabor filters and deep belief network. J. Electron. Imag. 26(2), (2017) https://doi.org/10.1117/1.JEI.26.2.023005

45. Joseph, R., Ali, F.: YOLOv3: An Incremental Improvement (2018) arXiv:1804.02767

46. Wu, D., Lv, S., Jiang, M., et al: Using channel pruning-based YOLO v4 deep learning algorithm for the real-time and accurate detection of apple flowers in natural environments. Comput. Electron. Agricul. 178, 2020, https://doi.org/10.1016/j.compag.2020.105742

47. Chen, W., Huang, H., Peng, S., Zhou, C., Zhang, C.: YOLO-face: a real-time face detector. Vis. Comput. 37(4), 805–813 (2020). https://doi.org/10.1007/s00371-020-01831-7

48. Proenca, H., Filipe, S., Santos, R., Oliveira, J., Alexandre, L.A.: The UBIRIS.v2: A database of visible wavelength iris images captured on-the-move and at-a-distance. IEEE Trans. Patt. Anal. Mach. Intell. 32(8), 1529–1535 (2010). https://doi.org/10.1109/TPAMI.2009.66

Detecting Scoreboard Updates to Increase the Accuracy of ML Automatic Extraction of Highlights in Badminton Games

Pei-Hsuan Hsieh[1]([⊠]) [iD], Hong Yi Chuah[1], and Qi-Xian Huang[2]

[1] National Chengchi University, Taipei 116011, Taiwan
hsiehph@nccu.edu.tw, 108703025@g.nccu.edu.tw
[2] National Tsing-Hua University, Hsinchu 300044, Taiwan
xiangg800906three@gapp.nthu.edu.tw

Abstract. In recent years, numerous studies have focused on the automatic detection of video highlights in different sports, including badminton. Auto-detection of highlights can save labor, money, and time when producing an abbreviated video of a game. It can shorten the viewing time of the audience by filtering out the less exciting scenes, thereby increasing the audience's interest while watching the game. This study examined different methods of capturing highlights and verified whether scoreboard updates can be used to improve the performance of a YOLOv5s auto-detection model in capturing highlights in badminton games. The model was trained to label the scoreboard correctly with different scores and different designs. The scoreboard was detected as the region of interest. Then, the right half of the scoreboard was divided into upper and lower halves to detect the scores earned by each team. Then, OpenCV's functions (grayscale, erode, eliminate noise, dilate, and find contours) were used to fine-tune the frame of the score. The area of interest (the number on the far right) was then compared to its immediate previous state, using the average hash algorithm to detect any differences between the two scoreboards. If there was a geometric change, the 10 s of videos immediately before the change that had been stored in the memory would be stored separately as a highlight segment. This study showed that this YOLO-trained model was more than 70% accurate in extracting highlight segments from all five videos that we tested.

Keywords: Badminton Highlights · Auto-detection · Machine Learning · YOLOv5s · OpenCV

1 Research Background

Since the emergence of COVID-19, the order of life has been disrupted all over the world, and the economies of all countries have been greatly affected. However, due to the impact of the pandemic, live broadcasting has become more and more popular. In Taiwan, more people have started to watch badminton matches online, and Taiwanese badminton players have also performed better in this sport. However, a badminton game

H. Degen and S. Ntoa (Eds.): HCII 2023, LNAI 14051, pp. 467–488, 2023.
https://doi.org/10.1007/978-3-031-35894-4_35

can be very long, with no fixed duration. Even two straightforward games can take more than 30 min, and three difficult games can take two hours or more. Not everyone has the patience or willingness to watch the matches in their entirety. Although the scoreboard on the screen helps the audience to quickly glance at the scores of the two teams during a badminton game, viewers would miss the events leading to the scores if they have not been watching the entire game.

Object detection technology is commonly used in everyday life, such as speed cameras and thermal imaging cameras [1–3]. For example, the speed camera calculates whether the speed of the car is above the speed limit by automatically detecting the time it takes a car to move from one point to another. In addition, it can also detect whether the vehicle has turned left or right in violation of the regulations or if it is parked in a place where it is not allowed. If a car speeds or parks illegally, object detection technology can also automatically detect the license plate and recognize the plate number to issue a ticket [1]. Another example is self-driving cars. When a self-driving car detects a vehicle or foreign object in front of it, it will automatically slow down and will not accelerate even if the driver steps on the accelerator. In addition, it can detect the lines that mark the lanes and drive inside the lane. This means that people do not need to spend as much energy to concentrate fully on their driving, rather, they just need to monitor whether the machine is faulty. Artificial intelligence cars also operate by using the Convolutional Neural Network (CNN) model, and in some cases, they can even detect things beyond what the human eye can recognize [2].

Object detection is also widely used in ball games [4] because it can detect people, balls, or anything on the field, such as counting the number of racket swings [5–7]. It can be used to detect the trajectories of players (characters) and balls (objects) to know what actions the players have made and where the ball is going. This allows us to learn the habits of players, as well as their strengths and weaknesses, to make strategic analyses or improve on any shortcomings. In addition, object detection can also be used to survey the venues of ball games. If the ball falls in a certain area, the technology can determine whether it is in-bounds or out-of-bounds. Automatic detection can save us time and achieve the desired effect [4].

Existing sports highlight models use the Gaussian Mixture Model (GMM), Long Short-Term Memory (LSTM), CNN, Recurrent Neural Network (RNN), and CNN + RNN [8, 9]. According to the literature on extracting sports event highlights, the "You Only Look Once" (YOLO) model can also be used for effective object detection [10, 11]. As the name implies, YOLO can quickly recognize the category and position of an object in an image, avoid mistakes, and learn the generalization characteristics of the object. However, it may be prone to false positives, object positioning errors, poor detection of small objects, and unstable accuracy.

Due to the small size of the badminton shuttlecock, the target object is easily confused with things like tissue paper or lines on the court. It is also difficult to detect when the shuttlecock is stationary for a prolonged period after scoring (a highlight) because as soon as the shuttlecock hits the ground, the camera usually turns to take a close-up shot of the players' movements or expressions, instead of continuing to give a panoramic view of the court. Therefore, GMM or LSTM models cannot be used to detect small-sized objects such as badminton shuttlecocks.

Since it is hard to detect the small white shuttlecock, the scoreboard can be used instead as a key object to determine the highlights in badminton matches. The scoreboard's size is larger than the shuttlecock. However, its size and location placed on the streaming site can vary during the match. Besides, the scoreboard consists of texts and numbers. During the match, only the numbers scored by the two teams are of interest to us. To effectively detect the highlight, this study employs the YOLO model since it only needs to see a feature once and does not depend on the image being consistent throughout the game.

2 Sports Highlight Models

Existing sports highlight models have used GMM, LSTM, CNN + RNN, etc. [8, 11]. GMM is an extension of a single Gaussian probability density function. It uses multiple Gaussian probability density functions to accurately quantify the distribution of variables, and it can decompose variable distributions into statistical models based on Gaussian probability density function distributions [8]. However, when the model has too little input data, it is more difficult to calculate, and the probability density will diverge [12].

LSTM is an RNN model suitable for time series research because of its ability to retain input data over an extended period. However, its scale of measure is too long, making the model very intractable and time-consuming [13]. LSTM has been used to predict the trajectory of pedestrians [5]. The human-human interaction function can design manual learning features according to the rules in specific scenarios and the distance between pedestrians. The activity forecasting function can learn motion patterns by clustering trajectories. It can simulate the interaction between people and space to infer the walkable path in a scene. The sequence prediction function of RNN models has proven to be very effective for intensive tasks such as semantic segmentation and scene analysis. RNN models can also learn the dependencies between spatially related data such as image pixels [5].

CNN and RNN are two important deep-learning models. CNN is mainly used to process spatially structured data, while RNN is mainly used to process time series data [9]. CNN uses shared convolution kernels to optimize the amount of calculation to train the weights of given features effectively. However, CNN requires that the researcher adjust the parameters; it also needs a large sample size, GPU, and other specific hardware [14]. RNN is suitable for time-series research that uses sequence data. However, it is difficult to save any long-term data after learning [13]. OpenCV is free, open source, and suitable for engineering practice, but it relies on complex programming and has a long development cycle [7, 8].

2.1 YOLO Model

The full name of YOLO is "You Only Look Once." It means that the model can identify the position and category of an object in a picture after one glance. YOLO is also known as the region-free method. Unlike the region-based method, YOLO does not need to find the regions that may contain the targets in advance, which is very convenient. Therefore, it is also called a single-stage or 1-stage model, whereas the region-based method is called a two-stage model [15]. Figure 1 shows the YOLO model.

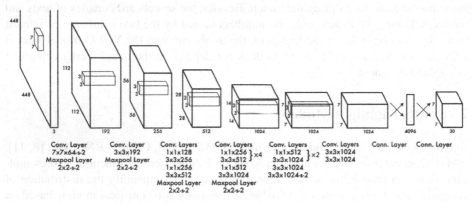

Fig. 1. YOLO model [16, p. 3].

2.2 Research on Sports Object Detection Models

In this section, we introduce several important studies that investigated sports object detection models. Some studies identified moving balls, while others identified sounds, words, and so on. Although their purpose differed from the highlights extraction of badminton matches discussed in this study, their rigorous modeling processes were referenced as machine learning-related knowledge as we developed our model. We describe chronologically and in detail a few studies that employed the most relevant approaches. We then summarize the other studies related to highlights of ball games in Table 1.

Watching lengthy videos in their entirety can be time-consuming and boring, so a previous study used a novel pairwise deep ranking model involving deep learning techniques to learn to analyze highlights [1]. The research designed a two-stream Deep Convolutional Neural Network (DCNN) architecture to independently train a DCNN deep ranking model on each stream in a pairwise manner and then represented the relative relationship within each pair, which contained a highlight and a non-highlight segment of the same video. The DCNN on each stream optimized the features and assigned a highlight score to each segment so that the highlighted parts had higher detection scores than the non-highlighted parts. Most of the 35 participants in that study preferred the video summary over the original video because the summary had better quality in terms of coverage (i.e., better content than the original video) and presentation (i.e., better extraction of the video's essence).

A previous study used visual features and text analysis to predict highlights in videos to save human resources and time [17]. Specifically, that study used a CNN + RNN model to automatically predict the highlights using multilingual feature-based models, deep learning-based vision models, and combinations of language and vision models. Their V-CNN mode used a pre-trained version of the features to directly predict the highlights of each frame. To exploit the visual video information, V-CNN-LSTM applied a memory-based LSTM-RNN on top of the image features to model long-term dependencies. The study also employed word-level LSTM-RNN models (a common method for embedding sentences), as well as an lv-LSTM model, which combined the best vision model (V-CNN-LSTM) and language model (L-Char-LSTM). The results showed that the L-Char-LSTM and V-CNN model training only worked best on the last 25% of frames of edited highlights. L-Char-LSTM outperformed L-WordLSTM by 22.3%. Although vision models generally outperform language-based models, this study [17] was able to build language models to help remove the more difficult cases in the vision models. These two models were most effective when working with multiple languages such as Traditional Chinese and English.

With the popularization of video platforms, there is an increasing demand for technologies to automatically extract video highlights. Therefore, important sub-events are identified by a trained recurrent autoencoder. A previous study leveraged web scraping data on videos in a specific domain and used that data to model the common characteristics or the foci of the videos [33]. This way, their original counterparts were not needed, allowing for easy scaling up and collection of more training data. The research proposed a scalable highlight extraction method based on unsupervised learning. The technique relied on an improved autoencoder with two major modifications: a novel shrinkage index loss that reduced the sensitivity to noisy training data scraped from the web and a repeated autoencoder configuration using LSTMs.

3 Methodology

This study established the model by using Python, a programming language widely used in various fields for deep learning, data analysis, machine learning, and artificial intelligence. Python is well accepted by researchers in data science-related fields, proving its importance and convenience. Python-related products are gradually appearing on the market, and a large amount of relevant information can be easily found on the Internet. Therefore, this study used Python to build a model. The following sections provide details about the data collection method, data processing method, model building procedures, model adoption and algorithm, and model evaluation method.

3.1 Data Collection Method

From the innumerable badminton games with scoreboards, this research selected videos of formal or large-scale events from YouTube, such as the Summer Olympic Games, BWF World Championships, the Thomas Cup, Uber Cup, etc. We captured 10,000 game frames with 1920 x 1080 pixels in png format. We then used a graphical image annotation tool called LabelImg to mark the scoreboard in the images, and then let YOLO learn.

3.2 Data Collection Method

Since YOLO directly resizes the video to a square, image distortion would be a problem. Therefore, we used the letterbox function to maintain the length-width ratio of the original image for scaling. After the image was resized to have the required length, the empty space that remained was filled with gray [34]. We divided the video pixel values in the range of 0 to 255 to convert them into real numbers 0.0–1.0. Most application programming interfaces (APIs) for image processing accept real numbers and integers as input. If the input is an integer, the API will convert it into a real number and then process it, and then output it as an integer. If there are too many processing steps, this constant conversion between real numbers and integers can reduce the precision significantly [35]. Therefore, we did a one-time pre-conversion of pixel values to avoid additional automatic conversions during the process.

Table 1. Relevant research on ball game highlights.

Purpose	Method	Model Evaluation
To improve highlight extraction of baseball programs so that viewing time can be reduced. [18]	The study used only audio and a combination of general sports features and baseball-specific features to extract the highlights, without relying on computationally expensive video track features	The model generated clips that matched 75% of human-labeled highlight clips
To bridge the gap between the system's need for low-level features and the user's preference for high-level semantic descriptions when identifying specific contents in sports videos. [19]	The method combined a variety of automatic techniques for feature detection with heuristic rules determined by manually observing sports footage. This generated a series of temporal models that automatically identified meaningful segments in basketball videos	Following the manual observations, the automatic analysis was able to capture most of the identified key events in basketball videos
To build a more complete summary of sports videos; to demonstrate that game plays, breaks, and highlights can be localized by detecting whistles and excitement sounds. [20]	This study used Unified Modeling Language to generate summaries by identifying semantic relationships of plays, breaks, and highlights in period-based sports. A detection algorithm was developed to segment plays and breaks and localize the highlights within each of them. The audio-based detection results during or after key sports events provided supplemental highlights	By combining whistles, text, and excitement sounds, the algorithm detected 90% to 100% of the highlights

(*continued*)

Table 1. (*continued*)

Purpose	Method	Model Evaluation
To automatically detect highlights using only the audio function and the browsing function of a video recorder. [21]	The audio classification module in the audio DSP used a low-complexity GMM to categorize each audio clip as applause, cheers, excited speech, normal speech, music, etc. The GMM classifier was trained using MDCT coefficients from various sports contents. During playback, the system obtained the importance level map and identified the highlight scenes by reading the metadata file before playing the target program	The technique could detect the highlight scenes from baseball, football, horse racing, sumo wrestling, etc., and the accuracy was sufficient to meet the needs of actual use
To provide an alternative approach to understanding video content based on human perception mechanisms, by generating an index of videos according to their importance ranking. [22]	This study used keyframe selection and video browsing extraction based on a user attention model that did not require complex heuristic rules and full semantic understanding. The study employed visual and auditory attention modeling approaches separately while addressing fusion schemes	The attention modeling process was significantly accelerated by effectively reducing the computational complexity. The satisfaction score also increased slightly
To propose a unified approach for video summarization based on the analysis of video structures and video highlights. [23]	The study used the structure of the film to ensure the content coverage of the summary. A motion attention model was employed to compute the perceptual quality of movie clips for content highlight selection. The information on the movie structure and the highlights were then efficiently encapsulated in a temporal graph	The proposed method could automatically detect scene changes and generate summaries

(*continued*)

Table 1. (*continued*)

Purpose	Method	Model Evaluation
To extract emotional highlight clips from drama films. [24]	The study integrated information from musical emotion, human faces, shot duration, and motion amplitude to extract highlights of dramatic films. A two-stage music emotion recognition scheme and a novel adaptive audio fingerprinting technique were used to improve the accuracy of incidental music emotion recognition. A novel distance metric was used to quantify the quality of the extraction	The evaluation results successfully demonstrated that high-level features, especially musical emotion, were effective for video highlight extraction
To extract time-synchronized video tags by automatically leveraging crowdsourced user comments on video sites. [25]	A model was proposed to enrich the knowledge of short reviews for videos and shots by collectively exploiting the preferences of multiple users. It also stripped the user interactions in time-synchronized comments to address the noisy comment problem. A case study was also conducted to demonstrate the capability of the proposed model in mining short and noisy reviews	The model outperformed the state-of-the-art baselines and could be applied to time-synchronized tagging of newsreels, videos, and social network-based events

(*continued*)

Table 1. (*continued*)

Purpose	Method	Model Evaluation
To automatically generate football video highlights using audiovisual descriptors. [26]	The method involved segmenting a film sequence into shots and analyzing their relevance and interest. For each shot, low-level (audio, color, and motion) and mid-level (people, whistle, zoom, perspective, and playback) audiovisual descriptors were linearly combined and weighted to score the segments, thereby generating customized highlights	The proposed framework was tested in specific scenarios and demonstrated satisfactory results
To improve the efficiency of standard video highlight extraction techniques using deep video features to encode various levels of content semantics. [27]	The study designed a deep neural network that mapped a video and description content to a common semantic space and trained it jointly with related video-description pairs. Deep features were extracted from video segments and cluster-based summarization techniques were applied. The highlights were evaluated using the SumMe dataset and baseline methods	The results demonstrated the advantages of incorporating deep semantic features in techniques for extracting video highlights
To assign temporal labels to highlighted film shots by combining bullet chatting reviews with timestamps. [28]	This study used the temporal deep structured semantic model to represent reviews as semantic vectors by exploiting their temporal correlation. Then, video highlights were identified and labeled in a supervised manner via semantic vectors	The framework labeled video highlights significantly more effectively than the baseline

(*continued*)

Table 1. (*continued*)

Purpose	Method	Model Evaluation
To propose a highlight detection technique in live e-sports matches using CNNs to learn the visual filters for highlight detection. [15]	The study first processed the scene type, and in the case of a game scene, applied a highlight processing classifier. The highlight classifier model was applied, followed by the highlight detector model	The technique achieved 18FPS on a single CPU with an average accuracy of 83.18%. This technology was also used in Yahoo Esports
To propose a novel framework for unsupervised video highlight detection and summarization based on crowdsourced time-sync comments. [29]	Global word embedding was used to carry out word-to-concept and word-to-emotion mapping by concentrating on lag-calibrated bullet comments for highlight detection and using a modified SumBasic algorithm for highlight summarization	The full model (Spike with lag-calibration step, emotion, and topic concentration) outperformed other methods (i.e., BLEU-1, ROUGE-1, and F1–1) in highlight detection and highlight summarization
To develop a machine learning model that predicts a large dataset of labeled and unlabeled videos. [30]	Feature extraction and augmentation were carried out to train on the video-level and frame-level data. Then, the best-performing video-level model, a mixture of Neural-Network Experts with 3 hidden layers in the expert part of the network, was trained. The frame-level models were trained by LSTMs and gated recurrent units. The ensemble model was evaluated by the Global Average Precision metric	Both video-level and frame-level models achieved a GAP of 0.834 level, and the ensemble exceeded 0.841. Models with larger sizes performed better. For video-level models of the same size, wider models performed better than deeper models

(*continued*)

Table 1. (*continued*)

Purpose	Method	Model Evaluation
To improve video understanding by designing a unified learning framework to embed videos using their audiovisual content in a metric space that preserves video-to-video relationships. [31]	This study used deep neural networks to extract images and audio features and created a graph to connect related videos with edges. Human viewers also were asked to determine whether edges existed between pairs of videos. The mapping of video content to collaborative filtering signals allowed for the identification of high-level semantic relationships between videos	The learned embedding was generalizable and transferable to various tasks, including personalized video recommendations and video annotation
To extract highlights or key points of videos using fewer comments. [32]	The study used biGRU-DNN to divide the entire video into several parts, then checked the comments to tag the keywords. The study used semantic segmentation technology to identify and classify specific objects in the pictures	The model outperformed several baseline methods. The accuracy rate of the highlight extraction was as high as 51.3%
To reduce time by automatically extracting highlights from a large number of recorded games. [4]	The study used LIGHTOR, including the Highlight Initializer to collect time-stamped chat messages and the Highlight Extractor to track how users interacted with these approximate highlight locations, then refined those locations to extract the highlights	LIGHTOR was able to achieve high extraction accuracy training datasets with low computational resources using two popular games on Twitch

4 Methodology

This study established the model by using Python, a programming language widely used in various fields for deep learning, data analysis, machine learning, and artificial intelligence. Python is well accepted by researchers in data science-related fields, proving its importance and convenience. Python-related products are gradually appearing on the market, and a large amount of relevant information can be easily found on the Internet. Therefore, this study used Python to build a model. The following sections provide details about the data collection method, data processing method, model building procedures, model adoption and algorithm, and model evaluation method.

4.1 Data Collection Method

From the innumerable badminton games with scoreboards, this research selected videos of formal or large-scale events from YouTube, such as the Summer Olympic Games, BWF World Championships, the Thomas Cup, Uber Cup, etc. We captured 10,000 game frames with 1920 x 1080 pixels in png format. We then used a graphical image annotation tool called LabelImg to mark the scoreboard in the images, and then let YOLO learn.

4.2 Data Collection Method

Since YOLO directly resizes the video to a square, image distortion would be a problem. Therefore, we used the letterbox function to maintain the length-width ratio of the original image for scaling. After the image was resized to have the required length, the empty space that remained was filled with gray [34]. We divided the video pixel values in the range of 0 to 255 to convert them into real numbers 0.0–1.0. Most application programming interfaces (APIs) for image processing accept real numbers and integers as input. If the input is an integer, the API will convert it into a real number and then process it, and then output it as an integer. If there are too many processing steps, this constant conversion between real numbers and integers can reduce the precision significantly [35]. Therefore, we did a one-time pre-conversion of pixel values to avoid additional automatic conversions during the process.

4.3 Model Building Procedures

The following is the process of building the model (also see Fig. 2):

1. Mark the scoreboard on the game picture and train YOLO to identify the scoreboard. ("What is the scoreboard?")
2. [f(x)] Let the YOLOv5s model train on the marked dataset 100 times to get the best model, and then set the detection frame (the area of the scoreboard) as the region of interest (ROI).
3. [g(x)] Set the right half of the area as the new ROI.
4. [h(x)] Split the new ROI into upper and lower halves to detect the score of each team.
5. [I(x)] Use OpenCV to convert RGB to grayscale; perform erosion ("erode") to eliminate noise and dilate ("dilate"); use cv2.findContours to find the contour of each object; use cv2.boundingRect to calculate the frame information of the outline (x, y, w, h).
6. [J(x)] Slightly adjust the frame selection result (ROI) from the feature map to make the framed numbers more complete; look for the rightmost number ROI; compare the previous number's ROI with the current one. The digital ROI is compared for similarity, and the intersection over union (IOU = area of overlap / area of union) is calculated to determine whether the frame positions of the preceding and following digital ROIs are numbers in the same position. Then, use the mean Hash algorithm to

compare the difference between the two images. Set the similarity threshold to 10 s. If the similarity calculation exceeds the threshold, it means that the ROI had a digital change.

7. Finally, if there is a geometric change (score change), 10 s of the video immediately before the score change is stored as a video segment.

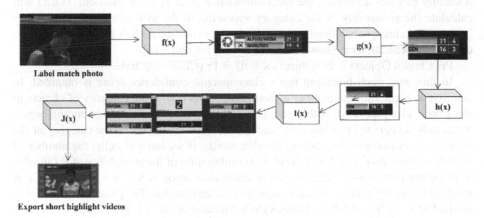

Fig. 2. Model building procedures.

Note: A successfully detected score change meant that a highlight had just happened. The scores were typically updated within 5 s after the shuttlecock hits the ground, so the 10 s before the update of the scoreboard was estimated to be the length of the highlights (scoring play). In this manner, the highlights were selected to let the audience watch in a very short amount of time all the exciting moments that led to the scoring of points throughout the game.

4.4 Model Adoption and Algorithm

The YOLO model only needs to look once, and there is no need to determine in advance the region that might contain the target. YOLO integrates the original scattered object detection steps into a single neural network, which predicts each bounding box through the features of the image and calculates the probability of each bounding box in each class [36]. YOLO needs to find an object in an image and detect its category and location. Each object contains five parameters: the center position (x, y), height (h), width (w), and class.

Assuming that the processed image is a square, the first step for YOLO is to divide the picture into a grid of s^2 (s × s) same-sized cells. An object does not have to completely fit within a grid cell; its location can be identified as long as its center is in a cell. This way, there is no need to design very large cells to fit the entire object. Suppose we want to predict B bounding boxes for each frame of s^2, and each bounding box has five parameters, which are the center position (x, y), height (h), width (w), and the confidence score of this prediction. To be noted, the thickness of each bounding box is different because the confidence scores are different. The boxes with high confidence scores are thicker, and vice versa.

A confidence score measures the accuracy of objects being contained in a given bounding box (i). It is calculated: *Confidence score = Pr (object) × IOU (ground truth)*. The ideal confidence should be the same as the IOU. If the native grid cell of the bounding box has no object, the ideal confidence is 0. Conversely, if the native grid cell of the bounding box has an object, the ideal confidence level is 1. In addition, YOLO will calculate the probability of the category appearing in the grid cell for each category (conditional class probabilities), and multiply the conditional class probabilities by the confidence predictions as shown in the following formula [16]:

Pr (Class-i| Object) × Pr (Object) × IOU = Pr (Class-i) × IOU.

In this way, each bounding box's class-specific confidence score is obtained. In addition to predicting the number of bounding boxes ("B"), the category of objects in this grid is also predicted. Although a grid cell may contain multiple bounding boxes, it can only recognize one object. So, each grid cell needs to predict the category of the object but not the bounding boxes. In other words, if we have s^2 cells, the number of bounding boxes predicted for each cell is a combination of the probability of B (number of bounding boxes) and C classes, so the tensor dimension is S × S × (B × 5 + C); B needs to be multiplied by 5 because there are five dimensions. The parameters of YOLO on the PASCAL Visual Object Classes (VOC) dataset are S = 7, B = 2, and C = 20, so the VOC final prediction is a 7 x 7 x 30 tensor.

YOLO Network Design. In this study, YOLO was mainly implemented and tested on the PASCAL VOC dataset and had 24 convolutional layers and two fully connected layers. We also used a faster version of YOLO that had only nine convolutional layers that also outputted a 7 x 7 x 30 tensor.

YOLO Training. The 2012 ImageNet 1000-class dataset was used in this study to pre-train the first 20 layers of the CNN, the average-pooling layer, and the fully connected layer. After about a week of training, it achieved an accuracy as high as 88% (ImageNet 2012 validation set). Both training and inference used the darknet framework. After training, four CNNs with random parameters and two fully connected layers were added to improve the model's performance. However, since object detection requires more detailed texture features, the number of pixels was increased from 224 × 224 to 448 × 448. Finally, the fully connected layer simultaneously predicted the probability and bounding box coordinates for each class. The width and weight of the bounding box were adjusted to a value between 0 and 1. The x and y values were also adjusted to between 0 and 1 for the grid cell. In CNN, the final layer used linear activation, and other neuron activations used leaky ReLU.

The loss function is a sum-squared error, which is relatively easy to optimize. However, localizing error weights equally will not lead to the best results during the optimization process because, during the training process, many grid cells do not contain any objects so the confidence level approaches 0, causing the grid cell error of some objects to become larger. As such, the model may become unstable and diverge during the training. To solve this problem, in our study, the loss weight of the bounding box prediction was increased and the loss weight of the confidence prediction without objects was reduced. In this method, we had to use two parameters, λ_{coord} (lambda-coordinates

= 5) and λ_{noobj} (lambda-noobject = 0.5) to finalize the solution [16]. At this point, the sum-squared error was the same for boxes of different sizes. However, given the same discrete value, a larger box should affect the error less. To accurately reflect the relationship between the size of the box and the error value, we further took the square root of the width and height. Since YOLO calculated several bounding boxes for each grid cell, during the training, the bounding box with the largest IOU for each identified object was selected as the bounding box predictor that represented that object.

Finally, the loss function was optimized during the training. The loss function would only consider the error of its classification when it contained objects in a grid cell during the training. Moreover, the bounding box error would only be considered if the bounding box was an object predictor. In summary, the training parameters were as follows (Fig. 3, [37]):

```
[TRAINING PARAMETERS]
135 epochs on training & validation from PASCAL VOC 2007/2012,
batch size = 64,
momentum = 0.9,
decay = 0.0005,
learning rate:
0-75 epochs = 10^-2,
75-105 epochs = 10^-3,
105-135 epochs = 10^-4,
dropout rate = 0.5
data augmentation by 20% or more
randomly adjust exposure and saturation up to 1.5x in HSV space
```

Fig. 3. Training parameters.

YOLO Inference. The test procedure was the same as the training procedure, and the result was obtained by directly running the image through the network. It was observed that YOLO was faster than the traditional classifier-based algorithm. Because slicing an image into a grid can cause its spatial information to be scattered, it is generally possible to know for certain which grid cell contains the object (even for large objects) and which ones are located next to the object. If a non-maximal expression were added to the model, the mean average precision could be increased by 2–3%.

Limitations of YOLO. YOLO's architecture limits the space of each grid to only predict two bounding boxes and one class for each grid. Therefore, it is difficult to recognize very small objects.

4.5 Model Evaluation Method

To calculate the accuracy, several indices could be used, such as IOU – the standard for detecting object accuracy, precision, recall, precision-recall curve, and average precision (AP) [15, 38]. In this study, we evaluated the accuracy of extracting highlights from the original live video, excluding any close-up replays. We used a confusion matrix (Table 2) to evaluate the accuracy rate of our model. Below are the four indices:

True positive (TP): There is a highlight, and the model can detect it.

True negative (TN): There is a highlight, but the model cannot detect it.

False positive (FP): There is no highlight, but the model detects it.

False negative (FN): There is no highlight, and the model does not detect it.

Table 2. Confusion matrix.

		Actual	
		True	False
Prediction	Positive	True Positive (TP)	False Positive (FP)
	Negative	True Negative (TN)	False Negative (FN)

The accuracy rate defined in this study is as follows:

$$\text{Accuracy rate} = \frac{\text{TruePositive}}{\text{TotalNumberofPredictions}}.$$

YOLOv5s generates correlogram plots to display the features of the supplied image (i.e., game pictures containing scoreboards) and bounding box. As shown in Fig. 4, ax[0] draws the histogram of the distribution of classes on the upper left; ax[1] draws all the real boxes on the upper right; ax[2] draws the histogram of the relationship between x and y on the lower left; ax[3] draws the width and height relationship histogram on the lower right. Clearly, this study has only one class, i.e., scoreboard. The scoreboard images contained about 1,750 instances, with x and y varying from 0.100 to 0.300, and the height and weight varying from 0.080 to 0.300, as seen in Fig. 5. Figure 5 displays the multivariate joint distribution histograms of x, y, width, and height in the marked dataset, including a visualization of the pairwise relationship between two or more variables. Overall, the marked datasets were normal and balanced and could be used to build a model.

5   Results

Tables 3–7 display all the test results. The computation time to process each video link is shown at the bottom of each table. Since the model did not give any value to non-highlights, the value of the TN cell was zero in every table. All results reached over 70% accuracy. They were obtained by dividing the value of the TP cell by the sum of all the predictions, i.e., the values in all the cells. The model's performance was regarded as acceptable, compared with another study using YOLOv4 [39]. The AP was about 72.12%. However, the computation time was not always efficient, ranging from 12.28% to 41.73%. The main reason was the resource constraints in training a model via internet using Google Colab (Python 3) of Google Compute Engine (GPU) instead of a GPU or a TPU supercomputer. Another reason that might have caused such unstable efficiency was the time necessary for video data stack exchange during the model training process. The accuracy rates for all the tests were as follows:

$$\text{Test 1 Accuracy} = \frac{70}{70+29} = 70.71\%$$

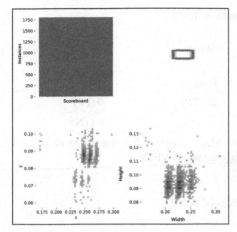

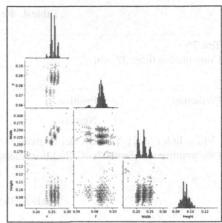

Fig. 4. Marked dataset (label: scoreboard for all collected game pictures).

Fig. 5. Distribution and correlation matrix of x, y, width, and height in the marked data (i.e., game pictures).

Computation time was 14.29% (42/49) of the original length of the video.

Test 2 Accuracy $= \frac{26}{26+11} = 70.27\%$

Computation time was 41.73% (32/54'55) of the original length of the video.

Test 3 Accuracy $= \frac{32}{32+12} = 72.72\%$

Computation time was 12.84% (43/49'20) of the original length of the video.

Test 4 Accuracy $= \frac{46}{46+19} = 70.77\%$

Computation time was 22.86% (54/70) of the original length of the video.

Test 5 Accuracy $= \frac{74}{74+30} = 71.15\%$

Computation time was 27.36% (60'03/83) of the original length of the video.

Table 3. Results of Test 1.

Test 1* Computation time: 42 min		Actual	
		True	False
Prediction	Positive	70 (TP)	0 (FP)
	Negative	29 (FN)	0 (TN)

* Video link ("2020 BWF Thomas Cup Men's Single"; duration: 49 min): https://www.youtube.com/watch?v=uXs4fI3CeHE&ab_channel=BWFTV

Table 4. Results of Test 2.

Test 2* Computation time: 32 min		Actual	
		True	False
Prediction	Positive	26 (TP)	0 (FP)
	Negative	11 (FN)	0 (TN)

* Video link ("2021 YONEX All England Open Men's Single"; duration: 54′55 min): https://www.youtube.com/watch?v=CZXQ_Joz69s&ab_channel=BWFTV

Table 5. Results of Test 3.

Test 3* Computation time: 43 min		Actual	
		True	False
Prediction	Positive	32 (TP)	0 (FP)
	Negative	12 (FN)	0 (TN)

* Video link ("2022 BWF World Championships Men's Single"; duration: 49′20 min): https://www.youtube.com/watch?v=c700deh2tCs&ab_channel=BWFTV

Table 6. Results of Test 4.

Test 4* Computation time: 54 min		Actual	
		True	False
Prediction	Positive	46 (TP)	0 (FP)
	Negative	19 (FN)	0 (TN)

* Video link ("2022 GR Toyota Gazoo Racing Thailand Open Men's Single"; duration: 70 min): https://www.youtube.com/watch?v=pp134m934s8

Table 7. Results of Test 5.

Test 5* Computation time: 60'03 min		Actual	
		True	False
Prediction	Positive	74 (TP)	0 (FP)
	Negative	30 (FN)	0 (TN)

* Video link ("2016 Rio Olympics Men's Single"; duration: 83 min): https://www.youtube.com/watch?v=Hf-n1yfd8II&t=480s

6 Discussions and Conclusion

This study used the YOLOv5s model to auto-detect sports highlights from badminton video clips by detecting the numbers shown on the scoreboard. Regardless of the scoreboard's location and size on the video clip, the model effectively detected the highlights (10 s before a player scores a point in the game). The test results from five video clips proved the model can extract the highlights with more than 70% accuracy to provide a highlight clip for badminton viewers, which is considered satisfactory. However, it was still time-consuming to detect the highlights by using the model. This study was limited by using only one model to carry out the scoreboard highlight detection, instead of comparing it with other models to determine which one was more accurate in detecting the changes in the scoreboard. Also, this study did not consider the teams' names (textual or word detection) in the model and treated both teams equally. Some viewers might prefer to see the highlights for their favorite team only. Future studies may consider including team names as a variable in their highlight prediction model. Note that while the model worked well with badminton games, it may not apply to other sports, such as basketball and volleyball. Lastly, the highlights defined in this study were the scoring segments during the game. However, there are many cases where beautiful and exciting plays happen in the middle of a rally that can be easily missed because the scoring doesn't happen until later. Therefore, we suggest that future studies can redefine the highlights in different sports, and they may need to be captured by using a completely different technology.

Different kinds of sports require different object detection models, and this can be achieved by revising the exemplar Python codes that prior studies have publicly released. The object of interest may not be the scoreboard, but the audio clips or other sports components shown in the video clips (i.e., the basketball slam dunking sound or cheerleaders' music or shouting). On the scoreboards, other than the numbers, the abbreviations of two teams' names might also be simultaneously detected. Other pieces of sensitive technology (e.g., MMOCR, a comprehensive and open-source toolbox for text detection, recognition, and understanding) are suggested to be implemented in future research [38]. Future studies are also suggested to use "State-of-the-Art" (SOTA) models (i.e., the best models for a specific task) to further improve the accuracy performance of object detection [40].

References

1. Yao, T., Mei, T., Rui, Y.: Highlight detection with pairwise deep ranking for first-person video summarization. In: 2016 IEEE Conference on Computer Vision and Pattern Recognition (CVPR), Las Vegas, NV, USA, 2016, pp. 982–990 (2016). https://doi.org/10.1109/CVPR.2016.112
2. Kulkarni, R., Dhavalikar, S., Bangar, S.: Traffic light detection and recognition for self-driving cars using deep learning. In: 2018 Fourth International Conference on Computing Communication Control and Automation, Pune, India, pp. 1–4 (2018). https://doi.org/10.1109/ICCUBEA.2018.8697819
3. Lee, J., Ryoo, M.S., Riley, M., Aggarwal, J.K.: Real-time illegal parking detection in outdoor environments using 1-D transformation. IEEE Trans. Circuits Syst. Video Technol. **19**(7), 1014–1024 (2009). https://doi.org/10.1109/TCSVT.2009.2020249
4. Jiang, R. Qu, C., Wang, J., Wang, C., Zheng, Y.: Towards extracting highlights from recorded live videos: An implicit crowdsourcing approach. In: 2020 IEEE 36th International Conference on Data Engineering (ICDE), 2019, pp. 1810–1813 (2019). https://doi.org/10.1109/ICDE48307.2020.00176
5. Alahi, A., Goel, K., Ramanathan, V., Robicquet, A., Li, F.F., Savarese, S.: Social LSTM: Human trajectory prediction in crowded spaces. In: 2016 IEEE Conference on Computer Vision and Pattern Recognition (CVPR), Las Vegas, NV, USA, 2016, pp. 961–971 (2016). https://doi.org/10.1109/CVPR.2016.110
6. OpenCV, https://docs.opencv.org/4.x/d1/d32/tutorial_py_contour_properties.html. Accessed 11 Feb 2023
7. LearnOpenCV. https://learnopencv.com/geometry-of-image-formation/
8. Azmedroub B., Ouarzeddine, M.: Polarimetric SAR images clustering with Gaussian mixtures model. In: 2015 Third International Conference on Control, Engineering & Information Technology, Tlemcen, Algeria, 2015, pp. 1–5 (2015). https://doi.org/10.1109/CEIT.2015.7233066
9. Zhang, Y., Lu, X.: A Speech recognition acoustic model based on LSTM –CTC. In: 2018 IEEE 18th International Conference on Communication Technology (ICCT), Chongqing, China, 2018, pp. 1052–1055 (2018). https://doi.org/10.1109/ICCT.2018.8599961
10. Buric, M., Pobar, M., Ivašić-Kos, M.: Adapting YOLO network for ball and player detection. In: The Proceedings of the 8th International Conference on Pattern Recognition Applications and Methods (ICPRAM), pp. 845–851 (2019). https://doi.org/10.5220/0007582008450851
11. Zhang, S., Lan, S., Bu, Q., Li, S.: YOLO based intelligent tracking system for curling sport. In: 2019 IEEE/ACIS 18th International Conference on Computer and Information Science (ICIS), Beijing, China, 2019, pp. 371–374 (2019). https://doi.org/10.1109/ICIS46139.2019.8940229
12. Park, C.H., Chang, J.H.: Revisiting skipped filter and development of robust localization method based on variational Bayesian Gaussian Mixture Algorithm. IEEE Trans. Signal Process. **70**, 5639–5651 (2022). https://doi.org/10.1109/TSP.2022.3224642
13. Massaoudi, M., et al.: An effective hybrid NARX-LSTM Model for point and interval PV power forecasting. IEEE Access **9**, 36571–36588 (2021). https://doi.org/10.1109/ACCESS.2021.3062776
14. Kido, S., Hirano, Y., Hashimoto, N.: Detection and classification of lung abnormalities by use of convolutional neural network (CNN) and regions with CNN features (R-CNN). In: 2018 International Workshop on Advanced Image Technology (IWAIT), Chiang Mai, Thailand, 2018, pp. 1-4 (2018). https://doi.org/10.1109/IWAIT.2018.8369798
15. Song, Y.: Real-time video highlights for Yahoo Esports. (2016) https://doi.org/10.48550/arXiv.1611.08780

16. Redmon, J., Divvala, S., Girshick, R. B., Farhadi, A.: You only look once: Unified, real-time object detection, CoRR (2015). https://doi.org/10.48550/arXiv.1506.02640
17. Fu, C.Y., Lee, J., Bansal, M., Berg, A.: Video Highlight Prediction Using Audience Chat Reactions. In: Proceedings of the 2017 Conference on Empirical Methods in Natural Language Processing, pp. 972–978 (2017). https://doi.org/10.18653/v1/D17-1102
18. Rui, Y., Gupta, A., Acero, A.: Automatically extracting highlights for TV Baseball programs. In: Proceedings of the Eighth ACM International Conference on Multimedia (MULTIMEDIA '00). Association for Computing Machinery, New York, NY, USA, pp. 105–115 (2000). https://doi.org/10.1145/354384.354443
19. Nepal, S., Srinivasan, U, Reynolds, G: Automatic detection of 'Goal' segments in basketball videos. In: Proceedings of the Ninth ACM International Conference on Multimedia (MULTIMEDIA '01). Association for Computing Machinery, pp. 261–269 (2001). https://doi.org/10.1145/500141.500181
20. Tjondronegoro, D., Phoebe Chen, Y.P., Pham, B.: Highlights for more complete sports video summarization. IEEE Multimedia 11(4), 22–37 (2004). https://doi.org/10.1109/MMUL.2004.28
21. Otsuka, I., Nakane, K., Divakaran, A., Hatanaka, K., Ogawa, M.: A highlight scene detection and video summarization system using audio feature for a personal video recorder. IEEE Trans. Consum. Electron. 51(1), 112–116 (2005). https://doi.org/10.1109/TCE.2005.1405707
22. Ma, Y.F., Hua, X.S., Lu, L., Zhang, H.J.: A generic framework of user attention model and its application in video summarization. IEEE Trans. Multimedia 7(5), 907–919 (2005). https://doi.org/10.1109/TMM.2005.854410
23. Ngo, C.W., Ma, Y.F., Zhang, H.J.: Video summarization and scene detection by graph modeling. IEEE Trans. Circuits Syst. Video Technol. 15(2), 296–305 (2005). https://doi.org/10.1109/TCSVT.2004.841694
24. Lin, K.S., Lee, A., Yang, Y.H., Lee, C.T., Chen, H.H.: Automatic highlights extraction for drama video using music emotion and human face features. In: 2011 IEEE 13th International Workshop on Multimedia Signal Processing, pp. 1–6 (2011). https://doi.org/10.1109/MMSP.2011.6093831
25. Wu, B., Zhong, E., Tan, B., Horner, A., Yang, Q.: Crowdsourced time-sync video tagging using temporal and personalized topic modeling. In: Proceedings of the 20th ACM SIGKDD International Conference on Knowledge discovery and data mining, pp. 721–730 (2014). doi: https://doi.org/10.1145/2623330.2623625
26. Raventós, A., Quijada, R., Torres, L., Tarrés, F.: Automatic summarization of soccer highlights using audio-visual descriptors. Springerplus 4(1), 1–19 (2015). https://doi.org/10.1186/s40064-015-1065-9
27. Otani, M., Nakashima, Y., Rahtu, E., Heikkilä, J., Yokoya, N.: Video summarization using deep semantic features. In: The 13th Asian Conference on Computer Vision (Asian Conference on Computer Vision, ACCV'16), pp. 361–377 (2016) https://doi.org/10.1007/978-3-319-54193-8_23
28. Lv, G., Xu, T., Chen, E., Liu, Q., Zheng, Y.: Reading the videos: Temporal labeling for crowdsourced time-sync videos based on semantic embedding. In: 2016 Thirtieth AAAI Conference on Artificial Intelligence (AAAI-2016). https://doi.org/10.1609/aaai.v30i1.10383
29. Ping, Q., Chen, C.: Video highlights detection and summarization with lag-calibration based on concept-emotion mapping of crowdsourced time-sync comments. In: Proceedings of the Workshop on New Frontiers in Summarization, pp. 1–11 (2017). https://doi.org/10.48550/arXiv.1708.02210
30. Skalic, M., Pekalski, M., Pan, X.: Deep learning methods for efficient large scale video labeling (2017). https://doi.org/10.48550/arXiv.1706.04572

31. Lee, J., Abu-El-Haija, S., Varadarajan, B., (Paul) Natsev, A.: Collaborative deep metric learning for video understanding. In: Proceedings of the 24th ACM SIGKDD International Conference on Knowledge Discovery & Data Mining (KDD '18). Association for Computing Machinery, New York, NY, USA, pp. 481–490 (2018). https://doi.org/10.1145/3219819.321 9856

32. Han, H.K., Huang, Y.C., Chen, C.: A deep learning model for extracting live streaming video highlights using audience messages. In: Proceedings of the 2019 2nd Artificial Intelligence and Cloud Computing Conference, pp. 75–81 (2019). https://doi.org/10.1145/3375959.337 5965

33. Yang, H., Wang, B., Lin, S., Wipf, D., Guo, M., Guo, B.: Unsupervised extraction of video highlights via robust recurrent auto-encoders. In: 2015 IEEE International Conference on Computer Vision (ICCV), Santiago, Chile, 2015, pp. 4633–4641 (2015). https://doi.org/10.1109/ICCV.2015.526

34. Jeong, J., Jeon, B.: A multiplierless letter-box converter for displaying 16:9 images on a 4:3 screen. IEEE Trans. Circuits Syst. Video Technol. 5(4), 363–366 (1995). https://doi.org/10.1109/76.465091

35. Theophilo, A., Giot, R., Rocha, A.: Authorship attribution of social media messages. In: IEEE Transactions on Computational Social Systems, vol. 10, pp. 10–23 https://doi.org/10.1109/TCSS.2021.3123895

36. Mahendru, M., Dubey, S.K.: Real time object detection with audio feedback using Yolo vs. Yolo_v3. In: 2021 11th International Conference on Cloud Computing, Data Science & Engineering (Confluence), Noida, India, pp. 734–740 (2021). https://doi.org/10.1109/Conflu ence51648.2021.9377064

37. Everingham, M., Eslami, S.M.A., Van Gool, L., Williams, C.K.I., Winn, J., Zisserman, A.: The Pascal visual object classes challenge: a retrospective. Int. J. Comput. Vision 111(1), 98–136 (2014). https://doi.org/10.1007/s11263-014-0733-5

38. Kuang, Z., et al.: MMOCR: A comprehensive toolbox for text detection, recognition and understanding (2021) https://doi.org/10.48550/arXiv.2108.06543

39. Bochkovskiy, A., Wang, C.Y., Mark Liao, H.Y.: YOLOv4: Optimal speed and accuracy of object detection (2020). https://doi.org/10.48550/arXiv.2004.10934

40. Naqvi, S.A.J., Ali, A.B. State-of-the-art Models for Object Detection in Various Fields of Application (2022). https://doi.org/10.48550/arXiv.2211.00733

A Drone-mounted Depth Camera-based Motion Capture System for Sports Performance Analysis

Martin Jacobsson[1]([envelope]) [iD], Jonas Willén[1][iD], and Mikael Swarén[2][iD]

[1] KTH Royal Institute of Technology, Huddinge, Sweden
{marjacob,jwi}@kth.se
[2] Dalarna University, Falun, Sweden
miv@du.se

Abstract. Video is the most used tool for sport performance analysis as it provides a common reference point for the coach and the athlete. The problem with video is that it is a subjective tool. To overcome this, motion capture systems can used to get an objective 3D model of a person's posture and motion, but only in laboratory settings. Unfortunately, many activities, such as most outdoor sports, cannot be captured in a lab without compromising the activity. In this paper, we propose to use an aerial drone system equipped with depth cameras, AI-based marker-less motion capture software to perform automatic skeleton tracking and real-time sports performance analysis of athletes. We experiment with off-the-shelf drone systems, miniaturized depth cameras, and commercially available skeleton tracking software to build a system for analyzing sports-related performance of athletes in their real settings. To make this a fully working system, we have conducted a few initial experiments and identified many issues that still needs to be addressed.

Keywords: Quadcopter · Drone · Motion capture · Skeleton tracking · Depth camera · Sports performance analysis

1 Introduction

Video-based analysis of sports performance is common practice today. Standard digital video cameras and smartphones are frequently used to record an action to later be analyzed by the athlete and coach together. However, this provides very little support for objective performance analysis. To overcome this, kinematic and force analyses in sports and health are performed indoors in specific laboratory settings due to the vast amount of required equipment and the need of a controlled environment for accurate data collection. There, motion capture systems are used to get a 3D model of a person's posture and motion. However, performing measurements in a laboratory always include adaptations to the actual situation and in many sports, it is almost impossible, such as sailing, rowing, the cornering in cycling, orienteering, and ski jumping.

H. Degen and S. Ntoa (Eds.): HCII 2023, LNAI 14051, pp. 489–503, 2023.
https://doi.org/10.1007/978-3-031-35894-4_36

There are solutions where multiple cameras are combined with sensors to provide kinematic data in e.g., track and field. However, these solutions are fixed and expensive installations in large sports arenas with the main purpose to enhance the spectator experience. Another possibility to capture 3D kinematics in the field, is to use inertial measurement units (IMUs) . The use of IMUs allows coaches, athletes, and researchers to collect kinematic data over a large area without any fixed installations. These existing solutions of in-field monitoring provide general information. However, there is a need for individual measurements of sport-specific techniques [21]. Even though today's IMUs are small, they still need to be attached to the athlete, which can interfere with borth the athlete and/or the equipment. They are also exposed to impacts that can cause them to fall off. The data from IMUs can also be difficult to interpret and connect with the athlete's action.

In this paper, to overcome these limitations, we propose an autonomously flying drone with subject tracking, a depth camera to capture the athlete, and to provide near real-time feedback to the coach or athlete based on AI-based skeleton tracking and kinematic analysis. Drones have become common, owing to the low cost and ease of operation. They are frequently being used in filming buildings, large objects, and large events, including sporting events. However, to analyze an athlete in motion, we also need further detailed information from the video camera, sophisticated data analysis, and processing as well as advanced flight control and guidance algorithms. Our proposed system would allow athletes to apply cutting-edge technological solutions to analyze kinematics in real settings for optimized performance in sports.

This paper is organized as follows. In Sect. 2, we begin with briefly discussing related work. Then, in Sect. 3, we introduce our prototype system. Section 4 covers our proposed application areas and initial experiments, whereas Sect. 5 lists identified challenges before we can realize our vision. Finally, the paper is concluded in Sect. 6.

2   Related Work

Markerless motion capture systems have recently started to develop and are now becoming more popular. A popular approach is to use a conventional digital video camera in combination with advanced computer vision algorithms [25]. Common approaches use standard RGB-images of a person and create a 3D model of the main human joints (e.g., ankles, knees, pelvis, shoulders, neck, elbows, and wrists), known as skeleton tracking. During the last decade, important improvements have been seen in both the techniques of video recording and how to analyze the video sequences with e.g., deep learning [6,26]. The technology can be used in many different application areas, including medical, film, animation, and sports.

Recent developments in depth camera technology have made them affordable and with increasing better accuracy. Every year, new and better cameras are released on the market. There is now also work in progress on creating better skeleton tracking algorithms based on depth camera input, instead of only the RGB-data. Examples include Cubemos [8] and NuiTrack [1].

Markerless motion capture systems have to some degree been used in sports. Recently, video-based marker-less motion capture based on one or more flying drones has been proposed (e.g., [7,17,24,27,29]). However, to the best of our knowledge, we are the first to propose the use of depth cameras on an aerial drone system for skeleton-based sports performance analysis.

In [29], a drone with a standard RGB-camera is used for skeleton tracking of a human performing sport-like activities. Another similar work is iHuman3D [7], where the authors are using a drone with depth cameras to do 3D human reconstruction. However, this work does not calculate a skeleton and hence is less useful for objective motion measurements of human athletes. Furthermore, a few examples exist where multiple drones with cameras are used to improve human pose estimation. Examples include Flycon [17] and AirCap [24] using standard cameras and FlyCap [27] using three flying drones with depth cameras. Finally, there is work on using skeleton tracking for mission planning, such as Domes to Drones [22] and ActiveMoCap [15]. However, their aim is to find the best position for the drone to improve the 3D human pose accuracy over time.

3 Our Prototype System

To make our vision a reality, a fully working system will include drones with depth cameras, 3D positioning and navigation, subject tracking, wireless networking, video analysis using 3D human pose estimation, human motion analysis, and feedback to the athlete or coach. Figure 1 depicts our vision of a complete system.

To initiate the journey towards our vision, we built an initial prototype. A photo of the fully equipped drone is shown in Fig. 2. In the following subsections, we introduce this prototype and motivate the choices that we made.

3.1 Drone Hardware

The drone frame is the NXP KIT-HGDRONEK66 [19], which is a self-assembly kit designed as a development platform for drone technology. It comes with a frame, motors, motor controllers, power supply control, GPS sensor, RC remote control, telemetry radio, and the NXP flight management unit (FMU) RDDRONE-FMUK66 [20]. The latter is an embedded system consisting of a microcontroller that is based on ARM Cortex M4, an IMU, a barometer, and connectors to motor controllers and additional sensors and other communication ports. It can run the popular open source PX4 Autopilot drone flight management software [23]. The drone was powered by a single LiPo 4S battery pack with a capacity of 2400 mAh, which gave us about 10 min of continuous flight time.

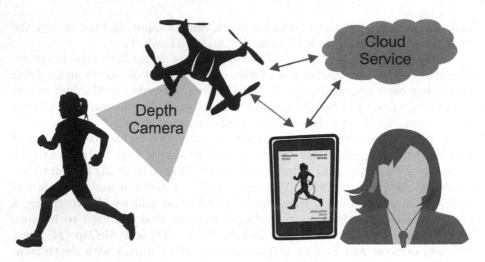

Fig. 1. Overview of a complete drone with depth camera system for sports performance analysis

Fig. 2. A photo illustrating the prototype drone system with all components mounted and highlighted

The drone is constantly moving and swinging during flight, even when hovering. To not obtain blurry images from the camera, we needed to stabilize the camera with an electromechanical stabilizer, a camera gimbal.

Finally, the drone is equipped with sensors guiding the flight and used by the FMU. In indoor use, the GPS/GLONASS sensor cannot be used. Furthermore, the barometer does not work well indoor as we experienced. The ventilation system in typical sports halls affects the air pressure, confusing the FMU, which might either crash into the floor or the ceiling as a consequence. Therefore, we equipped the drone with an altitude sensor based on a downwards directed time-of-flight (ToF) LiDAR-based ranging sensor.

3.2 Depth Camera

For the depth camera, we mainly experimented with the Intel RealSense LiDAR camera L515 [13], which was released in 2020. It is a combined Full HD color camera (RGB-camera) and a depth camera based on LiDAR-technology controlled by MEMS technology to scan the entire field-of-view with an IR beam. The camera is small and weighs only 100 g. It is connected by an USB-C 3.1 Gen 1 cable and can generate data up to 5 Gbps. One drawback of the L515 camera, when used in sports, is its low frame rate of only 30 fps. Another drawback is its difficulty to operate in outdoor daylight conditions.

We also experimented with the Intel RealSense D435i camera [14], which is based on active IR and stereo vision technology to obtain the depth information instead. However, the depth information has lower accuracy and works best with distances around 2 m, which is too close for our drone solution. On the other hand, the D435i supports frame rates of up to 90 fps and can be used outdoor in daylight conditions. An even better option for future prototypes is the newer Intel RealSense D455 camera [14], which allows for larger distances between the drone and the subject.

3.3 Onboard Computation

For the data analysis and video coding, we cannot use the FMU, but we need a powerful embedded computer. Our choice became LattePanda Alpha 864s, which is equipped with an Intel Core m3-8100Y 1.1 GHz dual-core processor. It has built-in eMMC-storage, but also PCIe 4x slots, where we connected an NVMe-based solid-state disk (SSD) with high writing performance for saving all the raw data generated by the camera.

3.4 Software

The FMU runs standard PX4 [23], which can easily be reconfigured for the NXP drone frame and RC remote control. To enable autonomous flight, we connected the FMU with the LattePanda. The LattePanda runs a standard Linux operating system and many of the tools were written in Python or C++ using OpenCV. The Intel RealSense cameras come with a library SDK called Intel RealSense SDK 2.0. This library has easy bindings for use in Python, C++, and other languages and works well together with OpenCV. From the library, we can control the camera configurations and receive data in the form of image frames and depth frames.

For our initial prototype, we tried two commercially available skeleton tracking software that use depth camera information, namely Cubemos Skeleton tracking [8] and Nuitrack Pro [1]. Both of them uses machine learning (ML) techniques on each of the frames to find the main joints of the human body. Nuitrack uses the depth camera data only, while Cubemos uses the color frame for joint detection and then the depth frame for extracting the third coordinate.

Figure 3 shows how the main software and hardware parts of the system are connected. However, we did not yet implement the control of the gimbal but controlled the yaw of the drone itself to point the camera in the right direction. The altitude of the drone was constantly measured by a LiDAR-based time-of-flight sensor pointing straight downwards and used to control the height over ground to about 2 m. Besides a few auxiliary software modules, the software was made up by two main parts: 1) the skeleton tracker analyzing the video stream, and 2) the mission control module that controls what the drone should do next. For each sensor and video input, the mission control would take the decision to move up, down, left, or right and send commands over the MAVLINK interface to the flight management unit (FMU) controlling the rotors.

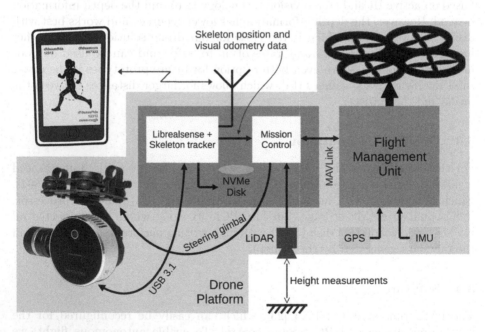

Fig. 3. Software and hardware architecture of our prototype drone platform

4   Application Areas and Initial Tests

In sports, video is an essential tool for performance analysis, to optimize player- and team-performance as well as for injury prevention. The rapid development in machine learning and computer vision, where specific metrics and kinematics can be obtained from video data, have increased the importance of video analyses even further. Video data is also important for enhancing the spectator experience as well as providing content to the spectators' second screen [5,9].

Today's video analysis software allows coaches to analyze kinematics as well as tactics. However, different sports need different camera setups to capture useful video data, e.g., a football field can be covered by a number of fixed cameras whereas it is difficult to cover a complete mountain bike course. There are also differences between sports regarding which metrics to analyze and the level of measurement accuracy. For example in football, common metrics to analyze are covered distance, running speeds, number of high-intensity sprints, the distance between team players, number of passes etc. [2,28] Whereas in athletics and kayaking, coaches often want to analyze specific joint angles, range of motion, contact times and center of mass movement [3,4,11,16,30]. Furthermore, explosive sports, such as javelin and long jump, demand a high video frame rate compared to tactical analyses of e.g., a football game. Hence a new drone-based camera system which can follow specific athletes, cover certain areas of interest, and provide accurate 2D and 3D data is of great interest for coaches, performance analysts, researchers, and commercial sports actors. Such a system could follow and capture accurate kinematic data of e.g., rowers, kayakers and eventing riders during entire races or analyze different lines in downhill mountain bikers and alpine skiing as well as sailing tactics during a regatta.

Another potential benefit with autonomous drones is the possibility to do skeleton tracking without a team of experts. This enables objective performance measurements with only the athlete him/herself and a coach or friend. Furthermore, the same system can be used as an easier and more accessible solution for skeleton tracking in film animation and gaming.

4.1 Use-case Evaluation

To test our system, we decided to start with simple sports in order to reduce the complexity. Therefore, we started with just jogging in an indoor sports hall. In this use-case evaluation, we did not have autonomous flying implemented. Instead, we tried to fly the drone manually with a remote radio controller. This meant that the drone pilot had to maneuver the drone at the right altitude, angle, and distance from the athlete. Due to near ground effects, and the lack of precise altitude sensors, this was very challenging, leading to the drone flying far too low and/or too close to the subject. This means that the full body will not always be visible in the camera's view.

Despite the challenges with manual flying, we could record short sequences of an athlete doing slow jogging in a sports hall. Based on these recordings, we experimented with two existing human pose estimation systems based on skeleton tracking software packages as can be seen in Fig. 4. In the left photo, we show the result of Cubemos Skeleton Tracker SDK [8], which used an 18-joints skeleton. Cubemos was a skeleton-tracker developed specifically for the Intel depth cameras, but has now been discontinued. In the photo, we draw the estimated skeleton by connecting yellow lines between the main joints. For each joint, we printed the three estimated coordinates.

In the right photo of Fig. 4, we show the result of a single video frame from the Nuitrack [1] software. Nuitrack uses only the depth camera information and estimates 19 main joints of the human body. The figure shows those joints marked as blue dots overlayed on the depth camera data, where different colors mean different distances. The yellow text accompanying each blue dot gives the distance (i.e., z-coordinate) to the joint.

Fig. 4. Examples of skeleton tracking from the drone and its Intel RealSense L515 camera using two different skeleton tracking software solutions. The left part shows Cubemos Skeleton Tracker SDK [8] and the right part shows Nuitrack [1] overlayed on the depth data. The two examples show the same subject, but different experiments.

In both these two examples, the distance to the athlete is very good and the full body is in the camera's view. Hence, we get fairly good results. With the RealSense L515 pixel resolution and at a distance of 3 m from the subject, one pixel off corresponds to an error in the order of 3 mm with the RGB and 5 mm with the depth frame in the XY-plane. As parts of the body leave the view, we loose the position of joints and if the athlete is far from the camera, the accuracy in the joint estimation reduces.

The next step is to use the skeleton data to do further analysis for the sport of interest. In the example of jogging, this can be how the ankle moves over time, the contact time with the ground, the length of each step, the symmetry between the left and right leg, the forward-leaning of the upper body, etc. In other sports, other analysis might be of interest.

Finally, we envision that real-time streaming and analysis of the depth camera recording will be made available, including an app for the coach and instantaneous feedback to the athlete, such as through tactile feedback. Furthermore, we foresee the need to complement the depth camera information with additional wearable sensors, such as force sensors and physiological sensors.

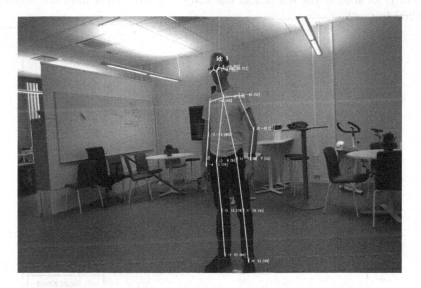

Fig. 5. Experiment setup for the validation of the accuracy of a skeleton tracking system based on a depth camera, from the thesis of Efstratiou [10]

4.2   Skeleton Tracking Accuracy

However, to be useful for sports applications, we need to know the accuracy of the skeleton-tracking systems. Hence, we created a simple experiment to get an initial understanding about the quality of current skeleton trackers [10]. We decided to use a static subject that keeps an identical pose while the depth camera circulates in a steady pace around the subject, as shown in Fig. 5. The subject is at standstill position with his knees fully extended (approximately 180°C) while the camera is tracking him in a semi-circular trajectory. The camera was positioned on a trolley and pushed around the subject in a steady and slow pace starting from right side of the subject, slightly behind and then moved around the subject counter-clockwise until reaching the position slightly behind the left side.

Figure 6 shows the knee angles of both the left and right knees as calculated from the skeleton tracking algorithm during the entire experiment. Each line derives from the same video and the x-axis represents the sequence of frames from the video, where the first frames are from the right side of the subject. Its duration is 43 s with 30 frames per second. The data has been filtered with a fixed-interval smoothing filter.

Self-occlusion is a large drawback of camera-based systems. Our qualitative observations confirm that. As we can observe in Fig. 6, when the camera is located at the right side of the subject (see the first 200 frames), the angle of the left knee is much further from the true value. The same holds true when the camera is located at the left side of the subject for the right knee angle (see the last 200 frames).

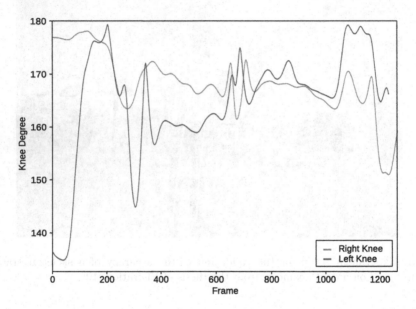

Fig. 6. The calculated knee angles by the depth camera-based skeleton tracking system as the camera moves around a static subject. The true value of both knees is approximately 180°C. The data comes from the thesis of Efstratiou [10].

Another issue added by the drone is the fact that both the subject and the camera are moving. Often, we wish to analyze how a subject move over the ground or floor, such as speed over ground or how long time a foot is on the ground. If the camera is on a flying drone, then the ground will move in the image and it becomes necessary to keep track of both the floor and the subject, which leads to bigger measurement uncertainties.

4.3   Autonomous Flying

In another evaluation, we experimented with getting the drone to do autonomous flying and following the athlete using the skeleton tracking software [18]. Due to hardware constraints by Cubemos, we had to base our solution on Nuitrack. 30 tests were conducted outdoor on a flat grass field during stable weather conditions (17–19°C, sunny, 4–8 m/s wind). In the tests, one person would walk at a slow pace in an L-shape movement pattern for about 10 s.

The drone was successfully able to follow the subject throughout the complete course in 20 of the performed tests. Four tests failed due to the drone being unable to complete its takeoff. The remaining six tests failed because the drone was unable to keep track of the subject due to either loss of tracking from Nuitrack or incorrect positioning commands sent to the FMU, which caused the drone to drift away from the subject. The drone performed its position adjustments without extensive delays based on the movements of the subject. Ignoring the takeoff and landing, the drone system successfully followed the walking person in 77%. However, we are aware of many improvements to these results. Details can be found in the thesis of Nordberg and Sjödal [18].

5   Challenges

The initial results are promising, but we are working on making the prototype system more robust and to implement missing features. We noticed several challenges that remains, not only in our prototype but in current state-of-the-art technology. In the following, we list them one by one.

5.1   Power and Weight

As with any aerial drone system, a big issue is to find the right balance between battery life and the weight of the drone. Currently, our drone is only able to collect data in the order of a few minutes. Hence, for an hour-long training session, multiple battery changes are required. This cannot be solved by more powerful batteries, since more weight is added. Instead, we need a smaller drone frame, smaller camera and gimbal, streamlined software and hardware, optimized calculations, and smarter battery management.

5.2   Computation, Storage, and Communications Capacity

This project aimed at providing real-time or near real-time feedback to the coach or athlete. To make this happen, we need a system that can do video coding (compression), analysis, and communication in real-time. The current camera generates several images per frame of uncompressed data: one RGB image, one depth data image, infrared images, and IMU data. The L515 camera can generate 30 frames per second yielding an amount of 1 GB of data per second. The generated data will exceed the bandwidth of most embedded systems. It will fill the memory very quickly. Furthermore, many types of persistent memories, including almost all SD-cards, will not handle the required bandwidth. In our prototype, we solved this with a high-speed laptop-grade NVMe memory.

5.3   Cameras and Optics

Currently, the drone is equipped with an Intel LiDAR L515 camera. This camera does not support the possibility to change the camera optics or to zoom. This is true for most LiDAR or stereo cameras, since they work with multiple cameras and lenses. Furthermore, a telephoto lens with a big aperture would be big and heavy while you need multiple such lenses. Hence, there is a need to fly at a given distance from the subject to capture the entire subject in the image and, at the same time, not being too far away since the image resolution would mean less granularity in the pose estimation. With the L515 camera, the optimal distance is about 3 m in order to capture a full-grown standing person, which is uncomfortably close to have a flying drone. However, the new Intel D455 depth-camera [14] allows for operation at distances up to 6 m from the subject, which would be a better choice.

Another unexpected issue that we encountered with the small camera and gimbal is the USB cable connecting the camera with the on-board computational platform. Due to the high data rate, we need USB cables supporting at least the USB 3.1 SuperSpeed standard. Unfortunately, such cables are very stiff. We needed to remove the outer protective layer of the cable and experiment with the weight balance of the camera and how to mount the cable in order to find acceptable configurations where the gimbal could perform without issues.

5.4   Skeleton Tracking Lack of Accuracy

The performance of today's skeleton tracking software has many limitations as demonstrated in Sect. 4.2. First, most systems based on machine learning have been trained on still images. Hence, the moving system that we have adds noise and jitter. Second, fast movements can cause motion blur if using lightweight optics in bad lighting conditions. When the drone is too far away, the spatial resolution of the subject becomes limited leading to problems with low granularity in the joint coordinates. Finally, skeleton trackers currently do not perform well from all angles and typically have problems with occlusions, such as when the arm is behind the body.

5.5   Autonomous Flight

Manually flying the drone via a remote radio control (RC) transmitter and following a moving athlete is extremely difficult as mentioned earlier. Hence, there is a need for autonomous flying or at least assisted flying. Furthermore, when flying indoors, the proximity to the floor, the ceiling, or walls make wind turbulence unpredictable and even harder to achieve stable flying. And outdoors, weather and wind can be a challenge.

In outdoor situations, satellite navigation receivers may enable stable flying. Indoors, however, other solutions are required, such as LiDAR-based altitude meters, visual odometery navigation [12], and feedback from the skeleton tracking system on where the athlete is located and in what direction and speed the athlete is moving.

Fully autonomous flying will also introduce new issues that need to be taken in to account, such as how to avoid obstacles, other drones, and other humans. Other challenges include the athlete moving into a tunnel, running over stairs and other uneven surfaces, and swimming in open water.

5.6 Time Synchronization with Other Devices

In some scenarios, recorded footage needs be complemented with key performance measurements, such as force sensors. However, we need to make sure that the measurements are time synchronized with the video so that it is possible to see in the film what exactly happened when a measurement gave a certain result. Another example is the use of multiple drones following the same athlete to solve the issues with occlusions of limbs and other body parts. Finally, there may be a use of IMUs to increase the accuracy of the skeleton tracking and that again means time synchronization between the video footage and wearable sensors.

6 Conclusions

In this paper, we introduced a system of an autonomously flying drone with a depth camera that perform skeleton tracking of a person by following the person at a close distance. This will enable efficient motion capture and performance analysis of many outdoor sports activities. The prototype was built using an off-the-shelf drone platform, miniaturized depth cameras, and commercially available skeleton tracking software. While the system already can perform some of the envisioned tasks, we have identified many issues that still need to be addressed to make this a useful working system.

Acknowledgments. We would like to thank Panagiotis Efstratiou for his help in working with the skeleton tracking software and analysis. Furthermore, we would like to thank Lucas Sjödal and Emil Nordberg for their work with the autonomous flying of the drone system.

References

1. Nuitrack Full Body Skeletal Tracking Software (2021). https://nuitrack.com/
2. Barris, S., Button, C.: A review of vision-based motion analysis in sport. Sports Med. **38**, 1025–1043 (2008). https://doi.org/10.2165/00007256-200838120-00006
3. Bjerkefors, A., Rosén, J.S., Tarassova, O., Arndt, A.: Three-dimensional kinematics and power output in elite para-kayakers and elite able-bodied flat-water kayakers. J. Appl. Biomech. **35**, 93–100 (2019)
4. Bulgan, C., Eroz, G., Bergün, Aydin, M.: Three-dimensional angular kinematics of 200m flat-water sprint kayaking. Acta Medica Mediterranea **33**, 129–132 (2017)
5. Centieriro, P., Romão, T., Dias, A.E.: Enhancing remote spectators' experience during live sports broadcasts with second screen applications. In: More Playful User Interfaces, pp. 231–261 (2015). https://doi.org/10.1007/978-981-287-546-4_10

6. Chen, C.H., Ramanan, D.: 3D human pose estimation = 2D pose estimation + matching. In: 2017 IEEE Conference on Computer Vision and Pattern Recognition (CVPR), pp. 5759–5767 (2017). https://doi.org/10.1109/CVPR.2017.610
7. Cheng, W., Xu, L., Han, L., Guo, Y., Fang, L.: iHuman3D: Intelligent human body 3D reconstruction using a single flying camera. In: Proceedings of the 26th ACM International Conference on Multimedia, pp. 1733–1741. MM '18, Association for Computing Machinery, New York, NY, USA (2018). https://doi.org/10.1145/3240508.3240600
8. Cubemos Skeleton Tracking SDK (2021). https://www.intel.com/content/www/us/en/internet-of-things/ai-in-production/partners/cubemos.html
9. Cunningham, N.R., Eastin, M.S.: Second screen and sports: a structural investigation into team identification and efficacy. Commun. Sport 5, 288–310 (2017)
10. Efstratiou, P.: Skeleton Tracking for Sports Using LiDAR Depth Camera. Master's thesis, KTH Royal Institute of Technology (2021). http://urn.kb.se/resolve?urn=urn:nbn:se:kth:diva-297536
11. Graham-Smith, P., Lees, A.: A three-dimensional kinematic analysis of the long jump take-off. J. Sports Sci. 23, 891–903 (2005)
12. He, M., Zhu, C., Huang, Q., Ren, B., Liu, J.: A review of monocular visual odometry. Vis. Comput. 36(5), 1053–1065 (2020). https://doi.org/10.1007/s00371-019-01714-6
13. Intel RealSense LiDAR Camera L515 - Datasheet (January 2021). https://www.intelrealsense.com/lidar-camera-l515/
14. Intel RealSense Product Family D400 Series (November 2022). https://www.intelrealsense.com/wp-content/uploads/2022/11/Intel-RealSense-D400-Series-Datasheet-November-2022.pdf
15. Kiciroglu, S., Rhodin, H., Sinha, S.N., Salzmann, M., Fua, P.: ActiveMoCap: Optimized viewpoint selection for active human motion capture. In: 2020 IEEE/CVF Conference on Computer Vision and Pattern Recognition (CVPR), pp. 100–109 (2020). https://doi.org/10.1109/CVPR42600.2020.00018
16. McDonald, C., Dapena, J.: Linear kinematics of the men's 110-m and women's 100-m hurdles races. Med. Sci. Sports Exerc. 23, 1382–1391 (1991)
17. Nägeli, T., Oberholzer, S., Plüss, S., Alonso-Mora, J., Hilliges, O.: Flycon: Realtime environment-independent multi-view human pose estimation with aerial vehicles. ACM Trans. Graph. 37(6) (Dec 2018). https://doi.org/10.1145/3272127.3275022
18. Nordberg, E., Sjödal, L.: Implementation of Video-based Person Tracking in a Drone System. Bachelor's thesis, KTH Royal Institute of Technolgy, Huddinge, Sweden (2021). http://urn.kb.se/resolve?urn=urn:nbn:se:kth:diva-296633
19. KIT-HGDRONEK66: NXP HoverGames drone kit including RDDRONE-FMUK66 and peripherals (2021). https://www.nxp.com/design/designs/nxp-hovergames-drone-kit-including-rddrone-fmuk66-and-peripherals:KIT-HGDRONEK66
20. PX4 Robotic Drone Flight Management Unit (FMU) - RDDRONE-FMUK66 (2021). https://www.nxp.com/design/designs/px4-robotic-drone-flight-management-unit-fmu-rddrone-fmuk66:RDDRONE-FMUK66
21. Pandey, M., Nebeling, M., Park, S.Y., Oney, S.: Exploring tracking needs and practices of recreational athletes. In: 13th EAI International Conference on Pervasive Computing Technologies for Healthcare - Demos and Posters. EAI (6 2019). https://doi.org/10.4108/eai.20-5-2019.2283726

22. Pirinen, A., Gärtner, E., Sminchisescu, C.: Domes to drones: Self-supervised active triangulation for 3d human pose reconstruction supplementary material. Advances in Neural Information Processing Systems 32 (Jan 2019). In: 33rd Annual Conference on Neural Information Processing Systems, NeurIPS 2019; Conference date: 08-12-2019 Through 14-12-2019
23. PX4 Open Source Autopilot for Drones (2021). https://px4.io/
24. Saini, N., et al.: Markerless outdoor human motion capture using multiple autonomous micro aerial vehicles. In: Proceedings of the IEEE/CVF International Conference on Computer Vision (ICCV), pp. 823–832 (2019). https://doi.org/10.1109/ICCV.2019.00091
25. Sarafianos, N., Boteanu, B., Ionescu, B., Kakadiaris, I.A.: 3D human pose estimation: A review of the literature and analysis of covariates. Computer Vision and Image Understanding **152**, 1 – 20 (2016). https://doi.org/10.1016/j.cviu.2016.09.002, http://www.sciencedirect.com/science/article/pii/S1077314216301369
26. Tome, D., Russell, C., Agapito, L.: Lifting from the deep: Convolutional 3D pose estimation from a single image. In: 2017 IEEE Conference on Computer Vision and Pattern Recognition (CVPR), pp. 5689–5698 (2017). https://doi.org/10.1109/CVPR.2017.603
27. Xu, L., et al.: FlyCap: markerless motion capture using multiple autonomous flying cameras. IEEE Trans. Visual Comput. Graph. **24**(8), 2284–2297 (2018). https://doi.org/10.1109/TVCG.2017.2728660
28. Yang, G., Leicht, A.S., Lago, C., Gómez, M.A.: Key team physical and technical performance indicators indicative of team quality in the soccer chinese super league. Res. Sports Med. **26**, 158–167 (2018). https://doi.org/10.1080/15438627.2018.1431539
29. Zhou, X., Liu, S., Pavlakos, G., Kumar, V., Daniilidis, K.: Human motion capture using a drone. In: 2018 IEEE International Conference on Robotics and Automation (ICRA), pp. 2027–2033 (2018). https://doi.org/10.1109/ICRA.2018.8462830
30. Čoh, M., Hébert-Losier, K., Štuhec, S., Babić, V., Supej, M.: Kinematics of usain bolt's maximal sprint velocity. Kinesiology **50**, 172–180 (2018)

General Agent Theory of Mind: Preliminary Investigations and Vision

Prabhat Kumar$^{(\boxtimes)}$, Adrienne Raglin, and John Richardson

US DEVCOM Army Research Laboratory, Adelphi, MD, USA
prabhat.kumar.civ@army.mil

Abstract. A Theory of Mind (ToM) is a mental representation one agent has of another's emotion, desires, beliefs, and intentions formed through their interactions which help the agent predict the other's behaviors. The concept comes from work in cognitive science which addresses questions about the mechanism for inferring motivations behind human behavior. We aim to apply this concept to understand the degree to which we can impart ToM capabilities to artificial agents. While we do not aim to resolve the depths of human emotions, desires, and beliefs, we hope to recreate a proof-of-concept from a recent machine learning application and later scale to more realistic contexts.

Keywords: cognitive science · machine learning · theory of mind · reasoning · artificial intelligence · artificial reasoning

1 Introduction

A Theory of Mind (ToM) is a mental representation one agent has of another's emotion, desires, beliefs, and intentions formed through their interactions which help the agent predict the other's behaviors. The concept was first presented in 1978 by Premack [12] where they attempt to answer whether chimpanzees infer mental states (purpose) from videos depicting humans facing some problem. In 1985, Baron-Cohen [4] applied ToM to learn that autistic children, specifically, may have a cognitive hindrance towards forming a ToM of other individuals, at least, until a bit later in life. They were the first to implement the Sally-Anne Test, Fig. 1, to ascribe to individuals the ability to infer false-beliefs.

Fast-forwarding, we come across works attempting to model the ToM process using inverse reinforcement learning by Ng [9], recursive-thinking by Yoshida [20], and most foundational to our work, using Bayesian techniques by Baker [3]. In the latter work, they use Bayesian inferencing on partially observable Markov decision processes (POMDPs) to model an agent's planning about its environment. An initial inspiration for our work came from Diaconescu's study [6], which builds on these Bayesian Theory of Mind ideas by considering a model known as a Hierarchical Gaussian Filter to account for the depths of one's understanding about the volatility and accuracy of another's information. Instead of asserting such a pre-existing Bayesian model, our interest lies in testing the extents

H. Degen and S. Ntoa (Eds.): HCII 2023, LNAI 14051, pp. 504–515, 2023.
https://doi.org/10.1007/978-3-031-35894-4_37

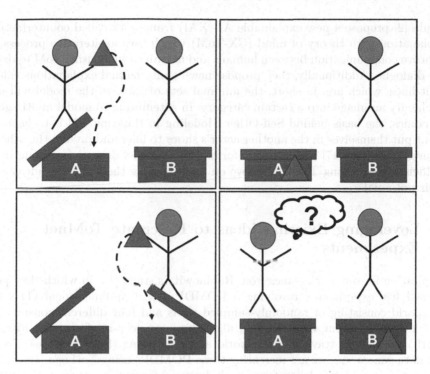

Fig. 1. The Sally-Anne Test was presented in Baron-Cohen [4]. Sally places an object in Box A, and leaves the room. While Sally is out, Anne switches the object to Box B. The idea is to have the test-taker infer where will Sally look for the object upon returning: Box A or B?

to which we can impart ToM capabilities to artificial agents using a machine learning model which has the flexibility to extend its learned representations.

Machine learning applications of ToM are still in their infancy with Rabinowitz's work [13] standing at the base of many recent studies. In this work, the goal is creating a neural network architecture, ToMnet, capable of modeling the mindset of the agents it observes. They perform experiments involving POMDPs of 2D gridworlds with an agent traversing the world and consuming objects within. We discuss the experiments in Sect. 2 and using the thoughts on scaling, presented in the paper, to inspire extensions of our own work in Sect. 4. To address a few more recent studies, Nguyen [10] and [11] builds directly off Rabinowitz, but uses a pre-supposed ACT-R cognitive learning model [16] as the observer rather than a blank-slate neural network architecture. In Chen [5], they use a convolutional network to predict behavior of robots based solely on raw camera input and using their own false-belief test they concluded the AI was able to separate its own perspective from that of the observed robots up to a degree determined by the physical attributes of the various objects the robot interacted with. There is also work on improving human trust in machines.

Akula [2] propose a new explainable AI (XAI) framework called counterfactual explanation with theory of mind (CX-ToM) which uses an iterative process to improve communication between humans and machines while using ToM to drive the dialogue. Additionally, they propose new counterfactual explanations called fault-lines, which are, in short, the minimal sets of features the model will use to classify an image into a certain category. In attempting to model multi-agent dynamics, the basis behind Self-Other Modeling in Raileanu [15] is to have an agent put themselves in the another actor's shoes to infer and predict the other's behavior. Sarkadi [17] contributes a formalism to model deception coming from artificial agents using ToM. We move on to leveraging these existing ideas and their potential.

2   Leveraging Existing Ideas to Re-create ToMnet Experiments

Inspiration for our work comes from Rabinowitz's study [13] in which they performed five experiments involving a POMDP of a two-dimensional (11×11) gridworld consisting of randomly-sampled walls and four different consumable objects and an agent with random, algorithmic or deep-reinforcement learned (DRL) policies for traversing the world and consuming the objects; see Fig. 2. For data generation, we are recreating these POMDPs using NetLogo [19] which is a programmable modeling framework designed for running these social simulations and other physical phenomena. In the initial stages, our ToMnet architecture will be based on Rabinowitz's work, but will adapt as we explore further. For example, data pipelines will adjust to accompany multiple agent trajectories, additional inputs and outputs to provide more reasoning perspectives and optimized embeddings; we discuss our work in Sect. 3 and expand further in Sect. 4 on scaling our work.

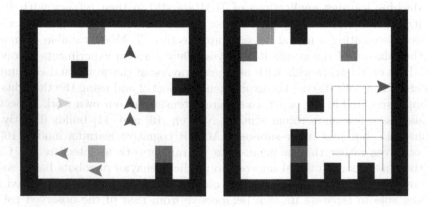

Fig. 2. Examples of POMDPs: 2D gridworlds and agents traversing each world, recreated in NetLogo [19] and based on work by Rabinowitz [13].

The five experiments included three for the each of the agent policies (random, algorithmic, DRL), one testing ToMnet's ability to infer false-beliefs with the Sally-Anne Test, and one to test ToMnet's ability to explicitly infer the mental states of the agents it observes. Even these "initial" experiments provide realistic insight. For the first three, it will be important for our system to be able to discern agent policies operating in the real world. If there is an agent following a more algorithmic trajectory (such as implementing classical wall-following or greedy algorithms), our own system could predict its path through space. Assuming full observer observability, the Sally-Anne Test could help our agents in the field avoid environmental shifts outside the agent's field of view, or help them create their own deceptions as needed. Finally, explicitly inferring the agent's mental states provides explainability to understand the motivations behind agent action. We aim to expand on these experiments to more closely model the real-world.

We hope to also build on ideas from some of the other studies mentioned in the Introduction. While Diaconescu [6] attempts to model ToM in human-human interaction, it inspires us in designing human-AI or even AI-AI experiments to unravel the "black-box" neural networks we implement while also helping us understand multi-agent interaction from a ToM standpoint. Nguyen [10] argues that their ACT-R observer model inherently assumes human neuro- and cognitive science which will be useful when attempting to infer on agents directly influenced by humans, but it also leads to its own philosophical explorations. For example, are artificial theories of mind derived from underlying theories of minds of their human developers, or are they (or do they become) independent? In other words, in our search of an artificial ToM are we really just searching for the human ToM? Raileanu [15] helps lay a foundation for experimenting with multi-agent interaction by having agents predict the behavior of other agents using their own policies and then updating those same policies accordingly through their interaction. This will be an interesting avenue to explore as our models may be able to impart agents with their current capabilities and optimize their policies in response to shifting agent behavior. Finally, Sarkadi [17] aims to address deception by artificial agents, which is another dimension of understanding intention.

3 Work Thus Far

Phase I of our work involves developing the experimental ground to test our models. This includes recreating the POMDP simulation within NetLogo, automating raw data and model input generation, and recreating ToMnet's neural network architectures based directly off Rabinowitz [13], to which we refer the reader to learn more about their experimental setup and background. Here, we describe experimental methods and provide more commentary on interpreting their design choices.

3.1 Simulation and Data Generation

As of this writing, we completed development of the first experimental simulation using NetLogo. The simulation is grounded in the POMDP setup described in Sect. 2. For this experiment, the gridworld contains a single agent with a random policy for traversing the space, and we attempt to train our model to predict the agent's next move. The stochasticity of an agent's policy can be adjusted from completely random (all moves are equally possible) to completely deterministic (agents favors one direction over the others.) For one stochasticity setting, we train our model on a number of agents sampled with such policies; that is, we do not train our model on a set of agents which have different levels of stochasticity. It is important to note, that when we set the policies to be completely deterministic, we do not assign a high probability to one direction for all agents. Rather, one sampled agent may prefer overwhelmingly to move upward, while another prefers overwhelmingly to go right, etc. These sampled agents are individually spawned into a randomly initialized gridworld and allowed to move until they consume an object or until a certain time limit. This completes one episode and we may record multiple episodes per agent. Figure 3 provides a visualization of a state (the environmental condition) and an action (agent behavior) and they are formalized to define the agent's trajectory in the gridworld.

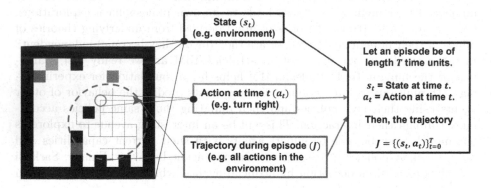

Fig. 3. Visualization of state and action in the gridworld and how they combine to form a trajectory.

We process the data using a custom, external Python package into an input state-action tensor as depicted in Fig. 4a, which represents one time step of one episode for a single agent. The reason we choose one time-step of an episode is because we are only interested in the model predicting the agent's next single time-step action. We record five episodes per agent. The POMDP is re-initialized randomly at the beginning of each episode, while the agent's policy remains the same. So, our gridworld is size 11×11 and we have K feature planes to capture different elements of the gridworld for the state tensor, resulting in a state tensor of shape $11 \times 11 \times K$. The action vector, a five-dimensntional vector with binary elements representing the agent's next step (up, down, left, right, stay), is spatialised (copied over space) so that its shape becomes compatible with two axes of the state tensor, namely $11 \times 11 \times 5$. Concatenating the action tensor with the state, we get our state-action vector with shape $11 \times 11 \times (K + 5)$. This would represent the data for one episode, and we have P episodes per agent and G agents. Therefore, our final input data shape will be $G \times P \times 11 \times 11 \times (K + 5)$; see Fig. 4b. It may help to think of a single state-action tensor as an image given its 3D structure. We have ToMnet train on the series of P such tensors for one agent to find connections within the series; namely the underlying agent policy.

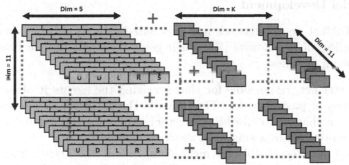

(a) State-Action input into the ToMnet model. (Left tensor) Action tensor, created by spatialising an action vector indicating an agent's next step. (Right tensor) State tensor created by parsing the gridworld into different features based on its components.

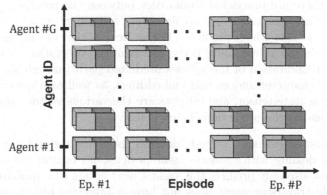

(b) A collection of state-action tensors for model input. Vertically, we are changing the agent's ID (total G agents) and horizontally we change the episode number (total P episodes). Final dataset size is $G \times P \times 11 \times 11 \times (K + 5)$

Fig. 4. Full dataset visualization for the first ToMnet experiment.

We also developed and automated the data-generation/model-input pipeline. NetLogo has a feature, BehaviorSpace, which helps automate parameter variation and, by extension, the experimental runs. For example, we can create a set of parameter values affecting the determinism of a random agent's traversal policies. Then, BehaviorSpace can loop through those parameter values, run the simulation, and record the gridworld state and agent trajectories in a CSV to externally process. NetLogo also has a Python extension which allows for embedding and running Python code within the simulation script, which is how we were able to incorporate the determinism setting for the agent policies.

3.2 Model Development

Our first ToMnet neural network model is based directly off the description in the Appendices of Rabinowitz [13]. Their general designs dictate that ToMnet has three main modules:

1. A character net, responsible for characterizing the agents it observes based on a series of past episodes. The input is the state-action tensors and the output is a character embedding (vector), which we will expand on shortly. (We interpret this as a long-term memory module.)
2. A mental net, responsible for mentalizing about the agent's mental state, given a more recent, past episode. (This can be interpreted as a short-term memory module.) Input is the character embedding from the character net and a recent episode's state-action tensor, and it outputs a mental embedding. We note there are functional similarities between the mental and character nets, but that their respective architectures will differ.
3. A prediction net, which predicts (1) the next action of the agent, (2) the agent's preferred object, and (3) the successor representation, which is essentially a representation of the agent's predicted path through the world. The inputs are character and mental embeddings, as well as a query state given simply by a state tensor, and outputs are the various vectors and other representations for the predictions listed before.

For the first experiment, we only develop the character and prediction nets; since we are dealing with random agent policies, no mental net is used. The prediction net also only predicts the agent's next action as a probability vector; the randomly traversing agent does not have a preferred object, and since we only predict the next step, we do not need to map out the agent's trajectory through the space.

Currently, our model is composed using TensorFlow's [1] Functional API, as this allows for much needed flexibility in multiple inputs and outputs, as well as non-linear data pipelines.

In developing our models, we treat each of ToMnet's modules individually, of course, but it is important to understand how these work together. Consider our current development of character and prediction nets. In the first module the model learns different agent characterizations based on their behavior, which are captured in the resulting character embedding passed to the prediction net. In a nutshell, an embedding is a machine's dense representation of some objects and their relationships and are typically formed as an intermediate step to a supervised machine learning problem, which is what we are working with given that we are comparing our model's prediction to the ground truth actions of an agent. One application is to extract the embeddings to use in a different context, i.e. transfer learning. For example, we could have a character embedding specifically trained using random agent trajectories, and another embedding for agents with more planned policies. These could be combined into a more general model which predicts on both types of agents. One advantage of using embeddings is to separate training on different types of instances reducing the need for a large variety of data for training on one model.

There are several considerations however. In our first experiment, our model is focused on attributing a tendency for agents to move in certain directions, which should not need more than a 2D learned embedding as per Rabinowitz [13]. As we increase agent capabilities to eventually plan out their trajectories using reinforcement learned policies and beyond, our embeddings will need to grow; Rabinowitz mentions use of 8D embedding spaces. They do not however mention any intermediate-dimensional spaces, so it will be interesting to explore the minimal embedding space rich enough to capture the agents' behaviors. We also need to understand how developed an embedding is before extracting and potentially transferring it to a different model/context. For higher-dimensional embeddings we will explore techniques to unravel the learned representations. Training our model through the full data pipeline from character net input to prediction output refines our character embeddings. For later experiments, we will also develop the mental net which produces a mental embedding from recent agent episodes. All in all, understanding and developing these character and mental embeddings will play an important, if not primary, role as we move towards our bigger vision.

4   Scaling and Potential Applications

Rabinowitz [13] mentions four ideas we also hope to leverage for scaling our simulation and models. Namely, (1) Expanding from 2D to 3D gridworlds, (2) Multi-agent dynamics, (3) Limiting the observer's field of view (FOV), and (4) Characterizing observed agents along different dimensions: animacy, reactive versus planned, social versus adversarial, natural versus artificial.

3D gridworlds will naturally allow generalizability to real-world situations; creating hills or valleys, vertical structures which may or may not be traversable, agents in the "air." While NetLogo has extensions to create 3D gridworlds, their website [19] notes that NetLogo 3D has less support than 2D at this time, so we will likely need to employ extensive testing or find another software solution. However, one workaround is using NetLogo's LevelSpace extension which allows one (parent) simulation model to open and run another (child) simulation and allows data transfer from the child to the parent model. This extension is still to be explored, but from initial investigation it will allow for simulations with more complex secondary tasks. For example, in video games there may "overworlds" in which the player directly traverses and interacts. The overworld may contain sub-areas which require the player to enter and complete tasks within (e.g. caves which have treasures.) The benefit of this is that we can conserve computational power for rendering the full sub-area simulation until our agent(s) enter it; see Fig. 5.

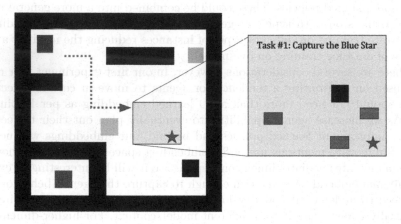

Fig. 5. Example visualization of how LevelSpace may be used in a NetLogo simulation to run a child simulation. To save on computational power, we can forgo rendering the Task Area simulation until the primary agent (blue triangle) enters it. (Color figure online)

Another potential for extension includes agents with different capabilites. Rabinowitz, for example, explores agents with different levels of perceptions (field of view size). What if agents could move more than one space at a time, what if they could go through obstacles, etc.? Further, what if multiple agents with different capabilties were included in the simulation?

Currently, we have programmed simple multi-agent traversal, where the agents do not interfere with one another, but we hope to expand to studying multi-agent dynamics and game theory more in-depth. Rabinowitz's study showed their ToMnet model has the potential to infer general and agent-specific theories of mind for various single agents, but can the model infer the mindsets of multiple agents in a situation? If so, how tightly-wound are the learned multi-agent embeddings?

Limiting observer FOV provides a sense a realism as the entire environment may not necessarily be accessible to the observer. We aim to answer how the learned representations with such a deficiency may differ from those of a panoptic observer.

We are interested in each of the dimensions to characterize agents along; namely animacy, having reactive or planned policies, being social or adversarial, and being natural or artificial. Animacy [18] deals with our perception of the observed agent being alive as opposed to causal. Is the agent actively taking in the environment and other actors? This also goes hand-in-hand with agents having reactive versus planned policies. Are they intentionally following their trajectory? In a multi-agent environment, are certain agents helpful to others or do they prevent other agents from achieving their goals. One delineation we will explore within the social agents is whether they are indeed helpful or neutral actors. The latter two dimensions will be experimented in conjunction with agents having DRL policies. Lastly, they mention characterizing agents as being natural or artificial. This dimension helps provide insight into the meaning behind an artificial agent having a ToM. The question is fairly philosophical, but it would be interesting to have our model compare behaviors of "automated" agents, as we are currently exploring, and agents controlled by human actors. NetLogo's HuBnet extension, for example, allows for "participatory simulation" so that live users can remotely control different aspects of a simulation [19]. It is not clear whether the user may control the NetLogo agent directly, but may be able to through control of the environment. This inspires us to developing a Theory of Mind model which infers on the live user's control of environment to affect the simulated agent's behavior.

Ultimately, the ToMnet machine learning model we are currently working with is being used to infer strategy and intention of the observed agent within a "board-game-like" context. Of course, this could impact areas like gaming if such systems could pre-train on a general gameplay strategy, say during development, and then actively adjust its difficulty as it captures a live user's gameplay in real-time.

Beyond this, the idea is to use ToMnet as a blueprint for machine learning models in other contexts. Autonomous vehicles, for example, need to infer intention of pedestrians and other vehicles on the road, see Girase [7] and Liu [8]. The former paper uses 900 h of video data taken in densely populated urban environments in the United States. Similar datasets could be used in training a ToM model adjusted to accommodate video data, as we plan for our later experiments involved in inferring on the NetLogo agents' full trajectory rather than a single timestep.

In addition, we will explore how ToM can be applied to agents representing various types of data sources with varying degrees of uncertainty. Given that uncertainty could lead to negative impact in various situations, recognizing this uncertainty and its evolves will assist in mitigating its effects. For this, we consider the work by Diaconsecu [6] with the concept of Uncertainty of Information (UoI) as presented in Raglin [14].

5 Conclusion

In this paper we reviewed a summary of the development of ToM research especially pertaining the machine learning. We provided insight into leveraging these various works and their potential applications, and provided commentary on our current progress in recreating Rabinowitz's [13] first experiment. Finally, we overviewed our plans to scale the simulations and models after initial development of the environments. As we mentioned, work in applying ToM with machine learning is still in its infancy; in the more immediate future we aim to illustrate more realistic proofs-of-concept and over time we hope this work will contribute to:

- Understanding the delineation, if any, between artificial and natural theories of mind.
- Improving machine learning data pipelines and model architectures geared towards exploration of, and use for, ToM capabilities.
- Game theory and models, even "black-boxed", of multi-agent and adversarial dynamics.
- Human-AI trust: XAI capabilities of ToM models which explicitly infer on agents' belief states.
- Methods to unravel complex learned representations to reveal unapparent agent capabilities.
- Uncertainty of information and causal reasoning: Looking beyond purely visual and symbolic data pipelines as well as metrological uncertainty; how can the system/agent reason when they do not have "the whole picture?"

These are a few of the bigger areas of interest we currently see. As we progress, we will surely experience and address many others.

References

1. Abadi, M., et al.: TensorFlow: large-scale machine learning on heterogeneous systems (2015). https://www.tensorflow.org/. Software available from tensorflow.org
2. Akula, A.R., et al.: CX-ToM: counterfactual explanations with theory-of-mind for enhancing human trust in image recognition models. iScience **25**(1), 103581 (2022). https://doi.org/10.1016/j.isci.2021.103581. https://www.sciencedirect.com/science/article/pii/S2589004221015510
3. Baker, C., Saxe, R., Tenenbaum, J.: Bayesian theory of mind: modeling joint belief-desire attribution. In: Proceedings of the Annual Meeting of the Cognitive Science Society, vol. 33 (2011)
4. Baron-Cohen, S., Leslie, A.M., Frith, U.: Does the autistic child have a "theory of mind"? Cognition **21**(1), 37–46 (1985). https://doi.org/10.1016/0010-0277(85)90022-8
5. Chen, B., Vondrick, C., Lipson, H.: Visual behavior modelling for robotic theory of mind. Sci. Rep. **11**(1), 1–14 (2021)
6. Diaconescu, A.O., et al.: Inferring on the intentions of others by hierarchical Bayesian learning. PLOS Comput. Biol. **10**(9), 1–19 (2014). https://doi.org/10.1371/journal.pcbi.1003810
7. Girase, H., et al.: LOKI: long term and key intentions for trajectory prediction. In: Proceedings of the IEEE/CVF International Conference on Computer Vision, pp. 9803–9812 (2021)
8. Liu, B., et al.: Spatiotemporal relationship reasoning for pedestrian intent prediction. IEEE Rob. Autom. Lett. **5**(2), 3485–3492 (2020)

9. Ng, A.Y., Russell, S., et al.: Algorithms for inverse reinforcement learning. In: ICML, vol. 1, p. 2 (2000)
10. Nguyen, T.N., Gonzalez, C.: Cognitive machine theory of mind, Technical report. Carnegie Mellon University (2020)
11. Nguyen, T.N., Gonzalez, C.: Theory of mind from observation in cognitive models and humans. Top. Cogn. Sci. (2021). https://doi.org/10.1111/tops.12553. https://onlinelibrary.wiley.com/doi/abs/10.1111/tops.12553
12. Premack, D., Woodruff, G.: Does the chimpanzee have a theory of mind? Behav. Brain Sci. 1(4), 515–526 (1978). https://doi.org/10.1017/S0140525X00076512
13. Rabinowitz, N., Perbet, F., Song, F., Zhang, C., Eslami, S.A., Botvinick, M.: Machine theory of mind. In: International Conference on Machine Learning, pp. 4218–4227. PMLR (2018)
14. Raglin, A., Metu, S., Lott, D.: Challenges of simulating uncertainty of information. In: Stephanidis, C., Antona, M., Ntoa, S. (eds.) HCII 2020. CCIS, vol. 1293, pp. 255–261. Springer, Cham (2020). https://doi.org/10.1007/978-3-030-60700-5_33
15. Raileanu, R., Denton, E., Szlam, A., Fergus, R.: Modeling others using oneself in multi-agent reinforcement learning. In: Krause, A., Dy, J. (eds.) 35th International Conference on Machine Learning, ICML 2018, pp. 6779–6788 (2018)
16. Ritter, F.E., Tehranchi, F., Oury, J.D.: ACT-R: a cognitive architecture for modeling cognition. WIREs Cognit. Sci. 10(3) (2019). https://doi.org/10.1002/wcs.1488
17. Sarkadi, S., Panisson, A., Bordini, R., McBurney, P., Parsons, S., Chapman, M.: Modelling deception using theory of mind in multi-agent systems. AI Commun. 32(4), 287–302 (2019). https://doi.org/10.3233/AIC-190615
18. Scholl, B.J., Tremoulet, P.D.: Perceptual causality and animacy. Trends Cogn. Sci. 4(8), 299–309 (2000). https://doi.org/10.1016/s1364-6613(00)01506-0
19. Wilensky, U.: Netlogo itself (1999). http://ccl.northwestern.edu/netlogo/
20. Yoshida, W., Dolan, R.J., Friston, K.J.: Game theory of mind. PLOS Comput. Biol. 4(12), 1–14 (2008). https://doi.org/10.1371/journal.pcbi.1000254

Trust Crisis or Algorithm Boost?
An Investigation of Artificial Intelligence
Divination Applications in China

Ying Lai$^{(\boxtimes)}$ ⓘ and Xing Zhou

Beijing Normal University, Xinjiekouwai Road 17, Beijing 100875, China
kroridge@outlook.com

Abstract. The study involves conducting in-depth interviews with 15 users of AI divination applications and analyzing texts in terms of their textual and interactive orientations to examine the underlying processes that influence AI consumption of specialty divination in China. The findings suggest that individual interpretation is significant in the process, from the creation of ritual sense in divination to the establishment of affective spaces online and the development of behavior cycles from online to offline. These individual experiences form the basis of personal feelings and interactive experiences, which are fundamental to the consumption of AI divination. The study concludes that a deeper understanding of the intersections between AI, cultural consumption, and social dynamics is essential to fully grasp the impact of AI on everyday life in modern Chinese cities.

Keywords: AI Divination · Religion Online · Interactive Applications

1   Introduction

The utilization of artificial intelligence (AI) in modern Chinese cities has resulted in a significant change in cultural consumption and social interactions. However, the impact of AI on cultural consumption has not been thoroughly investigated. Lustig and Rosner conducted research [1] into how the use of AI in divination has amplified existing patterns of cultural consumption and caused changes in consumer behavior. Specifically, individuals now ask targeted questions, use algorithms for divination, depend on AI-generated outcomes for divination results, and seek counsel from AI-generated responses, particularly in the area of tarot.

2   Digital Divination and Religious Culture

Digital religion refers to the intersection of technology and traditional religious practices. It is a growing interdisciplinary field of study that explores how religion is being adapted to digital environments and how digital culture is informing offline religious groups. As Campbell describes [2], digital religion is a "framework for articulating the evolution

H. Degen and S. Ntoa (Eds.): HCII 2023, LNAI 14051, pp. 516–524, 2023.
https://doi.org/10.1007/978-3-031-35894-4_38

of religious practices online which are linked to online and offline contexts simultaneously." This interdisciplinary field of research explores the relationship between online and offline religious contexts and how they become blended and integrated over time. Campbell introduced the theoretical concept of "networked religion" to describe the five core characteristics of religion in a digital age: networked communities, storied identities, shifting authorities, convergent practices, and multi-site reality. Other scholars, such as Hoover and Echchaibi [3] and Grieve [4], also discuss the unique character of digital technology and culture in relation to new expressions of religious practice and beliefs. Digital religion scholars study diverse technologies beyond just the Internet, including cell phones, digital gaming, and mobile apps, and face the challenge of studying constantly evolving phenomena with new theoretical and methodological approaches. They explore questions such as the impact of technology on religion, the connection between online and offline phenomena, and the challenges and opportunities that new media pose to religious groups and institutions. The interdisciplinary field of digital religion studies aims to understand how a "third space" [5] emerges, requiring new logics and evoking unique forms of meaning-making.

Current studies of digital religion go beyond manifestations of religion on the Internet and explore diverse technologies such as cell-phone use, religious intersections within digital gaming, and even religious practice facilitated via mobile apps. Digital religion scholars face the challenge of studying constantly evolving phenomena that demand new theoretical and methodological approaches to answer questions such as: Does technology shape religion (and vice versa)? How can scholars measure the impacts of digital culture on religion and the effects of religion on digital culture? What challenges and opportunities do new media pose to religious groups and institutions? What is the connection between online and offline phenomena?

This study focuses on the use of AI divination applications within China. China has developed numerous self-contained divination techniques [6] throughout its long history, one of which is the widely used Ba-Zi. These techniques are utilized in numerous aspects of daily life, ranging from naming, marriage, and house buying to selecting a car registration number. Religious rituals are extremely important in Chinese society [7], and personal emotions play an important role in the experience. People are more inclined towards experiencing the meaning of religion in their individual lives and sharing their experiences or events that have been influenced by religious rituals with others than understanding or learning the content of a uniform doctrine.

However, this does not imply that digital divination rituals are widely accepted in Chinese culture [8]. Traditional face-to-face divination rituals continue to be widely practiced, and multi-person congregational traditions such as pilgrimage and ritual remain essential features of traditional Chinese religious venues.

3 AI Algorithm and Interactive Divination Application Platform

Artificial intelligence (AI) has been traditionally categorized into two types: artificial narrow intelligence (ANI) and artificial general intelligence (AGI) [9]. ANI refers to the use of AI for classification and prediction tasks. Such tasks start with a dataset that is divided into training and test data. The model first learns from the training dataset, and then it is applied to the test dataset to classify or predict the data based on the type of model used. AI divination applications follow a similar model [1], in which valid data is derived from a fixed dataset, such as numbers, tarot cards, or horoscopes. The data is then extracted and recombined using some method, and all possible data combinations can be calculated exhaustively. Despite the novelty of AI divination applications, the use of a fixed dataset has limitations in that it may not capture the full range of traditional divination symbol meanings and interpretations. Furthermore, biases or errors in AI models can affect the model's prediction or classification accuracy [10].

Cece, an interactive platform for mobile devices that uses AI algorithms to complete online divination tasks such as horoscopes, astrolabes, tarot, numerology, hexagrams, and zhouyi, is one such AI divination application. Cece also provides a variety of consulting services, such as lucky color recommendations, marriage advice, and fun tests, which provide users with personalized insights and recommendations based on their specific preferences and circumstances.

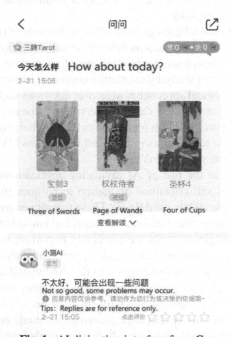

Fig. 1. AI divination interface from Cece

Cece's success can be attributed to its popularity among young Chinese internet users, who are drawn to its user-friendly interface (see Fig. 1), engaging content, and personalized recommendations. Cece's AI algorithms enable a highly personalized and accurate divination experience, as the application learns from user data to generate more accurate predictions and classifications over time.

4 Research Methods and Participants

This study uses a qualitative approach and draws on data collected through in-depth interviews with users of AI Tarot divination applications. We conducted 15 semi-structured interviews as part of our research, totaling approximately 20 h of data collection. To ensure a diverse sample of participants, we utilized the standard of random sampling. This involved selecting interviewees based on their usage frequency, degree of participation, and self-reported affection for artificial intelligence divination. The interviewees were born between the late 1990s and early 2000s, and the majority had been engaging with AI divination for three months or more.

We conducted the interviews via a variety of modes, including instant messaging, face-to-face conversations, and phone calls, to ensure flexibility and convenience for our interviewees. This allowed us to gather data from a broad range of participants who may have had different preferences for communication.

During the semi-structured interviews, we used a set of pre-determined questions as a starting point, but we also allowed for open-ended discussion and exploration of the participants' experiences with AI divination. This approach allowed us to gain a deeper understanding of the informants' perspectives and uncover insights that may have been missed with a more rigid questionnaire.

Through these interviews, we were able to gain valuable insights into the ways in which young people engage with AI divination and the role that it plays in their lives. The interviewees shared their AI divination experiences, beliefs, and opinions with us, providing us with a more nuanced understanding of this emerging trend.

However, we acknowledge that our sample size was small and that generalizing the findings to a larger population may be difficult. Further research with a larger and more diverse sample size could provide new insights into the role of artificial intelligence divination in modern society.

5 Digital Practice of AI Divination

5.1 Algorithm Boost in Online Environment

It is critical to consider practical verification and effective feedback of divination results when studying tarot divination. This concern was shared by the majority of participants in this study, who demonstrated a clear understanding of the steps involved in the tarot divination ceremony. They also acknowledged the limited possibility that the outcome of divination is made up of a fixed number of tarot cards. This realization prompts an important discussion of tarot divination from a spiritual standpoint (see Fig. 2).

Previously, religious and psychological research [11] attributed tarot divination's spiritual problems to the divination ceremony itself or the diviners' psychological implications. However, this article is not intended to analyze the source of spirituality or the problem of where spirituality is. Instead, it focuses on the understanding of the diviners (users) of spirituality in the AI divination instrument. The study involved a series of in-depth interviews where interviewees expressed different views on spiritual issues.

The interviewees recognized the finiteness and controllability of divination results. While this realization may help them further appreciate the powerful assistance of AI

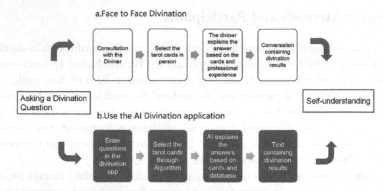

Fig. 2. Diagram of the process of face-to-face divination and AI divination

algorithms in divination rituals, it also raises a fundamental doubt about whether the divination ceremony, which is no longer controlled by people, can "sense" the diviner's spirituality or belief. This paper believes that both understandings have practical significance for AI divination, but there are also imaginations about technology (algorithms) or spirituality.

It is important to note that in traditional tarot card divination, the diviners attempt to interpret the same card or combination in a more diversified sense, but the effectiveness of the divination results still largely depends on the user's personal understanding of the tarot card combination. In face-to-face divination, most of the contents of the divination results are actually negotiated answers provided by the diviners to customers based on personal questions. To comprehend the AI tarot divination ceremony, it is critical to solving the problem of the card meaning rather than card selection.

5.2   Trust Crisis in Offline Environment

The study discovered that people who had been using AI divination apps for six months or longer had similar reasons for continuing to use them. They believed that these applications provided a higher level of privacy, lowering the risk of their personal information being disclosed. One interviewee mentioned that with AI divination, they could avoid disclosing personal information to strangers (see Fig. 2), including the diviner. They were especially hesitant to discuss sensitive topics like childhood, gender relations, and traumatic experiences. This reluctance to reveal information stemmed from concerns about the diviner's personal bias, which could affect the accuracy of the results. Inadequate information disclosure, on the other hand, could lead to inaccurate divination outcomes, and respondents acknowledged the need to strike a balance in this regard.

Participants in the study also expressed a preference for AI divination over face-to-face divination. They felt that face-to-face divination was constrained by their geographic location and limited range of activities, which could result in a diviner catering to their own preferences based on external factors such as income level and cultural background. Interviewees believed that this could undermine the credibility of the results, which depended largely on their trust in the diviner. Consequently, they were more likely to choose fortune-tellers who were strangers and had no prior connection to them, emphasizing the importance of loyalty and tolerance on the part of the diviner in establishing trust with the customer.

Surprisingly, a minority of respondents demonstrated a high level of trust in AI divination applications, far exceeding expectations. Despite high-profile data breaches involving internet users, these interviewees said they would continue to use AI divination apps. One person even stated:

"Nobody knows more about my life than my phone. I'd rather keep this secret on the internet than have to tell someone about my experiences every time I do divination, though information leakage is also a possibility. Plus, I'm not the only one whose secrets are being revealed when (information leakage) occurs."

The perspectives shared by the respondents challenge the traditional notion that face-to-face divination is a reliable means of divination. Additionally, the results of the study suggest that AI divination could potentially evolve into an Internet religion [12], as a significant proportion of the respondents expressed trust and confidence in this technology. They argued that utilizing AI divination applications with high privacy settings not only ensures the protection of their confidential information but also promotes a sense of comfort and willingness to accept divination insights.

5.3 Human or Non-human: Towards AGI

When we asked our participants if AI divination software should progress toward Artificial General Intelligence (AGI), we received a variety of responses. Their perspectives were heavily influenced by their levels of trust and comprehension of AI divination outcomes.

Some participants were excited about the possibility of AI divination progressing to AGI, believing that it would allow the software to provide even more accurate and personalized results. They believed that artificial intelligence (AGI) could improve the divination experience by allowing the software to learn from the user's previous behavior, preferences, and feedback, allowing it to provide even more insightful predictions. On the other hand, some participants were skeptical about the idea of AI divination moving towards AGI. They expressed concern about the potential loss of human touch and intuition, as well as the software becoming overly complex and unpredictable. These participants thought the current level of AI in divination software was accurate enough to provide meaningful insights and predictions [13].

However, we also found that there were participants who fell somewhere in between these two views. They expressed a desire for the software to continue evolving and improving, but not to the point of AGI. They emphasized the importance of striking a balance between prediction accuracy and human touch in the divination experience.

Overall, our findings indicate that there is no clear agreement on whether AI divination software should progress to AGI. The users' levels of trust and understanding of AI divination results influence their opinions. More research could be conducted to better understand the potential benefits and drawbacks of moving toward AGI in AI divination.

6 Conclusion and Discussion

According to a study of AI divination app users, the majority of participants lacked a strong religious background and did not regularly participate in religious rituals. Instead, they learned about divination through social media platforms like "Cece." Despite this, participants were willing to use AI-generated divination results as personal guidance because they believed AI algorithms were more accurate, objective, and reliable than traditional divination methods. This is due to the fact that AI does not prioritize any specific result based on the user's emotions, but rather provides direct and impartial answers to each question.

Interestingly, the study discovered that participants' use of AI divination reflects their lack of trust in offline social relationships. Users cited privacy, scandal, and personal experiences as the primary reasons they did not seek out real diviners for offline divination. This emphasizes the importance of distrust in real social and personal relationships, which leads people to prefer anonymous or even AI divination over traditional methods. This discovery highlights the impact of modern technology on shaping people's behavior and belief systems, where anonymity and objectivity are becoming increasingly valuable in a world where trust in human relationships is declining. And reveals how AI divination is changing cultural consumption patterns in modern Chinese society.

This study reveals significant findings about the use of artificial intelligence (AI) in divination applications in China, but it also has some limitations to consider. For starters, the short answers provided by Cece's AI system pose a challenge to users seeking more detailed responses (see Fig. 1). After using AI divination, many users seek additional guidance from traditional diviners. While this does not discourage users from using Cece for personal divination, the inability to obtain more detailed answers or pursue further questions continues to be a significant barrier to AI divination.

Second, Cece is not the only interactive application platform in China that provides AI divination services. Numerous interactive apps are attempting to offer distinct services in order to attract different consumer groups, with Cece's use of cute and colorful interface designs making it more appealing to the youth demographic. Some interviewees stated that they used multiple divination platforms and chose services based on their own strengths and weaknesses. Furthermore, the low cost of private divination services provided by AI algorithms has enticed people without long-term religious beliefs to participate in AI tarot rituals and become loyal users. While this has increased participation in tarot, divination, and religious culture, it has also resulted in a more gamified approach to divination. Some interviewees expressed concern that the fun test had diminished the importance of interpreting the results, claiming that the results appeared random and insignificant.

Finally, the gender ratio of this study's respondents was overwhelmingly female, reflecting the prevalence of divination in Asian female culture [14], where women are both consumers and providers [15]. This variation in gender may have influenced the study's analysis and conclusions.

Acknowledgements. Sincere thanks to all of the reference authors and the Beijing Normal University Department of Film and Media. The authors would also like to thank Chongqing Technology and Business University's Professor Quhai Shi for her invaluable assistance.

Funding. The author(s) disclosed the following financial support for the research, authorship, and/or publication of this article: This research was supported by the "A Sociological Study on the Foreign Communication of China's National Image" (1955012) project from Chongqing Technology and Business University.

Appendix

List of Interviews

ID	Year of birth	Gender	Interview Duration	Get started to use Cece	Method
1	1996	F	59 min	2021	Face-to -face
2	1998	F	1 h 21 min	2022	Face-to -face
3	1997	F	1 h 9 min	2022	Face-to -face
4	1992	F	1 h 15 min	2020	Instant messenger
5	1996	F	1 h 27 min	2020	Face-to -face
6	1997	M	1 h 13 min	2022	Instant messenger
7	2000	F	1 h 4 min	2022	Face-to -face
8	2003	F	1 h 16 min	2021	Audio recording
9	1996	F	1 h 11 min	2020	Instant messenger
10	1996	M	1 h	2022	Face-to -face
11	1998	F	1 h 2 min	2021	Audio recording
12	1997	F	1 h 30 min	2021	Instant messenger
13	1991	F	1 h	2021	Instant messenger
14	1997	M	1 h 20 min	2022	Face-to -face
15	1998	F	2 h	2022	Facc-to -face

This study's interviews were conducted using a combination of online and offline methods. The researchers used the chat software WeChat to conduct online interviews. Prior to participating in the study, all participants signed informed consent forms to ensure that ethical standards were met. To protect participants' privacy, any personal information obtained through screenshots or other relevant analyses was carefully anonymized.

References

1. Lustig, C., Rosner, D.: From explainability to ineffability?: ML tarot and the possibility of inspiriting design. In: Designing Interactive Systems Conference, pp. 123–136. ACM, Virtual Event Australia (2022). https://doi.org/10.1145/3532106.3533552
2. Campbell, H.A.: Surveying theoretical approaches within digital religion studies. New Media Soc. **19**, 15–24 (2017). https://doi.org/10.1177/1461444816649912

3. Hoover, S.M.: Religion in the Media Age. Routledge (2006). https://doi.org/10.4324/978020 3503201
4. Grieve, G.P., Campbell, H.A.: Studying religion in digital gaming. a critical review of an emerging field. Online - Heidelberg J. Religions Internet (2014). https://doi.org/10.11588/REL.2014.0.12183
5. Hoover, S.M.: The third spaces of digital religion (2015). https://doi.org/10.4324/978100304 8190
6. Lackner, M., Lu, Z. (eds.): The living traditions of divination. In: Handbook of Divination and Prognostication in China, pp. 502–536. BRILL (2022). https://doi.org/10.1163/978900 4514263_014
7. Smith, R.J.: Fortune-Tellers and Philosophers: Divination in Traditional Chinese Society. Routledge, New York (2021). https://doi.org/10.4324/9780429039799
8. Fu, H., Li, Y., Lee, F.L.: Techno-cultural domestication of online Tarot reading in contemporary China. Media Cult. Soc. **45**, 74–91 (2023). https://doi.org/10.1177/016344372211 04700
9. Reed, R.: A.I. in Religion, A.I. for Religion, A.I. and Religion: towards a theory of religious studies and artificial intelligence. Religions **12**, 401 (2021). https://doi.org/10.3390/rel120 60401
10. Kimura, T.: Robotics and AI in the sociology of religion: a human in imago Roboticae. Soc. Compass. **64**, 6–22 (2017). https://doi.org/10.1177/0037768616683326
11. Ivtzan, I.: Tarot cards: a literature review and evaluation of psychic versus psychological explanations. J. Parapsychol. **71**, 139–149 (2007)
12. Singler, B.: The AI creation meme: a case study of the new visibility of religion in artificial intelligence discourse. Religions **11**, 253 (2020). https://doi.org/10.3390/rel11050253
13. Dawson, L.L., Cowan, D.E.: Religion Online: Finding Faith on the Internet. Taylor and Francis, Florence (2013)
14. Miller, L.: The Divination Arts in Girl Culture. University of Hawai'i Press (2014)
15. Smith, R.J.: Women and divination in traditional china: some reflections (1992)

Human-Machine Learning Approach for Ejection System Design in Injection Molds

Johanna Lauwigi[✉][iD], Robert Jungnickel[iD], and Daniel Lütticke[iD]

Information Management in Mechanical Engineering, RWTH Aachen University, Aachen, Germany
{johanna.lauwigi,robert.jungnickel}@ima.rwth-aachen.de
https://cybernetics-lab.de/en/

Abstract. Designing the ejection system for injection molds is a time-consuming task that requires a significant amount of human involvement. In addition, the current shortage of skilled workers coupled with the increasing demand for customized products poses a major challenge to the ejection system design process and makes human knowledge essential to the design process. Thus, this work proposes a novel human-machine learning approach for an automated design process. To make the human knowledge readable for the machine, we quantify the knowledge and fit it into a positioning model. This model is the key component of the developed expert system that supports the human in the design process. In particular, the machine model recommends ejection element positions to the human who gives feedback on the proposed positions. This feedback is used for training the positioning model. By allowing the human to make the final decision, we also prevent the creation of an ejection system that fails to function. We show the benefits of our human-machine learning approach to enable an automated design process of ejection system design.

Keywords: Injection Molding · Automated Design · Expert System · Human-Centric Machine Learning · Mental Model · Positioning Model

1 Introduction

Injection molding is a widely used manufacturing process in the plastics industry. In this process, the injection mold determines the form and quality of the final product. One essential component of injection molds is the ejection system that ensures the removal of the product from the mold, which allows for the next cycle of production to begin. The precise positioning of ejection elements in the ejection system is a crucial step in ensuring that the finished product is removed without damage, and therefore, it is a critical factor in determining the overall quality of the final product in injection molding.

J. Lauwigi and R. Jungnickel—These authors contributed equally to this work.

© The Author(s), under exclusive license to Springer Nature Switzerland AG 2023
H. Degen and S. Ntoa (Eds.): HCII 2023, LNAI 14051, pp. 525–541, 2023.
https://doi.org/10.1007/978-3-031-35894-4_39

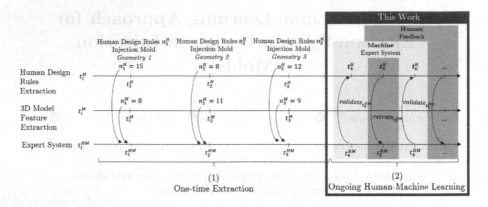

Fig. 1. The two-step human-centric machine-learning (HCML) process for ejection system design in injection molding, derived from [7]. This work focuses on the (2) ongoing human-machine learning as part of the framework.

Currently, the design of the ejection system is carried out manually by human designers using Computer-Aided Design (CAD) programs. While this approach allows for a high degree of flexibility and customization, it also leads to significant time and cost constraints. Over 70% of the total cost of an injection molded part is determined by mold design [4]. The design is a highly human-driven process as it depends on the experience of the designer. The design knowledge is saved in human mental models [13], reflecting a set of fundamental design rules to guide the design including the positioning of ejection elements like ejection pins or sliders. As a result, each molding part is designed manually, placing each ejection element separately one by one. Automation of ejection element positioning can reduce design time and cost.

The challenge is not only to extract and quantify human design knowledge and to integrate these rules into a human-centric machine learning (HCML) process but also to ensure that ongoing human-machine learning (HML) enables human feedback. This human feedback supports to optimize the positioning model. Note that knowledge in this work, as in [7], refers to human design rules and the human feedback to the ejection elements mentioned above.

In this work, we present an ongoing HML approach as part of the human-centric machine-learning framework proposed in our work [7]. In detail, these are our contributions:

1. We propose an ongoing human-machine learning approach that automatically positions ejection elements.
2. We develop a machine model for the automated positioning of ejection elements (positioning model) based on human design knowledge.
3. We propose a training process for the positioning model based on human feedback.
4. We validate our approach with ejection pins as one ejection element.

2 Previous Work

Prior work in injection mold design has mainly focused on an expert system for estimating injection mold costs [3], balancing algorithm for engineering ejector pins [14], numerical layout design of ejector pin size [9], multi-objective optimization of the injection molding process [1,10] and multidisciplinary framework that incorporates customer requirements [5].

Table 1. Qualitative comparison of prior and our work on ejection element positioning in injection mold design

Work	Ejection System	Pin Positioning	Human Knowledge
Kwai et al. 1995 [3]	✗	✗	✓
Wang et al. 1996 [14]	✓	✗	✗
Kwak et al. 2003 [9]	✓	✗	✗
Ferreira et al. 2014 [5]	✓	✗	✗
Alvarado et al. 2019 [1]	✓	✗	✗
Li et al.2019 [10]	✓	✗	✗
Mercado-Colmenero et al. 2017 [11]	✓	✓	✗
Jungnickel et al. 2022 [7]	✓	✓	✓
Our	✓	✓	✓

While the main research focuses on machine-generated numerical simulations, Kwai et al. [3] utilize human design knowledge for cost predictions of injection mold products, listed in Table 1. In particular, humans estimate whether an ejection pin is required and predict the total costs of the injection molding process. However, this work is not considering ejection systems or ejection element positioning in an automated design process. Ferreira et al. [5] propose a multidisciplinary framework to develop a platform that automatically analyses ejection systems and outputs ejection structure cost. Here, the diameter and length of ejection pins are taken into account. While this work includes ejection systems and ejection pins, the approach is neither based on pin positioning, nor on human knowledge [5]. The work most closely related to ours is [11], in which automatic ejector pins are calculated based on the discrete geometry of the plastic part. Still, this approach does not incorporate human knowledge.

Overall, while numerous works exist on ejection systems and pin positioning, the integration of human knowledge into the design process has rarely been considered.

In contrast to prior work, the proposed human-centric machine learning framework (HCML) in [7] integrates human design knowledge about ejection pin positioning into an automated design process. Based on the HCML framework, this work narrows down the ongoing human-machine learning part of the HCML framework, illustrated in Fig. 1. We propose a process that translates human knowledge into a machine-understandable model for positioning ejection elements. Additionally, we define the training process for the positioning model based on human feedback. Thus we allow the training of the machine-understandable positioning model using human feedback to optimize the positioning of ejection elements. We implemented this approach specifically for ejection pins as one of the ejection elements.

3   Concept

The concept for the automated positioning of ejection elements contains three main components: the **CAD program**, the **expert system**, and the **feedback system**, illustrated in Fig. 2. From the CAD program, the data is sent via the expert system to the feedback system and back. Each component can process the data to get insights for its calculation. While the human interacts directly with the CAD program and the feedback system, the expert system operates automatically without interacting with the human.

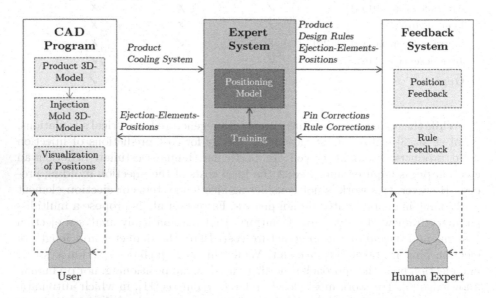

Fig. 2. Components and data flow of the automatic ejection element positioning concept

The **CAD program** is the design tool for human designers to develop 3D models. In this case, the 3D models are the plastics product to be produced in the injection molding process and the injection mold. The geometry and characteristics of the injection mold depend on the product. One part of the injection mold design is the design of the ejection system. The ejection system consists of different elements like pins and sliders. All these elements together remove the product from the mold. To support the human designer in developing the injection mold, this work aims to recommend positions for the ejection elements. The positions for the ejection elements are drawn from the expert system and visualized in the CAD program. The designer can decide whether to consider the recommended or choose different positions. Therefore, the designer or user only interacts with the CAD program to design the injection mold while using the automatic positioning of the ejection system for the mold.

The **expert system** is responsible for the automated positioning of the ejection elements using the model of the product. Therefore, the expert system takes as input the 3D model of the product and the information about the cooling system. The cooling system is responsible for cooling the product after the liquefied plastic is injected into the mold. This is essential for positioning the ejection elements, as the cooling system and the ejection elements compete for the positions in the mold. The information about the product and the cooling system is then used by the positioning model to calculate potential positions for each ejection element. To train this positioning model with human feedback, the expert system also includes a training module that influences the positioning model. With the connection to the feedback system and the CAD program, the expert system interacts automatically with the other components.

The **feedback system** receives input from the human. This system shows the results from the positioning model in the expert system to the human. The human returns the improved positioning of ejection elements to the expert system if necessary. To visualize the results, the feedback system shows the product, the positions of the ejection elements, and the design rules that lead to this position of the ejection element. Thus, the feedback system gets the model of the product, the ejection element positions, and the design rules from the expert system. These design rules were extracted in the one-time extraction of human knowledge [7]. The human can accept, delete, add, and change positions for ejection elements and evaluate the human design rules for each corrected ejection element position. Both, the ejection element corrections and human design rule corrections, are transferred to the expert system that utilizes the human feedback in the training module. With the described structure, the feedback enables the human to improve the positioning of ejection elements from the expert system and returns the necessary feedback to the expert system.

4 The Machine Model for Positioning Ejection Elements

The machine model for positioning ejection elements, further called the positioning model, is the essential module of the expert system. It is based on the one-time extraction of human design knowledge as mental models, illustrated in Fig. 1. Thus, it contains the human design rules about the positioning of ejection elements in a machine-readable language.

4.1   Process for Deriving a Positioning Model from Human Knowledge

For integrating the mental model of the human into the positioning model, we developed a process that translates the design rules in a machine-understandable way. This process contains five steps:

1. Redefinition of the design rules with parameters, if required
2. Characterization of the design rules
3. Analysis of the characteristics to identify inherent properties as well as relations between design rules
4. Identification of the required features from the 3D model to follow the design rules
5. Derivation of the positioning model based on the analysis and the additional information

The redefinition of the design rules with parameters is especially necessary if a design rule is expressed as a qualitative human feeling. This step includes experts as they need to define quantitative parameters for qualitative descriptions like "thick" or "small". After the redefinition, the characteristics of the design rules can be determined and compared. This enables an understanding of the relationships and the context behind the positioning of ejection elements in the following analysis. Based on the characterization and the analysis, it is possible to identify which features need to be identified from the 3D model of the product. If a design rule for example is based on the material thickness, the algorithm needs to identify the thickness while having the 3D model of the product as an input. With these features and including the analysis from step three, it is possible to derive the positioning model. This positioning model includes the human knowledge in form of design rules and works in a machine-understandable way.

4.2   The Positioning Model for Ejection Pins

As an example of translating human knowledge to a machine model, we defined the positioning model for ejection pins. Ejection pins are one ejection element that pushes the product out of the mold. The positioning model is based on the design rules from the mental model derived in Jungnickel et al. [7]. The mental model includes 15 design rules. The design rules are human knowledge that was extracted in the one-time extraction (see Fig. 1. By building the positioning model with the design rules, we ensure to include the human knowledge in the machine model.

For **redefining the design rules**, we included the experts who were already part in the one-time extraction of human knowledge. In cooperation with these experts, the design rules were specified. For instance, the design rule "Do not place a pin on thin material" was redefined to: "Do not place a pin on material thinner than 3/4 of the average material thickness". The result is a set of design rules that are clearly defined with parameters.

The **characterization of the design rules** for positioning ejection pins led to the following three characteristics that define each design rule:

1. Including criteria or excluding criteria
2. Point-specific properties or geometrical properties (of the product)
3. Design rules that correlate with one or more other design rules

Each design rule was characterized according to the three characteristics. For example, the design rule "Place pin on a corner" has the character *(Including, Geometrical, 0)*. This tuple shows that the design rule is an including criteria, as it describes a position where to place an ejection pin. Excluding criteria describe positions where no ejection pin should be placed. The second value of the tuple describes that the design rule is based on a geometry, in this case a corner, and not on a point specific value like material thickness. The correlation value 0 indicates that the design rule has no direct correlation to other design rules.

The **analysis of the characteristics** of the design rules showed that all design rules categorized as excluding are point-specific while all including design rules are based on geometrical properties. Additionally, some of the rules are contradictory, e.g., a position is defined as not suitable, while another rule defines the position as suitable. But all conflicts are between two design rules, where one design rule is including and the other is excluding. These findings need to be taken into account when deriving the position model.

Based on the redefined design rules, the required **features from the 3D model of the product** can be identified. The features are divided into point-specific features based on the point-specific properties and geometrical features based on the geometrical properties. The point-specific features are: material thickness, height of the product in this point, the existence of a cooling system and the existence of a visible surface. The geometrical features are: domes, corners, walls, and ribs.

The findings from the analysis in combination with the defined features were used to derive the **positioning model**. To avoid conflicts between including and excluding design rules, excluding design rules are ranked higher. To follow the design rules, we defined a positioning model that can position ejection pins and consists of three steps, illustrated in Fig. 3:

1. Definition of point-specific characteristics to determine the fitness of each point
2. Identification of geometrical shapes to determine positioning values
3. Positioning of ejection pins based on fitness and positioning values with dependencies on further positions

The first step defines the **point-specific characteristics** for each point of the 3D model, considering only the surface of the product from a view from the

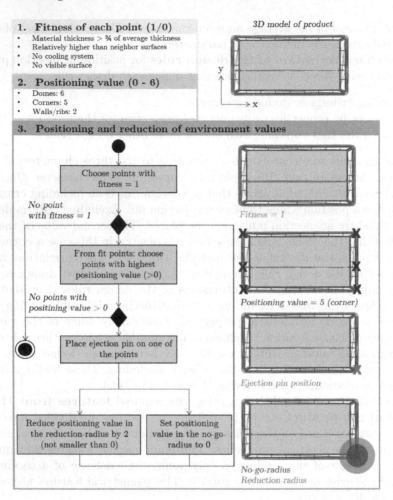

Fig. 3. Components and data flow of the positioning model for ejection pins

top. With that, a point is defined by Cartesian coordinates in x- and y-direction. Based on the point-specific characteristics, each point is defined as either fit or not fit for a possible positioning of an ejection pin. We define those points as fit that (a) do not have less than 3/4 of the average material thickness, (b) are relatively higher than the points on the neighbor surfaces, shown in Fig. 4, (c) have no cooling system and (d) are not a visible surface. With the definition of the fitness, each point can be evaluated as a potential ejection pin position.

The second step determines suitable options for the placement of an ejection pin depending on the **geometrical shapes**. As the geometries need to be evaluated differently regarding their suitability for positioning an ejection pin, we introduce the positioning value. While geometries with a high suitability get a high positioning value, geometries with a low suitability get a low positioning

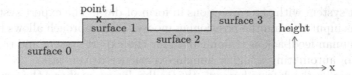

Fig. 4. Sectional representation of a product: Point 1 on surface 1 is relatively higher than the neighbour surfaces 0 and 2. Surface 3 is not a neighbor surface for point 1 and therefore not considered for the relative height.

value. In this case the positioning values range from six for domes, over five for corners, to two for walls and ribs.

The third step defines the **positions of the ejection pins** based on both fitness and positioning values. The ejection pins are positioned only on points that fit according to the first step and have an positioning value higher than zero according to the second step. As the positioning of ejection pins influence each other, the ejection pins are positioned successively. At first, ejection pins are set to positions with the highest positioning values. Each positioning has a direct influence on the positioning values of it's environment. Then, the positioning values of all points within the no-go-position, further called no-go-radius, are set to zero. The no-go-radius is a parameter of the positioning model that is set to 5 mm in a first instance. Beyond the no-go-radius and within the reduction-radius, the positioning values of the points are reduced by two. The reduction-radius is another parameter of the positioning model and is set to 50 mm. With the reduction in this radius, important geometries as domes and corners still have a high positioning value, while walls and ribs within this area will not be considered for positioning anymore. The given approach of the no-go-radius and the reduction-radius ensures that no ejection pins are placed too close to each other. At the same time, walls and ribs only serve as positions for ejection pins if no dome or corner is within the distance of the reduction-radius. Domes and corners also only serve as positions for ejection pins if the amount of other ejection pins positioned within the reduction-radius is to high.

Following the process described in Subsect. 4.1, the positioning model for ejection pins are derived. This model allows the positioning of ejection pins in a machine-understandable way and is based on human knowledge. Thus, the positioning model for ejection pins includes the human knowledge in a machine model.

5 The Feedback System

The feedback system acts as an interface between the human and the expert system. It ensures that the machine model for positioning the ejection elements can learn from the human. Therefore, it acquires human feedback and provides the expert system with the corrections in form of data. The expert system takes the data as input to train the positioning model. This approach allows the acquisition of human feedback as training data for the expert system and to meet the challenge of automating a highly human experience-driven task.

To obtain feedback from humans, the feedback system shows the results of the expert system to the human in an understandable language. Since the human, as well as the expert system, base their decisions on the 3D model of the product, the feedback system shows the 3D model of the product for which the ejection system was designed. Additionally, the feedback system also shows the positions of the ejection elements placed by the expert system. These positions are shown in relation to the product but also with the concrete Cartesian coordinates. Hence, the human can evaluate the positioning model in the expert system and thus the corresponding design rules. Through this evaluation, the human can understand which design rules led to each position of the ejection elements and make corrections to the rules.

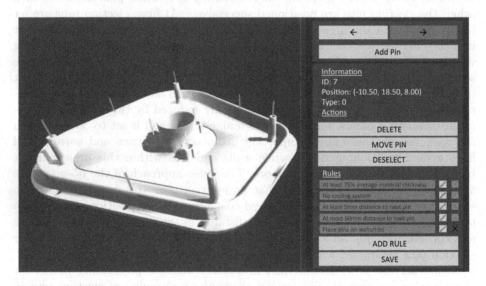

Fig. 5. Screenshot of the feedback system to acquire human feedback with the example of ejection pins as one ejection element

We designed a graphical user interface (GUI) for the feedback system to visualize the ejection elements and to acquire human feedback. As in the example for the positioning model, we implemented the feedback system for ejection pins as an example of the ejection elements. The GUI shows the 3D model of the product as well as the positions of the ejection pins in relation to the product in form of small cylinders, illustrated in Fig. 5. Ejection pins can have different shapes depending on their type. The type and the concrete Cartesian coordinates of an ejection pin are displayed as *Type* and *Position* in the dark blue box on the right side. This box appears when one ejection pin is selected. Additional information about design rules is also visualized specifically for the selected ejection pin in the box. In consequence, the human can get all relevant information for the positioning of one ejection pin without being overwhelmed by all the information that is available in the expert system.

The main purpose of the feedback system is to receive improved pin positions from the human to train the positioning model. Therefore, the feedback is acquired in two steps. First, the human evaluates the positions of the ejection pins and the design rules that led to the position of this ejection pin. Second, the human evaluates the design rules, shown in Fig. 6. This second step is only possible for those ejection pins that were modified in the first step. Given this approach, the acquired feedback is used for the training process of the positioning model.

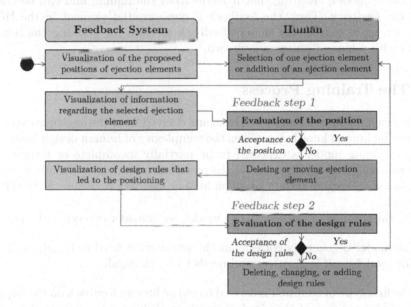

Fig. 6. Process of feedback acquisition

For the first step, the human can change a selected ejection pin by either deleting or moving it. A moved ejection pin is visualized by a yellow color and a deleted ejection pin by a red color. This allows the human to have an overview of all changes. Additionally, the human can also add more ejection pins. To enable the human to see which ejection pin positions were already evaluated, the user can also accept a position of an ejection pin and thus the pin turns to green color. Based on this, the ejection pins have the following color coding: grey for pin not evaluated, green for pin accepted, yellow for pin position changed or pin added, and red for pin deleted. This color coding allows the user to see whether all ejector pins were checked.

For ejection pins that the human changes (pin deleted or pin changed), the bottom part of the information box turns up. It shows the human design rules that led to the positioning of the selected ejection pin. Here, the human can perform the second step of the feedback and evaluate the design rules. Each of the design rules can be deleted or changed. The information about the evaluated design rules is part of the input data for the training process.

In conclusion, the proposed feedback system provides a unique approach for training a machine model with human feedback to automate a highly human experience-driven task. The feedback system interface allows the human to understand and evaluate the positioning model and the corresponding design rules by showing the results of the expert system in an understandable manner. The GUI allows for easy visualization and improvement of the positions of the ejection pins and the design rules. The acquired feedback is used to train the positioning model, ensuring that it learns from the human and can be trained with the feedback. Thus, the feedback is one essential element in the HCML approach as it collects the human feedback as data for training the machine model with a human-centered approach.

6   The Training Process

The positioning model for ejection elements derived from the one-time extraction is based on human knowledge. Given the complexity of human design knowledge, the positioning model is expected to be partially incomplete or incorrect. To meet this challenge and to improve the positioning model, we include a training process for the expert system based on human feedback according to the HCML approach.

For the training of the positioning model, we consider two types of adaptions:

1. The model is generally correct but the parameters need to be adjusted.
2. The model itself is incorrect and needs to be changed.

The first type of adaption is derived from the human feedback on the improvement of the position of the ejection elements. Taking into account the coordinates of the corrected ejection element positions, the parameters of the positioning model can be adjusted. For the positioning model presented in Sect. 4, the parameters are the no-go-radius and the reduction-radius. Both parameters are trained by the positioning corrections from the feedback system.

For the training of the no-go-radius, all ejection pin positions after the correction by the human are taken into consideration. The distance between all ejection pins and their closest neighbours are calculated. From all these distances, only the 10% shortest distances are taken into consideration. The new no-go-radius results from the average of these shortest distances. The calculation takes several short distances into consideration to counter potential outliers in the feedback data.

The reduction-radius mainly states the minimal distance between ejection pins. Everything out of the reduction-radius is not influenced by the positioning of an ejection pin. To train this radius the training process takes the larger distances between ejection pins into consideration. Therefore, it first determines the distance to the closest neighbours for each ejection pin. For calculating the new reduction-radius, it takes the 25% of the largest distances into consideration, which defines the upper quarter of the higher distances. The new reduction-radius calculates the average of the largest 25% of the closest-neighbour-distances between the corrected ejection pins.

For feedback that includes corrections of the design rules, we expect that the positioning model itself is changing. These changes can not be done automatically but need to be included within an assessment of the positioning model. The changed design rules are evaluated and included into the model in the same process to address the first definition of the positioning model, which is described in Sect. 4. With the introduction of the rule correction, it is possible to add previously unknown human design knowledge into the system.

The presented training process for the positioning model allows for the improvement of the machine model's accuracy and completeness. By considering two types of adaptations, adjustments to model parameters or changes to the model itself, the training process can accommodate various types of human feedback. With the inclusion of previously unknown human design knowledge, this system has the potential to expand the capabilities of the first version of the positioning model in the expert system by focusing on a human-centered approach.

7   Validation

The validation was conducted in two part: A validation of the positioning model derived from human knowledge and a validation of the ongoing machine learning including the human feedback. For the validation of the positioning model, we compared the ejection pins the machine model placed before it was trained with the improvements of the human. The HML was validated in cooperation with the human expert who worked with the feedback system. By validating the results from the one-time knowledge extraction and the concept for including human feedback to train the positioning model, we cover both parts of the HCML-approach where the human is involved.

The positioning of ejection pins by the positioning model was tested for six products that are produced with injection molding. The outcome was evaluated in the feedback system by two human designers with more than five years of experience in the field of design for injection molds. To evaluate the first, untrained version of the positioning model, the ejection pin corrections are considered. The positioning model proposed positions for ejection pins that were accepted by the human designers in five of six cases. In all cases, additional ejection pins were added. In two cases, the human deleted ejection pins from the proposed positions. Table 2 shows the results.

Table 2. Overview of ejector pin placements for each injection molded part

	Machine	Human			
Part No.	Pin placed	Pin accepted	Pin deleted	Pin added	Pin position changed
1	3	3	0	6	0
2	8	7	0	2	1
3	4	4	0	6	4
4	4	0	0	20	0
5	4	0	4	14	0
6	4	1	3	2	0
Total	27	15	7	50	5

The analysis of the added ejection pins shows that many additional ejection pins were positioned on domes. This geometry is considered as a relevant position for ejection pins in the positioning model but it did not recognize this geometry in step two (*Identification of geometrical shapes to determine positioning values*). Thus, an evaluation of the identification of the geometrical shapes is essential in the evaluation of the positioning based on these geometrical shapes.

The HML includes the feedback of the human and the processing of the human data in the machine model, that in the presented case is called positioning model. To validate the feedback system, we interviewed the two human experts that were generating feedback with it. Both of them agree that the feedback system is easy to use and intuitive. They appreciate the possibility to improve positions that are proposed from the expert system and with that helping the system to improve instead of trusting it blindly. The data that was created from their feedback (see Table 2 was included in the training of the positioning model. Especially the reduction-radius decreased significantly so that more ejection pins were placed. The trained positioning model shows a higher match of positions of ejection pins with the positions the human proposed in the feedback system.

8   Discussion

The feedback from the experts shows that the approach of the positioning model is suitable for the automated positioning of ejection pins. Additionally added ejection pins are mainly based on a faulty identification of geometrical shapes.

Also, the density of ejection pins is generally higher for the positioning of the humans compared to the positioning of the expert system. This problem can be resolved with an adjustment of the parameters no-go-radius and reduction-radius in the positioning model. Thus, the ongoing machine learning of these parameters gives an improved positioning model based on the human feedback. The positioning model does still not create positions as good as the humans. Therefore, training with more human feedback on more parts should bring even better results.

The design rule corrections show that two additional design rules need to be added to the positioning model. Hence, the manual adjustment of the positioning model based on the additional rules is crucial to reach an optimal outcome with the expert system. Additionally, the humans that used the feedback system, pointed out that a pure inspection of just the ejection pins does not meet the complexity of the overall system. It is relevant also to include the other ejection elements as the positioning influences each other. A further improvement based on the feedback to the design rules as well as including all ejection elements is crucial for a successful automated positioning of ejection pins.

Overall, the concept of the proposed expert system is a promising human-machine learning approach to automate the design process of the ejection system in injection molds. The machine model improves through training using human feedback and learns from the human knowledge. However, the expert system must identify the relevant features correctly, such as geometrical shapes. Additionally, it is necessary to include positioning models for all ejection elements to meet the complexity of the design task. Given this, the described approach can provide an automated positioning of ejection elements based on human knowledge.

9 Outlook and Further Research

The positioning of ejection elements is a first step towards an automated design system for injection mold design. Currently, we consider all steps as independent design steps. The positioning model takes a fixed configuration of the cooling system into account. However, it is essential to also include the design of the cooling system in an automated design as it influences the positioning. With these two aspects, the ejection elements and the cooling system, the designers of ejection molds would have an efficient support system to reduce time on repetitive tasks.

In addition, training the positioning model with more human feedback can increase the number of correct positioning of ejection pins. The current work proposes to use human feedback as training data. But the design process of injection molds can include further algorithms that produce data. For example, an essential aspect of the design is the process forces that apply to the plastics product when being demolded. As human designers experience these forces during the design process, additional human mental models and process force data can be extracted to optimize the positioning model that supports automating design processes. However, an additional approach is to include a Finite-Element-Method (FEM) simulation to calculate the process forces in each point of the product. With the data about these forces, the positioning can be based on a mix of human knowledge and technical machine data and therefore be improved.

Acknowledgements. This publication is part of the project "AutoEnSys: Automatisierte Auslegung des Entformungssystems von Spritzgießwerkzeugen auf Basis selbstlernender Algorithmen", funded by the Federal Ministry of Economics and Climate Protection according to a resolution of the German Parliament.

References

1. Alvarado-Iniesta, A., Cuate, O., Schütze, O.: Multi-objective and many objective design of plastic injection molding process. Int. J. Adv. Manuf. Technol., 3165–3180 (2019). https://doi.org/10.1007/s00170-019-03432-8
2. Bubeck, S.: Convex Optimization. Algorithms and Complexity. Foundations and Trends® in Machine Learning Ser, 26th. Now Publishers, Norwell (2015)
3. Chin, K.-S., Wong, T.N.: An expert system for injection mold cost estimation. Adv. Polym. Technol. **9**(4), 303–314 (1995). https://doi.org/10.1002/ADV.1995.060140404
4. Ehrlenspiel K., Kiewert A., Mörtl M., Lindemann U.: Kostengünstig Entwickeln und Konstruieren. Kostenmanagement bei der integrierten Produktentwicklung, 8nd edn. Springer, Heidelberg (2020). https://doi.org/10.1007/978-3-642-41959-1
5. Ferreira, I., Cabral, J.A., Saraiva, P., Oliveira, M.C.: A multidisciplinary framework to support the design of injection mold tools. Struct. Multidisc. Optim. **49**(3), 501–521 (2014). https://doi.org/10.1007/s00158-013-0990-x
6. Gary, M.S., Wood, R.E.: Unpacking mental models through laboratory experiments. Syst. Dyn. Rev. **32**(2), 101–129 (2016). https://doi.org/10.1002/sdr.1560
7. Jungnickel, R., Lauwigi, J., Samsonov, V., Lütticke, D.: Human-centric machine learning approach for injection mold design: towards automated pin placement. In: LOD 2022–8th International Conference on Machine Learning, Optimization, and Data Science (2022). https://doi.org/10.1007/978-3-031-25891-6_3
8. Kaluarachchi, T., Reis, A., Nanayakkara, S.: A review of recent deep learning approaches in human-centered machine learning **21**(7) (2021). https://doi.org/10.3390/s21072514
9. Kwak, S., Kim, T., Park, S., Lee, K.: Layout and sizing of ejector pins for injection mould desian using the wavelet transform. Proc. Inst. Mech. Eng. Part B J. Eng. Manuf. **217**(4), 463–473 (2003). https://doi.org/10.1243/095440503321628143
10. Li, K., Yan, S., Zhong, Y., Pan, W., Zhao, G.: Multi-objective optimization of the fiber-reinforced composite injection molding process using Taguchi method, RSM, and NSGA-II. Simul. Model. Pract. Theory **91**, 69–82 (2019). https://doi.org/10.1016/j.simpat.2018.09.003
11. Mercado-Colmenero, J.M., Rubio-Paramio, M.A., Vizan-Idoipe, A., Martin-Doñate, C.: A new procedure for the automated design of ejection systems in injection molds. Rob. Comput.-Integr. Manuf. **46**, 68–85 (2017). https://doi.org/10.1016/j.rcim.2016.12.006
12. Sperrle, F., et al.: A survey of human-centered evaluations in human-centered machine learning. Comput. Graph. Forum **40**(3), 543–568 (2021). https://doi.org/10.1111/cgf.14329

13. Sterman, J.D.: Business Dynamics. Systems Thinking and Modeling for a Complex World. Irwin/McGraw-Hill, Boston (2000)
14. Wang, Z., et al.: Optimum ejector system design for plastic injection moulds. Int. J. Comput. Appl. Technol. **9**(4), 211–218 (1996). ScholarBank@NUS Repository. https://doi.org/10.1504/IJMPT.1996.036339

A Weightlifting Clean and Jerk Team Formation Model by Considering Barbell Trajectory and LSTM Neural Network

Jin-Yi Lin, Yan-Ren Ban, Ching-Ting Hsu[✉], Wei-Hua Ho, and Pao-Hung Chung

Graduate Institute of Sports Equipment Technology, University of Taipei, Taipei, Taiwan R.O.C.
jingting@utaipei.deu.tw

Abstract. Clean and jerk is one category of Olympic weightlifting. The barbell trajectory including much kinematic parameters such as displacement, velocity and acceleration which provide coach and athletes to read and obtain athletes' performance. However, kinematic parameters in barbell trajectory is difficult to understand. Hence, in this paper, we propose a weightlifting Clean&Jerk performance evaluation model by utilizing neural network architecture. Considering barbell trajectory characteristics, the all kinematic parameters on trajectory are dependent and time-sequential, hence, long-short-term memory (LSTM) architecture is considered. We gather the domestic adult competitions from 2019–2021 in Taiwan and utilize video tracking scheme to obtain the barbell trajectory from Clean&Jerk competitions. From the results, our inference model archives 71% identify accuracy to indicate the performance of Clean&Jerk of the lifter. Our proposed model not only helps coaches and athletes evaluating their performance, it also shows neural network can assist sport science.

Keywords: Neural Network · Long-Short-Term memory · Weightlifting · Clean&Jerk

1 Introduction

Weightlifting is one of the focuses in Olympic game in Taiwan. Since the 2008 Summer Olympics, Taiwan's weightlifters could get many gold, silver or bronze medals in every acceding category. Taiwan's national weightlifting team has brilliant achievements, which attracted people's attention. Not only the professionals in weightlifting but also the general in Taiwan are following with interest in this program's scientific development on how to help coaches and athletes.

In daily training, coaches and athletes use mirror to adjust athletes' movement. The correct movement is important in bringing up a weightlifter. Mirror inflecting athletes' image in daily training provides real-time feedback, however, sometimes the athlete may forget their movement s in a while after finishing the practice. On the other hand, trajectory including much kinematic parameters such as displacement, velocity and acceleration provides coach and athletes to read and obtain sports' performance. Furthermore, weightlifting is a fast-paced competition. Every attempt has only two minutes. It means

© The Author(s), under exclusive license to Springer Nature Switzerland AG 2023
H. Degen and S. Ntoa (Eds.): HCII 2023, LNAI 14051, pp. 542–553, 2023.
https://doi.org/10.1007/978-3-031-35894-4_40

that coaches have to decide new weight for lifter's current attempt in about 30 s. It also indicates that the sport scientist should obtain opponents' performance in 30 s. To satisfy this issue, video analysis is a suit tool to obtain the sport performance for athletes and coaches to observe lifters' movement. Although video analysis efficiently provides accuracy kinematic parameters, however, the coaches or athletes should read and understand the meaning of kinematic parameters by their own experience. This may cause fault understanding the tiny difference of the kinematic parameters [1].

The barbell trajectory is a critical performance indicator to indicate Olympic weightlifter's performance since it including many kinematic parameters. Chiu *et al.* utilize trajectories to quantify successful lift's characteristics [2]. Nego *et al.* utilize trajectories to indicate the snatch movement successful of excellent male lifters in IWF (International Weightlifting Federation) World Championship and IWF Junior World Championship [3]. Barbell trajectory implies many important kinematic parameters such as barbell's displacement, velocity and acceleration provides to let coaches and athletes to indicate their sport's performance.

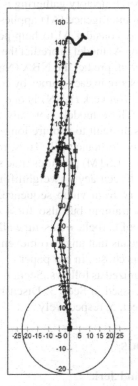

Fig. 1. Trajectories of three continues attempts

As can be seen in Fig. 1 we compare barbell trajectories of three different attempt of a lifter with three different weights on the bar. From this figure, we can observe that the three trajectories are similar. It represents that the lift performance is well down. As mentioned above, if coaches or athletes need to understand the meaning of kinematic parameters, it may need sport scientists to translate to coaches and athletes.

Kinematic parameters have been thoroughly researched in sports biomechanics and acceptably applied for sports performance evaluation. Motion Analysis system is one of popular kinematic analysis software to obtain the barbell trajectory. Not only Motion Analysis, there are also many software tools, such as Kinovea, which can obtain barbell trajectories from video sequences. However, the common problem with these software tools is difficultly operating and further consumes huge time by manual. Furthermore, after obtaining barbell trajectory, the kinematic parameters of barbell trajectory are also need experts to understand and translate to athletes or coaches.

Not only video sequence can obtain barbell trajectory, sensors are also good tools which provide high accuracy and high efficiency kinematic parameters. Sato *et al.* utilize the accelerometer to gather the trajectories of the barbell. However, when the weightlifter drops down the barbell after finishing the action, it can get a total weight is nearly 170G [1]. The sensor might be damaged. Sensors maybe easier operation then video analysis software, however, sensors cannot be suitable for the real competition. Non-contactable video analysis method for barbell trajectory gathering is the best way.

On the other hand, artificial intelligence (AI) applies in sport science in nowadays. Fialho *et al.* and Oluebube *et al.* consider AI to help people to solve mega-scale data analysis. They create and training AI model to predict the battle result in Premier League [4, 5]. Huang *et al.* and Chen *et al.* predict the NBA (National Basketball Association) team's total score and personal score in each games by considering official record information [6, 7]. Recurrent Neural Network (RNN) is one category of AI which good for handling time series material. These models not only decide the problem of weight exponential explosion, and it is difficult to capture long-term time correlation, but also archives excellent time series performance [8]. Thus, many pre-trained RNN models such as long-short-term memory (LSTM) provides time series material architecture [8].

In this paper, we create a high accuracy AI weightlifting movement evaluation model by considering barbell trajectory from video sequence. This model indicates lifters' performance not only in daily training but also for a real competition in real time. Considering the characteristics of barbell, we assume all movement information of the barbell is time-dependent. It means that any two movement points are interdependent. Therefore, LSTM architecture is chosen in our paper.

The rest of this paper is organized as follows. Section 2 introduces our LSTM model. The experimental result is discussed in Sect. 3. Discussion and conclusion result will then be shown in Sect. 4 and Sect. 5, respectively.

2   Materials and Methods

2.1   Motion Phase of Clean and Jerk

According to International Weightlifting Federation Technical and Competition Rules and Regulations, Olympic weightlifting can be divided into Snatch and Clean&Jerk categories [9]. In this paper, Clean&Jerk are considered to build the model to automatically evaluate lifters' movement. Our proposed Clean&Jerk movement evaluation model is aim to provide a high accuracy Clean&Jerk movement evaluation model for coaches and athletes to indicate the lifters' performance. Furthermore, we also like to provide an application of AI in sport science.

Both Snatch and Clean&Jerk are complex systemic movements and have high-strength muscular contractions. Lifters achieve more power outputs than other athletes [10]. Different from Snatch, Clean&Jerk is combined of clean followed by jerk. Refer to Storey *et al.*, the authors consider characteristics of Clean&Jerk and separate into twelve phases [11]. Figure 2 and Fig. 3 show each phase for clean and jerk respectively.

The motion phases are described as follows:

1. First Pull: Lifter raises up the barbell to the knee from the floor, as shown in Fig. 2 (a) and Fig. 2 (b).
2. Transition: The barbell is raised from the knee to hip joint, as shown in Fig. 2 (b) and Fig. 2 (c).
3. Second Pull: Lifter raises the barbell to the farthest with the body from the hip joint, as shown in Fig. 2 (c) and Fig. 2 (d).
4. Turnover: The barbell is lifted to the maximum vertical height from the farthest with the body, as shown in Fig. 2 (d) and Fig. 2 (e).
5. Catch: Lift catches the barbell from the maximum vertical height, as shown in Fig. 2 (e) and Fig. 2 (f).
6. Recovery from the Clean: The barbell is at the lowest position. Lifter stands up after catching the barbell, as shown in Fig. 2 (f) and Fig. 2 (g).
7. Start position for the Jerk: Lifter keeps legs straight and tiptoes parallel, and rests the barbell on lifter's collarbone, as shown in Fig. 3 (a).
8. Jerk Dip: Lifter starts squatting to the lowest position quickly, as shown in Fig. 3 (b) and Fig. 3 (c)
9. Jerk Drive: Lifter put his/her legs forth strength from the lowest position and keep legs straight finally, as shown in Fig. 3 (c) and Fig. 3 (d).
10. Unsupported split under the bar: Lifter powerfully raises the barbell to the highest position and keeps legs straight, as shown in Fig. 3 (d) and Fig. 3 (e).
11. Supported split under the bar: Lifter splits his/her legs and keeps the barbell at the highest position, as shown Fig. 3 (e) and Fig. 3 (f).
12. Recovery from the jerk: Lifter recover his/her legs to straight and parallel. Further-more, lifter's arms should always keep straight to finish, as shown in Fig. 3 (f) and Fig. 3 (g).

The phases mentioned above split continuous trajectory. These phases make scholars easily to gather kinematic information. From relevant research of Clean&Jerk by motion phase, scholars obtain many kinematics parameters that can efficiently indicate the sports performance of the lifter [3, 12–14].

| (a)Start the movement | (b)Barbell to knee. | (c)Barbell to hip joint. | (d) Furthest from the body. | (e) Maximum vertical height. | (f)Catching the barbell. | (g) Reply to standing. |

Fig. 2. Motion phase of Clean

| (a) Standing. | (b) Start to squat down. | (c) The lowest position | (d) To highest point when the legs straighten. | (e)The highest position. | (f)Supported split under the barbell. | (g)Recover the legs and stand. |

Fig. 3. Motion phase of Jerk

2.2 Experimental Procedure

In this paper, we create an AI model to evaluate the lifters' sports performance automatically. Our proposed AI model is shown in Fig. 4. In our proposed AI model, video sequence will be input and further extracted the barbell trajectory from each frame by data processing phase. In data processing phase, image pre-processing reduces the noise and blur each frame. The "classification of technical indicators" extracts barbell trajectory from video sequence and further calculate kinematic parameters of each movement phases which denotes in from the barbell trajectory [11]. The kinematic parameters are horizontal displacement and vertical displacement considered in this paper. Since movement evaluation should be in high accuracy, supervisor learning is considered in our proposed model. After kinematic parameters are gathered, the kinematic parameters will then be labeled by data labels which indicates the performance of each movement. All the video samples are randomly separated into training, validation and testing sets with 80%, 10% and 10%, respectively. Training and validation samples are utilized for neural network model training, and testing sample is used to evaluate the performance of our proposed model. We will adjust the parameters of neural network by training and validation samples, both of training lost and validation lost are considered to further provide a high accuracy model.

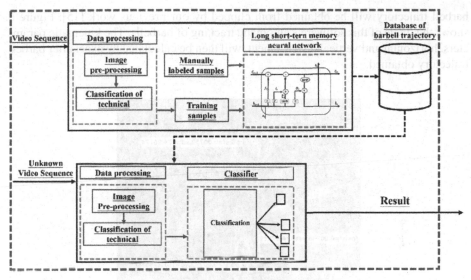

Fig. 4. Experimental procedure

2.3 Data Collection and Processing

All the video samples are gathered from Taiwan domestic adult competitions from 2019 to 2021. We select the men's 61 kg, 67 kg, 73 kg, 81 kg, 89 kg and 96 kg categories. As can be seen in Fig. 5(a), we installed the cameras in the spectator area for not affecting the game's progress. In addition, the camera is parallel to the weightlifting platform based on the collection principle by kinematics parameter. Since it is erected above the second floor, chose a nearly vertical direction to shoot, and the θ in the Fig. 5 (b) tends to be 45°.

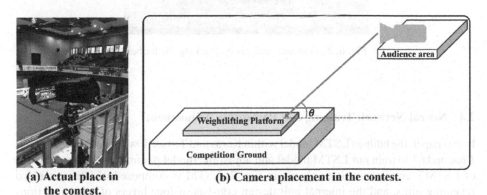

(a) Actual place in the contest.   **(b) Camera placement in the contest.**

Fig. 5. Instructions figure of data collection

After collecting the video sequences, we clip and obtain the barbell trajectory. The duration of the clipped video sequence is from barbell lift-up to dropped. In this paper, barbell trajectory will be obtained from clipped by our previous work [15]. Figure 6 shows the finale of this software's automatic tracking of barbells. The kinematic parameters, horizontal and vertical displacement, will then be calculated by excel after barbell trajectory obtained.

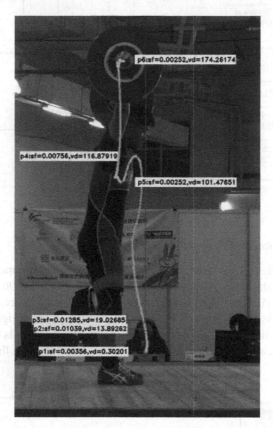

Fig. 6. Completed analysis by tracking the barbell

2.4   Neural Network Training and Parameter Adjustment

In this paper, the built-in LSTM model within Keras and Tensorflow is considered. We use Anaconda 3 to train our LSTM model and adjust the model parameters. The exhaustive of LSTM's architecture is as shown in Fig. 7. LSTM is composed of interconnected repeating units, and the internal unit design consists of four layers of logic functions (yellow rectangles in Fig. 7). One of the core concepts of LSTM is regulation through the gate (red circle in Fig. 7).

The first step is to decide which information to forget. Through the logic function, we can determine the proportion of the information brought in from the output of the

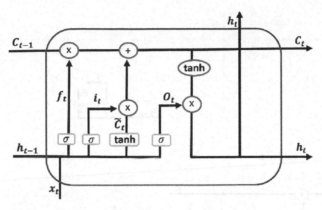

Fig. 7. LSTM neural network's architecture.

previous layer and the newly added input of this layer to be forgotten and not brought into the next layer (as can be seen in Fig. 8 (a)). The equation is shown in (1) as follows.

$$f_t = \sigma\left(W_f \cdot \left[h_{t-1}, x_t\right] + b_f\right) \tag{1}$$

The next step is to record the newly brought-in data into the central unit state. There are two steps: deciding what to record and updating the unit. Equations (2)–(4) and Fig. 8 (b)–(c) determine how much new information needs to be registered. Then the activation function (*tanh* function taken as example) calculates a vector to determine how much information C_t need to update the central unit.

$$i_t = \sigma\left(W_i \cdot \left[h_{t-1}, x_t\right] + b_i\right) \tag{2}$$

$$\tilde{C}_t = tanh\left(W_c \cdot \left[h_{t-1}, x_t\right] + b_c\right) \tag{3}$$

$$C_t = f_t \cdot C_{t-1} + i_t \cdot \tilde{C}_t \tag{4}$$

Finally, we decide how much information to output as Eqs. (5)–(6). From the result C_t of the previous step and the f_t by the forgetting measure, through the control of the logic function and *tanh*, it is determined that the central unit is to be output, such as shown in Fig. 8 (d).

$$O_t = \sigma\left(W_o \cdot \left[h_{t-1}, x_t\right] + b_o\right) \tag{5}$$

$$h_t = O_t \cdot tanh(C_t) \tag{6}$$

After LSTM model created, the model parameters such as numbers of neural, activation function, training times and data amount should be decided by each training. The model parameters will be shown as follows.

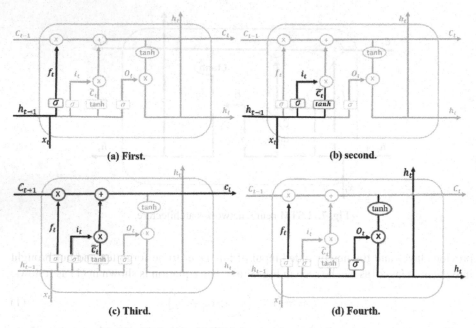

(a) First. (b) second.

(c) Third. (d) Fourth.

Fig. 8. Standard LSTM do at each step in the unit.

3 Result

In this paper, we only focus on good lift, therefore, totally 149 Clean&Jerk barbell trajectory with 2980 kinematic parameters are gathered. We labeled the barbell trajectory by considering the ranking of the Clean&Jerk competitions. The barbell trajectory of first three grade will be labeled as well-lift, otherwise will be normal-lift. The experimental results are shown in Table 1. Our proposed the model parameters of proposed LSTM weightlifting barbell trajectory performance evaluation model are decided by both considering training loss rate and validation loss rate. Our proposed model archives 71% for both accuracy and precision and recall rate is 59%. Table 2 is confusion matrix to present the sensitivity of our proposed model.

Table 1. Model performance index

	Value (%)
Accuracy rate	71%
Precision rate	71%
Recall	50%

Figure 9 shows the finale of the neural network's composition. As can be seen in Fig. 9, we have a LSTM with 64 output nodes connected by a dense layer as output with

Table 2. Confusion matrix

		Predict class	
		True	False
True class	True	71.4%	71.4%
	False	28.6%	28.6%

```
Model: "sequential_7"
_____
 Layer (type)                Output Shape              Param #
=================================================================
 lstm_7 (LSTM)               (None, 64)                16896

 dense_7 (Dense)             (None, 2)                 130

=================================================================
Total params: 17,026
Trainable params: 17,026
Non-trainable params: 0
```

Fig. 9. The final result of the neural network after adjustment.

2 output nodes. All of the parameters in each layer are shown in Table 3. Furthermore, we also revise the learning rate, epoch, and batch size to 0.00001, 2000, 10, respectively.

Table 3. Relevant adjustment parameters of each layer.

layer	Activation function	units
LSTM	Softsign	64
Dense	Softmax	2

4 Discussion

From the experimental results shown in Table 1, we can observe that our proposed LSTM weightlifting barbell trajectory performance evaluation model indicates the lifters' performance in high accuracy. Both referring to Table 1 and Table 2, our proposed model can archive accuracy and sensitivity. The proposed model provides lifters, coaches and sport scientists an efficient way to help the lifter to improve his/her skill. Lifters, coaches or sports scientists use a camera to capture the lifter's attempt video, and then the barbell kinematic parameters are obtained to evaluate this lifter's performance and technology quickly. This improvement reduces the operation procedure and efficiently utilizes sports biomechanics in daily training. The result of this model also can efficiently indicate the sport performance of the lifters [3, 16–18].

Weightlifting is a competitive sport that needs powerful muscle and excellent technique for a good lift attempt. As mentioned, observation kinematic parameters of barbell trajectory although can be gathered, however, the meaning of the kinematic parameters may need sport scientist translated to lifters and coaches. Otherwise, coaches and lifters may obtain the gesture with their eyes and their experience. From our LSTM weightlifting barbell trajectory performance evaluation model, the kinematic parameters from video sequence will be further evaluated to indicate lifter's performance in high accuracy. It shows that machine learning can be suit for sport data classification to further assist coaches or athletes in daily training course and competition information gathering.

5 Conclusion

An LSTM weightlifting barbell trajectory performance evaluation model is proposed in this paper. The result shows our proposed model both archiving efficiency and accuracy. This model provides evaluation of the lifters' performance of Clean&Jerk by considering kinematic parameters of barbell trajectory to lifters, coaches and sports scientists for adjusting the gesture and further deciding the tactic in competition. We can conclude that our proposed model not only provides an efficient and easy tool for kinematic analysis and further indicate that machine learning technique can be suited for sport science.

Acknowledgements. This research is supported by National Science and Technology Council, Taiwan, R.O.C. The project number is NSTC 112-2425-H-845-002.

References

1. Sato, K., Sands, W.A., Stone, M.H.: The reliability of accelerometry to measure weightlifting performance. Sports Biomech. **11**(4), 524–531 (2012)
2. Chiu, H., Liang, J.: BCH angles of young female weightlifters during snatch movement. In: ISBS-Conference Proceedings Archive (2010)
3. Nagao, H., Kubo, Y., Tsuno, T., Kurosaka, S., Muto, M.: A biomechanical comparison of successful and unsuccessful snatch attempts among elite male weightlifters. Sports **7**(6), 151 (2019)
4. Fialho, G., Manhães, A., Teixeira, J.P.: Predicting sports results with artificial intelligence–a proposal framework for soccer games. Procedia Comput. Sci. **164**, 131–136 (2019)
5. Oluebube, N.L., Chijioke, E.G., Oghenekevwe, E.H., Ifeanyichukwu, U.C.: English premier league scoreline analysis: a stochastic and game theory approach. Am. J. Theor. Appl. Stat. **10**(3), 136 (2021)
6. Huang, M.L., Lin, Y.J.: Regression tree model for predicting game scores for the golden state warriors in the national basketball association. Symmetry **12**(5), 835 (2020)
7. Chen, W.J., Jhou, M.J., Lee, T.S., Lu, C.J.: Hybrid basketball game outcome prediction model by integrating data mining methods for the national basketball association. Entropy **23**(4), 477 (2021)
8. Sherstinsky, A.: Fundamentals of recurrent neural network (RNN) and long short-term memory (LSTM) network. Physica D **404**, 132306 (2020)

9. Garhammer, J.O.H.N.: Power production by Olympic weightlifters. Med. Sci. Sports Exerc. **12**(1), 54–60 (1980)
10. https://iwf.sport/wp-content/uploads/downloads/2020/01/IWF_TCRR_2020.pdf
11. Storey, A., Smith, H.K.: Unique aspects of competitive weightlifting: performance, training and physiology. Sports Med. **42**, 769–790 (2012)
12. Kipp, K., Meinerz, C.: A biomechanical comparison of successful and unsuccessful power clean attempts. Sports Biomech. **16**(2), 272–282 (2017)
13. Harbili, E., Alptekin, A.: Comparative kinematic analysis of the snatch lifts in elite male adolescent weightlifters. J. Sports Sci. Med. **13**(2), 417 (2014)
14. Al-Khleifat, A.I., Al-Kilani, M., Kilani, H.A.: Biomechanics of the clean and jerk in weightlifting national Jordanian team (2019)
15. Hsu, C.-T., Ho, W.-H., Chen, J.-S.: High efficient weightlifting barbell tracking algorithm based on diamond search strategy. In: Arkusz, K., Będziński, R., Klekiel, T., Piszczatowski, S. (eds.) Biomechanics in Medicine and Biology, pp. 252–262. Springer, Cham (2019). https://doi.org/10.1007/978-3-319-97286-2_23
16. Garhammer, J.: Weight lifting and training. Biomech. Sport, 169–211 (2020)
17. Grabe, S.A., Widule, C.J.: Comparative biomechanics of the jerk in Olympic weightlifting. Res. Q. Exerc. Sport **59**(1), 1–8 (1988)
18. Hadi, G., Akkus, H., Harbili, E.: Three-dimensional kinematic analysis of the snatch technique for lifting different barbell weights. J. Strength Conditioning Res. **26**(6), 1568–1576 (2012)

Incorporating the Dynamics of Climate Change into the Deep Dive Virtual Reality Underwater Site Prediction System

Sarah Saad[1], Thomas Palazzolo[1], Chencheng Zhang[1], Robert G. Reynolds[1,2(✉)],
Ashley Lemke[3], John O'Shea[2], and Calien O'Shea[4]

[1] Wayne State University, Detroit, MI 48201, USA
robert.reynolds@wayne.edu
[2] University of Michigan, Ann Arbor, MI 48109, USA
[3] University of Texas, Arlington, TX 76019, USA
[4] North Dakota State University, Fargo, ND 58102, USA

Abstract. The procedural content of a virtual reality system is a key contributor to its success. However, it is often the case that the content needs to be adjusted. This may take place for a variety of reasons. This research investigates the possibility of the use of machine learning technology to facilitate the modification of a games content. Here, the Deep Dive system was designed originally to predict ancient site locations. Recently it was repurposed to be used as an educational tool to facilitate aspects of STEM education. This required the modification of the content to support this novel use. An evolutionary learning algorithm, Cultural Algorithm, is employed to facilitate the addition of the new content required for the educational application.

Keywords: Procedural Content Generation · Evolutionary Algorithms · Cultural Algorithms · Virtual Reality · Stem education

1 Introduction

The Deep Dive Land Bridge simulation system was initially developed to aid underwater archaeologists in the discovery of ancient prehistoric sites located underwater in Lake Huron, one of the Great Lakes in the United States [1–3]. It utilized Artificial Intelligence and Virtual Reality to recreate the archaic semi-artic landscape and has facilitated the discovery of several ancient underwater sites [4]. The Land Bridge was above the Lake Huron water level for about 2,000 years from 10,000 B.P. to 8,000 B.P. Figure 1 shows the location of the Land Bridge relative to the State of Michigan in the USA and Canada. The two cells on the bridge represent areas that are the focus of original exploration. They were initially selected due to their location relative to the widest part of the Land Bridge.

While the Land Bridge program was initially designed as an aid for the discovery of submerged prehistoric sites, the system's potential as a means for understanding

H. Degen and S. Ntoa (Eds.): HCII 2023, LNAI 14051, pp. 554–573, 2023.
https://doi.org/10.1007/978-3-031-35894-4_41

traditional hunting practices, its use as an educational tool became rapidly apparent in two ways. First, it could be used to record hunters' observations about potential uses of the ancient landscape. Traditional Alaskan hunters were invited to enter the Virtual World and describe what they saw. By tracking the hunter's movements over the virtual landscape and by listening to their commentary, insight was gained into how traditional hunters view and conceptualize the landscape in general. In addition, their assessment of locations that might have served as sites for hunting structures and activities in the distant past were recorded [5].

These results suggested that the system might be successfully repurposed to be a valuable educational tool. In order to test this theory out the system was used as part of the STEM high school curriculum in Alpena Michigan. The first group of high school students used the Virtual Reality system for two weeks. Their goal was to identify areas of potential hunter activity. During the process of using the system it became clear that the system was in need of more detailed procedural content. While there was sufficient content in the regions first surveyed by the Archaeologists as shown in Fig. 1, other portions of the bridge lacked additional detail about other biomes and geological features that were not present in the initial surveyed regions.

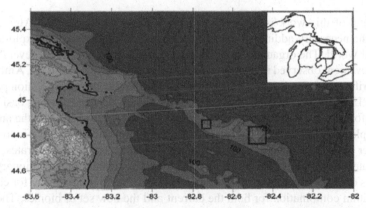

Fig. 1. Location of the Alpena-Amberley Land Bridge. The rectangles represent area originally surveyed by Archaeologists

Procedural content generation is not a new concept, but it is an important one. It can be a useful solution to a number of problems. It is capable of being performed using a variety of methods including evolutionary, random search, and nature based. The content generated will take the form of what is needed to solve the problem at hand. Some applications of procedural content generation can include virtual testing, simulation, and game design. Simulations can be a great asset in fields like archaeology where it is not always possible to directly observe the environment being studied due to physical restrictions.

The key component of the Virtual Reality system are the caribou herds and their migration patterns through various biomes. Ancient hunter behaviors would have related to their ability to predict herd movements and exploit those predictions. Figure 2 shows a caribou herd moving across the Land Bridge. The intended target demographic, High School students, needed to have more content available about caribou across the different biomes present on the Land Bridge.

Fig. 2. A caribou herd moving across the Land Bridge.

The goal of this work is to use Evolutionary Algorithms, Cultural Algorithms to generate the necessary additional content necessary to support student explorations of the Virtual World. The organization of the paper is as follows. In Sect. 2 several models of herd movement observed in the real world are described: Single Path A*, Ambush A*, and Dendriform A*. Each of them will be used to generate optimal migration pathways across the Land Bridge. Next in Sect. 2.1 simulations are performed using basic calorie content information to identify three categories of herd types based upon the amount of STRESS placed on the herd as it moves across the landscape. The goal is to identify the number of animals in herds with high survival rates, average survival rates, and low survival rates respectively. Then in Sect. 3 Cultural Algorithms, an evolutionary hyper-heuristic is described and the employed to generate an optimum pathway for each herd size algorithm combination for both the current and the new set of biomes. The results are presented in Sect. 4, and Sect. 5 gives the conclusion.

2   The Multi-agent Planning Framework for the Deep Dive Simulation Component

Figure 3 gives an overview of the overall Deep Dive system. It has three basic components: The Pathfinder MAP Simulation system; the Graphical User Interface (GUI) for the simulation system; and The Virtual Reality system.

The topographic data acquired from the National Oceanographic and Atmospheric database (*NOAA*) of the area was fed into the AI pipeline to *Generate* AI content via the Landscape. This created content includes the water level of various cells of the landscape to identify which areas of the Land Bridge were above the current water level or not for a given year between 10,000 and 8,000 B.P. For any given year height map data for those portions of the landscape was calculated along with derived slope. Hydrological

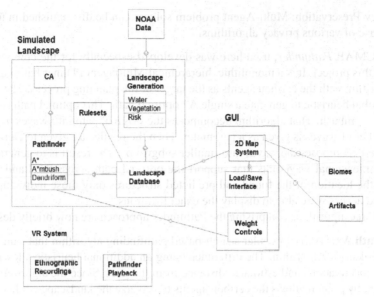

Fig. 3. The Overall Organization of the Deep Dive system.

information including the location of ponds, swamps, and rivers that are present in the location were then calculated. Given the location, water content, slope and sun angle the AI pipeline can predict the cells potential vegetation at each location on the Land Bridge. This information is stored in the *Landscape Database* for use by the *Pathfinder* system.

The basis for the simulation system is *Pathfinder*, a Cooperative Multi-Agent Planner (CMAPP). There are several deterministic general purpose MAP solvers available [9]. They include MAPR (MAP Planning by Reuse), CMAP (Cooperative MAP), mu-SATPLAN (Satisfiability based planning), among others. The different CMAP solvers are be classified by the mechanisms that they employ to address the planning process. The main features that can be used to characterize cooperative MAP solvers are:

1. Agent Distribution: The MAP process here involves multiple agents who are involved in the planning process either as active participants or as target for the planning process.
2. Computational Process: Whether the computational process is performed using a centralized monolithic processor or distributed among several processing units.
3. Plan Synthesis: This involves how and when the coordination activity is applied among agents. Coordination activities represent how information is distributed among agents and how their actions are combined together.
4. Communication Mechanism: How agents communicate with each other.
5. Heuristic Search: MAPs that use local heuristics to allow individual agents to assess their estimate progress towards their individual goals. Those with global heuristics calculate them for all the agents.

6. Privacy Preservation: Multi-Agent problem solvers can be distinguished in terms of their use of various privacy algorithms.

The CMAP, *Pathfinder*, used here was developed especially for the computational needs of this project. It is a monolithic, hierarchical Multiagent Planner based upon the A* Algorithm with the caribou agents as the target of the planning process. The planner uses a global heuristic to generate a single A* optimal path. This optimal path is used as basis for A*mbush. That algorithm decomposes the original path into waves of agents. The number of waves is given as a parameter. Then the results are given to Dendriform A* which decomposes the waves into smaller subgroups. The result is to generate a set of two-dimensional waypoints that support the optimal path across the Land Bridge. To keep the location of the found and predicted structures only those individuals with privileged access were able to display the exact locations.

The three algorithms comprising the Pathfinder approach are now briefly described:

Single Path A*: A* is a popular search-based pathfinding algorithm that's an adaptation of Dijkstra's Algorithm. The difference being an additional heuristic allowing it to attribute cost to actual and estimated distance from the goal. Since the algorithm calculated point by point it allows the caribou agents to traverse the landscape while focusing on effort, risk, and nutrition.

A Pseudocode*

```
Add pathStart to openNodes
    Initialize pathStart scores
    While (openNodes count greater than 0)
    {
            currentNode = openNodes [0]
        If (currentNode is goalNode)
        { assemblePath() and return true}
        Remove currentNode from openNodes
        Find currentNode's neighboringNodes.
        ForEach(neighboringNode) calculate f and g score
        If (neighborNode is not in openNodes) add to openNodes.
        Else {adjust neighborNode's position in the openList based on total score}
    }
```

Ambush: Another migration algorithm integrated into the system is A*mbush. A*mbush incorporates A* at its root. It uses the algorithm of A* but does so in separate waves instead of a single path. The number of waves are entered as a parameter, then the total herd size of Caribou is divided amongst the waves. The waves are then sent one after another with the nest wave entering the landscape as the last one completes its journey. Each wave consumes a certain proportion of available calories, leaving the remainder for the waves that follow.

Ambush Pseudocode:

```
for (generations=0; generations < ambushGenerations; generations++)

for (waypoint = waypoints-2; waypoint > 0; waypoint--)

{foundPath = AStar(waypoint, waypoint+1)

foreach(node in foundPath)

{Insert node in resultPath(generations) at index 0.}

} resultingHerd += calculateMigrationScore()

devourVegetation(foundPath)

}
```

Dendriform: Dendriform is the final algorithm used in the path planner portion on the Deep Dive system. It incorporates A* at its root but also allows for branching during the exploration of the landscape. This means as the line of Caribou is traversing, they can divide on the spot allowing some of the herd to continue their path while the rest look for a separate path. This allows for more complex paths to be generated like the example in Fig. 4.

Dendriform Pseudocode:

```
Calculate optimal A* path

Add starting point and ending point to node list.

While node list has more than two nodes {

checkForNewDivergencePoints

select last two nodes in node list and A*mbush Devour path section.

Remove last node in node list.

If last node in node list is not starting point:

    Calculate optimal A* path to ending point.

}
```

The Simulation system then communicates with the simulation GUI in two basic ways. First, the user interface displays a series of tabs through which the user may navigate to a given data set or select an experiment to run as shown in Fig. 5. Maps can be viewed in a variety of data styles, such as biome data, topographical data, archaeological points of interest, ruleset hotspots, and so on. Pictured below, the user has selected to run six iterations of the A*mbush pathfinder, each wave being made up of 1000 caribou. The weight priority wheel on the bottom left allows the user to manually set the weights for Effort, Risk, Nutrition, and Time in the performance function. The priority weights

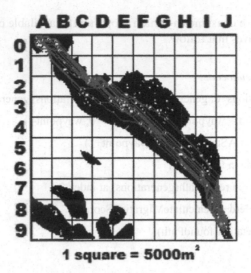

Fig. 4. Sample Run of Dendriform on the landscape.

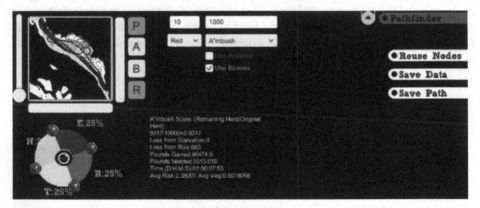

Fig. 5. The Current Deep Dive GUI. The upper left gives the path produced by an algorithm. Bottom left gives the 4 basic parameters for the optimization. (Color figure online)

control what will be important to the caribou in the current run. The green segment denoted by a "N" is the nutrition this will have caribou prioritize situations which will lead to an increase in calorie or food intake. The blue segment is effort ("E"). An increase in this priority will cause the caribou to avoid scenarios that lead to excess calories being spent for example going up a steep incline. The red segment is risk ("R") which influences caribou to avoid scenarios that lead to a higher percentage of deaths. The last weight denoted by yellow is time ("T"). This parameter prioritizes the amount of time it would take to cross the entirety of the portion of the land bridge simulated.

In the next section, the goal will be to simulate the three algorithms with different herd sizes and parameter weights over a subarea restricted by the largest of the two boxes in Fig. 1. The model will be used as the basis for expanding the optimization activities from the small area to the entire Land Bridge in Sect. 4. This will be necessary to address the challenges associated with the change of user groups envisioned here.

2.1 The Prototype Herd Movement Model

The DEEP DIVE system was originally targeted towards the prediction of sites in selected regions on the Land Bridge. Those regions are shown in Fig. 1. Now that the focus has expanded to include the entire bridge as part of the educational user experience, the model will need to be expanded to produce optimal paths over the entire Land Bridge. This will require the addition of new biomes and geological features not present in the original areas. Prior to doing this we need to generate as estimate of the number of animals that correspond to herds with high, medium, and low survival rates based solely on estimated calories content for the bridge. That is the goal of this section.

In the following, the model assumes a Fall migration pathway over the Land Bridge under the control of the four basic parameter components: Risk, Nutrition, Effort, and Time. Figure 6 below shows the effect that effort, time and nutrition can have on Caribou path planning. Part (a) of the figure shows the influence of nutrition on the created generated path. Instead of going straight through, they deviated toward the dark green area, indicating an area of high nutrition or food. In (b) there are two areas of higher elevation that the Caribou intentionally moved around, causing the path to move in a more circuitous way instead of straight through. Part (c) showcases the effect of incorporating both risk and time into the system. The generated path avoids the swamp areas which tend to take more time and are riskier. To better visualize the tradeoffs between the components STRESS charts were produced as a result of simulating the optimal path constructed by each algorithm for herds ranging in size from 50 to 300,000 across the Land Bridge. Herd size is plotted on the x-axis and the herd survival as a percentage is plotted on the y-axis. Figure 7 gives the chart for the Dendriform algorithm.

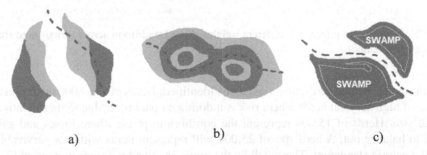

a)   b)   c)

Fig. 6. Example paths showing influence of Nutrition (a), Effort (b) and Time (c)

In Fig. 7 the STRESS curves for Dendriform are given for several different configurations of parameter weights. The Blue curve represents the scenario where the priorities are set to equal across the four priorities. The other four curves represent the scenarios where one of the components is set to 100% at the expense of all of the others. Notice that there are three basic phases. In the first phase, survival rates increase as herd size increases from 50 to around 1000. This reflects the principle of safety in numbers. The scenario that prefers risk over all other factors dominates in that phase. The next phase represents a plateau where the impact of adding new members is offset by an increase in members who are lost due to starvation. In the final phase the nutritional concerns start to dominate with herds above 8000. In that phase, the scenario that focusses only on nutrition is best able to ameliorate the observed reduction in survivability. On the other hand, it is the worst performer in the first phase relative to the others.

Figure 8 combines the STRESS curves for all three algorithms under the "all things being equal" assumption for the weights. In that Figure Ambush (1 wave) is the same as A*. As before, the more the herd is broken into waves the lower the slope for risk reduction. A* has the highest rate of reduction in risk since all of the individuals in a herd are used at once. Dendriform is a close second since it introduces all of the individuals into the simulation at once although they broke into groups. The plateau phase is the shortest for A* followed by Dendriform. For Ambush the more waves there are, the longer the equilibrium phase and the shorter the nutrition dominant phase.

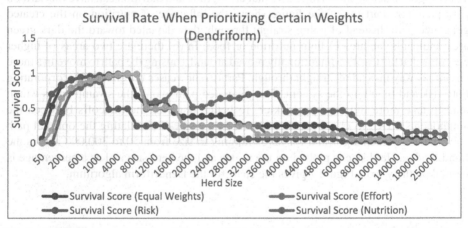

Fig. 7. Survival rates prioritizing different weights using Dendriform across various herd sizes. (Color figure online)

From Fig. 8 three herd categories can be identified. Herds of size 8000 are representative of high survival herds where risk is a dominant parameter due to their relatively small size. Herds of 15,000 represent the equilibrium phase where losses and gains tend to balance out. A herd size of 25,000 will represent herds with low survivabilty from a caloric standpoint. These will be the representative herd sizes to be used in the subsequent simulations.

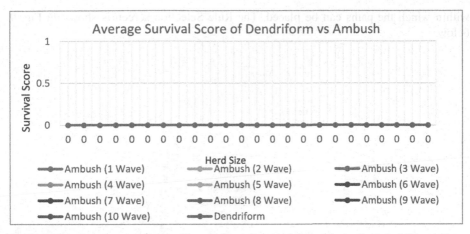

Fig. 8. Survival rates equalizing all weights using the A*, A*mbush and A*Dendriform algorithms across various herd size. Ambush (1 Wave) is the same as A*.

3   Using Cultural Algorithms to Generate Optimal Caribou Migration Paths

The goal is to identify those cells on the map that are visited by herds of all sizes and by all of the algorithms. These locations can then be used as reference points for the user exploration of the Land Bridge. This is particularly important for the STEM student repurposing. Since the representation consists of over a billion cells, this will make the task of exploration more feasible for the user. Of course, the optimal pathway will be different from one herd size to another. In addition, for any given herd size the optimization landscape can be very rugged. Finding the combination of weights that can produce optimal survivability for large herd sizes is a non-trivial task.

Here a machine learning algorithm, the Cultural Algorithm (*CA*) is employed to produce a set of weights that optimize group survivability. The Cultural algorithm is a socially motivated algorithm developed by Reynolds [9, 10]. It's a means to solve problems in a complex system like the ones posed to the Deep Dive's path planner. It is described graphically in Fig. 10. The CA is composed of a belief space and population space. Here the population is a set of experiments that employ different values weights for environmental parameters. The knowledge sources are housed in the belief space represent the knowledge of the population.

Individuals from the population are then influenced by belief space knowledge. Their resultant decision is evaluated by their relative fitness. Top performers are accepted into the belief space and used to update the knowledge there. Here the knowledge sources determine the optimal weights priorities of risk, nutrition, time, and effort can have on the system.

In addition, the user can place constraints on the generated pathways in two ways. First, they can require the path generated path to be constrained to pass through a set of manually set waypoints. Those points can be set by clicking on the map in the upper left-hand corner of the screen. Also, users can select rules that constrain the regions within which the paths can be placed. The Rule Selection screen is shown in Fig. 9 below.

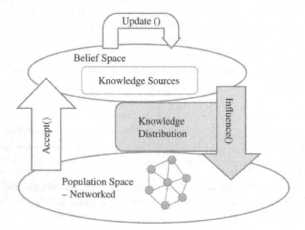

Fig. 9. Cultural Algorithm Representation.

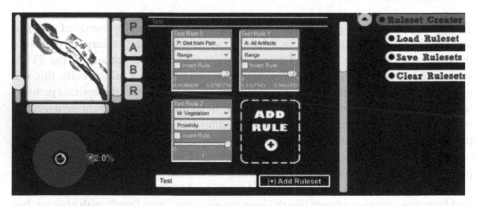

Fig. 10. The GUI screen used to display and modify heuristic constraints on generated paths.

The Cultural Algorithm will be applied to produce the optimum component weights for the three representative herd sizes determined earlier. One herd size will be selected from each of the three phases in the model. The Risk dominant phase is represented by a herd of population size of 8000. The plateau phase is represented by a herd of size 15000, and the Nutrition dominant phase is represented by a herd of size 25000. The caloric content of the Land Bridge cells are represented by biome that represents plant content on the Land Bridge while it was above water between 10,000 and 8,000 B.P.

The biome information used in these tests was the Sonnenberg Version 3 biome map, created from annotated biome map data, early predictions of the nature of areas, and later polygonal region data used to refine and correct the predicted areas. In Fig. 11 the original biomes from Sonnenberg are presented on the left. The figure on the right is the enhanced set of biomes that represent additional details that were needed to produce a more concise set of paths for use by the student users. Figure 12 gives the color-coded key for each of the biomes. The presence of water bodies are indicated in black. The white color is the plains, a low-hazard, easily-traversable biome. Green represents marshlands, abundant in nutrition but high in risk and requiring more time to move through. Yellow is the sandy beach biome, with relatively low risk but low nutrition and a time penalty for moving in soft sand. Orange represents the rocky biome, with lower vegetation and light risk and time penalties due to the uneven, rocky surface of the landscape. Gray represents the northern cliff biome, which is immediately adjacent to a vertical drop which would likely be fatal to any caribou that fell from it. The most recent version now contains eskers. Eskers are long ridges of gravel and other sediment with a typical winding course that are deposited by meltwater from a retreating glacier or ice sheet. Overall the enhanced version contains more detail about landscape features that can serve to constrain herd movement.

3.1 Original and Esker Update CA Optimized Runs Comparison

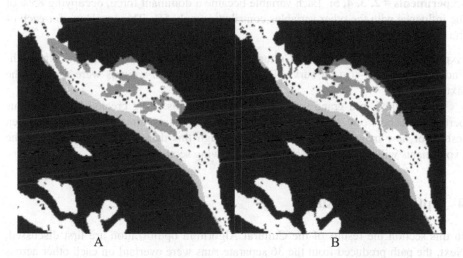

Fig. 11. On the left (a) is the original version of the biome data, comprised of a single piece of polygon data, and the hypothesized biome data from Dr. Elizabeth Sonnenberg. On the right (b) is the updated version of the biome data, comprised of the updated polygon data which includes the lake biomes, the lake-edge marsh biomes, and the esker obstacles.

The Cultural Algorithm was then applied to produce an optimal configuration of weights for each of the three representative herd sizes when run with Ambush and Dendriform. A* was omitted since it was a special case of Ambush with just one wave. In addition to the Cultural Algorithm runs, Optimal paths produced by A*mbush and Dendriform for scenarios where all weights were set to be equal, as well with where

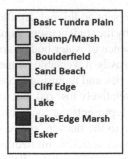

Basic Tundra Plain
Swamp/Marsh
Boulderfield
Sand Beach
Cliff Edge
Lake
Lake-Edge Marsh
Esker

Fig. 12. Color coded key to the biome maps from Fig. 11. (Color figure online)

each component was set to be dominant. The overall set of experiments to be run are given below:

Experiment #1: All things being equal, the four variables were in balance, each contributing 25% to the overall influence.

Experiments # 2, 3, 4, 5: Each variable became a dominant force, occupying 85% of the influence with the other variables contributing only 5%. This was done for each of the four variables.

Experiment #6: Utilizing the Cultural Algorithm to optimize the particular path-finder's given herd-size for survival, the resulting optimal weights were used for the sixth path.

This resulted in a grand total of 36 different paths being created by the various permutations between A*mbush and Dendriform. The datapoints of the map were then tested for how many times paths moved through this data point. The results of the experiments will now be discussed in the following section.

4   Optimization Results

In this section the results of the Cultural Algorithm optimization are first discussed. Next, the path produced from the 36 separate runs were overlaid on each other across the entire Land Bridge. The paths were generated by three different scenarios: all things being equal; one component dominant over the others; and the optimal paths produced by the Cultural Algorithm. Each scenario was viewed to provide a different perspective on the produced paths. The resultant paths are then described, and the new procedural content translated into the Virtual Reality presentation.

Table 1 gives the results of the optimized path parameter weights produced by the Cultural Algorithm. Each column represents the optimal configuration of weights for a given herd size, algorithm, and biome configuration. In the original biome risk is highest for small herds but becomes less important with increased herd size for both A*mbush and Dendriform. Likewise, the importance of nutrition as factor in determining the optimal path increases with increased herd size for both algorithms. However, is less important for Dendriform since the algorithm can distribute caribou over a larger area to

Table 1. The Effort Risk Nutrition and Time weight variables for the CA-Optimized paths, for the original biome data, and for the new polygonal biome data with eskers added.

Old Biomes: Did NOT include Eskers, Lake-Edge Swamps, or Lake Biomes.

	Am-bush 8000	Am-bush 15000	Am-bush 25000	Den-dri 8000	Den-dri 15000	Den-dri 25000	AVG	STD DEV
Effort	10	19	21	26	43	41	26.666	11.84155
Risk	73	12	7	40	31	13	29.333	22.69116
Nutri-tion	16	63	66	15	25	35	36.666	20.77392
Time	1	7	5	18	1	10	7	5.859465

New Biomes: Includes Eskers, Lake-Edge Swamp, and Lake Biomes.

	Am-bush 8000	Am-bush 15000	Am-bush 25000	Den-dri 8000	Den-dri 15000	Den-dri 25000	AVG	STD DEV
Effort	12	9	13	55	11	27	21.166	16.23183
Risk	31	40	10	11	38	9	23.166	13.45878
Nutri-tion	36	29	72	30	35	38	40	14.66288
Time	22	22	6	4	16	24	15.666	7.95124

insure access to more resources than A*Ambush. While effort essentially increases with increased herd size in both approaches it is clearly less important than risk and nutrition. Time is the least important of the four in both algorithms. However, it increases slightly with herd size for A*Ambush but actually is reduced with herd size for Dendriform. This is again due to the fact that the algorithm can distribute larger herds across a larger area so congestion at bottlenecks is less likely.

The new biome results exhibit a shift in priorities. First, while nutrition still increases with increased herd size for both algorithms it is overall less of a factor except for the largest of the A*Ambush herds. This is probably because each wave consumes some resources, leaving less resources available for the wave that follows. In Dendriform if there is reduced nutrition herds just break up. Risk still more important for A*Ambush the Dendriform and overall, still the second most weighted parameter on average. Effort is still the third ranked parameter but has an overall higher average weight across both algorithms. How the two algorithms Dendriform weighs effort more than ambush since the distribution of the herd now must encounter obstacles such as eskers and marshes that make distribution more work. Finally, time is now more of an issue for both algorithms. This again derives from the presence of the eskers and marshes that make it harder to from east to west without having to make a north or south detour.

The question now is how do these differential weights manifest themselves in the actual paths that are produced? Fig. 13 gives the set of all 36 paths generated including the CA Optimum paths. The different colors represent each of the 36 different configurations that were produced. What is important to note is that with the enhanced biome map, there are clearly more constraints on the caribou paths, regardless of the configuration. The new biomes clearly produce a bottleneck on the Alpena side going east but after the bottleneck the paths are more distributed. This might be due to the need for more resources after the bottleneck since there could be shortages there.

In Fig. 14 the paths generated by the CA-Optimizer for A*Ambush and Dendriform are displayed showing only those cells that are traversed by every single path by all algorithms over all herd sizes. Again, the paths produced for the old biomes are on the left and the enhanced biomes on the right. Notice that by adding in the additional biomes, there appears to be a singular path that all optimized herds are traversing regardless of algorithm or herd size. Any gaps in the path represent the fact that there is a choice to continue along the route using a secondary route. What this Means is that there is a singular optimal pathway along the bridge. This will be very useful in arranging explorations for STEM students since the pathway can be the start for local side trips and explorations.

Finally, in Fig. 15 the location of the three major features related to hunting activities on the bridge that have been found. Notice the two of those features bookend the westmost eskers. In fact, the overlook is located very near the southern region where all of the paths tend to converge. This choke point would then seem to be a good place for the positioning of related hunting activities. Figure 16 highlights a portion of the optimal pathways are shown in red. Those are the cells that a portion of all runs for all herd sizes and algorithm passed through. The colors are taken from the corresponding color scale used in Figs. 13 and 14. The view is towards the south east from a point near the Overlock.

Figure

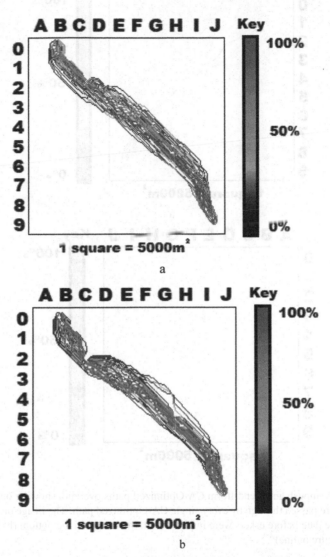

a

b

Fig. 13. The A*mbush and Dendriform CA-Optimized paths overlaid, showing the data cells colored based on what ratio of the total number of paths passed through the given data cell. The image on the top (a) is the older biome date before eskers were implemented, the image on the bottom (b) is with esker data. Note the dramatic deviation in area C2 on the bottom (b) image where an esker is located. (Color figure online)

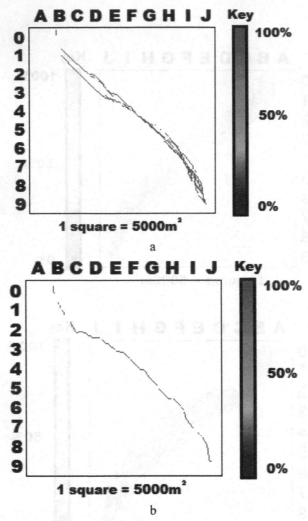

a

b

Fig. 14. The A*mbush and Dendriform CA-Optimized paths overlaid, showing only those data cells which were passed through by every single CA-Optimized path. The image on the top (a) is the older biome date before eskers were implemented, the image on the bottom (b) is with esker data. (Color figure online)

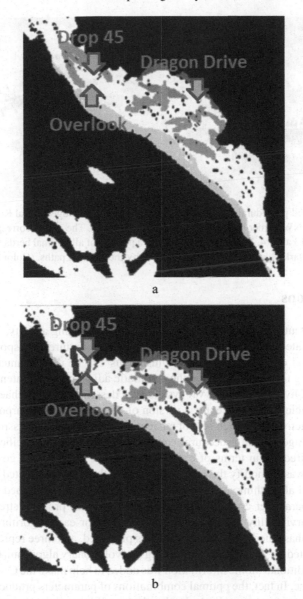

Fig. 15. The biome maps from Fig. 1 with three noted sites of interest denoted with arrows.

Fig. 16. Generated procedural content overlaid onto the Land Bridge Virtual Reality landscape. A view from the NW corner of Fig. 15 towards the southeast. The colors correspond to those in the key for Figs. 13 and 14. Red cells\are visited by a portion of all optimal herds for all herd sizes and algorithms. Dark blue cells are rarely traversed by the optimal paths. (Color figure online)

5   Conclusions

Procedural content generation is an important and challenging activity. Yet, even after content is generated changes in the game or system may require corresponding changes in the procedural content. While such adjustments can be done manually the use of machine learning techniques to aid in the automatic adjustment of content is promising. Here the Deep Dive Land Bridge VR system was designed to aid archaeologists in the prediction of ancient sites. Recently, a version of the system was repurposed to support STEM related activities by high school students. Initial use in the classroom suggested that certain changes in the procedural content were necessary. Specifically, the users needed more direction in terms of exploring the Land Bridge. The goal of the work described here was to modify the content to support those more directed activities.

Here several algorithmic models of herd movement were described and simulated using various parameter configurations. The result was to produce stress curves that showed how survivability was affected by herd size for each algorithm. From those curves a three-phase model of survivability was produced, and three representative herd sizes were selected for path optimization using an evolutionary algorithm, Cultural Algorithms. Then additional biome information was added to help make the CA-Optimization task more precise. In fact, the optimal combinations of parameters produced by the Cultural Algorithm suggest a singular optimal pathway of high activity that can now be used to help students explore the landscape in a more structured way.

References

1. Drikx, S., van der Meijer, J., Velden, A., Iosup, A.: Procedural content generation for games. ACM Trans. Multimed. Comput. Commun. Appl. **9**(1), 1–22 (2013). https://doi.org/10.1145/2422956.2422957

2. Amato, A.: Procedural content generation in the game industry. In: Korn, O., Lee, N. (eds.) Game Dynamics, pp. 15–25. Springer, Cham (2017). https://doi.org/10.1007/978-3-319-530 88-8_2
3. Reynolds, R.G., O'Shea, J., Che, Z., Gawasmeh, Y., Meadows, G., Fotouhi, F.: The agile design of reality game AI. In: Multi-agent Applications with Evolutionary Computation and Biologically Inspired Technologies: Intelligent Techniques for Ubiquity and Optimization. IGI Global Press (2011)
4. Fogarty, J., Reynolds, R.G.,Salamayeh, A., Palazzolo, T.: Serious game modeling of caribou behavior across Lake Huron using cultural algorithms and influence maps. In: O'Shea, J., Sonnenberg, E. (ed.) Archaeological, Ethnographic and Paleo-Environmental Perspectives on Caribou Hunting in the Great Lakes: Maps, Directions and Accommodations, University of Michigan Museum of Anthropology (2015)
5. Palazzolo, T., Reynolds, R.G., Stanley, S.: Exploring virtual worlds with cultural algorithms: Ancient Alpena-Amberley Land Bridge. In: Cultural Algorithms: Tools for the Engineering of Social Intelligence into Complex Systems, pp. 203–271. IEEE Wiley Press, Hoboken (2020)
6. O'Shea, J, Lemke, A., Sonnenburg, E., Reynolds, R.G., Abbot, B.: A 9,000 year-old submerged Caribou hunting structure in Lake Huron. In: Proceedings of the National Academy of Science (2014)
7. Palazzolo, T., Lemke, A., Zhang, C., Saad, S., Reynolds, R.G., O'Shea, J.: DeepDive: the use of virtual worlds to create an ethnography of an ancient civilization. In: Stephanidis, C. et al. (ed.) HCII 2021. LNCS, vol. 13096, pp. 615–629. Springer, Cham (2021). https://doi.org/10.1007/978-3-030-90328-2_42
8. The IB Learner Profile. https://www.ibo.org/globalassets/publications/recognition/learnerprofile-en.pdf
9. McLeod, S., Shareski, D.: Different Schools for a Different World. Solution Tree Press, Bloomington (2017)
10. Culturally Responsive-Sustaining Education Framework. http://www.nysed.gov/crs/framework
11. Reynolds, R.G.: Culture on the Edge of Chaos: Cultural Algorithms and the Foundations of Social Intelligence, 1st edn. Springer, Switzerland (2018). https://doi.org/10.1007/978-3-319-74171-0
12. Reynolds, R.G.: Cultural Algorithms: Tools for the Engineering of Social Intelligence into Complex Cultural Systems. Wiley-IEEE Press, Hoboken (2021)
13. Koenig, S.: Fast replanning for navigation in unknown terrain. IEEE Trans. Rob. 21(3), 354–363 (2005)
14. Millington, I.: AI for Games. 3rd edn. CRC Press, Boca Raton (2019)

Using Machine Learning to Model Potential Users with Health Risk Concerns Regarding Microchip Implants

Shekufeh Shafeie[1(✉)], Mona Mohamed[2], Tahir Bachar Issa[3],
and Beenish Moalla Chaudhry[1]

[1] University of Louisiana at Lafayette, 301 E. Lewis Street, Lafayette,
LA 70503, USA
{shekufeh.shafeie1,beenish.chaudhry}@louisiana.edu
[2] Towson University, 8000, York Road, Towson, MD 21252, USA
mmohamed@towson.edu
[3] San Jose State University, One Washington Square, San José, CA 95192, USA
tahirbachar.issa@sjsu.edu

Abstract. Understanding traits that are associated with users who are willing to accept microchip implants can help drive future microchip designs, but little is known in this space. We applied three Machine Learning classifiers, that are Decision Trees, Random Forest and XGBoost on demographic information (user characteristics) of 255 survey respondents. The aim was to recognize dominant features and characteristics that lead participants to be categorized as having "Health risk" concern regarding micro-chipping. Comparison of the classifiers in the prediction tasks demonstrated that XGBoost provides the best performance in term of accuracy, precision and recall. XGBoost also showed that "Migration status", "Race", "Age" and "Degree" are the most important and "Medical Condition" is the next important characteristic of potential users with "Health risk" concerns about micro-chipping. Further research is needed to classify other concerns and expectations of the survey respondents and to create a fuller understanding of the users willing to accept microchip implants.

Keywords: Machine Learning (ML) · Subcutaneous Microchips · Implantable · User Characteristics · Health Risk Concern · Classification Model · Future user · Prediction

1 Introduction

An implantable technology refers to a computational device that can be surgically inserted inside the human body [1]. Examples of implantable technologies include subcutaneous microchips, pacemakers, and cochlear implants [1–5]. Individuals can leverage the capabilities of implantable technologies to improve their health, enhance their innate capabilities and experience a better overall quality of life. For example, subcutaneous microchip implants can provide faster and more secure access to information [6], support health monitoring [7,8], and make daily tasks,

H. Degen and S. Ntoa (Eds.): HCII 2023, LNAI 14051, pp. 574–592, 2023.
https://doi.org/10.1007/978-3-031-35894-4_42

such as the operation of home appliances and devices, more convenient [7,9–11]. Similarly, brain implants, such as Neuralink [12], promise to improve medical treatments, restore or enhance sensory and motor functions, and ameliorate cognitive abilities. Although, currently, many claims around implants appear to be science fiction, it is hoped that, one day, these technologies will be advanced enough to propel humans towards intellectual and physical transcendence [13,14].

Given the invasive nature of implantable technologies, previous research has mostly focused on investigating the potential benefits, risks and ethical issues associated with these technologies [15–18]. For example, Foster et al. [16] have discussed various advantages of microchips for both health and non-health purposes. But they mention that the technology also raises ethical questions about issues such as privacy and the potential for forceful implantation in people. They stress the importance of promoting a public conversation to define the bounds of appropriate use of implantable microchips in people.

However, only a few studies investigate user characteristics that are accepting of implantable technologies. A user characteristic is a trait, attribute, or feature that describes or defines an individual who uses a product or technology [19–23]. It can include demographic information, such as age, gender, and education, as well as psychological and behavioral traits, such as attitudes, beliefs, and values.

With the recent advances in implantable technologies, it is becoming increasingly important to identify the characteristics of individuals who are likely to use and adopt these technologies. In the context of technology and product design, the knowledge of user characteristics can help developers create products that will meet the needs and preferences of the target market. Researchers can use this information to improve the user experience and increase the likelihood of product adoption and success. User characteristics can also inform the development of marketing and promotional strategies, as well as provide insight into potential safety and privacy concerns prevalent within certain populations. They can also be used to inform public policy decisions related to the regulation and use of a technology. Therefore, to ensure future success of implantable technology, it makes sense to explore this space.

Based on the aforementioned gap, this paper aims to identify the main user characteristics that are likely to exhibit health risk related concerns about microchip implants. We adapted data collected from our previous study [24], where the aim was to identify potential users' concerns and expectations about microchip implants. The contributions of this paper are as follows:

- Identification of user characteristics that were associated with health risk concern regarding microchip implants;
- Comparison of the accuracy of three machine learning techniques (i.e., decision tree, random forest, XGBoost) for the above mentioned task;
- Identification of a machine learning technique that might help predict characteristics of future microchip implant users with health risk concern.

The rest of the paper is organized as follows. Section 2 is Literature Review. Section 3 is Data Collection. Section 4 is Data Preparation. Section 5 is dedicated to Experimental Details. Section 6 is Experimental Findings. The last Sections are Conclusion, Future works and Limitation.

2   Literature Review

A few research studies report that the decision to adopt and attitude toward adopting microchip implants is influenced by users' personal and demographic characteristics, and intended use of microchips. Žnidaršič and Werber [25] found that age, gender, and frequency of social media use have an impact on people's intention to use microchips. In particular, they found that elderly were less open to using microchip implants than younger individuals, and men were less cautious about and more in favor of microchip adoption compared to their female colleagues. This result was confirmed by Gangadharbatla [26], who found that gender and age impact people's attitudes and willingness toward microchip adoption. Chebolu [27] reported that biological sex, education, race, religion, and spirituality of individuals do not play a significant role in altering people's perception towards the implantable technology. However, their findings is based on the responses from a homogeneous user group, i.e. students from one academic institute.

In 1999, a group of authors [28] conducted a study to explore the characteristics and attitudes of women who chose to use Norplant, a newly approved contraceptive implant, in southeast Texas. The study participants were 678 women aged 12 to 45 who visited a university-based family planning clinic, 8 Planned Parenthood clinics, or the private practice or health maintenance organization clinic of 8 physicians. The authors aimed to identify the factors that influenced the women's decision to use Norplant and their overall perceptions of the implant. After analyzing the collected data, they found that the reasons for choosing Norplant and the concerns about its use varied based on the age, education level, and racial or ethnic background of the users.

Some researchers have been more interested in exploring how users' psychographics impact their attitude toward microchip acceptance. For instance, Chebolu [27] considered the influence of personality traits, i.e. Extraversion, Agreeableness, Conscientiousness, Neuroticism, and Openness to Experience, as potential determinants of a person's intention to use microchip implants. Chebolu found no significant relationship between the (five) personality traits and intended use. But they concluded that there is a relationship between trust, motivation to use, and acceptance of microchip implants. However, the finding of their study was limited as it focused on a certain user group, i.e. students. Gangadharbatla [26] explored the role of self-efficacy and found that it can predict both attitude and willingness to get implanted.

Researchers such as Niemeijer et al. [29] pointed out that technology acceptance studies should also consider cultural contexts of the individuals. She notes notable cultural differences between American and European literature when it comes to technology usage. For instance, in Britain, there seems to be more ethical consideration and debate of human rights and privacy than in the United States. Following this line of thought, Cristina et al. [30] took into account five ethical dimensions: "Moral Equity," "Relativism," "Utilitarianism," "Egoism," and "Contractualism" and studied their impact on willing to accept implantables in 1563 young, digital native college students from seven different nations via a poll. The researchers came to the conclusion that ethical judgment is essential for the acceptance of wearables and insideables. Furthermore, among young individuals, insideables have a stronger explanatory power than wearables. They also discovered that "Egoism" (as opposed to "Altruism") has the best explanatory power for Intention to Use implantable devices, suggesting that the millennial generation is likely to accept implantable microchips in the future for self-enhancement. However, due to the imbalanced ratio of participants from different nations, the authors did not conduct a comparative analysis.

Researchers have also studied the impact of technical literacy and intended use of microchips on willingness to use them. In their 2014 survey, Werber et al. [25] found that survey respondents who used different kinds of Internet platforms such as social networking sites had more positive attitude toward microchip implant use. Moreover, people who bad experiences with stolen wallet or lost keys had more positive attitude towards microchip implants [31,32]. This shows that acceptance of microchips is highly dependent on individual's life experiences. In their 2017 survey [33], Werber et al. conducted a research to investigate people's readiness to use microchips in daily life such as home chores, shopping or payments, wellness monitoring and personal identification. The majority of research participants-almost half-said they intended to use microchips for medical purposes, which outnumbered other suggested uses including identification, shopping, or home use.

3 Data Collection

3.1 Methods

Approval for the study was obtained from the University of Towson's institutional review board (ID #1056). We used a qualitative survey technique to acquire rich, emotionally driven data from a bigger, more varied group of participants for a wider coverage of insights. The aim was to identify drivers and barriers of microchip adoption. Two open-ended questions that have also been utilized by Pettersson, were included in the survey to gather the public's individual viewpoints on subcutaneous microchips.

The survey was disseminated between March 2020 and May 2020, via mailing lists, social media sites, and online patient networks. The survey participants had to meet two requirements in order to qualify: they had to be at least 18 years old, and they had to be able to read and understand English. After reading the informed consent document and accepting it, participants willingly decided to take part. They had the freedom to skip any questions they chose not to answer and to exit at any time by closing their browser. The poll, on average, took 30–45 min to complete. Participants were not provided any compensation for completing the survey.

3.2 Survey Design

The web-based Qualtrics software was used to create the survey. Following completion of an informed consent, the participants had to watch a 10-minute educational video (https://youtu.be/Gu44w4yJmxI) regarding microchips. The video discussed microchip implants' history, present applications, and ongoing discussions. Participants then answered a few questions about their demographics, including their age, gender, race, religion, nationality, and any chronic illnesses they may have. However, no personally identifiable data, such as a name, email address, or mailing address, was gathered. We selected demographic variables and personality traits that are well-known to moderate the adoption of new technologies. Finally, participants provided their open-ended responses to the following: a) What are your top worries concerning microchip implants? b) What aspects of the development of implantable microchips interest you?

3.3 Participants

255 respondents attended the survey but we had to remove nearly 30% of them due to missing entries. In total 179 participants completed at least one of the open-ended questions and were considered in the analysis. American nationals made up the majority (54%, or 96 out of 179) of the respondents. 72 out of the total of 179 were foreign nationals living in the US, or 40%. 6% (11 out of 179) of the participants were living in the US at the time of the poll but did not disclose their immigration status. A total of 126 individuals were female, 50 were male, one was gender fluid, and two did not want to reveal their gender. The participants' ages ranged from 18 to 83 years, with 41% (73 out of 179) falling into the 18- to 29-year age range.

Most participants, or 30.2% (54 out of 179), had a bachelor's degree as their highest educational attainment. 14.5% (26 out of 179) of the participants reported having a disability, 3.5% (6 out of 179) had some form of an implant (such as a birth control or insulin pump), and 44% (78 out of 179) of the individuals had at least one chronic ailment. 36% (64 out of 179) of the participants selected Islam as their religion, 30% (53 out of 179) selected Christianity or Roman Catholicism, and 11% (20 out of 179) selected spirituality. Further participant details are summarized in Table 1.

4 Data Preparation

The data preparation process that we used in this paper is depicted in Fig. 1 below in general and explained with details in the following subsections.

4.1 Thematic Coding

The goal of this stage was to identify main concerns and expectations of the survey respondents by analyzing their responses to the two main survey questions. We applied thematic coding technique, which begins with the researchers reading and re-reading the qualitative data to prepare a set of codes using an inductive approach. Then over several meetings, the researchers met to go over

Table 1. Demographic Survey Questions and Responses

Demographic	Answer choice
Age	1. 18–29 years (n = 73)
	2. 30–49 years (n = 60)
	3. 50–64 years (n = 36)
	4. 65–79 years (n = 8)
	5. 80 years and above (n = 1)
	6. Unspecified (n = 1)
Gender	1. Male (n = 50)
	2. Female (n = 126)
	3. Fluid (n = 1)
	4. Prefer not to disclose (n = 1)
	5. Other (n = 1)
Race	1. African American or Black (n = 48)
	2. Asian or Pacific Islander (n = 14)
	3. Hispanic/Latino (n = 6)
	4. Native American or American Indian (n = 0)
	5. White or Caucasian (n = 86)
	6. Other (n = 18)
	7. Unspecified (n = 7)
Education	1. No schooling completed (n = 0)
	2. Nursery school to 8th grade (n = 0)
	3. Some high school, no diploma (n = 3)
	4. High school graduate, diploma or the equivalent (n = 26)
	5. Some college credit, no degree (n = 33)
	6. Trade/technical/vocational training (n = 2)
	7. Associate degree (n = 11)
	8. Bachelor's degree (n = 54)
	9. Master's degree (n = 34)
	10. Professional degree (n = 1)
	11. PhD or higher degree (n = 15)
Religion	1. Muslim (n = 67)
	2. Christian (n = 38)
	3. Roman Catholic (n = 15)
	4. Latter-Day Saint or Mormon (n = 2)
	5. Jewish (n = 4)
	6. Buddhist (n = 2)
	7. Hindu (n = 2)
	8. Sikh (n = 0)
	9. Agnostic (You are not sure if there is a God) (n = 11)
	10. Atheist (You believe there is no God) (n = 7)
	11. Spiritual, but not committed to a particular faith (n = 20)
	12. Don't give it much thought (n = 3)
	13. Any other faith-based identity (n = 8)
Immigrant?	1. Yes (n = 72)
	2. No (US national) (n = 96)
	3. Unspecified (n = 11)
Medical Conditions?	1. Yes (n = 78)
	2. No (n = 95)
	3. Unspecified (n = 6)
Disability?	1. Yes (n = 26)
	2. No (n = 148)
	3. Unspecified (n = 5)

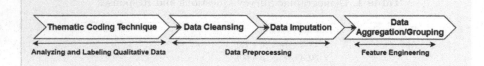

Fig. 1. Data Preparation Process Diagram before applying Machine Learning Classifiers.

and compare the evolving codes. The discussions mostly centered on finalizing the coding language and addressing coding disagreements. The researchers finally settled on a set of codes to code the remaining survey responses, that is, a deductive coding method was then used to direct a second round of coding and analysis. The two researchers met in multiple sessions to complete this. Following the coding, the researchers collaborated to arrange similar codes into categories, and combine similar categories into themes. Before a final report was produced, there were numerous meetings where discussion lasted. Microsoft Excel was used to document and code the interviews.

The thematic coding resulted in concerns related to data protection, health risks, knowledge, negative affect, ease of use, metaphysical dilemmas, monetary issues, and negative social impact. Expectations included medical and non-medical uses, dismissal of microchips, technical advances, human enhancement, regulations, and affordability [24]. In this paper, we limit ourselves to exploring user characteristics that were responsible for generating the "health risk" concern. This concern relates to a person's belief that utilizing subcutaneous microchips will result in physical harm. The participants were quite concerned about the health hazards associated with subcutaneous microchips, and many of them expressed anxiety and apprehension about having something implanted inside of them. The technology acceptance models put forth by Čičević et al. [34] and Werber et al. [35] also include "Health Concerns", having the same definition, as a direct determinant of microchip implant acceptance. Therefore, uncovering user characteristics of this concern will provide us with an insight into the kind of users who are willing to accept microchip implants.

4.2   Data Cleansing

Participants who did not respond to any of the two open-ended questions regarding concerns and hopes about microchip implants were removed before the preprocessing and analysis were performed. 255 respondents attended the survey but we had to remove nearly 30% of them. So, in total 179 participants who completed at least one of the open-ended questions in the survey were included in this study.

4.3   Data Imputation

Imputation means replacing missing data with substituted values. According to the literature there are different approaches that can be used to impute or compensate for missing values in a dataset [36]. We imputed features by replacing the missing data with the most frequently occurring value within each column. This statistical strategy works best when the features involved are categorical in nature. Indeed, all of the features or user characteristics (i.e., age, gender, race, medical conditions immigration status, disability condition, religion, education) were categorical variables.

4.4   Feature Engineering

We used data aggregation and grouping to generate features for our target variable (i.e. health risk concern). Data aggregation refers to the process of combining multiple individual data points into a single summary metric or value, such as computing the average or sum of a set of numbers. This process helps to reduce the complexity of data and make it easier to analyze and interpret [37].

Data grouping (or segmentation) refers to the process of dividing data into smaller, more manageable groups based on certain criteria, such as age, income, or geographic location. This process is often used to create segments or sub-populations of data that can be analyzed separately and in greater detail.

Since we did not have enough instances for all categories of the eight main features, it was crucial engineer features to balance the group sizes and improve the performance of the machine learning models. For example, "age" was grouped into the following categories: (a) 18–29 years (n = 74), (b) 30–49 years (n = 60) and (c) 50 years and above (n = 45). Other aggregated features are summarized in Table 2.

5   Experimental Details

Since every machine learning method has its own advantages and unique properties, we compared the performance of three distinct classifiers [38] for recognizing principal user characteristics that demonstrated "health risk" as a major determinant of intention to use a microchip. We chose the following three methods because they give reliable results with small categorical data sets.

5.1   Machine Learning Techniques

1. Decision Tree: A decision tree [39–41] is a supervised classification method that categorizes data based on certain criteria. It works by recursively splitting the data into smaller and smaller subsets based on the values of the attributes that best separate the data. The process continues until a stopping criterion is reached, such as maximum tree depth, or minimum number of samples in a leaf node. The final result is a tree structure where each leaf node represents a class label. The constructed decision tree can then be used to classify new instances of attribute values (user characteristics Table 2).

Table 2. Aggregated features (Demographic information)

Demographic	Answer choice
Age	1. 18–29 years (n = 74)
	2. 30–49 years (n = 60)
	3. 50 years and above (n = 45)
Gender	1. Male/Fluid/Other (n = 53)
	2. Female (n = 126)
Race	1. African American or Black (n = 48)
	2. Asian or Pacific Islander or Hispanic/Latino (n = 20)
	5. White or Caucasian/Unspecified (n = 93)
	6. Other (n = 18)
Education	1. No schooling completed/Nursery school to 8th grade (n = 0)
	4. High school graduate, diploma or the equivalent (n = 26)
	5. Some college credit, no degree (n = 33)
	7. Associate degree/Some high school, no diploma/Professional degree/ Trade/technical/vocational training (n = 17)
	8. Bachelor's degree (n = 54)
	9. Master's degree (n = 34)
	11. PhD or higher degree (n = 15)
Religion	1. Muslim (n = 67)
	2. Christian (n = 38)
	3. Roman Catholic (n = 15)
	9. Agnostic (You are not sure if there is a God) (n = 11)
	10. Atheist (You believe there is no God) (n = 7)
	11. Spiritual, but not committed to a particular faith (n = 20)
	13. Any other faith-based identity (n = 8)
	14. Don't give it much thought/Latter-Day Saint or Mormon/ Jewish/Buddhist/Hindu (n = 13)
Immigrant?	1. Yes (n = 72)
	2. No (US national) (n = 107)
Medical Conditions?	1. Yes (n = 78)
	2. No (n = 101)
Disability?	1. Yes (n = 26)
	2. No/Unspecified (n = 153)

Since decision trees are prone to over-fitting, a number of ways can be used to improve their accuracy and interpret-ability [42, 43]. In the context of classification, some common ones include pruning, using ensemble methods such as random forest, gradient boosting, bagging, and hyper parameter tuning.

In this research, we used pruning, which involves removing some branches of the tree that do not contribute much to the accuracy of the classification. Pruning helps to reduce the complexity of the tree and improve its generalization performance. There are two types of pruning: pre-pruning and post-pruning. Pre-pruning technique refers to ending the growth of the decision tree before it becomes fully developed. This is accomplished by adjusting the hyper-parameters of the model before the training process starts. Whereas, post-pruning involves trimming or merging the branches of the decision tree model after it has grown to its full extent.

2. Random forest: The random forest classifier [44,45] is used to address the over-fitting problem of decision trees. A random forest is an ensemble of multiple ($n = K$) decision trees. Each decision tree is trained on a random subset of the data and a random subset of the features. The output of the random forest is the majority vote of the individual tree predictions.

By building multiple trees on random subsets of the data, the model can capture more of the complex relationships between the features and the target variable. By randomly selecting subsets of the features at each node, the model can also reduce the variance and over-fitting that can occur in a single decision tree.

Random forests are often used in classification tasks, where the goal is to predict a target categorical variable. The random forest can handle both binary and multi-class classification problems, and it can also provide estimates of class probabilities.

3. XGBoost: XGBoost [46–48] stands for "Extreme Gradient Boosting". This model is responsible for generating gradient boosted decision trees (GBDTs) that consist of a collection of decision trees. Each tree is trained successively to minimize the residual errors of the previous tree (optimization). Unlike random forests, where multiple trees are trained on random subsets of the data, in gradient boosting, each subsequent tree builds upon the errors corrected by the previous trees.

The final prediction is the sum of the predictions of all the individual trees in the ensemble, weighted by their importance. The importance of each tree is determined by its performance on the validation data and the number of times it was selected during the optimization process.

5.2   Experimental Procedures

Three experiments were conducted - one for each machine learning technique. Each technique was used to first create a user model based on the training data. The models were then verified with the help of the test data set. The major concerns of the participants, which is "Health risk" were the target classes or labels in all three experiments. Python machine learning libraries such as sklearn.tree, sklearn.ensemble, xgboost (xgb.XGBClassifier) were used to run these experiments since Python offers imported libraries for multiple techniques and interpretations of statistical analysis of the data sets.

1. Experimenting with Decision Tree. In the first experiment, decision tree was applied to user characteristics associated with "Health risk" concern. We, first, split 75% ($n = 134$) of the participants for training the model and 25% ($n = 45$) for testing. We, then, used pre-pruning technique on the generated tree to reduce the size of the tree, improving the accuracy and interpret-ability of the generated decision tree, preventing over-fitting and making it computationally efficient and generalizable to the new data.

2. Experimenting with Random Forest. In the second experiment, we applied random forest on the most important theme of concern from potential user's point of view about microchip implants which is "Health risk". The training set consisted of 70% of the participants ($n = 125$) and test set was represented by 30% of participants ($n = 54$).

3. Experimenting with XGBoost. In the third experiment, XGBoost is used to see what dominant features of microchip implants potential users could lead them to select "Health risk" as their main concern. Again for this technique, 70% of the participants ($n = 125$) were chosen for training purposes and the remaining 30% for testing ($n = 54$).

6 Experimental Findings

6.1 User Characteristics Based on Applied Technique

1. Decision Tree

The achieved output after pruning show that the most three important factors that affected participants decision to choose "health risk" as their concerns for implantables are "Degree", "Medical condition" and "Religion" followed by "Age" and "Race".

Decision Tree visualization after pruning can be seen in the following Fig. 2.

The pruned decision tree shows the detailed characteristics of users who have "Health risk" concern. For example, participants with no faith-based identity (Religion $<= 12.5$), younger than 49 years old (Age $<= 2.5$), with some medical condition (Medical $<= 1.5$), with education not higher than Some college credit, but no degree (Degree $<= 4.5$) are the ones with "Health risk" concern. As another example, "Health risk" is not the major concern of participants whose Degree is above Some college credit, but no degree (Degree > 4.5), their Religion is Muslim or Christian (Religion $<= 2.5$), their Race is African American or Black (Race $<= 1.5$), with any immigration status (Migration > 0.5).

2. Random Forest

As visualized random forest shows in the following Fig. 3, the most significant factors that affected participants decision to choose "health risk" (Class1) as their concerns for implantables are "Medical condition", "Degree", "Religions" followed by "Race" and "Migration status".

3. XGBoost

As it can be observed in the following Fig. 4, "Migration status", "Race", "Age" and "Degree" are the four most important ones among all of the features and "Medical Condition" is in the fifth.

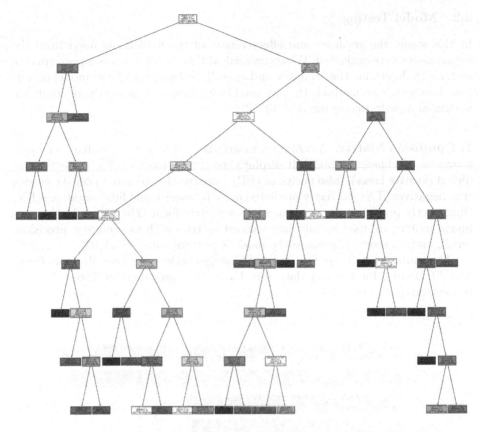

Fig. 2. Decision Tree visualization after pruning regarding Health Risk Concern.

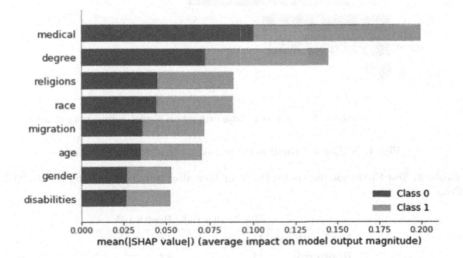

Fig. 3. Random Forest Visualization regarding Health Risk Concern.

6.2   Model Testing

In this stage, the accuracy and effectiveness of the models obtained from the experiments were evaluated. We accomplished this by using various performance metrics to determine the accuracy and overall performance of the model on our test data sets. Two methods that we used to evaluate our models were confusion matrix and performance metrics [49–52].

1. Confusion Matrix. A confusion matrix is a table used to evaluate the performance of a classifier model. It displays the true positives (TP) (correctly predicted positive cases), false positives (FP) (incorrectly predicted positive cases), true negatives (TN) (correctly predicted negative cases), and false negatives (FN) (incorrectly predicted negative cases) in a matrix form. The values in the confusion matrix are used to calculate various metrics such as accuracy, precision, recall, and F1 score to measure the model's performance [49–51,53].

The confusion matrices for the three classifiers (Decision Tree, Random forest and XGBoost), for the test data sets have been presented in Tables 3, 4, 5, respectively.

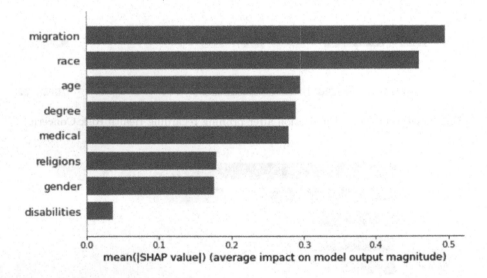

Fig. 4. XGBoost Visualization regarding Health Risk Concern.

Table 3. Test Confusion matrix for Decision Tree after pruning regarding Health Risk Concern

	Not health risk	Health risk
Not health risk	11	11
Health risk	11	12

Table 4. Test Confusion Matrix for Random forest regarding Health risk of Microchip users

	Not health risk	Health risk
Not health risk	16	6
Health risk	18	14

Table 5. Test Confusion Matrix for XGBoost regarding Health risk of Microchip users

	Not health risk	Health risk
Not health risk	14	7
Health risk	16	17

2. Performance Evaluation. We used commonly used metrics, i.e. accuracy, precision, recall and F1 score to evaluate our classifiers' performance.

a Accuracy: Accuracy refers to the fraction of correct predictions made by the classifier. It is calculated as the number of true positives and true negatives divided by the total number of instances.

Accuracy = (True Positives + True Negatives)/(True Positives + True Negatives + False Positives + False Negatives)

b Precision: Precision refers to the fraction of positive predictions that are actually correct. It is calculated as the number of true positives divided by the number of true positives plus false positives.
Precision = True Positives/(True Positives + False Positives)

c Recall: Recall refers to the fraction of positive instances that are correctly identified by the classifier. It is calculated as the number of true positives divided by the number of true positives plus false negatives.
Recall = True Positives/(True Positives + False Negatives)

d F1 Score: F1 score is the harmonic mean of precision and recall, and it ranges from 0 to 1, with a higher value indicating better performance.
F1 Score = 2 * (Precision * Recall)/(Precision + Recall)

The metrics associated with each model's performance on the test data has been shown in the following Tables 6 and 7 for both random run and with weighted avg. The comparative accuracy of the models is shown with the help of bar plots (Fig. 5).

Table 6. Performance Evaluation of Predictions for health risk as the most significant concern of Microchip users as predicted by three classifiers (Decision Tree, Random forest and XGBoost)

Classifier Method			
Evaluation Metrics	Decision Tree	Random forest	XGBoost
Accuracy%	51.0	56.0	57.0
Precision%	52.0	70.0	71.0
Recall%	52.0	44.0	52.0
F1_score%	52.0	54.0	60.0

Table 7. Performance Evaluation of Predictions for health risk as the most significant concern of Microchip users as predicted by three classifiers (Decision Tree, Random forest and XGBoost) (weighted avg)

Classifier Method			
Evaluation Metrics	Decision Tree	Random forest	XGBoost
Accuracy%	51.0	56.0	57.0
Precision%	51.0	61.0	61.0
Recall%	51.0	56.0	57.0
F1_score%	51.0	55.0	58.0

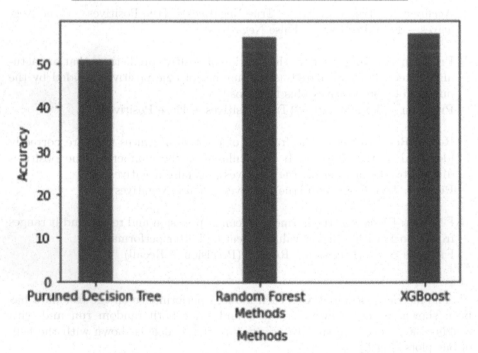

Fig. 5. XGBoost Visualization regarding Health Risk Concern.

7   Conclusion and Future Works

We used decision tree as the base model to identify the characteristics of individuals who are likely to show health risk concerns. We can say that compared to Random Forest and the baseline, XGBoost has the best performance metrics (accuracy, precision, recall and F1 score) and ability to predict whether "Health Risk" is a major concern of a potential user of Microchip Implants or not. XGBoost revealed that, among all of the features of users who show "Health risk" concern regarding microchip implants, "Migration status", "Race", "Age" and "Degree" are the four most important ones while "Medical Condition" is the fifth important one.

All three classifiers agree that education (degree) plays an important role in impacting users' view point towards Health Risk concern regarding microchip implant usage.

We plan to apply Machine learning techniques to determine user characteristics associated with other major determinants of microchip acceptance, i.e. themes of concerns and expectations that were identified in our previous work [24]. Future work can also focus on collecting larger sample sizes to improve model accuracy and predictive capability.

8   Limitation

Small sample size is a major limitation of this work. With larger sample sizes, it is possible to improve machine learning model performance and obtain more accurate models.

References

1. TODAY, D.K.U.: Implantable technology will get under our skin, March 2014. https://www.usatoday.com/story/tech/reviewed-com/2014/03/27/implantable-tech-is-the-next-wave/6914363/
2. NEWS, C.S.C.: Meet the humans with microchips implanted in them, June 2016. https://www.cbsnews.com/news/meet-the-humans-with-microchips-implanted-in-them/
3. CNN, S.W.: Is human chip implant wave of the future? January 1999. https://www.edition.cnn.com/TECH/computing/9901/14/chipman.idg/
4. Nsanze, F.: ICT implants in the human body-a review. In: The European Group on Ethics in Science and New Technologies to the European Commission (2005)
5. Sobot, R.: Implantable technology: history, controversies, and social implications [commentary]. IEEE Technol. Soc. Mag. **37**(4), 35–45 (2018)
6. Microchip, T.: Chipping away employee privacy: legal implications of RFID microchip implants for employees, 10 October 2019. https://www.natlawreview.com/article/chipping-away-employee-privacy-legal-implications-rfid-microchip-implants-employees

7. Burt, C.: Chip implants from Swedish developer support digital health pass storage under your skin, December 2021. https://www.biometricupdate.com/202112/chip-implants-from-swedish-developer-support-digital-health-pass-storage-under-your-skin

8. Bramstedt, K.A.: When microchip implants do more than drug delivery: blending, blurring, and bundling of protected health information and patient monitoring. Technol. Health Care **13**(3), 193–198 (2005)

9. Joannou, C.: Are microchip implants the future of ticketing? November 2017. https://www.forbes.com/sites/chrisjoannou/2017/11/06/are-microchip-implants-the-future-of-ticketing/?sh=31414f89426d

10. Lohrmann, D.: Chip implants: opportunities, concerns and what could be next, 16 January 2022. https://www.govtech.com/blogs/lohrmann-on-cybersecurity/chip-implants-opportunities-concerns-and-what-could-be-next

11. Ghormley, S.: The opportunities and fears of human microchipping, October 2021. https://medium.com/@sarah.ghormley/the-opportunities-and-fears-of-human-microchipping-ad77c1036e33

12. Choi, C.Q.: Wireless 'neural dust' could monitor your brain, 3 August 2016. https://www.popsci.com/tiny-wireless-implants-could-monitor-your-brain/

13. Hooijdonk, R.V.: BNR mindshift—chips in your body - sure, why not? October 2015. https://www.blog.richardvanhooijdonk.com/en/bnr-mindshift-chips-in-your-body-sure-why-not/

14. Bill Holton, V.R.: Four emerging vision-enhancing technologies: the implantable miniature telescope, the telescopic contact lens, the argus ii retinal prosthesis, and the artificial silicon retina, October 2015. https://www.afb.org/aw/14/9/15655

15. Michael, K., McNamee, A., Michael, M.G.: The emerging ethics of humancentric GPS tracking and monitoring. In: 2006 International Conference on Mobile Business, p. 34. IEEE (2006)

16. Foster, K.R., Jaeger, J.: Ethical implications of implantable radiofrequency identification (RFID) tags in humans. Am. J. Bioeth. **8**(8), 44–48 (2008)

17. Perakslis, C., Michael, K., Michael, M., Gable, R.: Perceived barriers for implanting microchips in humans: a transnational study. In: 2014 IEEE Conference on Norbert Wiener in the 21st Century (21CW), pp. 1–8. IEEE (2014)

18. Bazaka, K., Jacob, M.V.: Implantable devices: issues and challenges. Electronics **2**(1), 1–34 (2012)

19. Garson, G.D., Khosrow-Pour, D., et al.: Handbook of Research on Public Information Technology. IGI Global (2008)

20. Dictionary: What is user characteristics, May 2018. https://www.igi-global.com/dictionary/user-characteristics/31176

21. Kim, C.: User characteristics and behaviour in operating annoying electronic products. Int. J. Des. **8**(1) (2014)

22. Diener, E., Biswas-Diener, R., Diener, E.: NOBA Textbook Series: Psychology. DEF, Champaign (2019)

23. Diener, E., Lucas, R.E.: Personality traits (2023). https://nobaproject.com/modules/personality-traits

24. Shafeie, S., Chaudhry, B.M., Mohamed, M.: Modeling subcutaneous microchip implant acceptance in the general population: a cross-sectional survey about concerns and expectations. Informatics **9**(1) (2022)

25. Žnidaršič, A., Werber, B.: Adoption of RFID microchip for eHealth according to eActivities of potential users (2014)

26. Gangadharbatla, H.: Biohacking: an exploratory study to understand the factors influencing the adoption of embedded technologies within the human body. Heliyon **6**(5), e03931 (2020)
27. Chebolu, R.D.: Exploring factors of acceptance of chip implants in the human body (2021)
28. Frank, M.L., Poindexter, A.N., Johnson, M.L., Bateman, L.: Characteristics and attitudes of early contraceptive implant acceptors in Texas. Family Plann. Perspect. 208–213 (1992)
29. Niemeijer, A.R., Frederiks, B.J., Riphagen, I.I., Legemaate, J., Eefsting, J.A., Hertogh, C.M.: Ethical and practical concerns of surveillance technologies in residential care for people with Dementia or intellectual disabilities: an overview of the literature. Int. Psychogeriatr. **22**(7), 1129–1142 (2010)
30. Cristina, O.P., Jorge, P.B., Eva, R.L., Mario, A.O.: From wearable to insideable: is ethical judgment key to the acceptance of human capacity-enhancing intelligent technologies? Comput. Hum. Behav. **114**, 106559 (2021)
31. Žnidaršič, A., Baggia, A., Werber, B.: The profile of future consumer with microchip implant: habits and characteristics. Int. J. Consum. Stud. **46**(4), 1488–1501 (2022)
32. Žnidaršič, A., Baggia, A., Werber, B.: The profile of future consumer with microchip implant
33. Werber, B., Baggia, A., Žnidaršič, A.: Behaviour intentions to use RFID subcutaneous microchips: a cross-sectional Slovenian perspective (2017)
34. Dragović, M., et al.: Factors affecting RFID subcutaneous microchips usage. In: Sinteza 2019-International Scientific Conference on Information Technology and Data Related Research, Singidunum University, pp. 235–243 (2019)
35. Werber, B., Baggia, A., Žnidaršič, A.: Factors affecting the intentions to use RFID subcutaneous microchip implants for healthcare purposes. Organizacija **51**(2), 121–133 (2018)
36. Badr, W.: 6 different ways to compensate for missing values in a dataset (data imputation with examples), 5 January 2019. https://www.towardsdatascience.com/6-different-ways-to-compensate-for-missing-values-data-imputation-with-examples-6022d9ca0779
37. Wikipedia: Aggregate data. (wikipedia, https://www.en.wikipedia.org/wiki/Aggregate_data
38. Cho, E., Chang, T.W., Hwang, G.: Data preprocessing combination to improve the performance of quality classification in the manufacturing process. Electronics **11**(3), 477 (2022)
39. Team, G.L.: Decision tree algorithm explained with examples (2022). https://www.mygreatlearning.com/blog/decision-tree-algorithm/
40. Breiman, L., Friedman, J., Olshen, R., Stone, C.: Classification and regression trees. Wadsworth Int. Group **37**(15), 237–251 (1984)
41. Abu-Hanna, A., Hunter, J.: Artificial intelligence in medicine **16**, 201 (1999). Elsevier
42. Chase, R.J., Harrison, D.R., Burke, A., Lackmann, G.M., McGovern, A.: A machine learning tutorial for operational meteorology. Part I: Tradit. Mach. Learn. Weather Forecasting **37**(8), 1509–1529 (2022)
43. Kumar, S.: 3 techniques to avoid overfitting of decision trees (2021). https://towardsdatascience.com/3-techniques-to-avoid-overfitting-of-decision-trees-1e7d3d985a09
44. Breiman, L.: Random forests. Mach. Learn. **45**, 5–32 (2001)

45. Great Learning Team: Random forest algorithm in machine learning: an overview (2022). https://www.mygreatlearning.com/blog/random-forest-algorithm/
46. Natekin, A., Knoll, A.: Gradient boosting machines, a tutorial. Front. Neurorobot. **7**, 21 (2013)
47. He, Z., Lin, D., Lau, T., Wu, M.: Gradient boosting machine: a survey. arXiv preprint arXiv:1908.06951 (2019)
48. XGBoost developers: XGBoost tutorials (2022). https://xgboost.readthedocs.io/en/stable/tutorials/model.html
49. Hossin, M.: A review on evaluation metrics for data classification evaluations. Int. J. Data Min. Knowl. Manag. Process **5**(2) (2020)
50. Liu, Y., Zhou, Y., Wen, S., Tang, C.: A strategy on selecting performance metrics for classifier evaluation. Int. J. Mob. Comput. Multimedia Commun. (IJMCMC) **6**(4), 20–35 (2014)
51. Pepe, M.S.: The Statistical Evaluation of Medical Tests for Classification and Prediction. Oxford University Press, Oxford (2003)
52. Fielding, A.H., Bell, J.F.: A review of methods for the assessment of prediction errors in conservation presence/absence models. Environ. Conserv. **24**(1), 38–49 (1997)
53. Martínez-Meyer, E., Nakamura, M., Araújo, M.B.: A. Townsend Peterson Jorge Soberón Richard G. Pearson Robert P. Anderson

Measuring Human Perception and Negative Elements of Public Space Quality Using Deep Learning: A Case Study of Area Within the Inner Road of Tianjin City

Jiaxin Shi[1] and Kaifeng Hao[2(✉)]

[1] Tianjin University, Tianjin, China
yueer@tju.edu.cn
[2] Naikai University, Tianjin, China
haokaifeng@didiglobal.com

Abstract. Due to a lack of data sources and data processing techniques, it has always been difficult to quantify public space quality, which includes urban construction quality and how it is perceived by people, especially in large urban areas. This study proposes a quantitative research method based on the consideration of emotional health and physical health of the built environment. It highlights the low quality of public areas in Tianjin, China, where there are many negative elements. Deep learning technology is then used to measure how effectively people perceive urban areas. First, this work suggests a deep learning model that might simulate how people can perceive the quality of urban construction. Second, we perform semantic segmentation on street images to identify visual elements influencing scene perception. Finally, this study correlated the scene perception score with the proportion of visual elements to determine the surrounding environmental elements that influence scene perception. Using a small-scale labeled Tianjin street view data set based on transfer learning, this study trains five negative spatial discriminant models in order to explore the negative space distribution and quality improvement of urban streets. Then it uses all Tianjin street-level imagery to make predictions and calculate the proportion of negative space. Visualizing the spatial distribution of negative space along the Tianjin Inner Ring Road reveals that the negative elements are mainly found close to the five key districts. The map of Tianjin was combined with the experimental data to perform the visual analysis. Based on the emotional assessment, the distribution of negative materials, and the direction of street guidelines, we suggest guidance content and design strategy points of the negative phenomena in Tianjin street space in the two dimensions of perception and substance.

This work demonstrates the utilization of deep learning techniques to understand how people appreciate high-quality urban construction, and it complements both theory and practice in urban planning. It illustrates the connection between human perception and the actual physical public space environment, allowing researchers to make urban interventions.

Keywords: human perception · public space quality · deep learning · negative elements · street images

H. Degen and S. Ntoa (Eds.): HCII 2023, LNAI 14051, pp. 593–606, 2023.
https://doi.org/10.1007/978-3-031-35894-4_43

1 Introduction

Spatial perception refers to the vague definition of a spatial perception situation by humans, and the study of human spatial perception can help enrich spatial semantics [1, 2], and further help researchers under-stand the underlying urban heterogeneity and reveal the impact of urban functions [3–5]. In recent years, how to collect visual information about the surrounding environment of urban buildings and affect the observation space has attracted extensive attention in various fields [6, 7]. Early research methods mainly relied on traditional data collection methods, such as street interviews and questionnaires [8, 9], these methods have high time and labor costs, and more importantly, the early research methods greatly limiting the size of the research field, urban-level spatial research is difficult to generalize. With the modernization of the country, the scale of the city is constantly expanding, and the appearance and structure of the city are undergoing dramatic changes. It is of great significance to develop a comprehensive building knowledge system based on streets, localities and even cities. It is also important for researchers and urban planners to understand how citizens perceive and evaluate the physical environment in large urban areas. Therefore, the development of a low-cost and efficient urban spatial method is particularly important.

Thanks to the rapid development of geographic information technology and volunteered geographic information (VGI) [10–12], the Internet has released a large number of street view images with rich geographic information, which contain detailed descriptions of each street and corner of the city [13]. Street view imagery is important to the research of building environment. Moreover, computer vision based on deep learning has also made great progress in the field of image recognition, Its high accuracy and computing speed have been great successes in image feature extraction, image scene perception and image scene inference [14–16]. Therefore, many scholars use the massive data provided by the Internet and the deep learning technology to deal with series of emotional perception and behavior prediction problems.

2 Related Work

Previous researchers used low/medium dimensional image features in the research process, including Gist, SIFT Fisher vector, DeCAF feature, geometric classification map, color histogram, HOG2x2, Dense SIFT and Naik [17, 18]. However, these methods cannot fully extract high-dimension information about natural images. In 2014, support vector machines (SVM) and linear regression (LR) were used to predict image labels in Ordonez and Berg [19], while Ordonez [20] and others used methods based on convolutional neural networks. Among many image representations and models, the method based on convolution neural network (CNN) is much better than the conventional methods [21].

The statistical results of the research on street quality at home and abroad shows that the early research on street quality mainly focused on urban space and street quality. The researchers focus on public space and human behavior influence gradually after 2012. It is worth noting that since 2018, the research on street quality has begun to introduce depth learning and become the mainstream research direction in the big data time. The overall development trend is shown in Fig. 1. In general, the research on street space quality mainly focuses on the surrounding environment of the street, the overall state of the city and the impact of human activity (Fig. 2).

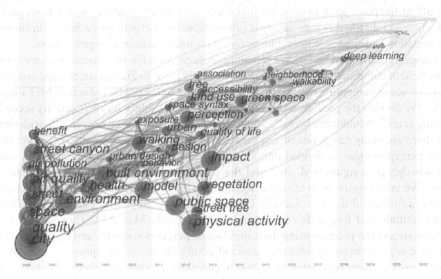

Fig. 1. Street quality document keyword time spectrum

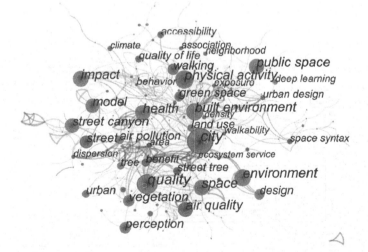

Fig. 2. Street quality literature keyword co-occurrence diagram

3 Approach

The surrounding environment of city streets affects the behavior and health of residents. In order to explore the humanistic perception of urban street scenes and the main factors that affect the perception results, we make a quantitatively analyzes scene perception elements, and divide this task into two sub-sections: scene perception based on image classification and scene element mining based on image semantic segmentation.

Image classification and image semantic segmentation are two mature technologies in the field of computer vision. In this paper we apply them to Tianjin streetscape images. First, the scene perception model is trained according to the public dataset of MIT Place Pulse. We divided the predict results into six categories: "safety score", "activity score", "boring score", "abundance score", "suppression score" and "beauty score", considering that there are many categories of tasks and classification is too difficult. Therefore, the scene perception task is divided into six binary classification tasks: whether it is safe and whether it is suppressed, etc., and the model output results is used as the final score. We take Tianjin as an example, the latitude and longitude coordinates of Tianjin streets are obtained through ArcGIS. Obtaining the corresponding pictures according to the latitude and longitude coordinates base on Baidu Map API. Then predict the crawled street view pictures using the trained scene perception model, and employ image semantic segmentation explores the factors affecting the scene perception semantically. Finally use the linear regression algorithm to calculate the specific relationship between the scene perception results and the influencing factors and visualization. We realize an urban scene perception experiment based on deep learning. The specific technical route is shown in Fig. 3.

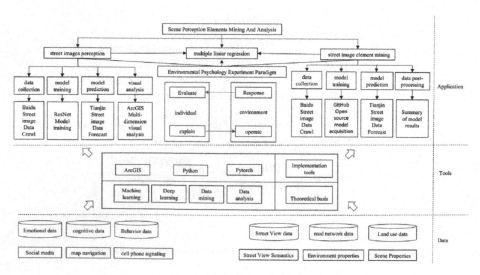

Fig. 3. Technology Roadmap

3.1 Acquisition of Tianjin Street View Data

In this paper we firstly complete Tianjin road network data visualization in ArcGIS, and then obtain WG1984 standard latitude and longitude coordinates through coordinate transformation in the software. Considering the geographical structure of Tianjin, the research site is selected within the bounding rectangle of Tianjin Outer Ring Road. In order to match the requirements of subsequent tasks, the conversion of WG1984 to BD09 coordinate system is completed by writing relevant programs in Python programming language (BD09 coordinate system is a special encrypted coordinate system for Baidu Maps), and then we use Python to access Baidu Maps API for crawling the corresponding pictures, considering that Baidu Street View is a panorama, so we divide the panorama and finally each coordinate point gets four pictures of $0°$, $90°$, $180°$, and $270°$ respectively, as shown in the Fig. 4, the resolution of each image is 960×720, and total of 38024 street view images are crawled.

Fig. 4. Tianjin Street View Data

3.2 MIT Place Pulse Data

In 2013, the MIT Media Lab launched the "Place Pulse 2.0" project, it's an online data collection platform for collecting public perceptions of the appearance of cities. On this data platform, two randomly selected street view images of a city will be displayed to the participants at a time, and then the participants will be asked to answer the following questions based on the displayed street view images: "Which picture looks more X?", Where X can be one of six choices: "Safe", "Active", "Boring", "Affluent", "Depressed" and "Aesthetic", participants can choose from three options from the left, right or equal as an answer, and the answer results represent their scene-aware judgment. The Street View Imagery dataset contains 110,988 Street View images collected between 2007 and 2012, covering 56 cities in 28 countries on 6 continents.

3.3 Scene Perception Based on Convolutional Neural Network

Predict human scene perception requires training a deep learning model, and we divide the task into six scene perception scores of street view images, namely safety score, activity score, boredom score, opulence score, depression score, and beauty score. In this study, we convert the six scene-awareness metrics into six binary classification tasks. Each binary classification task was trained and predicted by the ResNet model. The training data of each binary classification task is MIT Place Pulse. 5W pieces of positive and negative data were extracted from MIT Place Pulse, and the training set, validation set and test set were divided according to the ratio of 7:2:1, and finally we obtain 7W pieces of training set data, 2W pieces of validation set data, and 1W pieces of test set data. The experiments in this section use two NVIDIA Tesla V100 GPUs for model training. Part of the model training parameters are: {Batch size: 16, Learning rate: 0.0001, Dropout: 0.1, Epoch: 50}. The average accuracy of the final model on the test set is 83.2%. The input of the model is a complete picture, and the output is one of the six scene indicators, as shown in Fig. 5.

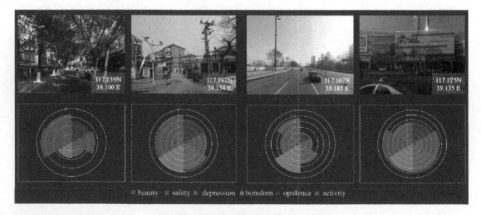

Fig. 5. Scene-aware output results

The trained model is used to predict the street view data in Tianjin, and ArcGIS is used to display the model prediction results. As shown in Fig. 6, the analysis results show that the roads with low safety score (safety score less than 4) account for 21.89%, and the visualization results show that they are mainly distributed in the boundary of the five districts in the center of Tianjin (Nankai District, Heping District, Hongqiao District, Hebei District, Hedong District), the overall safety value in the northwest direction is relatively high; the proportion of roads with a low activity score (activity score less than 4) is 20.97%. The visualization results show that the activity score is higher in the urban area and lower in the suburbs. The overall distribution is relatively uniform, and there is no local concentration area. Roads with a high boring score (boring score greater than 5) account for 39.05%; The visualization results shows that the boredom score in the peripheral edge of the four districts of the city center is higher; The boredom score in the urban center is lower; The proportion of roads with a low affluence score (the affluence score is less than 4) is 24.35%; The visualization results show that the affluence score also higher in urban area and lower in suburbs; The affluent score in the northwest of the suburbs is the highest; roads with a high depression score (a depression score greater than 5) account for 56.20%. The visualization results show that the overall depression score in Tianjin is high, and the depression score in the southeast suburbs is low, which may be related to the small urban area of Tianjin and the compact building structure; the proportion of roads with a low aesthetic score (aesthetic score less than 4) is 25.73%. The visualization results show that the aesthetic score is also higher in urban areas and lower in suburbs, and the aesthetic score in the northwest direction in the suburbs is the highest; comprehensively analyzing the six scene perception results. The positive perception results are mainly distributed in the urban area, and the negative perception results are mainly distributed in the urban area. The results are mainly distributed in the suburbs. It is worth noting that the suburbs in the northwest also have a relatively high distribution of positive perception results. It may be related to the neighboring capital Beijing. Data analysis shows that a large number of employees working in Beijing choose to Settle in the adjacent Wuqing District of Tianjin, which has driven the development of the local economy and changes in the urban structure.

3.4 Scene Perception Based on Convolutional Neural Network

To explore the visual factors that affect the scene perception results, we introduce a picture semantic segmentation-based method to identify visual elements related to the scene perception results. The experiment adopts the scene semantic segmentation technique [22] to calculate the area ratio of semantic objects in the scene. Semantic scene parsing is one of the key techniques for scene understanding, which aims to identify and segment object instances in a natural image. Giving an input image, the model is able to predict a class label for each lable. This paper adopts the mature Unet model in the industry for scene semantic segmentation task.

The Unet model is a relatively mature model in the field of image semantic segmentation. We use an open source Unet model based on the Github, which is the largest technical exchange platform for programmers. The accuracy of this model on the training set is 97%, and it can be recognized the elements include the proportion of buildings,

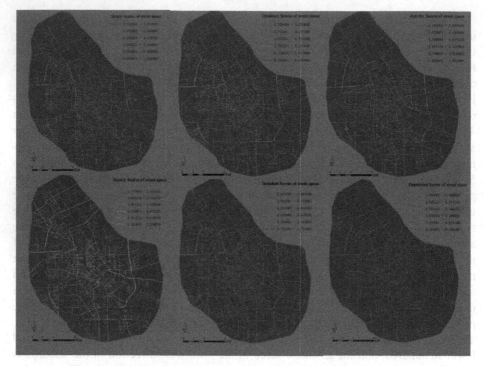

Fig. 6. Road distribution map of perception score

roads, sky and other areas in the picture, etc., which can better match the semantic segmentation task. Therefore, we use this Unet model to predict street view pictures.

The selected semantic segmentation extracts greening ratio, sky ratio, number of cars, number of shops, proportion of buildings, proportion of motor vehicle lanes, proportion of sidewalks, and number of pedestrians. The input of the model is a complete picture, and the output is the area ratio or quantity of corresponding 8 elements in the picture, The specific output results are shown in Fig. 7.

3.5 Correlation Analysis Between Perception and Physical Elements

The scene perception score can obtain the perception score from the scene perception model, and calculate the area ratio of each visual element in the image through scene semantic segmentation. Finally, the scene perception score and the area ratio of each visual element are regressed through multi-dimensional analysis, and obtain the main visual elements that lead to the perception of the local scene.

The linear regression model is a classic multidimensional regression analysis that analyzes each of the six perception indicators separately. The principle is to use a polynomial to fit the target problem.

$$f(x) = w_0 + w_1 x_1 + w_2 x_2 + \cdots + w_n x_n \tag{1}$$

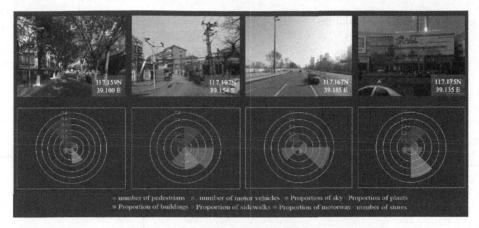

Fig. 7. Semantic segmentation output diagram

Among them, xi is called the weight of the polynomial, which is the final output result of the model, indicating the influence of each factor on the final result. The weight can be positive or negative, and the absolute value of the weight indicates the size that the factor has a positive effect or negative effect on the final result. This paper uses a linear regression algorithm to explore the importance of factors affecting scene perception, and visualize the final weight.

Using Python to extract 5K pieces of scene perception and semantic segmentation data from Tianjin street view data, divide training set, validation set and test set according to the ratio of 7:2:1, and finally get 3.5K pieces of training set data and 1K validation set data There are 0.5K pieces of data in the test set. In this section, two NVIDA Tesla V100 GPUs are used for model training. The training parameters of the model are {normalize: True, fit_intercept: True, copy_X: True}.

4   Experiment Results

It can be seen from the regression coefficient diagram of the safety score (Fig. 8) that the places with more modern factors such as the area occupied by buildings and the number of cars in the street view pictures are mostly urban centers, where the facilities are complete, the streets are regular, and the safety score is high, and the place with a high proportion of sky area is relatively empty, and the risk factors will increase, which will reduce the safety score.

From the regression coefficient graph of the activity score (Fig. 9), it can be seen that the places with a large number of cars and a high proportion of green vegetation in the street view pictures show the diversified characteristics of the street view, and more abundant and complex environmental factors are conducive to the increase of the activity score and the high proportion of the sky area will make the composition of the street view relatively simple, and the relatively monotonous factors will reduce the activity score.

From the regression coefficient graph of the boredom score (Fig. 10), it can be seen that the areas with high proportion of sidewalks or motor vehicle lanes in the street view

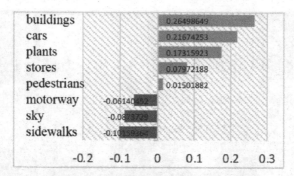

Fig. 8. Regression diagram of safety score

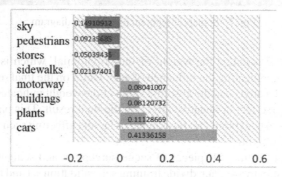

Fig. 9. Regression diagram of activity score

images are usually suburban ring roads. Relatively monotonous, increase the boredom score, while a larger vegetation area will make the picture full of vigor and vitality, increase the ornamental value, and thus reduce the boredom score.

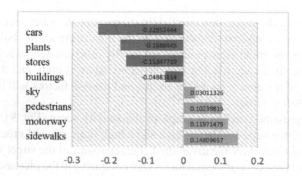

Fig. 10. Regression diagram of boredom score

From the regression coefficient graph of the wealth score (Fig. 11), it can be seen that the more vegetation area, the number of cars and shops in the street view picture will increase the wealth score, and the reason for the vegetation area is explained here, because the picture of the MIT Place Pulse dataset is large. Some of them are from abroad, and most of the pictures with a higher wealth score are villas of the wealthy and have a higher green area, so the model will give a higher weight to the vegetation area, while the open suburbs with a large proportion of motor vehicle lanes are It is considered sparsely populated and the affluence score is low.

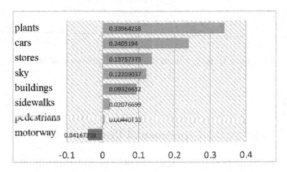

Fig. 11. Regression graph of wealth score

It can be seen from the regression coefficient diagram of the depression score (Fig. 12) that the higher proportion of building area in the street view picture will increase the depression score. More places are considered to have a relatively large flow, and a higher proportion of greenery will bring people a sense of visual comfort, which is conducive to the reduction of the depression score.

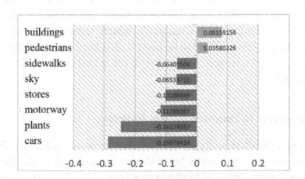

Fig. 12. Regression graph of depression score

It can be seen from the regression coefficient diagram of the aesthetic score (Fig. 13) that the high vegetation and sky proportions in the street view images are mostly in the suburbs, which are far away from the hustle and bustle of the urban area, while intersections with large traffic or suburban ring roads with a large proportion of roads are monotonous, lacking in viewing, and have a low aesthetic score.

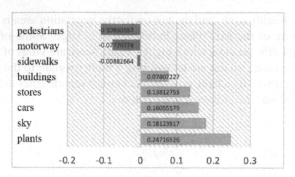

Fig. 13. Regression diagram of aesthetic score

5 Discussion

5.1 Measures to Improve the Experimental Process

The work conducts corresponding experiments on the mining and quantification of scene perception elements based on deep learning, and the efficiency has been greatly improved. However, review the entire experimental process, there are also points worth improving:

The scene perception evaluation model did not include Tianjin data in the training process, resulting in no learning experience of Tianjin street view pictures when the model landed in Tianjin City. Later, it was considered to add manually reviewed Tianjin street view pictures to the data set to improve scene perception and the model predict accuracy.

The scene element recognition model directly uses the open source model, which greatly shortens the experiment time. However, the scene elements which not involved in the open source model cannot be analyzed, which reduces the effect of the model. Later, the U-net model is considered to be used with a larger scale data sets which cover all elements of the street view, aiming to improve the actual predict effect of the semantic segmentation model.

5.2 Countermeasures to Improve the Six Indexes

This paper makes a detailed analysis of the specific factors affecting the six score of scene perception, and the test results have almost equal effect in the fields of environmental psychology and ecological land-scape science [23–27]. For example, the green vegetation in the street scene, such as trees, potted plants, grass, etc., can significantly reduce the individual sense of depression.

The appearance of cars and green vegetation in the street view increases the sense of vitality in the scene and improves the activity score. On the other hand, too many buildings in the streetscape often make people feel depressed.

Rational construction of man-made features to reduce the impact of manmade features on individual emotional perception is an optimization strategy worthy of attention, and controlling the ratio of man-made features to natural landscapes in urban landscapes is a key element in building a healing environment. For example, the safety score can be improved by reasonably reducing the proportion of the sky area of the street view, and the wealth score can be improved by reasonably increasing the green vegetation area, the proportion of cars and shops in the scene, and so on.

6 Conclusion

The surrounding environment of city streets affects the behavior and health of residents. More than a century, various fields of urban planning have discussed the importance of a city's appearance and the exploitation of visual factors that may contribute to human perception. We first use a method that combines big data and deep learning of street view imagery to determine scene awareness in large urban areas. Second, this paper quantitatively studies the connection between scene perception and scene elements. Through the above experimental, we mine and quantify scene perception factors from the perspective base on deep learning in Tianjin. These technologies have great potential and will directly support the theory and practice of urban design. Moreover, the research content of us can also provide reference value for research in related fields.

References

1. Salesses, P., Schechtner, K., Hidalgo, C.A.: The collaborative image of the city: mapping the inequality of urban perception. Plos One 8 (2013)
2. Schroeder, H.W., Anderson, L.M.: Perception of personal safety in urban recreation sites. J. Leisure Res. 16(2) (1984)
3. Downs, R.M., Tuan, Y.F.: Space and place: the perspective of experience. Geogr. Rev. 68(3), 375 (1978)
4. Morison, B.: On Location: Aristotle's Concept of Place. Oxford University Press on Demand, vol. 18(3) (2002)
5. Goodchild, M.F.: Formalizing place in geographic information systems. In: Burton, L., Matthews, S., Leung, M., Kemp, S., Takeuchi, D. (eds.) Communities, Neighborhoods, and Health, pp. 21–33. Springer, Cham (2011). https://doi.org/10.1007/978-1-4419-7482-2_2
6. Katz. The Experience of Nature: A Psychological Perspective (1991)
7. Nasar, J.L.: The evaluative image of the city. APA J. 56(1), 41–53 (1990)
8. Cresswell, T.: In place/out of place: geography, ideology, and transgression. Cineaste 51(4), 559–584 (1996)
9. Montello, D.R., Goodchild, M.F., Gottsegen, J., et al.: Where's Downtown? Behavioral methods for determining referents of vague spatial queries. Spat. Cogn. Comput. 3(2), 185–204 (2003)
10. Anguelov, D., Dulong, C., Filip, D., et al.: Google street view: capturing the world at street level. Computer 43(6), 32–38 (2010)
11. Goodchild, M.F.: Citizens as sensors: the world of volunteered geography. GeoJournal 69(4), 211–221 (2007)
12. Liu, Y., Liu, X., Gao, S., et al.: Social Sensing: A New Approach to Understanding Our Socio-economic Environments
13. Barabási, A.L.: Bursts: The Hidden Patterns Behind Everything We Do, From Your E-Mail to Bloody Crusades. Plume (2011)

14. Yu, D., Deng, L.: Deep Neural Network-Hidden Markov Model Hybrid Systems. Springer, London (2015)
15. He, K., Gkioxari, G., Dollár, P., et al.: Mask R-CNN. IEEE (2017)
16. Savchenko, A.V.: Intelligent Classification Systems. Springer, New York (2016). https://doi.org/10.1007/978-3-319-30515-8_1
17. Simonyan, K., Zisserman, A.: Very deep convolutional networks for large-scale image recognition. Comput. Sci. (2014)
18. Deep residual learning for image recognition In: IEEE Conference on Computer Vision & Pattern Recognition. IEEE Computer Society (2016)
19. Technicolor, T., Related, S., Technicolor, T., et al.: ImageNet Classification with Deep Convolutional Neural Networks (2008)
20. Russakovsky, O., Deng, J., Su, H., et al.: imagenet large scale visual recognition challenge. Int. J. Comput. Vis. 1–42 (2014)
21. Datta, R., Joshi, D., Li, J., Wang, J.Z.: Studying aesthetics in photographic images using a computational approach. In: Leonardis, A., Bischof, H., Pinz, A. (eds.) ECCV 2006. LNCS, vol. 3953, pp. 288–301. Springer, Heidelberg (2006). https://doi.org/10.1007/11744078_23
22. Ren, S., He, K., Girshick, R., et al.: Faster R-CNN: towards real-time object detection with region proposal networks. IEEE Trans. Pattern Anal. Mach. Intell. 39(6), 1137–1149 (2017)
23. Chen, Z.A., Zl, A., Hj, A., et al.: Deep learning method for evaluating photovoltaic potential of urban land-use: a case study of Wuhan, China - ScienceDirect. Appl. Energy (2020)
24. Fang, Z., Yang, T., Jin, Y.: DeepStreet: a deep learning powered urban street network generation module (2020)
25. Khryashchev, V.V., Pavlov, V.A., Priorov, A., et al.: Deep learning for region detection in high-resolution aerial images. In: 2018 IEEE East-West Design & Test Symposium (EWDTS). IEEE (2018)
26. Gunning, T.: From the Kaleidoscope to the X-Ray: urban spectatorship, Poe, Benjamin, and Traffic in souls (1913). Wide Angle 19(4), 25–61 (1997)
27. Kauer, T., Joglekar, S., Redi, M., et al.: Mapping and visualizing deep-learning urban beautification. IEEE Comput. Graphics Appl. 38(5), 70–83 (2018)

Multi-monitor System for Adaptive Image Saliency Detection Based on Attentive Mechanisms

Mariacarla Staffa(✉) [ID] and Paola Barra [ID]

Science and Techology Department, Parthenope University of Naples, Naples, Italy
{mariacarla.staffa,paola.barra}@uniparthenope.it

Abstract. One of the most powerful human-inspired cognitive processes adopted within robotics systems is visual attention to select salient information about the environment. The use of human-inspired cognitive processes has become an essential direction for the robotic research field, especially when robotics systems are deployed in complex and unstructured everyday environments where the limited computation capacity and the real-time requirements become the bottleneck of the system development. In the context above, developing a biologically plausible method must also meet the technical constraints needed to bridge the gap between bio-inspired influences and technical applicability. This paper proposes a bio-inspired visual attention system based on selective attention monitors to satisfy computational capacity constraints and identify semantically relevant information by prioritizing the visual stimuli based on both bottom-up and top-down information.

Keywords: Multi-monitor system · image salience detection · attentive mechanisms

1 Introduction

Developing cognitive/semantic abilities for technical systems have become a prevalent focus of robotics research.

Human cognitive mechanisms such as perception, attention, memory, action planning, and learning are taken as inspiration to build an efficient biologically inspired model for technical systems since it is envisioned that robots endowed with such abilities will be more adaptive, acceptable, reliable, and robust.

Vision is a powerful source of information among various sensory modalities and can provide a large amount of information about the world.

The mainstream approach to model focal visual attention involves the identification of saliency in the image and applying a search process to the salient regions. However, simultaneously identifying salient targets in the visual field is already a daunting task for the most sophisticated biological brains [27], let alone for robotic systems. In fact, due to the limited processing capacity or the real-time constraints imposed by automatic systems, not all the information can

The original version of this chapter was revised: The wrong author has been presented as corresponding author. This was corrected. The correction to this chapter is available at https://doi.org/10.1007/978-3-031-35894-4_45

H. Degen and S. Ntoa (Eds.): HCII 2023, LNAI 14051, pp. 607–617, 2023.
https://doi.org/10.1007/978-3-031-35894-4_44

be further processed in detail without leading to a prohibitive computational complexity. Typically, the solution is to select and process the relevant information at a higher resolution or earlier while concurrently inhibiting the others. This kind of visual information selection process is called visual attention, which plays an essential role in human perception and cognition.

Inspired by the neural model proposed in [16] and by the so called *Feature Integration Theory (FIT)* from Treisman and Gelade [26], in this work, we present a multi-monitor system for adaptive image salience detection, where a new way of calculating a salience map based on a particular model of attentive mechanisms is proposed. In this work, our attentional multi-monitor approach implements a similar parallel visual field analysis. Its purpose is to automatically detect the most relevant parts of a color picture. The general philosophy of this approach is to design a biologically-inspired algorithm based on an implementation of selective attention processes.

Compared to other approaches, the proposed method permits not only to orient the focus of the attention towards the salience part of the field of view, but it contemporary allows for to preservation of computational resources.

2   Related Works

In recent years computer vision has addressed the problem of sensing object detection through the use of deep learning: with network architecture, supervision level, learning paradigm and object/instance level detection [31].

The use of feed-forward neural networks for object detection is justified by several studies showing that a number of tests of visual salience can be implemented in a biologically plausible way [11].

Some trends concern a statistical signal-based approach [8], which automatically predicts salient regions of the visual scene by directly using image statistics at the point of gaze [22,24].

Observing human behavior makes it possible to describe models of visual attention; these models can use system block diagrams, mathematical models, natural language, or other calculations. A computational model of visual attention not only includes a formal description of how concentration is computed, but it is possible to see how the model behaves through a comparison through images [30].

Numerous computational models of visual attention have been proposed during the last three decades, dealing with different aspects of visual awareness such as visual salience, visual research, gaze, eye movements, or other behavioral patterns. The survey presented by Tsotsos et al. [29] analyze and compare these categories with each other.

One of the main approaches relies on analysing the visual information through parallel different salience maps, one for each early visual feature, organised according to locations in our visual field [1,13,14,18,28].

With respect to these works [1,18], while from the one hand we start from the same hypothesis that localized saliency computation serves to maximize information sampled from the environment, from the other hand these models do not explicitly reduce the computational burden further as our model does.

In particular, Koch and Ullman [16] proposed a framework relying on the concept of salience map which is a two-dimensional topographic representation of salience for every pixel in the image. This visual attention model has been widely used [12] in a number of computer vision applications, such as object tracking, image segmentation/compression, etc. [21].

This work also takes inspiration from the Koch-Ullman model, where different features are computed in parallel and their conspicuities are represented in several feature maps. A central saliency map combines the saliencies of the elements, and a winner take all network (WTA) determines the most salient location. In our model, different features are elaborated in parallel; some of them, such as color and movements, are prioritised. Priority depends on top-down stimuli coming from internal goals or expectations of the observer by adaptively changing the salience level of different areas of the visual field depending on both bottom-up and top-down stimuli [25]. Still, the global saliency map is determined by the superimposition of the feature maps generated by the multiple parallel monitors.

Furthermore, similarly to the *Feature Integration Theory (FIT)* from Treisman and Gelade [26], in the presented model the generated saliency maps specify where salient things are but not what they are in the display. Conversely, to the FIT approach, the proposed method does not mind storing descriptions to identify or classify objects.

3   The Selective Attention Mechanism

Selective visual attention is the mechanism by which we can rapidly direct our gaze towards interesting objects in our field of view [17]. Studies about human visual perception [15] show that selective visual attention is affected by two distinct types of attentional mechanisms, which guide where to look at based on both bottom-up (image-based) and top-down (task-dependent) cues [7].

In particular, top-down attentional selection refers to voluntary attention closely linked to the observers' experience and the task they have in mind. In contrast, bottom-up attentional selection is linked to involuntary attention reflecting the salience of the environmental stimuli, such as abrupt onsets [32] or local singularity [26]. The deployment of the attention towards bottom-up stimuli can be modulated and sometimes overridden by top-down factors [9, 19].

Within a robotic system, selective attention mechanisms can be used to direct sensors toward the most salient sources of information.

3.1   Our Selective Attentional Model

According to typical works on visual attention [19], our approach is concerned with the orientation of the attention in the space (i.e. the field of view). It also relies on the temporal distribution of attentional resources needed to monitor and control multiple salient objects [23].

These attentional allocation mechanisms have been successfully employed in applications of adapting control of robot interactive behavior [2,4–6,20]. In this work, we propose a frequency-based model of selective attention monitor for contemporary and adaptively regulating the salience level of different parts of the visual field. Such a particular attention mechanism can adaptively increase or decrease the salience level of each part of the image based on salient internal and external stimuli by changing the frequencies of the monitors' internal clocks. The values of the internal clock will be used to regulate the frequency of processing of the sub-parts of the image according to the salience level. The higher the salience, the higher the frequency at which that part of the image will be monitored and controlled.

The Attentive Monitor. The attentive monitors aim to drive the focus of attention on specific parts of the image where a certain saliency is detected. They are defined by setting the salient cue they aim at detecting (a particular color, or a movement of an object in the scene, etc.) and the frequency updating functions used to increase or decrease the processing rate of specific image zones based on their saliency degree. All the monitors (each defined on a particular feature) are distributed on the whole image. The monitors update when the image changes by changing the salience map accordingly. In particular, in addition to focusing on different areas depending on the salience, the monitors also have a distraction function to decrease the saliency of a specific area where there are no more salient features. The different monitors activate salience maps depending on the features they are in charge of detecting in the image. The overlapping of the salience maps of each monitor determines the degree of total salience for each area. The resulting global salience map will provide more frequent processing of the parts of the image where saliency is supposed to be by processing at a lower frequency than the other zones where no salient cues have been detected. This process permits not only to attentively move the focus of attention but also to reduce the number of sensors reading and processing by implicitly improving the computational costs. The computational costs mainly depend on the number of resolutions of the monitors on the image. The advantage of using this frequency-based model over the traditional ones is that the computational costs are drastically reduced since the mechanism subtending the model permits to avoid unnecessary sensor reading and processing while augmenting the precision in the salience zone of the image; this leads to an optimization of the resources distribution.

In Fig. 1, the Attentional Monitor (AM) model is shown. The AM is obtained as a frequency-based model of attention [3] endowed with an adaptive internal mechanism. This mechanism not only regulates in time the saliency level of a particular part of the image, based on both bottom-up stimuli and top-down influences, but it also can filter the available sensory input by efficiently deploying the robot's computational resources. It relies on the central concept that the parts of the image with a low saliency level will be cut off by the image processing task (i.e., they are processed at a lower frequency) until they reach a considerable value of saliency.

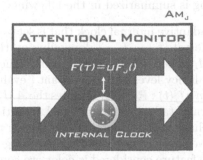

Fig. 1. Attentional Monitor.

Different types of AMs will be deployed depending on the particular feature we aim to consider. In this preliminary study, we consider two kinds of AMs for detecting a salient color (e.g., red, green) or moving objects in the scene. Suppose we assume the input image (from the video stream) is divided into N quadrants for each quadrant. In that case, all available types of AMs will be applied so that the final saliency value of that part of the image will result from the combination of a multi-features evaluation.

More precisely, the input image at each frame is divided in N sub-figures or quadrants and $N \times M$ AMs are used to detect the saliency of a particular zone of the image and to regulate the level of attention to dedicate to such a part of the image (see Fig. 2).

In particular, for each quadrant $i \in [1, N]$, M different types of AMs are deployed, for each external feature F_j we aim at considering (in this case $j = 1$ is for color and $j = 2$ is for movements, with $j \in [1, M]$).

Attentive Monitor Functioning. Each AM will be characterized by its own *monitoring strategy*, i.e. the process of changing the saliency level that can be associated with the increase or decrease of attention towards a particular quadrant of the image. Namely, the more salient the zone is, the higher the clock frequency and the resolution at which that zone should be monitored. Intuitively, the mechanism to focus the attention on a particular stimulus (i.e., increment of the frequency) can be different from the mechanism of distraction (i.e., decrease of the frequency). For this reason, we decided to distinguish two updating functions for the internal clock frequency of each AM: a *focus updating function* $fuf(t)$ and a *distraction updating function* $duf(t)$. Notice that the frequencies of the adaptive clocks also provide a divided attention mechanism. The monitoring activity is distributed over the concurrent part of the image; the current part depends on the frequencies of the clocks associated with the AMs working on that part. Following this approach, we can obtain different attentional mechanisms associated with each part once we define the associated *monitoring strategy* that balances the cost of monitoring a sub-part of the image against the risk of acquiring inaccurate/degraded information about the whole visual scene.

The AM functioning is summarized in the following:

- Each $AM_{i,j}$ has an adaptive internal clock that is set to a base frequency value f_b ranging in an interval $[f_{min}, f_{max}]$ depending on the particular feature j analyzed by the AM_i (where i is the quadrant reference number). This value also measures the saliency level of the quadrant i evaluated by the AM_j.
- An *updating function* $uf_j(t) : \mathbb{R}^n \to \mathbb{R}$ updates the AM_j internal clock according to both the internal state of the robot (goal, intention, motivation) and to the environmental changes. This function depends on the considered feature. In this case study, we consider the following updating functions:
  - $j = 1$: in case the feature considered is color; we consider a focus updating policy for the adaptive clock, which can increase the frequency value when a particular color is detected. Namely, the frequency f_t will be updated through the following focus updating function:

  $$fuf_1(t) = \alpha_1 * RATE$$

  where α_1 is the priority (weight) we want to give to this particular feature w.r.t to the others and depends on the task-dependent top-down influences; $RATE$ parameter identifies the Weber law of perception:

  $$RATE = \frac{\Delta\sigma(t)}{\sigma(t)}$$

  where, $\Delta\sigma(t)$ is equal to $\sigma(t) - \sigma(t - f_{t-1})$ that is the difference between the actual data perceived by the camera sensor $\sigma(t)$ and data received at the previous sampling step $\sigma(t - f_{t-1})$ and $\sigma(t)$ refers to current the camera percept, in order to measure how much the intensity of a particular color is changed with respect to previous readings.

  When the robot does not perceive the interesting color more, its clock frequency is relaxed according to the following linear function:

  $$duf_1(t) = f_{t-1} - \beta_1$$

  - $j = 2$: in case the feature to be detected is movements; we consider a focus is updating the policy for the adaptive clock, which can timely react to the movement speed (which can be associated with dangerous situations) must increase the attentional focus. In this case, the focus of attention on the clock frequency can be associated with the input percept rate of variation. More formally, the frequency f_t will be updated through the following focus updating function:

  $$fuf_2(t) = \alpha_2 * RATE$$

where, α_2 is the priority (weight) we want to give to this particular feature; and $RATE$ parameter identifies the first derivative of sensors signal w.r.t. time:

$$RATE = \frac{\Delta\sigma(t)}{\Delta(t)}$$

In particular $\Delta(t)$ is equal to f_{t-1}, that is the frequency at the previous clock cycle, $\Delta\sigma(t)$ is equal to $\sigma(t) - \sigma(t - f_{t-1})$ that is the difference between the actual data perceived by the camera sensor $\sigma(t)$ and data received at the previous sampling step $\sigma(t - f_{t-1})$. In this way, the attentional frequency, as well as the saliency level, will adapt not only to the environmental changes but also to the speed at which these changes took place. As in the previous case, the distraction updating mechanism can be implemented with a linear function:

$$duf_2(t) = f_{t-1} + \beta_2$$

For all the presented updating functions, a normalization process $\phi(uf_j(t)) : \mathbb{R} \rightarrow \mathbb{N}$ will be applied to map the generated values by the updating functions in the range of the respective allowed values $[f_j min, f_j max]$.

- Finally, a trigger function $\rho(f_t, f_{t-1})$, will be used to alert when a particular zone reaches a considerable salience level and have thus to be monitored. In this case that part of the image will be processed by the AM otherwise it will be ignored for a while, depending on the current frequency of the AM internal clock.

$$\rho(f_t, Tf) = \begin{cases} 1, & \text{if } f_t \geq Tf \\ 0, & \text{otherwise} \end{cases} \tag{1}$$

Hence, starting from the clock frequency at time 0 $f_0 = f_b$ (with $t = 0$ and $f_b \in [f_{min}, f_{max}]$), the clock period at time t will be regulated as follows:

$$f_t = \rho(f_t, Tf) * \phi(uf(t)) + (1 - \rho(f_t, Tf)) * f_{t-1} \tag{2}$$

That is, if the value of the frequency calculated at time t is not greater than a certain threshold Tf, the level of salience is not significant to attract the attentional focus on that part of the image. Consequently, that quadrant will not be evaluated for e period equal to $\frac{1}{f_t}$. Instead, when the value of the trigger function is equal to 1, the saliency level is high, and the corresponding quadrant must be processed and the frequency updated according to the current changes.

Conceptual Meaning of the Proposed Approach. Intuitively, the frequency of the monitor is interpreted as the degree of attention on that precise location of the environment. The higher the clock frequency, the higher the current saliency of that part of the image, and the higher the resolution at which that part of the environment should be monitored.

Namely, the more objects/persons in a specific part of the image are salient, the more the internal frequency of the monitor will be incremented, and the more that part of the image will attract attention in a bottom-up manner. In this case, let's think, for example, of a lone red object in a blue field). This bottom-up mechanism, characterized by well-defined visual features such as color or moving objects, will be combined with a top-down regulation (the α weights) introduced for biasing the selective attention mechanism based on internal goal-directed stimuli. In previous works [10], it has been shown that intrinsic motivations and goals directly affect the modulation and control of attentional resources. Hence, we will use these internal motivations to weight the monitor level of salience produced by the bottom-up stimuli.

4   The Multi-monitor System

The proposed multi-monitor system consists of a set of M AMs applied to the N location of an image (see Fig. 2). The different attentive monitors will code for the salience within a particular feature dimension.

To assess the overall salience of a location, we will combine the information of the individual AM into one global measure of salience by producing a *saliency map*. The frequencies of the AMs, will be combined as follows: for each quadrant $i \in [1, N]$

$$saliency_i(t) = \sum_{j=1}^{M} \alpha_j * f_{i,j}(t)$$

The higher the AMs frequencies, the higher the saliency of the corresponding location in the visual field. This saliency will account for all considered bottom-up stimuli and the top-down influences, which will weigh the intensity of the

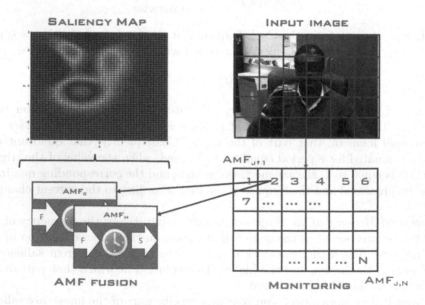

Fig. 2. The Salience Map generation Cycle.

features to emphasize internally motivated stimulation towards external objects or features.

The resulting global salience map will give a biased view of the visual environment, emphasizing exciting locations in the visual field. Namely, it will encode the saliency of part of the scene in terms of simple features such as color and motion. The salience of a given location is determined primarily by how different this location is from its surroundings in color, movement etc.

5   Conclusions and Discussions

Summarizing, in the porposed system, the attentive monitors are used with the aim of driving the focus of attention on specific parts of the image where a certain saliency is detected. They are defined by setting the salient cue they aim at detecting (a particular color, or movements of objects in the scene, etc.) and the frequency updating functions used to increase or decrease the processing rate of specific zones of the image basing on their saliency degree. Thanks to this mechanism, the monitored salient parts of the image receive an increased attentional weight balanced by combining external (bottom-up) and internal (top-down) factors. The visual processing resources are redistributed accordingly. The higher the frequency of the attentive monitor, the greater the salience of the corresponding position in the field of view. The different monitors activate different salience maps depending on the features they are in charge to detect into the image. The degree of saliency is represented by the summation of the outputs of the whole monitors which overlap on each zone to catch each for a particular salient feature. In order to evaluate the overall salience of a place, all the information from the individual attentive monitor is combined into a single global measure of salience producing a salience map. The resulting global salience map will provide a more frequent processing of the parts of the image where a saliency is supposed to be, by processing at a lower frequency the other zones where no salient cues have been detected. This process permits not only to attentively move the focus of attention, but also to reduce the number of sensors reading and processing, by implicitly improving in turn the computational costs.

The main issue of the presented approach is the setting of the updating function. In fact, while from the one hand we can benefit from the customization of the monitoring function for adapting the saliency level to particular objects or movements, from the other hand we need to pay attention to the choice of the updating function which should catch the velocity of possible changes in the image, since the updating frequency approach while from the one hand can decrease the computational cost could lose some details in between one reading and the other when abrupt event happens in a non-salient zone.

Acknowledgements. We acknowledge financial support from the project PNRR MUR project PE0000013-FAIR.

References

1. Borji, A., Itti, L.: State-of-the-art in visual attention modeling. IEEE Trans. Pattern Anal. Mach. Intell. 35(1), 185–207 (2013)
2. Broquere, X., Finzi, A., Mainprice, J., Rossi, S., Sidobre, D., Staffa, M.: An attentional approach to human-robot interactive manipulation. Int. J. Soc. Robot. 6(4), 533–553 (2014)
3. Burattini, E., Finzi, A., Rossi, S., Staffa, M.: Monitoring strategies for adaptive periodic control in behavior-based robotic systems. In: 2009 Advanced Technologies for Enhanced Quality of Life, pp. 130–135, July 2009
4. Burattini, E., Finzi, A., Rossi, S., Staffa, M.: Attentional human-robot interaction in simple manipulation tasks, pp. 129–130 (2012)
5. Burattini, E., Rossi, S., Finzi, A., Staffa, M.: Attentional modulation of mutually dependent behaviors. In: Doncieux, S., Girard, B., Guillot, A., Hallam, J., Meyer, J.-A., Mouret, J.-B. (eds.) SAB 2010. LNCS (LNAI), vol. 6226, pp. 283–292. Springer, Heidelberg (2010). https://doi.org/10.1007/978-3-642-15193-4_27
6. Caccavalebib6 Caccavale, R., Leone, E., Lucignano, L., Rossi, S., Staffa, M., Finzi, A.: Attentional regulations in a situated human-robot dialogue. In: RO-MAN, pp. 844–849. IEEE (2014)
7. Chun, M., Wolfe, J.: Visual attention. In: Goldstein, E.B. (ed.) Blackwell Handbook of Perception, pp. 2–335. Blackwell (2001)
8. Cormack, U.R.L.K., Bovik, A.C.: Point-of-gaze analysis reveals visual search strategies. In: Proceedings of SPIE 5292, Human Vision and Electronic Imaging IX, June 2004
9. Desimone, R., Duncan, J.: Neural mechanisms of selective visual attention. Annu. Rev. Neurosci. 18, 193–222 (1995)
10. di Nocera, D., Finzi, A., Rossi, S., Staffa, M.: The role of intrinsic motivations in attention allocation and shifting. Front. Psychol. 5 (2014)
11. Han, S., Vasconcelos, N.: Biologically plausible saliency mechanisms improve feedforward object recognition. Vis. Res. 50(22), 2295–2307 (2010). Mathematical Models of Visual Coding
12. Itti, L., Koch, C.: A comparison of feature combination strategies for saliency-based visual attention systems. J. Electron. Imaging 10, 161–169 (1999)
13. Itti, L., Koch, C.: A saliency-based search mechanism for overt and covert shifts of visual attention. Vision. Res. 40(10–12), 1489–1506 (2000)
14. Itti, L., Koch, C., Niebur, E.: A model of saliency-based visual attention for rapid scene analysis. IEEE Trans. PAMI 20(11), 1254–1259 (1998)
15. James, W.: The Principles of Psychology, vol. 1. American Science Series. H. Holt (1890)
16. Koch, C., Ullman, S.: Shifts in selective attention: towards the underlying neural circuitry. Hum. Neurobiol. 4, 219–227 (1985)
17. Koike, T., Saiki, J.: Stochastic guided search model for search asymmetries in visual search tasks. In: Bülthoff, H.H., Wallraven, C., Lee, S.-W., Poggio, T.A. (eds.) BMCV 2002. LNCS, vol. 2525, pp. 408–417. Springer, Heidelberg (2002). https://doi.org/10.1007/3-540-36181-2_41
18. Kong, L., Duan, L., Yang, W., Dou, Y.: Salient region detection: an integration approach based on image pyramid and region property. IET Comput. Vision 9(1), 85–97 (2013)
19. Li, J., Tian, Y., Huang, T., Gao, W.: Multi-task rank learning for visual saliency estimation. IEEE Trans. Circuits Syst. Video Technol. 21(5), 623–636 (2011)

20. Origlia, A., Iengo, S., Staffa, M., Finzi, A.: Attentional and emotional regulation in human-robot interaction, pp. 1135–1140 (2012)
21. Ouerhani, N., Hügli, H., Gruener, G., Codourey, A.: A visual attention-based approach for automatic landmark selection and recognition. In: Paletta, L., Tsotsos, J.K., Rome, E., Humphreys, G. (eds.) WAPCV 2004. LNCS, vol. 3368, pp. 183–195. Springer, Heidelberg (2005). https://doi.org/10.1007/978-3-540-30572-9_14
22. Parkhurst, D., Niebur, E.: Scene content selected by active vision. Spat. Vis. **16**(2), 125–154 (2003)
23. Posner, M.I., Snyder, C.R., Davidson, B.J.: Attention and the detection of signals. J. Exp. Psychol. **109**(2), 160–174 (1980)
24. Reinagel, P., Zador, A.M.: Natural scene statistics at the center of gaze. Nctw. Comput. Neural Syst. **10**, 1–10 (1999)
25. Theeuwes, J.: Top-down and bottom-up control of visual selection. Acta Physiol. (Oxf) **135**(2), 77–99 (2010)
26. Treisman, A.M., Gelade, G.: A feature-integration theory of attention. Cogn. Psychol. **12**, 97–136 (1980)
27. Tsotsos, J.K.: Is complexity theory appropriate for analyzing biological systems? Behav. Brain Sci. **14**(4), 770–773 (1991)
28. Tsotsos, J.K., Culhane, S.M., Wai, W.Y.K., Lai, Y., Davis, N., Nuflo, F.: Modeling visual attention via selective tuning. Artif. Intell. **78**(1–2), 507–545 (1995)
29. Tsotsos, J.K., Eckstein, M.P., Landy, M.S.: Computational models of visual attention. Vision Res. **116**, 93–94 (2015)
30. Tsotsos, J.K., Rothenstein, A.L.: Computational models of visual attention. Scholarpedia **6**(1), 6201 (2011)
31. Wang, W., Lai, Q., Fu, H., Shen, J., Ling, H., Yang, R.: Salient object detection in the deep learning era: an in-depth survey. IEEE Trans. Pattern Anal. Mach. Intell. **44**(6), 3239–3259 (2022)
32. Yantis, S., Jonides, J.: Attentional capture by abrupt onsets: new perceptual objects or visual masking. J. Exp. Psychol. Hum. Percept. Perform. **22**, 1505 (1996)

Correction to: Multi-monitor System for Adaptive Image Saliency Detection Based on Attentive Mechanisms

Mariacarla Staffa$^{(\boxtimes)}$ (iD) and Paola Barra (iD)

Correction to:
Chapter "Multi-monitor System for Adaptive Image Saliency Detection Based on Attentive Mechanisms" in: H. Degen and S. Ntoa (Eds.): *Artificial Intelligence in HCI*, **LNAI 14051, https://doi.org/10.1007/978-3-031-35894-4_44**

In an older version of this paper, the wrong author has been presented as corresponding author. This was corrected.

The updated original version of this chapter can be found at
https://doi.org/10.1007/978-3-031-35894-4_44

Author Index

Printed in the United States
by Baker & Taylor Publisher Services

Printed in the United States
by Baker & Taylor Publisher Services